SALES
Management

PRADIP KUMAR MALLIK

Professor, Department of Business Administration
The University of Burdwan
West Bengal

OXFORD
UNIVERSITY PRESS

OXFORD
UNIVERSITY PRESS

22 Workspace, 2nd Floor, 1/22 Asaf Ali Road, New Delhi 110002, India

Oxford University Press is a department of the University of Oxford.
It furthers the University's objective of excellence in research, scholarship,
and education by publishing worldwide in

Oxford   New York
Auckland   Cape Town   Dar es Salaam   Hong Kong   Karachi
Kuala Lumpur   Madrid   Melbourne   Mexico City   Nairobi
New Delhi   Shanghai   Taipei   Toronto

With offices in
Argentina   Austria   Brazil   Chile   Czech Republic   France   Greece
Guatemala   Hungary   Italy   Japan   Poland   Portugal   Singapore
South Korea   Switzerland   Thailand   Turkey   Ukraine   Vietnam

Oxford is a registered trade mark of Oxford University Press
in the UK and in certain other countries.

Published in India
by Oxford University Press

First published 2011
Digitally Printed in 2023

ISBN-13: 978-0-19-807202-7
ISBN-10: 0-19-807202-3

Typeset in Baskerville
by County Caramels, Ghaziabad
Printed at Manipal Technologies Limited, Manipal
and published by Oxford University Press
22 Workspace, 2nd Floor, 1/22 Asaf Ali Road, New Delhi 110002, India

I would like to dedicate this book to my mother

(*Late*) *Mrs Anandamoyee Mallik.*

She was my inspiration in life.

Preface

Selling has undergone a tremendous change since the age of the barter system. It has taken different forms through the upheavals of war, economic boom and slump, varying customers' needs and aspirations, unpredictable competition, globalization, and digital breakthroughs in the industry. Today, we see that the scope of pedalling by traders along the streets and lanes has shifted to door-to-door selling; selling from unorganized marketplace has found place in the retail shops; and selling by personal interactions with customers has changed to selling by the application of e-commerce.

It is important to understand that behind every transformation, there is an underlying cause. Industrial revolution at the end of the eighteenth century was one such cause that brought about these radical changes in the selling practices. Earlier, only a few producers ruled the market with ferocity of price dictation and inferior quality of products. Customers, in those days, could not make any choice because of the limited options available to them. Industrial revolution changed this phenomenon which triggered growth of industries, market rivalries among producers, sense of product quality among producers and customers, quality–price consistency, etc. Customers were gradually able to begin selecting products based on their expectations, demands, and satisfaction.

The World War II was another epochal phenomenon that temporarily stifled the journey of industrial growth and sales. First, the revival of the industrial world arousing from the traumas of war saw rejuvenation of agriculture, manufacturing industries, service sectors, etc. and selling came to a point of opening a new leaf. Identifying the needs and demands of the customers became the starting point of the selling process. Second, reaching the customers with the right product or service at the right price and quality also became essential for effective selling. Third, servicing the customers to the utmost to ensure repeat business and concomitant spreading of customer base expanded the horizon of selling activities. So, selling wore the mantle of marketing and was started to be adjudged as not only a profession but also as a discipline. Since then, selling has emerged as a new face having two important crowns—selling as a professional field and an academic arena. These two go hand in hand to bolster each other reciprocally.

The aim behind writing this book has been around projecting a sustained and nurtured correspondence between professional selling and its academic infrastructure. As selling is basically a human process of generating a mental congruence between a seller and a buyer before and after the exchange and transaction, a thorough knowledge of understanding of the buying and selling behaviour of the two parties is indispensable to consummate effective selling. Furthermore, salesmanship demonstrated by salespeople plays a pivotal role in mellowing the prospective customers from their indecisive stand. But salesmanship determining the means of artful but productive selling can be ingrained in the personal qualities of the salespeople only when sales managers choose the right salespeople, train and motivate them by managerial capabilities. Here, proper planning, organizing, directing, coordinating, and controlling the sales force are crucial managerial functions that on one side orient towards developing right sales force and on the other, formulate customer planning and customer relationship strategies to enhance the stability of the customer base.

Today's sales managers need to be futuristic and ambitious. Salespeople need to be complying and conscientious. The unison of sales managers as planners and salespeople as executors is definitely a decisive factor in shaping the success of the organization. As sales and marketing are the prime movers of the organization, rechristening of sales and marketing plans, strategies, schemes, and effectiveness studies is necessary to anchor the organization safely and securely whenever changes try to disrupt its smooth sailing. So, selling confronts a challenging sphere to tide over and time has come to inoculate new thoughts, insights, concepts, and ideas in the veins and arteries of selling.

Hence, developing a precise understanding of sales management in the context of the present environmental contexts and contingencies has become a necessity to help sales managers in order to meet new challenges and risks meted out by them. At the same time, it is crucial to generate new academic domain in order to instruct learners on the evolving discourses on personal selling and sales management with an aim to attain academic excellence. It goes without saying that selling can only get its academic and professional meaningfulness under pragmatic sales management.

About the Book

Although there are innumerable books on sales management available for students, the latter are still in a fix to find the right book that can raise to the level of their hunger for knowledge and applications in the arena of personal selling and sales force management. There is a dearth of books that fit well enough with the syllabi prescribed under undergraduate and postgraduate programmes in universities and institutes offering sales management as a part of their course curricula. With an aim to achieve that, this book on sales management is compiled

- to develop a lucid but comprehensive understanding of the subject matter and cases in sales management
- to generate all-round preparedness for examinations and interviews for students
- to gather industry-oriented exposure in this field for the budding and the present professionals in personal selling and sales management

The book in the real sense is a comprehensive textbook on sales management. It has made an attempt to cover every sphere of sales management along with the presentation of industry-oriented case studies that invariably complement the academic and professional interests of the learners. It would surely escalate the wisdom and pedagogy of the learners in this field.

Keeping the students' interests in mind, the author has consulted the present syllabi and detailed contents of sales management in post graduate level of professional courses thoroughly. Accordingly, the book has been designed, contents have been discussed, and cases have been inducted to present a methodical and curriculum-oriented deliberation on texts, issues, scopes, and applications of different aspects of sales management. The book is also composed keeping abreast of the twists and turns in the business environment. The book has left no stone unturned to detail out the modern approaches of sales management.

Students would definitely get a great reservoir of information on the past, present, and future scenarios in personal selling and sales management. Sales professionals would get vital inputs to equip themselves with the knowledge and applications of sales management too. It would boost up the confidence levels of salespeople and sales managers who want to shine in their professional fields. Thus, the book would cater to students, scholars, researchers, sales executives, salespeople, sales managers, and many others in the relevant arena.

Pedagogical Features

Special pedagogical features used throughout the book are as follows:

- *Authentic, comprehensive, and enriched coverage:* The book presents an authentic text covering the key areas of personal selling and sales management exhaustively and provides in-depth wealth of information.
- *Numerous examples and cases:* Each chapter presents a plethora of examples, illustrations, exhibits, and case studies in a comprehensive and vivid manner. This obviously gives the readers a thought-provoking experience and mind-absorbing learning.
- *Application orientation:* The book takes help of a plenty of examples from real-life situations as well as corporate dossiers to draw an extension of the theoretical

treatments in order to help the readers in tracking down from conceptual bases to their practical applications of the issues.

• *Lucid and learner friendly:* The book from the beginning has been contemplated to portray the texts and cases in a lucid and user friendly manner so that students can easily understand both. It aims to provide knowledge as well as confidence to the students to accept the subject at ease.

• *Modern issues with updates:* The book as far as practicable brings forth modern practices of selling such as e-business, e-commerce, and web-based selling, selling via social media, etc. with the latest and updated information as well as conceptual clarities and analytical understanding.

• *Critical and exhaustive:* The book makes an attempt to churn out critical issues of sales management and moulds it in a comprehensible manner without distracting from the original themes of the subject.

Coverage and Structure

The book is divided into five crucial parts, each part comprising a set of chapters.

Part I: Personal Selling

Chapter 1, *An Introduction to Personal Selling,* discusses the concept, meaning, and objectives of personal selling, along with the role of personal selling in marketing communication, importance of salesmanship, traditional and modern selling practices, types of selling, selling as a profession, and the ethical aspects of it.

Chapter 2, *Personal Selling: Approaches and Strategies,* discusses the theoretical perspectives of personal selling, the buyer–seller dyad and its implication in personal selling, and the factors influencing the buyer–seller dyad.

Chapter 3, *Personal Selling Process,* deliberates on the process, objectives, and the problems and its solutions in each step of personal selling. It also examines the dos and don'ts of each step and presents a detailed discussion on sales presentation and demonstration and after-sales services.

Part II: Organization of Sales Force Functions

Chapter 4, *Sales Force Management,* discusses the basic concept of sales management, role of planning in sales management, environmental issues in sales planning, role of strategic planning in sales management, and the role of sales managers in sales.

Chapter 5, *Sales Organization,* confers a detailed discussion on sales organization, its meaning, purposes, and types, the process of organizing the sales force, determination of sales force size, functional aspects of managing a sales force, and a few contemporary issues of sales organization.

Chapter 6, *Sales Territories,* discusses the meaning and definition of sales territory, its objectives and benefits, and the management of sales territories.

Part III: Managing the Sales Team

Chapter 7, *Salespeople and Sales Managers: Profiles, Roles, and Responsibilities,* gives a critical analysis of the role and responsibility of salespeople and sales managers in an organization. At the same time, it delves into the discussion of the factors determining the qualities of salespeople and the skills of sales managers.

Chapter 8, *Sales Force Recruitment,* presents the meaning and conception of recruitment in connection with salespeople, job analysis, job description and job specifications of salespeople, and the sources of sales force recruitment.

Chapter 9, *Sales Force Selection,* presents the selection process of salespeople, guidelines for effective selection, interview process, psychological tests, reference checks, and socialization process after induction of salespeople in the organization.

Chapter 10, *Sales Training,* discusses the objectives and benefits of sales force training, the procedural details of training process, and their types along with the training methods.

Chapter 11, *Sales Force Motivation,* deals with the objectives and benefits of sales force motivation, strategic issues of sales force motivation, and theoretical rationale of the motivation process. It also highlights the stress in salespeople's lives and the role of motivation to deal with stress.

Chapter 12, *Directing the Sales Force,* stresses on the concept and understanding of sales force direction, leadership, and its role in directing and motivating the sales force. The qualities of a sales leader, theoretical perspectives of leadership, and their practical implications in leading sales force is also discussed.

Chapter 13, *Sales Force Compensation,* elucidates on sales force compensation from conceptual and typical perspectives, and discusses the factors influencing compensation plans, criteria of sound compensation plan, other than discussing the steps and methods of sales force compensation.

Chapter 14, *Sales Force Performance,* examines the performance and appraisal of a sales force along with the criteria and benefits of sales force appraisal. This chapter also identifies the steps in sales force performance appraisal, sales force control, and its contribution to improve performance. Contemporary issues in sales force performance are also discussed.

Part IV: Financial Aspects of Sales

Chapter 15, *Sales Budgeting and Forecasting,* deals with the fundamentals of sales budgeting and forecasting along with their approaches. The factors influencing the steps and methods of sales budget, and sales forecasting are also discussed.

Chapter 16, *Sales and Cost Analysis,* discusses the concept, methods, and role of sales quota in sales analysis, and the objectives and methodical approaches of cost analysis.

Part V: Strategy and Modern Approaches

Chapter 17, *Sales Strategy,* focuses on the strategic orientation of selling, environmental analysis, and its importance in formulating sales strategies. The steps in strategic sales management, impacts of competition on sales strategy, social responsibility issues in sales strategy, customer relationship and retention as important prerogatives in sales strategy are also discussed.

Chapter 18, *Modern Selling Approaches,* delves into the modern approaches of selling, especially under globalization issues, ascendance of e-commerce and its application in contemporary selling, benefits and limitations of e-commerce, web-based selling, emergence of social media, and its role in facilitating modern selling.

Acknowledgements

Writing a book on sales management to generate a meaningful space amidst a plethora of personal selling and sales management books was an uphill task. A book on sales management of a different nature and perspective is easy to imagine but difficult to envisage, particularly at the present juncture when the globalization wave has already shaken the deepest root of sales management practices. Accepting the task from one of the world's largest publishing houses, Oxford University Press (OUP), New Delhi, was my greatest challenge and a great boost to me.

I would like to sincerely thank my teacher, Prof. Sankar Kumar Sengupta, whose blessings have been a great asset to me. I would also like to extend my thanks to Dr Uday Kumar Haldar, my scholar, who has always stood by me and encouraged me to work in the field of sales management. I thank my beloved students who have always inspired me to write new books. I must pay my deepest gratitude to the University of Burdwan for giving me the right teaching and learning environment to mould my knowledge and experience.

I would like to extend my heartfelt thanks to OUP to give me a platform and an opportunity to express my inner voice and knowledge in the area of sales management. Thanks are due to the editorial team of OUP for their relentless follow-ups and constructive criticisms during the course of writing this book.

Last but not the least, I would like to convey a special note of gratitude to my wife, Sima Mallik, and daughter, Rima Mallik, who have constantly inspired and encouraged me during the preparation of this work.

I would be grateful to receive any comments on my book to improve future editions. Readers can send their suggestions to mallik_p59@yahoo.com.

Pradip Kumar Mallik

Contents

3. Personal Selling process — **58**

Part II   Organization of Sales Force Functions

4. Sales Force Management — **89**

5. Sales Organization — **116**

Part III   Managing the Sales Team

Part V   Strategy and Modern Approaches

Part I

Personal Selling

Chapter 1: An Introduction to Personal Selling
Chapter 2: Personal Selling—Approaches and Strategies
Chapter 3: Personal Selling Process

1

An Introduction to Personal Selling

Personal selling is a promotional tool that has been contributing significantly to the sales in organizations since the industrial age. Earlier, firms used hawkers and peddlers for door-to-door selling, which still stands tall. But today many more modern approaches of selling are being adopted to bring in speed and effectiveness. Personal selling is now a matter of academic discussion, research, and profession. In this chapter, an effort has been made to focus on the conceptual issues, objectives, types, advantages, limitations, professional aspects, ethical implications, etc. of personal selling.

1.1 INTRODUCTION TO PERSONAL SELLING

An old adage says, 'Nothing happens until something is sold.' This means that until a seller and a buyer come to a point of exchange and do a transaction, no selling or buying can take place. The history of personal selling is dated back to 2000 BC. It originated in ancient Greece. Salespeople at that time were referred to as peddlers. Kurtz and Boone (2006) scripted that during the 1700s, Yankee peddlers pulled their carts full of goods from village to village and turn to turn, and helped to expand trade among the colonies in the US. The industrial revolution that began in the eighteenth century triggered the need of salespeople for the expansion of business.

Personal selling is an act of exchange of products or services between a buyer and a seller for a certain amount of money or its equivalent kind. It involves a one-to-one interaction

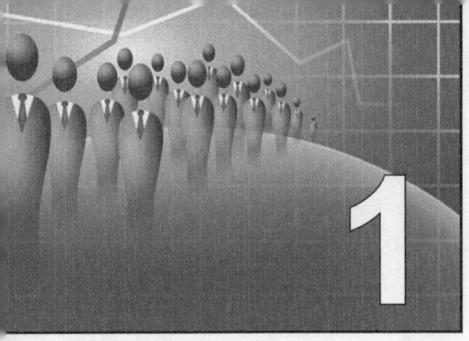

1 An Introduction to Personal Selling

Personal selling is a promotional tool that has been contributing significantly to the sales in organizations since the industrial age. Earlier, firms used hawkers and peddlers for door-to-door selling, which still stands tall. But, today many more modern approaches of selling are being adopted to bring in speed and effectiveness. Personal selling is now a matter of academic discourse, research, and profession. In this chapter, an effort has been made to focus on the conceptual issues, objectives, types, advantages, limitations, professional aspects, ethical implications, etc. of personal selling.

1.1 INTRODUCTION TO PERSONAL SELLING

An old adage says, 'Nothing happens until something is sold.' This means that until a seller and a buyer come to a point of exchange and do a transaction, no selling or buying can take place. The history of personal selling is dated back to 2000 BC. It originated in ancient Greece. Salespeople at that time were referred to as peddlers. Kurtz and Boone (2006) scripted that during the 1700s, Yankee peddlers pulled their carts full of goods from village to village and farm to farm, and helped to expand trade among the colonies in the US. The industrial revolution that began in the eighteenth century triggered the need of salespeople for the expansion of business.

Personal selling is an act of exchange of products or services between a buyer and a seller for a certain amount of money or its equivalent kind. It involves a one-to-one interaction between the salesperson representing a company and the prospective buyer, wherein the former informs, assists, and/or persuades the latter to engage in the exchange process to consummate the sales. In fact, the exchange warrants five types of flow between the buyer and the seller. These are as follows:

(a) Product flow
(b) Ownership flow
(c) Information flow
(d) Money flow
(e) Feedback that flows from buyer to seller after the use of the product, demanding after-sales service from the seller.

The salesperson communicates information about the features, characteristics, technical know-how, benefits, and conditions of sale of the product to the buyer before or at the time of delivering the product. In return, the buyer pays money to the seller, acquires ownership or title of the product, and apprises them on the experience of the product use.

Therefore, personal selling is a two-way form of communication. Most often, it is face-to-face where a salesperson representing a company makes an attempt to persuade the potential buyer to buy the company's offer. It is a promotional technique whereby salespeople use their knowledge and skills for engaging them and the buyers in some sort of an exchange relationship such that both the parties derive values. The value obtained from this transaction for the salespeople is the monetary reward while the customer receives benefits of the product. Personal selling is not manipulation as the salespeople cannot direct people to buy. They can only encourage, persuade, stimulate, influence, and allure people to buy.

But, personal selling is not just a facilitation of exchange. It encompasses identifying prospective customers, understanding their needs, communicating with them, disseminating the information at the pre-transaction phase, following up after-sales, and providing after-sales service and building relationships with the customers for future business at the post-transaction period. With the advancement in telecommunication, personal selling can also be performed using telephones, through videoconferencing, or the Internet. This interactive nature makes it the most convenient and effective means of promotional method for building relationships with the customers, particularly in business-to-business market. The purpose of personal selling is to facilitate exchange to the mutual advantages of both the buyers and the sellers.

1.1.1 Defining Personal Selling

Management thinkers have defined personal selling through various perspectives. Some of these are mentioned here:

Kotler and Armstrong (2006) defined personal selling as personal presentation by the firm's sales force for the purpose of making sales and building customer relationship.

Evans and Berman (1988) defined personal selling as the part of promotion that involves an oral presentation in a conversation with one or more prospective buyers for the purpose of making a sale.

Johnson et al. (1994) defined personal selling as the aspect of promotion that brings human elements into marketing transactions.

Belch and Belch (2006) termed personal selling as a form of person-to-person communication in which a seller attempts to assist and/or persuade prospective buyers to purchase the company's product or service.

Kerin et al. (2007) defined personal selling as a two-way flow of communication between a buyer and a seller, often in a face-to-face encounter, designed to fulfil the purchase decision of a a person or a group.

Thus it can be concluded that personal selling is a process of communication, interaction, persuasion, negotiation, and exchange between a seller and a prospective buyer whereby the former delivers something of value to the latter and the latter pays back the former the equivalent value in monetary or related terms. Through this process, both the parties are satisfied.

1.2   IMPORTANCE OF PERSONAL SELLING IN COMMUNICATION MIX

Personal selling is one of the major elements in the communication mix (also called promotion mix). It is a more direct, immediate, and personalized form of communication unlike other forms of communication, namely advertising, sales promotion, and publicity which constitute the other elements of promotion mix. Nowadays, the boundary of promotion mix has extended to include a wide range of promotional activities, such as trade show, point-of-purchase (POP) display and demonstration, direct mail, word of mouth communication, event marketing, etc.

In a communication programme, a firm can use one, two, three, or a combination of all the four basic types of promotion mix, including personal selling, advertising, sales promotion, and publicity. Different communication tools vary in their utilities and applications. Unlike personal selling, advertising is a non-personal communication. For mass promotion and mass distribution of a product, advertising is extremely useful. But it is believed that for certain customized products and where the number of potential customers is less, personal selling is a viable tool.

Advertising is effective in pre- and post-transaction phases of selling. In pre-transaction phase, it arouses the demands of the consumer and in post-transaction phase it reduces the post-purchase doubts. On the other hand, personal selling involves customers who are active during the transaction phase. In post-purchase phase, selling assumes the responsibility of handling customer complaints or the need for after-sales service. This is because, advertising is a one-way communication but personal selling is a two-way communication process. There is no scope for receiving any immediate opinion of people in case of advertisements, when they reach mass audience. But since personal selling is a one-on-one interaction between a buyer and a seller, there is more scope for getting first-hand opinion of the prospective users. Actual demonstration of the product in case of advertising is impossible. But, it is possible for the salespeople to show samples of the product, live demonstration, and performance. A comparative description of characteristics of these four major promotional elements is illustrated in Table 1.1.

Table 1.1 Comparison of promotional elements

Characteristics	Advertising	Personal selling	Sales promotion	Publicity
Definition	Paid but non-personal communication of products, services, of ideas through media by an identified sponsor.	A face-to-face conversation between sellers and prospective buyers with an aim to facilitate exchange between the two culminating in sales	Short-term incentives to encourage purchase or sale of a product or service	Non-personal stimulation of demand for a product, service, or business unit under identified sponsorship
Sponsor	Company	Company	Company	No formal sponsor
Major goal	To appeal to a mass audience to create awareness or favourable attitude to the offer of the company	To deal with individual customers with a view to create or activate demands and close the sale	To stimulate short-term sales or spur impulse purchases	To reach a mass audience with an independently reported message
Cost	Low per audience	High per customer	Moderate per customer	None for media space and time
Flexibility	Low	High	Moderate	Low
Credibility	Moderate to high	Moderate to high	Moderate to low	Very high
Effectiveness	Effective in pre- and post- transactional periods	Effective in transactional period	Effective in transactional period	Effective more in enhancing company image and encouraging future transaction
Managerial perspective	Both long- and short-term; in long-term, it builds the image of the company and in short-term, it stimulates sales	Long-term because it emphasizes on long-term relationship with buyers	Short-term; it entails immediate sales	Long-term; publicity is unparallel in building the image of the company

So, personal selling gives marketers the highest freedom to convey a message in their style and to satisfy the needs of the customer in comparison to other promotional tools. While personal selling is aimed at prospective customers, other forms of communication may or may not be targeted at prospective customers. Moreover, the results of personal selling can be measured easily. Sales managers can easily compare the performance of the salespeople.

1.3 SALESMANSHIP

As discussed, the word 'selling' denotes the act of transferring ownership from sellers to buyers. The word 'salesmanship' has been used to embrace broader perspectives of selling. Salesmanship is the ability of the salesperson to persuade prospective buyers to buy goods or services of a company. It encompasses all those efforts that are needed to convert a suspect (undecided buyer) to a prospect (expected buyer), and a prospect to an actual buyer. The suspect has no such awareness or interest to the company's offer whereas a prospect is a person who shows some interest to know the offer and its details.

American Marketing Association (AMA) defined salesmanship as 'personal or interpersonal process of assisting and/or persuading a prospective customer to buy a commodity or service and to act favorably upon an idea that has commercial significance to the seller'. The central concept of salesmanship is persuasion with a long-term goal of creating a cordial and beneficial relationship between the organization and the customer. Both the parties reap benefits from this relationship. For instance, a company wants to sell a washing machine. It sends its salespeople to a housewife. They talk to the lady and explain how a washing machine will greatly reduce her workload and how much she would like to have one; then they tell her about their own product and explain in detail about the functions and how it is better than other brand. They also mention the attractive price and the guarantee period. Applying all skills, they list out the advantages of buying the washing machine from his company. In some cases, they might even give a demonstration of the same. This is the skill which they use to persuade her to buy the product and this is termed as salesmanship.

Still et al. (1994) defined salesmanship as the art of successfully persuading prospects or customers to buy products or services from which they can derive suitable benefits, thereby increasing their total satisfaction. Salesmanship does not end at convincing people to act but also assists them to buy the product. Therefore, salesmanship is a process of stimulation or activation and fulfilment of the needs of the consumers by supplying the right product or service. Sometimes, the demand of the consumer may be expressed, latent, or unfelt and a salesperson should be able to identify and creatively deal with it. For example, a consumer's demand for an easy-to-wash detergent is expressed, the demand for less consumption of water during washing is latent or the demand for a surprise gift within the detergent pack is unfelt. In such a case, salesmanship digs in latent demand or sparks such unfelt demand by creatively thinking of a solution. It can thus be figured out from this example that salesmanship is also a creative process.

Therefore, from the discussion so far it can be inferred that selling is an operational activity whereas salesmanship is a strategic intent to integrate company, company's products or services with the customers, and bind them in a form of a relationship. In brief it can be said that personal selling is a method in which the salespeople use their salesmanship to make a sale, where both the parties, the seller and the buyer, obtain values that builds enduring relationship with each other.

1.4 OBJECTIVES OF PERSONAL SELLING

Personal selling starts with identifying the prospective customers and ascertaining their needs or helping them recognize the existence of needs or arousing a fresh need in case of a new product or a new market situation or both. Estimating the market demand and communicating it to the organization to take a production decision is also part of personal selling. It further embodies demonstrating the qualified prospects on how the product works and persuades them on how the product would fulfil their demands. Finally, motivating the target customers to take a buying decision in favour of their product is the culminating point of the job of personal selling.

But, selling does not always end with clinching a deal with the target groups. It should also understand the level of satisfaction of the customers and inform the organization of the customer experiences on the use of the product. It further assists the organization to invoke suitable changes to fill the deficient areas where the perceived experience levels of the customers are less than expected. So, following up after the sale, to elicit satisfaction or dissatisfaction levels of the customer is considered as a far-sighted objective of personal selling.

Broadly speaking, personal selling is designed to fulfil four major objectives. These are (a) informative, (b) persuasive, (c) relational, and (d) image building. These have been briefly explained as follows.

Informative objectives aim to provide information about the product or service attributes, features, benefits, values, and answer all the queries of the customers It provides an opportunity to create and increase awareness, interest, and the desire of the potential customers towards the firm's products/services and prompts them to take a buying decision favourable to the organization.

Persuasive objectives help to generate interest among prospects, instil conviction, and convert them to buyers. Persuasion aids in establishing superiority of the product over competitors.

1. It uses persuasive communication to stimulate target customers to move in for trial purchase of the company's products or services.
2. It motivates potential buyers to seek more information about the company and its offers.
3. It involves salespeople to support the push strategy to encourage intermediaries to buy and distribute the products to the customers. It, also, facilitates pull strategy by inducing the potential customers to tend towards intermediaries to buy the products of the organization.

Relational objectives are served by prompt delivery, customer training, installation, lenient credit terms, after-sales service, warranties, etc. Healthy customer relations lead to develop good company image and recognition.

1. It catalyses order getting, order taking, order influencing, order delivery and follow up after sales for the customers.
2. It aids the company in retaining old customers, creating new customers and achieving a respectable position in the industry and society.
3. It helps to reinforce the brand image and the reputation of the company—the two major sought after goals of the firm for stability and growth.
4. Personal selling can be intelligently used for new business development to augment the customer base of the organization.

Image-building objectives are aimed at creating a company's favourable image or goodwill in the eyes of the people.

1. It spreads the company's concern for social well-being.
2. It consolidates the confidence and trust of the stakeholders of the company.
3. It becomes a vital promotional tool for salespersons to deal with customers.

1.5 ESSENTIALS FOR EFFECTIVE PERSONAL SELLING

Personal selling is an essential promotional tool to communicate with the customers and achieve sales. An organization may have sound resources, well laid out corporate and marketing strategies, but ineffective and inefficient personal selling practices do not produce desired results for it. How the target customers are approached and dealt with, how their needs and demands are met, and how their problems are resolved are the fundamentals to link organizational goals and objectives with its performance. Indeed, the following factors are central for effective selling by the salespeople of a company:

1.5.1 Knowing the Company

Understanding one's company, its products or services, intermediaries, and customers are crucial for successful selling. A salesperson should know the corporate objective(s), marketing objective(s), sales objective(s), intermediaries handled, customers and their needs and demands, demographic, psychographic, and behavioural characteristics in-depth before moving on to the selling process. Therefore, knowing these objectives, the buying process, key decision makers in buying, and even the corporate culture and climate precisely are important adjuncts to effective selling.

1.5.2 Knowledge of Competition

It is seen that competition comes in the way of selling. Ignorance of competition is a threat to the organization. A salesperson should be aware of competitive climate surrounding the environment. Knowledge of competition means having an idea about the products and services of the competitors, their strengths and weaknesses, the superiority of their products against those of the competitors, relationship of the intermediaries with the competitors, including their terms and conditions, the future plans of the competitors, etc. This further helps a salesperson to defend and establish a product before prospective customers.

1.5.3 Knowledge of Selling Process

A salesperson should know the stages of the selling process before dealing with the prospects. Each stage is important for successful selling. Starting from prospecting to pre-approach, approach, presentation, and demonstration to closing the sale and follow-up after-sales, a salesperson should meticulously go through to convert a prospect to a customer. Similarly, getting the order, processing, and fulfilling orders without procedural expertise will prove a salesperson ineffective.

1.5.4 Selling Skill

Knowledgeable salespeople cannot perform their task of selling effectively unless they skilfully handle their customers. Selling skill implies adept variation and manifestation of selling behaviour depending on the type of prospect, selling situation, buying procedures, and strategies of target groups. Salesmanship, here, decides the ability of the salespeople to draw the prospective customer in their favour.

1.5.5 Sales Motivation

Sales motivation is also a precondition for successful selling. Salespeople, however informative and competent, if lack motivation can jeopardize their selling abilities and ruin the chances of winning the prospects. Indeed, a less motivated salesperson cannot participate in business interaction with the buyer and may frustrate the team effort in selling.

1.6 ADVANTAGES AND DISADVANTAGES OF PERSONAL SELLING

After discussions on the objectives and essentials of personal selling, it is important to note the advantages and limitations of personal selling. This will help to understand why a salesperson goes through repeated training sessions to get his act of personal selling right. Understanding the pros and cons of personal selling is also important for a firm because it helps in achieving organizational objectives. Though it is an expensive mode of promotion and involves setting up of special establishments under marketing department, but if properly planned and executed, it is incomparable to other promotional components. Advertising, sales promotion or publicity can spearhead the promotional campaigns but a company cannot turn promotional plans to its realization without personal selling. Let us now look at the advantages and disadvantages of personal selling.

Advantages

Following are the advantages of personal selling:

1. Personal selling is an indistinguishable type of direct, personalized, and persuasive communication that helps to come in close proximity with the potential customers and prepares a one-to-one interactive platform. Therefore, communicating information and getting immediate feedback happens almost simultaneously.

2. Personal selling has the flexibility of adjusting the sales message by inducting subtle modifications of the selling proposition in course of conversation with the prospect, depending on the trend of discussion and mental mapping of the prospect. For example, a price sensitive customer likes to listen more on the value for less money from a product. Orientation on quality may discourage him to cooperate in participative discussion.

3. Demonstrating the product and handling objections on the spot is a genuine advantage of personal selling. In some situations, salespeople find opportunity to give hands-on exhibition and demonstration of the product before the prospect to familiarize them with the product features and operations. At the same time, salespeople can answer the queries and remove doubts or suspicions of the prospects regarding the product or its allied features.

4. Person-to-person interaction assists in creating a personal relationship between the two and continuous nurturing of such relations provides ample commercial benefits to both. Personal selling is irreplaceable in developing a collaborative partnering with the customer and helps promoting a healthy business-to-business relationship.

5. Personal selling is often undertaken in a team or group where each member has a specific task to handle; for instance to solve different problems of the customer. Secondly, many a times, a sales manager accompanies a young salesperson to visit a customer, particularly when the customer is a major account. These team efforts build interpersonal relationships and bolster the morale of the sales force.

Disadvantages

Following are the disadvantages of personal selling:

1. Personal selling takes away a large pie of funds from the promotional budget because of the 'individualized' nature of communication. Cost per prospect is, therefore, extremely high. Travelling and dearness allowances are expenditure items in the cost of selling and in some selling situations these are quite high.

2. Even if the company spends huge sum of money for personal selling there is no assurance that the sales will be picked up and profitable accounts will emerge. So, the risk of selling is very high.

3. Recruiting, selecting, training, and development costs for salespeople are of extremely high order. However, even with the requisite expenditures and efforts all salespeople may not turn out to be competent.

4. The risk of turnover of a good salesperson is a serious threat to personal selling. Competitors are always on the prowl to draw away skilled salespeople and once it happens, the organization suffers badly.

5. Good and competent salespeople are difficult to find. For the lack of good presentation and problem-handling ineptitude, an organization fails to impress potential customers despite a well-designed product, reasonable price, and smooth distribution policies.

1.7 ROLE OF PERSONAL SELLING IN MARKETING

Selling has a crucial role in marketing. Selling objectives cannot be excluded from marketing objectives because without selling, profits are unattainable and organizations are unsustainable. A marketing manager in a for-profit organization cannot think of customer satisfaction at the sacrifice of profit. In such a case, it becomes important for the sellers to sell or rather meet with the customers at a personal level to clarify their doubts as well as satisfy them completely. Therefore, personal selling is an important part in a company's marketing plan and marketing strategy.

Selling in today's business environment has assumed a much bigger role than just simply coaxing the customers to join in relationships of exchange and transaction. Selling now starts from understanding the needs and demands of the customers, sensing the degree of competition, knowing the marketing information, and the strengths and weaknesses of the products of the competitors. Sales managers assign tasks of marketing research to salespeople because the latter can better appraise the former about the realities of markets, customers, competitors, and intermediaries. Organizations can gauge the pulse of the market from the salespeople as a source of information.

Personal selling occupies an important position in marketing mix and continually interacts with the other components of the mix to give full justification to marketing. In fact, marketing becomes inconsequential in the absence of personal selling. For instance, the marketing department needs support from the production centre to keep promises to customers for delivering the products at the right time or from the research and development wing that ensure quality assurance to the merchandises. Personal selling assumes a bigger role than just economic value addition. Salespeople provide valuable information of the markets to the business firms to take necessary measures and remain competitive and customer oriented. Both tangible (appearance, packaging, brand name, service supports, etc.) and intangible (warranty, quality, brand image, etc.) features become the discoursing points between the salespeople and the prospects.

Selling gets thrust under competitive pricing strategies. Not only the quoted price but also such price-related benefits like financing facilities, credit terms, allowances, discounts, leasing options, etc. are some of the attractive features of selling. Moreover, the selling cost should be suitably controlled to maintain price at the desired level. Personal selling becomes effective at the transaction phase with customers if advertising or publicity is meaningful to lend potential customers some sort of awareness or recognition of the products or services during pre-sale periods.

Last but not the least, selling finds some strong recommendations from the customers when the products are available at the right time and place. Short, hassle-free, and cost-effective distribution of the product is definitely a buying incentive for the customers. Selling gets the right momentum when the distribution channel helps both the buyers and the organizations to derive benefits from all types of logistical considerations. Channel members are also motivated to deal with such products where commissions or allowances that the organizations offer are profitable to them. Organizations maintain links with the channel members by using salespeople as conduits. In some selling situations, the salespeople of the distributors take vital role in dealing with the customers.

In the following sections, we will read about the traditional and modern selling approaches.

1.8 TRADITIONAL SELLING APPROACH

The history of selling is rooted in the aftermath of industrial revolution when producers themselves sold the products whatever they produced. As the numbers of production units were less, sellers did not require much effort to deliver the merchandises in the hands of the consumers. Output was limited and the producers devoted their efforts to the physical distribution of the products. So, organizations were, basically, production and distribution oriented. But, as competition crept in and many manufacturers started producing identical products, the need for some persuasive effort was felt before getting the consumers to agree to purchase their product.

Earlier, understanding the needs of the consumers was not a necessity and selling was primarily a one-sided communication. Sellers dictated the terms of purchase and the buyers simply accepted them without any objection. After World War II, industrial production gained momentum and spearheaded subtle modifications in traditional selling. This was because the demands for consumer goods shot up unexpectedly and thus, triggered high industrial production. Sellers realized that production planning should start from the consumers' end and the consumer needs should be given due importance in product innovations and designs. At the same time, apart from the demands of the consumers that was becoming the major focus of production volumes, delivering the right products in the right quantity to the right consumers also turned into a crucial factor to confront competition. Consumers emphasized on the ready availability and the low price of the products. Indeed, economic theory suggests that when supply exceeds demand, consumers begin to show buying inertia and an organization undertakes some persuasive promotional efforts to coax the consumers to buy. Some aggressive promotions are also resorted to lure target groups particularly for unsought goods. In fact, sales orientation underscores the need for increasing sales volume without delving into consumer expectations and satisfactions. Here, comes the utility of marketing concept.

Organizations understood that to do effective selling, it should operate within the gambit of marketing. Marketing focuses on the consumer-need assessment, formulate appropriate product, price and promotional policies, and develop suitable distribution networks to reach target consumers. Thus, marketing concepts paved its way to mend loopholes in the selling process. Short-term gains from selling gradually lost its sheen with marketing as an emerging means to build long term relationship with customers along with profit generation. Marketing plans, therefore, featured substantively in the corporate planning process.

Under the traditional selling approach, the situation of overcapacity in production and competitive clout in the market required the salespeople to interact and convince prospective customers with company-instructed canned sales pitch. The objective was to transform as many prospects as possible to being their customers. But during those days, the salespeople did not show any urge to gather detailed information from prospects about their needs or provide them with company and product information. They used to be mere narrators of product features and benefits. These sales conversations were lopsided where salespeople did the bulk of talking treating prospective customers as mere receivers of information. Talk and transaction were the art of business. Traditional salespeople were made to believe in selling a product and not serving the customers. They were need creators rather than need soothers. They, even, took manipulative ways if prospects showed inertia or resistance in buying. Following up after the sale was non-existent. Building professional relationship with customers was ante-culture to the organization.

1.9 MODERN SELLING APPROACH

Connie (2007) noted that modern personal selling got its start during the first part of the twentieth century. Selling has experienced a major turnaround in conceptualization and application particularly in recent times. Economy, today, is characterized by global marketing environment, sizzling competition among market players, both domestic and multinational, changing tastes and preferences of customers by the grace of media explosion and deregulation of economic barriers of nations. 'Customer focus' has become the nerve centre of present day selling. Understanding customer needs, translating them to offers, assisting customers in acquiring these offers, and putting a major thrust on post-sell alliance with customers are the seeds of win-win selling for both—sellers and buyers. Modern selling basically hinges on serving the customers with the best possible solutions of their purchasing problems in a much efficient manner than its competitors. In fact, it is seen that, today customer problems find a route of redress by getting optimal benefits from the product/service if not maximum, at a minimum of their sacrifice including the cost.

Today's customers are far more informative and discerning unlike the ones in earlier years. Their ability to contrast and compare identical or similar products of different companies cannot be underestimated. Therefore, salespeople of the day should have an in-depth knowledge and the expertise to persuade customers to ascent their offers. Modern selling distinguishes the customers of the same product and focuses on individual transaction approach rather than on approach for all customers. So, *customerization*, and not customization, is the benchmark of modern selling. It gives total attention to individual requirement of the customer, need fulfilment, commitment to serve in future because holding a customer for an infinite time period is the core of the success in selling. Also, building customer loyalty is central to establish long-term and never ending relationship with customers.

Today, competition among organizations is not based on core or tangible features but on augmented or peripheral benefits. The more a company can differentiate its products on augmented features, the more attractive will be its offer and the possibility of customer acquisition. For example, usually some companies marketing refrigerators do not focus on providing any different cooling solutions, other than simply providing frost free facility, but focus more on presenting their products in different sizes and colours. This acts as the USP of the product. Product differentiation followed by most organizations is strategically made based on the warranty on the component parts, follow up after-sales, etc. For machines, helping the customer in installation, educating the customer, and adaptation may give an edge to the company in reaching its sales goals. Johnson et al. (1994) termed it as value-added selling. It implies provisioning of customer services that exceeds the expectations of the customers.

Now, telephonic selling, teleshopping, web-based selling, teleconferencing with customers are some of the major changeovers in contemporary selling. Information technology has come to fore to take a lead role in customer interaction management (CIM). Use of electronic data interchange (EDI) system has made the access of interacting with customers easier and quicker. Automated order placing and processing replenishment, inventory management, sales forecasting, etc. are being done at ease. Doubts and uncertainties of customers are sorted through customer information systems. Customer complaints are easily addressed through SAP solutions or e-CRM (Electronic Customer Relationship Management) system.

To support these discussions, refer to Exhibit 1.1.

Exhibit 1.1   Technology leads company to success

Amazon.com Inc.

Amazon.com Inc. is a multinational electronic commerce company, which is also one of the largest online retailers in America. It started as an online bookstore, but today, because of its success it has diversified into selling CDs, DVDs, computer software, video games, kitchen tools, and many more.

Amazon has established separate websites in Canada, the United Kingdom, Germany, France, Japan, and China and also provides international shipping to certain countries for some of its products.

Bharti Airtel

Similarly, *Bharti Airtel,* India's largest cellular service provider faced dropping average revenue per user (ARPU). It needed to find a solution to come out of this mess. Bharti Airtel's SMART SOA™ solution with IBM WebSphere technologies enabled the company to outsource its IT to IBM and other strategic partners to integrate its systems in order to automate routine transactions and hone customer service. This resulted in its ability to provide flawless service to 110 million customers at low margins. The employee productivity improved using business activity monitoring real-time responses to customer requests as well.

Sources: http:en.wikipedia.org/wiki/Amazon.com, accessed on 23 August 2010; http://www-01.ibm. com/software/success/cssdb.nsf/CS/SJHA- 83ZKF6?OpenDocument&Site=wsportal&cty=en_us, accessed on 23 August 2010.

Modern selling directs salespeople to act as consultants, problem solvers, partners, and collaborators to customers. Customers are treated as insiders of the business today. Often the advice of loyal customers for the development of marketing mix and associated services are sought for the improvement in the product quality or service characteristics or customer relationship.

1.10 TYPES OF SELLING

The type of selling varies across customers, situations, and the nature of commodity dealt in, i.e., product or service, and the resources and objectives of the company. When customers are end users of the products, the products are sold through retail markets. For industrial products, the salespeople of a company or distributors are appointed to deal with customers. These customers may be direct consumers, retailers or agents.

Again, selling situations might also vary according to the involvement of the customers with the products. For high involvement buying situations where products are high on unit value and technically complex, e.g., electronic equipments, computing machines, etc. generally a company does business with customers engaging technically qualified salespeople. For low involvement situations, a company appoints dealers or retailers who are entrusted in reselling the products based on commissions or profit margins. For mass consumption items, selling through marketing intermediaries is a common place. For shopping goods, like fashion shoes or designer shirts, selling through independent or franchised retailers are effective.

In situations, where purchase is deliberative in character and potential customers need enough product information, specification compliance, and the need to consider selling terms and conditions; direct selling through company hired salespeople or experienced distributors are given the responsibility to handle the customers. Again, selling a product is different from selling a service. But one common feature of both product and service is saleability. Both should be of value to the customers and both should satisfy customer demands. Besides, service has some specific characteristics like intangibility, inseparability, variability, and non-storability. So, services cannot be seen, touched or smelt but can be felt and consumed.

Ownership of service can never be transferred from service provider to customers. It has a high degree of heterogeneity and its variability is more complex than products. Services cannot be stored or warehoused unlike products. Most importantly, service creation and its utilization take place simultaneously. Finally, a company's financial strength, manpower, relationship with intermediaries, desire for market control and legal compulsions affect the type of selling emphatically. Based on the discussion so far, selling can be categorized into the following types:

(a) Industrial selling
(b) Service selling
(c) Retail selling

1.10.1 Industrial Selling

Under industrial selling, marketing transactions take place between at least two companies, both of which seek to generate favours from the business. That is why industrial selling is also termed as business-to-business selling. Industrial selling is more complex and time consuming because a sales-person has to negotiate with a number of individuals representing the buying organization, particularly in large firms. Needless to mention, goods that are dealt in this selling are industrial in nature.

In large industrial units, buying decision may not be entrusted with a single individual but with a number of individuals who take the buying decision jointly. But in some cases, each of them may want to satisfy their personalized needs. For example, a purchase manager of a firm may be more interested in price, distribution scheme, credit terms, etc. as compared to the manufacturer or the research and development manager who would focus more on the quality of the product. The production manager veers on the uninterrupted supply of the product. So, when these three constitute the decision making body of the firm for buying, a salesperson often faces difficulty to satisfy all the three parties. Price may not be an important criteria in industrial buying, rather vendor reliability, quality of the product, periods of warranty, and after-sales service form the major criteria in industrial buying. For installations, importance is given to lifecycle costing constituting purchase cost, start up cost, and post-purchase cost. (Forbis and Mehta 1981) Moreover, buying strategies of the firm influence the selling mechanisms of the industrial firms. Morris (1992) illustrated three types of buying strategies, namely speculative buying, forward buying, and hand to mouth buying. In *speculative buying*, an organization purchases quantities of goods in excess of its projected or foreseeable requirements. *Forward buying* involves purchasing in excess an amount of material of what is currently required but not beyond anticipated future requirements. Under *hand-to-mouth buying*, a buyer purchases a product or service in quantities that would just satisfy their immediate operating requirements. Different buying strategies demand different logistical operations and sellers must accommodate effectively and efficiently to inventory policies, material handling, production scheduling, and support services of the customers to ensure continuity of business.

Both central and state government departments, government undertakings and agencies (e.g., railway, telecommunication department, etc.) are bulk purchasers of industrial goods where the scope of industrial selling is enormous. But, procedural complexity of buying in government firms is immense and involves huge formalities. For example, a seller has to be registered with the government firms before it can take part in the selling process. Tendering is a popular method of buying from government firms. Tendering is the usual process where the government unit invites registered sellers to submit quotations where it applies bidding process and supplies the desired product to the party who quotes the lowest price of a particular commodity.

Institutional buying is a special category of industrial buying. Public and private institutions such as colleges, universities, hospitals, prisons, etc. deemed as institutional customers have their own buying policies. An industrial salesperson should rigidly follow the selling guidelines as determined by the buying procedures of these firms to be effective in institutional selling. One common problem of industrial selling is that often the salesperson tends to involve in overselling to the buying organization. They overpromise the customer about product qualities, options for life which are often difficult for these selling firms to attain.

1.10.2 Service Selling

Service selling has some distinctive properties vis-à-vis product selling. One major characteristic feature of service selling is that of service creation, where selling takes place simultaneously. In product selling these two are separate incidents. A doctor or a lawyer advices and suggests remedies to their clients simultaneously. An insurance agent selling insurance products to a customer persuades him to purchase and only then sells it. This is because service is more of an activity or performance designed to evolve and solve specific problems of customers.

Selling service encompasses a number of features and customer satisfaction depends on getting the expected results in performance of all these features. For instance, a transport company can satisfy a customer only by packaging, labelling, delivering, risk taking, insuring, and offering various logistical services. Service selling involves a lot of variability and needs careful manoeuvring of each selling operation. A courier firm provides multiple services like dispatching letters, money orders, delivering parcels, managing cargo operations, etc.

Colleges, universities, hospitals, insurance companies, tourism companies, hotels, etc. are major service organizations. Each renders specific type of service and the selling mechanism for each is unique. Increase in competition in this sector has increased the need for differentiation in service attributes and quality improvements to win and hold customers for a longer time. As service cannot be displayed or demonstrated, need for promotion before selling is very crucial. However, once a set of satisfied customers is created, word of mouth communication takes a lead role in spreading the information of a service to potential customers. Excellent customer relationship also plays a catalytic role in ingraining a sense of trust amongst present customers. Experiences and credentials of service providers encourage potential customers to buy services and ease selling efforts.

Today, the service sector has achieved a thrust in the economy as it has contributed much more to the national income and employment of our country than a product sector. In this respect, service selling has gained importance because of a large customer base and competitive clout. Here, customer satisfaction is not only determined by service quality or functionalities but also by human centric or emotional value addition in selling and servicing.

Indeed, service quality is judged both by the technicalities of service and human factors in relation to selling. For example, a patient in a hospital expects reliability in service, assurance from doctors and nurses, personal care, cleanliness of environment, hygienic ambience in addition to quality treatment. Selling a satisfying health care service has a long drawn impact on the image of the organization. In insurance or tourism selling, creating awareness and interest among potential buyers and converting them to customers depend a lot on the communication skill, conceptual clarity, and the ability of the seller to infuse conviction among the customers. At the same time, monitoring service quality and measuring service satisfaction should be a continuous process also.

1.10.3 Retail Selling

Retail selling, popularly known as retailing, involves activities both in selling goods as well as services. Thus, it aims to deliver the finished goods to the consumers for personal or business use. Retailing is the last stage of distribution. It facilitates the adoption process of products/services by consumers and aids in creating value-addition to the merchandise to make it more attractive and acceptable to the consumers.

Retail selling may take the form of store retailing or non-store retailing. In store retailing, selling takes place from a physical location in a market whereas non-store retailing is based on door-to-door selling, mail order selling, telephonic selling or selling through the Internet. Some of the common services attached to retail selling involve procuring needed items, arranging transportation, storing and assorting the goods, grading and packaging, labelling, risk taking, selling, servicing, financing, complaints, and returns handling. Retail selling includes the total bundle of benefits offered to consumers in terms of locational advantage of the store, parking facilities, retail ambience, in stock position, shelf spacing given to brands, product availability, product quality, imparting adequate information to consumers, product customization, logistics support to customers, building customer relationship, and after-sales service where needed.

Direct selling is a kind of non-store retailing. It is an interactive system of selling that uses one or more ways to arouse the demands and encourage the customers to contact sellers to buy. These ways vary from marketing through sending catalogues or sales letters, flyers, foldouts, etc. to prospective buyers, soliciting the prospective customers to buy products or services contacting them over the phone or subsequent face-to-face interaction, web conferencing, hawking the product on radio or television (teleshopping), web-based selling, or multi-level marketing or network marketing or multi-tiered marketing where selling of products depend on the people in the network.

1.11   SALES AS A PROFESSION

Sales, as a profession, has shown immense potential to attract aspiring youth. Selling has always been a challenging assignment because of the intricacies of market dynamics and behavioural complexities of buyers. Moreover, competition in today's competitive landscape is so intense that to win a customer is very difficult. Therefore, vagaries of marketplace demand salespeople to be creative, assertive, resilient, and persevering to consolidate their positions in highly vibrant, slippery, and tenacious sales profession.

Kurtz and Boone (2009) cited that sales professionalism is defined as a customer-oriented approach that employs truthful, non-manipulative activities to satisfy long-term needs of both the customer and the selling firm. Selling constitutes a well-organized and defined body of knowledge and principles on the basis of which selling decisions are made. Rookie salespersons after selection undergo rigorous training to acquire knowledge and insights for practical applications in real life situations. But, natural sales talents and skills are important for any person to join sales. Effective training can further sharpen the ability and competence of those born to be good salesperson.

Forceful acceptance of selling as a profession can frustrate one's career growth. On the other hand, if a person is interested in it, selling can provide a great opportunity for personal development. It also endows salespeople to earn a decent living. Of course, performance is a sole criterion to endorse such growth. High sales performance is linked to attractive financial rewards, personal satisfaction, personal affiliation, upward career mobility, social status, and recognition.

Selling, today, is a multifarious job. A lot of diversity shapes modern selling process. In fact, the interdependence between selling and marketing functions coalesce to modify the job profiles of a salesperson. Salespeople, apart from selling the product, also undertake marketing research, cultivate the strengths and weaknesses of the products of the competitors, help in product development, and engage in public relations at present.

Graduates from different academic disciplines are drawn to the job of selling because they find ample opportunity to earn money on salary, commissions, bonuses, and other financial and non-financial benefits. Kerin et al. (2007) viewed that a selling career offers benefits that is hard to achieve in any other field. The reasons are as follows:

(a) The opportunity for rapid advancement into management, new territories, and accounts

(b) The potential for extremely attractive compensation

(c) The development of personal satisfaction, feelings of accomplishments, and increased self-confidence

(d) The independence that the salespeople have including complete control over the time and activities

Systematic and well-designed training programmes help in creating a base of professionalism. Salespeople acquire knowledge on products, company, competing firms, and marketing environment. They gather preliminary ideas about customers, ways of dealing with customers, handling selling aids like samples, brochures, test reports, previous successful case histories of the company, and techniques of closing the sales. Since, salespeople are the mouthpiece of the organizations, their success or failure directly affects the organizations. Hence, it is vital for them to learn how to attract customers, how to establish a large customer base, and retain them for long with strong customer relationship. Again, the zeal of learning, power to control emotions in case of defeat, abounding confidence, foresight to predict future changes, persistence in jobs, achievement motivation are the other essential characteristics required in a professional salesperson. From the clients' sides, warmth, cooperation, empathy, concern for the problems of the customers, rapport, and a sense of ethics of salespersons are deserving qualities. Moreover, loyalty and a sense of belongingness to the firm act as a great motivator too.

Selling is a profession that can get sincere salespeople to the pinnacle of their career graphs. In fact, the career progression of a salesperson ultimately merges with company's growth and stability. The amount of earnings for a performing salesperson knows no income ceilings. So, selling is fun for achievers and doomsday for defeatists.

1.12   ETHICS IN SELLING

Ethics are the building blocks of a business that are based on moral principles and values. It lends honesty and transparency in dealings between buyers and sellers. A buyer-seller dyad is not only governed by economic relationships but also by social institutions, legal procedures, and ethical principles. Responsible organizations feel it is imperative for them to cater to the customers with the 'right' combinations of marketing mix. The word 'right' should have the same or different meaning to different customer groupings. Right implies the actual product which the consumer demands, the right price which the customer expects, the availability and accessibility to the product should be as the consumer wants, and the right information that the customer needs.

A customer may have certain queries about the advantages and disadvantages of the product or the money that they are paying which must equate with the value of the particular product. It is important to keep in mind that the sacrifice(s) a customer concedes should be paid back by optimal product benefits both in quality and/or quantity. A customer calls for total commitment from the seller in ethical and legal terms to protect his interests with no space for aberration. Ethics in business draws out both parties to strike a healthy and congenial deal free from all sorts of doubts and uncertainties. Thus, ethics consolidates the relationship between the buyer and seller on the plank of truth and trustworthiness.

Ethical principles are somewhat different from legal codes. Ethics imply accomplishment of task with moral justification where an organization's virtues and integrity take the lead role to persuade customers whereas legal codes demand compliance to business laws and social standards constituted by the government of a nation.

The following are some of the unethical practices followed by organizations:

(a) Delivering inferior quality product that does not commensurate with the price paid

(b) Variation between promised and actual specification levels of the product

(c) Price discrimination amongst buyers

(d) Showing wrong test reports and promoting false stories of product success to certify product quality

(e) Use of unsafe packaging materials

(f) Providing wrong information on the labels of the product

(g) Condemning competitors harshly before customers wilfully and wrongly

(h) Failing to supply the product at right time and place without any prior intimation

(i) Disregarding the complaints received from customers on earlier supply of products

Any deliberate wrong doing with an aim to garner myopic interests is unethical for a selling organization. Similarly, unscrupulous policy decisions to dupe innocent customers in the hands of the salespeople definitely stigmatize the ethical disciplines. Salespeople should be advised to furnish a complete description of the product to the prospective customers. Concealing any fact on product information (e.g., life, safety standards, handling difficulties, etc.) or price components (e.g., value added tax, service tax, sales tax, etc.) warranty guidelines (e.g., specific mention of warranty of component parts, policy after the expiry of warranty period, etc.), replacement policy in case of defects, financing facilities culminates in unethical business dealing and may subject to legal intervention if customers desire. Quality of the product supplied to the customer not consistent with the price is condemnable.

Again, if the actual specifications of the product do not correspond with the agreed specifications decided at the time of the pre-sale contract, the customer cannot get the actual performance. This is a major move away from ethical standards. Some sellers are also accused of passing on redundant selling costs or promotional costs or packaging costs unreasonably to customers causing a high mark up at the price level. This is also a variation from ethical norms.

Healthy business culture can keep unethical practices at bay. Salespersons should drill themselves to inherit the marketing culture that operates within the boundary of ethical and legal limits. Business culture is a set of core values, ideas, and attitudes that an organization inculcates and shares among its members in the organization. An organization culture tutors employees to learn ethics and value systems that involve total commitment to the organization and total protection of the interests of the customers.

Salespeople as boundary spanners of the organization take up a huge responsibility to spread the embedded culture and inoculate a sense of trust and confidence in the customers. One primary condition of unblemished culture is to always disseminate the right information and respond to all the queries of customers with actual information. False or misuse of business culture spoils the relationship with customers and erode the sanctity of the organization. An organization as a result loses its credibility to the customer's fraternity. For example, salespeople are often instructed to go overboard to engage in clandestine collection of trade secrets or corporate information of competitors. If the malpractice of the firm is publicly exposed, the organization may suffer from image problem. Deceptive promotion making tall and exaggerated claims about product features, showing forged documents to customers, etc. ominously violates the ethical and social principles.

Consumers have every right to get complete information about products or services. Salespeople are also bound to provide specific business related information to customers regardless of outcome. This is known as *moral idealism*. It is a philosophy, which should be followed by organizations, of speaking the truth in the interest of customers even if a particular business is threatened. Indeed, submission of the correct message can help an organization to build its image on the pedestal of trust and reliability.

The relationship between the costs and benefits to the customers is a major determinant of the buyer and seller relationship. This principle is known as *utilitarianism*. It means 'the greatest good for the greatest number' If the benefits exceed, the cost of the behaviour is ethical otherwise is unethical. Moreover, consumers should be safeguarded from all forms of hazards or side effects of the product. Today, consumer protection laws and acts are being practiced widely to protect consumers from illegal business dealings. In fact, since 1960s, consumer movement and attention to get free and fair business was started to protect them from unethical business activities. In March 1962, US President John F. Kennedy took up the consumer protection and interest programme that emphasized upon:

Right to safety To safeguard consumers from the hazards and side effects of products that may endanger them.

Right to be informed To protect consumers against fraudulent, deceitful or grossly misleading information, advertising, labelling or other malpractices.

Right to choose To assure access to a variety of products and services at competitive prices. It further includes that the market offer for consideration will be fairly priced and of satisfactory quality.

Right to be heard To assure full and sympathetic consideration in the formulation of government policy and to provide fair and expeditious treatment in the administrative tribunals in the interest of the consumers.

At present, consumerism has gained momentum to dissociate manipulative businessmen from all illegal marketing practices. This is because today's consumers are more literate and judgemental unlike in the previous years. This is further bolstered by their rising income level, purchasing power, and influence of the media. They are more aware of legal implications of infringement of consumer rights.

SUMMARY

Personal selling is basically a two-way communication process, mostly in a face-to-face situation between buyers and sellers. It is an act of exchange from which both buyers and sellers derive their benefits. It is one of the major components of the promotion mix. It is a more direct, immediate, and personalized form of communication that lends an edge over the effectiveness of other forms of communication, such as advertising, sales promotion, and publicity. Personal selling involves identifying prospective customers, understanding their needs, communicating with them, carrying out the transaction, following up with after-sales service, and taking care of the customers' post-transaction problems.

Salesmanship is the nerve centre of personal selling. Salesmanship is the ability of the salesperson to persuade prospective buyers to buy the product(s) or service(s) of a company. Personal selling aims at building awareness, creating interest by persuasive communication, and kindling intent to buy among prospective buyers. It also helps in establishing a healthy relationship with customers and building a positive company or product image in the society. Effective selling precedes sound knowledge of the company, product/service, competition and selling process. It also requires selling skills and sales motivation of the salespeople.

The traditional approach of selling relied more on selling rather than serving customers. It focused more on generating sales volume rather than customer satisfaction. The modern approach, on the other hand, assumes a more collaborative relationship with the customers. Here, salespeople are projected more as problem solvers and consultants to the buyers. Building a career in selling is quite a commonplace among young people. Selling must follow ethical discipline and moral code of conduct.

KEY TERMS

Communication Mix/Promotion Mix   It is a blend of personal and non-personal promotional tools that the company constitutes to achieve promotional objectives.

Modern Sales Approach   This type of selling which is being followed today involves, serving customers with the best possible solutions for their marketing problems in a more efficient manner than the competitors.

Personal Selling   It is a process that involves interaction between a buyer and a seller where a product or a service is exchanged in return for a price or its equivalent kind.

Salesmanship   This is the ability of the salesperson to motivate and convince a prospective buyer to purchase the goods or services of a company.

Traditional Sales Approach   This was the kind of selling which was mainly in vogue before World War II, where a few sellers dictated the terms of purchase and the consumers had to accept it.

CONCEPT REVIEW QUESTIONS

1. Define personal selling. Under what circumstances personal selling should be recommended?
2. How does personal selling fit within the marketing mix of the firm?
3. How does personal selling differ from other modes of communication?
4. What is the role of salesmanship in personal selling?
5. Explain the merits and demerits of personal selling.
6. What are the essentials of personal selling?
7. Distinguish between the traditional and modern approaches of selling.

8. Selling as profession has come of age. Discuss.
9. Ethics is an indispensable part of sustainable selling. Critically review.

CRITICAL THINKING QUESTION

Choosing a career in selling is getting more challenging today. The company also understands that transaction-based selling has gradually lost its gloss and instead, relationship selling, consultative selling, and team selling have come on centre stage. A company still holding the traditional path finds the task more difficult to cope with competition.

1. Trace out the evolutionary progression of selling since its inception till date.
2. How has selling become an interesting career option for youths and how does a company fit in young salespeople in the moulds of modern selling techniques?

PROJECT ASSIGNMENTS

1. Go online and research a multinational firm engaged in selling food and beverage products through intermediaries to find the role of personal selling for its various brands. Then, visit a few retail store handling such products and review the role interacting with retail salespeople. Prepare a note on it combining information from two different sources.
2. Meet a sales executive of an FMCG firm and enquire about the application of advertising and personal selling by means of questionnaire. Review how two forms of communication complement each other to reach target customers.

REFERENCES

Belch, E.G. and A.M. Belch (2006), *Advertising and Promotion: An Integrated Marketing Communications Perspective*, 6th ed., Tata McGraw-Hill Publishing Company Limited, New Delhi.

Connie, D. (2007), 'Marketing', http://conniegold typepad.com/mkt_by_connie_d/2007/01/history_of_pers.html, accessed on 10 March 2009.

Evans, J.R. and B. Berman (1988), *Principles of Marketing*, 2nd ed., Macmillan Publishing Company, New York.

Forbis, L.J. and T.N. Mehta (1981), 'Value-based Strategies for Industrial Products', *Business Horizons*, May–June, pp. 32–42.

Johnson, M.J., L.D. Kurtz, and E.E. Scheuing (1994), *Sales Management—Concepts, Practices and Cases*, 2nd ed., McGraw-Hill Inc., New York, Toronto.

Kerin, A.R., S.W. Hartley, E.N. Berkowitz, and W. Rudelius (2007), *Marketing*, 8th ed., Tata McGraw-Hill Publishing Company Limited, New Delhi.

Kotler, P. (1988), *Marketing Management: Analysis, Planning, Implementation and Control,* Prentice-Hall, Englewood Cliffs, New Jersey.

Kotler, P. and G. Armstrong (2006), *Principles of Marketing*, 11th ed., Prentice-Hall of India Private Limited, New Delhi.

Kurtz, D.L. and L.E. Boone (2006), *Principles of Marketing*, 12th ed., South-Western Cengage Learning, Australia, United States.

Morris, M.H. (1992), *Industrial and Organizational Marketing*, 2nd ed., Maxwell Macmillan International, New York.

Still, R.R., E.W. Cundiff, and N.A.P. Govoni (1994), *Sales Management: Decisions, Strategies and Cases*, 5th ed., Prentice-Hall of India Private Limited, New Delhi.

CASE STUDIES

1. Reebok

Reebok, the second largest athletic shoe manufacturer, focuses on three crucial aspects of selling:

(a) Building trust between the salesperson and the retailer
(b) Sharing enough information with retailers about product varieties, features, and marketing objectives
(c) Supporting the retailers with promotional aids, commissions, shelf displays, and other promotional kits

In fact, Reebok has an illustrious sporting goods line and concentrates its resources on getting its footwear and sporting goods distributed through athletic footwear speciality stores, other departmental stores, and large sporting goods stores. The company's good relation with the retailers has been evident from the statement of the employee of MVP sports, one of Reebok's major retailers. An excerpt of his comment is 'Reebok is the only company that comes in on a regular basis and gives us information. Reebok comes in every month to update us on new information on products. They tell us about technology, so we can tell the customers'.

Reebok's ultimate goal is to reach to a large customer base by using retailers as partners. To achieve this, Reebok organizes selling in teams consisting of account representatives, who do the actual selling to the retailers and the vector representatives, who spend their time in the store training the store's salespeople and providing feedbacks to the account managers. The selling teams are organized geographically so that the salespeople live and work in the same area. On an average, the Reebok salespeople spend seventy per cent of their time in preparing for a sales call and thirty per cent on actual selling. Reebok has also provided laptops to its salespeople to check inventories in the warehouses, procure store orders in time with an objective to expedite order preparation and implementation.

Discussion Questions

1. How does Reebok integrate distribution and promotional policies to create and maintain a satisfied customer base?
2. How has Reebok prepared its salespeople to utilize personal selling for a bigger purpose of business development?

(*Source*: Kerin et al. 2007)

2. Selling Strategy at ABC Inc.

ABC Inc., which is located in Glasgow, is a manufacturer of electrical components for automobiles and has the reputation of manufacturing high quality products. Car manufacturers are the major accounts, its sales force calls upon. But, recent economic meltdown has made a serious dent in the automobile industry and most of the car manufacturers have slowed down the pace of their production and opted for quick disposal of cars from the inventories. So, more attention is being given to the clearance of stored vehicles rather than on further production. Therefore, sales of the ABC Inc. have tumbled down automatically to quite a short of target in the 2008–09 financial year.

The company has a blend of new and senior sales personnel who have created an effective sales network with quite a few automobile companies. The company, however, is following a dual distribution network:

(a) Reaching large customers through the sales team
(b) Catering to medium and small customers consisting of automobile dealers, service centres, maintenance firms, etc. through territorial distributors

Surprisingly, response at channel (b) level is more impressive as compared to channel (a) after the recent recession hit.

At this point of time, when automobile manufacturers are busy in offloading their warehouses, the dealers and service firms have chosen friendly incentive schemes for customer such as easy financing, flexible annual maintenance contracts, free automobile check up programmes to induce present and prospective customers not to lose hearts and go for buying with added interest and zeal. So, after scrutinizing the situation, the company has intensified its selling effort to build more rapport with dealers and service firms. Sales personnel have also been instructed to pay more attention to develop an extended distribution network with an intensive liaison with car dealers and service firms. The principal objective is not to hurt the sales growth drastically but to keep the momentum going until the situation is reversed.

Discussion Questions

1. Comment on the selling strategy of ABC Inc. under crisis situation to combat recession.
2. Explain the role of personal selling in building a renewed distribution network and relational proximity with car dealers and service firms.

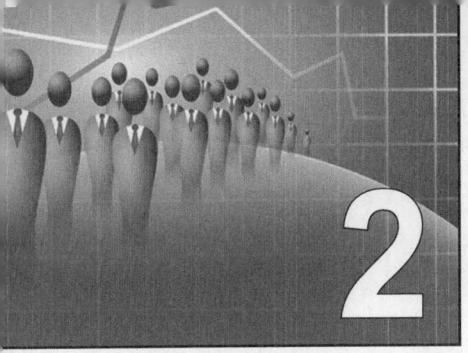

2 Personal Selling—
Approaches and Strategies

Today, selling is regarded as an academic discipline. Like any other theoretical discipline, this too follows certain concepts, principles, theories, and approaches. Selling, being an important adjunct of business, often lends theoretical inputs and rationales to make it more productive and effective. So, while we search for new and innovative applications of selling, we should also develop its academic treasures.

2.1 SELLING APPROACHES—A THEORETICAL PERSPECTIVE

Since the industrial age, selling has been regarded as the most potent promotional tool to entice the target customers to buy products and services. Whichever approach has been evolved, they all speak about creating awareness for the customers, generating interests, and enhancing the buying intentions as the main objectives of personal selling.

With the passage of time, increase in competition, and customer demand, the approaches have taken recourse to customer relationship, partnership, collaboration, etc. to justify the sustainable issues in selling. Keeping this in mind, an attempt has been made to discuss the various approaches to illustrate the journey of selling on theoretical routes which also gives us a brief understanding of the evolutionary transition of selling practices.

Following are the approaches of selling that are discussed in this regard:

(a) AIDAS approach
(b) Right set of circumstances approach
(c) Buying formula approach
(d) Behavioural equation approach
(e) Need satisfaction approach

(f) Consultative approach

(g) Customer relationship-based approach

(h) Problem-solving approach

(i) Team selling approach

In the following paragraphs, we will discuss these approaches in detail.

2.1.1 AIDAS Approach

AIDAS (attention, interest, desire, action, satisfaction), a popular acronym in the lexicon of selling, stands for the universal concept of selling and for guidelines for the sales training programme since the late 1950s. It is prescribed as an updated version of AIDA (attention, interest, desire, action) which was introduced in the 1920s as a communication model to depict the structure of the selling process (Strong 1925). AIDA, in fact, was coined from the term AIDR (attention, interest, desire, resolve), a selling formula sequence that evinced from the works of Arthur Sheldon, published in 1902. Figure 2.1 shows the schematic flow of AIDAS approach.

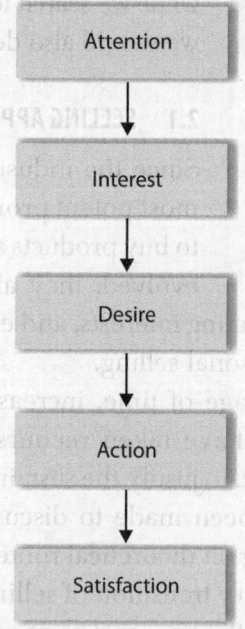

Figure 2.1 AIDAS approach

AIDAS theory of selling suggests that a prospective buyer passes through five mental stages of attention, interest, desire, action, and satisfaction. These are arranged sequentially to complete the buying process. It, thus, directs the selling process to design as well as implement the communication programmes that are consistent with the needs of each mental stage. A customer demands an effort from the salesperson to kindle an urge in the former for learning and understanding the features and attributes of the products or services. A salesperson is supposed to generate the right cognition and knowledge in customers that can lead them to traverse through the successive stages in a stepwise manner. Therefore, AIDAS selling is also known as formula-selling approach.

Following are the five mental stages of AIDAS:

Attention

Getting the customer's attention fruitfully sets the ball rolling automatically along the mental hierarchy, which is evident from the subsequent reactions of the customers. In fact, this leads to the customers wanting to know more about the products or services and buying privileges. Therefore, it is said that the initial session with the prospects is vital for salespeople as that is the stage where the customers can be motivated and an enthusiasm can be built towards selling. The entire discourse is expected to be adroitly managed by the salespeople with conversational skill, openness, assertiveness, risk-taking propensity, rapport-building ability coupled with physical appearance and mannerism. Then this takes a positive turn to facilitate continuity of discussion with the fullest cooperation and support from the prospects.

The aim of the salespeople is not merely to project the tangible and the intangible features of the products/services but also to emphasize on their abilities to solve problems of the prospects, as well as, render adequate benefits to them.

Interest

The second mental stage is to get the prospect interested to know more about the sales offer. It is believed that if the stage of attention is going successfully, then interest building is spontaneous. Sometimes, the prospect may overtly express interest to ease the job of the salesperson. In other cases, a covert attitude of the prospect needs to be understood from non-verbal cues and body language. Demonstration of the product by handing a sample of product or showing illustrations, pictures, flipcharts or videos can also enhance the degree of interest amongst prospective buyers, and intensify their eagerness and earnestness for the offer.

Desire

The prospect then reaches the third stage of mental process, i.e., desire. This is a step closer to the buying decision. Gaining interest and instilling a desire should be sequenced intelligently by the salesperson. This can be achieved by handling objections and enquiries of the prospects and by predicting more about the conviction in their minds.

Action

Salespeople should clearly manifest all the selling points to remove even miniscule doubts that the prospects might have and reply to all questions with confidence. A complete control over the sales presentation incites the prospects to take the buying decision. This leads to the fourth stage of mental buying, which is satisfaction.

Satisfaction

A customer's first time acceptance of a product is no assurance of a second or successive buying. Indeed, customer satisfaction of the product or service also sets the tone of opportunities of future buying or selling for the same organization. Often, a psychological strain of having taken a wrong or a right decision puts the customer into an anxiety syndrome known as cognitive dissonance. This dichotomy of the customer should be delicately warded off by the salespeople so that no sense of negativity may creep in the minds of the customers. A customer's satisfaction of a product or service depends on the match between the actual and the expected performance. If the expected level of performance is not met by the product, the customer is dissatisfied. In contrast, if the actual performance exceeds the expected level, the salesperson gets a delighted customer.

2.1.2 Right Set of Circumstances Approach

The right set of circumstances approach is also known as the situation-response theory. According to this theory, the circumstances prevailing in a given situation leads a prospect to behave in a particular way. This means that a situation is the psychological driver which evokes a response (positive or negative) from the customer. The theory suggests that a persuasive-selling situation should be created by salespeople to influence the prospects in their favour.

Creating and managing a situation is the building block of this theory. Some prominent internal and external factors or stimuli may act as facilitators to evolve a selling situation. Figure 2.2 exhibits a schematic overview of the theory. Both internal and external factors create circumstances that influence the customers to take a buying decision. A buying decision directs buying behaviour. Most salespeople are able to exchange information on external factors quite easily but find it difficult to highlight information on internal factors. As a result, a responsive sales situation does not emerge.

It also propounds that all factors are not equally persuasive and they contribute differently in stimulating customers. Salespeople should be trained to learn the efficacies of various factors to manage the selling situations and treat them in the selling process accordingly. An experienced and skilled salesperson does not find it difficult to create the right circumstances favourable to the prospects in taking a buying decision. This is a seller-oriented theory because the success of selling depends entirely on the deft handling of circumstances by the salespeople.

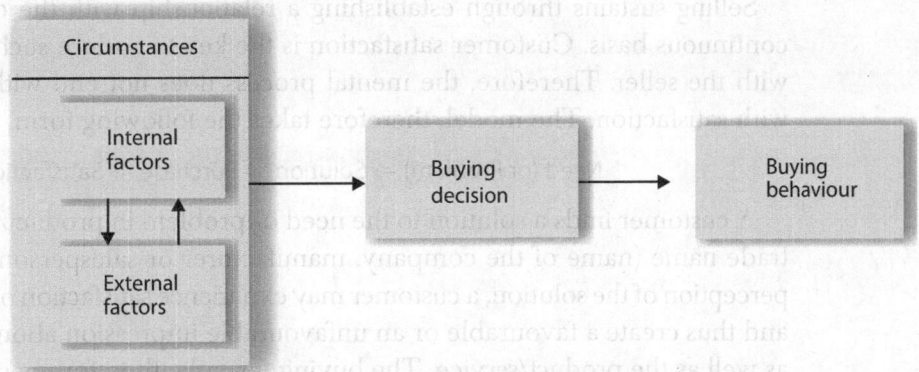

Figure 2.2 Right set of circumstances approach

Assume a situation where a company allows one of its salesperson to invite a major prospect for dinner being organized in a banquet hall of a five-star hotel. The external factors affecting the buying decision include the salesperson himself, the invitation for dinner as well as the ambience of the dinner hall. All these factors are quite conducive to spearhead a nice sales conversation between the prospect and the salesperson. The internal factors are the acceptance of the invitation, whether the customer is accompanied by the salesperson to go to the hotel or take dinner or is interested to take part in the sales conversation during dinner.

Both the internal and the external factors are important in building the right sales situation. But there are a few problems that are quite common in these situations.

First, the external factors may not create the right circumstances, if the internal factors are under-emphasized.

Second, the internal factors are very difficult to identify in many selling situations.

Third, all factors are not equally important. Salespeople should know which factors are to be given major thrust and which ones moderate or minor.

Fourth, managing and controlling the sales situation needs subtle handling by the salespeople, otherwise a good sales opportunity may be lost.

2.1.3 Buying Formula Approach

The buying formula theory suggests that the prospective buyers take initiative to fructify a buying–selling intercourse. The needs or problems of the buyers are the starting points of this theory where the salespeople can assist them in finding suitable solutions to their problems. The second assumption is that the the buyer passes through stages that are the step-by-step occurrences of mental events to finally reach the buying decision. A generalized model of the approach is represented below:

Need (or Problem) → Solution → Purchase

Selling sustains through establishing a relationship with the customers on a continuous basis. Customer satisfaction is the key to endure such a relationship with the seller. Therefore, the mental process does not end with purchase but with satisfaction. The model, therefore takes the following form,

Need (or Problem) → Solution → Purchase → Satisfaction

A customer finds a solution to the need or problem in product/service and/or trade name (name of the company, manufacturer or salesperson). Again, upon perception of the solution, a customer may experience satisfaction or dissatisfaction and thus create a favourable or an unfavourable impression about the company as well as the product/service. The buying formula, therefore becomes,

Need or (Problem) → Product Service/ and/or Trade Name → Purchase → Satisfaction

Both the product or service and the trade name must be adequate for the prospective buyer to take or rather confirm their decision. The feeling of anticipated satisfaction on the adequacy or inadequacy of the product or service and/or trade name (name of the supplier) to solve their problem guides the prospect's buying behaviour. Adequacy can be viewed as a matter of liking or disliking.

In many situations, adequacy ensures a pleasant feeling but it is not always true. A product or service may appear inadequate to a customer in comparison to a competing product but is still liked. Similar explanation is applicable to the trade name as well. With adequacy and pleasant feeling, the buying formula is restructured as follows: In fact, presence of adequacy of product features and benefits, patronage of trade name and consequent present feelings of customers enhances the probability of purchase.

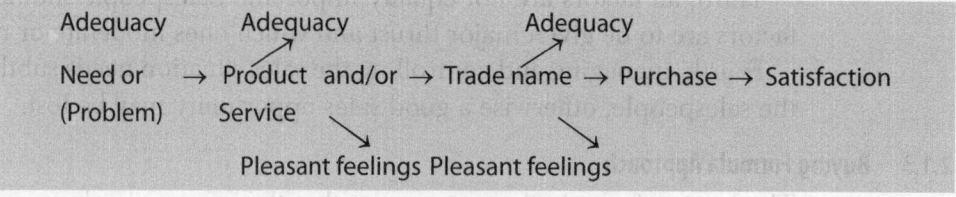

Buying formula approach

Once the decision to buy a product/service is taken, that product/service then becomes a habit. This ultimately leads to a pleasant feeling as well as an adequacy about that particular product or service and/or trade name. These feelings are cemented psychologically in the buyer's mind. Both create a defensive aura surrounding the product or service and/or a trade name which cannot be distorted by products of any competitor, their presentation or advertisement.

Adequacy and a pleasant feeling in the buyer's frame of reference can complement each other to facilitate repeat buying behaviour so long as these act upon the minds of the buyer. These two are represented by dotted lines to show the effects in the buyer's psychological world. The major elements in the buying formula are connected by solid lines/arrows.

Few implications of the buying formula theory are discussed below:

1. In some situations, buyers may not be concerned about the need or problem. In such cases, if some products or services satisfy their needs, companies should emphasize more on them during the sales presentation.
2. If a prospect feels or recognizes a problem but does not have any idea about the product or service, then the companies should highlight the association between the needs or problems and the products or services.
3. The situation mentioned in point (b) is also applicable for trade name. This means that the prospects have needs or problems but no idea about trade names. In such cases, companies should focus on the relationship between the needs or problems and their trade names.
4. Once the association between products or services or trade names, and needs or problems are well-established, efforts should be made to facilitate the purchase and use of such products or services.
5. Under competitive situations, emphasis should be laid upon adequacy of products or services and their trade names to provide solutions to problems and pleasant feelings of the prospects.
6. For selling products or services to the prospects, every element in the buying formula should be highlighted in the sales presentation.
7. Old customers of the company should be reminded of every element in the buying formula, if the company wants more sales from them.

2.1.4 Behavioural Equation Approach

The behavioural equation approach is based on J.A. Howard's (1963) stimulus-response model of buying behaviour where the buying decision process was envisaged as phases of learning process. Four essential elements of the learning process are drive, cue, response, and reinforcement.

Drives are strong internal stimuli that propel a buyer's response. They are of two kinds–innate drives and learned drives. Innate drives source from psychological needs, e.g., hunger, thrust, pain, etc. Learned drives arise from the striving for the fulfilment of social needs such as status, social recognition, etc.

Cues are weak stimuli that determine the responsive patterns of the buyer. Cues are of two types—triggering cues and non-triggering cues. Triggering cues are the stimulators of the decision process for any purchase situation. Non-triggering cues do not activate the buying decision process but influence them. It may operate at any moment even at a time when a buyer is not thinking of a purchase. Non-triggering cues are further divided into two kinds–product cues and informational cues. Product cues are external stimuli of the product that are directly perceived by the buyers, e.g., colour, size, price, etc. Informational cues are also external stimuli but symbolic in nature of the product. Such stimuli come from advertising, interaction with salespeople, etc.

Response is the buying action of the buyer.

Reinforcement is the psychological event that consolidates the efforts of the buyer to take a particular responsive action.

These four elements, when combined generate the act of buying or endorsing a supplier's product or service. J.A. Howard (1963) combined the four elements in a form of multiplicative equation.

$$B = P \times D \times K \times V$$

where,   B = Response, i.e., act of buying a product or patronizing a supplier

        P = Internal response tendency or force of habit

        D = Present drive level or the level of motivation

        K = Value of the product or its potential satisfaction to the buyer

        V = Intensity of all cues, triggering and non-triggering

Some corollaries can be deduced from the equation:

1. If any independent variable assumes a zero value, B will be zero and there will be a null response.

2. For unmotivated buyer (D=0), B will be zero, irrespective of internal response tendency or force of habit (P).

3. Whenever a purchase gives a buyer enough satisfaction (K) leading to yield reward, the internal response tendency (P) will increase and enhance the possibility of future purchase. It means satisfaction leads to reinforcement of learning that triggers future action or behaviour.

4. A salesperson influences the buyer in terms of the aforesaid equation. A salesperson influences P or internal response, also called pre-disposition directly through interaction with the buyer in ways rewarding the buyer. However, the greatest effect on P comes from usage experience.

5. A salesperson tries to influence the level of motivation (D) of the buyer. The tendency of a buyer to seek more information indicates the success of the salesperson to motivate the buyer.

6. Triggering cues are more meaningful to influencing buyers.

7. When the buyer has few sellers under consideration, a salesperson should emphasize more on merits of the company's brand and in the process influence the value of the product or the potential satisfaction (K) of the buyer.

8. A salesperson can vary the intensity of the efforts and thus make differences in the intensity of cues.

2.1.5 Need Satisfaction Approach

The need-satisfaction approach is based on the notion that a buyer buys a product or service in order to satisfy a specific need or a set of needs. The approach intends to meet

(a) need identification,

(b) need fulfilment, and

(c) need satisfaction.

A salesperson should actively listen to the need(s) of the prospective customer. If the prospects are not able to express their needs but show need-oriented anxiety or tension, a salesperson should help the prospect to articulate their needs. Suppose a human resource manager finds it difficult to maintain the payroll of employees in an organization. In such a case, a salesperson of a software company that designs and develops software packages for financial accounting can advise him on how to avert such a crisis of payroll development, maintenance, and updating. This is known as need development or identification.

Proper presentation of goods or services and handling objections of the prospects by the salespeople can fructify sales objectives of the firm. This is known as need fulfilment. Need satisfaction denotes getting expected benefits from the product or service. A salesperson can also assist a customer on how to get maximum benefits from the product or service. For example, an insurance agent should properly explain to the customer about how to carry out a full term of the policy and how a nominee can make claims in case of necessities. Thus, the presentation skills and demonstration ability of a salesperson resolves all sorts of concerns and queries of the prospects.

The need satisfaction approach is customer-oriented. How a salesperson adds value and benefits to the customer by least affecting their financial interests is the crux of this approach.

2.1.6 Consultative Approach

The consultative approach of selling is based on the philosophy that salespeople act as consultants to the prospects/customers and help them achieve strategic goals. Consultative selling emphasizes on giving solutions to the problems of the customers. Helping the prospects to identify and meet their needs, and handle problems in post-purchase situations are the tasks of consultative selling.

Proper diagnosis of the needs of the prospects is the starting point of consultative selling. A salesperson examines the needs and wants of the prospects and understands the various dimensions of their problems to find suitable solutions to their crises. For example, a retail salesperson in a garment store can guide a potential customer, who is in quandary to select dress materials that are best suited and are within budget.

Under consultative selling, a salesperson helps a prospect to solve the following problems:

(a) Need problem (A salesperson identifies the need deficiency that is known or unknown to the customer.)

(b) Choice problem (A salesperson directs and advises the customer to choose the right offer.)

(c) Helping in deciding the choice criteria (Knowing the problem, a salesperson helps the customer to select products with those buying criteria that will obviate the problem.)

(d) Product installation (A salesperson looks at the proper installation of a product in the customer's premise.)

(e) Product-use problem (A salesperson stands by the side of customer when the customer encounters difficulties on product application.)

(f) Product-maintenance problem (A salesperson offers after-sales service at regular basis.)

(g) Customer-feedback problem, e.g., future communication, reporting to the company, etc.

(h) Problems related to quick redress of defects in products within and beyond warranty periods.

2.1.7 Customer Relationship-based Approach

Customer-centred personalized approach is the major thrust in this approach. It emphasizes more on relationship building between salespeople and prospects rather than over transactions in buying–selling dyad. Selling is not just a process of engaging in economic relationship with the buyer but is also means to generate social and psychological relationships with the buyer. A customer's service on a continuous basis obviously helps to prolong such relationship. Service is a link of relationship. A customer does not buy a product but a set of benefits. A product gives no meaning until it renders service to the customer.

For instance, a vacuum cleaner is a mere showpiece if it does not remove dirt effectively. Thus, a value-added service from the seller to the buyer and earnest response from the buyer to fulfil all the conditions of buying binds the two in an enduring relationship. A relationship helps in

(a) eliciting fullest information and quarries from both sides,

(b) reducing doubts from both sides,

(c) driving out or marginalizing communication barrier,

(d) handling future problems at ease,

(e) reducing post-purchase anxiety of customers,

(f) diminishing media expenditure,

(g) staving-off competitive action, and

(h) meeting future requirements of both sides easily.

Rapport building is the key to customer relationship approach. Acceptance of each other's points of view, problems and prospects, concerns and consents, appreciation and criticism, treating each other as part of the business condense the relationship between the two. Social relationship overrides business relationship. Mutual gain is the basic string of a relationship.

2.1.8 Problem-solving Approach

Problem-solving approach is the extension of need satisfaction approach. It starts not with the identification of needs but with the root of the problems. Problem definition is the basic aspect of this approach. For example, a problem of the security and safety of employees in an organization is a core problem for the owner of a firm. He feels a need for insuring the employees under a suitable insurance scheme. In such a situation, a salesperson of an insurance company can solve his problem by helping them to purchase a group insurance policy for the employees.

In some cases, solutions provided are for more than one particular problem. Working women can solve their problem of washing clothes either themselves, sending dirty clothes to the dry cleaners or buying a washing machine. The salesperson selling washing machine should understand the exact nature of the problem and persuade them to buy the product. The salesperson should explain how a one-time investment can economically and effectively help solve their problems. With high-quality washing, the machine also dries clothes adding value to the product.

Similarly, a salesperson representing an insurance company dealing in mutual funds may guide and incite an individual to invest in the right scheme where returns can be high at minimum risk. A salesperson representing a radial tyre manufacturing company can apprise customers to get friction resistant, resilient, high-shelf life tyres for tensionless and smooth driving on the road.

Therefore, solving problems is a thinking process and is the intellectual part of selling. Problem-solving skills of the salepeople help to resolve the problems of the customers. Expertise and knowledge on products or services sharpens this skill and facilitates better dealing with the buying decision of the customer.

A salesperson with problem-solving skills helps a prospect:

(a) To identify genesis of a buying problem
(b) To define a buying problem
(c) To provide alternative solutions to the problem
(d) To help in evaluating alternative solutions to the problem
(e) To help prospects in selecting a specific solution, i.e., purchase decision

2.1.9 Team Selling Approach

Team selling is a coordinated selling effort that uses multiple personnel to solve complex buying problems of the customers. Team selling is appropriate when customers have complex needs that demand an all-round servicing in which an individual salesperson is incapable of fulfilling all the need deficiencies. It finds large use in case of highly technical buying situations.

Furthermore, team-based selling is advised when handling national or key accounts of the company. Team effort is needed to maximize the value of the customers when dealing with complex selling situations. A team may consist of company salespeople, technical support people, research and development personnel, product use experts or application specialists, representatives of manufacturing units, representative of purchase departments, etc., who are expected to provide solutions to the varying need problems and multiple objections of the customers. With a team consisting of members from all departments, the team is able to respond to production, marketing, technology, purchase, service, logistics, warranty, finance, and insurance-oriented questions.

Depending on the nature of questions, a member representing a specific functional unit of the organization can rise to the occasion and respond to the customers. It places the right people to tackle the specific need(s) of the customers. However, the team composition may change during post-selling when maintenance and service-oriented personnel are required more to address the post-purchase activities including operational problems, repair and overhauling, and provide after-sales service to the customers.

Team selling, if intelligently executed, can solve many complex problems of the customers that individualized selling may not be able to provide. It gives a holistic view of the company-customer interface and lends competitive advantage to both parties. It is a powerful means to win customers if managed correctly. But, coordination among team members is very important to make it successful. Otherwise, the team will lose its credibility.

Boress (2007) advocated ten rules of effective team selling. These are as follows:

1. Select team members carefully.
2. Have an orchestrator. In fact a team leader must act at the helm of the team, who moderates the team effort.

3. Stage a pre-briefing session. This is important because a pre-briefing or pre-meeting session specifically defines the job for each member and helps in knowing the sphere of interaction. It also creates a sense of liaison and cooperation among team members.

4. Hold a debriefing. After interaction with the customers, members must appraise what worked and what did not work. It helps to ease the following sessions with the customers.

5. Be prepared with questions. Questions are prepared during pre-briefing.

6. Keep the number of members to a minimum level. A sales team should consist of only those who are absolutely necessary.

7. Succulently answer questions of the customers.

8. Be flexible in the agenda.

9. Team members must be at the same wavelength. There should be an absolute mental cohesion and team spirit. Do not include members in the team who do not like each other.

9. Sell something. This should be the goal. The team should be committed to sell something every time.

After discussing the various approaches to personal selling and understanding their differing views, we will now focus on recognizing the relationship between a buyer and a seller, and its importance for any successful personal selling process.

2.2 BUYER–SELLER DYAD

Buyer–Seller interaction is the architect of personal selling that needs a medium to take place and a situation to occur. The medium is a face-to-face interaction between the two in most occasions of personal selling, although it can be a telephonic discussion, via the Internet, video conferencing, etc.

MONASH marketing dictionary defines the buyer–seller dyad as the two-way flow of communication between the buyer and the seller. Situation is a necessary condition for personal selling to take place. A situation entails that a potential customer has a need to be satisfied. A seller has a solution in their product or service that meets the need of the customers. Sociologists termed it as dyad, which means interaction between the two.

Dynamics of the buyer–seller dyad is a subject matter of discourse for understanding the factors and variables that impinge on the interaction. Interaction leads to building a relationship, if both parties feel a sense of dependency on each other. This relationship is not static in nature and varies with time. Time may further induce change in the volume of business, buying/selling conditions, transaction costs and uncertainty, and benefits sought for and rendered. So, the dyad has a situation perspective. It will not be out of place to discuss the conditions of selling situations that impact on dyadic relationship.

Some of the factors that influence the buying–selling dyad are listed below:

1. There should be an interaction between the potential customer and seller either directly or indirectly. A company salesperson can perform personal selling directly or can interact with the prospect by conversing with them on telephone or exchange information electronically.

2. The interaction should be acceptable to both parties in terms of participation and exchange of views. Both should accommodate each other to a meaningful conversation for a win-win situation for both.

3. A seller's anticipation and understanding of the customer needs, efforts to fulfil the needs to satisfy the customer on one side and patient listening to the sales pitch by the customer, recognizing, evaluating, and selecting the seller's offer on the other hand completes the dyadic interface efficaciously.

4. Selling the product or service at a price that accomplishes the selling objectives such as gross margin, net margin, return on investment, profitability is one half of the dyad. Buying the product at a right specification, price, place, and information consistent with the buyer's demand is the other half of the dyad.

5. A seller's effort to prove the superiority of a product over its competitors and a potential effort of the customer to get the best offer at a price that suits optimally with the budget gives resilience to such a relationship.

6. A seller's ability to modify the product/service according to the changing requirements of the customer gives fluidity to the relationship between the buyer and the seller.

7. Apart from the requirements of the buyer in terms of quantity and quality, the seller should also understand the inventory policy, production planning and scheduling, marketing policy of the buyer, etc. The buyer should know about the offer in detail, distribution planning, logistical support, pricing terms and conditions, etc. of the seller so that there is no communication gap in the dyadic framework.

8. A seller's initiative to establish a relationship with the buyer includes an effective installation of the product at the chosen place of installation, imparting buyer's education on product use, applications, etc., consistency in product quality, uninterrupted supply schedules, carrying out warranty promises, after-sales service, etc. A buyer should also complement the seller by taking the delivery of products, adhere to payment terms, routinely sending feedback to the seller about the performance of the product.

9. The orientation of the seller's organization should be customer-centric. A customer's problem is not only a matter of concern for the salesperson but for all employees of the seller's organization. For example, while manufacturing a product a production employee should keep in mind the technical and quality specifications specified by the buyer.

10. Similarly, the buyer's organization should always accommodate clearly to the salespeople representing the seller's organization. A salesperson often gets confused as to whom to deal with and satisfy in the buyer's organization. Also decision making in buyer's organization is complex, particularly for industrial products and involves dealing with multiple people across departments.

11. The buyer–seller relationship is the key to perpetual business between the two. The relationship should not limit to economic issues only. Social and psychological relationships are also instrumental in furthering the relationship. Acceptance of each other's social values, customs, culture, emotional components, and ethos definitely strengthens the relationships.

2.2.1 Determinants of Buyer–Seller Dyad

The dyadic relationship between a buyer and a seller is a complex web of associations including a number of variables that flow along the transactional conduit and signify the economic aspects of business interface. But, marketing in today's business parlance, does not only mean veering around economic pursuits of business as it hardly fulfils the promise of long-term sustainable relationship between a buyer and a seller. A seller's success to get a buyer to behave in an expected manner is a result of sound selling strategies and well-knitted approaches.

In consumer product markets, the relational economics is not so complex or imperceptible, as in the case of industrial markets. Here, the product is often developed to satisfy the need(s) of a particular market segment. Like for instance, Blackberry that targeted corporate office goers today sees people of all age groups using it. The target audience for them has become wider. Today, a consumer's claim for the right product at the right price, popularly known as value for money rules the marketing game in consumer marketing. It is important to note here that meeting all individual need(s) cannot be thought of from an economic standpoint, whereas, in industrial or business marketing, products are made according to the directed specifications of the buyers. The customized nature of the products demand more personalized interaction and long term buyer–seller relationship.

Thus, in the industrial product-market scenario, the buyer–seller interaction has a much wider connotation and a simple give and take equation is inadequate to explain the two-way communication. Here, selling starts much ahead of the actual transactions and its effect continues for an unlimited time period till both the buyer and the seller fulfil their unfulfilled terms. The role of personal selling in industrial markets is a pervasive issue because of the broad perspective of industrial selling involving enormity of the buying criteria and complexity of the user's selection procedures. It also includes many formalities and conditions of selling/buying where relational justification for growth and survival of both the selling and buying firms is also an important issue.

From selling items such as operating supplies like lubricants, nails, pins, etc. to more important ones such as capital goods like boiler, furnace, fabricator, etc. i.e. dealing with low-cost to high-cost customers, the relational amity or incongruity depends a lot on the fulfilment of promises on both sides. This cannot be explained simply with the help of traditional marketing theory. Buying and selling are the two sides of the same coin. So, a mark of symbiotic determinism needs to describe the dyadic interdependence of the two. Kotler and Armstrong (2001) suggested that the 4Ps concept reflects the seller's view on marketing decision but not the buyer's. Kotler (2004) referred to Lauterborn (1990) to mention the need for 4Cs in place of 4Ps to justify the marketing decision. 4Cs are customer cost, customer solution, customer convenience, and communication.

Thus, the buyer–seller dyadic relationship, if effective, can yield productive outcomes for both of them in the long run. Business goals, strategies, performance indexes, values, relationships with stakeholders and customers, etc. are all time dependent. Time decides the contextually of a goal, strategy or relationship. Also, an organization gears itself to change and accommodates with time by redeploying its resources on sustainability grounds. Therefore, the symbiotic relationship between the buyer and the seller depends more on need-based makeover with time so that link between the two firms can remain unperturbed amidst business fluctuations.

Dyadic approach, thus, entails a proper management of exchanges of products/ services, information, money, legal obligations and commitments that affect each other and adds benefits leading to the mutual satisfaction for both. Besides conditions and constructs of exchange, dyadic relationship is influenced by a host of dimensions that saliently mould and shape the dynamic of the dyadic game. Alternatively, to understand the dyad that exists, it is helpful to examine the major components that operate within the dyadic interface. The dimensions of the buyer–seller dyad affecting the relationship are exhibited in Figure 2.3.

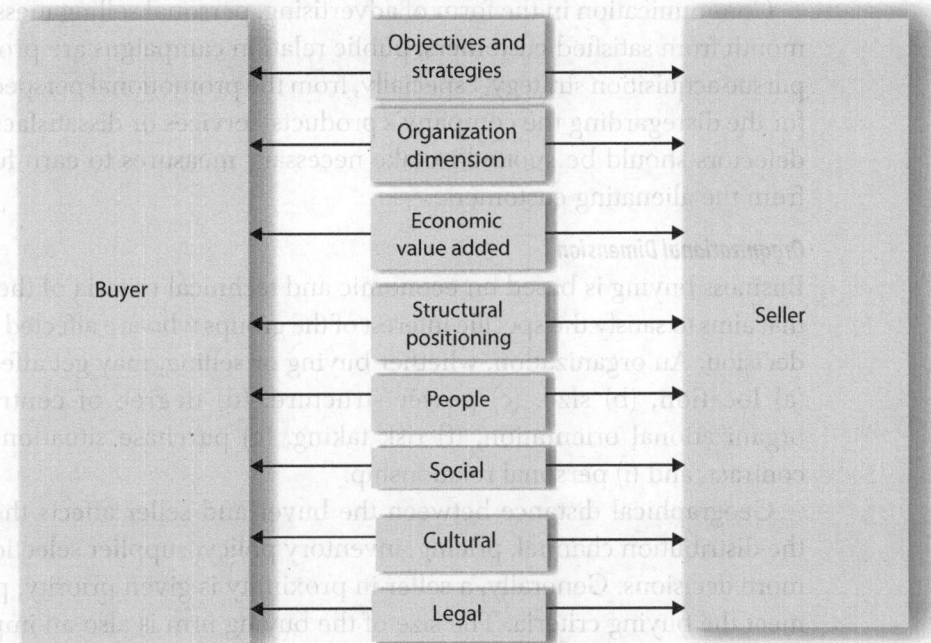

Figure 2.3 Buyer–seller dyad

A brief description of the factors is discussed in the following paragraphs.

Objectives and Strategic Dimension

The basic notion of personal selling objectives and strategies should be in line with the corporate objectives and strategies. Clearly defined target market, prospective customers, product/service specifications, channels of distribution, communication strategies, and pricing mechanisms should be at the roots of objective formulations and strategic initiations. Moreover, quantitative objectives such as sales volume by product, customer group and territory, gross and net margins, target return on investment, sales growth, etc. and qualitative objectives such as healthy customer relationship, conveying an image, public welfare, etc. should build destination points for the organization with personal selling as the major thrust to achieve.

Strategies are blue prints to accomplish objectives. An organization can devise personal selling strategies for present customers, future customers, and defectors. Some of these strategies are as follows:

1. *Retention strategy* is the suited and tested one for the existing customers.
2. *Relational marketing* has an important role to play in holding on to the existing customers.
3. *Acquisition strategy* is ideal for the prospective customers.

Communication in the form of advertising, personal selling message, word-of-mouth from satisfied customers, public relation campaigns are proven means to pursue acquisition strategy, especially, from the promotional perspective. Reasons for the disregarding the company's products/services or dissatisfaction in case of defectors should be spotted to take necessary measures to earn further respect from the alienating customers.

Organizational Dimension

Business buying is based on economic and technical criteria of the organization that aims to satisfy the specific interest of the groups who are affected by the buying decision. An organization, whether buying or selling, may get affected by (a) location, (b) size, (c) power structure, (d) degree of centralization, (e) organizational orientation, (f) risk taking, (g) purchase situation, (h) types of contract, and (i) personal relationship.

Geographical distance between the buyer and seller affects the decision on the distribution channel, pricing, inventory policy, supplier selection, and many more decisions. Generally, a seller in proximity is given priority, provided they meet the buying criteria. The size of the buying firm is also an important factor that influences buying decision. In general, large firms are difficult to manage for sellers because of the involvement of stakes of a number of individuals and the interest fragmentation is much larger. For example, a purchase manager and a production manager in a buying organization may have conflicting purposes as far as choice of the critical selection criterion to evaluate potential sellers is concerned.

Power positions of the buyer and the seller affect the degree of dependency or independency on each other. A single source of supply for the buying firm reduces the bargaining space of the buyer and makes it dependent on the seller. But, in a competitive market, sellers are always on their toes to satisfy buyers. Buyers, therefore, enjoy the power of authority to oblige the sellers to come to their (buyer) terms. The degree of centralization of the buying organization moderates the selling approaches of the seller's firm.

For a centralized buying decision, a single party takes (or is permitted to take) a buying decision and so the selling task is minimized. But in a decentralized situation, the selling task multiplies for the seller as they need to satisfy a number of individuals. An organization that is focussed on the customer always gets leverage in winning the selling contracts. And, in a customized product marketing situation, the customer specific product design and development enhances the chance of a seller to gain long-term selling contracts. The orientation of a firm aids in evolving a well-defined decision criteria and influence the seller's marketing strategies. For example, an investment banking firm entrusts more on financial experts to deal with the selling firms. Similarly, a scientific research laboratory depends more on technical experts to handle sellers.

Again, where risk taking in a purchase situation is high, what matters most is the commitment of the seller for the buyer's firm. Here, decision making in the buying firm is more formalized and rigorously evaluated. However, in routine buying situations, where the purchase situation is repetitive in nature, continuing with the existing seller is a common practice of the buyer. In a modified re-buy situation, the buyer contemplates changing the existing seller and joins hands with another for the same product. The objective is to lessen the dependence on one source.

Another possibility that might be seen is of a new buying situation when a new seller is appointed to start a fresh business transaction. The situation has a time perspective also particularly for buyers. Under emergent-buying situation, say sudden shortfall of raw materials impacting production process badly, the buyer has a limited choice for the selection of the seller and engages in the one who is readily available with reasonable accuracy of product specifications. Types of contract also determine the business relationship between a buyer and a seller.

For an annual-plan contract, a seller feels more confident to work with especially large buyers and the buyer also becomes more confident of the assurance of supply. But in spot contract or blanket-order situation, the seller and the buyer get together for a single contract. The relational depth from the business perspective is comparatively less and at times breached due to a mismatch between the expectation of the buyer and the contribution of the seller. Personal relationship between the buying and selling firms or between one or two personnel in two firms affects business development. Matching family backgrounds, educational backgrounds, life styles, affiliation to clubs or associations outside business boundaries, social status, etc. between the seller and buyer or their representatives also often play a defining role in establishing healthy business connections.

Economic Value-added Dimension

Value refers to the worth that the sellers create through products or services that they manufacture for the buyers; the buyers receive it as a cost. Buyers judge the value of the product by comparing the perceived benefits of the same against the actual costs that they incur. A seller can enhance the value of a product or service by adding more tangible or intangible features or supplementary services at the same or at an increased cost. Buyers, too, perceive these incremental benefits at the same or a somewhat higher price. For instance, a hotelier can enhance the accommodation comforts for the customers at the same or a slightly higher rent. Buyers weigh this value by the incremental benefits against the earlier incremental price and benefits that they received before making the actual purchase. Here, the economics of exchange rests on the premise that buyers obtain some value from the sellers in return of some values that is acceptable to the sellers.

Assessing value is linked to the evaluative criteria of the buyer. These are known as buyer's consideration set. Buyers have a choice set particularly for competitive markets. Only after evaluating each of these choice options and benchmarking them on evaluative criteria do the buyers reach a buying decision. Buyers today are value-oriented. Their consciousness on value is best reflected in their demands for getting the best quality with special features and effective performance. Sellers should always respond to the new orientation in buying behaviour and explore innovative ways of product development, market development, market penetration, market extension or diversification ventures to remain steady in the otherwise vicious market.

Structural Positioning Dimension

By structural dimension, here, we mean the formal position of the decision makers in the buying and selling organization. These are the bodies which are meant to influence the purchasing/selling decision significantly. In fact, the decision inclines a lot upon the relative horizontal and vertical differentiation of the positions of seller and buyer or their representatives in their respective organizations. When a rookie salesperson having a formal position in the lower rung of the hierarchy is asked to interact with the technical manager of the buying firm, the interaction so happened has a vertical discordance. This vertical gap can be reduced when the sales manager of a firm meets the research and development manager or the financial head of the buying firm.

However, one problem still persists. The functional difference between a non-technical salesperson and a technical manager of a firm in terms of technical knowledge and skill, business directions, goals, and values impedes successful selling/buying. This is known as horizontal gap. So, vertical and horizontal gaps are impediments to a dyadic relationship. Such a difference can be minimized to a great extent by having the interaction between two personnel of more or less similar or same formal positions and functional orientations in their respective organizations.

Presence or absence of interdependence or cohesion amongst various departments in the buying firm impacts the selling approach. Salespeople find their task easy when the departmental head acts towards fulfilling the common goal by shedding off minor departmental interests. This leads to causing conflicts in the buying decision in the buyer's organization. In contrast, if opposing phenomenon happens, the selling situation might be grave. Same explanation is applicable to a selling firm also. A buyer always wants a team effort amongst departments in the selling firm so that the product or service they get is not short of any specification criteria–technical, commercial, service level, etc.

People Dimension

Human element in personal selling is central to dyadic relations. Interpersonal force of inducement to talk, discourse, convert dissension to acceptance, and finally consolidation of relations is the root of the buyer–seller coalition. But to reach a state of union, a number of conformities between the buyer and the seller in the interest of the dyad is required. Following are some of the areas of conformities between the buyer and the seller.

First, the ability of the product or the service to satisfy the specific needs of the customer should be the prime focus of the seller. The seller must obey the customer's expected benchmarks in product specification and fulfil them.

Second, a complete cognizance of the buyer's personal profiles such as educational back ground, age, experience, life style, gender, race, and personal goals with that of the seller induces them to expect more or less from the seller. Similarly, economic (e.g., customer's buying power), social (e.g., the social status of the buyer and the seller), and the cultural (e.g., both have a common preference for films, sports, etc.) factors may implicitly play a salient role in fructifying business relationships too.

Third, an ardent desire of the salesperson to recognize the personal agenda of the prospective buyer can bring them to a point of confidence where, they can easily win the mind of the prospect. It is believed that besides technical and commercial solicitation, a buyer and seller are also involved in the mind game where personal and personality characteristics of both play a viable role to reach a point of communion.

Fourth, group dynamics between the organizations of the buyer and the seller often come to fore to steer the journey of selling/buying towards the goal. This is particularly relevant in case of group decision making in the seller's organization or team selling on behalf of buying firms. Here, matching a group's pooled personnel and personality equation with that of the others is important to fructify business dealings.

Social Dimension

Personal selling is a vehicle to establish a social link between a buyer and a seller. As selling is basically a human behaviour, social ingredients of selling/buying assume a significant role, particularly, at the pre-relationship phase of the selling/buying process. Both the selling and the buying organizations have their own social spheres where people absorb and nurture specific organizational culture that ultimately shapes their beliefs, values, norms, customs, expectations, accepted practices, etc.

As two organizations expectedly impregnate with different social systems, social inequality is a handicap to the process of socialization. So long as the social disparity lasts, the two organizations find it difficult to stave off relational distance and set interpersonal (between buyer and seller) and/or inter-organizational (between two organizations) bonding. Personal selling is a kind of promotion where both sides get tremendous opportunity to make social exchanges, remove relational obstacles due to social grounds and create an environment of trust, friendship, and affinity.

For example, acceptance of a junior salesperson by the prospective buyer during the encounter stage is often difficult, as the latter believes in the social convention of expecting a sales manager during the first meeting. Cold calling to the buying organization may be treated as a discourteous affair and adversely affects the dignity of the selling firms. One party believes and follows strict official protocols while the other party does not follow such an austere official decorum in every deal. So, role expectation is a normative affair in social interaction that cannot be ruled out.

Social ties are established through information exchange, learning, and recognition of each other's social systems and concerted efforts to establish social compatibility. Once it is established, it percolates down the subsequent stages of selling. Morris (1992) reviewed the role of relational variables, social structural variables, social actor variables, and normative variables in determining the course of social relationships between a buyer and a seller. Sense and manifestation of need, dependency, certainty, and empathy characterizes the relational con-sistency between the two firms. This also leads to evincing in pre-selling, relation exploration and development, negotiation, and even tactical games between the two.

Structural variables focus on positional existence of organizational actors and concomitant power structure, authority, and decision-making latitudes. Difference between selling and buying organizations in this regard distorts the social symmetry. In the same way, social actor variables like age, sex, life style, education, personality, charisma, communication styles, and other characteristics of organizational actors impacts social relationships. Last but not the least, normative variables like practicing social customs, value systems, organizational culture, rule of the game, etc. have an effect on social correspondence between the two firms.

Cultural Dimension

In the same connotation of social relationship, it can also be said that cultural propinquity is a gracing factor to cause healthy interaction between the buyer and the seller that leads to goal achievement. Cultural milieus governed by shared values and beliefs are supposedly different between two organizations. Employees grow up in a definite organizational culture and therefore, hone up particular types of organizational values, customs, norms, ethos, and ethics. An organizational culture of a firm is expressed in the core values of their product/service, brand image, homogeneous attitude, and activity patterns of organizational actors at micro level and corporate missions, governance, tradition, and legacy at the macro level.

A salesperson, being nurtured in an organizational culture, may find a different culture in the buying organization. Conversely, acceptance of a salesperson by the buying organization may not be palatable due to cross-cultural insufficiency leading to cultural void spaces between the two firms. A salesperson during pre-selling stage is looked upon as a stranger by the buyer and the vice versa which leads to anxiety. This relationship anxiety leads to misperceptions, misinterpretations, and misevaluations. For example, a buyer may not like a salesperson who at the time of interaction verbosely dwells on positive features of the product and claims no such negativity. Exaggeration supersedes cultural boundary and mars the spirit of cross-cultural spirit. Information exchange, knowledge sharing, persuasion, problem-solving attitude, and finally commitment can drastically iron out cultural gaps and bind the two on a relational axis.

Legal Dimension

Business culture provides a foundation for understanding the moral and ethical behaviours in business practices. Selling is an important business activity which involves exchanging of products/services, as well as moral and ethical values between the buyer and the seller. This also means that both the parties look for peace of mind by getting the actual value or worth from the transaction. Legal disciplines are regulators of moral and ethical behaviour. Protection of interests of both buyers and sellers are of vital legal interest and the laws and regulations concern both the liabilities of the buyer and the seller, their warrant morals, and ethical practices in business. Any departure from quality specifications of products/services, logistical inappropriateness, price discrimination, deceptive promotions, dumping, tariffs and tax treatments, non-compliance to pollution controls, violation of health and safety standards, etc. are treated as gross infringements of legal jurisdictions.

Legal enactments define and control the respective rights and obligations of both buyers and sellers. This is the watchdog of free and fair business, and trade practices, healthy competition, consumer's rights and duties, manufacturer's duties and responsibilities to consumers, societies, and governments. In India, Consumer Protection Act, 1986, Competition Act 2002, Trade Mark Act, 1999, Standards of Weight and Measure Act, 1976, and many more acts are enacted. Legal machineries like regulatory agencies, consumer courts, and administrative support systems are given total juridical power to prevent illegal trade activities. The legal concept of caveat emptor—let the buyers beware—became a slogan in the consuming fraternity in the US prior to 1960s.

Legal principles are equally applicable between buyer and seller. Laws demarcate and defend their roles and responsibilities in business transactions. In case of any discrepancy, they are free to seek the assistance of law.

SUMMARY

Selling has various approaches to fructify and find its meaningfulness. Selling approaches are not of recent origin. Since the industrial age, selling has been aiming to win target customers; it has both theoretical rationales and practical ramifications. AIDAS approach of selling is regarded as a traditional one that acts as a major basis to understand the communication objectives at various stages of selling. AIDAS suggests that a prospect passes through five mental stages such as attention, interest, desire, action, and satisfaction in sequence to complete the buying process.

Right set of circumstances approach advocates that situation or circumstances prevailing in a given situation lead a prospect to behave in a particular way. Buying formula approach vouches for identifying the needs and problems of the customer and finding a suitable solution for it. Behavioural equation approach, also known as situation-response model of buying behaviour envisages

buying decision process as the phases of learning process. Need satisfaction approach is based on the notion that a buyer buys a product/service to satisfy a specific need or a set of needs. Consultative approach suggests that a salesperson acts as a consultant to the prospect and helps the customer achieve strategic goals. Customer relationship approach centres more on relationship building with the customers rather than on transaction economics. Problem-solving approach starts from the root of the customer's problem whereas team selling is a coordinated selling effort using multiple personnel to solve the complex buying problem of the customer.

Buyer–Seller dyad is the backbone of personal selling. A dyad, in selling context, is a two-way flow of communication between the buyer and the seller. This dyadic relationship is a more prominent issue in industrial selling.

KEY TERMS

AIDAS Approach AIDAS approach suggests that a prospective buyer passes through five mental stages of attention, interest, desire, action, and satisfaction that are arranged sequentially to complete the buying process

Behavioural Equation Approach The behavioural equation approach portrays the buying behaviour where the buying decision process was envisaged as phases of the learning process. Four essential elements of the learning process are drive, cue, response, and reinforcement that characterize behaviour.

Buyer–Seller Dyad The buyer–seller dyad entails a

proper management of exchanges of the products/services, information, money, legal obligations, and commitments between the buyer and the seller, and adds benefits leading to the mutual satisfaction for both.

Buying Formula Approach The buying formula approach suggests that the prospective buyers take initiative to fructify a buying–selling intercourse. The needs or problems of the buyers are the starting points of this theory where the salespeople assist them in finding suitable solutions to their problems.

CONCEPT REVIEW QUESTIONS

1. Briefly illustrate the AIDAS approach in personal selling. How does it resolve the communication objectives of a firm?
2. The buying formula approach of selling focuses on the thinking process that happens in the prospect's mind to shape buying decision. Discuss.
3. What are the major elements of behavioural equation approach of personal selling? How do these affect a buyer's response to buying?
4. Compare the role of the salesperson as a problem-solver and a consultant to the buyer.
5. Under what circumstances is the team approach of selling recommended?
6. Define buyer–seller dyad. What are its major dimensions?
7. Explain the economic, social, cultural, and legal dimensions of buyer–seller dyad and how do these affect the relationship between the buyer and the seller?

CRITICAL THINKING QUESTION

Choosing the right approach of selling is a difficult proposition for any selling firm. In many situations 'everything is right for the sale' does not produce successful results. A favourable situation for selling may prove wrong for a company to achieve sales goal. A sales expert may point towards the lack of good quality salespeople, who do not live up to the expectations of the firm to meet the demands of the situation. Sometimes, an efficient salesperson can turn stubborn towards a genuine customer.

1. Explain the favourable situations for selling. Give examples to support your answer.
2. Do you think that only the quality of salespeople speaks for the selling success under favourable circumstances? Please elaborate.
3. Motivating an indifferent prospect to buy is a tough task. Motivating a customer of a competing brand to switch flank is tougher. The toughest is breaking the loyalty domain of a hardcore customer of another brand. Choose the appropriate selling theory for each of the selling situations and explain how that helps to generate a win-win dyadic relationship for the seller and buyer.

PROJECT ASSIGNMENTS

1. Contact a prospective buyer of a laptop and research the following:
   (a) Why is he buying?
   (b) When is he buying?
   (c) Where is he buying from?
   (d) How is he buying?
   (e) What attributes is he looking for in the product?
   (f) What is his budget?

   Collect information and prepare a selling model where all the questions above are used as inputs. The answers you obtain will be used as outputs. What are the components that facilitate balancing between the the inputs and outputs? Also project these balancing elements in the model. *Hint*: For example, quality of the product or company reputation may act as facilitators in the buying decision.

2. Visit a Pantaloon shopping mall and follow the interaction between the retail salesperson and a male customer of dress materials. List the points for the salesperson and the customer separately. Fit a stimulus-response model of selling based on the course of interaction between the two.

REFERENCES

Boress, A. (2007), 'The Ten Rules of Effective Team Selling', http://www.accountingweb.com/item/104060 accessed on 31 December 2010.

Howard, J.A. (1963), *Marketing Management, Analysis and Planning*, Revised ed., Richard D. Irwin, Homewood, Ill.

Kotler, P. and G. Armstrong (2001), *Principles of Marketing*, Prentice-Hall, New Jersey.

Kotler, P. (2004), *Marketing Management*, Prentice-Hall, New Jersey.

Lauterborn, R. (1990), 'New Marketing Litany: 4P's Passe; C–words Take Over', *Advertising Age*, 1 October 1990: 26.

Mathur, U.C. (2008), *Business to Business Marketing*, New Age International (P) Limited, Publishers, New Delhi.

MONASH University, http://www.buseco.buseco.monash.edu.au/mkt/dictionary/sss.html, accessed on 14 May 2009.

Morris, M.H. (1992), *Industrial and Organizational Marketing*, 2nd ed., Macmillan Publishing Company, New York.

Still, R.R., E.W. Cundiff, and N.A.P. Govoni (1994), *Sales Management: Decisions, Strategies and Cases*, 5th ed., Prentice-Hall of India Private Limited, New Delhi.

Strong, K.E. (1925), *The Psychology of Selling*, McGraw-Hill, New York.

http://www.slideshare.net/Ukabuka/behavioural/formula-theory-editttt accessed on 02 September 2010.

CASE STUDIES

1. A Turnaround Story

Walt University has a challenging task ahead to attract graduates to its newly launched post-graduate curriculum in business administration. The university, in its 20 years of existence has acquired a name to produce good quality students, particularly in the fields of engineering and technology. The university has a sprawling campus spreading over 2.8 square kilometres bestowed with lush greeneries and panoramic lakes. The natural environment surrounding the university lends a community prestige to this educational fortress. The university is also equipped with rich libraries, labs, teaching faculties, infrastructure and IT supports health care unit, gymnasium, and other facilities.

In spite of all this, the university has failed to pull enough students unlike other universities in the same state. Few problems can be cited to this regard:

(a) Admission procedure is too rigid and competitive
(b) Advertisements for admission to various courses are posted only in two regional news papers
(c) A common perception of high academic standard debars ordinary students to show enthusiasm in getting admission tickets

Recently, the university has opened a public relation cell engaging a senior public relation officer that has started campaigning with

(Contd)

advertisements in newspapers, cable TV, and outdoor hoardings in solus positions to drive out misconceptions among students and their guardians. Announcement of few scholarships for top-ranked students and waiving of the tuition fees up to fifty per cent for poor but academically deserving students is also a part of this promotion. The campaign at the same time focuses on social orientation, value system, performance, and other positive features. This promotion programme has, indeed, enabled the university to attract a large chunk of students from different socio-economic strata and improves the roll strength significantly. A good communication programme obviously has helped to reach target groups and build conviction amongst potential students.

Discussion Questions

1. Apply AIDAS model to examine the effects of its components to reach the communication objectives for Walt University.
2. Good public relation calls for 'good deeds followed by good words'. How far is this observed in public relation campaign?

2. Eureka Forbes Ltd

Eureka Forbes Ltd. (EFL), Asia's largest direct sales organization, is a leader in domestic and industrial water purification systems, vacuum cleaners, air purifiers, and security solutions. The company is the world's largest manufacturer of ultraviolet-based water purification with over twenty products. The 2006 'Mera Brand' award to Aquaguard water purifier has glorified the company and the brand is being treated as India's most preferred one amongst domestic users of water purifiers.

The ascent of EFL has found reason in its overwhelming success in direct selling which connotes direct communication with carefully selected customers serving them without any involvement of intermediaries. EFL uses a team of young salespeople to give in-house product demonstrations and persuade customers about the 'must have' importance of water purifiers and other products. These salespeople, using direct selling, have to overcome the prospect's inertia through effective presentation, hand-on demonstration, and handling prospect's objections through customized explanations.

Direct selling is becoming popular nowadays. In fact, here, the salespeople apprise customers of a need that they do not feel otherwise. It is the best personalized and interactive form of selling that gives a

(Contd)

(*Contd*)

salesperson an opportunity to spot out any query of the customer and give an immediate feedback. It offers a high degree of selectivity in identifying customers, reaching to them directly and sharing information with them based on personal sales message using sales tools. After all, the objective of direct selling is to get immediate customer response and develop enduring customer relationship. In the process, they prevent the apprehension of a lot many lost calls experienced as in conventional selling efforts.

Discussion Question

Generate a buyer–seller dyadic framework on EFL customer interaction model for direct selling, taking cues from problem solving, consultative, and customer relationship approaches of selling

Source: http://www.idswater.co.in, accessed on 1 October 2010.

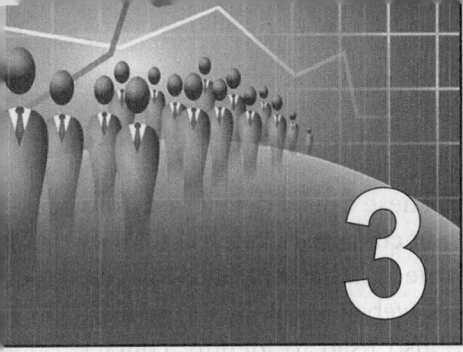

3 Personal Selling Process

LEARNING OBJECTIVES

After reading this chapter, you will be able to

- understand the components and steps of personal selling
- explain the role of prospecting and how it helps in identifying and locating customers
- appreciate the importance and process of pre-approach and approach as steps to start interaction with prospective buyers
- understand ways of identifying the needs of the prospects
- identify the different presentational techniques and ways of handling customer objections
- learn the importance and techniques of closing the sales
- get insights of how to make follow-up calls after selling

Personal selling is an integral part of sales management and its importance is well regarded by a lot of industrial firms. It is an art which consists of a series of steps that a salesperson should learn and follow to attain marketing goals. Personal selling is also considered as an indispensable promotional tool because of its flexibility in its administration, control over content of the message, and the ability to enhance customer relationship.

3.1 SELLING PROCESS—A STEPWISE APPROACH

Personal selling begins with identifying customers and ends with ensuring satisfaction to them. The series of steps that are followed in between the two are diverse, complex, and knowledge-based. Salespeople need to learn and understand the objectives, importance, and intricacies of each step before taking a stride to perform the task of personal selling. Keeping in view the need for understanding the procedural formalities and complexities, this chapter aims to discuss the steps of personal selling in detail as shown in Figure 3.1.

Step 1: Prospecting

Prospecting is the first stage of the process of personal selling that involves searching for a potential customer, also known as a prospect, and making him qualified for the product. A qualified prospect is a person who has an unsatisfied need, an ability to pay, and a willingness to buy. A person before being classified as a prospect is known as a 'lead' to a salesperson.

It is the task of the salespeople to generate leads. These can be developed from various sources such as company given leads, current customers, referral sources like distributors, suppliers, commercially available databases, yellow pages, telephone directories, trade associations, trade shows, websites, etc. Advertisement with coupon or toll free telephone numbers are also used to identify contact prospects.

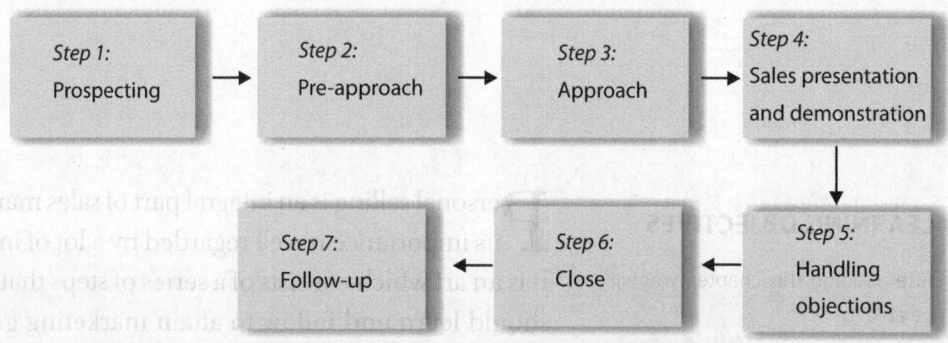

Figure 3.1   Process of personal selling

Leads are qualified to be either hot or warm, having a long-term potential or no potential. Hot leads are the ones who are highly prospective and intend to buy immediately. Warm leads take some time to take a decision before purchasing the product. Long-term potentials have no plan to purchase within the foreseeable time period but have all the potential to be buyers. No potential is a category of buyers who cannot be buy at all, whatsoever the product or buying situation.

So, one can say that prospecting is a process of locating or identifying and qualifying prospects. The usual qualification criteria used for identifying prospects are location, accessibility, volume of business, time period of purchase, time period of payment, continuity of business, etc.

Since, this is the first step of the process, it is very important for salespeople to develop skills for prospecting. They should also have the ability to work hard and manage time.

Step 2: Pre-approach
Once the salespeople have identified a group of potential customers, they should learn as much as possible about these prospects along with their names and contact details. In case these prospects are organizations, details of the organizational demographics such as location, type of organization, organizational size, business activities, and their marketing information such as sales volumes, market shares, market position, present suppliers, the final authority in the organization to take a decision to buy, and their personal traits need to be acquired. Having collected all such information, a salesperson should seek appointments with these prospects and formulate a plan with the best procedure, place, and time to meet them.

Step 3: Approach

After fixing an appointment with the prospect in the pre-approach, a salesperson gets a chance to prepare himself with how to introduce himself and the product to the client. It also enables him to carry a useful and interesting discussion, which would be vital to establish an initial connection. Here, the appearance, attire, communication, and gestures of a salesperson are important to attract the willingness of a prospect to witness the presentation.

The objective here is to gain the attention of the prospects, arouse their interest, and stimulate a desire that encourages them to take part in the sales presentation. Therefore, creating a first-hand impression on the client is critical for the salesperson to be able to build an interactive environment. This prompts the prospect to start a working relationship with the salesperson.

Step 4: Sales Presentation

Once the salespeople gets an approval through verbal or non-verbal cues from the prospects, they can begin with the presentation of the product. In general, a salesperson follows a conventional selling model, AIDA (gaining attention, arousing interest, instilling desire, and prompting action) as a presentation technique to influence the prospective customer.

A comprehensive and precise explanation about the features and benefits of the product should be given to the prospects. The language used in the presentation should be simple and comprehensible. During the conversation, a salesperson should always try to establish a link between the product and the needs of the prospect. This can further be used to highlight the importance of the product in satisfying the prospect's need.

Generally, a sales presentation is planned beforehand. A planned sales presentation is a standardized sales talk with little or no modification made by the salesperson. In most situations, tailored presentation is recommended where a salesperson is prepared to make a customized presentation in case of discussion on the specific needs of the prospect. The presentation should be managed keeping in mind the prospect's interest on the offer being presented and the time schedule for the presentation.

After its completion, the salesperson goes for a product demonstration which consolidates the points of presentation. In case of small products, showing a sample is not a problem. For larger products, visual aids can be used for display. To avoid confusion and disinterest, the points of demonstration should be consistent with that of the presentation.

Step 5: Handling Objections

Salespeople may face objections from potential customers during the presentation. These objections are viewed as resistance to selling. But objections are welcome in selling because these are clear indications of the interest of the prospects on the offer and their intent to know more about the offer. Objections may be rational or psychological. Rational objections are raised on product features, price, quality, delivery schedule, etc. where as psychological objections are preference for competing brands, indifference to sales persons, affinity to distract from the discussion, etc.

Salespeople should not be perturbed by objections; rather, they should be mentally prepared to accept them. They should stay positive and ask the prospects to clarify their objections by asking questions. The objective is to know whether the prospect has an actual interest to listen to the message of the salesperson or wants to avoid citing pretext. If objections are genuine, the salesperson should answer them carefully, if otherwise, i.e., objections have no real basis, they can negate the objections supplementing adequate reasons and references.

Salespeople need an in-depth training to handle customer objections. Adequate knowledge about the products being presented, along with information about the company and its past history can help them counter objections confidently. Salespeople should be familiar about the industries manufacturing these products, competitors' products, prevailing price and distribution policy of the competitors, etc.

Step 6: Closing

During this stage, the salesperson attempts to close the sale by asking for an order. A nice presentation and deft objection handling leads to a successful closing of the sale; otherwise all efforts are futile. The salesperson should learn various closing techniques. For example, either a salesperson can recapitulate the points of discussion or may help the prospective customer in taking a buying decision or offer few alternatives to help the prospect to choose from. A salesperson can also offer company-sponsored incentives, say discounts or gifts to persuade the prospect in taking a buying decision. A sale finally closes when a salesperson acquires an order and makes the delivery.

Step 7: Follow-up

Sales do not end with closing, rather, this is the starting point of future sales with the same customers. A salesperson should make arrangements to complete all the formalities of delivering the product and related facilities like user's guide, manuals, supportive literature, etc. This stage is important for further continuation of business with that customer. Enquiring about a customer's feedback, i.e., due delivery of the product, proper installation of products, customer instruction, servicing, any hazard(s) of product handling, level of satisfaction or dissatisfaction are the major objectives of follow-up calls, which should be made every now and then. Repeated follow-ups help the salespeople to know experience of the customer with their product and if the functioning of the product is to their expectation. The salesperson should take proper measures to remove all sorts of post-purchase problems of the customers. In fact, he should prepare a follow-up schedule after the initial order is procured. This boosts the customer confidence and moral, and aids in building long-term relationship of the customer and the salesperson, as well as, between the buying and selling firms.

Now, we will discuss all these stages in greater detail.

3.2 PROSPECTING—MEANING, OBJECTIVES, AND SOURCES

The term 'prospecting' relates to locating and qualifying new customers. Prospecting is necessary because

(a) finding customers is a business compulsion for a new and existing product,
(b) there is a decline in the existing customer base as customers are taken away by competitors, and
(c) it helps in strengthening the existing customer base.

The objective of prospecting is to identify qualified potential customers. An organization or an individual has to fulfil certain conditions to become a prospect. The qualification criteria for being a prospective customer requires them to have

(a) a need for the product/service,
(b) the willingness to buy,
(c) purchasing capacity,
(d) The authority to buy, and
(e) accessibility to the salespeople.

If any of the above conditions are not met, no new customer is generated however industrious or efficient a salesperson might be. Therefore, qualifying the prospect is very crucial, otherwise a salesperson's valuable time and effort is wasted. Identifying or locating the prospective customers involves the following steps:

(a) Identify potential customers
(b) Generate sales leads
(c) Screen out weak leads
(d) Select a group of qualified prospects
(e) Define the target customers

Target customers are one or more specific groups of potential customers that a firm proposes to serve with a particular marketing programme. Developing a profile of prospective customers is the starting point of the selling process. To do so, one should start with defining the market segment and end with identifying the target market.

Segmentation involves classifying or dividing the market into clear subsets of customers with comparable need patterns and those who behave or act in the same way. If one wants to sell an encyclopedia, college and university libraries should be treated as market segments. Target markets are those where the salesperson finds accessibility, demand situation, intention of the recommending authority (e.g., head of the library), and support of departmental heads as influencers. Students and libraries in the management institutions, for instance are the target markets for publishers of marketing books. Classifying the entire student community into pure science, engineering, arts, law and management, etc. helps a marketer reach a definite market segment.

After this, the marketer evolves the potential market within the segment. Potential market consists of a set of customers who profess some level of interest in a defined marketing offer. But, only a section of people of the potential market have the interest, financial power, access, and qualification to accept a specific market offer. They are known as qualified available customers and the market, so evolved, is known as the qualified available market.

Target customers are those parts of the qualified available market which the company decides to pursue. A company can treat a whole set of qualified available customers as target customers. The company selects a target market depending on the geography, size, characteristics and interests of the qualified available customers. Figure 3.2 shows the evolution of target market, on a whole.

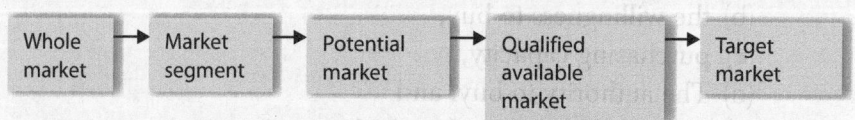

Figure 3.2   Evolution of target market

The result of good prospecting is a number of qualified prospects. It is advisable to get a small number of qualified prospects who are sure shots for the salesperson to explain large volume of sales. In fact, these prospects become the major customers. Hovering on a large number of weak or unsolicited prospects is disastrous for a salesperson as no such significant sales get generated.

Below are presented a set of questions that salespeople should ask a lead to identify them as a prospect. The questions are grouped under three heads:

1. Have the prospect perceived their need and expressed it to the salespeople?
2. Have the salespeople identified their need?
3. Do the salespeople have any solution to fulfil the need?

Qualifying a prospect is more important than locating one. It is mere wastage of time and energy if salespeople spend their efforts on poor or no potential leads.

After identification, the prospects should be subjected to the test of qualification to define them as valid prospects. Here, comes a set of questions a salesperson can introspect upon to judge the qualification of prospects.

1. Will the prospect buy?
2. Does the prospect have the buying capacity?
3. Does the prospect have the authority to take the buying decision?
4. Will the prospect buy from your company?
5. Whether the prospect will buy it now?
6. How is the given offer a demand for the prospect?
7. Will the volume of business with the prospect be profitable?

Prospects can be generated from many sources and some of the common sources and ways of identifying prospects are discussed below.

Present Customers

Existing customers are the best source of prospecting. Present customers can be a good source of information about the names and whereabouts of their acquaintances, relatives, neighborhoods, etc. who can be capable prospects. For instance, the departmental head of an arts faculty in an institution, a customer of a desktop computer company can suggest the name of the same in a different department to the salesperson of the computer firm as a potential customer for the product.

Former Customers

The database of a company can provide sufficient information about the whereabouts of their former customers. They can be traced, approached, and reasoned for their departure. Their current need levels for the same or new products can also be studied and they can finally be brought back to the company as present customers.

Centre of Influence Approach

This method is based on obtaining the names and identities of prospects from people who are well-known in a society or hold responsible positions in organizations, civic or local administration or have high social recognitions due to extraordinary accomplishments. They are known as centre of influence and their recommendations can help salespeople to get acquainted with unknown potential customers.

Personal Contact Method

By interacting with friends, relatives, neighbors or acquaintances in seminars, conferences, social programmes, travelling, etc. a salesperson may develop plenty of opportunities to identify prospects.

Endless Chain Method

A satisfied customer is requested to provide names of friends, business associates or any known acquaintances who may be potential customers. This procedure of generating a number of customers from them is repeated several times. So, this method implies a continuous cultivation of referral sources.

Direct Mail or Telephonic Contacts

By using telephone directories or yellow pages, salespeople can personally contact prospective buyers. They can also send letters along with product or service leaflets or booklets to the prospective buyers. Mass mailing gives a lot of exposure to the salespeople, company, and its products. Sometimes, a reply card or a similar format is attached with the letter for prompt response.

Cold Calling

It is yet another approach used to identify potential customers without any reference. Salespeople can call strangers in anticipation of getting a prospective customer, introduce themselves, and gather information about the presence of need for their product. Making cold calls is encouraged among salespeople when they find time between their scheduled appointments.

Electronic Mail Campaigns

Contacting prospective customers by sending them electronic mails along with attachments of product or service descriptions can also help generate a host of prospects for the salespeople. Besides, a firm can create blogs or use online social media channels to promote itself and/or its products.

Exhibitions and Trade Shows

A company can use exhibitions and trade shows as media to generate connections with prospective customers. A salesperson can distribute literature, pamphlets, free samples or exhibits to draw the attention of the prospects and approach them with their sales offer.

Non-competing Sales Force

Salesperson of non-competing firms often provide useful information about prospects for different product/service types as well. They are rich sources of information on new business opportunities. A salesperson selling LCD projectors in universities can be a good source of information for the demand for laptop or desktop computers in the universities.

Media

Many organizations advertise their requirements in newspapers or local television networks. These become a source of information for the customers.

Intermediaries

Intermediaries includes distributors, retailers or agents who work directly with customers, and can exchange valuable information about prospects to the sales-people.

3.3 PRE-APPROACH—A STEP TOWARDS SALES PLANNING

Pre-approach is a stage of collecting detailed information about prospects and deciding on the best sales method to reach them. Pre-approach is the fact-finding stage. Information about the needs of the prospects, their likes and dislikes, demographic characteristics, preferences, buying behaviour, personal behaviour, economic and social status is gathered, analysed, and used as a tool to lay down sales plan. In an organizational setting, pre-approach is more extensive. Box 3.1 furnishes the type of information a salesperson collects about prospective organizations.

Box 3.1   Information collected by salespeople on organizations

(a) Location, (b) type, say engineering firm, service firm, etc., (c) size, (d) present market position by sales volume, market share, etc., (e) present suppliers, (f) present competitors, (g) business goals, (h) buying criteria, (i) key buying authority, say purchase manager, (j) key influencers in buying, say, quality control manager has an influence on purchase manager in taking buying decision, (k) users of the product, (l) future business trend, (m) chief provider of information called gatekeeper who controls the flow of information, say secretary, receptionist or administrative staff, etc.

In a small organizations, a single person may act as buyer and influencer. Therefore, sale planning is comparatively easy. In large firms, a salesperson has to work out on more number of factors stated above to formulate a sales plan. A sales plan is a concise description of sales objectives, sales budget, and sales strategy of getting the product/service sold to the customers.

While planning a sales call, the following should be kept in mind to achieve best results:

1. Decide on the mode of appointment with the prospect, say sending an e-mail, writing a letter or telephonic contact, etc. Be particular on the kind of words used when taking an appointment. Words should be pre-planned or else a business opportunity may be lost forever.

2. After fixing the mode of appointment, a salesperson should go for call planning. This includes:

    (a) Whom to call? (prospect)
    (b) Where to call? (place)
    (c) When to call? (date and time)
    (d) How to call? (calling method)
    (e) At what expense to call? (sales budget)

Call planning should be made in a manner that allows salespeople to spend maximum possible time with major prospects because the latter are expected to account for large volume of business to the seller.

3. Prepare the sales talk, say, introductory message, points to be discussed, samples to be shown, probable objections from prospects to be faced during the presentation, replies to those objections, closing techniques, etc. should also be prepared.

4. Deciding on the sales strategy is another issue that should be tackled in the very beginning. It focuses on the means to reach the target customers successfully by matching the needs of the customers to the product or service.

5. It gives clear indication of the sales budgets, sales targets for salespeople within a time period, estimated sales revenues and profits, expected returns on investment, etc.

6. A sales plan suggests the type of salespeople who will be responsible to achieve the sales goals. It is important for them to be conversant with product or service attributes—characteristics, knowledge on company profiles, the strengths and weaknesses of the company, technology, growth prospect, profitability, future goals, etc.

7. A sales plan also has a provision of comparing actual versus target performance of the salespeople and prescribe different incentive schemes for high, medium, and low performing salespeople.

Selling strategies also varies according to different types of customers, organizations or even the products. The salespeople feel that sales transactions can only be effective if certain points are kept in mind. Some of these points are discussed below in Box 3.2.

Box 3.2   Selling strategies

For variation across customer groups, salespeople emphasize more on the following:

(a) Value for money for price-sensitive buyers
(b) Novelty and exclusiveness for prestige-conscious buyers
(c) Heritage and tradition for conservative buyers

For variation across products, salespeople emphasize more on the following:

(a) Product installation, knowledge of the customer, technological know-how, operations and maintenance support in case of a high-unit value products, e.g., boiler, milling machine, etc.
(b) Economy, quality, the image of the distributor or retailer in case of low-unit value products, e.g., toiletry products

Selling strategy varies across organizations. Salespeople representing large organizations emphasisze more on the image of the organization, research and development supports, reliability and financing, etc. Customer attention at individual level and customer relationship, etc. are more prioritized in small organizations.

The first impression is very crucial for the salespeople to begin a conversation with a reference or a common acquaintance or a referral. A salesperson should design the sales talk in a manner that can help him/her establish rapport with the prospect during the initial phase of approach itself. Non-business talks for a reasonable time are quite helpful to build a rapport. The objectives of this approach are as follows:

(a) To capture the attention of the prospect

(b) To create a favourable impression on the prospects so that they can accept the salesperson

There are certain tips which can help salespeople to fulfil these objectives effectively. Some of these are listed below in Exhibit 3.1.

Exhibit 3.1 Tips for effective results

1. The salespeople should introduce themselves and the company.
2. They should elaborate the purpose of the visit in a concise manner. They should not spend much time if the purpose of the visit has already been communicated to the prospect.
3. They should try an establish rapport by
   (a) Citing the names of common acquaintances, if any
   (b) Mentioning the names of referrals, say a current customer. It stands in good stead, in case the prospects know the current customer
   (c) Spending some time on non-business talk particularly on the areas of interest of the prospects
4. They should pronounce the name of the prospects correctly.
5. They should speak gently in a pleasing tone.
6. The salespeople should wear neat and tidy formal clothe and avoid dressing in loud colours. They should be smartly dressed and knot the tie properly, if wearing one.
7. They should hand a clean business card to the prospects. The cards should be well-designed and made on glossy stocks.
8. They should wait for the prospects to take the initiative to shake hands.
9. The salespeople should not to be seated until requested to.
10. They should take the initiative to start off a conversation and allow time to the prospect to talk. They should listen patiently and constructively to know what the prospects have in mind.
11. The salesperson should be seated in a normal posture while leaning forward towards the prospect.
12. They should avoid making hasty and excited gestures and interactions. Salespeople should be soft spoken, well-mannered, and should try to follow a pre-designed route of discussion.
13. They should concentrate on building relations at the preliminary stage as it removes the initial barrier of relational tension between two strangers.

(Contd)

(Contd)

14. They should remember to congratulate the prospect for any achievement or recent promotion.

15. They should not lose an opportunity to mention the name of a satisfied company or customer, whose identity will impress the prospect.

16. The salespeople should look at the belongings, furniture and fixtures, books, statues, photographs in the prospect's room to get an idea of the prospect's taste, preference, and culture.

17. They should try and gauge whether a prospect has
    (a) a real need for the product,
    (b) is dissatisfied with the present supplier,
    (c) the grounds of dissatisfaction with the present supplier, and
    (d) has an actual buying criteria in order of importance.

18. Salespeople should not get disheartened in case of rejection. Believe that every lost opportunity can bring forth a new opportunity in future. They should not forget to say thank you even in case of rejection.

After discussing certain tips that a salesperson should be familiar with, we will now list out a few techniques that can be used for approaching prospects:

Use a name of a referral   The name of a satisfied user of a product is an effective starting point.

Cite the company or brand name   Citing the name of a company or brand can be a major influencer to draw the attention of the prospect.

Compliment the prospect   A compliment is a novel way of establishing rapport with the prospect. By giving full recognition to him for some achievement or special award that the prospect acquires could be helpful as well.

Offer a gift   By presenting a gift or novelty to a prospect, a salesperson may gain a complete attention of the prospect.

Give the prospect a feel of influence   Salespeople reiterates the authority of the prospects in taking a buying decision. This helps the prospects feel how important they are.

Ask a planning question or statement   A good question (intelligent discussion) may open the prospect for discussion. For example, a sales person of UPS (uninterrupted power supply) equipment may ask a prospect. 'would you please lend a share of your mind of how you solve the crisis of frequent power cuts'.

Demonstrate the innovativeness in a product or service   A salesperson with an innovative product or service should not lose the opportunity to create an immediate impression by mentioning its features and benefits to the prospect and how it will be a better option than the existing product or service.

3.4 CUSTOMER'S NEED DISCOVERY—A PRIME CONCERN FOR SELLING

Uncovering the perceived needs of a customer should be the first and the foremost concern of the selling process. To fructify it, a salesperson should ask questions and listen intently to know what the prospect is saying. The objective should be to gain as much information as possible on the prospect's present buying problem. Thorough probing helps the prospects to understand their needs. In case, the prospect has full recognition of the need situation, he/she can decipher these to the salesperson and in this regard, logical questioning to the prospect would definitely elicit his/her need. However, questions should be designed, sequenced, and asked in a way that the prospect does not feel uncomfortable in responding to these questions.

The few initial questions of the salesperson should aim to build trust and rapport with the prospect so that getting them to cooperate is not a problem. Showing urge, interest, and positive attitude enthuses the prospects to speak about their need situations But what is crucial is that the salesperson should allow the prospect to talk more in the initial phase of discussion and listen ardently and sympathetically to find out how the prospect is affected by the need deficiency.

Gaining confidence of the prospect is the primary motto of the salesperson. This is needed because:

(a) A salesperson is a stranger to the prospect. It should not be expected that the prospect will easily disclose the problem to an unknown person.

(b) A prospect may not psychologically accept the salesperson as a problem solver, i.e., the prospect may have preconceived notion that the salesperson has no problem-solving ability and, therefore, discussion is of no use.

(c) At the initial stage, the prospects seldom consider a salesperson as an empathizer to mitigate their problem.

So the basic task of the salesperson is to help the prospects feel free and uncluttered, and instil a sense of confidence in them. Questions here act as effective selling tool to ease out the relational infidelity and bring out the unexplored domain of the prospect's mind.

Getting Information

Questions are of two types, open-ended questions and close-ended questions. Open-ended questions are the ones that are used to instruct the prospects to answer in their own words. An unidentified problem area finds much additional information by open-ended questions. For example, a sales person may ask a prospect about how the current economic slowdown may be affecting his buying policy? From the prospect's response, the salesperson can get an idea about the prospect's point of view and get some ideas about any selling opportunity that can generate. Close-ended questions provide response options to a question. For example, 'Are you in search of a new supplier for raw materials?' Salespeople should use both open- and close-ended questions depending on the type of information they want to elicit from the prospects. Open-ended questions are helpful to get insights of the problem whereas close-ended ones fulfil the fact-finding purpose.

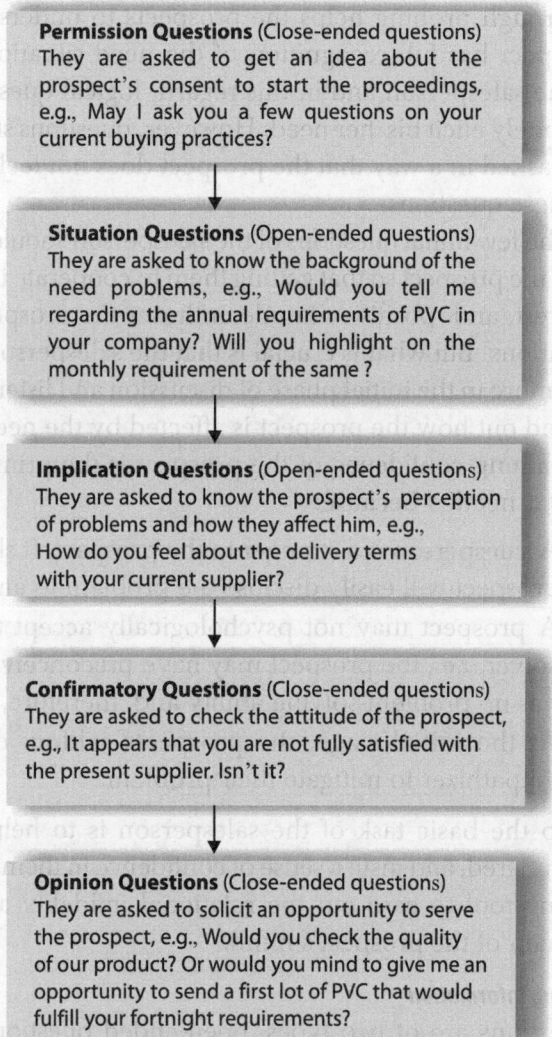

Permission Questions (Close-ended questions)
They are asked to get an idea about the prospect's consent to start the proceedings, e.g., May I ask you a few questions on your current buying practices?

Situation Questions (Open-ended questions)
They are asked to know the background of the need problems, e.g., Would you tell me regarding the annual requirements of PVC in your company? Will you highlight on the monthly requirement of the same ?

Implication Questions (Open-ended questions)
They are asked to know the prospect's perception of problems and how they affect him, e.g., How do you feel about the delivery terms with your current supplier?

Confirmatory Questions (Close-ended questions)
They are asked to check the attitude of the prospect, e.g., It appears that you are not fully satisfied with the present supplier. Isn't it?

Opinion Questions (Close-ended questions)
They are asked to solicit an opportunity to serve the prospect, e.g., Would you check the quality of our product? Or would you mind to give me an opportunity to send a first lot of PVC that would fulfill your fortnight requirements?

Figure 3.3 Guidelines for questions

Salespeople should ask questions in a systematic and a stepwise manner. They should start with a broad question and gradually narrow down to the specific one to get a clear picture of the needs and demands of the prospects. Figure 3.3 represents a guideline to the sequence and pattern of the questions that are asked.

3.5 SALES PRESENTATION—SCOPE AND METHODS

A sales presentation is a central part of selling. A good sales presentation, sometimes, even moves an indifferent prospect to a point of purchase. It also softens the stand of loyal customers of competing products to try out the new offer. The mode of presentation should conform to the nature of product or service, the prospect's need situation, interest, buying criteria, buying authority, and time schedule for presentation. The presentation relates product(s) or service(s) features with benefits which, in turn becomes a solution to the prospect's problem. Simply, presenting the product/service attributes without linking their benefits generates a listless presentation.

A presentation is a vivid description of product/service features and associated benefits that satisfies the requirements of the prospects. Presentations can be made lively and believable, if claims of feature-benefit relationships are evinced by substantive proofs and documentary supports. Therefore, if presentation is coupled with display of product-in-use demonstration, visual aids, test reports certified by recognized authority, etc. salespeople can get an opportunity to justify the claims and persuade the prospects to act in their favour.

Dos and Don'ts

The presentation should focus on customer and centre around how the product or service would solve the customer's problem. So, during a presentation, a salesperson should:

1. Specify the unique features and benefits that competitors cannot or do not offer.
2. Always create an association between the features and customer benefits.
3. Combine verbal deliberation with demonstration. Use charts, graphs, flip-charts, pictures, models, videos, slides, product samples as aids to establish a sense of trust with the customer.
4. Ward off doubts and confusions of the customers by a judicious combination of presentations and demonstrations. In this regard, testimonials (e.g., reports from satisfied customers), examples by citing evidences, pay-back assurances in case of non-compliance between whatever promised by the salespeople and the actual experience of the product/service can be resorted to.
5. Do not indulge in one-sided presentation. Illustrate the key points of offer and allow the customers to participate in the discussion.
6. Do not undermine your competitors by criticizing them unnecessarily in front of the customers.
7. Make your presentation animated so that it can appeal to the senses of the customers. Uninteresting and dull presentations may destroy chances of selling even innovative products or services.

8. Do not involve in any argument with customers during presentation. Patiently listen to the problems/complaints/suggestions of the customers and answer them point wise after the presentation.

9. If the product or service being offerd has any demerits, do not hide them. But, do not forget to mention how the company has taken measures or will take care to counter these demerits. Otherwise, try to outweigh the demerits by merits of the product/service.

3.5.1 Presentation Methods

Broadly, organizations decide on the method of presentation based on the type of customer, type of salesperson, and products or services dealt in. For major customers, efforts are made to make customer-specific presentations that demand special attention from the sales managers or senior sales personnel. For other customers, salespeople are asked to follow the organization-sponsored common form of presentation, with no variation from the prepared message.

Senior salespeople are given more freedom to design their own presentations whereas juniors follow the presentation guidelines given by the company. For technically complex products, presentation should be more demonstrative and document-oriented. A generalized presentation is quite helpful for mass or standardized products. Based on the above discussion, three types of sales presentations can be suggested to sell products or services effectively. These are as follows:

(a) Canned presentation

(b) Organized presentation

(c) Tailored presentation

Canned Presentation

Canned presentation is a structured presentation where a company prepares the contents of the presentation exactly in a manner the way it is to be presented. During the presentation, salespeople memorize it and convey the same message with little or no modification in the script. New or junior salespeople feel comfortable with this type of presentation. However, senior sales personnel may not feel compatible with memorized presentations because over their years of experience, they are confident of interacting with customers in their own styles. Moreover, for handling a wide range of products, canned presentation becomes a tedious affair. This is because a different presentation has to be prepared for every product. This technique is often dull and uninteresting, and fails to arouse any enthusiasm amongst customers.

Organized Presentation

In organized presentation, salespeople are given a checklist containing all selling points and are permitted to prepare the message of presentation based on those points. This method is highly flexible because salespeople can prepare the wordings of the sales message and present it in their own style. The only caution in this method to be remembered is that no selling point should be missed during the presentation. Utter care should also be taken not to digress from the company's marketing or sales plan at the time of deliberation. Both new and experienced salespeople can use it but experienced salespeople can better manage this method.

Tailored Presentation

Tailored presentation is a specially prepared sales presentation message for an individual customer where a customer's requirements, preferences or personal goals are found to be unique. It emphasizes on the fulfilment of specialized needs of the customers. Only senior sales personnel are allowed to apply this presentation technique.

3.6 HANDLING OBJECTIONS—A NATURAL EXPERIENCE IN SELLING

Objections are viewed as a natural part of a sales presentation. Objection, in fact, is resistance from the prospective buyers to block the completion of selling. But, objections are welcomed in the selling process because these are clear indications of a prospect's interest in the offer as they await satisfactory replies from the salespeople. Therefore, an objection is more of an opportunity than an obstacle to sales. The prospects raise objections due to the following reasons:

(a) Instinctive concern or fear of taking or not taking a decision to buy.
(b) Prospects want more information from the salespeople.
(c) Prospects do not find a suitable match between their perceived needs and the ability of the offer to satisfy their needs.
(d) Prospects want to know more about the product/service and here, the knowledge of the salesperson about the product or service is put to test.
(e) Prospects want to be sure whether the promises claimed by the salesperson have any real basis or not.
(f) Prospects do not know much about the company being represented by the salesperson. In fact, they want to be categorical about the identity or image of the company.
(g) Prospects want to buy some time to take the buying decision. They are not confident about the product/service having met all the buying criteria despite being satisfied on some characteristics of the offer.
(h) Prospects need more assurance on the quality of the product/service.
(i) Prospects want to bargain on price.

(j) Prospects want more facilitating functions from the salesperson, say, customer training on the product.

(k) Prospects want to compare the product/service of the existing supplier and the current product/service proposal in hand.

In fact, objections are triggers for getting more information from the salespeople. A salesperson should not think that a prospect who has not raised any objection and remained calm will be a genuine customer. Often, non-interactive prospects do not want to take any buying decision or they refuse to buy. Thus, objections are questions demanding more explanation from the salespeople. Objections reduce the mental barriers between the prospects and the salespeople and get them closer and acceptable to each other. Responding to objections build a rapport between the two. Following Exhibit 3.2 discusses some of these objections through examples.

Exhibit 3.2   Examples of some objections

Time Objection

Many prospects take time for buying decisions and therefore, do not agree to act immediately. The real reason for delaying the buy is an enigma to the salesperson. A salesperson finds solution to such an objection by finding the real reason for it.

Strategy to be used by the salespeople: Salespeople show the cost of delay for taking a late buying decision to the prospective buyers. It means, if the prospects fail to take the decision immediately, they will have to suffer by cost enhancement, i.e., losing some advantages that may not be present in future, etc. In many situations, some implicit reasons are hidden behind time objection. By asking questions a salesperson can identify the real reasons. Suppose the budgetary provision does not allow the prospects to take a buying decision immediately. In such cases, it is better to take an appointment with the prospects in the nearest future as per the prospect's convenience.

Examples: The prospects say something like the following, when they do not want to buy immediately.

(a) 'Your offer appears to have meaning, but I have to discuss the matter with VP.'

(b) 'Sorry, I can't take any decision right now.'

Need Objection

During the presentation, a prospect expresses no need for the product or service, that the salesperson is promoting.

Strategy to be used by the salespeople: Converting 'having no reason to buy' to 'a reason to buy' is the technique to entice dogged prospects to the company's offer. The salesperson, here, should explain to the customer about the severity of future circumstances.

Example: During conversation between a salesperson of an insurance policy and the prospect

Prospect: 'I have no need for such a policy. Moreover, I can't afford it.'

(Contd)

Salesperson: 'You need a policy. God forbids, if any misfortune happens with you, who will look after your family? Your kids? At a negligible premium per annum, you can have a safe future.'

Competition Objection

A prospect may express satisfaction with the present supplier. He feels no need to change the present supplier.

Strategy to be used by the salespeople: In such circumstances, the salespeople can invite the prospects to have a trial of the new product or take part in the demonstration, free of cost.

Example: During a conversation between a seller trying to sell a new brand of washing machine to the prospect.

Prospect: 'Why should I change the present supplier? Moreover, I don't feel right to change the present supplier.'

Salesperson: 'I respect your decision, sir. I am not suggesting you to change the present supplier. I am just asking you to try out these free samples of our product.'

Source Objection

This type of objection has its origin in the past buying/selling situations when the customer was left unhappy. The customer has developed a negative mindset about the company.

Strategy to be used by the salespeople: The salesperson should identify the reasons for dissatisfaction and show the prospect how the situation is different now. But, if the prospect's logic has no valid ground, the salesperson can refute it gently by citing the case histories of the product.

Example: A dialogue where a salesperson is trying to cover-up their previous mistake.

Prospect: 'Last time your salesperson made a lofty promise about the product quality, which was simply a lie.'

Sales person: 'Your concern is totally valid. But this time our company has given special attention to the products to match their quality with the customer's expected quality standard. Please give me an opportunity to prove the worth of my product.'

Service Objection

The customer has a negative concern regarding the service part of selling. The customer has reservations on the delivery policy, credit policy, return policy in case of defective items, etc.

Strategy to be used by the salespeople: One can claim to provide service policies to be customer-friendly by either citing references or by compensating an apparently rigid policy by the flexibility of another. For example, a customer may be asked to join an annual maintenance contract on a purchased machine for an initial investment of a certain sum but the customer will have no worries for maintenance of that machine for one year.

Example: A salesperson of a transport company interacts with the prospect.

Prospect: 'Your delivery policy is too tight.'

Salesperson: 'Apparently true! But our customers are immensely benefited by punctuality in our delivery.'

Price Objection

Price is a common objection in selling. Here, the prospects feel that the price of the offer is high and they cannot afford it. The prospect draws comparison with the competitor's price to complain about the high price of the salesperson's product/service.

(Contd)

(Contd)

Strategy to be used by the salespeople: Make a counterclaim of product quality and/or other benefits to handle price objection. Secondly, liberal credit policy on purchase can help the prospect feel comfortable on higher price.

Example: A negotiation between a salesperson and a prospect.

Prospect: 'Everything is all right but the price of the product is too high.'

Salesperson: 'True, but you can't juxtapose any of the competitor's product by ours on quality and added features.' (Here, the salespeople can proclaim higher quality or more features about his product by sidewise comparison of their product with the competitors, presenting literatures and manuals. The quality certification by any recognized scientific body or association can establish the salesperson's point.)

Pseudo-objections

These are mere pretexts of the prospect to avoid a salesperson. In fact, the prospect poses lame excuses to abstain from any discussion with the salesperson. Few reasons are:

(a) The prospect is not interested to change the present supplier.

(b) The prospect has a dearth of fund.

(c) The prospect is in a tight situation, i.e., low on cash on personal grounds.

(d) The prospect does not like the salesperson due to some reasons. (For example, the prospect does not like the approaching style of the salesperson.)

Strategy to be used by the salespeople: Follow the body language of the prospect and if reasons appear to be baseless, continue the discussion. But if the prospect is obstinate, leave but show promptness to meet soon and even request to decide on a date of future appointment.

Examples: In such situations, the prospect presents excuses such as,

(a) 'I'm very busy now.'

(b) 'I have an urgent meeting to attend.'

(c) 'I will get back to you.'

(d) 'We can't accommodate you this financial year.'

3.7 CLOSING THE SALE

The efforts of the salesperson culminates only by getting an order from the prospect. This is the final attempt of the salesperson to make the prospect agree to the business proposal and place for an order. Therefore, this is a crucial step in the selling process. Success in selling or buying is meaningful only when the prospect decides to buy at the agreed terms and conditions that satisfy both the buyer and the seller.

'Closing the sales' refers to a situation when the salesperson reaches an agreement with the prospect. But, the vital points to be remembered during the closing are the selection of the right time and the way to close the sales. It is important to keep in mind that at the time of closing, the prospect should be rationally and/or psychologically moved to strike a business deal. An early close or a late close can end a delicate approach and sound presentation in vain. Many salespeople make blunder in the closing stage by becoming hesitant or lazy thus proving them unsuccessful. Therefore, they are trained to know two important issues in closing. These two are:

(a) When to close
(b) How to close

When to Close

Here, the ability of a salesperson to gauge the buying signal from the prospect is of utter importance. This buying signal is not necessarily a verbal statement or question from the prospect, but can be non-verbal also. A prospect can signal ascent by affirmative eye movement, facial expression or positive gestures through physical actions by which the salesperson can judge the mood, attitude, and intention of the prospect and request an order immediately. Therefore, in many situations, understanding the non-verbal communication from the prospect can help a salesperson to take initiative in closing the sales.

But, in order to handle the closing part of the selling process safely, a salesperson applies a trial close before the actual close. Trial close is a confident and polite statement or question from the salespeople to the prospects that induce them to reflect an opinion on the offer in verbal terms; the actual close, on the other hand, indicates the decisive mind of the prospect to accede to the request for sale.

Examples of trial close statements/questions are as follows:

1. I think the proposal matches your requirement.
2. I think the proposal sounds good to you.
3. How important do you feel in our offer?
4. Is this what you have been searching for?
5. I think this was in your mind.
6. Is this consistent with what you have been contemplating?

How to Close

Salespeople apply their judgment to decide which closing technique to use. However, a salesperson is trained and instructed to study the selling situation and the prospect, and only then choose a technique to pick an order. Of course, it also depends on the type of product/service, company policies, incentive schemes to the salespeople and discounts, commissions or allowances for customer's impact on the closing techniques. Implications of these situations can be better understood if we discuss different closing techniques that are applied to seal the final buying agreement with the prospective buyers. Some useful closing techniques are described below:

Alternative close   Alternative closing finds sense when a particular offer (product) has few alternatives, say colour, size or capacity variations available. The salesperson requests the prospect to choose among the alternatives. For example, the salesperson of refrigerators can ask a prospect 'Do you prefer green or violet?

What's your choice, 165 or 230 litres capacity?' Offering options facilitate the prospects to reach to a buying conclusion shortly.

Assumption close   The salesperson takes an assumptive stance that the prospect has agreed to buy. He takes an initiative to write a buying order and requests the prospect to sign it. Here, the mood and perception of the prospect is very important. If the salesperson is able to generate a sense of confidence in the prospect, assumption close can be a worthy closing technique.

Concession close   Concession closing is a kind of deal where the prospect is enticed to come to buying/selling terms in exchange for some monetary concession. Here, the salesperson is given the liberty from the company to offer incentives to the customers for prompt response to buying decision.

Gift close   Gift closing is a type of additional inducement to the prospects to make them take a buying action immediately. The salesperson may request the prospect as, 'If you sign the buying order right now, we will deliver the product to you at no transportation cost. Our company offers this policy for a short term to encourage new customers to buy.'

Balance sheet close   Salespeople sum up the discussion between themselves and the prospects by noting the pros and cons of taking a buying decision where the reasons for acting now are listed on one side and the same for pending decision on the other. The salesperson always weighs the pros side to outdo the cons with persuasive arguments and incite the prospect to go for signing the order form.

Direct close   In direct closing, a salesperson plainly asks the prospect to take a decision. This technique is extremely useful when the product or service has strong merits or the buying signal from the prospect is too positive. The salesperson should not hesitate to directly request a prospect to take an immediate action.

Action close   A salesperson takes an action to close down the sales, particularly when the prospect hesitates to take an immediate decision. For example, a salesperson can request the purchase manager of an engineering firm intending to purchase switchgears, 'In fact, quality specifications are the major points of your buying decision. May I talk to R&D manager on the details of the product specifications?'

Bonus close   The salesperson promises to offer some attractive incentives along with the purchased items that may lure the prospect to clinch the deal. Say, the selling firm will take charge of full maintenance of the machine for three years at no cost involvement of the buying firm.

Best-time close   Persuading prospective buyers to take immediate decisions to buy else they might face purchase difficulties in future is also a useful technique. The salesperson says, 'From the next month the present scheme will not be effective and you will have to pay 20 per cent more to buy our items.'

3.8 FOLLOW-UP AFTER SALES—IMPORTANCE AND METHODS

Following up after sales is a very important stage of the selling process. Salespeople should not believe that the selling process is complete once the transaction is over. Rather, first time selling is the beginning of the sales cycle. Follow-up is not less important in creating satisfied customers. Only a satisfied customer approaches again for a second time buying and the process continues. Moreover, they help to create a number of new customers for the selling firm by word-of-mouth. So, ignoring follow-up is a serious drawback in selling.

Follow-up refers to the after-sales activities that are undertaken to provide service to the customers and build a growing and a lasting relationship with them. It is used to describe all the efforts that are made to keep the customers content with the purchased item. In fact, follow-up starts immediately after closing the sale. The salesperson takes the responsibility of delivering the product or service at the predetermined place and time. On receipt of the product by the customers, the salesperson should provide sales support by supervising proper installation, customer training, supplying user's manuals, sales proceeds, etc. The salesperson should also get in touch with the customer in case a customer is dissatisfied with the product.

The objectives of the 'after-sales activities' are as follows:

(a) To complement the customer for taking a purchase decision in favour of the company. By showing gratitude to customers, which is the maiden step during follow-up, leads to future sales.
(b) To prove that the responsibility of the company is not over after selling, the company takes care of a customer's convenience.
(c) To affirm that the customer has taken the right decision in choosing the item. This is needed to even out any post-purchase doubt of the customer. Moreover, selling the same item to other customers and bringing this information to a customer builds their confidence on the buying decision.
(d) To bind both the buyer and the seller in a relationship of trust, dependability, and integrity.
(e) To generate more referrals from the present customers. Satisfied customers lessen the task of the salesperson by influencing others to buy from the same firm.

Methods of Follow-up

Following are the methods that can be used to follow-up after sales:

(a) Sending a message of complement immediately after the purchase through letters, e-mails, notes, etc. with a request to inform the company in case the customers comes across any problem with the product or service.
(b) Getting feedbacks from the customers regularly (e.g., monthly, quarterly) and taking prompt action against any complaints received from them

(c) Sending in house magazines, newsletters, gifts, gritting cards, communicating good wishes on customer's birthday, inviting them to company socials, offering lunch or dinner on special occasions, etc. carry significant message of the selling firm's concern for customers.

(d) Keeping the technical or service personnel always informed and solicitous to take an action when customers confront troubles that demand technical attention or immediate servicing.

An earnest intent to serve customers can bring the salesperson in the confidence of the customer that opens the door of future possibility of businesses with the present customers. Furthermore, the present customers can be a good source of identifying new customers.

Therefore, it can be said that selling is a stepwise process. Each step contributes to the success of selling. A salesperson should have all round ability to identify and qualify prospects, display right attitude and attention to instil confidence in the customers, exhibit mental preparedness to confront questions from the customers, convert a prospective buyer to an actual buyer and keep in constant touch with customers to solve post-sale problems with the products. A salesperson must have the capacity to read a selling situation, the expectations and attitudes of the customers towards product quality, price, frequency of buying, credit buying, payment schedules, etc. and treat each customer separately.

SUMMARY

Selling is a sequential process. It encompasses prospecting, pre-approach, approach, sales presentation, handling objections, closing the sales, and follow-up. Prospecting involves search for qualified potential customers. Common sources of prospecting are present customers, former customers, cold calls, centre of influences, etc. Pre-approach is a fact finding stage of collecting detailed information on prospects and deciding the best method of approach.

Approach means meeting the customers and making goal-directed conversations with them. Some common approaching techniques use a name of a referral, cite the name of the company or brand, complement the prospect, etc. Need discovery of prospect is also an important part of approach. A salesperson should proceed on a logical question sequence to identify the need of the prospect. The sequence involves beginning with a permission question, followed by situation question, implication question, confirmatory question, and opinion question.

Effective presentation follows the AIDA approach, i.e., drawing the attention of the customer, arousing interest, stimulating desire, and prompting customer action. Common presentation techniques are classified into canned, organized, and tailored presentations. Handling objections is commonplace in sales presentation. Salespeople face objections on time, need, competition, source, etc. Each objection should be addressed by appropriate selling strategy.

A sales effort culminates with closing the sales, i.e., getting the order. Close is preceded by trial close. Some common closing techniques are alternative close, assumption close, concession close, gift close, etc. Follow-up is a post-sales activity. It aims to provide service to the customer and reduce post-purchase dissonance. The objective is to create an enduring relationship with the customer. Success in selling depends on proper execution of the stages of selling.

KEY TERMS

Canned Presentation Canned presentation is a structured presentation where a company prepares the contents of the presentation and directs the salesperson to follow it.

Organized Presentation Organized presentation is a technique where the salespeople are given a checklist containing all the selling points and are permitted only to prepare the message of presentation based on those points themselves.

Prospecting Prospecting is the first stage of personal selling which involves searching for a potential customer, also known as prospect, and making him qualified for the product.

Tailored Presentation Tailored presentation is a specially prepared sales presentation message for individual customers where the requirements, preferences or personal goals of the customer are found to be unique.

CONCEPT REVIEW QUESTIONS

1. Briefly illustrate the steps in the selling process.
2. What is prospecting? What is its importance? Mention some sources of prospecting.
3. Why pre-approach is must before approach to prospect?
4. What precautions should a salesperson take during approach to the prospective customer?
5. Why is it important to undergo need discovery of a prospect? How is it undertaken?
6. What are the different sales presentation techniques?
7. Illustrate the importance of handling objections during sales presentation. How are time, need, and source objections handled?
8. What do you mean by closing the sales? What are the different closing techniques?
9. Why is follow-up regarded as an important step in selling? Explain two follow-up methods.

CRITICAL THINKING QUESTION

AMZ Corporation manufactures and sells vacuum cleaners. It primarily depends on its salesperson to push the product through the distribution channel. Omkar Corporation, its main competitor and market leader, adopts a dual channel policy, selling the product through distributors and reaching the customers through salespeople directly using the door-to-door selling approach. In the first situation, the salespeople of the distributors do the personal selling and in the second, both salespeople of the distributors and salespeople of the company undertake it.

1. Do you think personal selling objectives vary from the salespeople of the distributors to the salespeople of a company?
2. Do you think the role of personal selling would be different for single and dual distribution strategies?
3. What are the personal selling problems which the salespeople confront under these two selling strategies?

PROJECT ASSIGNMENTS

1. Interview a group of ten salespeople selling credit cards regarding the problems they encounter during prospecting. How much support do they get from the company in prospecting?
2. Meet ten housewives of moderate economic strata who have an experience in meeting and purchasing from these door-to-door salespeople of two to three well-known organizations pursuing direct selling (e.g., Amway). Interview them and collect information on the following:

(a) Their attitude towards door-to-door selling and salespeople

(b) Their attitude towards such organizations

(c) Reliability of the product

(d) Satisfaction or dissatisfaction with price

(e) Apprehension of future service, if any

(f) Mental satisfaction

Prepare a 5-point attitude scale where 1 indicates extremely bad and 5 represents extremely good to show the average views of the housewives on door-to-door selling.

REFERENCES

Johnson, E.M., D.L. Kurtz, and E.E. Scheuing (1994), *Sales Management: Concepts, Practices and Cases*, 2nd ed. McGraw-Hill Inc., New York.

Kotler, P. and G. Armstrong (2006), *Principles of Marketing*, 11th ed., Prentice-Hall of India Private Limited, New Delhi.

Still, R.R., E.W. Cundiff, and N.A.P. Govoni (1994), *Sales Management: Decisions, Strategies and Cases*, 5th ed., Prentice-Hall of India Private Limited, New Delhi.

CASE STUDIES

1. Success in Insurance Selling, in Search of Causes

Zip Inc., a private insurance company, is headquartered in Mumbai. Taking privilege of liberalized economic policy in India and entry of private insurance players in the financial markets, the company expands its operation in other parts of India as well. The company has recently engaged two hundred salespeople and instructed them to join an intensive training programme for two months. The training emphasizes more on:

(a) Developing customer awareness on insurance products

(b) Identifying the needs of the customers

(c) Educating the customers on the need for insurance

(d) Suggesting the customers on the specific policy that will best match their income level, age, and benefits sought from the policy

(e) Assisting the customer to buy the policy

(f) Cooperating with customer in maintaining the policy for the stipulated time period

In this regard, salespeople are also advised to note:

(a) Needs of the customer

(b) Purchasing power

(c) Liking/disliking to insurance policy

(d) Specific reasons to buy or not to buy the policy. For example, a customer buys the policy that will fetch him a house-building loan

The company also warns the salespersons that they will confront problems from customers of the following types:

(a) Customers express the needs but does not mention anything else.
(b) Customers express needs but lack buying power.
(c) Customers express need and have the buying power but are not interested in the buying policy.
(d) Customers have need, buying power, and interest but are confused about choosing the right policy.
(e) Customers have all such qualities mentioned in point (d) but have apathy toward investing money in private insurance firms on safety and security grounds.

Discussion Question

Being a sales manager of the insurance company, how do you prepare your salespeople to face different situations?

2. Genesis of a Selling Problem

A software company confronted a problem of indifference from the customers towards dilatory practices of decision-making and finalizing terms and conditions. The company was in a quandary of how to tackle this selling situation. The company appointed a marketing research firm to investigate the crisis. Upon surveying the situation, the firm made it clear that the salespeople had no problems in building awareness and interest about the product amongst prospective buyers. In fact, salespeople were quite successful in product presentation and in establishing points of technological edges of the product over competitors.

Secondly, the research also revealed that customers were not alike in their reasons for resentment. For example, a section of customers felt that offers of competing products were far more attractive on price factors while another group felt that price was not commensurate with quality. A detailed probing of the issue finally settled that price was the major problem for the customers to come to terms with. Though the company knew about it, it could not afford to reduce price. The company, instead, resolved the problem by the following:

(a) Counterbalancing the higher price by providing a feeler of less replacement cost compared to the competitors.
(b) Mediating a financial firm to offer credits to the customers keeping the pricing terms intact. This was also unique compared to competitors.

(c) Washing out wrong notions of customers on quality-price mismatch by hands-on demonstration of the product.

The results were outstanding. The sales picked up steeply and the company outsmarted the competing firms convincingly.

Discussion Questions

1. List the pros and cons of the company's software that influence the responses of the prospective buyers.
2. Do you think the measures the company adopted would pay in the long term? Does it not have too much indirect cost implications?

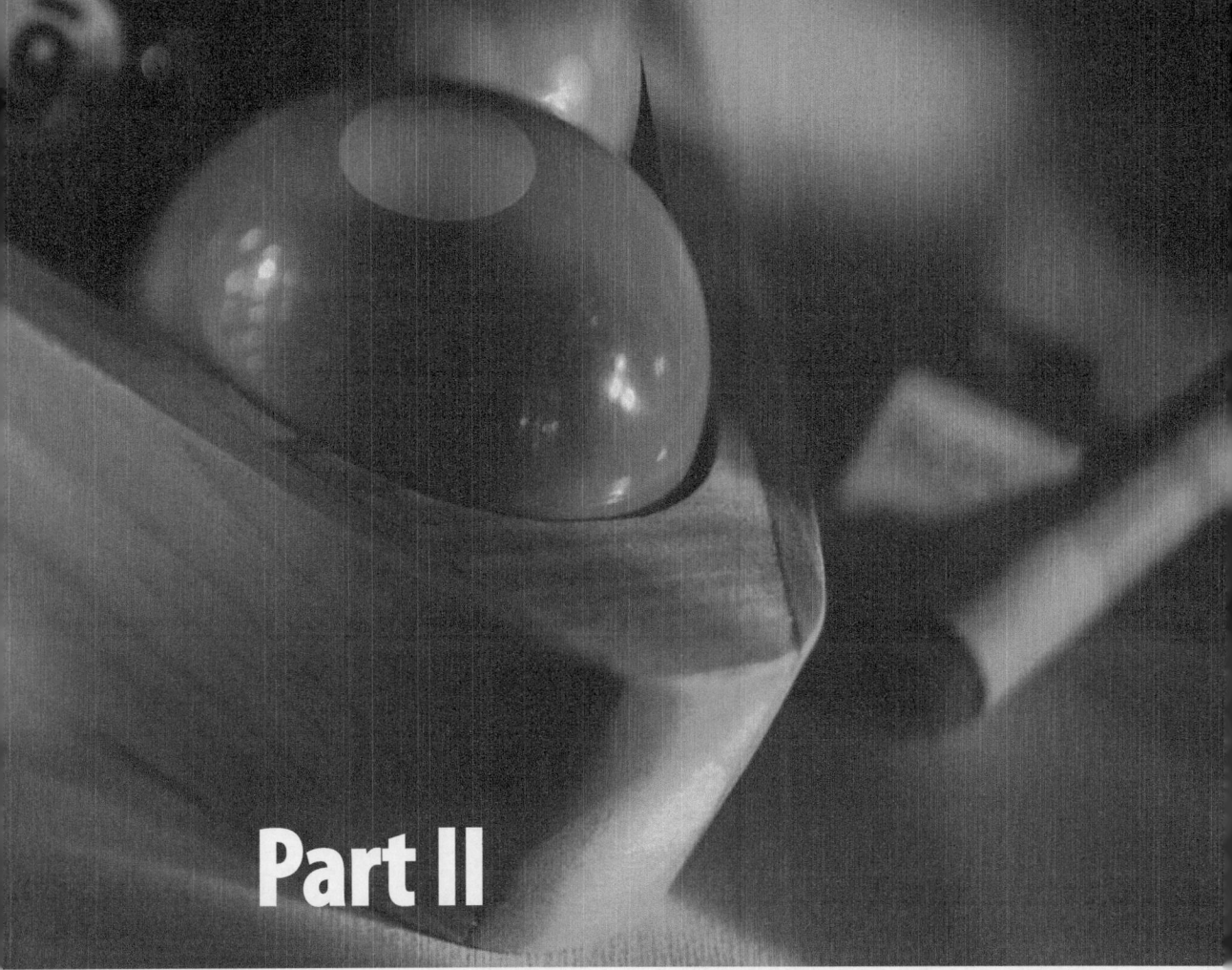

Part II

Organization of Sales Force Functions

Part II

Organization of Sales Force Functions

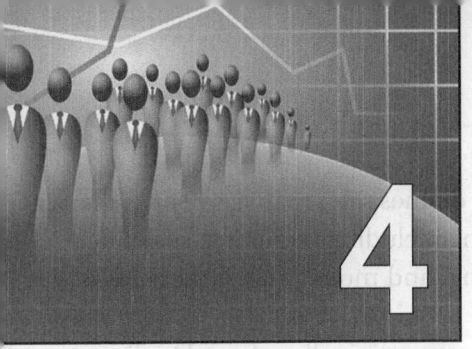

4 Sales Force Management

LEARNING OBJECTIVES

After reading this chapter, you will be able to

- provide insights into the conceptual framework of sales management, its task elements, and functional orientations
- understand the guidelines for planning a sales operation, its implementation, evaluation, and controlling issues
- explain the environmental impacts on sales planning and the benefits of understanding the environmental issues in formulating the sales plan
- discuss the guidelines to plan a sales operation
- discuss the role of strategic planning on sales management
- give valuable inputs on the tasks and roles of sales managers
- appreciate the essential qualities of a sales manager

4.1 SALES MANAGEMENT—AN INTRODUCTION

It is important for organizations to develop and maintain an effective sales force. This is because a sales manager is not only entrusted with managing the sales force to derive target-based sales outcomes but also perform managerial functions comprising planning the sales efforts and organizing, directing, motivating, coordinating, and controlling the sales force to achieve sales goals. Sales management operates within the periphery of marketing management. In a broad sense, marketing management decides the role of various promotional activities including personal selling.

Sales management is assigned the task of managing the personal selling activities, the results of which ultimately affect the marketing department. Sales management specifically contributes to achieve the marketing objectives of a firm. In fact, sales managers set their personal selling objectives and formulate the personal selling policies and strategies. They prepare the sales budget as components of marketing plans, taking in confidence the broad objectives of the marketing department.

Sales management covers planning and organizing personal selling activities. It further performs sales force recruiting, selecting, training, assigning, routing, directing, motivating, remunerating, evaluating, and controlling functions of personal selling. Sales management implements the marketing plan to generate sales performance.

Ingram et al. (2007) noted that sales managers are involved in both the strategy (planning) and people (implementation) aspects of personal selling, as well as evaluating and controlling personal selling activities.

The American Marketing Association (AMA) defines sales management as the planning, direction, and control of personal selling including recruiting, selecting, equipping, assigning, routing, supervising, paying, and motivating as these tasks apply to personal sales force.

Still et al. (1988) illustrated that sales management, originally referred to direction of sales force, later assumed a broader description in addition to management of personal selling to include advertising, sales promotion, marketing research, physical distribution, pricing, and product merchandising. In time, it became more popularly known as marketing management which described the broader concept. So, in simpler terms, sales management is the managerial process of utilizing people and other resources optimally to achieve the goals of an organization in a cost-effective way.

Indeed, the role of sales management becomes more pervasive by finding its importance both within and outside the firm. Within the firm, it builds an organizational structure which allows both formal and informal communication amongst sales and other departments. This also helps in establishing a distribution network outside the company encompassing salespeople and/or intermediaries that serve as a medium to reach target customers. Box 4.1 summarizes the major tasks of sales management.

Box 4.1 Task elements in sales management

Following are the task elements in sales management:

(a) Determining personal selling objectives that can give direction to the sales force as to what is to be achieved

(b) Formulating sales policies which can set guidelines for selling

(c) Mapping out sales strategies that can draw up action plans to accomplish personal selling objectives

(d) Developing sales budgets based on sales forecasts and estimated selling expenses within an estimated period of time

(e) Deciding on the structure of the sales network

(f) Designing sales territories and deciding the size of the sales force

(g) Fixing up target sales for each territory in terms of sales volume or in monetary value

(h) Recruiting, selecting, and training the sales force (staffing)

(i) Assigning salespeople to their respective territories, offering them their targets (sales quota), supervising and motivating them, coordinating their activities, evaluating their performance, and controlling their actions in case the performance does not corroborate with the sales objectives

(j) Designing compensation packages for the sales force

(k) Providing feedback to the marketing department

4.2 FUNCTIONS OF SALES MANAGEMENT—A REVIEW

Selling must be managed if it aims to fulfil the marketing objectives of a firm. A firm's marketing objective is also to enter a new market segment and inspire customers to buy their product/service through personal selling efforts. As selling is an intervening step in marketing, therefore, sales management is at the core of the fulfilment of the marketing objectives. But, selling becomes an unaccomplished task without the aid of effective distribution and promotion. Therefore, management of distribution and promotional tools bolsters sales management, which in turn, weaves the roadmap of success in marketing. Therefore, one can say that sales management, broadly, is the management of personal selling functions. Therefore, to understand the tasks of sales management and how it attains the sales goals of an organization, it is important to know the functional components of sales management. It basically consists of three interrelated functions.

First, management must decide what functions the sales managers should perform. This includes defining the role and objectives of the sales force, organizing the sales force, and formulating an account (customer) for the management policies. Collectively this is known as *sales plan formulation.*

Second, sales management should think of how to implement the sales plan. This involves recruiting, selecting, training, and deploying the sales force along with directing, motivating, and compensating the salespeople. This is known as *implementation of sales plan.*

The third function is *evaluating and controlling the sales operations* on a continuous basis so that performance gaps can be identified and rectified.

Planning sets the tone for any managerial activity. Its utility is understood by its performance in the organization. Sales management fructifies only in the presence of the right plans being efficiently implemented and regularly evaluated for its operational effectiveness.

Figure 4.1 depicts these interrelated functions of sales management. Also, these functions are explained in greater detail in the following paragraphs.

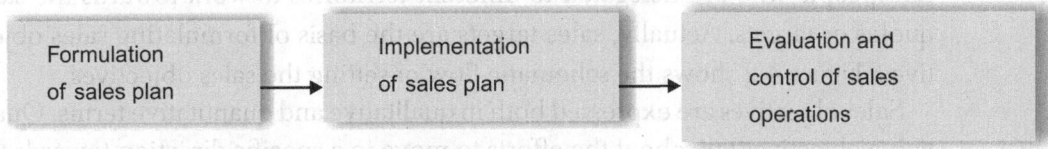

Figure 4.1 Planning—pivotal steps in sales management

4.2.1 Formulation of Sales Plan

As planning precedes any purposeful action, it is essential for successful sales management too. Planning involves three steps as follows:

(a) To determine the direction of the business by setting objectives

(b) To lay down strategies and tactics to implement the action plans

(c) To develop the sales budget in order to meet the expenses of sales plans implementation

Effective planning acts as a guidepost for a firm to move in the right direction. It also acts as a hedge against risk and uncertainty in business. Setting objectives specifies the tasks, as well as, the goals that are to be achieved. Objectives are also essential in evaluating and controlling the sales efforts. Sales force objectives should be consistent with marketing objectives of the firm which, in turn, should reciprocate with the firm's business objectives. Baker (1987) defined sales force objectives as pre-determined tasks set by management for salespeople in terms of fulfilling organizational goals.

Determining sales objective is a thought provoking process. Mandell and Rosenberg (1983) viewed that objective setting is a chain-wise process that originates from the understanding of the sales potential in a geographic area Sales potential of a product is a measurement of the maximum sales revenue or units of sale of that product that a firm can generate within a given time period. From the sales potential, the firms get an idea of the attractiveness of the market. But, sometimes actual sales may not equate with or fall short of sales potential. This is why firms need to develop sales forecast, which is based on sales potential that can give an idea about the attractiveness of the market. Based on sales forecasting, the sales budget is determined. The budget also allocates selling costs among salespeople, selling process, and logistical expenses. It should also be kept in mind that the sales budget must always be lower than the anticipated sales revenues to earn profit.

So in short, once the sales objectives of the entire geographic area as well as its subdivisions known as territories is determined, the firms may start with estimating the sales potentials, sales forecasts, and the sales budgets at micro-level, i.e., at the territorial level. After which, the sales quotas can be determined for salespeople who are delegated to different territories to work towards the sales quotas or targets. Actually, sales targets are the basis of formulating sales objectives. Figure 4.2 shows the schematic flow of setting the sales objectives.

Sales objectives are expressed both in qualitative and quantitative terms. Qualitative objectives talk about the efforts to move in a specific direction towards the

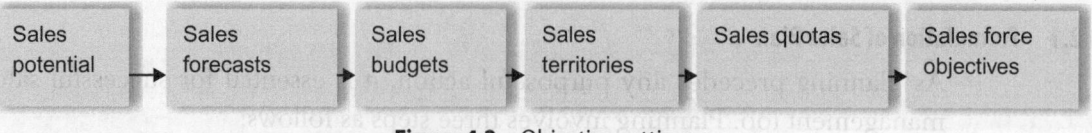

Figure 4.2 Objective setting

goal whereas quantitative objectives are specific target outcomes expressed in numerical terms that set the criteria for goal attainment. Some of its examples are cited in Box 4.2 below.

These objectives should be

(a) quantifiable,
(b) time dependent,
(c) achievable,
(d) flexible, i.e., can be changed with changing objectives,
(e) communicable to salespeople, and
(f) treated as performance standards.

Box 4.2   Examples of objectives

Examples of qualitative objectives are as follows:

(a) To increase customer awareness
(b) To develop new accounts
(c) To develop distribution network

Examples of quantitative objectives are as follows:

(a) To achieve thirty per cent of return on investment (ROI) in the coming year
(b) To increase customer base by ten per cent within the present year
(c) To add two more distributors within the distribution network

---

The sales objectives should not be restricted only to the sales targets. Craven et al. (1987) suggested that the major areas on the basis of which the objectives of sales management are set include (a) market performance, (b) contribution to profits, (c) customer relations and services, (d) development of sales personnel, and (e) marketing programme support. In fact, sales managers use these as criteria to set performance objectives for individual salespeople such as sales quotas, volume of sales orders in quantity and monetary terms, sales revenues, customer services, etc.

Organizing the sales force is the second priority, while formulating the sales plan, the first being determining sales objectives. It ensures systematic coordination of functions, namely planning, implementation, and control essential to achieve the objectives of the organization. It works on setting structures and procedures for smooth and effective implementation of the sales plan. It facilitates effective supervision of the sales force and evaluates their performance against set standards. For example, a geographic area may be the basis of organizing the sales force. Depending on the size of the sales force, different units (territories) can be established in the area and salespeople can be allocated among units to serve customers intensively.

Yet another important aspect is to classify accounts into major, moderate, and minor accounts that not only vary in terms of purchase volumes but also demand planning attention of different degrees. Accounts management plan, as this is technically referred to, is about channelizing the focus of the organization more on major accounts because they contribute higher sales. They also look forward to building long-term, cooperative relationship with them by special planning, directing, and control efforts.

4.2.2 Implementation of Sales Plan

Implementation of sales plan, in simple terms, refers to turning plans into action. The major functions under implementation of a plan involve recruiting, selecting, and training, deploying, motivating, and compensating the salespeople towards achieving goals, as have already been mentioned.

Recruiting means identifying potential pool/candidates and attracting them to the firm. It is a procedure of locating a sufficient number of job applicants for a job.

Selection involves picking and hiring a few candidates by screening out the rest who do not meet the hiring criteria.

Training plays a key role in imbibing knowledge, skill, and values to the salespeople that are essential for performance of their jobs.

Deploying entails assigning suitable sales territories to salespeople and instructing them to take charge of executing sales from customers.

By *motivating* the salespeople, sales managers enhance their willingness to exert effort to achieve the goals of an organization. However, the organization must pay attention that in the pursuit of fulfilling the goals of the organization, the individual needs of the salespeople are satisfied as well.

Compensation is an important motivating factor for salespeople and relates to how salespeople are financially rewarded for their efforts. Detailed discussion in this regard is made in Chapter 11.

4.2.3 Evaluation and Control of Sales Operations

The evaluation of performance of the salespeople is part of the controlling function. Evaluation involves assessing the performance of salespeople and then making a comparison between the planned and actual results. Evaluation suggests the areas a salesperson need to improve or whether there requires a change in the sales objectives or strategies. Control of sales operations means identifying reasons for discrepancies between the two results and taking corrective measures to sort out the differences. Here, sales objectives are treated as performance standards and comparisons of actual sales performance are made against these pre-determined objectives. Major discussion on this issue is found in Chapter 12.

4.3 SALES PLANNING—AN ENVIRONMENTAL PERSPECTIVE

Planning is an organizational function and it is believed that any company's success is mostly owed to its right planning. Planning plays the key role in getting results for the company. If planning is done properly, the company can safely act upon by avoiding risk and uncertainty. It is the prerogative of the marketing department, which guides the organization to move on the stated course of action.

Sales planning involve studying the past phenomenon, the present situation, and anticipating future changes in market demands, sales, customer behaviour, competition, economic conditions, regulatory policies, etc. It includes deciding on objectives and developing action programmes to fulfil them.

Planning is essential to cope with environmental changes (which are external to the organization). Sales managers start the planning process with identifying those environmental factors that impact on the selling process. This process of gathering information on the environmental forces, which influences the organizational activities and helps in analysing it to discover opportunities and threats evolving in the environment is known as environmental scanning. So, environmental analysis is important for sales managers to deal with a host of environmental factors that take up significant part in the sales planning process.

An organization has to deliberate on environmental forces before shaping the sales plan. Because of the dynamic nature of the environment, an organization is constantly engaged in studying swings and movements of the environment, and reflects them in the planning process. This is the reason why an organization should be flexible and adaptive in its structure, system, process, and decision-making so that it can plan for any contingencies that might occur due to a change in the environment.

Environmental forces affecting organizations have both internal and external orientations. Resources within the firm such as financial, sales force, technical, organizational, and types of products or services offered are the elements of internal sales environment. The external environmental forces include inflation, government regulations, interest rate fluctuation in banking sector, movement of share prices, technological development, changing tastes, preferences of customers, etc. All such external factors operate within the economic, technological, social, cultural, and legal environments. For example, in the age of nanotechnology, rapid production, and precision in design is the benchmark of car manufacturing. Quartz revolution in wrist watches by Titan has brought forth metamorphic changes amongst users. Earlier people never thought of using wrist watches as lifestyle companions.

Today, an organization cannot survive the competition if it does not upgrade its core processes in line with the technological innovations. This is because in today's cutting-edge competition, only zero defect product or service can expedite sales. Continuous innovation and precision management has become the key to existence.

The success of sales depends on a firm's ability to respond to the changes in its environment. Selling as a function signals the effect of any change in the marketing performance more accurately as compared to other functions. It is seen that an organization can manage and control forces of internal environment but external forces are beyond control. Internal resources can be generated, deployed, and utilized depending on the capability and support from the top-level corporate managers.

Prediction of effects of external forces is deemed to consolidate the strategic planning process of the firm. It helps sales managers formulate sales planning for territories and allocation of sales force. For example, the prediction about how an organization will react to certain cut in the competitor's price should be based on scientific estimation and not on hunch or assumption.

Analysis of environmental opportunities and threats is the pivotal aspect of sales planning. An opportunity is a positive stimulus to the firm. For example, frequent power cuts enables the inverter manufacturers to sense an opportunity to sell their gadgets to households. Contrarily, threat is a negative situation to the firm, and if not mellowed down by suitable action, can severely afflict sales performance. For example, sales force turnover is a threat to the firm and if reasons for separation are not addressed, the firm ebbs awkwardly on performance. Opportunity creates potentially favourable circumstances and threats beget challenge.

4.4 PLANNING SALES OPERATIONS—A USEFUL GUIDELINE

Sales plans are far more difficult to implement than to preach because there are certain inherent premises within and outside the firms that may act as stumbling blocks to the fructification of these plans. Broadly, these premises are related to resources and functions within and outside the firm. The major difficulties within the firm that confronts the sales managers are lack of skilled and knowledgeable sales force, financial support, availability of finished goods in time, adequate information and assistance from other departments of the firm, etc. that act as bottlenecks in executing plans. Needless to mention, these are treated as constrains of resources within the firm too. As sales determine the ultimate success of the organization, absence of functional cooperation between sales and other departments may jeopardize the financial health of the organization. At the same time, sales department should work in tandem with the other functional units. A sales plan must corroborate with production plan, inventory plan, distribution plan, and the entire supply chain plan and operations to yield effective results in sales. For example, if the production department does not act in tandem with the marketing or sales department, the promise of fulfilment of the customer's order in time remains unaccomplished. This is a functional disorder within the firm. In the same way, externally if the sales manager is not able to generate expected results from the salespeople or get complete cooperation from the distributors or other intermediaries, the implementation of plans remain in the dossier and do not find operational meaningfulness. Besides, uncertainties in certain environmental factors like economic, social, political or legal may stand as impediments in implementation. So, a sales plan can be executed completely only when a

(a) firm assures the sales manager with the availability of optimal resource base that is needed in the process, and

(b) sales manager can make proper utilization of resources.

In this regard, capability of the sales manager is of extreme importance. They should know the right way that initiates the right use of resources to put a plan into action. They should ensure that all resources are used to their best advantage. At the same time, the organization should see that the sales manager is given the support from other departments to facilitate action programmes.

Planning answers three basic questions. They are as follows:

1. What are directions of the business? This relates to objective setting.
2. How will the organization reach there? This is the planning process.
3. How will the organization know that it reaches the goal it aims to achieve? This involves the process of control.

Wilson (1985) termed it (finding answers to the above three questions) as the objective–planning–control continuum. This continuum is essential for a company to move forward purposefully. Synchronization among objective setting, planning process, and process of control–all are necessary if the company is to balance between its internal and external operations. Otherwise, the company would bear unexpected pressures from both the sides, internal and external, and plunge into crisis. For example, the company may face variable competitive and market pressures from the external environment and respond to it by making suitable variations in the internal operations to pre-empt negative consequences in company performance.

A sales manager begins planning by considering the overall marketing objectives. Marketing objectives are backed by information on future trends of market in terms of sales, revenues, profits, return on investment, etc. It means a sales manager makes allowances by forecasting the sales by volume and monetary units, gross and net profits, costs and an expense budget ceiling. Sales forecasts influence the sales objectives of the overall firm directly. Also, sales objectives are formulated at unitary levels, i.e., territories separately based on sales targets supported by forecasted sales in each unit.

After having set the target, the next plan of action is how to achieve it. Sales managers explain their sales team about the plans and suggest a course of action to implement them. At this juncture, a sales manager should contemplate operational description of the plan and express it in written statements so that the salespeople can clearly understand it. Categorically, sales managers should instruct the sales persons on the following:

1. What is to be sold?
2. Who are the customers, present and prospective?
3. What methods are to be chosen?
4. At what price? How much price variation can be accommodated?
5. What are the terms of selling, e.g., payment terms, distribution schedules, warranty conditions, etc?
6. What are the expense or cost ceilings for selling in various territories?

In this regard, a company should ensure the following before it sends the salespeople for contacting customers.

First, a sales manager should leave no effort untried to make the salespeople aware of the sales objectives, policies, and strategies. Further, they should educate them on features of saleability, profitability, utility, demand characteristics, uniqueness, range, price, transaction policy of products/services, etc. so that interaction with customers do not pose any hurdle to the salespeople.

Second, the knowledge about the profiles of present and prospective customers is a basic pre-selling preparation that the salespeople should have before they finally get engaged in field selling.

Third, salespeople should have the knowledge about the selling process such as prospecting, researching the customers to know their demands, buying criteria, sales presentation techniques, objections and complaint handling of customers, closing methods, and follow-up actions. A salesperson should learn the use of tactical moves that overcomes a customer's logical and psychological barriers at the point of sale provided that is endorsed by the sales manager. For example, if on the spot there is a five per cent price reduction, it can change the mind of the prospect to take a positive decision that benefits the salesperson.

Fourth, salespeople should have a total understanding on the elements of marketing mix so that they feel no difficulty while interacting with customers. Information on product features and benefits, information on price or price-oriented company policy such as discount or commission offers on the quoted or list price, distribution policies of the firm, promotional supports, etc. should be quite within the reach of the salespeople as well.

Fifth, salespeople should be concerned with the expense of selling that should never exceed the sales budget. Cost has a direct bearing on profit, and salespeople always try to keep field sales cost at a level that should result in cost-effective sales operation.

Sixth, the company should set standards, so that the actual performance of the salespeople can be compared. The company should analyse sales productivity on a regular basis to identify whether the performance of the salespeople is up to the expectation of the sales goals. Exhibit 4.1 shows some key ratios measuring sales productivity that the sales managers can examine.

Exhibit 4.1   Productivity ratios

Following are the productivity ratios:

(a) Selling Expenses: Sales volume—What is the trend?

(b) Gross margin: sales volume—A positive indicator?

(c) Sales volume: Sales targets in a territory—What is the variance?

(d) Number of order procured: Number of calls made (Batting Average)—Variance between expected and actual?

(e) Number of new accounts: Number of Total Accounts in a year—A Significant Number?

(f) Field sales cost: Total sales cost – Too much with respect to order procured?

(g) Average size of order by an individual salesperson—Is there a big difference between average order procured by salesperson and an actual order collected by a salesperson?

(h) Number of customers lost: Total number of customers in a year—Too much customer erosion?

(i) Percentage of salespeople turnover: Stability of the sales force is in question?

(j) Non-selling expenses (such as advertising, sales force training, etc): Direct selling expenses— What is the average industrial trend?

Only after studying these key ratios, can a sales manager realize the present performance level of the firm and the areas where status quo are to be maintained and where improvements are to be made. A firm should always compare these ratios with the same of a highly successful firm, if possible the market leader and modify the present standards of performance. Accordingly, the changes are reflected in the planning process.

4.5   STRATEGIC PLANNING—A BUILDING BLOCK TO SALES MANAGEMENT

A business plan should always have a strategic face. Strategy gives a specific focus to the plan. It throws light on how the plan gets into action. This is the reason why an organization dwells on strategic planning. Without strategic planning, the organization cannot cope with the vagaries of the market situation, insulate it from competitive thrust and attain targeted sales and profits. It aims to equilibrate corporate objectives and resources in perfect synchronization.

Kotler (1988) defined strategic planning as the managerial process of developing and maintaining a viable fit between the objectives and resources of an organization. The aim of strategic planning is to shape and reshape the businesses and products of a company so that they combine to produce satisfactory profits and growth.

Strategic planning finds development at three levels. These are as follows:

(a) Corporate level
(b) Business level
(c) Product/Functional level

4.5.1 Corporate Level Strategic Plans

These strategic plans are the ones that are chalked out at the helm of the organizational ladder where the top brass of management is entitled to decide about (a) corporate mission, (b) strategic business units (SBUs), (c) allocating resources to SBUs, and (d) filling up strategic planning gaps for existing and new businesses. These issues are discussed briefly as follows:

1. A mission is a stated sense of purpose for an organization. It answers the following questions:
   (a) Who are the organization's stakeholders?
   (b) Why and how does the organization serve them?
   (c) Where does the organization intend to reach by serving its stake holders?

   Through mission statements, a workforce can understand the shared sense of purpose, scope, values, direction, opportunity, and achievements of the business. Both sales managers and salespeople operate within the framework of corporate mission statements. Moreover, these statements are the bases of corporate guidelines that are observed by sales management. Exhibit 4.2 illustrates an example of a corporate mission.

Exhibit 4.2   Example illustrating mission statements

Mission statements of Holiday Inns

Stakeholders	Statements
Customers	To provide quality food and lodging services to business and vacation travellers
Employees	To provide unlimited career opportunities for productive employees
Owners	To provide a consistent and attractive return on investment

Source: Reproduced from Pearce II and Robinson Jr (1989). Originally developed from 1985 and 1986 Annual Reports of Holiday Corporation.

---

2. Most organizations are multi-business centres, manufacturing more than one product or service. Each of these businesses deal with at least one product

or service and serves a definite customer group. So each business unit has a specific product/service-market combination with a definite strategic purpose. Each unit is called SBU.

Each SBU has its own objectives, strategies, profit motives, budgetary allocation because each unit is an independent business centre having its own target markets, customer groups, competitors, modalities of serving customer needs, and capacity to contribute profits to the organization. So, the principle underlying the business-level planning is that all related products or services are grouped under one SBU. For example, the BPL group with more than one hundred products in its portfolio constituted six SBUs. These are entertainment electronics and appliances, components, telecom, power, soft energy, and financial services.

3. The third activity of allocating resources to various SBUs is based on the business potentials and market demands. Resources add strength to the unit to become equal to or to surpass the competitors. Resources are needed to make further development (Build), maintain current position (Hold), reap short-term benefits regardless of long-term effects (Harvest), as well as, sell or liquidate the business because of no attractiveness (Divest).

   Sales managers under the 'Build' strategy advise their subordinates to increase their efforts to increase sales volume and distribution network. The objective here is to increase market share of SBU and consolidate the business on financial fundamentals. 'Hold' makes sense when sales managers want to maintain their sales volume by securing the present sales force and distribution network. The objective is to concentrate on the present target market(s). Maintenance of a steady cash flow is the smart way to stay uncluttered in the 'Hold' strategy. 'Harvest' involves the efforts of the sales managers to target profitable accounts and reduce selling costs. So, limiting ties with customers where business prospect is dim and shift attention to profit-making customers under the 'Harvest' approach is the strategy used by managers. Fourthly, when an SBU finds no hope, both in short- or long-term business accruals, the company decides to sell it off or terminate the operation. Sales managers in the 'Divest' strategy suggest stopping all the selling activities except making desperate bids to clear off inventories. The 'Divest Strategy' also recommends expansion of present business in new geographical areas, if possible or establishment of new businesses to fill the strategic planning gap.

4. In selling parlance, sales managers call for greater market expansion, penetration or development (intensive growth) or suggest ways to strengthen the supply chain by forward integration (e.g., pursuing exclusive distribution network to firm up customer service), backward integration (e.g., acquiring one

or more businesses of the suppliers) or horizontal integration (e.g., acquiring one or more competitors). The company, as an alternative move can also choose the diversification strategy that entails where and how it should venture out to explore other business opportunities not akin to the existing businesses. Sales managers need to bother more about intensive growth because they are to operate under varied product-market situations. Each situation evolves an opportunity for improving the performance of the organization.

Ansoff's Product-market Expansion Matrix

Ansoff (1957) in his work proposed a framework to explore various product-market situations that offer opportunities to a company for intensive growth. He termed it as product-market expansion grid. Figure 4.3 exhibits it. It believed that each opportunity deserves a right strategy to conquer. Ansoff suggested four such strategies and each strategy fits in a particular product-market situation. These strategies are as follows:

(a) Market penetration strategy
(b) Market development strategy
(c) Product development strategy
(d) Diversification strategy

Market Penetration Strategy

Market penetration strategy is a marketing decision where the company centres its attention on the present market with the existing product. For example, P&G introduced lower priced variant of its existing Ariel detergent (e.g., Ariel Super Soaker) to serve the existing market.

Market Development Strategy

Market development strategy is resorted to when the company develops new markets for current products. Videocon in television market introduced models for both high-end (Videocon Bazooka) and low-end markets (Videocon Budget line) thus developing both economy and premium market segments.

Product Development Strategy

Product development strategy is a strategic selection when a company deals with the new product in the existing market. LCD television with high-definition features with networking facility with computers is meant to attract the existing customers who want multimedia support from their television.

Diversification Strategy

Strategy for getting a new product in a new market situation is known as *diversification strategy*. Companies like GE, ITC, BPL, etc. have diversified in various dissimilar business arenas.

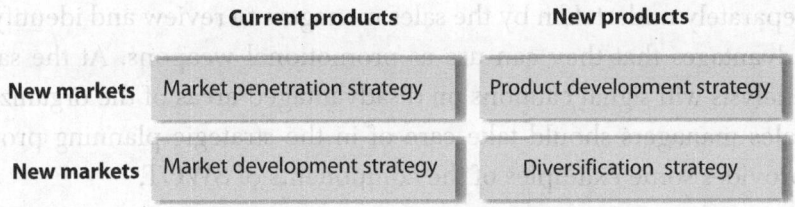

Figure 4.3   Product–market expansion matrix

4.5.2   Business Level Strategic Plans

An organization consists of a number of SBUs. Each SBU develops its own missions, objectives, and strategies to achieve. Each SBU explores its marketing opportunities separately and analyses its external threats as well. It lays down its own strategic plans which must not contradict the overall corporate plan. The components of the SBU's strategic plan, in general, are:

(a) Defining the business mission

(b) Analysing the external environment for identifying opportunities and threats

(c) Analysing the internal environment for introspecting strengths and weaknesses

(d) Developing business objectives and goals

(e) Developing business strategies

(f) Preparing programmes or action plans

(g) Implementing action plans

(h) Monitoring feedbacks and take corrective actions

These are discussed briefly in the following paragraphs.

Each business unit within the organization has its own mission to develop. The mission statements for the business covers up the market segment and the target market for a company that they will serve. For example, mission for a pharmaceutical business that manufactures paediatric medicines is to spread goodwill amongst parents by taking care of their children's health.

How better an organization can fulfil its mission depends on how better it can manage its resources and control its impediments in its way to success. This means the ability of the organization to capitalize on strengths by keeping weaknesses at bay and exploit business opportunities by thwarting threats convincingly. SWOT (strength, weakness, opportunity, and threat) analysis is an important strategic planning tool that helps the organization to do a critical review and compare its strengths and weaknesses with opportunities and threats. SWOT analysis can be separately undertaken by the sales managers to review and identify the strategic advantages that they can use as promotional weapons. At the same time, the analysis will signal cautions on disadvantaged areas of the organization that the sales managers should take care of in the strategic planning process. Box 4.2 provides some examples of the components of SWOT.

Box 4.2   Examples of SWOT components

Strengths	Cost advantage
	Skilled and knowledgeable salespeople
	Customer loyalty
Weaknesses	Too much indirect cost
	Distribution network is poor
	Customer awareness level is low
Opportunities	Product line addition
	The company enters new market
	The company adopts a new Customer Relationship Management (CRM) tool
Threats	Customer base is receding
	Competition is soaring up
	A new government policy adversely affecting the business

After the business mission is defined and the SWOT analysis is over, the sales manager decides on the objectives of the business dealing with specific product(s) or product line. Multiple objectives are set to cover up the major points of destination. Kotler (1988) viewed that most business units should pursue a mix of objectives including profitability, sales growth, market share improvement, risk containment, innovativeness, reputation, and so on.

Strategies lay down the activities and distribute resources with a long-term plan of how to compete with the designated products and markets zeroing in on business objectives and goals. A business strategy, in the same lines, suggest the plan of action which should be pursued by a business unit to accomplish objectives in a cost-effective manner. In this regard, Porter's strategic thinking is worthy of discussion because, according to him all strategic routes are condensed into three generic strategies. According to Porter, these generics provide food for strategic thoughts for managers to steer businesses towards accomplishment of objectives. Following are the generic strategies:

(a) Cost leadership
(b) Differentiation
(c) Focus

Cost Leadership

Cost leadership can be achieved by lowering the cost of production and distribution, and pricing the product cheaper than the competitors with a hope to attain the largest market share. This strategy can pay dividends only when the organization performs superbly on the quality of inputs (vendor analysis in stricter sense should be pursued), critical allocation path between inventories and production centres (time management is crucial), ergonomically effective and technologically valued production facilities, and last but not the least, adding marketing skills and efficiency to satisfy customers on acquisition, transaction, and perception of values at a price that benefits the organization to maximize its returns.

Differentiation

Here, the organization strives to stand out from its competitors in terms of value additions to the product or service which the competitors cannot offer. The organization integrates with one or more specific features of the product or service that can keep off competitors behind on performance. For example, unmatched service quality or high technological sophistication definitely gives service leadership or technological leadership to the firm.

Focus

Whenever the organization narrows its focus on one or two niche markets rather than pervading the whole market, it can go in for all efforts to serve the particular market segment. Within the limited sphere of the market, an organization can strategize on cost leadership or differentiation.

The role of sales management at SBU level is to do the following:

1. Analyse the market in terms of market potential, nature of competition, prevailing marketing mix, etc.
2. Identify the market segment, target market, competitive advantage, and market positioning strategy.
3. Set the selling objectives.
4. Decide on the marketing mix strategies that include product line decisions, pricing strategies, promotional policies, and distribution mechanisms.
5. Co-ordinate the marketing mix elements.
6. Take market entry decisions.
7. Develop organizational structures to implement the plan.
8. Allocate resources.

4.5.3 Product/Functional Level Strategic Plan

A strategic plan provides the framework for preparing marketing strategies for a specific product or service. These product/functional level strategies should be consistent with the business strategies. Two important aspects of marketing strategy are as follows:

Target market selection The method for the selection of target market is discussed in Chapter 3.

Marketing mix decision Marketing mix development is the central part of a marketing programme. A marketing programme should be designed in a manner that always surpasses that of competitors, which is termed as the competitive advantage. The development of marketing mix takes place basically in its four components, namely product, price, place, and promotion. Information on market potential, market size, growth, level of competitor's activity, level of tastes and preferences of the customers, economic behaviour of customers, key buying influencers, cost factors for market entry, etc. are other factors to be studied before taking entry decisions.

Marketing mix decision is geared towards developing the marketing mix elements–product, price, place, and promotion in a way that meets the needs and preferences of specific target market. Kumar and Meenakshi (2006) advocated that competitive advantage can be built in the marketing programme by the following:

(i) Being better: Superior quality or service
(ii) Being faster: Anticipate and respond to customer needs faster than the competitors
(iii) Being closer: Establishing close long-term relationships with the customers

The objective is to create a clear competitive advantage over rivals. Box 4.3 presents 'fit' as critical issues. A higher fit amongst the dimensions of the marketing programme, as compared to other competitors, can bring competitive advantage to the organization.

Box 4.3   Best fits

Following are the best fits:

(a) A positive cost-quality-price association for the product/service offered
(b) Pursuing fundamental business economics, i.e., quantity demanded must equate quantity supplied
(c) Objectives must commensurate with the resources available
(d) Quality of resources and requirements of the marketing programme should me be a worthy combination
(e) Business growth and customer welfare should be a proportional relationship

---

4.6   SALES MANAGERS—TASKS AND ROLES

By the very definition of management, we designate a manager who plans, organizes, directs, motivates, coordinates, and controls the activities of an organization. The role of a sales manager basically revolves around activities in relation to selling. They define the tasks, assign it to the salespeople, monitor the progress, and complete its accomplishment successfully. The tasks of the sales manager are broadly as follows:

First, before he starts the managerial function, he must perform the role of a researcher who analyses the present situation of the firm and checks minutely issues such as sales records—present and previous, availability of resources—particularly financial and human resources, strengths and weaknesses of the salespeople, and market trends and conditions, competition, customer demands and preferences, government regulations, and other environmental forces relevant to sales.

Second, the sales manager ascertains what should be the future activities to help the organization attain corporate objectives. This means that they should develop separate sales plans for the products or services that would work towards the achievement of the corporate plan. They develop sales objectives, strategies and procedures as the steps in planning, prepares the sales team with the selling tasks and customer handling techniques, and asks them to act upon the stated objectives and strategies.

Third, the sales managers organize the sales team to achieve objectives. They divide the selling task into some unitary selling jobs and assigns salespeople of each unit to perform on their units. A unit here means a specific customer group or geographic territory, known as target market. So allocation of salespeople to sales units and managing their performance are slated to be one of the major roles of the sales manager.

Fourth, manpower planning and supervision is also undertaken by the sales manager. Writing the job specification, recruitment, selection, training, and socializing the salespeople with organizational culture is also entrusted with the sales manager. Collectively, it is known as staffing.

Fifth, the sales manager arranges training for newly recruited (at times, existing as well) sales force. It is important for salespeople to be given formal and informal training for them to be equipped with the knowledge and skills required for the sales jobs.

Sixth, they inculcate the spirit of group dynamics within the sales team by group counselling, rapport building, motivation, effective compensation, and reward package for the salespeople so that they can equivocally perform as an individual and a member of the sales team.

Seventh, the sales manager oversees the sales operation, guides and controls the salespeople in both on the field and off the field sales activities, measures their performances, and takes evaluative actions to direct the performance in the right direction.

Eight, the sales manager must continually review the progress of the salespeople to determine the effectiveness of sales units within the sales organization and that performance of the salespeople gravitates towards business mission, objectives, and goals. He must take measures to correct the actions of the salespeople where they have made mistakes while executing the sales plans or have faltered in achieving sales goals.

Figure 4.4 illustrates a schematic view of the functions of a sales manager.

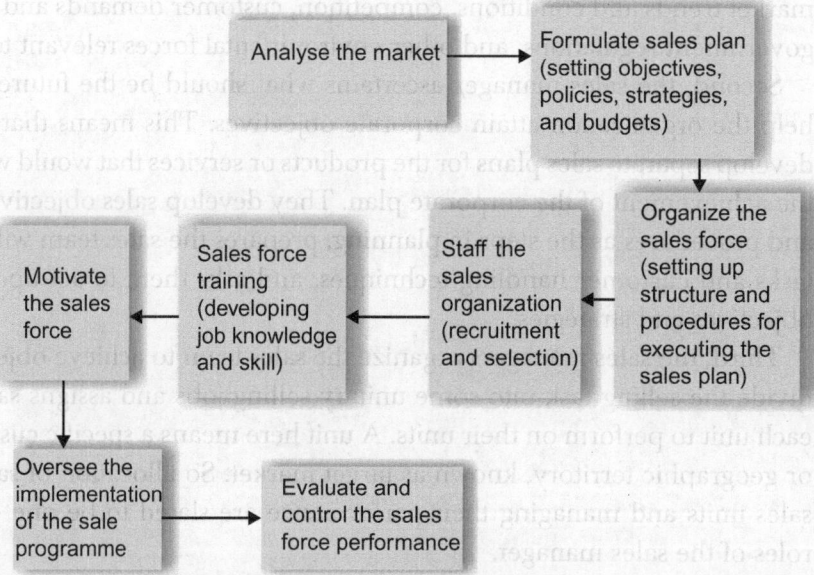

Figure 4.4 Task sequence

Sales managers, are required to take vital decisions that are then carried out by their sales force. Hence, whatever decisions they take should translate into objectives, and the strategies must carry adequate meaning. These decisions and strategies must take into consideration the capacity of the salespeople, namely their knowledge level, technical competence, and social skills of the sales force. As these qualities vary from one person to another, a sales manager divides the sales job amongst them in such a way that the more efficient salespeople are entrusted to deal with major clients and less efficient ones are directed to smaller accounts/customers.

Needless to say, major customers are generally fewer in number but they account for the bulk of the sales. In contrast, smaller accounts/customers, though large in numbers, explain less sales volume for the company and loss of a small customer does not bear much impact on the target sales volume unlike a large customer. Wilson (1985) noted that for most companies, sales exhibit 80:20 tendencies, i.e., a small percentage of large customers taking the bulk of sales and vice versa. Therefore, sales managers extend special planning attention and deft handling of major customers. Again, it is advisable that sales managers need to consult the sales force on the sales forecasts and sales targets while chalking out the plan because it is the sales force that experiences the requirements of the customers and the activities of the competitors better than the sales managers. Their opinions can be valuable instruments in designing the sales plan.

The role of a sales manager in the present era has changed considerably from being the 'boss' to the 'leader' of the salespeople who are not only involved in planning and decision-making but also guides them by taking part in actions along with the salespeople or allowing them to work in their presence and assisting them when they make any mistake. The participatory role of the sales managers definitely boosts the morale of the salespeople and brings more success to the firm.

Sales managers not only have to work with the sales team but also various other people, both inside and outside the firm. Internally, for example, the sales managers maintain liaison with the production heads to get outputs in time with the right quality and quantity and/or gives feedback about any variation in product planning or designing. They make regular contact with the finance managers about the availability of funds that are needed to meet the selling expenses. Externally they need to have contact with the customers, opinion leaders, distributors, government authorities and public to organize effective sales operations, widely and reliably.

Haynes and Mukherjee (2001) referred to Mintzberg's study of closely observing the day-to-day activities of a group of Chief Executive Officers (CEOs) who suggested that the formal authority accompanied with the status provides three basic roles for managers to perform. These are as follows:

Interpersonal role   It facilitates interpersonal relationship with superiors, peers, and subordinates.

Informational role   It helps to gather and disseminate information that is important for decision-making.

Decision role   It facilitates managers to take rational decisions.

The managerial task of the sales manager, in fact, veers around the above three roles. In their interpersonal role, they establish and maintain a working relationship with the salespeople and people outside the organization. In their informational role, they collect information of value from internal and external environments of the organization and use it for important strategic decisions. The sales managers have to choose the right information while planning, resource allocation, handling problems, negotiation, etc. in their decision-making role.

The role of the sales managers can be better understood from Box 4.4.

> ### Box 4.4   Multifaceted role of a sales manager
>
> *Roles of the sales manager:*
>
> | | |
> |---|---|
> | (a) Market analyst | (b) Planner |
> | (c) Decision-maker | (d) Forecaster |
> | (e) Budget maker | (f) Organizer |
> | (g) Resource allocator | (h) Communicator |
> | (i) Recruiter | (j) Selector |
> | (k) Trainer | (l) Motivator |
> | (m) Leader | (n) Adviser |
> | (o) Problem solver | (p) Coordinator |
> | (q) CONTROLLER | (r) CONTROLLER |

4.7   QUALITIES OF A SALES MANAGER

Sales managers are first and foremost leaders of the salespeople. Clear understanding of what is to be managed, who is to be managed, how is it to be managed, and what should be the cost effectiveness to manage it are some of the important qualitative requirements of a sales manager. They must recognize the need, skill, knowledge, talent, ability, motivational level, etc. of the salespeople and take appropriate measures, when these are found wanted by training, coaching, counselling, leading, motivating, and setting examples by actions.

To perform multipurpose roles, a sales manager should have all qualities of physical strength and stamina, abounding mental energy, passion, vigour, tact and self-respect, adequate educational, and technical expertise to shoot problems. Ability to understand others, willingness to accept responsibility, judgmental ability, initiative, integrity and commitment to the organization, empathy, and adaptability to different kinds of business situations are deemed as essential qualities of a successful sales manager.

Moreover, having interpersonal skills, communicability, organizational skills, sense of social responsibility give them a commendable position in the firm. They should have a rational mind to think and act out of the box in a crisis situation. So, analytical ability, leadership and managerial quality, assertiveness, emotional intelligence, and team management skill always lend them a firm hand to control any situation adroitly. They must have the ability to earn admiration, trust, and support from the salespeople. According to Monalastas (2008), a successful sales manager is one who consistently pursues and achieves through his people, the company's vision, mission, objectives, strategies and operational targets of the organization in the context of serving and delighting the customers.

SUMMARY

Sales management encompasses planning and organizing personal selling activities. A sales manager is entrusted with setting personal objectives, formulating policies, mapping out strategies, and preparing sales budgets under the planning process. Besides, organizing, recruiting, selecting, training, assigning, routing, directing, motivating, remunerating, evaluating, and controlling are the other important functions of sales management. Objective setting is backed with investigating sales potential and sales forecast. The major areas on the basis of which objectives are set include market performance, contribution to profits, customer relation and services, development of sales personnel, and marketing programme supports.

Implementation of the sales plan, and evaluation and control of sales operations are action programmes in sales management. Sales planning have environmental implications too. Sales planning involve studying the past phenomenon, present situation, and anticipated future changes of the market factors. Estimating important productivity ratios can provide useful information on cost effectiveness of sales operations. Strategic planning is an important building block of sales management too. It is a process of developing a viable fit between the objectives and resources of the organization. The tasks ans roles of sales managers span over various functional activities of sales management. The quality of a sales manager speaks a lot for successful sales planning and execution of sales plan.

KEY TERMS

Build Strategy Sales managers under it advise their subordinates to increase their efforts to increase sales volume and distribution network.

Cost Leadership A strategy by which a company lowers the cost of production and distribution, and prices its products cheaper than the competitors with a hope to attain the largest market share.

Divest Strategy Divest strategy refers to selling or liquidating the business because of no attractiveness.

Diversification Strategy Diversification strategy is used for introducing a new product in a new market situation.

Hold Strategy Hold strategy makes sense when sales managers want to maintain their sales volume by securing the present sales force and distribution network.

Harvest Strategy Harvest strategy comes into picture when a firm reaps short-term benefits regardless of the long-term effects.

Market Penetration Strategy A company centres its attention in the present market with the exist-

ing product, while using the market penetration strategy.

Market Development Strategy Using the market development strategy, a company develops new markets for current products.

Productivity Ratio The volume of output per unit of input expressed in terms of capital, work force, machine, etc. is referred to as productivity ratio. It aids a sales manager to realize its present performance level and move towards accomplishing goals.

Product Development Strategy Product development strategy refers to the strategic selection when a company deals with a new product in the existing market.

Strategic Business Unit A multi-business firm consists of several business units and each of these units have a specific product/service-market combination with a definite strategic purpose. Such a unit is called SBU (Strategic Business Unit).

CONCEPT REVIEW QUESTIONS

1. Define sales management. What are its tasks?
2. What are the functions of sales management? Illustrate.
3. How is sales planning affected by environmental changes?
4. Sales plans are far more difficult to implement than to preach. Examine.
5. How is sales productivity assessed?
6. Discuss the role of strategic planning in facilitating the role of sales management.
7. Briefly explain the tasks and roles of sales managers.
8. What should be the qualities of sales managers?

CRITICAL REVIEW QUESTION

Strategic planning appears to contribute towards significant economic and behavioural advantages in a business with potential customers. Economic advantages are felt in terms of financial indices. But what matters most is how far is the selling organization able to invoke developments in the relationship with customers, team-based strategic decisions, enhanced motivation of salespeople, better co-ordination of marketing department with other departments, and coping with environmental stressors.

What are the specific issues in strategic planning that need careful diagnosis, analysis, and prognosis in order to make a strategy fit for a sales organization with an ever-changing marketing environment?

PROJECT ASSIGNMENTS

1. Imagine that you are going to formulate strategic plan for your company engaged in the production of digital cameras. Having a domestic firm, you have to survive the scary competition from the reputed multinational firms. Technically your product is no less than theirs, but what you lack is a distribution network. As digital camera is a popular choice of the young generation; a well-knit distribution network for this is required to reach the urban as well as the semi-urban youths. You have a sales team that is quite capable of generating a distribution network. How would you develop a distribution system as a part of your strategic plan and advise your salespeople to work on it.

2. Visit the website of a MNC manufacturing consumer durables and collect detailed information on sales and marketing programmes. Collect annual reports of the company for the last three years and understand its performance on sales. Also, gather information on market position, market share, competitive positioning, etc. from secondary sources including websites. You can, even, interview the company's dealers/ distributors in this regard.

   Based on these two sets of information, i.e., corporate sales and marketing programmes and performance reports evolve the possible selling objectives and strategies for the company. Can you predict the economic prospect of the company? Match your results with the renowned consumer durable company––LG.

REFERENCES

Ansoff, I. (1957), 'Strategies for Diversification', *Harvard Business Review*, September–October, pp.113–24.

Baker, J.M. (1987), *Macmillan Dictionary of Marketing and Advertising*, Macmillan Press, London.

Cravens, D.W, G.E. Hills, and W.B. Woodruff (1987), *Marketing Management*, Richard D. Irwin Unc., Illinois.

Haynes, W. and S. Mukherjee (2001), *21st Century Management*, New Central Book Agency (P) Ltd, Calcutta.

Ingram, T.N., R.W. LaForge, R.A. Avila, C.H. Schwepker Jr, and M.R. Williams (2007), *Sales Management—Anlysis and Decision-making*, 6th ed., South-Western Cengage Learning, Australia.

Kotler, P. (1988), *Marketing Management: Analysis, Planning, Implementation and Control.* 6th ed., Prentice-Hall Inc., Engelwood Cliffs, New Jersey, USA.

Kumar, A. and N. Meenakshi (2006), *Marketing Management*, Vikas Publishing House Pvt. Ltd, New Delhi.

Mandell, I.M. and L.J. Rosenberg (1983), Marketing, 2nd ed., Prentice-Hall of India Private Limited, New Delhi.

Monalastas, R.C. (2008), 'Associated Content–Business & Finance', http://www.associated content. com/article/867335/qualities_of_a_successful_manager.htm?Cat=5, accessed on 22 May 2009.

Pearce II, J.A. and R.B. Robinson Jr (1989), *Management*, McGraw-Hill Book Company, New York.

Still, R.W., E.W. Cundiff., and N.A.P. Govoni (1988), *Sales Management: Decisions, Strategies and Cases*, Prentice-Hall of India Private Limited, New Delhi.

Wilson, M. (1985), *Managing a Sales Force*, 2nd ed., Gower Publishing Company Limited, England.

CASE STUDY

Dell's Success Story

Dell Computer Corporation, a renowned name in designing and developing a wide range of computer systems intelligently, has adopted a direct selling model as part of its successful strategic innovation to outmanoeuvre competitors. The principal aim was to keep intermediaries at bay and sell the product directly to the customers. In this process, they undercut their competitors on price, established an intimate link with their customers, and satisfied their shareholders with handsome returns that appeared to be quite large as compared to the average returns prevailing in the financial markets. Dell's success has been attributed to the creation of product specifications tailored to meet individual and business applications. Moreover, a narrow lead time of procuring an order and fulfilling it by assembling, installing software, testing, packing and delivering to customers, managing inventory level efficiently, etc. are some of the operational strategies that have further added to the popularity of Dell. Besides timely adoption of seasoned management, new structure, process, and design have bolstered the strategic efficiencies of the firm.

Dell found three important strategic areas for growth. These were

(a) focusing on the largest corporate customers,
(b) reaching the pinnacle of service level quite unparallel in the personal computer industries, and
(c) expanding direct selling model to global level.

Dell, however, later moved partly to retail chain, offering its product through power retailers, PC superstores, etc. This was adopted due to the expansion of product line (e.g., inclusion of notebook computers) and better service provisions in the niche markets.

Dell initially coined its strategy based on growth as a determinant of profitability and liquidity, and later refocused on cash conversion cycles consisting of inventory, payables, receivables, and cash-flow operations. Cash-conversion cycle was quite consistent with direct sales model because selling directly to customers brought advantages of limited or no finished products inventory. Secondly, just-in-supply of components and spares further strengthened the low inventory maintenance policy. Thirdly, the payment cycle of customers at times superseded the pace of cash flows to suppliers. So, satisfactory cash flow, low or zero inventories, and any reduction in component costs were rapidly converted to gain customer advantages, thus, deriving strong competitive positioning in the computer markets.

But one particular problem that stared Dell's operations with intermediaries was that any change in the price level of any product had cascading effects in the chain with the urge of price protection and compensation of middlemen for price reductions. To make subtle adjustment of such price variations was not very easy for the company because of the possibility of aggrandizement of inventory levels and difficulty to reach customers on time with price-related advantages. So, instead of retail chains, the company enabled field selling to serve large organizations and telephone selling to cater to small businesses and consumers.

Dell, with worldwide divisional networks, shifted from a functional structure to regional structure and spread everything across regions other than product development. This was necessary as the size of the business and customer base was increasing rapidly. Though, it expanded its business along geographical boundaries, later it segmented its market customer-wise with the addition of new customer sets. Besides, having large customers like corporate sectors, it also started business with federal, state, and local governments, enterprise accounts, small and medium business houses, consumers, etc. The noticeable feature of the customer-based segmentation was that the customer-based corporate units in charge of handling these accounts were empowered to run independently, had their own forecasting and product mix to optimize their efforts to meet customer expectations.

At the same time, every customer had the opportunity to contact through Dell's toll free number or through Dell's websites. Any service call received had its resolution instantly recorded. In fact, the exact configuration of the service caller's machine along with the purchase documents, since the first buy, was at the fingertips of the Dell's representatives. Dell's service and support systems provided direct access to the diagnostic tools used by Dell techniques. Dell's information system was also robust to record each user's configuration. The objective was to provide customized solution and experience to the customers.

Discussion Questions

1. List the success factors that have brought Dell Computer Corporation to a respectable position in computer markets.
2. What are the unique features of Dell's direct selling model? Highlight the major strategies adopted by Dell which helped it gain the vast market share worldwide.

Source: Fisher, L.M. (1998), 'Inside Dell Computer Corporation: Managing Working Capital, Strategy+Business' http://www.strategy-business.com/article/9571?gko = d8c29 accessed on 30 December 2010; http://www.business.com/directory/computers_andsoftware/dell_computer_corporation/, accessed on 20 August 2009.

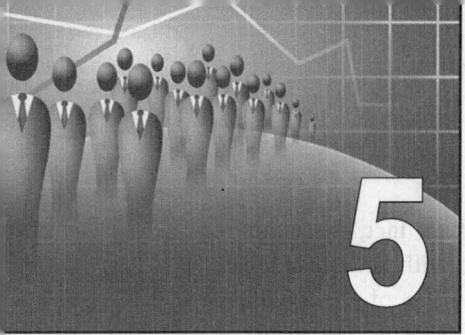

5 Sales Organization

LEARNING OBJECTIVES

After reading this chapter, you will be able to

- illustrate the meaning, purposes, and types of sales organizations
- delineate various structural perspectives of sales organization and make a comparative review of the different structural organizations
- examine the criteria and principles of developing a sales organization
- understand the procedure of organizing the sales force
- present a methodological study on the determination of the size of the sales force
- examine the functional orientation of the management of the sales force
- integrate the sales force within an organization

5.1 SALES ORGANIZATION—MEANING, PURPOSES, AND TYPES

An organization is referred to as a web of management functions in a firm with each function having its own goals and purposes to fulfil to contribute towards the goals and missions of the firm. It is a network that defines the essential relationships amongst people, tasks, and activities with an aim to optimally utilize and coordinate resources to achieve the goals of the organization. It is also a framework of authority–responsibility relationships through which managers can implement their plans. It is sometimes even compared to the neural network in a human system that integrates all the organs in a coherent manner. Here, organs are akin to units, divisions, or departments in a business organization.

Organizing is a multitask activity that involves allocation of tasks amongst business units, distribution of resources, assignment of authority, and delegation of responsibility to carry out respective work functions. This, if conducted properly, works towards organizational growth and prosperity.

A sales organization entails in organizing its sales force to facilitate the act of selling and distributing a product or a service. It also involves speeding the process of transferring the ownership of the product or the service from the seller to the buyer. This is one of the vital units that enable a company to accomplish its objectives as a whole by fulfilling the sales objectives in a more effective and efficient manner.

An effective sales organization conceives a structure to implement strategies that show a set path of accomplishing a firm's objectives. An organization rests on its structure to divide the activities into distinct tasks, coordinate them, and finally direct all efforts towards the sales goal. So, structure is the roadmap to execute the strategies of an organization. It helps in passing the information and commands from the sales managers to the salespeople more effectively, undertakes the entire selling process, completes the workflow, and aids in providing performance feedback to the salespeople from their managers. It also helps the salespeople to understand their specific activities which they have to implement, supervise, and control. In other words, the structure of an organization provides a clear indication of what are the precise sets of activities and by whom are these activities to be performed.

At the same time, people in a sales organization consciously co-operate to work towards achieving a common goal. Sales organizations are the engines for the translation of strategic plans to selling operations. Exhibit 5.1 illustrates the role of sales organization in Hindustan Unilever Limited (HUL) and how it has been shaped in the rural sector.

Exhibit 5.1 HUL's rural sales organization

HUL, a pioneer distribution network in India, is constantly on the way of reinventing the process of distributing its products to serve rural segments. In this process of reinventing, HUL has revamped its sales organization in the rural markets that has helped in fulfilling all the needs of the people there. This has increased the purchasing capacity of rural customers and is satisfying their needs as well.

The company has brought all the 'markets' with a population below 50 thousand under one rural sales organization. This team consists of an exclusive sales force and redistribution of stockists under the charge of responsible managers. The team stresses on excellent availability of the products and building superior brand preferences in the rural interiors. With this strategy, HUL's distribution network in the rural sector has already covered 50 thousands villages, reaching 250 million consumers through 6000 stockists.

Source: Jadhav (2009).

Similarly, sales organizations can also help in upgrading the technological aspects and making the company more technologically savvy. Exhibit 5.2 demonstrates how an organization can develop successful electronic information network to facilitate faster business transactions.

Exhibit 5.2 ITC's e-choupal

ITC has revolutionized agricultural marketing by modernizing the agro-business. It has brought in computer-aided agricultural information network across villages to interact with farmers. This modern IT-based system helps farmers to access immediate information to weather conditions, soil status, price movements, improved farming practices, etc. via the Internet. The system helps farmers to sell their products faster and get timely payments through electronic transactions.

Source: Saravani (2005).

The major premise of an organizational structure is work specialization. It encompasses breaking down the overall task into smaller component units where each unit demands a specific method and skill to cater to the completion of the overall task. The best example of this is the automobile assembly line where components of different types are added one-by-one in a conveyor system by cost-effective logistical operations to produce a finished car.

In a sales organization, emphasis on work specialization permits the salespeople to apply their individual skills and expertise. For example, a salesperson, who has developed good customer relationship skills, could engage in servicing customers for a prolonged period of time. A technically efficient salesperson can look after the installation and customer training for equipment selling. In geographical context, area specialization is highly prominent with respect to selling. Salespeople by virtue of being residents of a state are expected to deal with the customers of that area quite comfortably because they are expected to know the economic behaviour, spoken language, social customs, cultural ethos, etc. This helps them to meet and treat customers better than salespeople belonging to other states. Thus, specialization helps the organization to achieve growth and productivity in financial and social terms.

It is clear from the above discussion that sales organizations, in general, make the lives of the sales managers easy and more convenient. Some of these benefits are listed as follows:

1. Sales organization bestows the firm with distinct structures, roles, tasks, and responsibilities for salespersons, sales managers–sales and marketing department as a whole.

2. It defines the formal authority and responsibility of the sales force and the sales managers.

3. It determines the sales activities that have to be performed to achieve organizational goals.

4. It divides the entire work into smaller manageable units (e.g., territories) and assigns salespeople to each unit to carry out selling jobs.

5. The sales force structure spells out the job description and helps to decide the type of sales personnel to be selected for a particular task.

6. It helps in undertaking managerial functions such as recruitment and selection of manpower, training, and supervision of work force.

7. It paves way for the all kinds of communication–upward and downward, horizontal and vertical, for flow of sales-related decisions, delegation of tasks and responsibilities, information sharing, and receiving performance-related information smoothly.

8. It helps the sales managers to separate the results from each work unit and later evaluate and control the salespeople with a view to improve their performance.

9. It assists sales managers to compare performances of the salespeople and devise incentive schemes that can be used to reward successful salespeople.

10. It aids the salespersons to know what to perform. As a result, they would have no misconceptions or confusions about their work activities.

11. Salespeople can work with a definite goal to reach, purpose to serve, and ways to obtain the target results.

12. It allows salespeople to take charge of specific units and thus generate a sense of work involvement and commitment towards work.

13. Customers can thus be better served. Customers can get better product availability, brand communication, brand experience, and after-sales service.

14. It prevents duplication of efforts (e.g., customer duplication, product duplication, etc.) and thus save time and money in expending sales efforts to enhance sales productivity.

5.2 SALES ORGANIZATIONAL STRUCTURE—DIFFERENT TYPOLOGICAL PERSPECTIVES

Sales organization mobilizes the operations of a firm through sales force structure. Sales force structure refers to assigning sales responsibilities amongst different salespeople, keeping in mind varied aspects to reach the target customers. For example, globally dispersed organizations such as Nestle, P&G, etc. distribute selling tasks amongst sales personnel to gain quick access to the customers. The objective is to ensure adequate attention to the product lines and brands at the customer level. This is an example of the territorial sales force structure.

The division of selling tasks can be implemented in different ways depending on the following:

(a) Number of geographical locations to cover up (known as territorial sales force structure)

(b) Number of products or services to deal with (known as product sales force structure)

(c) Number of customers to approach (known as customer sales force structure)

(d) Number of functional specializations (known as functional sales force structure)

(e) Combination of the above (known as complex sales force structure)

Let us now discuss the various structures separately.

Territorial Sales Force Structure

When a company follows geographical divisions to allocate tasks amongst salespeople, the territorial sales force structure develops. Here, each salesperson is assigned an exclusive geographical area to sell a company's full range of products or services to all customers located in that particular territory. Setting up a territorial structure implies sizing the sales tasks down to manageable units. The company benefits from such a structure when customers characteristically vary across geographical locations. Customers can vary in numbers, size of the orders, attention seeking, etc. across territories. Sometimes, potentially attractive territories ask for a delegation of more number of salespeople who can continually keep abreast with the requirements of the customers.

A company clearly mentions the jobs and accountabilities of salespeople. It increases their initiative to cultivate local business and personal bonding. It encourages the salesperson to build customer relationships in the respective geographical area which finally improves sales effectiveness. This type of sales structure is helpful when a company has a wide geographical dispersion of the customer base and each customer group deserves special attention from the salespeople.

Coordination and controlling of operations amongst territorial units is a major concern for the company. Generally large FMCG firms such as manufacturers of foods and beverages, toiletry products, etc. follow territory-based sales organization. The general structure of territory-based sales organization is shown in Figure 5.1.

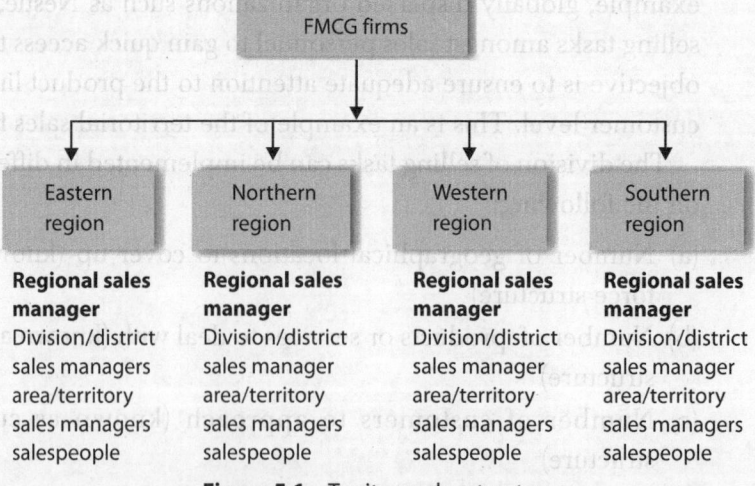

Figure 5.1 Territory sales structure

Coca-Cola (http://en.wikipedia.org/wiki/Departmentalization), the global leader in the beverage industry has achieved the summit of success because of its efficient territory sales structure. The organizational structure of Coca-Cola indicates that the company runs its sales operations in two broad geographic areas–the North American sector and the international sector, which includes the Pacific Rim, the European Community, Northeast Europe, Africa, and Latin American groups.

Product Sales Force Structure

Product sales force structure represents a sales organization where salespeople are asked to concentrate on only a part of the company's products or product lines. The company defines the job of salespeople based on a few products or product lines and they are directed to specialize in selling those products only. This type of sales structure is effective when a company deals with a number of unrelated products or lines, and each product demands a special planning attention and strategic actions. But, in this type of structure, coordination amongst several lines might be a problem for the company.

Companies such as ITC, HUL, Kodak, etc. are quite successful with product-oriented sales structure. Figure 5.2 depicts the product-based sales organization of an agricultural inputs manufacturing firm.

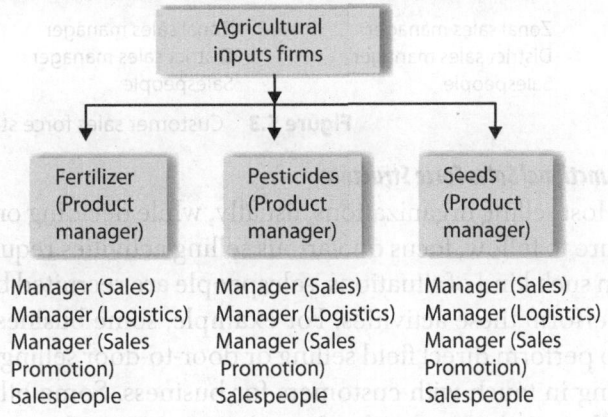

Figure 5.2   Product-based sales structure

Customer Sales Force Structure

Customer sales force structure involves sellers that sell their products only to a selected number of customers or customer groups. The company organizes and designs its structure in such a way that the sales force has to carry out selling activities only for specific customer groups. The objective of such a structure is to divide the sales force into groups where each group serves one customer group or industry. So, separate sales forces are set up to treat different industries and customer groups. Organizing the sales force along with the customers help to build intimate relationships with them. Customer-based sales organizational structure of a pharmaceutical firm is shown in Figure 5.3.

A pharmaceutical firm manufacturing medicines, medical equipment, and medical supplies has customers in government and non-government hospitals, health care centres, NGOs, medicine distributors, etc. A section of these customers buy drugs, another segment buys medical equipments, etc. A customer sales force structure at this pharmaceutical firm, thus, involves salespeople focusing on different product lines and so different customer groups.

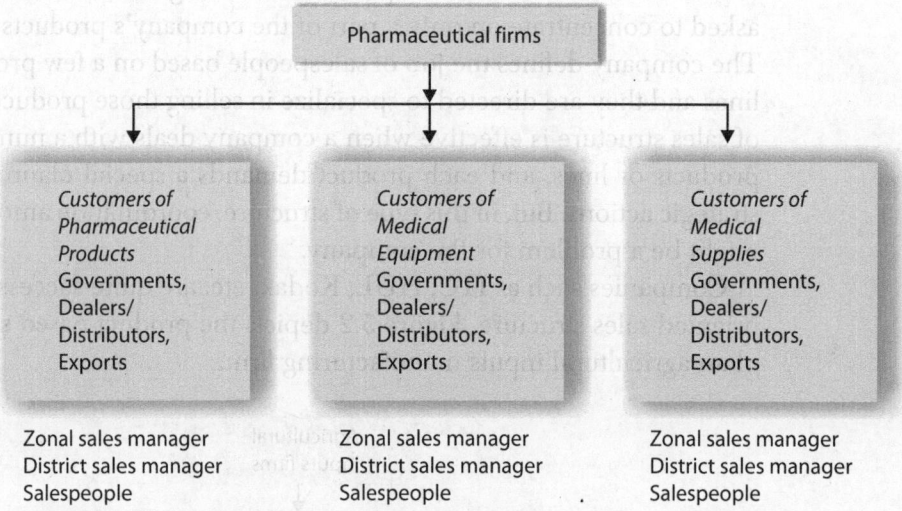

Figure 5.3   Customer sales force structure

Functional Sales Force Structure

Most selling organizations, usually, while deciding on the kind of sales force structure to follow, focus on various selling activities required in selling their products. In such kind of situations, salespeople are recruited based on their special skills to perform these activities. For example, some businesses may require salespeople to perform direct field selling or door-to-door selling, which involves directly getting in touch with customers for business. Some other businesses might require salespeople to provide after-sales-services to the customers.

Salespeople can also be required to specialize in retail selling activities, such as merchandising, shelf management, order taking and processing, billing, etc. For instance, salespeople working in computer manufacturing firms need people with some expertise on computers in order to succeed in direct selling, technical support, servicing, retailing, etc. Being specialized in a job can distinguish a salesperson from the others. Similarly, a salesperson can be an expert either in hardcore selling or missionary selling to spread goodwill amongst present and prospective customers.

The organizational structure of a typical functional sales organization of firms is presented in Figure 5.4.

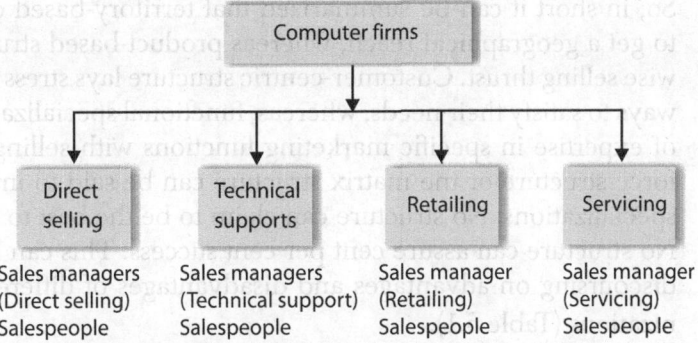

Figure 5.4 Functional sales force structure

Complex Sales Force Structure

Complex sales force structure advocates organizing the sales force on a wide variety of products and customers over a broad geographical area, i.e., complex sales force structure manages a number of product-market-customer variants. Large organizations producing different products for different customers spreading across large geographical areas may opt for such sales structure. Salespeople can specialize in territory–product, territory–customer, product–customer or all the three combinations. Complex sales force organizational structure for any multi-product firm is represented in Figure 5.5.

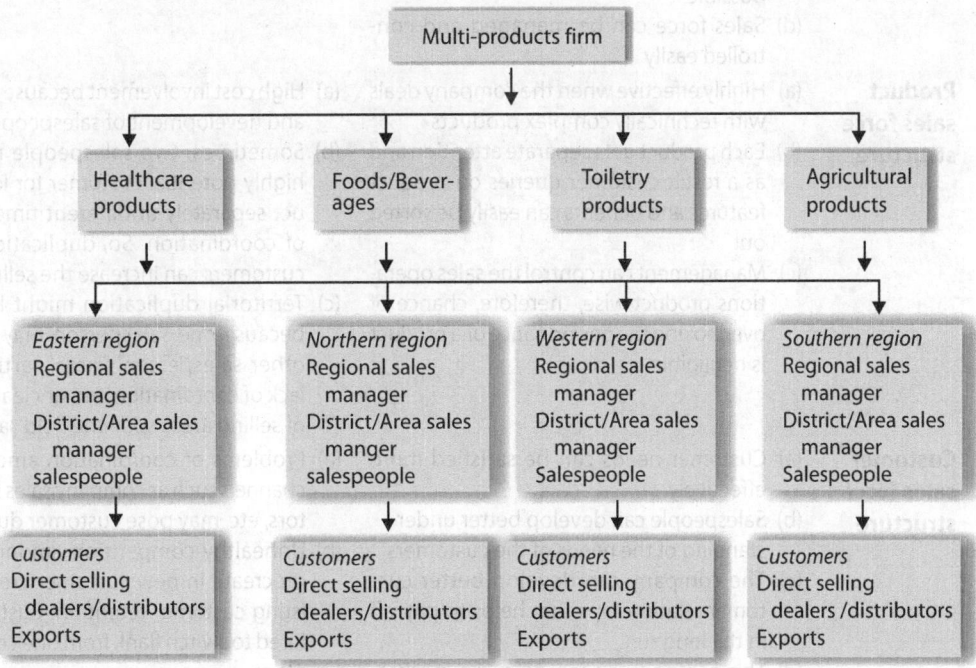

Figure 5.5 Complex sales force structure

So, in short it can be summarized that territory-based organization is designed to get a geographical reach, whereas product-based structure provides product-wise selling thrust. Customer-centric structure lays stress on customer groups and ways to satisfy their needs, whereas, functional specialization involves integration of expertise in specific marketing functions with selling efforts. Complex sales force structure or the matrix structure can be said to involve a hybrid of multi-specializations. No structure can claim to be the best to organize the sales force. No structure can assure cent per cent success. This can be better understood by discoursing on advantages and disadvantages of different structural sales organizations (Table 5.1).

Table 5.1 Advantages and disadvantages of different sales organization structures

Sales force structure	Advantages	Disadvantages
Territorial sales force structure	(a) Local problems of customers can be-handled speedily and adequately (b) Salesperson can adapt with local conditions such as climate, culture, customs, market sentiments, competition, behaviour of the customer, etc. to act comfortably (c) Intensive market coverage at low cost is possible (d) Sales force can be managed and controlled easily	(a) Specialization is underemphasized (b) Coordination of multiple geographical operations might be a problem (c) As salespeople deal with all types of products in a territory, they can ignore difficult selling items
Product sales force structure	(a) Highly effective when the company deals with technically complex products (b) Each product gets separate attention and as a result customer queries on product features and benefits can easily be sorted out (c) Management can control the sales operations product-wise, therefore, chance of overlooking the performance of a product is negligible	(a) High cost involvement because of the training and development of salespeople (b) Sometimes, two salespeople may pursue a highly potential customer for identical product separately at different times due to lack of coordination. So, duplication of calls on customers can increase the selling cost (c) Territorial duplication might be a problem because one salesperson may transgress to other salesperson's area particularly when lack of coordination and unclear demarcation of selling areas spoil the field sales efforts
Customer sales force structure	(a) Customer needs can be satisfied more effectively (b) Salespeople can develop better understanding of the needs of the customers (c) The company can develop better customer relationships that helps to pay off in the long run (d) The company becomes more market-driven and customer-oriented	(a) Problems of coordination among multi-tier channels such as company sales force, distributors, etc. may pose customer duplication (b) Unhealthy competition amongst firms may procreate in new customer creation and existing customer retention. Customers can be lured to switch flank from one company to the other

(Contd)

(*Contd*)

Sales force structure	Advantages	Disadvantages
Functional sales force structure	(a) Organizing the sales along functional specialization is simple to implement and administer (b) Efficient operations of each function is possible (c) Division of labour encourage salespeople to focus more on their functions and precision, which speeds up the selling of technical products	(a) Geographical duplication is possible (b) Customer duplication might be a problem. (c) Lack of coordination amongst functions may jeopardize selling efforts
Complex sales force structure	(a) Specialization combining territories, products, customer, and functions is possible thus leading to more effective results (b) Each specialization is given due weightage by the management	(a) High cost involvement (b) Management may face organizational problems (c) Confusion amongst salespeople may occur and they may be at a fix to obey the guidelines and show accountability (d) Territorial and customer duplications might be major hurdles

5.3 CRITERIA AND PRINCIPLES OF DEVELOPING A SALES ORGANIZATION

Before a sales organization is developed, the management should know the criteria for setting a successful sales organization. These are as follows:

1. Sales organization should specify precisely the functions of the sales department and plan and coordinate the activities of the salespeople and superiors in a coherent manner.

2. Proper allocation of resources should be made with a view to reach customers with the right marketing mix. The goals are—customer satisfaction and target return on investment.

3. Sales organizations should lead to a sales force structure that can effectively and efficiently control the sales operations. This means whatever the sales structure is, it must adequately cover the market and control the cost of selling operations.

As discussed earlier also, a sales organization is established on some important organizational principles very much akin to the principles of the whole organization. These principles are like software guiding and controlling the smooth functioning of the organization. Principles help the organization to explore market opportunities and move towards their goals. It protects the organization to stray from the pre-determined course of actions. Fundamentally, these principles are worth considering while developing a sales organization. These are as follows:

(a) Span of control
(b) Unity of command
(c) Stability and continuity

(d) Centralization and decentralization
(e) Line and staff positions
(f) Coordination and integration
(g) Specialization

Span of Control

Span of control refers to the number of subordinates that a sales manager can supervise at a particular time. It is related to a manager's ability to control to coordinate the activities of salespeople working under him and integrate them with other activities of the organization. A narrow span of control endorses tall structures of organization with more layers of supervision where only the field salesperson can reach to the level of end users. A wider span of control encourages a flat organizational structure with lesser levels of supervision. Coordination between the lower- and higher-level employees is a bonus to such structure. Depending on the span of control, a sales manager has the capacity to manage his subordinate sales staff.

Unity of Command

The unity of command principle says that no subordinate should be responsible to more than one supervisor. Each person should report to only one superior. However, this is too rigid to fit well with the modern organization where horizontal communication has a major role to play particularly in multi-specialty organizations such as multi-speciality hospitals, IT firms, etc. Moreover, flexibility in work culture is crucial to get warm cohabitation of managers and subordinates. For example, a territory manager is given a free hand to decide a sales budget for a particular project in a particular territory. It has been seen that an organization thrives more where the role of the superior leads the salespeople from the front rather than directing them to carry out the instructions.

Stability and Continuity

It is suggested that jobs should not be assigned without giving due regards to the talent and preferences of the current employees. Managers should distribute job responsibilities according to the specializations of the salespeople where the latter has the knowledge and skill to execute the task. To maintain stability in a firm, this becomes the key to an organization's perpetual success and continuity which steadies the growth of business. For example, in a customer-based sales organization, salespeople are assigned to deal with customers where they have an experience to handle both new and existing customers.

Similarly, in a computer firm, a salesperson, experienced in retail selling, is deputed to take up selling responsibilities with dealers whereas a salesperson who has knowledge in institutional selling is asked to sell computers in educational units, banks, hotels, etc.

Centralization and Decentralization

The concept of centralization and decentralization refers to the degree to which control and authority are vested to the top management in an organization. Centralization means that authority and control are concentrated to the top of the organization and decentralization indicates the same has been distributed from the top to the lower levels of working units. In a centralized operation, staffing, training, motivating, compensating, and evaluating sales performance are controlled by a core management group located at the upper rung of the organization, whereas, in a decentralized firm the field sales managers are given the authority to perform these activities.

Absolute centralization and decentralization hardly exists in any firm. Organizations typically centralize some activities and decentralize the others. For example, recruiting and selecting, training, fixation of sales targets, territory distribution, and performance appraisal of the field sales staff is vested with middle-level managers in some firms. Decentralized firms allow more freedom of action and result in more motivated sales force. On the other hand, centralized firms provide more coordination and integration of work activities, behaviour of employees, and efforts.

It is seen that firms emphasizing on specialization are more successful with decentralization. Also, advances in technology enhance the scope of electronic communication and demands more decentralization for regional and branch units to perform businesses independently in distant corners of a nation.

Line and Staff Positions

A line of authority is exercised by immediate superiors over their subordinates and a chain of command is directed downwards through various levels of the organization. One subordinate is responsible only to one person on the next higher level. The chief executive officer takes the decision and this decision flows down the line for implementation. So lines of authority move vertically down the structure and the members at the organizational level are independent of all others on that level. This type of organization is known as line organization. In line sales organization, sales managers control a number of subordinates and report directly to the next higher level in the organization.

On the other hand, a staff authority is directed to specialized staff that is associated with their areas of specialization. Staff sales organizations are bereft of a direct chain of command. Those in staff positions do not manage people directly but are entrusted with managing certain functions such as recruiting and selecting, training, sales promotion, servicing, etc. Staff sales managers do not have the authority to delegate orders or directives. The recommendations of staff managers are submitted to the top-level executives. If these are approved by the executive officers, instructions are run down to the line organizations. Both line and staff positions may coexist in the same organization.

Figure 5.6 represents the line authority downwards from the CEO. The marketing research manager and sales training manager as staff authorities assist the line managers in taking managerial decisions.

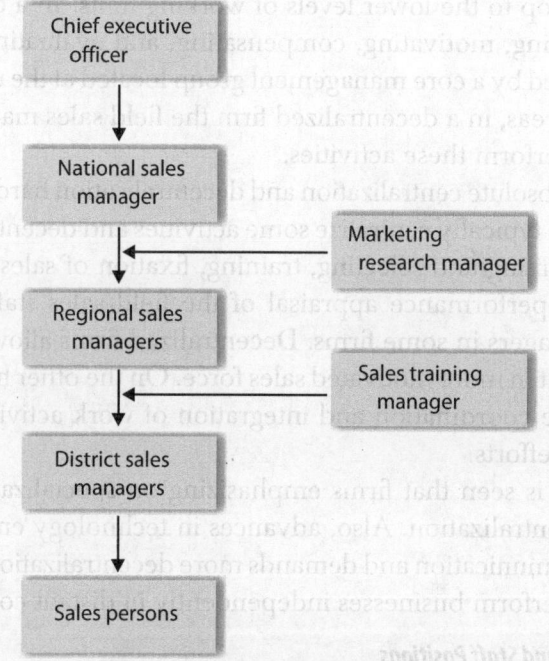

Figure 5.6 Line and staff positions

For example, a sales organization with geographical specialization can entrust the chief executive officer, national sales, and regional sales managers to perform staff functions. District sales managers and salespeople are the other members in the line positions where salespeople report to district sales managers. District sales managers report to regional sales managers who send information to the national sales manager. The national sales manager, finally, submits the reports to the chief executive officer of the company.

Marketing research manager and sales training manager are the staff positions. Marketing research managers give feedback of all the market-related information to the line authority. A sales training manager located in between regional and district sales managers, looks after the training of salespeople and prepares them to handle selling jobs. As have been suggested in the figure as well, the marketing research manger sends research reports and recommendations to both the regional and district sales managers. Training of salespeople is conducted by sales training manager at the regional level in cognizance with district sales managers.

Coordination and Integration

Traditional sales organizations relied more on direct communication with customers through the sales force. The sales department in these traditional firms acted as the front office where they could deal with customers directly and assistance from the other functional areas such as R&D, production, finance, etc. could be called for whenever required . Flow of communication was more or less unidirectional and no coordination amongst functional areas was ever felt.

But, modern organizations prescribe different roles for different departments. For instance, the sales department is responsible for solving customer problems. The communication flow, here, in these organizations is a two-way process between sales and other departments.

The sales force explores the needs of the customers and sends information to other functional departments. In usual cases, the R&D department develops the product; the production department gives physical shape to the product concept; the finance department decides on the sales budget and the company's credit policy; the marketing department frames the advertising and distribution policies and decides the price of the product in consultation with the finance department. Finally the sales department takes charge of handing the products to the customers.

Therefore, it can be seen that coordination amongst different functions is extremely imperative. And integrating all the value-added activities together, to develop an offer that meets the expectations of the customers is also important.

Specialization

A sales organization is a combination of different sales and marketing activities and requires the presence of managers and sales personnel with specializations in their respective fields. A sales manager is said to be capable of making call plans, prepare routing, and work scheduling for the salespeople. It is important to note that salespeople should be efficient in treating customers and handling their problems as well. For example, a financial firm needs salespeople with knowledge in accounting and finance. And a technologically oriented firm requires salespeople with technical qualifications.

So, the basic idea behind specialization is using the expertise and knowledge of the sales managers or people, so that a firm can understand the needs and expectations of the customers better, share information with other departments, shoot the problems of the customers professionally, and provide after-sales service with ease. So, specialization leads to improved performance of the organization.

5.4 ORGANIZING THE SALES FORCE—A DESCRIPTION

The starting point of building a sales organization is identification of their objectives, which in turn, indicates the type of sales force structure required. Once the structure has been zeroed in, the organization defines the task keeping in mind the objectives and the sales force structure. The sales force task is specified in order to fulfil the long- and the short-term objectives of the organization and the marketing department.

A sales organization, usually, acts upon corporate level strategies in which the market-level strategies are embedded. For example, if corporate-level strategy involves expansion of business in a region, the marketing strategy would involve mapping out ways to add more distribution outlets or ways to engage more salespeople to augment selling activity. So, marketing strategies should be precisely articulated to underpin specific action plans that will achieve the sales objectives.

Operationally, the sales objectives are expressed in terms of sales quotas that the salespeople target in a given period of time. But the decided strategy, further decides on how prospective customers will be explored, targeted, communicated, persuaded or how the resources will be allocated to achieve targets. For existing customers, the basic objective is to retain and provide the service to them which requires them to use a direct strategy.

Objectives are also guideposts that determine the type of sales force, their, tasks and size along with ways to manage them. It also helps in finding the approaches that can be used to control the performance of the sales force and also, as to how a sales organization can be integrated with the marketing department and the entire company.

Zoltners et al. (2001) mentioned three objectives of the sales force structure. These are

(a) adaptability,
(b) efficiency, and
(c) effectiveness.

Adaptability

Adaptability leads an organization to react quickly and effectively to any change in the product or market without any major structural overhaul. An adaptive firm can easily accommodate to the changes in the selling process resulting from product or market fluctuations with the present sales force structure.

Efficiency

Efficiency reflects the rate at which the sales force converts its money investment into actual calls.

Effectiveness

Effectiveness represents the response of the buyer to the calling level (or the number of calls) in a selling organization. A highly effective sales force has high impact per call which generates high level of sales too.

Objectives point out the necessary activities to be performed by the organization and its design facilitates the performance of such activities. Objectives, also, precisely determine the tasks of the sales force.

Traditional sales organization treated salespeople as mere order takers. So, the primary objective of all salespeople was to increase sales directly by interacting with customers. But this is an oversimplification of the salesperson's task in relation to today's business scenario characterized by a rising customer base, the demands of the customer for quality products and services, market competition, and need for long-term relationship with the customers. So, classical selling theory which suggested that the salespeople are agents of an organization who meet and collect orders from the customers and sales managers, and are engaged in managing the sales operations, actually do not pay much dividend to the company today. Indeed, often the buyers, especially larger ones, wish to set some terms and conditions of buying with the organization prior to carrying out the actual deal. In some cases, a buyer may want to negotiate the price or logistical formalities with the top level of marketing department.

Modern sales organizations advocate participation of salespeople in sales management. For example, salespeople in territory-based sales organizations are solely responsible for every sales activity that happens in their territories. Similarly, in customer-based organizations, salespeople can develop sales performance by managing the demands and relations of the customers. Salespeople are also responsible for managing resources such as promotional budgets, products or services that are allocated to them for selling, various service supports. etc. Some companies entrust senior salespeople to handle only major accounts and sales representatives to sell medium- or small-sized forms. But certain big national or international customers may be interested to work with senior (regional or national) level of the suppliers. In some other selling situations, territory sales managers and their subordinates handle medium- or small-sized buyers who completely exist within their territories.

Another trend, which is being noticed, divides the salespeople into two groups, one handling the existing accounts and the other, cultivating new accounts. A company catering to various segments of the market for the same product or product line works with different distribution outlets. So, a salesperson working in a customer-centric structural design is quite comfortable to deal with a wide spectrum of customers. For example, a company manufacturing crockery needs to serve different customers of two major market segments. One is the institutional market such as hotels and the other is retail market. Company salespeople can deal with the former and the latter may be fed by specialized wholesalers. Even within the same market segment, a company can adopt unique structural decisions. Senior salespeople may be engaged in order taking whereas the juniors can be involved in merchandising.

Organizing the sales force means organizing the sales effort. Organizing the sales effort implies distribution of selling activities in such a way that alleviates the needs and demands of the marketplace in time. The sales force structure delineates the working relationship between sales managers and salespeople. Before sales efforts are laid out, a thorough research of customer profiles such as their economic behaviour, demographic compositions, culture, social customs, linguistic, lifestyle, etc. are needed to be known. Also, the following qualities about the customers should also be looked into as follows:

(a) Level and quantity of customer service
(b) Geographical locations of customer
(c) Buying behaviour of customer
(d) Structural composition of the customer, in case the customer is an organization
(e) Buying authority of the customer
(f) Buying capacity of customer
(g) Centralization or decentralization in the buying organization, etc.

The decision to choose a particular type of sales organization (territorial, product, etc.) depends on the distribution of customers, range of products dealt with, specialization of customers (e.g., insurers, bankers, hoteliers, etc.), the functional orientation of customers (e.g., retailing, advertising, financing, etc.) or the combination of two or three specializations. A specialization suggests a specific architecture of organizational design that can fulfil the needs of a customer by selling the products and services of a company.

Organizational design aims to align the sales force structure with the purposes of the sales organization. Indeed, organizational design is a strategic exercise setting guidelines for specific actions and meeting the missions, purposes, and core philosophies of an organization. Many people equate organizational design with organizational structure. In fact, organizational design is much more than just an organizational structure. Organizational design is the process of integrating an organization's structure with its mission. This means relating tasks, workflow, responsibility, and authority synergistically to support the fulfilment of objectives (http://www. mindtools.com).

5.5   DETERMINING THE SIZE OF THE SALES FORCE—A METHODOLOGICAL STUDY

After building the organizational structure, the company needs to decide the size of the sales force to match the manpower requirements of the organization.

This decision has been further influenced by the company's desire to gain sales volume and profit level. The size of the sales force should be optimal to get the best of the results, i.e., lesser than the actual size will lessen the manning of sales territories and extensive customer coverage whereas a higher size will unnecessarily increase the operating expenses.

Some of the methods that are used to determine the sales force size are as follows:

(a) Workload approach

(b) Sales potential or breakdown method

(c) Incremental method

Workload Approach

The method is based on two salient assumptions. All salespeople should have equal workloads. The workload defining the amount of work a salesperson renders should encompass covering customer size, potential, and travel time.

The method includes the following steps:

1. Classify the present and prospective customers into groups according to their sales potentials, generally large, medium, and small customers. The number of accounts to be visited by the salespersons should be listed. It is comparatively easy to identify present customers by name, address, number, and type. Prospective customers can be generated by telephone directory, yellow pages, referral sources, cold calls, etc. Details on prospecting are discussed in Chapter 3. Let us suppose, a company researches out the presence of 250 large (Type A), 500 medium (Type B), and 800 small customers (Type 3) of both the types.

2. The call frequency per type of customer must be assessed. As a general rule, the larger the size of customer, the more frequent is the call. Assuming, the number of both the present and the prospective customers is given with time per a sales call and the call frequencies are the same. The following distribution of time and call frequencies can be decided.

   Type A: 60 minutes per call × 40 calls a year = 40 hours/year

   Type B: 30 minutes per call × 30 calls a tear = 15 hours/year

   Type C: 20 minutes per call × 18 calls a year = 6 hours/year

3. Estimate the total workload needed to reach the entire market which can be calculated by multiplying the number of customers with the number of years in the following way:

   Type A: 250 customers × 40 hours/year   = 20000 hours

Type B: 500 customers × 15 hours/year   = 7500 hours

Type C: 800 customers × 6 hours/year   = 4800 hours

             Total   = **22,300 hours**

4. Decide on the number of working hours available to the salespeople

Total days in a year = 365 days

    Sundays = 52 days

    Holidays = 10 days

    Sickness = 5 days

    Training = 10 days

    Meetings = 10 days

   Conferences = 5 days

Total days lost = 92 days

So, the number of working days = 273 days = 273 × 8 hours = 2184 hours

(Assuming each salesperson spends eight hours a day on their respective activities)

So, each salesperson has 2184 hours per year for selling and non-selling activities (waiting time, travelling time, etc.)

5. Divide the total working hours into selling and non-selling activities

Say, Selling activities = 40 per cent of total selling hours = 873.6 hours

Non-selling activities = 60 per cent of total selling hours = 1310.4 hours

6. Calculate the number of salespeople required

This is calculated by dividing the total number of workload by the total selling activity hours per salesperson.

Therefore, the number of salespeople needed = 22300/874 = 25 salespeople

This method is simple and conceptually accurate. Sales force size depends on the selling efforts allocated amongst accounts of varied types. The method is applicable to all types of selling situations. However, it needs accurate information about the number of present and prospective customers and their sales potentials. A major drawback of this method is that it disregards profits and costs as explicit factors influencing different levels of customer service.

Also, call frequencies used in the approach are based on mere judgment. It does not give optimal size of the sales force because it is not clear whether the call frequencies set maximizes the sales profits or not. It does not consider sales productivity in terms of sales per salesperson or salesperson turnover.

Sales Potential Method

The sales potential method is based on the assumption that on an average, a salesperson is able to fulfil all the requirements of a job description. The performance for a set of activities contained in the job description is equal to one sales personnel unit. An excellent salesperson is supposed to exceed the one sales personnel unit. A mediocre salesperson does not achieve the same unit. If all salespeople work according to the conditions of job description, then the number of salespeople is equal to the number of sales personnel units. The method should also take into account attrition of some salespeople within an year.

The basic formula is as follows:

Sales force size = Forecasted sales/Estimated sales productivity of the average salesperson

The method considers the following three factors:

(i) Annual sales forecast for the company (S)

(ii) Estimated productivity of the average salesperson (P)

(iii) Estimated percentage of annual sales turnover (T)

Say, the number of salespeople needed = N

The formula is reduced to

$$N = S/P + T (S/P)$$

It is simplified to,

$$N = S/P (1 + T)$$

The basic premise of this method is that an accurate forecast of sales is available. The forecast is then broken down into estimating the number of salespeople needed to produce the forecasted level of sales volume. This is also known as the breakdown method.

Suppose, a firm's sales forecast is ₹40 million in the next year, estimated sales productivity per sales personnel unit is ₹2 million and an estimated annual rate of sales turnover is 10 per cent, then the number of salespeople will be:

$$N = 40,000,000/2,000,000 (1 + 0.10) = 22$$

The method is also simple and straightforward. Thus, estimation of salespeople is easy. But, the method is conceptually weak because the sales forecast determines the number of salespeople needed. It should be the other way around as the number of salespeople should determine the volume of sales and the sales force size should control the sales forecast.

The estimate of sales productivity of one sales personnel unit depends on the accuracy and completeness of the job description. Again, estimating the turnover rate of salespeople is a matter of anticipation. Furthermore, a lead time is needed to recruit and train the salespeople in order to attain the desired level of productivity. Despite the limitations, the method is quite applicable to relatively stable business environment where sales do not fluctuate much and whatever changes happen are predictable.

Incremental Method

The basic concept of this method is to compare marginal profits with marginal selling costs with the addition of a salesperson. Salespeople are added in case incremental sales revenues exceed the incremental cost incurred so that the net profits increase. An example of the incremental approach is illustrated in Table 5.2.

Table 5.2 Financial statement

Number of salespeople (A)	Sales volume (₹) B)	Cost of goods (₹) (C)	Gross margin (D) D = B – C	Salaries (₹) (E)	Commissions (₹) (F)	Travel and expense allowances (₹) (G)	Profit contributions (₹) H = D – (E + F + G)
20	6,00,000	3,60.000	2,40,000	100,000	15,000	12,000	1,13,000
21	5,00,000	3,00,000	2,00,000	100,000	10,000	12,000	78,000
22	4,50,000	2,70.000	1,80,000	100,000	9,000	12,000	59,000
23	3,00,000	1,80,000	1,20,000	100,000	6,000	12,000	2,000
24	2,50.000	1,50,000	1,00,000	100,000	5,000	12,000	–17,000

Table 5.2 shows an example of a company's record of sales volume, cost of goods sold, gross margin, salaries of the salespeople, commissions, travel and expense allowances, and profit contributions. It is evident from the table that sales volume varies directly with the number of salespeople engaged in selling the products of the company. Cost of the goods sold remains same at 60 per cent of sales. Usually, salespeople are given a salary of ₹1 lakh plus commission of 2 per cent on sales volume every year. Each salesperson also receives travel and expense allowance of ₹12,000 a year, i.e., ₹1,000 per month. At present, the company has 19 sales people and wants to determine whether more sales staff would be required or not. Sales managers wants to estimate the increase in sales volume, cost of goods sold, selling costs, and profit contributions.

From Table 5.2, it is clear that a sales manager can add four more salespeople to the existing 19. An addition of the fourth salesperson results in 23 salespeople fetching an additional profit contribution of ₹2,000. But, adding fifth salesperson would yield in a negative profit contribution of ₹17, 000. Thus, the optimal size of the sales force is 23.

This method is conceptually sound and expresses the quantitative relationship among sales force size, sales, costs, and profits. It shows the impact of incremental sales force size on potential sales and profits. But the method is difficult to develop in the absence of historical data of the company. Also, for new joinees, this method is not applicable as no historical data is available.

5.6 MANAGING THE SALES FORCE—A FUNCTIONAL ORIENTATION

Once the sales organization is developed, the next step on the cards is how to manage it. A successful company develops an effectively designed sales structure and efficiently managed sales force. Definitely, managing starts at the helm of the organization. A manager has to be engaged in line function or staff function or both. Modern sales organization deserves the involvement of sales managers in both staff as well as line functions. So, the division of a sales manager's job and responsibility in field sales management and staff functions such as recruiting, selecting, training, marketing research, sales promotion, etc., is crucial. An effective sales organization needs feeding of active and potential salespeople. Therefore, sound *recruitment* policy and *selection* of the right salespeople is a part of managerial process.

An imperative process for managers is *training* in order to make salespeople knowledgeable and practical. However, the degree of training depends on the type of salespeople and sales jobs. Particularly, a new sales force requires more time for training, otherwise it is difficult for them to be successful in this field. Similarly, supervision is closely linked to managing a pioneering sales team. Wilson (1985) viewed that a pioneer sales force is likely to need much more time from the manager than a routine order taking team. Similarly, Washington (2005) said that the salespeople working on commission basis do not require much supervision time from the sales managers.

Motivation is another aspect of management. Even senior salespeople need motivation at some point of time in their careers because of fatigue and lethargy crippling their performances. This happens due to continuous mental involvement with travails and travesties of the business. There is nothing more hectic than 'selling' as a profession. Whims and speculative nature of the business are the bane of the selling profession.

Designing the *compensation* package for a sales force is a significant area of management because this is a major motivator for the sales team. This should be evolved judiciously so that efficient salespeople are duly rewarded and less efficient ones get their reasonable dues.

Evaluating and controlling salespeople is yet another important area for managing the sales force. Managers should continually check sales reports submitted by sales supervisors and follow the sales proceeds to locate the deficient areas in sales performance and work on them. This also involves cost analysis and auditing the sales and cost documents. Control is necessary to curb the decline in performance and help improve the future sales efforts.

Managing a sales organization further entails close *coordination of all plans*, from bottom line to the top, from account to territory, from regional to national, and from strategic to operational. Whatsoever the plan is, it should be customer focused, including responding to customer needs and meeting their expectations on real time. Poor management of sales organization leads to the following problems:

(a) Loss of sales productivity and organizational inefficiency

(b) The organization will be highly susceptible to competition and may find it difficult to withstand the heat of competition

(c) The organization will lose its revenue-generating capacity

(d) Customers may develop a negative bent of mind and switch over to other organizations

(e) Sales force will be highly demotivated and this will result in high attrition of salespeople

(f) The organization will tarnish its image in front of its stakeholders

5.7 INTEGRATING THE SALES FORCE WITHIN THE ORGANIZATION—A NEED-BASED APPROACH

The organization should develop a collaborative environment within it by linking the sales force with the management. The objective is to reduce the communication barriers between the two where salespeople can distinctly understand the goals and missions of an organization, plans and procedures, and responsibility and accountability. Present day organizations emphasize more on team efforts combining sales managers and sales force where salespeople are kept abreast of the marketing plans and are consulted on the efficacy of the plans and the likelihood of their implementation. Because of their involvement in plan formulation, goal setting, and strategic actions of the organization, they feel more committed to achieving the objectives. There should not be any place of confusion or ambiguity amongst salespeople so far as their contribution to managing and executing the selling functions is associated with sales productivity.

Box 5.1 lists plausible reasons that create confusion and distract salespeople. This is further aggravated by miscommunication from top authority, inadequate training, and lesser induction of salespeople about organization's goal, functional orientation, and organizational structure. This demands clarity and specificity for the sake of sales performance.

> **Box 5.1 Areas triggering confusion among sales force**
>
> Following are the areas triggering confusion amongst sales force:
>
> (a) Improper definitions of the missions and objectives of an organization
> (b) Incomprehensible sales planning and procedures
> (c) Incomplete description of customer profiles
> (d) Vague order taking, delivering, financing, and transaction policies of the firm
> (e) Unclear reporting authority, wrong sales forecast, unachievable sales target, and quota
> (f) Complex performance appraisal procedure
> (g) Unclear compensation policies and promotional scopes.

Delegation of authority and responsibility to experienced salespeople is quite common in sales organization. Authority and responsibility stay side-by-side. Salespeople cannot accept a responsibility unless they are given the authority to accomplish it. By empowerment, administrative costs can be lowered provided it promises results. In contrast, new or inexperienced salespeople could be treated as implementing machineries, being involved in dealing with customers at the operational phase, such as order taking and processing, arranging supply of finished goods to customers, collecting cheques or overdue debts, etc. For new salespeople, management needs to exercise close supervision and control of their activities. So, here, delegation of task rather than authority is the principal issue.

In many sales situations, sales managers personally accompany inexperienced salespeople to conduct personal selling. Basically, the objectives here are two fold. The first is to train the salespeople as to how to manage field selling. Second, many customers, particularly large ones, demand a large degree of involvement of higher-level managers, if not individually, as leaders of the sales team. For capital equipment selling, this is quite prevalent.

SUMMARY

Organization is like a neural network in a human system integrating all the organs in a coherent manner. Sales organization entails organizing the sales force to facilitate selling the product or service, distribute it to the customers, and transfer the ownership from the seller to the buyer. An effective sales organization conceives a structure to implement strategies that show the set path of reaching the objectives of an organization. So, the structure is the roadmap to execute the strategies of the organization.

The major task of organization structure is work specialization. It encompasses breaking down the overall task into smaller component units where each unit demands specific method and skill to cater to the completion of the overall task. On a sales organization, the emphasis is also paid on work specialization. Specialization helps the organization to achieve growth and productivity in financial and social terms. Sales organization mobilizes its operations through sales force structure. Different

(Contd)

types of sales force structure are (a) territorial sales force structure, (b) product sales force structure, (c) customer sales force structure, (d) functional sales force structure, and (e) complex sales force structure. Different structures have their advantages and disadvantages. Sales organization is established on important organizational principles very much akin to the whole organization. These are (a) span of control, (b) unity of command, (c) stability and continuity, (d) centralization and decentralization, (e) coordination and integration, and (f) specialization. The starting point of building a sales organization is the recognition of objectives that in turn, indicate the type of sales structure. Accordingly, the organization develops and specifies the tasks and the sales force fulfils the marketing goals.

Three important objectives of sales force structure are adaptability, efficiency, and effectiveness. Traditional sales organization treated salespeople as order takers. Modern sales organization advocates participation of salespeople in sales management. Organizing the sales force means organizing the sales effort and organizing the sales effort implies distribution of selling activities in such a way that it alleviates the needs and demands of the marketplace in time. After building the organization structure, the company needs to decide the size of the sales force. Three major methods of determining the size of the sales force are (a) workload approach, (b) sales potential or breakdown method, and (c) incremental method. Once the sales organization is developed, the next step is how to manage it. Moreover, the integration of the sales force within the organization is important for developing collaborative sales environment.

KEY TERMS

Customer Sales Force Structure Customer sales force structure involves focusing on specific customers or customer groups to sell products. The company organizes and designs its structure in such a way that the sales force has to carry out selling activities only for specific customers/ customer groups.

Complex Sales Force Structure Complex sales force structure advocates in organizing the sales force on a wide variety of products and customers over a broad geographical area. This type of structure manages a number of product-market-customer variants simultaneously.

Functional Sales Force Structure The functional sales force structure type refers to organizing the sales force structure on the basis of various selling activi-

ties which are required in selling an organization's products. In such kind of situations, salespeople are recruited based on their special skills to perform these specific activities.

Product Sales Force Structure The product sales force structure represents a sales organization where salespeople are asked to concentrate only a part of the company's products or product lines.

Sales Organization A sales organization entails in organizing its sales force to facilitate the act of selling and distributing a product or a service.

Territorial Sales Force Structure The territorial sales force structure is a type of structure used when a company follows geographical divisions to allocate tasks amongst salespeople.

CONCEPT REVIEW QUESTIONS

1. What do you mean by sales organization? How organizational structure assumes a significant role in sales organization?
2. The major premise of organizational structure is work specialization. Examine it with respect to sales organization.

3. What are the purposes of a sales organization?
4. What are the different types of sales force structure? Explain at least two such structures.
5. What are the merits and demerits of territorial and product sales force structure?
6. Explain the criteria for developing a sales organization.
7. State the organizational principles that guide the setting of organizational structure. Extend your answer considering sales organizational structure.
8. How is a sales force organized?
9. How is the size of the sales force determined? How is workload approach used to determine the size of the sales force?
10. An effectively designed sales organization facilitates the task of sales management. Examine.
11. Prepare a note on integrating the sales force within the organization.
12. Estimate the number of sales persons required in a sales territory where,
    (a) Number of major customers = 200 and call frequency = 8 per annum
    (b) Number of moderate customers = 450 and call frequency = 6 per annum
    (c) Number of small customers = 600 and call frequency = 4 per annum

CRITICAL REVIEW QUESTION

While going from local to regional, regional to national, and national to transnational level of sales operations, an organization should intelligently leverage on experience in management practices, knowledge and skill, marketing mix, sales strategies, advertising appeals, etc. The company needs to mobilize its resources to take opportunities for growth and expansion. Again, the company should aim at maximizing sales volume to obtain advantage of scale economies.

As the chief executive officer of the company, how would you bring effective changes in organizational structure, strategies, and its implementation in order to facilitate continuous expansion of your operations from a micro-level geographical unit to global scale? Do you think that for the treble time increase in business potential from national to global level, the size of the sales force should be increased at the proportionate rate?

PROJECT ASSIGNMENTS

1. Visit a pharmaceutical company either personally or on websites to know the organizational structure especially the sales organization. Determine the type of organization and find its merits and demerits. Mention how the sales organization maintains coordination with other functional departments.
2. Find an MNC and an Indian firm engaged in software businesses. The Indian firm works on projects both within the nation and abroad. Study their sales organizational structures and sales operations. Compare and contrast the difference in structural architectures of the two firms. Based on it, predict the architecture of an ideal sales organizational structure that will be effective for both national and international business operations?

REFERENCES

Jadhav, S. (2009), 'Supply Chain Management at Hindutan Lever', http://www.mindtree.com, accessed on 28 September 2010.

Jindal, S. Er (2003), 'Cross Border Enterprise—A Paradigm for Food and Agribusiness Sector', *Prabandh*, December, pp. 36–46.

Saravani, V. (2005), 'ITC's E-Chaupal: Taking E-Business to Farmers', *Marketing Mastermind*, vol. V(2), February, pp. 64–76.

Washington, S (2005). 'Designing and Managing a Sales Force', *Business & Finance*, http://www.associatedcontent.com/article/11540/designing_and_managing_a_sales_force.html?cat=3, accessed on 21 July 2009.

Wilson, M. (1985). 'Managing a Sales Force', 2nd ed., Gower Publishing Company Limited, England.

Zoltners, A.A., P. Sinha, and A.G. Joltners (2001), 'The Complete Guide to Accelerating Sales Force Performance', http://toostep.com/insight/supply_chain_management_at_hindusthan_unilever, accessed on 05 June 2009.

http://books.google.co.in/, accessed on 11 September 2010.

http://en.wikipedia.org/wiki/Departmentalization, accessed on 24 January 2010.

http://www. mindtools.com/pages/article/newPPM95htm, accessed on 20 July 2009.

CASE STUDY

Selling Phenomenon under Cross Border Enterprise

In today's changing world, the goal of a sales organization is to devise a structure that enables a firm to respond to the requirements of the customers in a better way than its competitors. Diffusion of corporate information on product or service, acquisition of knowledge and experience of product or service applications in local, regional, national and global markets, and expansion of business from local level to regional and global market is the thrust of the present day organizations. But, to operate on such a large volume, a firm finds it hard to respond to varied differences in marketing environments and set up suitable marketing approaches to match such conditions. Secondly, dearth of resources constricts a firm to extend the boundary of operations. Moreover, resource allocation on an equitable basis is not an easy proposition due to distance and time factors. Thirdly, often companies lack strategic experiences to gain competitive advantages on equal merits in various geographical units. But the exigency of running a business on a national and global platform cannot be overruled from the point of view of survival of the firm.

Strategic partnership is quite common among two or three firms to add gravity in the resources and momentum in operations. For example, Nokia Telecommunication, the infrastructure arm of Finland based Nokia group and BPL Telecom Ltd. of India have inked a deal for distribution and service agreements covering Nokia's Private Mobile Radio (PMR) Actionet and related terminal products. BPL will provide full customer service capabilities to support the Nokia Actionet Compact customers in India.

In the fast changing global market, corporations are always looking for new and creative ways to organize. New types of flexibility, cohe-

(Contd)

siveness, and efficiency are requited from firms to meet the demands of the customers. Need for being cost effective, customer driven, quality consciousness, and delivering the quality faster than competitors are the determinants of performance. The challenge for the organization is to develop new concept(s) of conducting business. One such way is to form a network of individual enterprises that work together in a value chain in order to meet the demands of the customers satisfactorily. So, under network structure, an organizational structure cannot sustain in isolation. Manufacturers do not perform all the functions singularly. Indeed, these operate as nodal agents connecting suppliers, distributors, customers, facilitating agencies such as insurance and financial firms, stockholders to produce a supply chain that works smoothly to the satisfaction of all the participants.

The concept of cross border enterprise has grown to synthesize resources, skills, and knowledge of multifunctional organizations into a product or service that suits the expectations of the customers gracefully. Extended enterprise (EE) and virtual enterprise (VE) are the offshoots of cross border enterprise. The extended enterprise is designed to fulfil market-driven requirements by utilizing external resources without owning them, whereas VE is a subset of units and processes within the supply chain that acts like a single enterprise through strong coordination among units. EE provides a permanent cohesiveness among enterprises where as VE is a temporary network of enterprises to deliver a product quickly to the market. Advanced technology and information systems are used to integrate enterprises under virtual systems. In agribusiness, the application of virtual enterprise is not uncommon. For example, in the production of canned food, the supply chain consists of farmers or fruit growers, suppliers of food ingredients, processors, wholesalers, retailers, can producers, transporters, and deliverers act in a unified manner.

VE concept in sales organization is gaining popularity to serve customers who want speed and responsiveness without impairing quality of the product. This finds relevance because salespeople are spread throughout the country. Virtual interactions of salespeople with customers, salespeople with organizations, and organizations with customers do not know geographical distances, time gaps or pauses in the supply chain. These supply chain problems can find virtual- and real-time solutions for the firms, vendors, and its customers. An organization following virtual selling model can generate CRM (customer relationship management) applications, SFA (sales force

(Contd)

automation), web-based campaigns, lead tracking, etc. Sales meetings can be organized by multiple virtual links that create a real-time collaborative session drawing an end to endless e-mail interactions. Virtual workspaces improve sales productivity, reduce cost of selling, limit the requirement of additional staff, and improve the value delivery systems. Sales teams can work together easily and securely irrespective of time pressure and distance barriers.

Discussion Questions

1. What is virtual enterprise? State its application in selling.
2. What are leading the present-day organizations to adopt virtual workspace in selling efforts?
3. Name some benefits of virtual sales organizations.
4. Do you think salespeople will not be so demanding in future due to induction of virtual selling approach in organizations?

Source: 'Building the virtual sales office', http://www.microsoftt.com/canada/midsizebusiness/business value local/virtualsales.mspx, 9 October 2007, accessed on 22 August 2009.

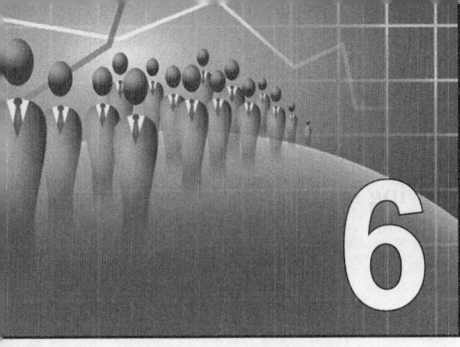

6 Sales Territories

6.1 SALES TERRITORY—MEANING AND DEFINITION

A territory is usually perceived as a geographical area. But sales territory does not necessarily mean a geographical area. It may consist of a group of present or potential customers assigned to a salesman usually in a particular geographical area. The concept of sales territory revolves around developing certain geographical units in a way so that customers residing there can be effectively served. The presence of customers means the presence of sales opportunities. So, the principal objective for the creation of sales territory is to match the sales opportunities with the selling efforts in a most productive manner. This is necessary because usually different territories have different market potentials. It creates varied kind of opportunities for different firms with respect to their respective abilities to utilize the market potentials. In some territories, the buying capacity of the customer is high and in others, it is low.

Firms are also seen to be behaving differently from situation to situation. In some cases, firms are able to put a challenging situation in front of their competitors but in others act only as a weakening force with no teeth to frustrate the competitors. In simple terms, there are certain factors that facilitate firms to exploit opportunities whereas the others simply pose threats.

The management should understand all these factors, set different sales objectives for different territories and allocate resources according to the requirements of the territories. Management must capitalize the strengths of a territory and overcome its weaknesses by proper territory management to get productive results.

So one can say that a territory can have the following forms:

(a) A geographical area
(b) A group of prospective and present customers
(c) An industry-based territory (e.g., textile industry)
(d) A market (e.g., an insurance market)

Johnson (1994) defined a sales territory as a configuration of current and potential accounts for which responsibility has been assigned to a particular sales representative.

Venugopal (2008) defined a sales territory as the number of present and potential customers located in a geographic area that are assigned to an individual salesperson.

Dalrymple (1995) illustrated that sales territory represents customers located in a geographic area that is assigned to an individual salesperson to perform. Therefore, in the context of a geographical area, a salesperson is entrusted to deal with customers located in that geographic unit. But in case a set of customers is treated as a territorial unit, a salesperson may not restrict the operation within that area. Rather he may have to pursue customers in more than one geographical area. For example, insurance salespeople never restrict their operations within a geographical territory. Sometimes, when an industry is conceived as a territory, a salesperson is instructed to meet the key buying authorities of the customer organizations where the geographical territory has nothing to do with the selling efforts. For example, a company dealing in medical supplies instructs its salespeople to meet government hospitals where, literally, the concept of geography as a territory is meaningless.

Again in many other companies, salespeople are given charge to handle their territories as if they are the managers there. In such case, they plan and execute all the sales operations themselves. Johnson et al. (1994) rightly pointed out that salespeople are scales down sales managers of their territories. Salespeople are instructed to focus on the sales opportunities and goals in the territories where they are assigned.

Exhibit 6.1 shows how a globally acclaimed company like Nestle has been utilizing its sales force to perform territorial responsibilities.

Exhibit 6.1   Nestle—gearing salespeople to bear fruit from sales territories

Salespeople shoulder the responsibility for the growth of a territory, both in terms of value and volume of the company's products. They are geared to perform sales tasks in their respective sales territories in line with the territory objectives and goals. New recruits are trained to understand the dynamics of the territorial environment and contribute to the plans for growth. Salespeople also undertake promotional jobs in the territory in order to

---

(Contd)

(Contd)

provide maximum visibility of the products in their defined territories and handle distributors. Salespeople get help from promotional supports such as point of purchase (POP) display, sampling, branding activities in different locations to improve their performance.

Source: 'Freshers Job Mumbai, Nestle India Requires Sales Trainees', www.nestle.com and http://blogs.mybandra.com/2009/11/26/freshers-jobs-mumbai-nestle-india-requires-sales-trainee-www.nestle.com/, accessed on 05 September 2010.

6.2 OBJECTIVES, BENEFITS, AND IMPERATIVES OF SALES TERRITORY

The sales territory is a subdivision of a large geographical unit or represents a group of customers of the total customer unit. A company sets the sales objectives as well as the objectives of the sales territory. But while laying down objectives of the sales territory, the broad objectives of the company must be kept in mind. In no occasion should the sales territory objectives act in opposition to the company's sales objectives. So, sales territory objectives are formulated towards meeting the sales goals and objectives of the territory in specific and company at large.

Again it is true, if a territory is properly designed, it can facilitate fulfilment of its objectives. Therefore, the company must consider good territory design as one of the major objectives, otherwise achieving territory objectives as well as the company's objectives will be disdained. Moreover, all the objectives must aim at how customers can be better managed and served keeping the sales and profit goals in focus. The main objectives of the sales territory are presented below in Box 6.1.

Box 6.1 Objectives of sales territory

Following are the objectives of sales territory:

(a) To formulate sales plans, policies, and strategies around the company's products, also services that are reflected accurately in the marketing programmes designed for a territory

(b) To analyse territory sales potentials and plan marketing programmes around the company's products/services and the key potential customers

(c) To analyse the strengths and weaknesses of competitors more precisely and lay down strategies to subvert competition

(d) To help in the identification and classification of accounts according to their potentials and chalk out call plans for each segment justifiably

(e) To organize sales force, allocate sales efforts, and implement sales plans more effectively

(f) To review the performance of its sales force at regular intervals and take prompt measures when it does not work up to the company's expectations

(g) To quickly redesign sales plans, policies, and strategies in case a firm finds changes in the market trends and in the territory business environment

A company's sales objectives are set to serve benefits to the customers and the company itself. In other words, sales territory objectives are formulated strictly in line with the company's overall sales objectives. Their objectives, mainly, aim to make extensive coverage of it to develop as many new customers as possible and hold the old customers intact. Again, accomplishment of objectives means distribution of benefits to customers as well as the company. A well-structured territory definitely helps to fructify sales territory objectives and yield benefits to both the company and the customers. Indeed, sales territory objectives aim to cater to multiple benefits. Some of these benefits are listed as follows:

1. Sales territory creates big opportunities for adequate customer coverage. Each customer deserves and gets sufficient time from the salespeople for interactions and services.
2. Sales territories, if properly designed, aid sales managers to distribute more or less equal workload among salespeople. Therefore, the evaluation and comparison of performance of salespeople as well as decision on rewards, both monetary and non-monetary becomes easy to sales managers.
3. A well laid out sales territory can reduce travel time of salespeople. Reduced travel time is related to reduced selling costs and increased length of customer interaction.
4. Sales territories also act as great motivators and morale boosters to the salespeople. Salespeople can clearly identify and understand their areas of operations, sales potentials, sales targets, number of customers to interact, sales budgets, and the competitive environment of the territory easily.
5. Sales managers can better manage and control sales force, take decisions of allocation of resources and modify sales tasks and marketing tools quite comfortably when the marketing situation changes.
6. Sales territories help in getting quick customer feedback, understanding customer experiences and satisfaction/dissatisfaction, and hasten providing the after-sales services and redressing customer grievances, if any.
7. Giving more personalized attention to the customers is possible. As customer fragmentation is clear in terms of major and small customers, therefore, call plans, call frequencies, and call rates can be easily adjusted to attend to customers depending on their buying potentials.

The construction of sales territory cannot be done arbitrarily. Certain formalities are followed to overcome them, else the objectives of sales territory will become attainable. Certain imperatives of sales territory development are furnished as follows:

1. Sales managers should properly map the sales territories to create fairly equitable sales opportunities for the salespeople. A sales territory with lesser number of accounts and less workload may frustrate a salesperson, particularly one who is efficient or working on commission basis.

2. Care should be taken while allocating territories amongst salespeople. In such cases, sales managers entrust experienced salespeople to handle territories with high competition and young salespeople in less competitive territories. Also, senior salespeople are given charge to deal with territories having the presence of most of the major customers who make the bulk of the sales and contribute to profits and whose loss significantly impact the sales revenues. In contrast, inexperienced salespeople are asked to handle comparatively less profitable customers.

3. A company should depute the right number of salespeople in a territory to carry out the workload. The workload should be commensurate with the sales potentials vis-à-vis sales opportunities. A large territory with few salespeople or a small territory with many salespeople is considered as a poor territory design. Too few salespeople for large sales territory is an impractical proposition to cash in sales opportunities and too many salespeople for small territory leads to underutilization of the sales force.

4. While designing a sales territory, analysis must be made on the expected costs and benefits (revenues specially). It should be made sure that benefits must outweigh the costs to render a territory profitable.

6.3 MANAGEMENT OF SALES TERRITORY

Management of a sales territory refers to the management of resources and processes in a territory. Sales territories are structured in such a manner that helps the sales managers to exert proper planning efforts and control of sales activities. Sales territory management can be defined as the planning, implementation and control of sales efforts, and the activities rendered by the salespeople in a sales territory to meet the sales and profit potentials of the organization. It is the process of designing sales territories, planning sales operations, organizing sales force, coordinating sales operations, and evaluating and controlling the sales force performance in a territory. Its major features are as follows:

1. It begins with the analysis and goal setting of the sales of the company's products or services.

2. It rests upon the proper understanding of the sales potentials and the sales opportunities in the territory.

3. It takes the right strategic initiatives to counter competitive threats in the territory.

4. It suggests the right allocation of resources amongst sales territories.

5. It directs the sales force to act upon territory plans and pre-assigned sales budgets.

6. It ensures smooth communication between the salespeople and the sales managers.

7. It helps in the formulation of optimal travel plans for the salespeople in the territory.

8. It decides the sales target for each salesperson and sets performance benchmarks for comparison of the actual and expected sales performance.

9. It guides salespeople to chalk out account planning and scheduling. The former one relates to account management and the later to time management.

10. It clearly suggests the total workload and its proper division amongst salespeople. Workload involves the number of customers to meet, call frequency, average daily call rate, number of orders to procure, volume of sales to earn, etc.

11. It keeps a close check on the selling costs, promotional costs, and distribution costs of the products.

12. It also involves managing relationships with the customers. Salespeople are properly trained and motivated to establish enduring relationships with customers to ensure future sales.

Sales territory management (STM) involves total supervision and control of sales territories. Organizations appoint sales territory officers, managers or executives to take charge of territories who are given responsibilities to plan, organize, and control salespeople and sales operations. Apart from this, they also have to keep abreast with the regional sales departments or the corporate head offices of every plan and action they take in their territories. Exhibit 6.2 gives some ideas about the roles and responsibilities of territory sales officers of one of the most premier organizations in India, HUL.

Exhibit 6.2   A sketchy outline of STM in HUL

The roles and responsibilities of an HUL's territory sales officers are as follows:

(a) Achieving sales target with personal selling

(b) Monitoring competitive activities intensively and taking appropriate actions

(c) Using improved customer services as a tool to consolidate competitive positioning

(d) Developing salespeople on managing customers to acquire more business

(e) Monitoring performance periodically and systematically

(f) Keeping the selling expenses within budget limits

(g) Giving feedback to branch heads

Source: Hindusthan Unilever Limited, Territory Sales Officer, https://recruitment.unilevervices.com/ MAIN/careerpotal/Job Profile.cfm?szOrderID = 3189&szUniqueCareerPortalID=afdd2675-ae2f-4e9-97-e5-84fd3llaf5fl, accessed on 24 December 2010.

Exhibit 6.3 reveals the delicacy of the sales territory management of a company that has been regarded as a household name across the globe.

Exhibit 6.3 Gaxosmithkline—success owes to state of the art territory planning

Glaxosmithkline, a world leader in consumer and healthcare products makes all-round efforts to develop high-level empowered and motivated medical representatives, and offers superior performance. The district managers to whom the salespeople report shoulder the responsibility to meet the sales targets, sales growth, and achieve market share objectives in their territories. Efficient territory plans, optimal utilization of resources to fetch maximum returns on investments, and persuading target groups to choose the company's products and services are some of the striking features of territory management.

Indeed, sound territory plans linking resources allocated to the territory consistent with the sales goals and target returns on investment are the hallmarks of the company's success in selling. Each sales territory according to its potential in terms of customer demands and growth prospects deserve prior plans to allocate the optimal number of salespeople and arrange organizational (e.g., setting a subdivision of the company) and financial support (e.g., supporting promotional expenses). Sound territory plans can only bolster territory management. In this regard, developing annual territory business plans, arranging clinical meetings, consistent call plans, developing market intelligence on customers and competitive activities, performance reviews are the key factors that can strengthen territory management. The company's commendable success owes much to superb distribution of sales tasks amongst salespeople and sound management of territories.

Source: GlaxoSmithKline Jobs: Medical Representatives, Current Jobs, http://alwaysme2u.com/jobs/medical-sector/glaxosmithkine-jobs-medicalrep–resentatives/, posted on 26 August 2010, accessed on 06 September 2010.

Territory planning is a significant part of territory management. It involves understanding the sales potentials and forecasting sales trends, establishing sales objectives, estimating sales budgets, and mapping out strategies that facilitate optimal utilization of resources to accomplish sales objectives.

Territory management is essentially done for effective planning, implementation and control of territory plans, strategies, and performance of sales territories. Moreover, managing costs of sales territory operations are also a part of territory management.

The implementation part of territory management implies taking actions for sales-goal achievement and the control part involves making comparisons of actual performance with the expected and taking appropriate action to bridge the differences.

Salespeople shoulder the responsibilities of managing accounts in their territories. They are held accountable for the good or bad sales performance, profits or losses, and control or decontrol of selling expenses within the territories.

Generally, sales strategies are formulated at the regional or national level of the organization regardless of territories but sometimes, subtle changes are needed in these strategies to respond effectively in order to meet the specific needs of a territory. A high competition-prone territory definitely claims more strategic attention compared to the less competitive one.

Salespeople due to their physical associations with territories can better recognize themselves and advise sales managers on mapping the sales strategies. Again, formulation of sales strategy should make room for its execution. So, it must be seen that salespeople can properly comprehend it and perform in the right direction. Salespeople also need to create the right customer awareness and interest activities, and stimulate positive customer-buying decisions.

6.4 DESIGNING SALES TERRITORY

Designing the sales territory is the building block of effective territory management. Territory design determines the boundary and contour of a territory within which the salespeople operate. It initiates the identification of sales tasks that are assigned to salespeople.

While designing a sales territory, the following conditions might be kept in mind:

1. All territories have equal sales potentials for the firm.
2. Salespeople are given equal sales targets to achieve.
3. Salespeople are given equal opportunities to reach their goals.
4. Salespeople are given equal workload.
5. Sales managers can supervise and control the sales force without any difficulty.
6. As salespeople perform towards attaining common sales goals, their performances are comparable.

But in real life, the ideal situation rarely exists. Differences in market and sales potentials across territories are quite common and therefore, equal workload for salespeople is a difficult proposition. Designing sales territories is not an easy task, particularly, under varying market conditions. So, efforts to redesign the sales territories with changing market conditions is essential for sales managers.

The differences in sales potentials and workload of salespeople are quite obvious but sales managers should design the territories in such a way that differences in sales potentials can be minimized. Second, they should assign sales quota to salespeople proportionate to the sales potentials and distribute workload accordingly so that workload is commensurate with the sales goals and targets to achieve.

Figure 6.1 shows the steps in designing sales territories.

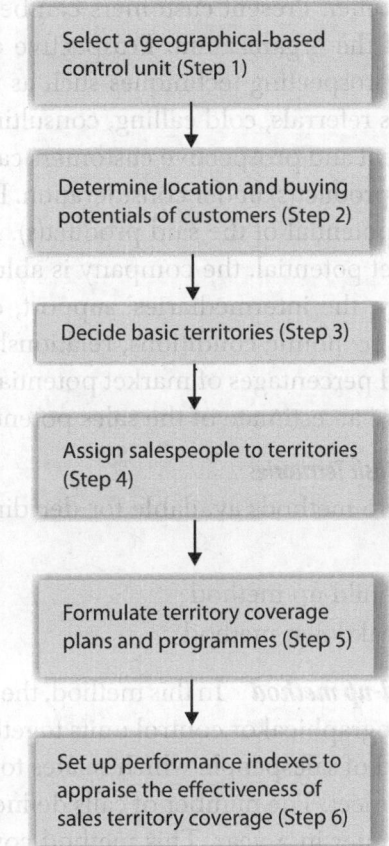

Select a geographical-based control unit (Step 1)

Determine location and buying potentials of customers (Step 2)

Decide basic territories (Step 3)

Assign salespeople to territories (Step 4)

Formulate territory coverage plans and programmes (Step 5)

Set up performance indexes to appraise the effectiveness of sales territory coverage (Step 6)

Figure 6.1   Flowchart depicting the steps in sales territory design

Step 1: Select a Geographical-based Control Unit

The first and the foremost step in designing a sales territory is to select a territorial base called the control unit. The states, regions, divisions, districts, postal code areas, metropolitan cities, etc. can be treated as control units. A control unit may consist of several subunits. For example, a region consists of several divisions, subdivisions, districts, etc.

Size is an important index of a sales territory design. A company should select a territory size so that information relating (i) market potential, (ii) market opportunities, (iii) number of prospective customers, (iv) number of salespeople to be assigned the job, (v) allocation of sales tasks to salespeople, (vi) comparison of sales force performance, (vii) adjustment of the size of the territory in future, and (viii) adaptation with the market conditions of the territory are easily ascertainable. In this way, a manageable number of sales territories can be obtained.

Step 2: Determination of Location and Buying Power of Customers

After identifying the sales territories, the management should find the location of customers, both present and prospective, and estimate the demand potential of each customer. Present customers can be well-recognized from the customer databases of the organization. Prospective customers can be located by taking help of the prospecting techniques such as telephone directories, using present customers as referrals, cold calling, consulting trade associations, etc.

The present and prospective customers can be contacted to know their annual demands of product(s) under consideration. From it, the sales managers can assess the market potential of the said product(s). A company can find out how much of the market potential, the company is able to cater depending on the production capacity, the intermediaries' support, competitive resistance, government regulations, economic conditions, relationship with existing customers, etc. So, the expected percentages of market potential that the company can convert into sales can give an estimate of the sales potentials.

Step 3: Decide Basic Territories

There are two methods available for deciding on the basic territories. They are as follows:

(a) Market build-up method
(b) Sales breakdown method

Market build-up method   In this method, the territories are developed by combining small geographical or control units together. The method calls for equalizing the workload of salespeople which relates to the number of calls a salesperson is expected to meet. The number of calls defines the number of times a salesperson visits a customer in a year. This method covers the following steps as depicted in the Figure 6.2.

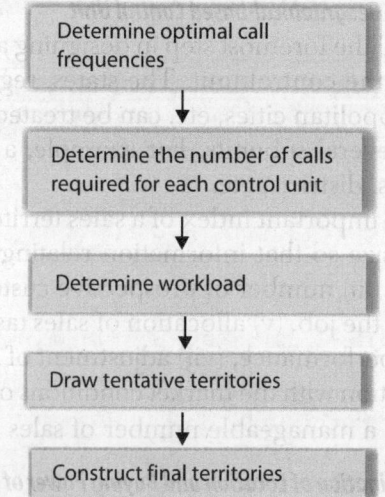

Determine optimal call frequencies

Determine the number of calls required for each control unit

Determine workload

Draw tentative territories

Construct final territories

Figure 6.2   Flowchart of market build-up method

(i) **Determine optimal call frequencies:** The call frequency should be set at an optimal level so that a salesperson is able to realize the sales potential. Besides this, the nature of the market, buying behaviour of the customers, average cost per call, nature of competition, and the support of the distributors influence call frequencies. Again, customers vary in terms of revenue or profit potentials and therefore deserve more call frequencies for some customers and less for the others. Based on marketing research, the annual requirement plans of customers on a product or a group of products and by studying the sales history of the present and prospective customers, customers are grouped into major (high-sales potential), moderate (moderate-sales potential) and minor customers (low-sales potential).

Covering the sales territory effectively stands on the premise of attaching the right importance to the right customer groupings. It goes without saying that high-sales potential customers need maximum attention from salespeople and vice-versa. A customers' attention, basically, relates to the number of visits or calls a salesperson makes to the customers. These call frequencies are decided according to the customer groups. Each group is treated as a control unit.

(ii) **Determine the number of calls required for each control unit:** The number of calls for each control can be determined as follows.

Number of calls for each control group = Number of accounts in each unit × Call frequency

Table 6.1, through an example, gives an idea of the distribution of customers, call frequencies, and number of calls to meet for each type of customers.

Table 6.1 Numerical example

Customer	Call frequency per annum	Control Unit 1		Control Unit 2	
		No. of customers	No. of calls per annum	No. of customers	No. of calls per annum
Major	8	100	800	150	1200
Moderate	6	150	900	250	1500
Minor	4	600	2400	700	2800

The above table represents that call frequencies for major, moderate, and minor customers are the same for both the control units. Control unit 1 has 100, 150, and 600 major, moderate, and minor customers respectively and for control unit 2, these figures are 150, 250, and 700.

(iii) **Determine workload:** By workload, we mean the total number of calls that a salesperson makes in a year. Thus,

Workload = Average number of calls a salesperson makes in a working day
 × Number of working days in a year.

So, if a salesperson needs to make 4 calls in a day and the number of working days available are 240; then, workload = 240 × 4 = 960

At the time of assigning workloads, the following factors are to be kept in mind:

- Average travel time per call
- Average waiting time per call
- Average face-to-face time with customers
- Time needed for salespeople to perform other activities such as attending sales meetings, preparing call reports, doing marketing research, missionary selling, etc.

It is found that if a salesperson works for eight hours a day, three hours on an average are spent on other activities besides doing selling jobs. It is usually seen that if each call requires one hour, then a salesperson can cover five calls a day.

(iv) **Draw tentative territories:** According to this technique, a company adds on neighbouring territorial control units which share common borders with it. This process continues until the yearly number of calls needed in these units equate to the total number of calls a salesperson is able to make, i.e., total workloads of the salespeople. From table 6.1, it is seen that the total number of calls of two control units is 800 + 900 + 2400 + 1200 + 1500 + 2800 = 9600. For 4 calls a day and 240 working days for a salesperson, the workload is 960. So, if a company hires 10 salespeople, they can adequately cover two control units.

(v) **Construct final territories:** Territories need reconstruction when workloads of salespeople are not equal. Here, adjustment of territories is made by adding or eliminating the control units until the workload becomes more or less equal for all the salespeople. But simple quantitative considerations may not be the guiding principles for adjusting tentative territories. Here, the intensity of competition, customer demands, willingness of the customer to purchase, spreads of customers across a territory, etc. are also considered. For example, in a territory with wide distribution of customers, a salesperson has difficulties in meeting workloads compared to territory with geographically concentrated customers. Similarly, in a territory, competition is one of the vital factors in shaping workload. A strong competition in a territory demands higher workload compared to that where it is weak. In fact, more customer attention and servicing can keep competitors at bay.

Sales breakdown method Breakdown method is another option for designing the sales territory. In fact, this method is the opposite of the market build-up method. Here, the exact projection of market potential and the company's probable share of it, i.e., the sales potential is vital. Then, the company depending on its available resources and impending market situations (e.g., economic recession is imminent or anticipating an entry of multinational company in the business fray) makes the prediction of the sales forecasts. Thus, the procedure begins with calculating the sales potential being derived from market potential and then forecasting the sales potential for each control unit being derived from the total sales potential.

Next, the method estimates the average sales per salesperson in order to ensure the desired profits from the sales operations. After which the average figure is distributed into overall sales potential to determine the number of territories. The steps in this method are indicated in Figure 6.3.

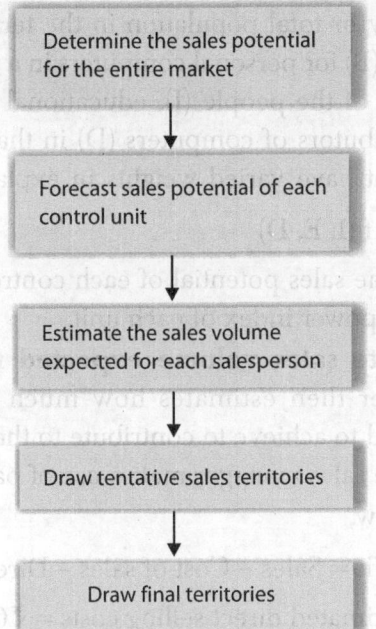

Figure 6.3 Flowchart of breakdown method

(i) **Determine the sales potential:** It stems from the estimation of the total market potential of the industry where the firm belongs and what percentages of market potential the firm is likely to share. Depending on the maximum demand responses of a product (i.e., the buying power), the firm estimates the market potential of a product. Secondly, depending on the availability of the resources and objectives of the firm, it decides the sales potential of a territory. Both the market and sales potentials may vary from one time period to the other subject to the environmental conditions and the competitive environment. A simple measure of the sales potential is shown as follows:

Say S = Sales potential

N = Number of prospective buyers for the firm

V = Estimates sales units (obtained by applying forecasting procedures)

P = Price per unit

So, **S = NVP**

(ii) **Forecast sales potential of each control unit:** The total sales potential is multiplied by a factor called the market index of each control unit. A market index is expressed as a percentage of a base of the total market. For example, buying power can be treated as a market index that varies across control units. Buying power is a multiple factor index because it is governed by a number of factors such as disposable income of people in a territory or total population in the territory. For instance, buying power of people (B) for personal computers in a territory is determined by the average income of the people (I), educational level of the people (E), and number of distributors of computers (D) in that unit. There are some other factors, too, that have varied weights in explaining buying power. So we can say,

B = f (I, E, D)

Thus, the sales potential of each control unit can be estimated by using the buying power index of each unit.

(iii) **Estimate sales volume expected from each salesperson:** The sales manager then estimates how much sales potential each salesperson is required to achieve to contribute to the targeted profits of the company. For this, the sales manager makes use of past sales experience and cost analysis. We know,

Profit = Sales – Cost of sales – Direct selling costs

Say, Estimated direct selling costs = ₹60,000

Estimated cost of products sold and distribution costs = 50 per cent of sales

Estimated profit = 20 per cent of sales

Assume Y= sales

So, we can write

0.20Y = Y – 0.50Y – 60,000

So, Y= ₹2,00,000

Using the above estimate, a sales manager can estimate the average volume of sales which a salesperson should achieve in a territory.

(iv) **Drawing tentative territories:** A sales manager begins tentative construction of sales territories with the preconception that each salesperson will be given more or less equal workload and therefore territories should be developed with more or less equal potentials. By applying step 3, the sales managers have already gathered an idea of the sales potentials of each control unit. Now, making suitable adjustments to the contagious territories by expansion or contraction of boundaries, they can arrive at a suitable number of control units with close sales potentials.

(v) **Draw final territories:** Sometimes, more modifications on the boundaries of sales territories are needed while considering factors such as the number of customers, distances amongst customers, control and supervision of salespeople, climatic situations, topographies, etc. to reach the final territories that are covered by the company's salespeople.

Territory construction and modification is a continuous process. The changing characteristics of the market in terms of fluctuations of the market potentials, market demands, competition, addition of new customers, deletion of some customers, etc. forces sales managers to revise the territories. Adjustment of territorial boundaries is needed at times. If this is not done, the company can lose sales and fall short of the sales targets.

Managers can effect modifications by observing the recent past sales trends and researching market changes. Application of GIS (geographical information system) is valuable to study spatial or geographical information to the proper reallocation of territories. GIS is a computer technology to gather, store, analyse, manage, interpret, and deliver valuable information of territorial geographies that can include population, demographics, topographical descriptions, and important spatial inputs. So, GIS is helpful for location mapping and planning. Modern method of GIS advocates the creation of geographical data in digital format where a hard copy or survey plan is converted into digital medium by using CAD (computer aided designs) programme. For designing the sales territories, sales managers are increasingly making use of GIS. Definitely, it gives more accuracy than traditional breakdown or build-up method in territory developments.

Step 4: Assigning Salespeople to Territories

After the territories are built, salespeople are assigned to different sales territories. A sales manager must apply his prudence to distribute sales territories amongst salespeople. While allocating salespeople to different territories, a salesperson's knowledge and skill, market information, acquaintance with geographies of the territory, past performance, ability to understand and communicate local language, etc. are given importance. Salespeople who have the abilities on most of these are assigned to the territories where they can meet these criteria. Generally, new salespeople are assigned to softer territories where competition is less and customers can be easily dealt with. Experienced salespeople are sent to territories where market rivalry is strong and the most profitable customers are located.

Step 5: Formulate Territory Coverage Plans and Programmes

Designing sales territories and allocating salespeople are the primary tasks of territory management. Following this is to make a sound coverage of territories and generate expected sales from these territories. So, planning territory coverage plans and programmes is important to justify the essential purposes of constructing sales territories.

The territory coverage plans and programmes include the following steps:

  (i) Analyse the territory
 (ii) Set territory sales plans
(iii) Decide on the tactical territory plans
 (iv) Implement the plans
  (v) Control the tasks of territory sales force

These steps are discussed briefly as follows:

Analyse the territory   Proper analysis of a sales territory is important to identify the prospective customers, competitive environment, market and sales potentials, marketing opportunities, etc. So, we can list the following steps in Box 6.2. These steps will gradually unveil the location of customers, understanding their demands, market opportunities and threats, buying capacities of customers, and the need for company support services to cover the territory profitably.

Box 6.2   Steps for analysis

Following are the steps for analysis:

(a) Locating prospective customers
(b) Identifying their needs
(c) Estimating the market potential
(d) Estimating the sales potential
(e) Analyse the marketing opportunities and threats. Opportunities include untapped customers, weak competition, poor distribution network of competitors, dissatisfaction of present customers, etc. Threats include market saturation, strong market rivalry, economic instability, etc
(f) Understanding the customers' buying patterns, elasticity of demands, frequency of buying, buying procedures (say, through distributors), etc
(g) Need for support services such as promotions, distribution, transports, etc. to reach customers profitably

Set territory sales plans It involves understanding the sales opportunities in the territory and consciously choosing the future course of actions. It talks about the action plans that focus attention on the sales objectives and expected results. Sales plans provide the right road map so that the salespeople can act in the right direction. Formulating territory sales plans include the following as depicted as follows in Box 6.3:

Box 6.3 Points to remember in territory sales plan

Following are the points that need to be kept in mind while developing the territory sales plan:

(a) Deciding territory sales targets
(b) Number of salespeople needed
(c) Assigning the sales tasks and quota to salespeople
(d) Determining the course of actions (strategies) to achieve territory objectives
(e) Deciding on the promotional and logistical support to fructify territory plans
(f) Prepare customer planning. It entails identifying the large, medium or small customers (in terms of sales volumes) and chalking out separate plans (e.g., call plans, promotional plans, etc.) for each group

---

Decide on the tactical territory plans Tactical plans to execute the specific course of actions are decided on as the strategy suggests. In fact, with broad course of actions (strategies), some specific actions are mapped in line with the master plans to respond to the current situations which demand subtle reorientation of actions. Box 6.4 shows the elements of tactical plans in sales territory management.

Box 6.4 Points to remember in tactical plans

Following are the points to remember while formulating the tactical plans:

(a) Determining call frequencies expressed in customer visits per a definite time period, usually one year
(b) Determining call rates per salesperson
(c) Routing: Determining the pathway to visit customers in sequence covering the shortest possible distance
(d) Scheduling: Fixing appointments with customers demands allocation of time in a way that fulfils target call rates and at the same time customers are adequately covered.

Implement the plan This is the action stage where the salespeople act according to the territory plans. Box 6.5 shows some of these activities in the action stage.

> **Box 6.5   Action steps**
>
> Following are some action steps:
>
> (a) Meeting the present and prospective customers
>
> (b) Preparation of sales reports and submission to the reporting authority
>
> (c) Scrutiny of reports and discussion in sales meetings
>
> (d) Taking feedbacks from customers
>
> (e) Customer servicing

Control the tasks of the sales force   It is vital to know whether the salespeople are working according to the territory sales plan. It involves the following steps:

(i) Compare actual sales against target

(ii) Analyse the variances, if any

(iii) Taking corrective actions

Step 6: Set up Performance Indexes

This is done in order to appraise the effectiveness of sales territory coverage. Sales performance of a territory contributes to the overall performance of the organization. It also gives indication of the extent of coverage of a territory with respect to its sales potential. Moreover, comparisons amongst territories, salespeople, costs involvement, growth prospect, etc. help sales managers to develop future marketing plans. Box 6.6 lists some of the indexes to judge the sales effectiveness of territories.

> **Box 6.6   Performance indexes**
>
> Following are the performance indexes:
>
> (a) Sales: Sales costs
>
> (b) Gross profit: Sales
>
> (c) Net profit: Sales
>
> (d) Field sales costs: Total sales costs
>
> (e) Order: Call
>
> (f) Number of new accounts developed
>
> (g) Average order size
>
> (h) Number of customers: Number of contacts made per salesperson
>
> (i) Return on assets managed (Ratio of profit contribution to assets managed)
>
> (j) Number of customers lost: Total number of customers
>
> (k) Sales performance of best salesperson: Average sales performance of salespeople

6.5 ROUTING AND SCHEDULING

These two are essential aspects of tactical territory plans. Routing helps to identify channels through which salespeople move to meet customers as per the expectations and scheduling, adjust the time distribution among customer interaction time, travel time, etc. A brief description of the two is given as follows:

Routing

Routing refers to identifying the itinerary of salespeople in their respective sales territories. It is the assignment of paths through which a salesperson travels in sequence to meet the present and the prospective customers. The sequence is chosen in a way that minimizes travel time and cost, and maximizes interaction time with the customers. So, routing is a method of finding a road map being included in the travel plan of the salesperson from his office or home to the destination and back to the same. An effective routing should yield maximum sales productivity and lead generation for salespeople.

So, routing is an essential part of territory management. In fact, it fosters territory management. The importance of routing is expressed as follows:

1. It facilitates the implementation of territory plans.
2. It minimizes the travel time hazards and the wasted time en route.
3. It shows the best sequence of meeting target customers.
4. It improves the scope for more communication between salespeople and the customers.
5. It works for getting the maximum customer coverage.
6. It suggests optimal allocation of resources (monetary resources, salespeople, promotional materials, etc.).
7. It helps to attain optimal distribution of sales calls to customers. For example, highly profitable customer should get maximum calls.
8. It helps salespeople to report feedback of the customers to sales managers.
9. It eases logistical operations. It entails smooth implementation and control of physical flow of goods and services from the point of origin to the point of customers. It helps in orderly completion of the calls.
10. It prevents overlapping of sales force activities.
11. It helps to provide services to the customers on time.
12. It helps in distributing equitable workloads to the customers.

So in short it can be said that routing is a map for connecting customer locations and sales offices indicating travel paths. It must ensure the following:

(a) Minimum travel time between two consecutive meetings with the customers

(b) No criss-crosses en route. Meeting a customer by travelling along a travel path and then going back on the same route to meet another customer is a bad routing

(c) The starting point of the journey, i.e., whether the journey begins from the office or home of the salesperson should be decided in advance

(d) Topographical features of a place, climatic conditions, availability of transport, etc. should be given importance in routing

A few popular route designs are mentioned as follows. These routes are popularly used by managers to get the best results.

Straight line design   A salesperson starts from the home/office point and goes to the customers located at the farthest distance and then comes back meeting customers positioned on the same route or interior portion of the route. The design is shown in Figure 6.4. The large rectangle is salesperson's starting point. The small rectangles represent customers.

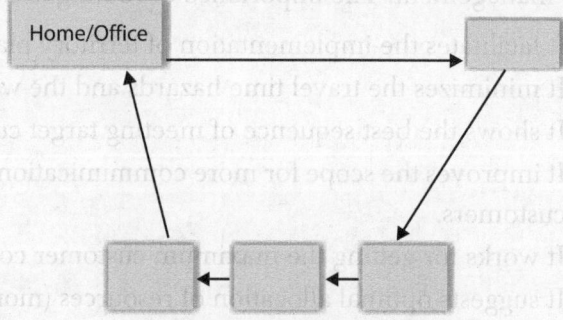

Figure 6.4   Straight line design

Cloverleaf design   The entire territory is a circular geographical unit where the circle is divided into equally sized territories with each sub-territory originating from the centre of the circle, indicating the salesperson's starting point. The salesperson chooses one sub-territory and covers it within a day or a week. Then he moves on to another sub-territory and covers it within the same time period, from where the process continues. After completion, he again comes back to the first sub-territory and the process rotates in sequence. In every journey, he moves along a track and comes back on different track to make intensive coverage of the geographical unit. Figure 6.5 represents the cloverleaf design.

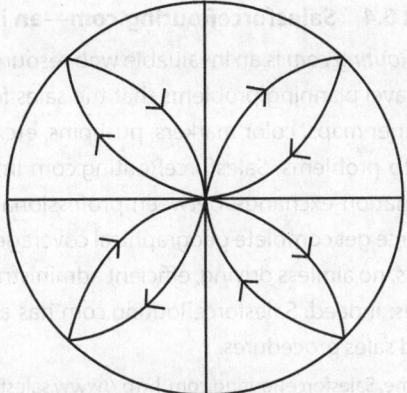

Figure 6.5 Cloverleaf design

Hopscotch design Hopscotch design is similar to the cloverleaf design but the sub-territories have jig-jag patterns instead of regular shapes. There is a central point from where the salesperson starts his journey and covers each sub-territory in a specific time period. After completion of all territories, he restarts his coverage again from the first territory where he covered the earlier one. Figure 6.6 shows the hopscotch design. Each small rectangle represents a customer.

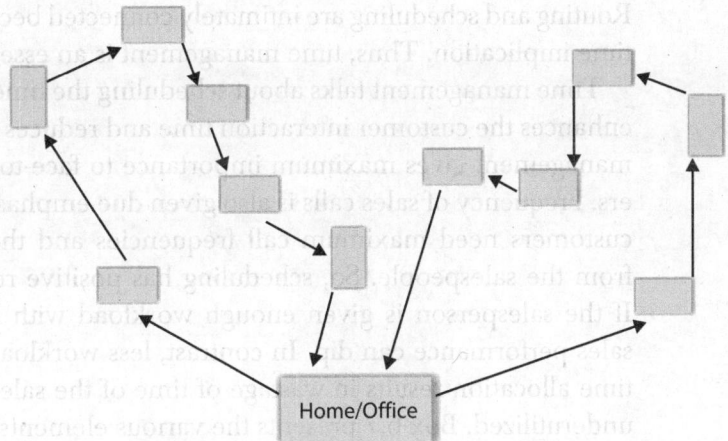

Figure 6.6 Hopscotch design

Automated lead routing This type of routing introduces sales force automation (SFA) in the company. From the 1980s and onwards, SFA has developed a commendable place in the sales organizations to replace traditional route mapping that is done manually. SFA generates travel plans and gives optimized solutions to routing and scheduling problems and minimizes lag in sales operations drastically. SFA provides computer-aided designs of travel plans and route schedules. Exhibit 6.4 illustrates one such popular web resource, i.e., Salesforce Routing.com

---

Exhibit 6.4   SalesforceRouting.com—an ingenious route to sales planning

SalesforceRouting.com is an invaluable web resource giving solutions to routing, scheduling, and travel planning problems that the sales force face. In fact, this has proved tools such as paper maps, color markers, pushpins, etc. inadequate and obsolete to carry out solutions to problems. SalesforceRouting.com imparts education, knowledge transfer, and information exchange between professionals managing sales force. Users of this web resource get complete geographical coverage, no missed appointments, productive travel plans, no aimless driving, efficient administration, no hidden costs, and many more advantages. Indeed, SalesforceRouting.com has added a new dimension in the field of automated sales procedures.

Source: Home, SalesforceRouting.com, http://www.salesforcerouting.com, accessed on 27 November 2010.

Scheduling

Scheduling refers to the optimal allocation of time on selling and non-selling activities made by salespeople. The objective of scheduling is to ensure the best use of a salesperson's time resource in the sales territory. Where, routing relates to travel plans, scheduling relates to optimal allocation of time amongst customer interaction time, travel time, waiting time, time lag between two appointments, etc. Routing and scheduling are intimately connected because covering a distance has time implication. Thus, time management is an essential aspect of scheduling.

Time management talks about scheduling the time resources in a manner that enhances the customer interaction time and reduces the travel time. Proper time management gives maximum importance to face-to-face time with the customers. Frequency of sales calls is also given due emphasis because highly profitable customers need maximum call frequencies and therefore deserve more time from the salespeople. So, scheduling has positive relationship with workloads. If the salesperson is given enough workload with less than appropriate time, sales performance can dip. In contrast, less workload with comparatively more time allocation results in wastage of time of the salespeople and they would be underutilized. Box 6.7 presents the various elements of time resources available to salespeople.

Box 6.7   Time resources

The various elements of time resources available to the salespeople are as follows:

(a) Face-to-face time with customers
(b) Travel time
(c) Sales report preparation and reporting time to sales managers
(d) Lead (prospective customer) generation time

(Contd)

(Contd)

> (e) Telephone contact time
> (f) Time for preparation of sales calls
> (g) Time between two sales calls
> (h) Customer servicing time
> (i) Time to participate in the sales meetings
> (j) Time to participate in conferences and seminars

6.6 SALES FORCE AUTOMATION (SFA)—OPENING A VISTA IN LEAD MANAGEMENT

Sales force automation (SFA) has brought forth radical changes in customer relationship and management. It has automated process of lead generation, identification of prospects, presentation and demonstration to prospective customers, digital communication with customers, lead routing and scheduling, customizing sales procedures, better customer planning, developing resourceful customer database, customer counselling and problem handling, and many more personal selling activities. SFA has been transforming paper heavy sales-related process and systems to its paperless formats with the upsurge of less dependence on human resource in selling and leaning more towards advanced information technology.

SFA stands instead to track the actions of the competitors and aids a company to spot sales and marketing opportunities. It speeds up faster transaction of information, reporting, getting feedback, etc. So, in a ward, SFA has revolutionized sales operations and management activities. Use of personal computers, net books, internet, fax, laptop, etc. are increasingly being used that have reduced the need for prolonged face-to-face interaction and communications between sales force and customers.

Today, many SFA softwares are available to boost sales activities. For example, customer relationship management (CRM) software is being used to follow and manage customer relationships through effective utilization of customer databases. A CRM programme uses information technology as its platform. The important task is choosing the right CRM solution to specific sales and marketing problem. The e-CRM (electronic CRM) is an advanced CRM technology, also called CRM online. The e-CRM is more customer friendly than CRM. Mohamed and Sagadevan (2002) viewed that e-CRM provides more interactive personalized and relevant communication with the customers across both electronic and traditional channels.

Therefore, traditional selling is gradually getting passé and SFA is taking its place. Companies like Hewlett-Packard, Levi Strauss, Dupont, etc. have made selling and sales management activities automated. In India, Maruti Suzuki is a big player to invoke sales automation in its unit. Panda and Sahadev (2005) reported that the company has all its dealers connected to its network linking production process at its Gurgaon plant.

SFA has reduced the hassles of routing and scheduling by paper and pencil. Today, many softwares are available (e.g., SalesforceRouting.com) that can optimize the travelling problems of salespeople. Unica, an IBM company, headquartered in Waltham, Massachusetts, a leader in marketing software solutions with offices in various parts of the world introduced Unica Leads ™, a user friendly, comprehensive platform and a complete end-to-end lead management software to cater to the all-round lead management solution coupled with marketing ROI of high order. The software solutions have eased reaching high quality lead at the right time. Besides, it contributes delicately to the automated lead routing, timely follow-up after sales, automatic reassignment of sales tasks on entry of new lead or exit of old customer, etc. In fact, the software is a huge guide to lead management.

So, it is evident that, the traditional way of developing and managing customers is on the way of oblivion. As time is a precious asset to sales managers, every second is given priority and for the slightest of delay in reaching a lead may prove disastrous to the firm. Optimization of resources is a now a stricter corporate practice. In the same way, optimization of sales force, sales efforts, customer visibility, market coverage, training costs, routing, and scheduling is a challenging task for sales managers.

SUMMARY

Sales territory can assume different meanings. It might be a geographical area, a set of customers, an industry or a market. A sales territory is a configuration of the present and potential accounts or a number of present and potential customers located in a geographical area for which responsibility has been assigned to particular salespeople. The main objective of a sales territory is to accurately formulate sales plans, programmes and strategies, analyse territory potentials, organize sales force, and allocate sales responsibilities. A well-planned sales territory creates big opportunities for salespeople, distribute more or less equal workload to them, and reduces travel time. Moreover, its helps the sales managers to supervise and control the sales force more effectively. They can direct the sales force to act in their territories within pre-assigned sales budgets.

Territory management is essential for effective planning, implementation, and control of territory plans. The steps involved in designing sales territory are selecting a geography-based control unit, determining locations and the buying potential of customers, deciding basic territory, assigning salespeople to territories, formulating territory coverage plans and programmes, and setting up performance indexes to apprise the effectiveness of sales-territory coverage. Two important methods of deciding sales territory are market build-up method and sales breakdown method.

Routing and scheduling are the two issues one faces in territory management. Routing is the assignment of paths through which a salesperson travels in sequence to meet the present and prospective customers in a way that can minimize travel time to the most and maximize customer interaction time to the highest. Scheduling refers to the allocation of time line between selling and non-selling activities made by salespeople and more specifically distribution of a salesperson's time on customer interaction, travel time, waiting time, time lag between two appointments, etc.

KEY TERMS

Breakdown Method Breakdown method is used to divide the entire market into approximately equal sales territories in a way so that it can ensure more or less equal sales potential of territories.

Market Build-up Method In the market build-up method, territories are developed by combining small geographical or control units together.

Routing Routing refers to identifying the itinerary of salespeople in their respective sales territories. It is the assignment of paths through which a salesperson travels in sequence to meet the present and the prospective customers.

Sales Territory Sales territory is the combination of current and potential accounts for which

responsibility has been assigned to a particular sales representative.

Sales Territory Management Sales territory management can be defined as the planning, implementation, and control of sales efforts and activities rendered by salespeople in a sales territory to meet the sales and profit potentials of the organization

Scheduling Scheduling refers to the allocation of time between selling and non-selling activities made by the salespeople and more specifically distribution of a sales person's time with regard to customer interaction time, travel time, waiting time, time lag between two appointments, etc.

CONCEPT REVIEW QUESTIONS

1. Define sales territory. What are its objectives?
2. What are the benefits of sales territory?
3. What are the imperatives of sales territory?
4. What is territory management? What are its major features?
5. Briefly illustrate the steps in designing sales territories.
6. Illustrate market build up method in designing sales territory. How is it different from sales breakdown method?
7. What is routing? How it is important in territory management?
8. What is scheduling? How does it help in effective allocation of time between a salesperson's selling and non-selling activities?

CRITICAL REVIEW QUESTIONS

1. Do you think that factors governing the development of sales territories for consumers and industrial products are the same or different?
2. Managing non-selling time is extremely crucial in fructifying territory plans. Justify.
3. A company selling its products through multi-channel distribution policy encounters difficulties in designing the sales territories. Analyse.

PROJECT ASSIGNMENTS

1. Investigate the sales territories of a global pharmaceutical company and identify how it attains coordination of sales operations between salespeople and distributors. Collect information from company sales managers, salespeople, and distributors to substantiate your information.
2. Find out a company practising SFA (sales force automation) in territory management. Investigate:
   (a) How does it run SFA programme?
   (b) How does it train salespeople in SFA?

(c) How has sales efficiency improved?

(d) What further changes the company would like make in SFA?

REFERENCES

Dalrymple, D.J. and W.L. Cron (1995), *Sales Management: Concepts and Cases*, 5th ed., John Wiley & Sons. Inc., New York.

Havaldar, K.K. and M.V. Cavale (2008), *Sales and Distribution Management: Text and Cases*, Tata McGraw-Hill Publishing Company Limited., New Delhi.

Johnson, E.M., L.D. Kurtz, and E.E. Scheuing, (1994), *Sales Management: Concepts, Practices and Cases*, 2nd ed., McGraw-Hill Inc., New York.

Mohamed, H.P. and A. Sagadevan (2002), *Customer Relationship Management: A Step-by-Step Approach*, Vikas Publishing House Pvt Ltd., New Delhi.

Panda, T.K. and S. Sahadev (2005), *Sales and Distribution Management*, Oxford University Press, New Delhi.

Venugopal, P. (2008), *Sales and Distribution Management: An Indian Perspective*, Response Books, New Delhi.

Wilson, M. (1985). *Managing a Sales Force*, 2nd. ed., Gower Publishing Company Limited, England.

http://www.unica.com/about-unica.htm, accessed on 21 November 2010.

http://www.unica.com/lead-management.htm, accessed on 21 November 2010.

CASE STUDY

Performance Paradoxes

Tomas Benedict, the chief marketing officer of Faridabad-based Sundaram Pipes Ltd, was totally non-plussed to find a remedy of the awkward situation in sales performance of his two trusted and efficient sales officers. He had the long cherished notion that experience positively reinforces performance. So if experience is any indicator of good sales performance, the results shown by two sales officers would speak otherwise. Astonishingly, the performance of the junior sales persons is quite satisfactory. So this is a sharp contradiction of the hypothesized relationship between years of experience in selling and sales performance.

Before going into the details of the problems, let us collect some useful information about the company. The company is in the manufacturing and marketing of PVC plastic pipes of various diameters to serve domestic and industrial sectors. The company has established its reputation in terms of the quality of its products and cost control in manufacturing, and the prices of its products are competitive.

The company has its marketing network in north and eastern regions. In north India, it has its branch office in New Delhi and in eastern region the branch office is located in Kolkata. Each city is treated as a territory. Each region has a sales officer at its top and three salespeople to run the

(Contd)

sales operations. The company has two pronged distribution channels to reach target customers. One, industrial and institutional customers consisting of automobile industries, hotel industries, block development offices, etc. that are covered by company salespeople and two distributors to cover domestic customers. Sales officers are in charge of dealing with distribution outlets in addition to overall supervision.

The company till 2008–09 financial years was running its business in both the sectors—industrial and domestic quite satisfactorily but the sales results of 2009–10 showed somewhat a rosy picture of the industrial sector and a shadowy picture of the domestic front. Tables A and B clearly demonstrate that there is a steady rise in industrial sales and decline in domestic sales

Table A Industrial sector

Sales (in ₹)	2007–08	2008–09	2009–10
Target	670	750	820
Actual	635	728	800

Table B Domestic sector

Sales (in ₹)	2007–08	2008–09	2009–10
Target	345	412	456
Actual	336	389	375

The anomaly in sales brewed a storm in the Mr Benedict's cup of tea. He felt pride with the sales results in industrial sector where a narrow variance was being maintained between target and actual sales steadily. But what worried him was the widening gap between the target and actual sales in the domestic sector in the year 2009–10. He convened a meeting with the sales officers and salespeople to discuss the problems. He sat separately with the sales officers. What transpired to Mr Benedict was the low motivation level of the sales officers unlike salespeople. The meeting with the salespeople separately furthermore, revealed lack of right leadership from the sales officers. Mr Benedict apparently believed in it. He knew that a post of a senior marketing officer was lying vacant and both the sales officers were aspiring for it. It might be so that ill-competition between the two might sap the spirit of both. But he was not sure of it. Therefore, he made a subtle change by reshuffling the allocation of sales tasks and duties with a risk temporarily. He brought in salespeople to look after the domestic sector and sales officers to handle industrial sector.

(Contd)

After six months since April 2009, he reviewed the sales results of the two sectors and to his astonishment, the sales in the industrial sector somewhat declined whereas in the domestic sector, a sign of recovery got noticed. So, Mr Benedict became clear that the problems had its root in the mind games of the two sales officers that had adverse impacts on their motivation levels and consequently on the sales performance.

Discussion Questions

1. What should Mr Benedict do with the sales officers?
2. Do you think the sales officers need retraining to recharge them with motivation?
3. What, according to you, are the reasons for success of salespeople despite poor leadership qualities of sales officers?

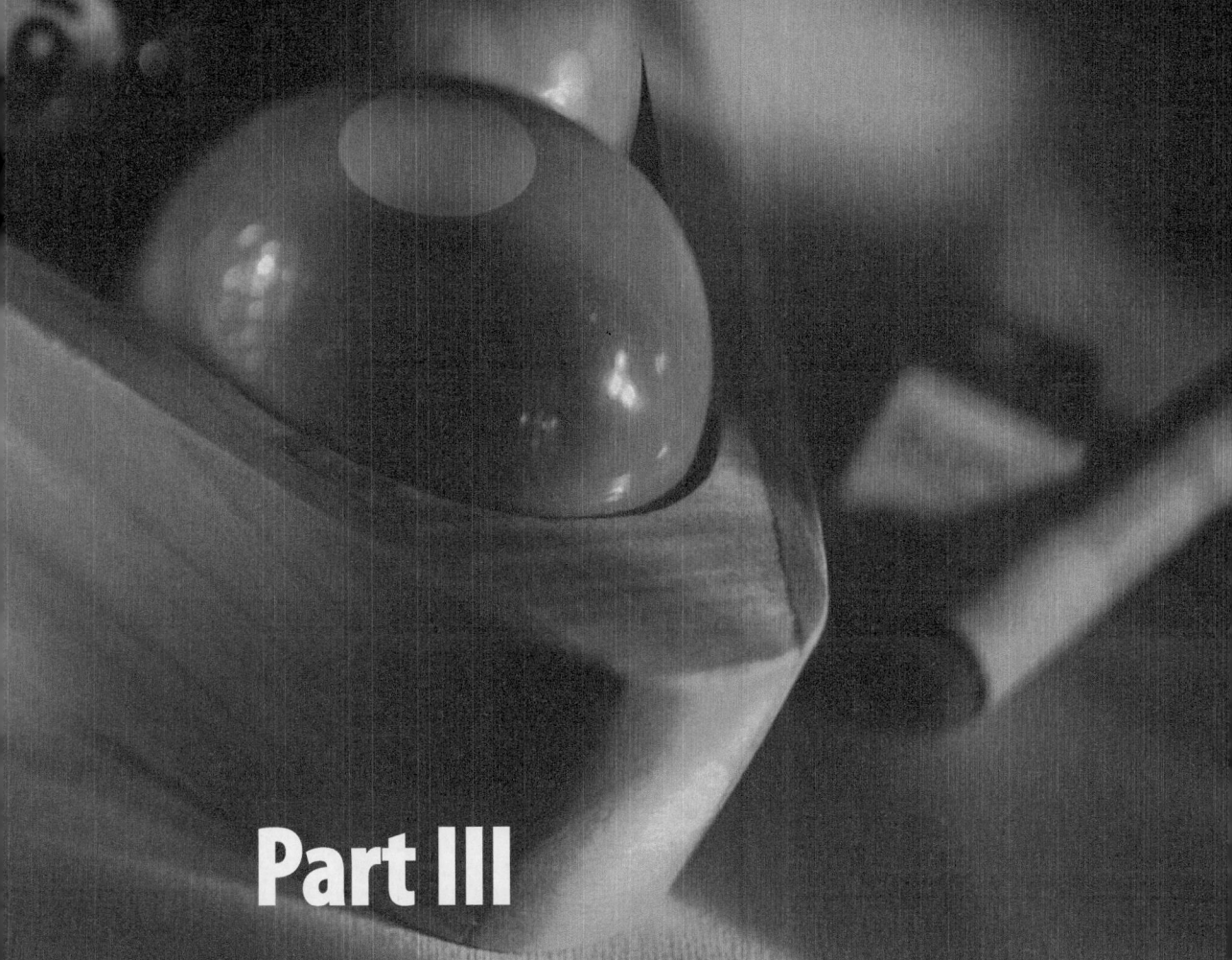

Part III

Managing the Sales Team

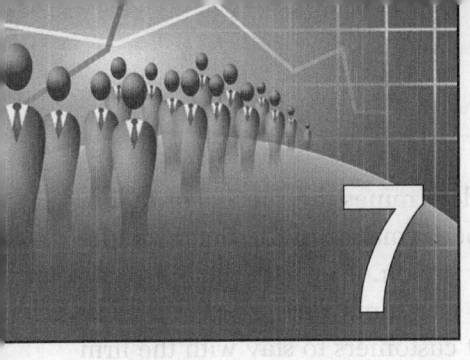

7

Salespeople and Sales Managers—Profiles, Roles, and Responsibilities

7.1 SALESPERSON—A CRITICAL HUMAN RESOURCE

Human resource is the livewire of all the organizations. It is the driving force that propels an organization amidst varying environmental situations. Every organization needs a human resource department to carry out all its activities. Similarly, it needs a sales force as a critical human resource to undertake business with customers. An organization demands line managers who supervise and manage production and distribution activities, and staff managers who act in the advisory capacities to formulate plans and programmes and set guidelines for action programmes. Salespeople are treated as valuable resources to the organizations because they are responsible for delivering the outputs of the firm and generate revenues.

7.1.1   Who is a Salesperson?

A salesperson is an individual whose fundamental job is to sell a product/service. They are people who are predominantly engaged in personal selling activities on behalf of the company with a view to generate business connections that culminate the salespeople in delivering the product or service to the customers. This is the description of salespeople that was portrayed in traditional selling. However, in modern selling, a salesperson's role extends much over than just delivering the product to the customers. Today, the bigger role of a salesperson lies in the post-selling period.

The job of the salesperson apparently sounds simple in ideation but intricate in execution. Selling is an all-important task of an organization. It is the wheel of the organization that gives mobility to it. It determines the success or failure of the organization. It guides and controls the performance of the organization. Salespeople are the drivers of the 'organization' wagon.

Salespeople are the human factors in selling that stimulates prospective customers to be the real customers and the present customers to stay with the firm and opt for higher rate of consumption. Salespeople also act at the operational ambit of the organization. Success in sales plans, policies, strategies rely heavily on the personalized selling demonstrated by salespeople. A salesperson can work on behalf of a manufacturer, wholesaler, distributor, retailer, institution, franchisee, etc.

In the traditional selling format, salespeople held a 'pushy' image. They used to coax and cajole innocent customers into buying their products. Even for narrow interests, salespeople did not hesitate to cross ethical lines of business and dupe naïve customers by swallowing over-priced products or inferior-quality products. Tall talk and lofty claims were often used as means to persuade customers to lean towards their products. Often, these salespeople were talkative and deceptive. They persistently used to flatter less or non-informative customers to join hands by pressure tactics.

But gone are the days of nightmarish experiences of the customers in the hands of the overboard salespeople. In fact, professional selling does not endorse pressure tactics in selling. And on top of it, it advocates the need for etiquettes in selling and advises salespeople to learn it for greater interests. Selling is a legal profession. Therefore, salespeople strictly observe legal laws and regulations during business. Selling is also an ethical profession. Honesty and integrity to the profession vouch for ethics in business. Truthfulness and devotion to the profession exhibited by salespeople delineate the ethical characters of selling. Salespeople are often haunted with ethical complexities during selling. This is because they are of the opinion that winning a customer is almost certain if a few ethical truths are hidden or suppressed. For example, claiming high quality of a product without any real basis is a breach of ethics. Salespeople often behave so because of the pressure of fulfilling sales quota. But once the truths are unveiled, salespeople lose their credibility forever and put the organization in a precarious situation.

Selling is a social profession. Courtesy, humility, decorum, and empathy towards customers and society extend the social chord of selling. Selling involves the social learning process also. Salespeople need to learn the needs and wants of the customers. Salespeople often converse with customers on non-business issues only to create meaningful rapport with them. Offering dinner, presenting a gift, inviting to a social programme, etc. are common from salespeople to potential customers that help to establish a social tie between the buyer and the seller. So, salespeople should learn how to build social network in their relevant fields.

Selling is a mental process. A salesperson may drift a customer to move through a sequence of mental stages before taking a purchase decision. A prospective buyer goes through cognitive, affective, and behavioural stages to complete the buying process. In cognitive domain, a buyer gathers knowledge and information on the product. In affective stage, the buyer is influenced by reasons, rationales, emotions, sentiments, beliefs, preconceived notions, etc. to find adequate justification behind the purchase. At the behavioural stage, the buyer enters a state of mind of taking a buying decision. So, salespeople seek to influence the behaviour of the customers.

Today's selling believes in an unwritten partnership building between salespeople and customers that prompt the customers to generate a business alliance between the sellers on a physical as well as psychological planes. If salespeople are instructed to work on economic relationships with the customers encompassing exchange and transaction alone, the long-term sustainability of the organization would come under question.

A salesperson should understand that he is the face of the organization. An organization finds its identity to the outside world through the salespeople. The dignity of the company depends largely on the salespeople. Salespeople can brighten the image of the firm by projecting themselves as real problem solvers, friends, and guides to the customers. A salesperson can demolish the image of a firm by procreating distrustful, false, and immoral stands. Due to these reasons, selling is said to be a sensitive profession where well-bred, educated, and good natured salespeople are always in demand. Salespeople should transmit confidence amongst customers and express goodwill to ensure an enduring business relationship with them. Box 7.1 shows the multifaceted sides of a salesperson.

Box 7.1 Different sides of salespeople

Following are the different facets of salespeople:

(a) Salespeople are a critical link between the buyers and the sellers

(b) Salespeople are a personal link between the buyers and the sellers

(c) Salespeople are the human factors in selling

(d) Salespeople are important parts of an economic system who contribute to the economic growth of a firm and the nation as a whole. They help to keep the economy moving

(e) Salespeople are social people who can move to the different strata of society to engage in beneficial exchanges with the customers

(f) Salespeople cater to the enhancement of the quality of life of the people

(g) Salespeople are the human face of the organization who act as the interface between the buyers and the sellers

(h) Salespeople are order getters, order creators, and order takers on behalf of the sellers

(Contd)

(Contd)

(i) Salespeople are missionaries who spread goodwill of the firm they belong to

(j) Salespeople are the providers of creative solutions to customer problems

(k) Salespeople act as consultants to the buyers

(l) Salespeople act as constant watchdogs of the customer needs and demands

(m) Salespeople are the executors of a firm's marketing strategy

(n) Salespeople are the mouthpiece of both the organization and the customers and act as mediators of information exchange between the two

(o) Salespeople are visionaries who can understand the changes of future marketing environment in advance

7.2 ROLE OF A SALESPERSON

Salespeople perform multiple roles as representatives of a company. They act as an interface between the company and the customers, and look after every fine detail of selling from the company's side and of buying from the customer's side to ensure value for money for the customer and profitability for the company. They aim to contribute maximum profits to the company which in turn affirms their future prospects and benefits including promotions, attractive compensations, social status, affiliation, etc. Salespeople by their sales performance can satisfy customers and build long-lasting relationships with them. Salespeople have the following roles:

1. Salespeople should know their company, customers, markets, demand and supply patterns, competition, and in general the economic environment where the company operates.

2. Salespeople should have detailed knowledge on the products they deal in, its qualitative attributes, specifications, application areas, side effects, etc.

3. Salespeople should always try to establish a good match between the company's products and customer needs. It also helps the company to attain it by communicating the expectations of the customers in advance.

4. Salespeople should identify customer problems patiently and suggest suitable solutions where the products they deal in can act as healers to the problems.

5. Salespeople should develop new customers and retain the existing customers to lend growth and stability to the firm. They should also look at how to prospect new customers and maintain liaisons and provide services to the existing customers.

6. Salespeople should delicately present and demonstrate the products in front of the customers, answer their queries, address their doubts, and incite them to place their orders.

7. Salespeople should always keep a check at the inventory position in the company, stock position with the distributors or retailers, make necessary arrangements to maintain the right quantities of goods in order to ensure a smooth flow to the customers.

8. Salespeople should help sales managers in mapping out sales plans, policies, and strategies. As they work at the grass-root level of the market, they can provide valuable information on various market or product factors, economic and other environmental factors, the strengths and weaknesses of the competitors, etc. to the sales managers to draw out strategic plans for the company.

9. Salespeople may engage in missionary selling activities on behalf of a company. It implies building goodwill or image of the firm outside the company by imparting adequate customer care, customer learning, customer service, and addressing customer inconveniences.

10. Salespeople should act as order takers or order getters for the firm. As order takers, they process routine orders, reorders, and execute them for the current buyers. But they do not need to persuade customers to buy. They just book orders and send instructions to the company. As an order getter, they are instructed to identify new customers and influence them to buy the company's products. Salespeople can be order takers or order getters. Both these acts can be from within the company or from the company-established sales and marketing offices.

    For example, a retail salesperson is an inside order taker who hands over the products to the concerned party and receives payments from the sales counters. Under the inside order taking situation, the company may have a policy to provide toll free telephone numbers to customers so that they can avail it to get more information and place orders. This activity is known as inbound telemarketing. As an inside order getter, the salesperson interacts with customers through telephones.

11. Salespeople can impart technical advice to the customers. A company generally appoints sales engineers who can act as technical consultants to the customers. They solve technical problems of the customers. They even guide prospective buyers to take the right purchase decision and persuade them to agree to the company's terms and conditions.

12. Salespeople should pay attention to their own professional development. They should attend sales meetings, training programmes, sales conferences, tradeshows, etc. to update themselves with the current state of the industry, knowledge on selling and marketing, business regulations, ethical practices of business, opportunity for overseas markets, etc.

13. Salespeople also participate in financial matters such as collection of payments, arrangement of credits, advising clients to join the financing schemes, brokering on financial terms, and conditions between the company and customers, etc.

14. Salespeople assist the company on product development, new product design, process development, territory development, formulating sales plans, and marketing mix development.

A distinction between an order taker and an order getter is exhibited in Table 7.1.

Table 7.1 Order taker vs order getter

Order taker	Order getter
Engages in collecting and processing orders and reorders	Generates leads and develops prospects
Performs routine jobs that are clerical in nature	Performs creative jobs
Does not require extensive training	Requires extensive training
Earns less compensations	Earns high compensations
Requires less energy and enthusiasm in their jobs	Requires a lot of energy and enthusiasm in their jobs

7.3 DUTIES AND RESPONSIBILITIES OF SALESPEOPLE

Different salespeople differ in their duties and responsibilities depending upon the types of company they serve, products they deal in, and the customers they handle. This is because with different products or services, customers have different kinds of expectations. An engineering firm appoints more sales engineers rather than ordinary sales representatives because of the technical intricacies of its products. A tour and travelling organization is likely to appoint salespeople having knowledge in tourism administration, histories, foreign languages, etc. But in general, salespeople are discharged some common duties and responsibilities in every organization. Certain general duties and responsibilities of salespeople irrespective of the nature of firms they represent are presented as follows:

1. Salespeople make an initial contact with the customers, introduce the company's product, explain its merits and demerits, argue how the merits outweigh the demerits and instill conviction within the customers to take purchase decisions in the favour of the company.

2. Salespeople must decipher complete information on the different constituents of the marketing mix to both the prospective and the present customers.

3. The primary duties of the salespeople is to inform, create interest in the products they handle with the customers, execute sales, and finally make arrangement to send the merchandises from the producer's end to the customer.

4. Salespeople must describe the products, conduct demonstration, articulate benefits, handle the questions raised by the customers and close the sales by requesting an order (for new customers) or reorder (for existing customers).

5. Salespeople must keep abreast of the information on product use, conveniences and inconveniences, changing requirements of the customers, and the need for after-sales services.

6. Salespeople must make arrangements for proper installation of the product in the customers' premises, train customers about the functioning and maintenance of the product, do occasional follow-up calls after the sales, enquire about the operational problems, and give useful tips on the upkeep of the products.

7. Salespeople must inform the customers properly about the availability of the products in case the products are sold through distribution outlets and extend a helping hand to buy it from the distributors or retailers at the right price and quality. They should also ensure that the middlemen comply with the agreed upon terms and conditions while dealing with the customers.

8. Besides regular selling, salespeople do some ancillary duties such as preparing call reports regularly, analyse sales data and finds discrepancies, schedules appointments, attend sales meetings, monitor market changes such as the competitors' activities, changing customer needs and wants, economic conditions, etc.

9. Salespeople assist the company in forecasting sales and preparing the sales budget, maintain selling expenses with budgetary limits, and maintain expense accounts.

10. Salespeople must know the inventory positions in the company warehouses and stock positions in the distribution outlets, and keep the management informed of the positions. He must make arrangements for the replenishment of positions if stocks are below the required levels. This is important to ensure the right time and place utilities for the customers.

11. Salespeople need to look after the delivering of goods to and from the warehouses, shipping of goods, unloading of goods at customer points, total protection of the goods during transportation, handing over the invoices to customers, and arrange disbursement of payments from the customers as per the predetermined conditions.

12. Salespeople must maintain regular contact with the customers, render customer services, offer suggestions, take suggestions from the customers on product development, and ingratiate customers with gifts, calendars, and greeting cards. Thus, they develop good cordial relationships with the customers that will pay off in the future.

Exhibit 7.1 presents the qualification criteria and job responsibilities of sales specialists of a well-known biotech company in a nutshell.

Exhibit 7.1   A bird's eye view on qualification and job responsibilities of sales specialists

MedImmune, LLC, a recognized biotech company engages in biotech sales specialists (BSS) who are responsible for the promotion of the company' products and achievement of the assigned sales goals. A BSS is desired to act as community-based sales specialist catering clinical/scientific/managed care expertise for all the company's promoted products. The company looks for BSS with a background of four-year college degree preferably in a scientific/medical or business discipline along with a minimum of 2–3 years tested, successful sales experience in the field of pharmaceutical, biotechnology or medical product industry. Travelling requirements of BSSs vary across sales territories and they are expected to attend company meetings and make use of the company mandated forms of transportation.for these, both to and from.

Source: 'Biotech Sales Specialist: MedImmune, LLC', http://www.pharmaopportunities.com/Jobs/Biotech_Sales_Texas_21415.aspx, accessed on 10 January 2011.

7.4   QUALITIES OF A SALESPERSON

Qualities of a salesperson are crucial in the success of personal selling. Before going to select an efficient salesperson, sales managers should gather important information on the quality traits of the salespeople and prepare a checklist for it. This checklist can be used during the selection process to screen out unqualified candidates and choose the qualified ones. An attempt is made to discuss the important quality traits of salespeople as follows:

Appearance   This is vital because a good appearance makes the salespeople approachable and acceptable to the customers. Appearance creates a first-hand impression of the salespeople and the company they represent. This is reflected through their height, weight, look, neatness in attire, gesture, posture, body language, eye movement, etc. It initiates their social acceptance to a customer. Good physical health is the precondition of sound mental health. Mental health is important because salespeople have to bear hectic schedules of selling and must be fit enough to withstand the drudgeries, toils and pangs of extensive sales tours, and accommodate in different environmental conditions. Moreover, gritty mental health leads to rejection, loss, dissension, etc. off and on during their sales career. Impressive appearance enhances the likelihood of winning target customers.

Communication skills   As buying–selling is a two-way communication process, communication skill is important for salespeople to demonstrate an effective sales presentation, have productive discussions with the customers and solve their problems, report to their managers, etc. Strong vocabulary, control over speech, voice quality, command over word selection, listening skill, writing ability, etc. determine the communication skill. A sound communication skill helps salespeople to understand both verbal and non-verbal expression of the customers. In fact, interpretation of verbal and non-verbal messages, thoughts, and ideas of customers need strong intelligence and confident minds. Moreover, a high remembrance power, paraphrasing capacity, rebutting ability, and reflexive stances of the salespeople augment their communication skill.

Communication skills that enhance interpersonal skills, listening skills, negotiation skills, conflict resolution skills, leadership skills, etc. are known as soft skills. The professional skills of salespeople that help them to fulfil the technical requirements of the job and lend proficiency in sales operations are known as hard skills. The efforts of the salespeople to make their customers agree to the terms and conditions of the sale and generate consensus is not possible without soft skills. Salespeople must understand the proper use of sales kits such as samples, test reports, power point presentations to exhibit graphs, charts, past-sales records, etc. and apply them for presenting and demonstrating the saleable items. It also requires deft articulation of product technicalities where hard skills come into play.

Creativity   Here, creativity mainly means the problem-solving ability of salespeople. How quickly can they identify the problems of the customers correctly, analyse it, and offer solutions to satisfy both the customers and accomplish the goals and objectives of the organization reflect their creativity. Creative salespeople always find ways to improve their sales operations, serve customers better, and show higher sales performances than before. They are able to differentiate the problem of one customer from the other meaningfully and adjust the selling techniques according to the buying motives and objectives of the customers.

Self-monitoring   It is a characteristic by which salespeople continually track the changes of the environment and adjust behaviour according to the demands of the situation. It makes them highly responsive to any buying–selling situation which they can handle both in pressing and favourable situations with no difficulties.

Ego strength   Ego is a combination of those traits that help salespeople tolerate pain, despair, defeat, loss, mental injury, etc. and overcome such crises. Salespeople with high ego strength possess persistence, self-esteem, competitiveness, unyielding mentality, emotional stability, and cope with work stresses cleverly and intelligently.

Ego drive   It determines the ability of the salespeople to hold high self-esteem and competitive instincts to influence, incite, stimulate, and convince customers to take a positive buying decision. High ego drives motivate salespeople to stay high on self-confidence and desire to succeed compared to those with low ego drives. It also makes salespeople ambitious and combative under any other sales situations.

Risk-taking propensity It is crucial for salespeople to be able to assume risk or avert risk during sales deals. It determines their willingness to take chances even in uncertain situations. Risk taking is a common phenomenon in sales profession because salespeople are often seen to be working on limited information about market situations and customers. It is a type of behaviour that incites salespeople to take faster decisions under uncertain or unknown selling situations.

Sociability Salespeople often need to act in a team or group where cooperation, coordination, morale, group cohesion, gregariousness are vital amongst team members. Salespeople should be flexible, trusting, amicable, and organized in order to get along with their team and work collectively towards common goals.

Empathy It a quality of the salespeople that makes them concerned for other members of the organization. It is the capacity to share the feelings and emotions, situations, motives and identify their problem situations, understand their views, emotions, feelings, etc. of other individuals and explicitly express willingness to stand by their side.

Emotional intelligence It is a capacity to understand and handle one's own and others' emotions with whom a salespeople deal and interact in their professional and social lives. It helps one to manage misunderstanding, fear, anxiety, opposing situations, sorrow, etc. that detract one to apply one's full potential and perform in the working environment.

Decision-making ability It is the quality that helps salespeople gauge a situation, make up their minds, and apply their judgment even under critical selling situations. Salespeople have to confront varying customer needs, expectations, claims and motivations to buy, etc. in their daily life. Therefore, decisiveness is highly important for salespeople to offer the right solutions to the customers and convince them to take positive buying decisions.

Initiative It is the ability of salespeople to take a proactive stand in selling by taking actions at an earliest opportunity. A salesperson who has initiative shows zeal to identify the problem areas of the customers even before being directed to do so. It is a kind of readiness behaviour of salespeople that shows enterprise, energy, and positive mental attitude to embark on the sales tasks with a desire to complete it with agility and determination. Both organizations and the salespeople are benefitted with this.

Sense of urgency Salespeople should be able to prioritize their tasks in order of their importance and show the right attitude to take up those tasks according to their importance. They must first focus on those jobs that require immediate accomplishments and attention. No sense of complacency should prevail in their mind and they should concentrate first on those jobs that should be completed immediately or within definite time period. In many occasions of selling, faster reaction of salespeople is required as compared to their competitors.

7.5 WHO IS A SALES MANAGER?

A sales manager is a person who is engaged in planning, organizing, staffing, motivating, and leading a sales team to achieve an aggregate performance level that corresponds to the sales objectives and goals. To make fruitful actions on the activities mentioned, a sales manager is supposed to

(a) take correct decisions on sales target, sales plans, sales strategies, sales operations, etc. and

(b) combine and coordinate the resources (human, financial, and information) to convert decisions into actions to reach the sales goals and objectives.

Box 7.2   Decision areas of sales managers

Following are some decision areas of sales managers:

1. What are the sales objectives?
2. What should be the sales budgets?
3. What are the sales plans, policies, and strategies?
4. What are the job descriptions and job specifications for the salespeople?
5. How would salespeople be selected, trained, motivated, coordinated, and compensated?
6. What are the standards of sales performance?
7. How performance of sales force would be measured?
8. How sales territories are formed?
9. How salespeople are distributed in the sales territories?
10. How would the sales force be controlled?

As decision-makers, sales managers are faced with a variety of issues where they have to take decisions. Box 7.2 pinpoints those decision areas.

Sales managers combine and coordinate human, financial, and information resources effectively to respond to each decision component. Human resources, here, include sales force that are guided and instructed to implement decisions. Financial resources with regard to sales management are needed to properly allocate funds to meet the expenses under different heads in the sales budget such as territory development, sales force recruitment and selection, training, compensation, etc. Information, too, is a vital resource to sales managers for managing sales. Sales managers are hungry to collect updated information on markets, products, competition, distributors, overall economic conditions, etc. to review their decisions and invoke changes within these to consolidate the firm's position.

So, the sales managers guide, lead, and control the efforts of the salespeople who act upon their decisions. They further distribute tasks amongst salespeople, allocate resources, coordinate their activities, and evaluate their performance at regular intervals to know whether the salespeople work towards the stated goals. Sales managers achieve results through the performances of the sales force. Therefore, it is essential for sales managers to do the following:

(a) Take decisions on the allocation of the sales tasks at all levels of salespeople. For example, senior salespeople are given the charge to handle major customers and the young salespeople are delegated to do the order taking.

(b) Delegate authority at all levels of salespeople and define their responsibilities

(c) Participate in personal-selling activities whenever needed. Some industries (e.g., capital industries) ask for larger participation of personal-selling efforts. Wilson (1983) viewed that it is essential for sales managers to lead a team of salespeople on important sales projects.

7.6 ROLE OF SALES MANAGERS

Sales managers are the wall behind the salespeople to provide the necessary instructions and support to carry out sales operations successfully. A sales manager formulates sales plan and assumes charge of implementing it by the salespeople. A sales manager continually tracks down sales force performance to steady the course of sales actions according to the sales plan and take measures when the performance slackens from its expected level. In fact, sales managers are the planners of sales operations and salespeople are the performers of such jobs. Decision-making in sales is completely entrusted with the sales managers and the salespeople are the executors of such decisions. But, at times a sales manager puts himself in the shoes of salesperson and performs personal selling for some lucrative customers. There are enormous variations in the activities of sales managers and such variations are seldom present with other functional managers of the firm. Box 7.3 portrays some major roles of sales managers.

Box 7.3   Role of sales managers at a glance

Following are the various roles of sales managers:

1. Sales managers show the route map to the salespeople on how to achieve sales target by properly implementing sales plans and programmes.

2. Sales managers prepare job specifications to delineate the profiles of salespeople to be recruited. They also develop job specifications to characterize the roles, duties, and responsibilities of salespeople.

3. Sales managers need to spot potential sales talents from a group of applicants for different sales positions.

(Contd)

(*Contd*)

4. Sales managers maintain close liaison with marketing research, finance, production, distribution sections of the organization to get cooperation for the smooth functioning of the sales functions.

5. Sales managers, in today's contexts are more apt to provide support and cooperation rather than directing and controlling salespeople. Spiro et al. (2003) viewed that the role of sales managers has changed subsequently with that of the salespeople. Salespeople today are more empowered units who are responsible for managing their own territories. So, sales managers unveil the role of a boss and take up leadership roles to coordinate the sales team.

6. Sales managers develop a flexible learning environment in which salespeople move on with unending learning experience on modern approaches of selling. For example, sales managers teach salespeople to be adaptive with teleselling, web-based marketing, direct marketing, etc. Inside selling is getting popular nowadays in view of extensive distribution of the customer base.

7. Sales managers hone a sales culture that continuously inculcates a sense of team spirit and belongingness amongst salespeople. They educate salespeople to behave responsibly and ethically in business. Sales managers inculcate self-motivation, discipline, devotion to the jobs, and dedication to serve both the organization and the society.

8. Sales managers teach salespeople a sense of purpose and vision to uphold the image of the organization. They educate salespeople to show more urges on customer training, development, relationship, and inclination to adaptive selling behaviour.

Exhibit 7.2 portrays the job profiles of sales managers of a stellar FMCG company such as P&G

Exhibit 7.2   P&G—a brief outline of recruiting criteria for sales managers

P&G (Procter and Gamble), a global corporation operating in over 80 countries across the world offers tremendous scope for career growth and development for all its employees. It recruits section sales managers with MBA in marketing from well-recognized institutes with 2–4 years of experience in the FMCG/Sales industry. P&G looks for the following basic requirements with prospective managers:

(a) Creativity and ability to innovate   (b) Proven track record of performance
(c) Initiative   (d) Leadership quality
(e) Goal setting and accomplishments

Duties and responsibilities include

(a) delivering sales volume,   (b) distribution and merchandizing,
(c) establish good will, and
(d) assist in operating efficiency of the retailers.

Source: Ascent, The Times of India, Kolkata, 11 August 2010, p. 4.

7.7   DUTIES AND RESPONSIBILITIES OF SALES MANAGERS

Sales managers perform administrative functions in the sales and marketing departments. Their principal goals are getting the selling activities done by salespeople effectively and efficiently, and obtaining best outputs from them so that the company can attain its sales goals. Sales managers perform all the managerial functions in their units that are common in the organization as whole. Their duties and responsibilities range from decision-making on goals, strategies, market positions, etc. to rendering key managerial functions such as planning, organizing, staffing, coordinating, motivating, and controlling the sales organization. Evans and Berman (2007) opined that sales managers outline the sales philosophy of the sales organization and determine selling tasks, characteristics of the sales force, methods of customer contacts, etc. Sales mangers are also responsible for monitoring and controlling sales targets, sales territories, sales and distribution expenses, advertising expenses, etc. The key functional areas where the sales managers have to basically concentrate their duties and responsibilities are discussed as follows:

Planning

Planning prompts sales managers to set goals and objectives of personal selling, formulate policies, establish sales budgets, determine resource requirements for sales units (product, customer, territory, etc.), allocate resources amongst these, and communicate the plans to all levels of the organization. Sales managers, in fact, delineate the blueprint for sales operations by the sales plans. Sales managers must anticipate future market requirements, analyse the pros and cons of market situations, forecast sales, and choose future plan of actions.

Organizing

By organizing sales force around products, customers, territories, etc. sales managers handle and manage different products, customer groups, and sales territories effectively and efficiently. Sales managers establish a framework for integrating various activities performed by salespeople to work towards a common goal. They clearly define and group the activities, establish channels for the flow of command and instructions, give directions to the sales force, and also accept feedback. Thus, by organization, they achieve coordination amongst activities between the salespeople and themselves.

Staffing

Sales managers determine the future sales force requirements and formulate plans on how to identify the right potential candidates, draw their attention, attract them to approach the organization, and finally select the right candidates for the jobs.

They also search out potential candidates within the organization and promote or transfer them to the respective job positions. Understanding the knowledge and skill requirements of the salespeople are the starting points of the staffing process. Based on it, the sales managers prepare job specifications and man profiles for different job positions. Moreover, they must also understand the nitty-gritty of the marketing environment to keep themselves informed on the manpower needs, competitors' staffing process, etc. In fact, staffing is a way to maintain the optimal human resource requirements of the organization. Before distribution of the tasks, duties, and responsibilities to salespeople, formal training is imparted to develop salespeople with technical knowledge and skills, right mental attitudes needed for the job so that they can work up to the company's expectations.

Coordinating

Coordination has several underpinnings as follows:

(i) Coordination of activities of salespeople working within and along different territories

(ii) Coordination of sales force activities with those of the other elements of the promotional mix, elements such as advertising, sales promotion, etc.

(iii) Coordination of sales force activities with that of the sales managers

Better coordination gives improved mobility in sales operations and brings cohesion in the sales efforts. It removes psychological barriers between sales managers and salespeople and brightens the prospect of sales productivity and efficiency.

Motivating

By motivating salespeople, sales managers want to induce the salespeople to apply their potentials to the fullest in order to achieve sales goals and objectives. Sales managers use financial incentives (raise in salary, commission, etc.) and non-financial incentives (recognition, reward, etc.) to motivate salespeople to exert persistently high physical and mental efforts in the planned course of actions. By motivation, sales managers ignite the willingness of salespeople to work even surpassing their capacities. Sales managers can stimulate them to feel that they will not only meet the company's sales goals but also satisfy personal goals.

Controlling

Sales managers periodically or on a regular basis appraise sales force performance with a view to check to what extent the salespeople comply with sales plans and achieve sales targets. They also take corrective actions when the actual sales performance is below the threshold level of performance that is expected from the salespeople.

7.8 SKILLS OF SALES MANAGERS

Sales managers today are not just involved in directing and controlling the sales force but they work with them and show the way by assuming the role of sales team and lead them from the front. They provide strategic inputs to the salespeople on how to edge past the competitive inroads, keep the selling expenses within budgeted levels, and develop sustainable relationships with the customers. In fact, sales managers require multifaceted skills that are necessary in managing sales force, taking accurate decisions, nurturing the sales force, outwitting competition, retaining existing customers, augmenting customer base, and many challenging roles. Today's sales managers need to be more dynamic, flexible, transformational compared to those of few years back.

People Skills

Sales managers need to communicate continually with the salespeople, lead, motivate, and control their activities. So sales managers must possess interactive skills, interpersonal skills, leadership quality, motivational ability, and should be open to accept new ideas even from subordinates, proactive minds to confront challenges, etc. Sales managers must comprehend skill variations amongst salespeople and assign responsibilities keeping them in mind. For example, a salesperson with high technical skill may be asked to look after the maintenance and servicing of customers.

Managerial Skills

Sales managers should be experienced in planning, budgeting, forecasting, strategizing, organizing, staffing, directing, motivating, and controlling functions to manage the sales force. They should understand the corporate goals and determine the sales goals in line of corporate perspectives. They should keep a constant vigil on the selling expenses and keep it in check within the budgetary estimates. They should judiciously construct sales territories, allocate selling resources based on territory sales potentials, and continually evaluate sales performance to control sales operations.

Analytical Skills

Sales managers need to know both the qualitative and quantitative techniques to estimate and analyse market conditions, customer demands, market and sales potentials, strengths and weaknesses of his own firm vis-à-vis competitors, environmental threats and opportunities, etc. They should estimate the opportunity costs of decision alternatives and their expected outcomes. So, sales managers should have aptitudes to select and use mathematical models, statistical techniques, operations research techniques, etc. to suitably diagnose the problems and evolve solutions.

Conceptual Skills

Sales managers should have the theoretical backgrounds on organizational theories, organizational behaviour, functions and roles of the management, corporate social responsibility in general and understanding of the marketing and sales management, consumer behaviour, market segmentation, product positioning, etc. specifically before they go for practical applications of it.

Technical Skills

Sales managers should have the knowledge on technical areas of sales force management such as development of sales plans, sales force recruitment and selection policies, performance appraisal, designing compensation packages, etc. Besides, they must know the bargaining and negotiation skills, addressing customer problems, use of information technology for faster customer interaction, etc.

7.9 FACE OF SALES FORCE TODAY

Salespeople are the fulcrum of the company. They are the face of the organization who acquaint customers to the firm they represent. Salespeople act as mediators between the buying and selling in the firms. They act on behalf of the firm where they pump in sales revenues and profits from the customers. They also look after the customer needs and uplift their current states by addition of product, service, quality of living standards, and satisfaction.

Salespeople educate, advice, guide, pacify, and reform customers. Both economic and psychological relationships integrate salespeople and customers. Salespeople perform multifarious roles keeping in mind the onus on the sales targets, where economic relationships come into play. But to assure financial success of the firm, physiological relationships are used to prepare the podium to incite the customers to join hands with the salespeople. Salespeople need to operate within the cost and budgetary constraints so as to acquire profits. Wherever, retaining customers is crucial, psycho-social relationship tops over economic ties. Salespeople may be amicable, friendly, and sociable in their demeanours during customer handling but they will be empty vessels with too much sound if they do not contribute financially to the firm.

Salespeople were once considered lone men. They were instructed to work in isolation and the concept of team selling was not even dreamt of. But their performances are always under scanner as in the past and in the present. Salespeople are always on their toes to serve the organization and the customers, and their personal will and woe, happiness and misery, trouble and travesty are no considerations. They know two extremes—either to perform or to perish. When they perform, they are worshipped like demigods and when they falter, they become the subject of scorn and curse. Such upturns and downturns are seldom observed in any other career.

Despite all such eventualities, salespeople are gaining importance and honour in today's organizations. Salespeople, today, are not treated as order getters or delivery boys. They are now treated as consultants to the customers. They are advised to operate within a sales team. They are given different accessories (e.g. laptop, hand-held computing devices, web technologies, etc.) to interact better with the customers, prepare call schedules, analyse and forecast sales, furnish sales reports, quickly consult databases, etc.

Kumar and Menakashi (2008) referred to Gentech, a biotechnology firm that has marketing consultants who are always supported with technical information from the company and can use laptops to access the latest medical information and update their knowledge. Salespeople are also using customer relationship management (CRM) software more effectively. Kotler and Armstrong (2006) cited that Ownes-Corning has integrated its sales force to field sales advantage (FSA) system that provides salespeople with constant supply of information about the company and the customers.

So, salespeople today are not the object of ridicule and neglect. They are all-important members of the organization. Their personal needs and developments are adequately taken care of. They are no strugglers but battlers behind whom the organization stands tall. Their commitment, involvement, empowerment are valuable resources to the organization.

SUMMARY

Salespeople are treated as critical resources in all organizations. A salesperson is one who is predominantly responsible for personal selling activities. In traditional selling, salespeople were used to apply pushy or different kinds of aggressive efforts to perform selling. Today, salespeople are responsible not only for generating sales but also for establishing long-term relationships with the customers. Salespeople act as links between the buyers and the sellers. Salespeople also act as order takers or getters. Salespeople can contribute to the enhancement of the quality of life of the customers. They contact customers, share information, persuade them to buy, make arrangement for the proper delivery of products or services, and perform after-sales services. It is also important for salespeople to possess qualities such as presentable appearance, communication skill, creativity, self-monitoring, etc.

A sales manager, on the other hand, is one who is engaged in planning, organizing, staffing, motivating, and leading a sales team to achieve aggregate performance levels that correspond to the sales objectives and goals. Sales managers combine and coordinate human, financial, and information resources effectively to respond to each decision component. They guide, lead, and control the efforts of the salespeople who act upon their decisions. They need people skills, managerial skills, conceptual skills, and technical skills to manage salespeople and sales functions successfully.

KEY TERMS

Order Getter   Order getters are individuals who identify new customers and influence them to buy the company's products.

Order Taker   Order takers are individuals who process routine orders and reorders, and execute it.

Sales Manager   Sales manager is a person who is engaged in planning, organizing, staffing, motivating, and leading a sales team to achieve an aggregate performance level that correspond to the sales objectives and goals.

Salesperson   Salesperson is an individual whose fundamental job is to sell a product/service.

Traditional Selling   Traditional selling is a method whereby salespeople coax and cajole innocent customers to buy their products.

CONCEPT REVIEW QUESTIONS

1. How would you characterize a successful salesperson? Briefly, illustrate the role of salespeople.
2. Mention the duties and responsibilities of salespeople.
3. Explain the types of skills a sales manager should possess.

CRITICAL REVIEW QUESTION

1. Critically compare and contrast the role of a salesperson and a sales manager.
2. Salespeople in a team can conceal their deficiencies in selling qualities and gain advantage, whereas a bright salesperson in a team cannot find opportunities to excel because of the repressors, i.e., poor performers. Critically review the statement.

PROJECT ASSIGNMENTS

1. Meet sales managers of two noted soft drink companies and conduct a discussion on the duties and responsibilities of their salespeople.
2. Interview salespeople of a (i) food and beverage, and (ii) biotechnology companies and discuss on how they view their sales managers. Orient the discussion on organizational, psychological, and social relationships of salespeople with sales managers.

REFERENCES

Evans, J.R. and B. Berman (2007), *Marketing Management*, Cengage Learning, Australia.

Kotler, P. and G. Armstrong (2006), *Principles of Marketing*, 11th ed., Prentice-Hall of India Private Limited, New Delhi.

Kumar, A. and N. Meenakshi (2008), *Marketing Management*, Vikas Publishing House Pvt. Ltd, New Delhi.

Spiro, R.L., W.J. Stanton, and G.A. Rich (2003), *Management of a Sales Force*, Tata McGraw-Hill Publishing Company Limited, New Delhi.

Wilson, M. (1983), *Managing a Sales Force*, 2nd ed., Gower Publishing Company Limited, England.

=== **CASE STUDY** ===

Profile of Sales Executives

TPI Food Products Ltd, a subsidiary of TPI group of industries, established in 1990, has been engaged in the manufacturing of snack foods, spices, chillies, organic herbal-enriched health foods, livestock foods, fisheries, etc. At present, the company has 150 professionals on its payroll working all over India. The company is in search of more professionals to expand the business in north-eastern region. It has recently invited applications from potential sales professionals for filling the vacancies of sales executives. The company plans to recruit 10 sales executives soon. The following are the details of qualification criteria for selection:

Post: Sales executive

Necessary Qualifications Candidates, male or female, must have an MBA degree in marketing from recognized institute. They should have a maximum age of 28 on 01 January 2011. They should have a minimum experience of four years in selling foods and beverages or relevant consumer products division. The candidates should be fluent in English, Hindi, Bengali, and regional languages of the north-eastern states. They should also be conversant in computers and high-speed internet operations, and have experience in handling logistical functions and intermediaries.

Desired profile of the candidate

Following are the desired profiles of the candidates:

(a) Should have sound physique and pleasing appearance
(b) Should be dynamic in handling territories independently
(c) Should be ambitious to move up the managerial ranks by consistent sales performance
(d) Should be assertive to hold courage and determination even under depressed market situations
(e) Should have emotional flexibility to cope with the ups and downs of the business
(f) Should have the ability to work in a team
(g) Should take initiative to identify profitable leads and convert them to actual customers

Job profile

Following is the job profile of the sales executive:

(a) To fulfil sales targets every month
(b) To plan, organize, and coordinate sales activities. These include prospecting, customer call preparations, making cold calls, prepara-

(Contd)

(Contd)

tion of sales kits, handling customer objections, customer follow-up calls, getting in touch with customer stock positions, replenishing the customer stocks as soon as it is at reordering level

(c) To open an account at least for five new customers a month

(d) To make at least five calls a day

(e) To type call reports everyday and send it by e-mail to territory managers

(f) To attend sales meetings every fortnight convened by territory managers

(g) To attend at least two conferences (one national and one international) in sales and marketing areas in a year

(h) To prepare route plans and time schedules independently and get it approved by territory managers

(i) To ably perform sales presentations and product demonstrations

(j) To be able to properly negotiate and close sales independently

(k) To resolve customer complaints on emergency basis and manage customer relationship convincingly

(l) To be equipped with sales brochures and other promotional materials, and distribute them amongst prospective/existing customers

Performance evaluations used

Following are the performance evaluations used:

(a) Target sales: Actual sales

(b) Order: Call

(c) Number of customers contacted: Number of prospects developed

(d) Sales: Sales expenses

(e) Field sales cost: Total sales cost

Remuneration   Basic ₹20,000 plus 20 per cent DA and 15 per cent HRA on basic salaries. Yearly increment is decided on sales performance. Company sponsored TA and DA will be provided on sales tours.

Promotional opportunities   Based on merit

Probations   One year probation after joining and then confirmed on the basis of performance

Discussion Questions

1. Prepare a brief outline of the sales force plans the company is targeting.

2. As a sales executive what more can you expect from the company? Do you think that the company will be able to develop a stable sales force?

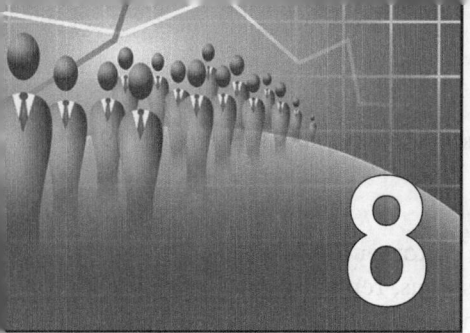

8 Sales Force Recruitment

8.1 RECRUITMENT—MEANING AND CONCEPTION

Recruitment is the process of obtaining qualified candidates for a job. It is a process of searching candidates with an objective to stimulate them to apply for jobs in the organizations. The searching process ends with discovering potential applicants who can best fit the vacancies of the organizations. So, it can be said that recruitment is an effort of bringing together those with job offers and those seeking jobs.

Recruiting basically involves two steps. First is identifying the manpower requirements. Second is filling the gap of manpower by sourcing it from various pools of resources. It is process of searching the right human resources and attracting them to apply for those jobs that need employees in the immediate future. It generates a qualified pool of candidates to enable the selection of the best people for the organization. The objective is to stimulate more number of potential candidates than the required manpower to apply from which selection of the best people is made. Recruitment is a positive process because it attracts suitable applicants to apply for vacant jobs. Selection, on the other hand is a negative process because it eliminates a good number of candidates from the resource pools developed during recruitment choosing only the best who are given the job offer.

Spiro et al. (2008) defined recruiting as the inclusion of all activities in securing individuals who will apply for the job.

Ingram et al. (2007) defined recruitment as a procedure of locating a sufficient number of prospective job applicants.

Chhabra (2002) refers recruitment as the attempt of getting interested applicants and providing a pool of prospective employees so that the management can select the right person for the right job from the pool.

Recruiting is an essential and the most important step in human resource planning. Recruitment does not mean placing of ads or contacting employment agencies, the results will then be disastrous. The company, in that case will suffer from non-availability of suitable candidates or wring placement of unfit candidates. In fact, it helps in the process of sales force planning. Results from two surveys are discussed below which are quite indicative of how important recruitment efforts are.

1. If company's successful salespeople were put in a territory by replacing the average ones, twenty per cent increase in sales should be expected in two years (Kumar and Meenakshi 2006).
2. The top twenty seven per cent of the sales force brought in over fifty two per cent of the sales (Kotler 2003).

Therefore, recruitment and selection are deeply seated at the core of the sales force management. Precisely, the process must include how, why, and when of the recruitment efforts and these are most clearly mentioned in the sales force planning statements. Moreover, it is a challenging job for the sales managers to select people which will collectively determine how effective the sales managers are. Recruitment and selection of sales force is an important activity because of the following reasons:

1. If properly undertaken, it provides a solid foundation of a sound sales organization and sales management.
2. It helps to employ and maintain an effective sales force which is beneficial for the stability of the organization.
3. Good recruitment is the starting point of selecting a number of efficient sales forces who can greatly improve sales performance.

8.1.1 Staffing—Achieving the Right Fit

With recruiting, the word staffing is also heard in the organizations in the human resource department. Staffing includes planning for the needs of future employment and fulfilling them through recruiting, selecting, promoting, laying off, transferring, etc. which aids in bringing the manpower to the needed quantity. So, the process of staffing is broader in perspective than the process of recruiting. Staffing starts with human resource planning and mediates through recruiting, selecting, and hiring the right human resource and ends with socializing the new recruits with the organization.

Staffing is an important activity in sales and marketing department particularly for the sales force because it is directly responsible for generating revenues for the organization. Product planning and strategic marketing schemes might be flawless but, wrong selection of the salespeople nips the expectations of the company to achieve marketing objectives and destabilizes its economic health. For example, service-oriented firms such as hotel and hospitality industries need to hire such sales force that can provide excellent customer care and develop good customer relationships. So, while staffing the sales force, skill to communicate, and deliver quality is given supreme importance.

For selection of senior marketing executives in packaging industries, knowledge and skill in formulating promotional strategies, resource allocation, territory planning, etc. are the other reckoning issues. This is why, staffing the marketing and sales department is considered as integral to strategic marketing planning. Sales force planning is part of strategic marketing planning.

A staffing process in the marketing wing of the organization consists of the following steps:

Planning

It further comprises of the following steps:

(a) Formulating the staffing objectives
(b) Forecasting the sales force requirements. Accordingly, the size of the sales force is determined
(c) Developing the staffing procedures. It involves how the sales force is to be recruited, identifying the recruiting sources, designing the recruiting format, and placing the recruiting material in the right medium
(d) Accepting and scrutinizing the applications, screening out unsuitable applicants, and inviting the potential applicants for the selection process

Select the Most Qualified Applicants

It involves the following steps:

(a) Formulating the selection objectives. The guiding principles are job descriptions and job specifications. These are discussed in Section 8.3
(b) Deciding the selection tools. For example, structured interview followed by psychological tests
(c) Conducting the selection process
(d) Selecting the right candidates

Assimilate the New Hires

It involves assimilating the new hires into the company by induction and socialization processes. These are discussed elaborately in Chapter 9.

Figure 8.1 represents the stages in the staffing process. The objective of staffing is to maintain a band of effective employees. Recruiting is also different from selecting the candidates. Recruiting facilitates a company to tap resources of manpower whereas selecting is choosing the right candidates to fill the deficient positions of human resource. Recruiting draws both suitable and unsuitable candidates to the firm, and selecting eliminates unsuitable ones and appoint the suitable ones who show some potential on knowledge, skills, creative abilities, talents, aptitudes, communication levels, and other characteristics that fit with the qualification criteria established at the beginning of the staffing process.

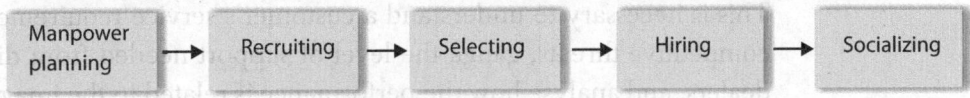

Figure 8.1   Stages in staffing

Manpower planning is the maiden step in the staffing process of the sales force. Planning illustrates the type, number, job responsibility, utilization, and preservation of the salespeople that the organization pursues in order to reach a desired manpower position that can work as per the expectation of the organization. It aids in setting the acquisition criteria for the sales personnel. At the same time it makes assessment of present manpower positions. So, how an organization moves from present human resource position to the desired level is the essence of manpower planning.

Desired number of sales personnel can be easily estimated by forecasting future requirements of the salespeople in terms of workload analysis or the application of incremental methods discussed vividly in Chapter 5.

The objective of manpower planning is to relate the future human resource requirements to the future projection of sales volume and return on investment. However, the sales managers must keep in mind the future uncertain economic scenario, unavoidable labour turnover, invasion of new technology, business expansion or reduction programme, etc. for developing a specific contingency plan to address exigencies. For large organizations, manpower planning helps to identify the surplus sales personnel on one territory and deficit sales personnel on the other. So, redeploying sales personnel by downsizing the overstaffed territories and rightsizing the understaffed ones can be effectively implemented by sales force planning. For an individual salesperson, it acts as a major boost to improve the skills and capabilities and an organization benefits from the efficient application of sales personnel.

8.2   JOB ANALYSIS—A PRE-REQUISITE FOR RECRUITMENT

Job analysis is an important pre-requisite for manpower planning, recruitment, and the selection processes. It involves deciding on the type of tasks, duties, and responsibilities of the selling jobs. Pearce II and Robinson, Jr (1989) defined job analysis as the identification of specific activities performed in a job and the characteristics of the person, the work situation, the materials or equipment necessary for performing the job effectively. It encompasses systematic and in depth research on the job with a view to identify the nature and characteristics of people to be employed for it. With respect to personal selling, it involves the following:

1. Analysis of the marketing environment in which the salespeople will work. This means analysis of customers, competitors, intermediaries, and people. This is necessary to understand a customer's service requirement, tide over competitive threats, gauge the level of support needed from distributors or dealers, and analyse how the performance is related to the image outside the firm.

2. It precisely defines the sales objectives and what salespeople and sales managers do to reach it. It states what product(s) the salespeople will sell, to whom to sell, how much to sell, the criteria for sales performance, how to furnish sales report as well as to whom do the salespeople report, etc.

3. Selling activity includes methods of selling and management of sales. In fact, the workload distribution between salespeople and sales managers, and duties and responsibilities that are expected from the both is thoroughly scrutinized.

4. It helps to generate recruitment and selection norms of salespeople, selection criteria, skill levels and personality characteristics of the applicants, training needs, and details of the training manuals, measures of training effectiveness, motivational packages, compensation schemes, performance benchmarks, and evaluation procedures for the sales force performance.

5. It gives an overall idea about the work environment and the work culture that is needed to facilitate selling activities and encourage salespeople of different skill levels to be involved with their jobs. For example, flexible work atmosphere with more authority delegation may make salespeople more responsive to their jobs.

So, job analysis vouches for the creation of a particular job in the organization. At the same time, it gives a clear indication of job goals and job behaviours. It precisely draws the relationship of a specific job to the others. For example, the job of pharmaceutical salespeople clearly specifies how they will coordinate their jobs with sales supervisors in terms of getting required instructions, sales target fixation, reporting to the higher level, etc. It further leaves space for further improvement of job environment and criteria. For example, salespeople may be provided with laptops in course of time for quick recording and retrieval of sales reports, sales letter preparation, and sending immediate feedback to the seniors via electronic modes.

8.2.1 The Process

Job analysis involves a careful and objective-oriented study of the job under scrutiny. Before a company goes for recruiting salespeople, it conducts a job analysis. It is basically undertaken through the following activities:

1. Company records the past activities and performances related to a specific job. For example, a company keeps the records of its sales proceeds, nature and extent of competition by market shares held by competitors vis-à-vis the same of the company, number of salespeople needed in previous selling occasions, types and traits of salespeople appointed in past circumstances, past performance of the sales force in terms of sales targets and actual sales proceeds, the then general business environment conditions such as demands of the customers, market situation, economic conditions, where salespeople worked, etc.

2. Interviews with the existing salespeople performing the jobs, their supervisors will give clues of the problems felt, opportunities that exist, job criteria that need moderation or extension, ways of improving job performance, etc.

3. Observing the behaviour of the sales force at work aids in understanding the nature of the job. Closely watching the salespeople when they are engaged in selling activities to identify the necessities in terms of qualification, skill, and attitude (QSA) is needed for the job accomplishment.

4. Self-appraisal and reporting by the salespeople through questionnaires, diaries, etc. gives information about the job. Analysing it will reveal the details of the job both from qualitative and quantitative achievements compared to their expected levels.

5. Consulting various secondary information sources such as government reports, trade association statistics, etc. on critical issues such as business trends, industry sales, future sales projection, etc. may be of great use in analysing the pros and cons of a job.

A sales manager collects the following information through analysis of a salesperson's job (Exhibit 8.1).

Exhibit 8.1   Outcome of job analysis

Following are the outcomes of a job analysis:

1. **Work activities:** A sales manager collects information about a salesperson's actual work activities such as prospecting, information gathering, order processing, delivering the goods/services, servicing, collecting payments from the customers, etc. The how (how these activities are to be undertaken), why (reasons behind each activity), and when (time and place contexts of each activity) are categorically stated.

(Contd)

(Contd)

2. **Human requirements:** A salesperson's educational background, physical appearance, job-related knowledge and experience, intelligence, aptitude, interests, etc. that are needed for jobs in selling.

3. **Human behavior of the salesperson:** Information on the type of human being the sales-people should be and the behavioral facets that they should possess are collected by the sales manager. Generally, it includes information on communication skill, decision-making ability, report writing ability, capacity to build customer relationship, perseverance, emo-tional stability, job motivation, personality, need for achievement, etc.

4. **Tools, equipments, and working aids:** A salesperson needs free samples to demonstrate, literature supports, performance-supporting documents, illustrations for machines or installations, user manuals, services to be rendered (such as customer counseling, repair or maintenance services, etc.)

5. **Performance specifications:** Information on sales territories, sales targets, quantity of orders to be procured, number of sales calls to be met, number of prospects to be generated, number of customers to be developed, etc. All these criteria have specific time limits.

6. **Job contexts:** Information on routing and scheduling for the sales operations, travelling and waiting times to be allowed, job schedules, reporting times, reporting schedules, organi-zational and social contexts of the job, information on remunerations and other incentives for the job holder, etc.

8.2.2 Outcomes—Job Description and Job Specification

The information collected through job analysis is classified into two. One relates to the requirements of the job and the other concerns with the qualities required of a salesperson. The former is known as job description and the latter job speci-fication. Job analysis provides the information inputs for writing job descriptions, as well as, job specifications.

Job Description

Job descriptions are organized written statements of the duties and responsibilities of the job, working conditions, reporting relationships, performance standards, and compensation packages for the respective job titles. Preparation of a job description is a must before a recruiting drive is undertaken. It specifically dis-closes three things as follows:

1. What is to be done?
2. Why it is to be done?
3. How it is to be done?

It defines the job title, the reporting authority, and the tasks the particular job contains.

Sales description on the other hand details on what is expected in terms of sales performance of the salesperson. So, job description at a glance indicates the following:

(a) List of duties and responsibilities linked with the job
(b) Working conditions that the salespeople strictly has to observe
(c) Selling kits, samples, etc. to be used in the job.

It is a checklist for sales managers to know whether all the tasks mentioned in the job description are totally covered or not. Based on it, the appraisal of the sales force performance is made. So, job description is the watchdog for the salespeople to examine whether they work in the right quantum and direction or not. It becomes a motivational influence for the salespeople as they feel assured of the limits and boundaries of the jobs. They may be encouraged to see the opportunity for further career development if they fulfil the requirements of the present job profile. Box 8.1 presents a generalized format of the job description.

Box 8.1   Job description format

1. Job title
2. Primary objectives
3. Secondary objectives
4. Reporting authority
5. Duties and responsibilities
6. Performance criteria
7. Remuneration

Job Title
It should be short and should predict the nature of the job. It also indicates the hierarchical position of the job holder. It is essential to distinguish various types of job in an organization. For example, sales representative, service engineer, etc.

Primary Objective
Primary objective is the definitive statement and the major focus of the job. It directly represents the major reasons for the existence of the position. It should be categorical and quantifiable so that job holders can follow the goals of the job. For example, the primary job objective of a sales manager is to sit together with representatives of one territory at least once in a fortnight to review the sales situation with sales target as a reference point.

Secondary Job Objective
While primary job objectives prioritize the essential aspects of the job, secondary job objectives highlight on lesser important components of the job but job holders are instructed to follow the subsequent for the fulfilment of primary job objectives. For example, the secondary objective of a sales representative is to generate at least four new accounts every month.

Reporting Authority

Reporting authority clearly specifies to whom the salespeople will report and to whom they are responsible to account for their work activities. For example, a territory sales representative reports to district sales manager.

Duties and Responsibilities

Duties and responsibilities lists the tasks of the job holder they should perform and the degree of responsibility and authority. While listing the tasks, the order of importance should be followed and secondly, the tasks framed should be consistent with the primary and secondary job objectives. For example, a sales representative is entrusted with call planning on a day, selling, prospecting, information gathering, payment collecting, report writing, communicating, etc. Each task should be stated in objective manner. Say, a sales representative should make eight effective calls a day on present customers.

Performance Criteria

Efforts are made to furnish performance measures in specific terms for the evaluation of job performance. Once the criterion is set, performance evaluation is based on comparing actual vs. stated performance levels. For example, actual vs. target sales per month or actual vs. stated new accounts development per month can be yardsticks to measure performance of the sales representatives.

Remuneration

The remuneration should be commensurate with the tasks performed. For example, salary-based remuneration is practiced for the performance of primary job objectives and commissions for the secondary job objectives. This should be designed in such a manner that efficient salespeople are not deprived of monetary gains or incentives. So, each element of remuneration such as salary, commission, bonus or other fringe benefits should be highlighted as a whole package under remuneration head.

A typical job description of a sales representative of a FMCG company is presented in Exhibit 8.2.

Exhibit 8.2   Job description of salespeople in the FMCG sector

Job Title: Sales Representative

Primary Job Objective: To call on retailers at least once a month and wholesalers bimonthly to verify the stock situations. Introduce and describe the new products to retailers and wholesalers.

Secondary Job Objective: To call on the household in your territory on sampling basis and get back responses about the consumption rate and customer satisfaction. Also, sell directly to consumers on door-to-door basis.

Responsible To: Territory Manager

(Contd)

(Contd)

> **Duties and Responsibilities:** Act on the laid down call schedules. Meet at least ten retailers a day. Arrange shelf display in the retail shop. Collect information on stock situation and listen patiently to any problems such as storing, logistics, consumer complaints, retailer satisfaction, etc. Meet wholesalers as per tour plan and collect information on inventories and hear the problems patiently, if any. Collect payments by cheque or cash or bank draft as per the company policy and hand it over to territory manager. Prepare reports on a regular basis and get it signed by the territory manager. Attend weekly meetings on every Saturday in the branch office as per the time and place scheduled.
>
> **Performance Criteria:** Actual sales vs. target sales, actual calls a day vs. target calls, new product trial rate, actual payment collection, door-to-door sales volume vs. expected sales volume, addition of new retailers in the distribution channel, desired stock position with wholesalers vs. actual stock position, and rate of stock replenishment.
>
> **Remuneration:** Salary: ₹10,000/month + for every percentage increase of actual sales 2 per cent commission on the basic salary. ₹75 TA & DA allowance per working day.

Job Specification

A job specification is a document that prescribes the minimum acceptable quality of the salesperson that is necessary for a job to be done in a desired way. Job description leads to the preparation of job specification because duties and responsibilities mentioned in the former will guide the organization to decide on knowledge, skill, aptitude, and personality profile requited to perform the job accurately. So, job specifications convert the job descriptions to job qualifications which are also known as hiring specifications.

Job specifications portray the characteristics of the person (the job holder). Job specifications are expressed in terms formal education of the salespeople, age, experience, physical statistics, character traits, emotional maturity, etc. So, in short, job specification is the profile of the salesperson that will fulfil the requirements of job description. Profiling is a technique that organizations use to identify desired job qualifications.

Johnson et al. (1994) viewed profiling as a benchmark technique to evaluate sales candidates by comparing their qualifications with those of high achievers or high-performing salespeople. Job specifications categorically answer what human traits and qualities are needed to complete the job satisfactorily. The items to be inserted in the job specification depend on the type of job description. In general, job specifications relate to the following:

(a) Demographic features such as age, education, sex, experience, language known
(b) Physical characteristics such as health, strength, stamina, height, weight, endurance, eye sight, voice quality, etc.

(c) Personal characteristics such as appearance, manners, dress sense, communication skill, listening ability, memory capacity, intelligence, decision-making skill, technical skill, analytical ability, innovativeness, etc. Character traits are mostly personal characteristics.

(d) Behavioural characteristics such as extroversion, emotional stability, self-reliance, ability to get along with others, personality, assertiveness, adaptability, achievement needed, leadership quality, competitive spirit, etc. Job motivations and emotional maturity are the predictors of behavioural characteristics of the salespeople.

Box 8.2 illustrates a specimen of job specifications of the salesperson to be employed at the junior level in a pharmaceutical company.

Box 8.2   A job specification format

Following are the job specifications:

Job Title: Junior sales executives

Age Limit: 25–30 years

Formal Education: Must be a graduate in commerce or business administration. Postgraduate degree in commerce or business administration is preferred. Working on computers is an added qualification.

Experience: Minimum two years work experience in selling pharmaceutical products

Language Spoken: Regional language, English and Hindi

Intelligence: Above-average (measured by IQ test)

Appearance: Pleasing

Physique: Physically strong, weight proportionate to height

Character Traits: Stability (maintaining same job and interests), communication skill, personality, perseverance, empathy, leadership quality, willingness to work, loyalty to the employer, sociability, assertiveness—high order.

Motivational Influencers: Money, security, power, status, competitiveness, innovativeness—Act upon in moderate to high order

Emotional Maturity: Capable of accepting job responsibility, social responsibility, self-starting, adjustable, and flexible—high order

---

An organization first considers the demographic traits of the candidates—age, education, experience, and even marital status in some jobs are vital considerations because these fulfil the initial requirements of the job description. Education is supposed to cater to the knowledge base. Appropriate age provides the physical vitality and mental stability, and experience offers skill and experience in the relevant field of work. Marital status in sales profession is an issue because of the touring nature of the job and staying out of home for long periods demand finer adjustments with the family members. Striking a balance between the family life and working life is essential to achieve success in the selling profession.

8.2.3 Basic Traits of a Successful Salesperson

Special qualifications of the candidates are added advantages to the organization as it reduces a lot of training cost and secondly a salesperson can utilize more expertise in the job. Similarly, candidates knowing two/three languages including the language of the region where they will work, intelligence, physical health are verified cautiously as these stimulate a candidate's ability to work on his duties and responsibilities. In this profession, a salesperson has to deal with customers of different *linguistic abilities* and, therefore, conversing under different selling situations asks for communicability in more than one or two languages. *Intelligence* is a necessary trait for the salesperson because this enhances trainability of the candidate. Secondly, while in selling warfare, intelligence boosts tactical acumen that is needed to cope with complicated selling situation.

Character traits are the yardsticks of a person's human quality. Selling as a profession demands the coexistence of both basic human qualities as well as self-earned or acquired qualities, that can be acquired through education and experience. Basic human qualities are honesty and integrity to the job, perseverance, industriousness, loyalty to the employer, empathy, i.e., ability to identify with the wants or problem situations of another person, personality, competitive attitude, etc. These qualities generally stay dormant in the salesperson in the initial stages of the selling career and gradually become expressive with age and experience.

Some *psychological traits* such as emotional balance, willingness to accept responsibility, capacity for self-discipline, communication skill, understanding of problems, leadership quality, sociability, etc., is gradually acquired with time. Basically, for highly potential rookie salespeople with a strong presence of basic human qualities can achieve the learnt qualities easily. Sales managers should also have the insights to recognize the qualities of the job applicants.

The top management also examines the motivational influencers of the potential sales candidates. For high-flying selling jobs such as selling capital goods/installations or motor cars, etc. where the unit cost of the product is high and returns are also substantive, prestige or status associated with the selling is naturally high. So the company always looks for experienced and dynamic salespeople who link status, power, and perfection with the selling profession. Security is connected with the remuneration pattern of the sales positions. An organization often appoints sales agents or salespeople who will work on commission basis and security of the job is less. However, for successful achievers, payment knows no limits. Therefore, candidates with risk-averting mentality, low-competitive spirit or less achievement do not find place in such selling situations.

8.3 METHODS FOR DEVELOPING JOB SPECIFICATIONS

Job specification is the other aspects of job analysis. While job description is concerned with the characteristics of the job, job specification pins on the characteristics of the person undertaking the job. The former actually provides the backdrop of the latter. The methods for developing job specifications are as follows:

Review the job description   A carefully prepared job description provides ample scope to develop the job specifications. Managers should study introspectively each clause of the job description and set the minimum acceptable standards for employment and performance of the job. So, items to be included in the job specifications should strictly adhere to the guidelines in the job descriptions.

Study the personal histories of existing or past salespeople   These are valuable reservoirs of information to construct job specifications. First of all, the organization prepares a checklist of traits or characteristics of the salesperson that are needed to perform a particular job. It goes without saying that high-performing salespeople stay or score on the favourable sides of the traits and vice-versa. The company, based on the traits of high-performing salespeople, establishes a minimum level of each trait that the selected salesperson should possess.

Say, for 'experience' a minimum of 2 years is the cut-off point for selection and for personality, a minimum of 4 on the scale of 1 to 5, where 1 indicates minimum presence of the attribute and 5, maximum. The company can prepare a pre-recruiting questionnaire to set evaluation criteria for pre-placement advertisements, scrutinizing the application forms, and selecting the salespeople.

Box 8.3 shows a specimen of standard questionnaire with a few attribute sets. The questionnaire is given to senior sales managers, senior company executives in marketing, and senior salespeople with ten to fifteen years experience to suggest the minimum acceptable standards for the job applicants. Given their feedbacks, the full-fledged job specification or qualification formats for a specific job title are prepared.

Box 8.3   Job specifications of a sales executive

Following are the job specifications of a sales executive:

Quantitative Traits

Age: 20–25, 26–30, 30–35 (choose the appropriate age)

Experience: 1 year, 2 years, 3 years (choose appropriate year)

Education: Graduate or Postgraduate (select)

Professional Qualification Needed: Yes___ , No___(Put a tick mark)

If yes, Type of Professional Qualification (select)

Bachelor of Business Administration:

Masters of Business Administration:

Height:

(Contd)

(Contd)

Minimum Height:

Weight: What is the range?

Qualitative Traits

(Put your opinion on 1 to 5 attitude scale)

Traits	Very important (5)	Important (4)	May be considered (3)	Unimportant (2)	Not required (1)
Mental stability					
Personality					
Self-reliance					
Dominance					
Communication skill					

Interviewing the customers   Customers are a valuable source of information of the expected qualities of the salespeople. How customers evaluate salespeople, therefore, is of valuable input to determine job specifications. Customers expect sincerity, promptness, personal care, and actuarial capacity form salespeople working in insurance industries.

8.4 SOURCES OF SALES RECRUITS

Recruiting activities begin with identifying the sources from where to attract a pool of potential candidates to apply for the jobs. Generally, the various sources of recruitment are classified into two categories:

(a) Internal sources

(b) External sources.

Internal sources means recruitment within the organization and external sources denote recruitments from outside. Figure 8.2 shows the various sources of recruitment under these two categories. Before the process starts, identification of the suitable source of recruitment is an important task. Next is the ability of the source to attract the maximum number of job applicants. So, potentiality of the source is a vital consideration. Therefore, a number of sources are first chosen and then a selection is made based on the strength of the sources. Strength means the ability of the source to spread the information of job vacancies to the maximum number of potential candidates, after applications are invited from the prospective candidates for the jobs.

So recruitment process includes

(a) exploration of different sources of work force,

(b) study the strength of these sources in terms of reach,

(c) choose the most suitable source(s) of recruitment, and

(d) execute the recruitment process.

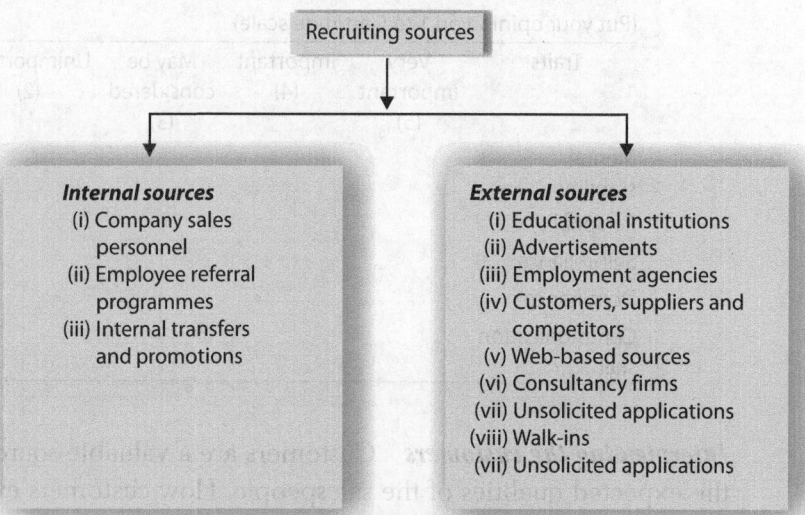

Figure 8.2   Sources of recruitment

Internal Sources

Internal sources exist within the company. Filling up vacancies for higher posts by utilizing organization's own employees is quite popular and common. Some of these internal sources are discussed as follows:

Company sales personnel   Present sales personnel are often potential candidates for higher sales positions. Recruiting within the organization helps the organizations in the following ways:

(i) The company does not require much investment for recruitment

(ii) The cost of training is very less because salespeople are quite familiar with the company's products or services, policies, and methods of operations

(iii) The policy improves the morale of the salespeople because they know they will be preferred first over candidates outside the organization when any job vacancies occur. It also promotes a sense of loyalty amongst present salespeople

(iv) Risk of selection is less as the employer can easily evaluate the abilities of the internal candidates

However, the method has loopholes also. The company in no way can learn whether more talented and knowledgeable prospective candidates are available or not. Many a time, right candidates may not be chosen.

Employee referral programmes   Recommendation by present employees can be a valuable source. Because of experience in the relevant field and social connections, managers or senior sales executives may have acquaintances with prospective salespeople who might work with competing firms or customers. Even they can recommend freshers, who have the right academic background and appear to be suitable for the sales positions. However, these recommendations need careful scrutiny and appraisal particularly when junior sales staff recommends outsiders.

Internal transfer and promotions   Salespeople can move to higher positions through promotions or can be transferred from one job to the other or one territory to the other (lateral movement). At the time of transfer, it should be certain that the shifting salesperson is capable of handling the new job or territory.

External Sources

In external sources, the salespeople are recruited from outside sources. The company wants to inject new blood in the sales department in the vacant positions to strengthen the existing human resource with more knowledge, skill, and experience particularly at senior positions. At the junior level, the company wants to get more dynamicity and energy in the manpower and recruits from academic institutions through advertisements. Here, discussed are some of the prominent external sources of recruitment:

Educational institutions   Colleges and universities are good sources of students who can match well with expected requirements of job qualifications set by the company. Professional institutions have placement cells where complete curriculum vitae and other particulars of the students are easily available. Campus interviews are often undertaken in the institutions where senior personnel from two/three departments of the organizations including sales and marketing are present to interview students in the final year.

Apart from the knowledge level, recruiters judge the aptitude, communication skill, analytical ability, leadership quality, etc. and last but not the least compatibility with the job qualification and the organization as a whole is also looked at. College or university students are good sources of salespeople because first, they are very young and generally possess natural exuberance and energy to work hard for the company. Second, training cost is less as they have the formal education. This can be reduced more if salespeople doing professional courses in marketing are employed. That is why, candidates from professional institutions, particularly premium ones, are in demand in top-notched organizations.

Advertisements   These are popular means of attracting suitable candidates for the job. The company publishes job vacancies either in a classified section or in the appointment pages of a well-circulated newspaper(s) to invite applications from the potential candidates. One specific problem of advertising is that it draws a large number of applications from the candidates and screening of applications often becomes a tough task for the human resource department to eliminate applications of poor candidates. Moreover, involvement of processing cost, time, and energy is a deterring effort to spare for eliminating unqualified applications. Inserting advertisements in newspapers and business magazines are very expensive. So, if the right placement does no not take place, this will put a huge burden on the company budgets.

Employment agencies Employment agencies are rich sources of information of potential unemployed youths in large volumes. These unemployed youth register their names in established employment agencies along with submission of their biodata and other relevant information. Organizations can contact these agencies to collect names and addresses of the prospective candidates who fit in with job specifications after which the applicants are called for written tests and/or interviews.

The basic advantage the recruiting organizations enjoy by working with employment agencies is the availability of huge database on candidates in the agencies. This saves cost of advertisements to the company as well as time of laborious screening of candidates. The agencies charge a fee to the employer which is significantly lower than the advertisement costs in the media. In fact, the fee is nil or nominal for government agencies. Private agencies charge a fee for supplying the database and even arranging interviews between the employer and the candidates. Private agencies also claim fees from candidates once employed, ranging from ten to twenty per cent of the first month's salary.

Consultancy firms, similar to employment agencies, also assist organizations to recruit at various levels of the organization, be it technical, managerial, and other professional levels. These firms, such as employment agencies, maintain a data bank of people with various qualifications, experience, and present working status. Whenever consultancy for selection is sought, they provide the relevant stored information from the human resource inventories to the recruiting organizations and also conduct interviews and facilitate the selection process on behalf of the employing forms at a cost.

Customers, suppliers, and competitors Good salespeople can be sought from the references of customers and suppliers, particularly those who have a long association of working with the organization. In fact, they can understand what are expected from salespeople who work well with the organization.

Pulling the competitor's salespeople is quite common in the industry though the practice appears to be not good for a healthy competition in the industry. In the process, a company can get a trained and experienced salesperson at a higher cost. But ethical controversies arise blamefully in the industry because of the possibility of divulgence of the old employer's secret information and strategic moves. That possibility also lies with drawing the employees of the customers. This recruiting practice is common in computer industries, insurance firms, office equipment companies, stock broking firms, retailing and trading houses, etc.

Web-based sources Many firms maintain their own websites and use it to attract candidates to apply for jobs electronically. Some companies even approach web-based service providers who advertise for the vacancies by webpages at a cost. The advantage is quick access to the particulars of the candidates. The particulars can then be sent quickly to the scrutinizers and interviewers for ready reckoning. So, interview can be arranged quickly and selection can be done promptly.

Today, companies are working with internet recruiting website providers frequently to search for potential applicants. By the process, the company can avoid hazardous workings on recruitment process and save much time. For example, websites such as www.naukri.com, www.jobsearch.com, etc. are well-known sources of information for both recruiters and candidates to come in close proximity to ease the selection process.

Unsolicited applications Many organizations accept forced applications and allow casual callers to submit their curriculum vitae and take interviews. Applicants contact the firms personally or send applications by hand or electronic mails. Often suitable candidates are found by this method. The merit of the method is the negligible cost of recruitment.

Walk-ins Walk-ins is yet another external source of recruitment. Though, this has been discussed under advertisement, many medium- and small-sized firms entertain walk-ins for identification of candidates. This is especially true for freshers and people joining at lower levels. The merits are that the cost of recruitment is less and for immediate selection of candidates, the method is quite useful.

The following Exhibit 8.3 shows the recruitment practices in one renowned company that earned high reputation by bringing changes to the recruitment practices.

Exhibit 8.3   General Electric Company

The *General Electric Company* or *GE* is an American multinational conglomerate corporation incorporated in the State of New York.

General Electric (GE) brought in a revolution by bringing GE's MBA recruitment project into the world of virtual space. This project aimed to educate and attract savvy marketing personnel, graduating MBAs around the world for them to take up an opportunity of working with GE. In essence, GE's plan was to effectively use the second life 3D platform for global marketing recruitment. This was an innovative recruitment drive from GE.

(Contd)

(Contd)

In this process, the potential candidates would start their exploration of virtual GE not at the standard Second Life download page, but rather at the GE careers website, where they could do a virtual exploration on GE's own virtual land. This would bypass the standard entry points and confusing orientation areas and assure that the candidates would never get lost along the way.

Upon arrival in virtual platform, the candidate would enter the welcome pavilion for an orientation experience that would let them customize to the company environment and policies. After this, they would go through an innovative interactive time line which involves a series of connected diorama style environments each outlining historic highlights of specific business units. A diorama is a three-dimensional visual projection of the subject to impact more meaningful understanding on it. In fact, this sort of interaction could deepen the liaison between the potential candidates and their employers.

Source: http://www.involve3d.com/begin/cases_ge.html, accessed on 11 June 2010.

Employees are the most important resource for any company and recruitment is a vital process for a company to succeed as, it deals with the critical process of identifying the right pool of potential employees. This serves as inputs to the next stage of selecting the right people for the organization, which will be discussed in the next chapter.

SUMMARY

Recruitment is the process of obtaining qualified candidates for the job. It involves two steps (a) identifying the man power requirement and (b) filling the manpower gap by sourcing it from various pools of resources. So, recruitment is the process of searching the right human resources and attracting them to jobs. Recruitment facilitates a company to tap resources of manpower whereas selection is choosing the right candidates for the jobs. Staffing means planning for the needs of future employment and fulfilling them by recruiting, selecting, promoting, laying off, transferring, etc. Manpower planning is an important step in planning.

Job descriptions and job specifications are two outcomes of job analysis. Job analysis is identification of specific activities in a job, characteristics of the person, the work situation, the materials or equipment necessary to perform the job effectively.

Job description relates to the requirements of the job and job specification is concerned with the qualities required for the salespeople. Job description is an organized written statement of the duties and responsibilities of the job. A job specification is a document that prescribes the minimum acceptable qualities of the salespeople necessary to do the job, in the desired way. Various methods for developing job specifications are (a) review the job specifications, (b) study the personal histories of existing and past personnel, and (c) interviewing the customers.

The various sources of recruitment are classified into two—internal sources and external sources. Internal sources mean recruitment from within the organization and external sources mean recruitment from outside the organization. Today, many organizations are bringing innovative changes in the recruitment process.

KEY TERMS

Job Analysis Job analysis involves identifying the type of tasks, duties, and responsibilities for a particular job. It also identifies the nature and characteristics of people who would be best suited for these jobs.

Job Description Job description is an organized written statement of tasks and duties, the working conditions, reporting relationships, performance standards, and compensation packages for the respective job title. It specifically discloses what, why, and how a job is to be done.

Job Specification Job specification basically involves a list of characteristics and qualities required in a candidate for the job to be carried out successfully.

Recruitment Recruitment is a process of searching and obtaining qualified candidates for the job. It is an effort of bringing together those with job offers and those seeking jobs.

Staffing Staffing is a broader perspective which includes planning to fulfil the needs of future employment through recruiting, selecting, promoting, laying off, transferring, etc. It ends with hiring the right human resource and socializing him with the organization.

CONCEPT REVIEW QUESTIONS

1. What do you mean by recruiting the sales force? What are its objectives?
2. What is job analysis? How is it effective in the recruitment of a sales force?
3. What is job description? How is it effective in the recruitment of a sales force?
4. What is job specification? What are its requirements?
5. Write the job specifications of sales representatives of a FMCG company.
6. Examine the methods for developing job specifications for sales people.
7. Briefly explain the different external sources of recruiting the sales force.
8. When is it beneficial to recruit sales force from internal sources?

CRITICAL REVIEW QUESTION

Treating competing firms as a recruiting source, widely known as poaching, is often looked down upon in the industry. Taking away experienced salespeople from competing firms do not create a healthy business climate. Rather, it often breeds a cold war between the recruiting and affecting firms. Furthermore, the outflow of key personnel means breaking the confidentiality barriers of ideas, thoughts, strategies, policies as well as customer information. Even the exit of a key salesperson may cause migration of customers from old company to new company where the salesperson joins. So from all extents, the practice appears to be unethical and immoral. But knowing the full implications, industry authorities and associations remain mum on the sensitive issue believing this is quite natural in the job market. As a sensible practitioner of personal selling how would you see this as a recruitment method?

PROJECT ASSIGNMENTS

1. What ought to be the recruiting sources of large scale FMCG firms and why? Now approach two such FMCG firms and collect information on the recruiting sources. Compare your views with actual practices.
2. Prepare a job description questionnaire for sales representatives working in a software company. Meet sample representatives (HR managers) of each company and show them the questionnaire. Identify the areas where you need to make corrections to prepare a fresh questionnaire for job description.

REFERENCES

Chhabra, T.N. (2002), *Human Resource Management: Concepts and Issues,* 3rd ed., Dhanpati Rai & Co. (P) Ltd, Delhi.

Ingram, T.N., R.A. LaForge, R.A. Avila, C.H. Schwepker Jr, and M.R. Williams (2007), *Sales Management, Analysis and Decision-making,* 6th ed., South-Western Cengage Learning, Australia.

Johnson, E.M., D.L. Kutrz, and E.E. Scheuing (1994), *Sales Management: Concepts, Practices and Cases,* 2nd ed. McGraw-Hill Inc., New York.

Kotler, P (2003), *Marketing Management,* Pearson, New Jersey, United States.

Kumar, A. and N. Meenakshi (2006), *Marketing Management,* Vikas Publishing House Pvt. Ltd, New Delhi.

Pearce II, J.A. and Richard, B. Robinson Jr (1989), *Management,* McGraw-Hill Book Company, New York.

Spiro, R.L., W.L. Stanton, and G.A. Rich (2008), *Management of a Sales Force,* Tata McGraw-Hill Publishing Company Limited, New Delhi.

CASE STUDY

Recruitment Consultancy

XYZ Ltd has recently developed a geographic organizational structure and engaged area managers in different divisions in regions. The objective is to expand the operations in different micro-markets where customers, so far, have remained unaware of the company's product. The area managers are instructed to recruit salespeople in their areas. XYZ Ltd empowers them to take up sole responsibilities for staffing the area offices. Before these area managers assume charge, the company organizes a one day workshop where a human resource (HR) consultant of a reputed consultancy firm is invited to tutor the area managers on recruitment policies and techniques.This type of a workshop usually consists of two sessions. The first being the lecture session and the second being the interactive session. Given below is an excerpt of the interactive session. Questions raised by the area managers at different times are furnished in a general way:

HR Consultant: So, now do you understand that recruiting is sourcing the right person for the right job? It is an effort to find a best match between an individual and a job?

Area Manager: Sir, would you please explain this again?

HR Consultant: Let me use an example to explain this. Say, the HR manager of a software company wants to recruit some sales executives at junior level of the firm. The things he should keep in mind are as follows:

First of all, the job profiles mentioned in the job description and the man profiles in the job specification should be clearly understood.

(Contd)

(Contd)

Secondly, the responsibilities and the authorities to be assigned.

Thirdly, the number of new accounts to be developed and the number of old accounts to be maintained should be categorically stated.

Fourth, the nature of problems of the clients to be dealt with should be clearly indicated.

Fifth, the preparation of journey plan and call schedules, and frequencies needed to be mentioned according to customer type and size.

Sixth, the performance criteria should be detailed out.

An area manager can develop a job description based on what a salesperson should do and the job specification describing the expected characteristics and traits of the salesperson by specifying the particulars that the recruiters are looking for. For instance in the software company, a manager might be looking for a candidate with a BTech in computer science or MCA (Masters of Computer Applications), with two years experience in the relevant field with an age group of twenty-five to thirty. So, from this information, a manager should be able to deduce the job description and specification.

Territory Manager: Sir, from where can we get the right information regarding the job description and the job specification?

HR Consultant: Well, you could find an ad copy and/or template of job description from the old files of your company. You could research your competitor's advertisements for the same or similar job titles also. But, if you are not familiar with what your salespeople do, don't risk. Request your regional office to send you the details of the job and qualification of the salespeople. Again you could cultivate ads of your competitors and other sources of recruitment.

Territory Manager: Sir, how can performance of the current salespeople help in this regard?

HR Consultant: This is an intelligent question. In this unique approach star salespeople are used as models. You can either analyse the performance factors of the star salespeople or study their qualifications. You can even sit down with them and have discussions. If possible, join them in the field and watch them perform. Find out what qualities they possess that make them successful salespeople. What are their attributes, etc.?

Territory Manager: What if you are not satisfied with current sales-people?

HR Consultant: In that case, you explore the performance factors of the top salespeople who once worked in your company or company such as yours, i.e., companies that sell similar types of products or services or customers. If found, contact them and take their views.

(Contd)

(Contd)

> **Territory Manager:** What if you need to appoint someone to a role that does not currently exist in the firm?
>
> **HR Consultant:** In that case, you search out organizations where such roles exist. Then, collect the information on elements that characterize the role. Also, find some personnel who have excelled in that role. Gather adequate information on the attributes of those people. Understand the personal and professional qualities that are important to accomplish the role.
>
> **Territory Manager:** Thank you, Sir.
>
> **HR Consultant:** Welcome. See you later for more discussions in other human resource areas.
>
> ### Discussion Questions
>
> 1. Highlight on pre-recruitment efforts made by sales managers of a firm.
> 2. Do you think studying the characteristics of present and past star performer's job or man profile can be accurately delineated?
> 3. What is the impact of the current business conditions on sales performance? How does it decide the qualitative requirements of a prospective salesperson?
>
> *Source:* Texnovek, Anna Johnson, http://www.gogojobs.ru/howtorecruit.htm, accessed on 1 October 2010.

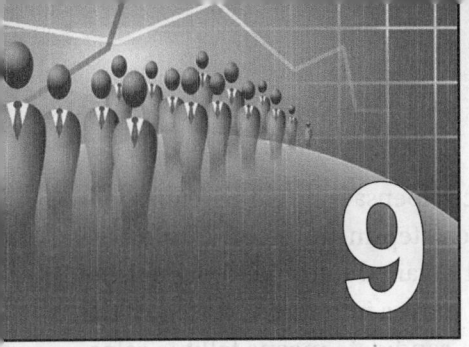

9 Sales Force Selection

LEARNING OBJECTIVES

After reading this chapter, you will be able to

- get insights into the selection process of salespeople
- understand the steps of the selection process and the intricacies of the interview process
- set guidelines for the selection of the right candidates
- equip potential sales candidates with the knowledge, skill, and attitude before the interview
- identify various psychological tests of the selection process
- understand the importance of reference checks
- examine the need and techniques of the socialization process of the salespeople

9.1 SELECTION—AN INTRODUCTION

Recruitment is the process of generating a pool of potential individuals, whereas selection is the process of choosing the best which can fulfil the needs of a particular company. So, selection is the process of eliminating the less fit candidates and hiring the best. The best candidates when inducted into the organization will help it to reach the desired goals. Selection of a salesperson involves a series of steps that are performed to complete the staffing process of the organization.

Dessler (2007) opined that selecting the right candidate is important for three main reasons as follows:

1. Performance of superiors (say, sales managers) always depends on the performance of the subordinates (say, salespeople). Salespeople with right skills and attributes perform better to satisfy the objectives of the sales managers. If this does not happen, it adversely affects the reputation of the sales managers as well as the company.

2. Staffing implies substantial cost involvement. For a wrong selection of employees, the financial loss cannot be compensated. Also, it leads to huge loss in terms of time and effort.

3. Legal implication of incompetent or negligent hiring can really be critical. Cases of lawsuits against the recruiting company by aggrieved candidates are plenty to lay emphasis on right and proper selection of employees.

Proper selection of sales force not only helps to improve sales performance but also keep the rate of attrition low.

One can say that selection is a vital process in any organization, which if not conducted properly can lead to selection of the wrong candidates coupled with wrong investments of money in training and compensation, which can result in huge loss to the organization. Therefore, each step in the selection process is critical and should be suitably planned to get detailed information about the candidates so that not a single wrong candidate moves into the next step of the selection procedure. Infiltration of an unsuitable candidate means fallible selection procedure and it spoils the balance of the sales team and efficiency of their sales efforts.

Selection is basically a screening process. Screening is a judgmental procedure to evaluate the knowledge, abilities, and skills of the candidates. A thorough review of the merits and demerits of the candidates on different job qualification standards is made. It further involves verifying the cognitive, physical, and psychological fitness of the candidates for the job under consideration. Selection, in fact, demands a careful analysis of the characteristics and traits of the sales candidates. Selling is one of the major deciders of success of an organization. That is why selection of the sales force is very critical.

The key areas of selection where the sales managers ought to take sufficient precautions are as follows:

Wrong prediction   A candidate may have all the qualifications necessary for a given job. But, at last, selection turns out to be evaluating the workable qualities of the people that will serve the purpose of the organization. Candidates may narrowly differ on educational qualifications and physical traits. But the psychological traits of people are not easy to judge in one or two interview sessions. A candidate's honesty, integrity, tact, and belongingness to a firm are difficult to evolve. The decision of experienced interviewers on selection is based on an aggregate or collective interpretation of the candidates' qualifications as effective for induction in the firm.

Suppression of facts   Astute candidates know well how to veil their negative features. For example, a candidate, who is terminated from his previous job, declares that he is presently working. They might even have the habit of suppressing the present positions held, salaries drawn, different facilities provided, etc. in the present organizations. Keeping the interviewers guessing and working on their intuitions are their objective. Selection of these deceptive candidates can prove to very harmful to the firm.

Selection tools   The selection tools that are used should be carefully chosen and used. The tools vary from one interview situation to the other. Selection test for rookie salespeople is different from that of senior ones in terms of job qualifications. At junior level, technical knowledge, aptitude, mental ability, emotional quality, etc. are judged. For the selection at senior positions, experience, skill, expertise, mental agility, recognition, professional affiliation, etc. are given a major thrust. So, proper selection of measurement tools is definitely a key aspect of a successful selection process.

Judgmental ability Putting the right candidate at the right job is the sole objective of the selection process. This absolutely depends on the ability of the interviewers to justify the pros and cons of the characteristics of the candidates. A wrong selection has long-term negative impacts on the profitability and image of the organization. A right selection helps an organization to perform satisfactorily. The members of the selection board should be chosen carefully and systematically. Interviewers having capabilities to judge and different selection criteria should be called for to constitute the interview panel.

One interviewer can gauge the communication skills and reasoning of the candidate. The second interviewer can ask technical questions to understand the candidate's depth of knowledge and clarity of ideas. The third interviewer might check the ability of the candidates to examine their industry orientations, corporate awareness, and the required job flair. So, weighing the merits and demerits of the candidates on the appropriate benchmarks on both qualitative and quantitative selection tools helps to justify the selection process.

9.2 SELECTION PROCESS—A STEPWISE JOURNEY

After short listing a pool of potential sales candidates, authorities in an organization start the selection process. The procedure varies from one organization to the other according to hiring policy and the kind of job vacancies that are to be fulfilled. It also depends on the number of applicants who are shortlisted after the recruitment stage.

In the selection for a higher position, a one-on-one interaction or personal interview is undertaken before finally deciding on the job offer. This is a practice in the selection of executives or managers at senior ranks in the organization. Whereas, candidates for lower posts, specially where the number of candidates shortlisted are more, these candidates go through a number of stages in the selection process including group discussions and group activities apart from a number of interviews.

Usually, job applicants differ along many dimensions. Some of these dimensions include educational or work experience, personality characteristics, or any special innate ability, and motivation level. While selecting a candidate, the interviewers like to assume that at least some of these individual differences must be relevant for a particular job. Thus, during the employee selection process, the panel tries to determine these relevant individual differences that would be helpful and needed in the job.

The organization must achieve these tasks in a way that does not illegally discriminate against any job applicants on the basis of race, colour, religion, sex, national origin, disability or veteran's status (www.referenceforbusiness.com). Figure 9.1 exhibits a standardized flow diagram of the selection process.

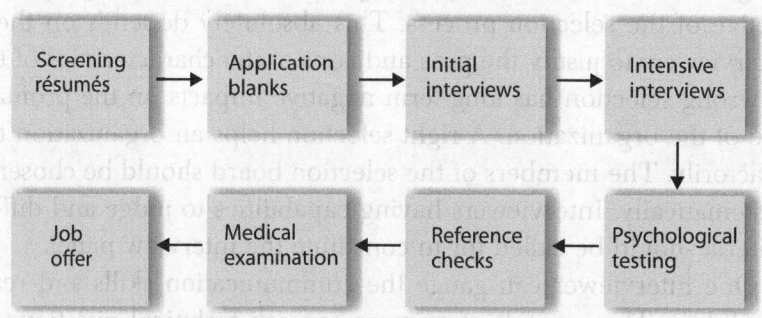

Figure 9.1 Selection process

9.3 INITIAL SCREENING—THE MAIDEN STEP

Preliminary screening of résumés of the applicants is made by the authority when it receives a large number as an outcome of a recruiting process. Résumé, also called curriculum vitae, are personal datasheets that applicants prepare according to the instructions in the advertisements in the recruiting stage and submit it to the company. These résumés help sales managers to get an initial impression about the applicants and they use it to eliminate unqualified candidates who do not fit the minimum criteria of selection at all.

Application blank, on the other hand, is the formal application designed to record pertinent information of the candidates in a way the company wants. The information includes educational background, physical and personal characteristics, work experience, present and past employment records such as job responsibilities, position held in the present organization, reasons for leaving the present organization, last salary drawn as well as expected salary, membership with social or professional organization, special interest areas or hobbies, etc. The application forms are filled by the applicants themselves. Looking at the filled application blanks, the company is able to make a quick review of the personal history of the candidates as well as compare the datasheets. As data is presented in the same order by the applicants, managers can proceed for an initial evaluation of the fitness of the candidates on different criteria of the job qualifications.

The difference between résumé and application blanks is that information furnished in a résumé may not be complete in all respects as expected by the organization. Application blank is a standardized format of recording all the necessary information about candidates that an organization sets to understand for the suitability of the candidates. This helps it to undertake an initial screening. Based on it, the managers decide which candidates to be called for an interview and whose applications to be turned down. Generally résumés or vitae resemble on only a few points of the completed application forms.

Dessler (2005) underlined the utility of the filled application forms. It helps one to judge whether the applicant has the right educational qualifications and the experience to do the job. Second, the applicant's previous progress and growth can be known. Third, the applicant's stability based on previous work experience can also be gauged. Lastly, from the comparative study of information, one may predict which applicant would succeed and who would not. Box 9.1 illustrates the kind of information that may be asked in the application blank.

> ### Box 9.1   Brief sketch—application blank
>
> **Applicant's biographical data:** Name, father's name, date of birth, nationality, sex, present and permanent address, identification mark, any physical disability, marital status, number of dependants, etc.
>
> **Educational background:** Name of academic and professional courses attended, name of institutions and universities attended, year of passing, grades or divisions acquired, percentage of marks, etc.
>
> **Work experiences:** Name of the past employers, present employer, designations held, salaries received, present salary drawn, expected salary, reasons for leaving the present firm, etc.
>
> **Memberships in organizations:** Memberships in clubs, societies, and professional associations, etc. along with offices held.
>
> **Extracurricular activities:** Sports, cultural activities, hobbies, etc.
>
> **References:** Name of individuals (2 or 3) with whom the candidate has worked earlier and who can be contacted for recommendation/cross-checking.

9.4   INTERVIEWS—BACKBONE OF THE SELECTION PROCESS

Interviews are a critical part of the selection process. It is a procedure to conduct an oral interactive session with the candidate involving inquiries and responses with a view to obtain information. It is a method of acquiring maximum amount of information from the candidates and judge their suitability for the job under question. In a way, it is a search process to discover the inner potential of a candidate which necessary to fulfil the requirements of the job.

Generally interviews are divided into four types. All four are discussed as follows:

Structured interview It employs a checklist of questions prepared beforehand. The checklist covers all the relevant questions on personal and academic qualifications that are asked to the interviewee in the same sequence that is maintained in the checklist. In a structured interview, all the candidates face the same questions. Therefore, scoring the questions for candidates, making comparisons, and drawing conclusions is not difficult.

The merit of this method is the uniformity in the questions asked across all the interviewees in every interview situation for similar positions. Controlling the session is also easy. The confidence level of the interviewer generally stays high and even a less experienced interviewer can conduct this type of interview. But the demerit of the interview is that depending on the replies from the candidates, changing the questions or their sequence is not allowed. Therefore, flexibility for the interviewers is less. The interview proceeds in a stereotyped manner. Despite demerits, standardization of the administration of questions has made this type of interview popular and widely used.

Unstructured interview This involves discussion between the interviewer and the interviewee on various issues not following any checklist or pre-assigned sequence of questions. So, there is no set format to proceed in such kind of an interview. Interactions can move in any direction. Discussions can take on various issues but the interviewer has to control the session in a way that never digresses from the objective of the interview. Therefore, the interviewer must have skills to control the session.

The flexibility in this approach allows the interviewer to ask follow-up questions and probe on some points where more detailed information is needed. The major demerit of this method is that different interviewees may or may not face identical or similar questions. Therefore, making comparisons on the positive or negative features of the candidates is difficult and drawing concrete conclusions on the ranking of the candidates is problematic.

Semi-structured interview It allows the interviewer to ask questions based on an outline of specific issues to be discussed and is prepared before the interview begins. The interviewer has full freedom to go in depth on some issues. For example, the interviewer may be interested to know more about the present organization of the candidate. The method enjoys the flexibility of an unstructured interview and aims to maintain some rigour that is present in a structured interview. Definitely, deft handling of the session demands the presence of an experienced and a skilled interviewer in the process.

Stress interview It is applied to examine how the interviewees cope with negative situations and how they overcome the tiring situations. The candidate's emotional reaction in an uncomfortable situation is judged. For example, putting the candidate before a rapid fire questioning session (asking a series of questions and telling him to reply instantly after each question) is the practice. Sometimes, the interviewer feigns an aggressive stand and watches the responsive behaviour of the candidate.

Interviewers may rudely tell the interviewees that they are a mismatch for the organization. If the candidates emotionally burst out at such a comment, they may prove unworthy of the position under question. But if they refute the statement logically by proving their abilities equating the demands of the job, the interviewer's purpose would come to a useful conclusion. In some cases, the interviewers apply stress interview technique to place the candidate deliberately in uncomfortable situations. The objective is to know how a candidate copes with stress-related situations. This proves the endurance of the candidates in tiring situations and application to come out with a solution.

Preliminary interview is another filter (first is the scrutiny of filled-in application blanks) to eliminate unsuitable applicants. This interview is arranged to clarify the applicant's personal history, job qualifications, knowledge on the relevant subject areas, knowledge on the relevant job positions where one will be appointed, duties and responsibilities in the present job, knowledge on computers, present salary drawn, expected salary, personal achievements, personal goals, etc. The interviewer's basic objective is to examine the match of the profile of the candidate with the job description and job specification. Some firms even conduct initial interviews through telephone. Today, interviews via video-conferencing are not uncommon, especially where long distance and expensive travel is involved. Proper conduct of preliminary interviews may save cost and time for the next stages of the selection process.

The candidates selected in the preliminary interview are called for the intensive interview. Intensive interview is conducted to get an in-depth impression of the candidate. This is necessary to iron out any doubt about the selection of the right candidate(s). It is a face-to-face interaction with candidates by higher-level managers, constituting a panel or is held in a sequential manner where a candidate has to meet and satisfy each interviewer in a series of interviews. In the latter, a candidate is interviewed in succession. Intensive interview specifically wants to evolve and understand a candidate's attitudinal ingredients, motivational components, and compatibility issues that are important to decide on the selection of the candidate.

Here, discussion is mainly centred on the duties and responsibilities of the job in question and candidate's knowledge, skill, experience, motivation, confidence, personality, attitude, etc. to fit in with the job title. Also, the interviewers judge the possible compliance of the candidate's traits and characteristics, and the organization's culture and mission. The objective is to get an assertion that the candidate will be a viable resource to the organization. Besides, discussion on the starting salary and other emoluments are made to steer clear of compensation-related doubts of the candidates. Some of the pertinent objectives are illustrated as follows:

Attitudinal level

(a) Positive mindset to join the new organization
(b) Ability to socialize quickly in the new setup
(c) Competitive attitude
(d) Mental capacity to transform the skill level to task performance

Motivational level

(a) Ready to apply themselves to the defined job
(b) Degree of psychological commitment to fulfil the requirements of the job
(c) Responsiveness to shoulder the specific duties and responsibilities in the new organization
(d) Willingness to make self-improvement

Compatibility issues   (This arises when the interviewers decide to make an initial selection of the candidate)

(a) Settling down the remuneration and other incentives including perks particularly in selection of senior positions.
(b) Resolving other terms and conditions excluding remunerations. For example, permissible travelling and dearness allowances for salespeople when they go for field trips.
(c) Minding the candidates about the terms and conditions in the probationary periods and confirmation clauses that the candidate needs to fulfil.
(d) Date of joining the organization

9.4.1   Interview Process

Figure 9.2 represents the steps in an interview where by a company after preliminary screening of the application blanks or résumés of the candidates invites applicants for an initial interview. It eliminates the unsuitable candidates and asks the qualified ones for intensive interview. Finally, the company takes a selection decision based on placement analysis.

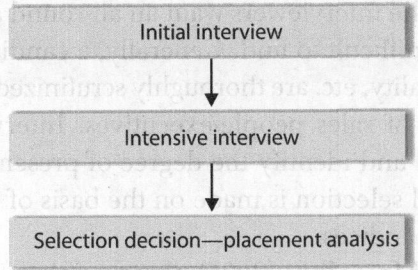

Figure 9.2 Steps in interview—a continuous filtering process

Initial Interview

The initial interview basically comprises of checking the general health and appearance, dress and cleanliness, present employer and working status, experience, technical questions on sales and marketing, communication skills, motivation levels, personality, and reasons for leaving the organization where the candidate is working.

For the new sales recruits, points about the present employer, their experience, and reasons for leaving the current organization are irrelevant.

Intensive Interview

The intensive interview uses certain psychological tests such as intelligence, interest, aptitude, and personality to check the various personality characteristics including their interpersonal skills, which is very important for a person to survive in the field of sales. Interviewers also try to judge or rather interpret the career growth and their ambition along with their expected remunerations and other benefits. The panellist also gauges the expected performance of the candidate if selected. This will be discussed in detail later in section 9.6.

Placement Analysis

The placement analysis is the last and the final stage where it is finally decided if the candidate would be selected to work in the company or not. It is inferred from the earlier interviews if the candidate is worthy enough of being given the job immediately. It is also considered if a candidate deserves to be kept on the job on a trial basis.

9.5 GUIDELINES FOR SELECTION—IMPORTANT DIMENSIONS AND ISSUES

For selection of a rookie salesperson, interview mainly emphasizes the candidate's educational attainments, experience in any industrial training, business flair, knowledge of present business trend, appearance, communication skill, honesty, personality, etc. Exhibit 9.1 presents a checklist that acts as a guideline for the interviewer. The checklist contains what the interviewer is required to know from the candidate. The interviewers want an all-round ability of the candidate which in most cases is difficult to find. Generally, a candidate's current working status, aptitude, personality, etc. are thoroughly scrutinized during interview particularly in the selection of sales people/executives. Interviewers follow a checklist of selection criteria and identify the degree of presence or absence of those in the candidates. Final selection is made on the basis of the rank of the candidates on those evaluation indices.

(a) Kumar and Meenakshi (2006) observed the top ten qualities sought in the salespeople by sales managers of large companies. These are educational background, appearance, communication skill, personality, determination, intelligence, motivation/self-motivation, product knowledge, resilience, and tenacity.

Exhibit 9.1 Selection criteria

Following are the selection criteria for a candidate to be selected:

Appearance and mannerism: Health, dress, poise and bearing, speech and voice, body language, facial expression, neatness and cleanliness, calmness, nervousness, and confidence.

Educational attainment and knowledge base: Degrees and/or diplomas obtained, class or rank, courses taken, area of specialization, reasons for choosing the specialization, knowledge on the subject area, knowledge of the practical applications of the areas where the selection is sought, creativity, analytical ability, any recognition or award received, etc. In senior sales positions, knowledge on applications of sales principles and practices, in depth knowledge of clients, sales forecasting skills, practical knowledge of developing markets, distribution network, marketing strategies, global marketing orientations, etc. are comprehensively scrutinized.

Previous work experience: This is important in selection of candidates for senior positions. For selection of new salespeople, attitude and enthusiasm towards the job, learning intentions, industry exposure, industry awareness, etc. are studied. For selection of senior sales personnel, ability to develop prospects, sales presentation and objection handling skills, sales closing techniques, customer relationship skills, etc. are thoroughly examined.

Personality and social adjustment: A polished human being, emotional stability, emotional maturity, self-confidence, assertiveness, sincerity, initiative, motivation level, ambition, attitude towards associates, ability to work in a team, sociability, need for achievement, etc.

Vocational skills: Industry and company knowledge, managerial flair (organizing ability, decision-making skill, leadership quality, etc. interpersonal skill, persuasive ability, empathy, i.e., ability to get along with others, sensitivity to the feelings of others, etc.), proven track record in the respective occupation, any special achievement, etc.

Spiro et al. (2008) identified the following major categories of traits for which specifics should be developed. These are as follows:

Mental capacities (planning and problem-solving ability) These set of qualities include a salesperson to be mentally active and score high on logical reasoning and analytical reasoning.

Physical characteristics (appearance and neatness) A salesperson should be presentable and should appear friendly and approachable.

Experience (sales and other business experience) A company always seeks for an employee with some experience in the same field. This is always an added advantage as the company does not have to invest much in training him.

Education (number of years, degrees, majors) A person with higher qualifications is any day suited over an individual with lesser qualifications. Higher education means more knowledge. A person has to be strong in his theoretical concepts to be able to succeed as a professional.

Personality traits (persuasiveness and adaptiveness) A salesperson has to be high on characteristics such as persuasiveness and adaptiveness to be able to convince the prospective clients to buy their products.

Skill (communication, interpersonal, technological and job specific) Salespeople can achieve their targets only if they have good communication and interpersonal skills. Of course, they need to be thorough with their technological and job-specific knowledge as well.

Socio-environmental factors (interests, activities, membership in organizations) A company, while recruiting a candidate is also interested to know about the interests and activities of the candidates.

McMurry and Arnold (1968) cited six major attributes that should be present in the interviewees. These are (a) high level of energy, (b) abounding self-confidence, (c) a value system marked by a chronic hunger for money, an improved standard of living, more status, and prestige, (d) established habit of working hard and without close supervision, (e) habit of perseverance, and (f) natural tendency to be competitive.

Exhibit 9.2 provides a few tips to the interviewees before they appear for the interviews.

Exhibit 9.2 Interview tips for the interviewees

Following are the interview tips for the interviewees:

1. The interviewees should do a background research on the company. Consulting yellow pages, websites of the company or friends, neighbours or friends who are familiar with the company to collect information on the company's background, its missions and objectives, market positions, types of products or services dealt in, customer base, any major innovations, global exposure, any major achievement, etc. The objective should be to take part in

(Contd)

(Contd)

the discussion and throw some insights on further development whenever the interview panel members desire to brief the candidate about the company.

2. Always wear conservative clothes with traditional attires. The candidate should be well-groomed and be careful of any slackness in the dress. The candidate should wear ties with perfect knots. The first impression definitely has a bearing on the interviewer's minds.

3. The candidates should prepare themselves mentally a day earlier of the date of interview (called pre-planning for interview) and inculcate thoughts and ideas that centre on the company and position or job title (for which the candidate is called for) with a very relaxed mind.

4. The interviewee should reach the place of the interview at least half an hour before the scheduled time and show the call letter to the receptionist. The idea is to prepare the mind and feel at ease.

5. The candidate should enter the boardroom after he is called in and should enter with permission. The candidate should wish good morning or good evening according to time of interview and should not be seated unless instructed to. He should not shake hands unless the interviewers take the initiatives. But always be smiling.

6. While answering any question, the candidate should not try to answer the question at one shot, else it will appear memorized. Answers should be given in parts by trying to draw attention to each member of the board.

7. For a question, whose answer is not known, the candidate should confess it gently and not beat around the bush. But, if they are called to try, then they can express their views. A good interviewee always tries to drift the discussion to the subject area relevant to the topic under discussion where they are strong.

8. The candidate should never look at the watch or other belongings in the interview room while talking. They should not shake legs or raise their hands when trying to explain anything and try having an eye contact with members more or less uniformly.

9. Before leaving the interview board, the candidates must never ask the probability of their selection. They should express their gratitude to the members for giving an opportunity to appear at the interview.

9.6 PSYCHOLOGICAL TESTS—A CRITICAL STEP IN SELECTION

Corporate recruiters use various types of tests to measure the ability of a person to fit in with the desired qualifications. Psychological tests are most effective in this regard to judge the behaviour of the candidate, particularly basic psychological attributes and socializing capacity that are important for success in a specific job. Most specifically, psychological tests examine a candidate's aptitude, mental ability, intellectual capacity, personality, etc.

Psychological tests help to uncover talents of the candidates that may not be identified in a direct personal interview. It explores a lot of information on the aptitude and mental ability of the person within a short period of time. It eases the selection procedure by differentiating right candidates from the wrong ones.

Interviews may overlook the good qualities of right people and poor qualities of the misfits. Tests also reduce the time of selection because a large number of candidates are evaluated within a short period of time. It further eliminates bias in the judgement of the quality of the candidates. Therefore, psychological tests have more objectivity for the evaluation of candidates.

Tests are crucial selection tools to apply in order to eliminate unsuccessful candidates who fail the tests and choose them who successfully qualify. But, what is vital is proper development of the testing procedures. Selection of suitable tests is a challenge to the human resource division of an organization; otherwise these will measure the wrong qualities of the candidates and misdirect selectors to predict a candidate's ability.

Exhibit 9.3 illustrates key aspects of a standard test which can be used in the selection process.

Exhibit 9.3   Reliability and validity of a test

Before improvisation, a testing instrument needs information on the validity and reliability. Without these two, applying the testing techniques is baseless. A test is called valid when it measures what it intends to measure. It reflects the true differences in scores of two respondents on the same attribute(s) that a testing instrument is designed to measure. A barometer is said to be valid if it measures the atmospheric pressure accurately. No systematic error should be present in the machine. A performance measurement scale measures the efficiency of the employees. If it predicts wrong results, it will be disastrous for the good employees and the organization. The validity of a test can be checked by highly experienced professionals in the respective fields and an initial administration of the test on a sample of respondents. It helps to revise the test instruments to bring in more validity in the application of the tests to the subjects. Two important conditions to prove the validity of the performance measurement test are:

(a) The items that are needed to measure the job performance should be in the test (content validity).

(b) The scores that the items measure are correlated to the job performance.

By reliability, we mean consistency of the test results for repeated measurement of the same characteristics of any person or object under identical conditions. Reliability can be judged by the following methods (a) test–retest reliability and (b) split–half reliability.

Test–retest reliability is the measurement of the objects at two different points of time using the same instrument and checking the correlation of these two measures. If the correlation is high, as suggested by the correlation coefficient, the instrument is said to be high on reliability.

In split–half reliability, an effort is made to divide a set of items constituting the measuring instrument into two equal parts and then apply these two halves to measure the object and examine the correlation of the two measures. If the correlation is high, the testing instrument is supposed to have high reliability.

Following categories of psychological tests are quite popular in the selection of salespeople:

Intelligence test   This test is used to study a candidate's reasoning ability and/or overall intelligence. It also adjudges a person's ability to learn, understand, and comprehend a situation. A person's intelligence quotient (IQ) is a good indicator of the aforesaid qualities. The test is very useful to examine the intelligence of salespeople because some specific intellectual abilities are needed to perform the job of personal selling. In personal selling, communication efficiency, memory capacity, reasoning power are important attributes needed to generate new customers as well as retain the existing ones. Besides, a strategic frame of mind, tactical decision-making and quick responsiveness to buying/selling problems are essential for salespeople to address a selling situation.

Aptitude test   This helps in judging the capacity/ability to perform a job by measuring a person's aptitude and understanding on a specific area of study. For selection of a salesperson, the test tries to explore the candidate's level of knowledge on selling. Knowledge on practical selling is essential to run selling operations successfully. A person with selling experience is assumed to have deep aptitude in selling. Aptitude tests explore a person's learning skill and expertise of handling any problem in the respective field.

Personality test   This is conducted to measure the personality traits. The basic personality traits of salespeople that are needed to fulfil the criteria usually include extroversion, conscientiousness, emotional stability, assertiveness, etc. It tells about how people interact with supervisors, subordinates, and peers within an organization and stakeholders outside. Many of the personality tests are projective in nature. For example, Thematic Apperception test, Sentence Completion test, etc. Besides, personality inventory tests are used to measure the personality of the candidates such as Minnesota Personality Inventory, Guilford-Zimmerman Temperament Survey, California Psychological Inventory, etc. are some tests. However, personality tests are difficult to apply and the results may not be always accurate if these tests are not skilfully controlled.

In fact, because of the qualitative nature of most of the personality traits, accurate measurement is a problem. Interpretation of the results is difficult. Findings of the tests also require careful analysis. Personality tests are important for sales recruits because research says that there is a high degree of association between personality and job performance of a person. If selection is narrowed on personality traits of a candidate, this may confound the ability and experience of a person.

Interests test   It determines the willingness of a person to do a job. It predicts how a candidate differs from the others in terms of motivation, values, act, and behaviour that would benefit the organization and also the candidate. Interest inventories are designed to compare the interest of a person with the interest of a successful person in a particular occupation. A candidate with low interest cannot provide full potential despite having high knowledge, intelligence, and personality levels. Interest is an indication of the motivation level of a person. A person with high interest level may offset weaknesses in intelligence and other attributes.

Achievement tests   These are conducted to measure the proficiency of the candidates that they are expected to acquire after a sales training programme. These tests are also applied for the selection of senior sales personnel or sales managers at higher positions where previous track records in sales profession is an important criterion. These tests find use in the promotions of employees.

Assessment centres   It usually consists of a battery of tests and exercises. It involves intensive testing situations where ten or twelve candidates are asked to perform in a situation that simulates a real world sales situation. An assessment centre can also be designed to replicate an original sales job. Various techniques such as group discussions, role-playing exercises, management games, case presentations, etc. are used for the selection of suitable salespeople. This also finds use in the training of salespeople, their promotions, and identification of their leadership potential.

Indeed, these tests are applied to understand the communication and social skills of the salespeople. How do salespeople behave in a group, how they maintain rapport with others and overcome conflicts and dissensions within group are noted by the judges in the assessment centres. One popular test of assessment centre is the in-basket exercise. In this exercise, a candidate is given an accumulation of memos, letters, reports, etc. that are kept in a basket in a simulated test situation and the candidate's action with respect to each is closely observed.

9.7   ESSENTIAL FORMALITIES OF SELECTION

This is the final stage of the selection process. Candidates undergo this stage only if their suitability (in terms of knowledge, aptitude, and skills) to be employed in a particular organization has been established in the earlier stages. It includes some essential formalities of selection such as reference checks, medical check-ups, and the official document discussing the job offer.

Reference Checks
Reference checks help to check the background information and references of the candidates who qualify the rigours of the selection process. These are verified and checked by the employers. Generally, an applicant is asked to provide few names of the people called references that have academic and professional recognitions

as well as are familiar to the candidates. They are also required to submit their postal addresses, phone numbers, e-mail addresses, etc. of the references who are contacted by the employers to justify the information furnished by the candidate in the application blank. A candidate's academic records, professional experience, honesty and integrity to the society, and the organization where one works are verified by the authority of the recruiting organization.

But often the references supplied by the candidates promote biased information. Therefore, the selectors search for such references whose names are not given by the salespeople but who are quite known for their expertise and behaviour of the recruiting candidates. Previous employers in this regard are the best references to obtain actual information of the candidates. Even customers previous organizations can share valuable information about the candidates.

Medical Examination

Medical examination is a part of the selection process to check the physical ability and stamina of a salesperson. Selling is a strenuous activity involving extensive travelling and visiting numerous customers. Vitality and tact are needed to cope with the stresses of the highly dynamic nature of the selling jobs. Therefore, the organization asks the initially selected sales recruits to go for medical examinations such as height and weight measurements, blood pressure, ECG test, ENT test, urine test, neuro-psychiatric test, etc. Medical examinations are important to ensure that the candidate is not physically disabled, mentally disordered, has ailments of the heart, has respiratory troubles, is addicted to drugs, etc. The disqualified candidates are simply rejected from the preliminary selected salespeople.

Job Offer

The candidates who are finally selected are provided call letters or appointment letters that are handed personally or sent by post to the respective candidates. In these letters, they are informed about their selection and asked to complete formalities before joining. Upon production of documents and scrutiny of the same, the candidates are asked the suitable dates for joining. It also carries details about the job title, terms and conditions of the organization, and salary structure.

9.8 SOCIALIZATION—AN IMPERATIVE

Socialization is a process by which the new recruits acquire culture and values which already prevail among the working class of the organization. The process starts as soon as the selected candidates join the firm and learn about the norms, values, and customs of the organization and start behaving in a way that is quite consistent with the behaviour of the employees of the organization. It also involves an employee finding an identity within it, both physically and psychologically. Socialization finds meaning when the employee finds recognition through the following:

(a) Accomplishment of tasks assigned to him

(b) Acceptability within the group

(c) Performance of tasks that prompts the organization to achieve its goals

(d) When an employee becomes a complete 'person–organization fit', i.e., the employee is comfortable working in the company and the company heads are also happy with the performance of their employees. It is also important for the employee to like his job profile. This is applicable to a salesperson who starts working in a company.

Socialization process, in fact begins before an employee joins a company. Getting enough information about the company and the jobs to perform, skills to demonstrate, and efficiency to exhibit are the sole prerogatives of socialization. Indeed, during the final phase of intensive interview, the interviewers should apprise projective employees about all these characteristics so that the candidate gets time to preview the new organizational environment. Reputed organizations (e.g., American Express, P&G, etc.) pick students from high-grade business schools for summer internships. The objective is to acclimatize those students with the organization before providing the job offer. Researches reveal that more an employee accustoms with the company and its culture, the greater will be the job involvement and more the job satisfaction.

The general trend of hiring an employee is to appoint him on probationary basis for six months to one year before being confirmed in a job. The objective is to provide the new employee some time to know, understand, and become comfortable in the working environment. This even helps organizations to eliminate the long-term risk of hiring a wrong (or misfit) candidate. Once the socialization of the candidate is successfully completed, the groundwork for conducive and productive working relationship is said to have been established.

Rookie salespeople are sent for training and development immediately after the selection. During this session, trainees are asked to attend classroom lectures, on-the-job programmes where the new recruits find ample scope to know the organizational culture and job situations, and their specific roles to contribute to the organization's progress. Therefore, it is also said that socialization is a continuing process until the total match between the employee and the organization happens, otherwise, a cent per cent involvement and commitment from the employee is not achievable.

So, through socialization, the organization presents a clear picture of its expectations from a salesperson. The salesperson also gets an opportunity to understand the exact nature and task of the job to perform. Senior managers ought to extend efforts to project the cultural insights of the organization that transcends across the management, working community, and the stakeholders of the organization and tries to flow the same ideology among the new employees too.

Socialization occurs in three phases as follows:

(a) Pre-entry socialization
(b) Onset of socialization
(c) Person–Organization fit

The stage begins with the appearance of the candidate for the final interview and the psychological tests for the new job. As the process of selection proceeds towards the final stage, the candidate starts thinking about the possible environmental situations in the new set up and undergoes mental preparation of how to adjust with it.

This is further aided by information gathering. First-hand information given by the interviewers during interviews and secondary sources of information such as friends or any acquaintances working in the organization, internet search, business reports, annual reports, etc. may provide sufficient inputs to the prospective employee to know about the recruiting firm. Candidates, who get all these cues, start to compare and moderate their personal goals and values with that of the organization so that at the encountering phase difficulties of assimilation can be minimized. The effort of the candidates to pre-socialize get intense as soon as they receive the call letter to join. This entire process is known as pre-entry job preview [stage (a)].

Actual socialization [(stage (b)] sets forth when the new recruits steps in the organization and confronts (i) new organizational environment, (ii) new job situation, (iii) new peers and subordinates, and (iv) new managerial functionaries. The company usually has a policy to prepare the trainees through training them particularly for green horn salespeople. The freshers get a reasonable time to induce themselves in the new business atmosphere. In the process, they acquire knowledge on the contexts and contents of the job, learn technical and social skills, and develop interpersonal relationship skills. So, mentoring gets underway when they are engaged in a training session. The act of socialization is part of mentoring with the inculcation of knowledge, skill, attitude, culture, and behaviour that the salespeople must inherit to think the organization as their second home.

Some companies come out with interesting programmes of socialization to help new employees adjust within the organization. One of these types is presented below in Box 9.2.

Box 9.2　Interesting programme of socialization

Trainees are divided into small groups and a game like treasure hunt is organized. The treasure is positioned at different locations of the city or the organization and the groups of trainees are given a set of clues to try and find it. These set of clues send the trainees to different parts of the city or departments to find the answers, which give them an opportunity to not only use their intellect but also meet different employees of the organization.

In this process, the newly appointed candidates have already learnt a lot about the organization, as well as, each other.

Finally the integration [[stage (c)] begins between the salespeople and the organization. Salespeople start to feel a part of the organization. The organization believes them to be the insiders of the business. Salespeople become comfortable with the new situations. Employers start reposing faith on them. A salesperson on being placed is given an opportunity to fit in a new territory. The salesperson is made aware of the rank, power, status, aims and objectives, boundary of operations, sales targets, etc.

So, socialization ends with the arousal of the sense of confidence and trust on the job and the organization per se in the minds of the salespeople. An effective socialization makes a salesperson feel at ease in the new organization.

SUMMARY

Selection is a process of choosing the best from the potential applicants who appear for the interview for a job. It is a process of eliminating the less fit candidates as compared to the better ones. It is a vital process for any organization which is true for the selection of salespeople also. If wrongly conducted, it can lead to huge loss of money, time, and effort. Steps in the process of selection are screening résumé, application blanks, initial interview, intensive interview, psychological testing, reference checks, medical examination, and job offers. Curriculum vitae and application blanks are two important means to gather first-hand impression of the candidates. Application blanks are more precise than vitae because they are company-prepared standardized formats for recording all necessary information on the candidates that the company sees to judge the suitability of the candidates with respect to the particular job.

Interview is a procedure to conduct an oral interactive session with the candidates. Interviews are of four types, namely structured interview, unstructured interview, semi-structured interview, and stress interview. Interview leads to the selection of candidates through initial interview, as well as, intensive interview. Psychological tests are unparallel to uncover talents and skills of the salespeople that are not possible to find through direct personal interviews. Four major psychological tests are intelligence tests, aptitude tests, personality tests, and achievement tests.

Assessment centre is an intensive-testing situation where ten to twelve candidates are asked to simulate real life sales situation. Reference checks are crucial to verify the authenticity of the information given by the candidates. Medical examinations are undertaken to check the physical and mental dis-

(Contd)

(Contd)

abilities of the candidates. Socialization is a process of assimilating newly selected employees with the organizational culture, customs, norms, and values.

Socialization takes place in three stages. These are pre-entry socialization, onset of socialization, and person–organization fit.

KEY TERMS

Application Blanks Application blanks are designed by a company for applicants to fill in order to check a candidate's background and personal profiles that best fits the company's requirement for initial screening of the candidates.

Assessment Centres Assessment centres are intensive testing situations where ten to twelve candidates are asked to perform in a situation that simulates a real world sales situation.

Curriculum Vitae Curriculum vitae are personal data-sheets that applicants submit with the applications for the job

Interview Interview is an interactive session between at least two people with the aim of obtaining as much information about the interviewee as possible and judge if the candidate is qualified enough for the post or not.

Psychological Tests Psychological tests help to uncover the talents of the candidates to explore a information on a person's aptitude and mental ability that remain uncovered during the personal interview.

Selection Selection is the process of choosing the right employees for the organization.

Semi-structured Interview Semi-structured interview allows the interviewer to ask questions based on an outline of specific issues to be discussed and is prepared before the interview begins.

Socialization Socialization is a process by which the new recruits acquire the culture and values which already prevail amongst the employees of the organization.

Stress Interview Stress interview is an interview situation planned to put the candidates in a psychologically stressed situation to observe how they act in such situations.

Structured Interview Structured interview uses a list of questions that are asked to the candidates during the interview in the same pattern and sequence.

Unstructured Interview Unstructured interview involves discussion between the interviewer and the interviewee on various issues not following any checklist of questions or pre-assigned sequence of questions.

CONCEPTUAL THINKING QUESTIONS

1. Distinguish between recruitment and selection. How is selection a vital function in an organization? State its relevance for the selection of the right salespeople.
2. Briefly state the steps of the selection process.
3. Distinguish between personal vitae and application blanks. Which one is more effective to the organization?
4. Define interview. What are its types?
5. What are the qualities of a potential sales candidate being judged before selection?
6. How can candidates project a sound impression in front of the interview board?
7. What are psychological tests? How are they useful for selection?
8. What is the importance of reference check?
9. What is socialization of a salesperson? Why is it important? How does it take place?

CRITICAL REVIEW QUESTIONS

1. A new sales recruit is hired from a competitive organization. He has an experience of five years in the previous organization and has proved himself as a successful salesperson. He is advised to contact the major customers of the previous organizations and distract them from the products of the competitors. The objective is to persuade them to switch over to the present organization. Put yourself in the shoes of the sales recruit and comment on how you would react to such a situation.

2. You, being a sales representative working in an organization for last two years appear for an interview in a business firm. You possess good academic records. After twenty minutes of interview, you are told on your face that as a salesperson you are good for nothing. How would you respond?

PROJECT ASSIGNMENT

Contact placement officers of two reputed B-schools and collect information on the following:

(a) Name of the school
(b) Address
(c) Number of students in the final semester
(d) Name of the specializations offered and the number of students in each
(e) What were the placement situations last year
(f) Number of companies visited for campus interview last year
(g) Management specializations on demand from the recruiters. Write in order of demand.
(h) Dates of campus interviews this year.

Be present on one or two dates of interview. Interact with the students after they come out of the interview board. Based on the responses, prepare an interview questionnaire.

Note down the responses of a sample of students. Contact some professionals and academicians in respective specializations of the management field and request them to understand the best answers of the questions. Then compare and contrast the responses of the students and experts and do a qualitative evaluation of the students of how they performed in interviews You can choose IIM and any UGC-recognized university running an MBA programme to conduct the survey.

REFERENCES

Dessler, Gary (2005), *Human Resource Management,* Pearson Prentice-Hall, New York.

Dessler, Gary (2007), *Human Resource Management,* PHI, New Delhi.

Kumar, A. and N. Meenakshi (2006), *Marketing Management,* Vikas Publishing House Pvt. Ltd, New Delhi.

McMurry, Robert. N. and S. James Arnold (1968), *How to Build a Dynamic Sales Organization,* McGraw-Hill Co., New York.

Spiro (2008), *Management of a Sales force,* Irwin/McGraw-Hill, Boston, Massachusetts.

Spiro, R.L., W.L. Stanton, and G.A. Rich (2008), *Management of a Sales Force,* Tata McGraw-Hill Publishing Company Limited, New Delhi.

http://www.referenceforbusiness.com/management/EM-Employee-Screening-and-Selection. html#ixzz0wkPo8kty, accessed on 16 August 2010.

===== **CASE STUDY** =====

Narratives of an Interview Session

The company *Trogers Engineering Ltd* is planning to recruit a few senior sales executives to look after the marketing of injection moulding machines. Below is an excerpt of an interview session.

Question 1: Introduce yourself.

Answer: I am Ashok Chandra. I was born and brought up in Chandigarh. I am a science graduate. I have completed my MBA with specialization in marketing from S.N. College of Commerce and Management, New Delhi. Currently, I am working with Eskon Engineering Pvt. Ltd, New Delhi as a junior sales executive for the last five years.

Question 2: What motivated you to apply to our company?

Answer: Well, I saw your advertisement in *The Times of India*. Since then, I have an urge to apply to your esteemed company for a number of reasons. First, my present selling job has stabilized to a great extent because in the area, New Delhi, where I have been currently serving has reached a level of saturation. The scope of new customer development has lessened. It impacts adversely to my incentives from commissions earned. Second, the present salary that I draw is not satisfactory considering the number of years of experience I have. In this regard, your advertisement attracted me. Third, I want to function in more number of sales territories which I am not able to fulfil in my present company.

Question 3: What makes you think that you are suitable for this position?

Answer: Sir, I can furnish some salient causes to prove my worth in this position. First of all, I have more than five years of experience in the related field. After working for this long, I desire to be promoted to a senior position. My present company does not show any interest to my promotion. In fact, a few junior executives queue up for promotions every year, yielding in unhealthy competition amongst us. Last but not the least, I have heard that the working atmosphere in your company is quite congenial and the opportunity to grow is very high.

Question 4: How can you contribute to our organization?

Answer: As a junior sales executive, I have closely watched senior managers and executives and learnt their supervisory operations and leadership styles. Moreover, I can utilize my knowledge and experience in selling to develop new customers and maintain relations with the present ones too. I possess a great deal of customer relationship skill which I can utilize for the retention of customers. If I get a chance, I will leave no stone unturned to contribute positively for the sales turnover of the company.

(Contd)

(Contd)

Question 5: What makes you feel qualified for this position?

Answer: Well, I think that I have the desired qualifications which you have mentioned in your advertisement. I have five years of experience in the field of marketing of moulding machines. In the process, I have also prepared a significant customer base by my own efforts. I have also developed an ingenious persuasive capacity and customer relationship skills that are essential for personal selling in present day. In fact, I have a good rapport and personal relationship with many customers.

Question 6: If you are asked to utilize your present customer base in the favour of our organization, how will you feel?

Answer: Well, this is a question of ethical importance. The present customers that I have generated are of my present company. I should not act in a way that harms the image of that organization. In fact, it is a matter of credibility and my personal image in the industry. If I join your organization, I will again work towards developing a marketing network where new customers would join our business. But, if the situation is such that our quality and price of the products are not competitive and do not excel over others, in future, I would approach my present customers as well. Healthy competition is good for the industry as such.

Question 7: Your esteem for your present organization is high. Then why are you thinking of leaving it?

Answer: Sir, I have cited my reasons earlier. Above all, I am not getting many opportunities to utilize the potential that I have. Therefore, I am looking for a change.

Question 8: How would you analyse the present business opportunity of plastics moulding machine?

Answer: Sir, The demand for plastics is increasing at a rapid rate. As you know, the prices of metals are steadily on the rise and it has been proved that plastics are gradually replacing metals in many applications such as automobiles, aircrafts, luggage, writing aids, toys, etc. Moreover, a report from the Plastics Manufacturing Association reveals that there is a growth of a whopping 8 per cent in plastics manufacturing units every year. So the situation has escalated the demand of plastics moulding machines. Also, import dependence of moulding machines is reducing as Indian firms are getting technologically strong to manufacture moulding machines indigenously. So, the plastics moulding machine has a great future ahead.

Question 9: How do you see the overall industrial climate in India?

Answer: Well, at present, India is one of the strongest developing nations in the industrial climate. India has been progressing in the businesses

(Contd)

of steel, cement, fertilizer, food grains, defence equipments, cars, two wheelers, steadfastly. India, being the second largest nation in the globe in terms of population, has an enviable consumer base, burgeoning middleclass as well as affluent segments. Demands for FMCGs, consumer durables, real estates, health care, and tourism products are increasing exponentially.

India is also an attractive market for telecom and education sectors. During recessionary phase, which is still hovering to some extent, India was the least affected nation because of the huge consumer demands within and strong money and capital market structures. So, the industrial scenario of India is very bright.

Question 10: What are your weak points?

Answer: Sir, I should not hesitate to state that I have a tendency to repose faith in a person very soon which often puts me in trouble. Secondly, sometimes I have to compromise with a number of odds in my family life due to the hectic nature of my profession. Thirdly, I often feel distressed thinking of the plights of thousands of have-nots in our society but I cannot do anything for them.

Question 11: What are your career goals?

Answer: Well, I am trying my best to move upwards in my sales career. I want to improve and achieve much more than what I already have. I intend to see myself in the top-level managerial rank. I want to be at the helm of the marketing department of a company. Lastly, I dream to be the CEO of a company.

Discussion Questions

1. Critically review the responses of Mr Chandra and draw his personality profile.
2. Analyse the above situation and identify the weak responses, if any. Provide a better response to these weak responses.
3. Comment on the probability of his selection in the new company.

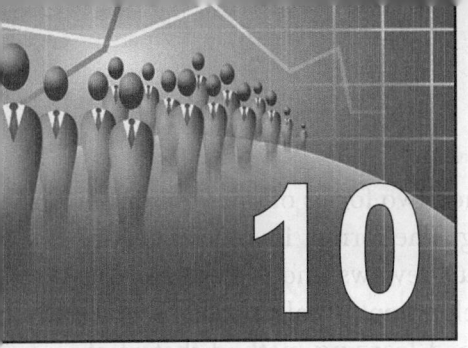

10 Sales Training

LEARNING OBJECTIVES

After reading this chapter, you will be able to

- understand the meaning, objective, and importance of sales training programmes
- understand the benefits of sales training
- explain the steps and ways to design a training programme
- appreciate the importance of place, duration, and budget on training
- identify the various training methods suitable for sales force training
- appreciate the effectiveness of the sales training programme

10.1 TRAINING

Training is an activity to derive the best possible efforts from an employee that contributes successfully to the performance of a job in an organization. It is a method to induct skills, knowledge, and attitudes amongst new or present employees with a view to extract needful performance from them. Salespeople are trained to develop their selling abilities with a view to sell the products and the services of a company and to reach the expected sales target. A newly recruited sales manager is trained to oversee the sales operations, manage sales force, and achieve predetermined sales objectives. So, the basic objective of a training programme is to convert the recruit into a productive employee.

Rao (2009) defined training as the act of increasing the knowledge and skill of an employee for doing a particular job. In fact, training churns out the employee's knowledge, skill, behaviour, aptitude, and attitude towards the requirements of the job and the organization.

Armstrong (2001) termed training as the formal and systematic modification of behaviour through learning which occurs as a result of education, instruction, development, and planned experience. Training is an investment to enable people to perform to the best of their abilities.

Havaldar and Cavale (2008) iterated sales force training as an effort that an employer makes to provide salespeople with job-related knowledge, skills, attitudes, and culture that should result in improved performance on sales, productivity, and profits.

Johnson et al. (1994) categorically distinguished two forms of sales training—formal sales training and informal sales training. The former involves categorically planned sales training programme, systematic reviews, and evaluations. The latter involves the continuous professional development of salespeople.

Sales training is a step-by-step programmemed learning method that, if effectively conducted, generates a sequence of behaviour from the salespeople leading to a smooth performance of the desired sales activities.

An effective training programme should be flexible enough to cater to training to all types of salespeople. These include people who are good, mediocre or comparatively less talented; without making any differential treatment in terms of attention or psychological support. But, it is welcome if a satisfactory training process arranges special allowances to uplift the knowledge and skill of less merited employees during training. Here, lies the need for experienced trainers who can keep a watch on the conduction of the training programmes so that equitable treatment is ensured. At the same time, training under the experienced trainers can make the less potential employees improve to a great extent.

Training is different from development. Training helps the employees to learn the actual methods and skills to perform a task whereas development means learning not only the knowledge and skills for the job but it also leads to an improvement in the mental faculties and personal characteristics. Chhabra (2002) used the term training as regards to teaching of specific skills whereas development denoted the overall development of the personality of an employee.

The two broad objectives of sales training are as folows:

(a) To make salespeople totally fit for the job for which they have been selected

(b) To motivate them to improve their sales productivity and earn profits for the organization

Some of the specific objectives of a sales training session are presented in Exhibit 10.1.

Exhibit 10.1   Objectives of sales training

(a) To supplement knowledge, skill, attitude, and culture to the salespeople that are consistent with the requirements of the job

(b) To arouse a deep interest in the job that finally sets in high sales force motivation

(c) To instill a sense of job involvement and commitment in the employee towards their job

(d) To awaken a feeling of job security and zeal for the advancement in job

(e) To develop a positive attitude towards the job and amiable feelings towards peers, subordinate staff, and higher authorities

---

(Contd)

(Contd)

(f) To reduce the turnover of the salespeople. In fact, building a sense of trust and belong-ingness reduces the attrition rate of the salespeople

(g) To fulfil the manpower requirements of an organization in both quantity and quality

(h) To prevent the obsolescence of skill and knowledge of the current employees when they start to under-perform

(i) To bestow a participative work culture amongst employees. In the selling context, this creates the right chord for team selling

(j) To reduce the level of supervision

(k) To reduce the cost of sales operations

(l) To help the employees gain self-confidence and morale that finally prepare them to be self-starters in many future sales assignments

(m) To help the salespeople to understand the nature and characteristics of the business environment where they are to operate. It includes understanding the nature of competition, market developments, social customs of the customers, legal conditions, etc.

(n) To teach salespeople the importance and ways of developing long-term relationships with the customers

(o) To teach salespeople how to beat competition. They learn the strategic components of personal selling

(p) To know how to increase the sales volume, sales productivity, and profit margins

(q) To learn the right working environment and habits required to be successful. In fact, this helps them to identify (i) their sales territories, (ii) the target markets and customers, (iii) their competitors, (iv) how to prepare a sales plan, (v) ways to conduct a sales operation, (vi) how to make sales calls, (vi) how to approach prospective customers, (vii) how to handle their customers, (viii) how to prepare sales reports, (ix) how to present sales reports in the sales meetings, and (x) how to maintain sales budgets, etc.

(r) To reduce the chances of detraining. Detraining involves learning wrong things on previous occasions and experiences

10.2   SALES FORCE TRAINING—A STRATEGIC ORIENTATION

Sales training is a systematic procedure to prepare salespeople with techniques, skills, and the right temperament for higher proficiency in their jobs. Through the process of training, salespeople learn conceptual skills, persuasive ability, communication skills, problem-solving abilities, analytical power, and many more to help them perform in lieu with the expectations of their organization.

Effective sales training is a part of strategic marketing plan. In today's cutting edge business climate, unless salespeople develop customer development plans, high demonstrative abilities, strong persuasive capacities, and long-lasting customer relationship skills, an organization cannot sustain in the competition.

Each selling situation is unique in nature as customers vary. In case, one cus-tomer hinges more on after-sales service, the other might demand extension of credit terms. As salespeople are spokespersons on behalf of the organizations, they need to understand the customers. Customers are more interested in those products that not only solve their problems that seem more beneficial as compared to the competitor's product. It is important for them to learn and understand the distinction between different selling situations. This enables them to serve customers in a manner that not only fulfils the needs of the customers effectively but also becomes cost effective and profit making for their firms. Salespeople, in some cases, work as a team where interpersonal skills are necessary. Training in such cases imparts this skill to the salesperson to function as an empathetic team member.

Training should be organized to enlighten the trainees with the strategic aspects of selling. It helps them to develop the ability to understand the requirements of their customers. It also aids them to choose the right customer-specific selling strategies which would help them to generate a win-win situation for both the company as well as the customers. It is also important for the product or the service to go through a continuous technological innovation to stay commendably in the market. If the company's offer does not keep pace with the demands of the market, the result could be horrendous for the company. Hence, it is important to have a strategically oriented salesperson who can track down the upswings and the downswings of the market and inform the company about the importance of changes in the offer along with their associated features.

Sales training also helps the existing salespeople, particularly, when the company faces a decline in the sales of a product for reasons linked to none other than the performance of the salesperson himself. Lack of motivation or complacency might be the reasons that should be identified by the firm and sorted out. Under such circumstances the salespeople are given retraining to gain their lost morale and confidence.

10.3 BENEFITS OF SALES TRAINING

Sales training imparts many benefits to the salespeople and the firm. This is possible only when the training programme rightly identifies the training needs and the firm designs a suitable programme to respond to it. The following list furnishes the salient benefits of a well-planned training programme:

1. It hones the right knowledge, skill, attitude amongst salespeople necessary to accomplish sales and bring in an improved sales performance.
2. It helps to develop the functions and activities in the selling jobs.
3. It helps to develop objectivity in the thinking process of a salesperson and nurture an analytical mind on the observed phenomena.

4. It tutors them to balance their time, effort, and money while planning and executing a sales operation.

5. It educates the salespeople on how to inform the customers about the product/service features, benefits, and usages.

6. It teaches them the language of competition and how it may affect the company.

7. It inducts a sense of competitiveness, spirit and vigour amongst salespeople so that they remain steady in awkward selling situations, such as a sudden loss of genuine customers to a competitor.

8. It motivates them to work hard and counsels them to be self-starters in the absence of any supervision.

9. It encourages them not to break any tie with the company.

10. It inculcates flair of managerial task and responsibility amongst future sales managers.

10.4 SALES TRAINING—A PROCEDURAL DISCOURSE

Like recruitment and selection, training is also a managerial function. The management is responsible to induct, socialize, train, develop, and make new employees who can work in the company. Training, as discussed earlier, is an organized process to extract the best from the employees and to use it for the success of the organization. Sales training is a systematic process consisting of a number of steps to achieve training goals. Figure 10.1 exhibits the steps of a training process.

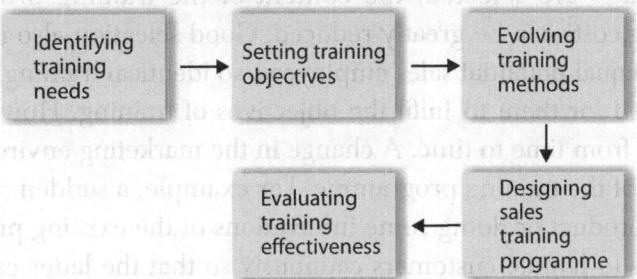

Figure 10.1   Steps in training

The steps are discussed as follows:

Identifying Training Needs

This is the starting point for designing an effective training programme. Identifying the training needs refer to determine the weaknesses of new as well as existing employees that affect the performance negatively and to find out the gap between the actual and the desired performance of the current employees. It aims to identify the specific knowledge, skills, attitudes, and behaviour that are lacking amongst employees, particularly at the entry point. Identifying training needs, therefore, entails analysing the latches amongst employees that prevent the organization to attain its goals.

The strengths and weaknesses of the employees are adjudged against the parameters of job descriptions and job specifications that are set before the recruitment process begins in the organization. Therefore, one can say that training guidelines are outlined based on the criteria contained in the job descriptions and job specifications. For example, a job description for a senior sales executive demands socialization and motivation as the major areas of the training programme rather than knowledge and skill development. But for rookie salespeople, training starts from scratch where knowledge on the business environment, company, job, peers and management, technical skills, personality development, etc. are given a major thrust. Personality correlates positively with communication skills and therefore, nurturing of communication skills is important to develop personality.

Training also bridges the gap between what salespeople know and what they need to know. A job analyst collects information from the newly engaged sales hires through interaction or observations of their selling behaviour on a trial run. Psychological tests such as aptitude or personality tests also help in providing the dearth areas of the salespeople.

Selection of a salesperson is also very important because if appropriate candidates are selected, the content of the training programme as well as training costs can be greatly reduced. Good selection also means inviting more or less equal potential sales employees, so identical training programmes can be prepared for them to fulfil the objectives of training. However, training needs to vary from time to time. A change in the marketing environment can alter the course of the training programme. For example, a sudden rise in the price level of the product or doing some innovations of the existing product requires sales persons to handle customers cautiously so that the latter can admire the cause for such changes.

The company, sometimes, feels the need for retraining of the existing employees to cope with unknown market situations. For current salespeople, if performance analysis indicates any discrepancy between the desired and actual sales performance, it is corrected through retraining. Exhibit 10.2 illustrates some points of the sales training need assessment programme of a large multinational firm, Avon.

> ### Exhibit 10.2   Avon's unique sales training programme
>
> *Avon's sales* training programme is unique in the sense that it designs to cater training needs for each type of salesperson. The training programme includes in-person training, job aids, self-paced courses, virtual classes, and e-learning. The company uses a combination of instructional strategies and technologies to buttress the training programmes. With this, the company is able to reduce training-related costs, increase the availability of training and access to experts, and make training more accessible. In fact, the training aims to enhance revenue generation through the knowledge of how to increase (a) the size of the salespeople, (b) number of customers served, and (c) the size of the orders of the representatives.
>
> *Source:* The Brandon Hall Research, 'Focus on Sales Training', http://www.barndon-hall.com, accessed on 25 January 2010.

Setting Sales Training Objectives

Assessment of training needs is the starting point of setting the training objectives. Training objectives are formulated on the basis of the types of product or service to sell, nature of selling jobs, types of salespeople that undergo training, types of customers to deal with, and environmental conditions that the salespeople will confront.

Suppose, the product to be sold is a fire extinguisher. This is an emergency product, where the salespeople need to teach the customers the importance of the product and necessity of owning it for one's safety. Here, it is important for the seller to know all the legal and safety norms, technological developments, etc. of the product. This would help them sustain against the competition better. The nature of selling job also depends upon the type of customer the product is to be sold to. For an industrial or institutional customer, the urgency of having the fire extinguisher and having more than one in number is immediate. At the same time, the business potential with such customers is high. So knowledge, experience, and persuasive skills of the salesperson become very vital to facilitate the increase in sale as well as customer size.

Sales training objectives are laid down to make salespeople comfortable with different selling situations. Indeed, they should gear up to make customers feel that they are getting value for money by taking purchase decisions. Moreover, they are also expected to put a positive image of the company in front of the customers. And hence, it is important that the salespeople should learn the company's core missions, values, philosophies, and goals during training so that during practical selling, they can raise the company's image high by popularizing the company's cherished image.

Before assigning territories to salespeople, they should also learn how to manage and handle their territories. So, understanding basic principles of management and organizing capacity is also a part of the training objectives. Again, measuring the market potential, sales forecasting, mapping out sales strategies, analysing the strengths and weaknesses of competitors, etc. are the operational aspects of sales management that salespeople need to learn during training.

Training objectives should be goal-directed and performance-oriented. Successful accomplishments of training objectives allude the generation of a well-trained salespeople who require no major supervision or management control to perform their jobs. Moreover, they emerge to be polite, emotionally balanced, and enthusiastic human beings who can apply their best potentials. At the same time, they can derive job satisfaction both from the company's internal environment (job context) and sales performance (job content).

Setting training objectives require deft handling from the sales managers. Right training objectives can serve the purpose of the firm to produce the right type of salespeople who bring success to the firm through the 'right performance'. Besides, these objectives are formulated to develop competence among salespeople while using different marketing tools such as customer-relationship management software, sales forecasting techniques, marketing research, etc. Training objectives are also purported for salespeople to learn certain functions such as planning, organizing, directing, and controlling with a view that they will be entrusted to manage the sales territories and become the future managers of the organizations. Setting up the training objectives is the guide post for designing the sales training programmes.

Deciding on the Training Methods

Once the company has decided on the objectives of the training, they need to evolve appropriate training methods to fulfil them. A suitably devised training method also entails how the training will be conducted. For example, for imparting knowledge about a product or service, lecture methods are most useful. To understand the applications of a product, demonstration is an ideal method. Places where salespeople work as team, methods such as group discussion or role playing are quite useful.

A company can choose either a single training method or a set of methods to carry out the training sessions. It is important to note that the methods chosen should be coherent with the training objectives and should be executable as well. For instance, financial resources, infrastructural support, cost effectiveness of training, etc. are major points to consider while deciding about the economic viability of training. Keeping the training objectives in mind, few training methods are initially chosen and training costs along with its consulting effectiveness of different methods are compared before a right training method(s) is suggested. The details of the training methods are discussed in subsection 10.7.

Designing the Training Programme

After analysing the training needs, determining objectives of training, and suggesting training methods, designing the training programme is a critical step for the success of training. The benefits of sales training cannot be achieved, if there is a flaw in its programme or is not correctly laid down to satisfy any one of the training needs. The essential aspects of designing a sales training programme are depicted in Figure 10.2. A training designer should always keep in mind the following facets while designing a programme to achieve best results.

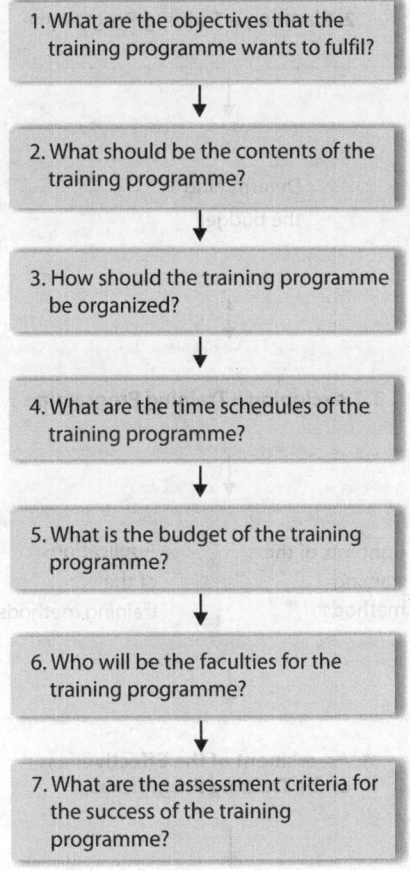

Figure 10.2   Essentials of a training programme

Based on the issues of the training programme, a full-fledged training programme is laid out. Figure 10.3 portrays the structure of a well-planned training programme.

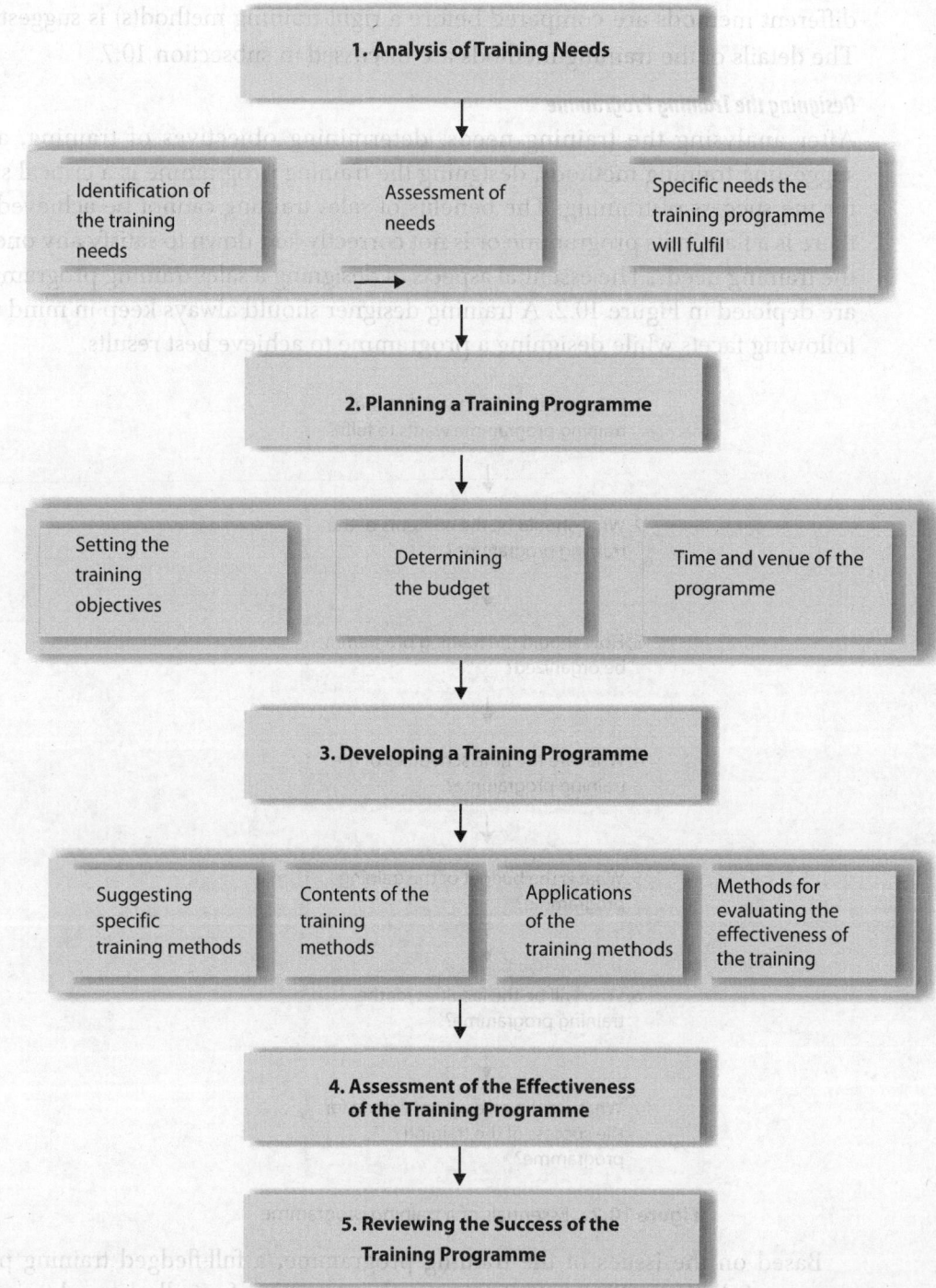

Figure 10.3   Structure of a training programme

Career Cycle

Planning a training programme is preceded by accurately analysing the training needs. This is required, both, for newly recruited salespeople and employees already working at different stages of their career cycles. Apart from this, it is important for sales managers to track the movements of their employees along their career cycles. A career cycle is a stepwise progression of the career of a salesperson covering four stages. These stages are initial training or grooming, development, maturity, and diminution. Figure 10.4 depicts the shape of the career cycle.

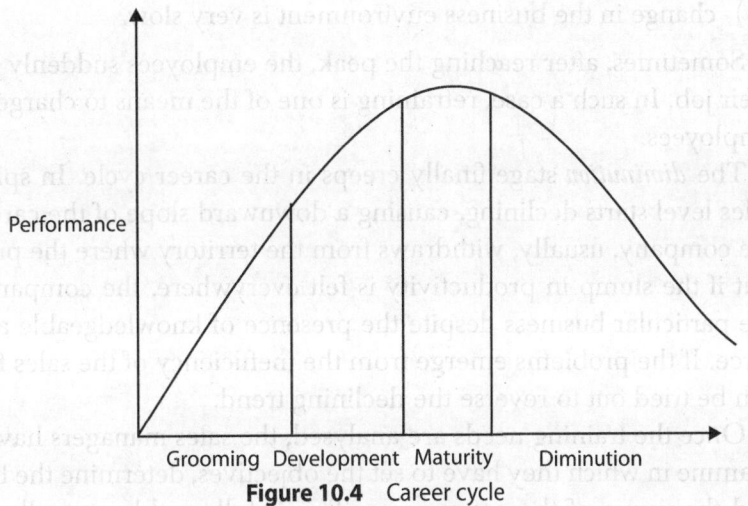

Figure 10.4 Career cycle

Grooming is the starting phase of a salesperson's career. It begins with an orientation of the salesperson with the company. During this stage, the salespeople are made aware of the corporate mission, their objectives, marketing goals, products/services portfolio, products/services to sell, markets to cover, selling expenses to incur, selling techniques to follow, sales budget, performance criteria, etc. The time period for this orientation depends on the type of salespeople hired (experienced or new), company training policy, budget allocation for training, types of customers to interact with (say, industrial customers), market situation to confront (say, oligopolistic market), etc.

After his induction/orientation, a salesperson is assigned a sales territory and asked to engage in the sales operation. As the salesperson starts generating sales, sales productivity begins to move upward. However, the salespeople need to monitor and control their performances closely. Whenever faults are identified, corrective actions must be taken by managers. This is the *development* stage where a person gets to know about his job profile and learns from his mistakes.

Maturity refers to a salesperson reaching the peak of their performance. Further increase of productivity in their performance is not observed. The sales level at this point remains steady. These problems occur with the old employees of the organization also. It happens when

(i) the market is saturated,

(ii) the market is not saturated, but no new customers are developed for the company,

(iii) intentions of the current customers are to continue business at the same volume as earlier, and

(iv) change in the business environment is very slow.

Sometimes, after reaching the peak, the employees suddenly loose interest in their job. In such a case, retraining is one of the means to charge up the existing employees.

The *diminution* stage finally creeps in the career cycle. In spite of all efforts, sales level starts declining, causing a downward slope of the career cycle. Here, the company, usually, withdraws from the territory where the problem is grave. But if the slump in productivity is felt everywhere, the company can liquidate the particular business despite the presence of knowledgeable and skilled sales force. If the problems emerge from the inefficiency of the sales force, retraining can be tried out to reverse the declining trend.

Once the training needs are analysed, the sales managers have to plan a programme in which they have to set the objectives, determine the budget, the time and the venue of the programme. This is followed by actually developing the training programme. During this phase, the manager must decide on the contents, applications, and methods for evaluating the effectiveness of the programme. Accessing the effectiveness and reviewing the success of the training programme completes the finalizing of the structure of the training programme.

Evaluating Training Effectiveness

Unless, a person evaluates the training process, it is difficult for anyone to judge the effectiveness of the programme. Also, this helps in coming up with a more comprehensive programme for the next time. This is discussed at the end of the chapter.

10.5 CONTENTS OF A TRAINING PROGRAMME

As discussed earlier, training the employees is a significant part to achieve success for any organization. Training, basically, covers the following:

(a) Product knowledge

(b) Company knowledge

(c) Knowledge on customers
(d) Knowledge on competition
(e) Sales techniques
(f) Industry orientation
(g) Management principles

Now we will discuss all these aspects one by one.

Product Knowledge

Salespeople learn about the attributes of the product that they are supposed to sell, including its characteristics, core and tangible features, production techniques and technology, technical specifications of the product, strengths and weaknesses of the competitor's products, product applications, customer benefits from the product use, selling features of the product, etc. Disseminating product information is a significant part of the selling message. However deft the sales presentation could be, lack of product knowledge can prove the entire effort futile. Today many salespeople store product information on laptops or notebook computers that they carry for meetings with the customers. This makes it easy for them to demonstrate the details of the product without much oral presentation.

Company Knowledge

A salesperson is made aware of the corporate histories, mission, goals and objectives, organizational structure, policies, strategies and procedures as a whole. Salespeople need to learn the workings and goals of the marketing departments. Training is also imparted on human resource policies, delegation of duties, tasks of the marketing functions, sales histories of the company, promotional policies, compensation schemes, etc. Trainees are also instructed regarding whom to report, whom to guide and whom to contact, whenever they find problems.

Knowledge about company definitely helps them to share company-related information with others. This is important because in the present scenario, the customers such as to know more and more about the company before they buy their product.

Knowledge on Customers

This is a crucial dimension which helps to attract customers, both prospective and present, towards the company's products/services. A thorough knowledge about the customers is essential for the salespeople to work out their selling approaches and optimize their selling efforts.

The purpose here is to sensitize the participants about the critical aspects of understanding the customers. Collecting information about the customer's name, addresses, and other demographic information, helps the salesperson in generating appropriate routing plans to meet them. In case these customers are organizations, knowing the details of the organizational demographics such as the type of organization, registered office, buying authorities of the organization, purchase criteria, etc. should be kept in mind to plan a win-win situation. Understanding the needs of the customers and the benefits they are looking forward to help in creating a step forward to building an appropriate conversation and rapport with them. It is always better for the salespeople to take a prior appointment with the prospective client. It gives a good impression.

After meeting the customer/client, the next important point to be kept in mind is to decide on the prospective procedure that could be used to sell to that particular group of customers. Understanding the personality of the customer along with identifying their ordering procedures, and order-closing procedures can help in building a lifelong relationship.

Also, it is always suitable for salespeople to do a proper follow up with the customers to make sure that they stay loyal to their company. Training programmes are designed to include making the salespeople aware about all these issues.

Knowledge on Competition

A salesperson should always know the products and services of the competitors, their prices, distribution schemes, promotional efforts, etc. They should be aware of the strengths and weaknesses of their products or services vis-à-vis that of the competitors. The more they are acquainted with the competitive offers, the more delicately they can establish superiority of their products. Also, it aids them to handle the competitive pressures easily and persuade the target customers not to switch over to the products of the competitors.

Selling Techniques

Salespeople should be aware of the important techniques to be used to be able to convert the prospects into customers. These are also needed to prolong the business with the existing customers. Through various training programmes, new sales recruits learn the art of prospecting, how to prepare before a sales presentation, knowing the techniques of the sales presentation, how to demonstrate product features and benefits, how to handle customer objections, how to close the sales, and how to build relations with customers. Moreover, how to make cold calls, preparation of time scheduling for customers meetings, preparation of route plans in a way that helps salespeople to meet customers with less travelling costs and time, recognition of a selling situation, sequencing the sales procedures are considered vital for the salesperson to know to achieve greater success.

Industry Orientation

It helps the salespeople acquire knowledge about any industry and the nature of the demand of products/services that is to be sold. This information also includes factors affecting customer behaviour, general economic conditions of the industry, legal and ethical issues of buying and selling conditions, and competitive environment. Technological development in related product or service field, innovations in sales force training and development, a brief idea about the size and location of the prospective and present customers, exposure to international market, if the company has any business or desires to foray in such markets in future, source of raw materials, information on suppliers, etc. are other types of information that can be shared. In fact, the objective should also render that the salespeople are knowledgeable about the industry-oriented information. This helps them become more confident, make more elaborate discussions, and share profuse information with the customers.

Exhibit 10.3 presents an example of LGEIL that brings in innovations in training programme for its sales cum service dealers. Apart from the proven quality of the product, the success of the company in a major way hinges on the development of its sales force.

Exhibit 10.3   LGEIL's innovative training programme

LG Electronics India Pvt. Limited (LGEIL), a renowned name in homes of many Indian families for consumer durables, rolled out an innovative training programme for the sales dealers called 'Sales-cum-Service' dealers (SSDs). In fact, the company has been conducting service training workshop that has focused on equipping the sales force with service knowledge. The objective is to serve consumers successfully and reach deep inside the country. The programme is designed to train, qualify, and authenticate their sales dealers.

Source: 'LG Introduces Training Program for Dealers', posted on November 05 2007 by itVAR news Staff, http:www.itvarnews.net/newsphp? = 6450, accessed on 25 January 2010.

Management Principles

Salespeople are expected to be the future managers of the company. So, they should learn the general management principles on planning, organizing, directing, and controlling functions. During management of territories, they need to apply management techniques and take a decision for effectively handling the territories. Besides, they also need to know the economic principles such as demand estimation, market forecasting techniques, inventory policies, queuing methods, statistical methods such as time series analysis, data analysis, etc. financial fundamentals such as profitability ration, sales turn over ration, sales expense ratio, etc.

Contents of the training programme should include all of the above discussed points for it to run successfully. They also vary from company to company. A brief outline of the general contents of the training programme that is usually followed by most of the firms is shown in Box 10.1.

Box 10.1   Training programme

Following are the contents of the training programme:

(a) Knowledge on the industry

(b) Knowledge on the company

(c) Knowledge the products/services that the company deals in

(d) Knowledge on customers

(e) Knowledge on competition

(f) Selling methods

(g) Territory development methods

(h) Territory management skills

(i) Persuasive communication skills

(j) Customer relationship skills

(k) Sales performance indicators

(l) Routing and scheduling techniques that include travelling plans and time management

(m) Managerial skills

(n) Legal and ethical aspects of selling

(o) Application of computers in selling

10.6   TRAINING PROGRAMME—TIME AND PLACE PERSPECTIVES

Training programme, as have been discussed earlier, is a programme which is developed in order to work towards achieving the set goals. It helps in getting the employees more motivated and willing to fulfil their objectives. Various companies design different kinds of training programmes for its employees for them to be efficient and achieve their targets. The type of training programme to be used is dependent on the time and place of conducting the programme.

Length of the Training Programme

The length of the training programme is an important decision area for the company. It principally depends upon the type of salesperson recruited (budding or moderately experienced salespeople), cost factor, urgency of selling situation, and availability of professional trainers. Generally, the company designs the training programme that runs from three months to one year depending on the management policy. Commonly, sales recruits are subjected to interviews or written examinations from time to time during training to decide on the effectiveness of the programme. They may be asked to show audio-visual presentations on sales cases or projects having associations with the future job assignments. Getting assured of the results, the training programme is completed.

Venue of the Training Programme

Location of the training programme depends on the company policy. The policy is guided by the availability of right infrastructure, financial supports, cost of the training programmes, efficient trainers, etc. Generally, the company chooses any one from the following two training programmes from the locational standpoint:

  (i) Centralized training programme
 (ii) Decentralized training programme
(iii) Combination of centralized and decentralized training

Centralized training programme All salespeople are asked to report to one particular location, say, the organization itself, the manufacturing plants, hotels or training centres or institutes. Location of the training programme depends on the company policy. The policy is guided by the availability of infrastructure, financial resources, cost of the training programme, availability of professional and qualified trainers, etc. In a centralized location, it is expected that substantial training aids such as spacious lecture rooms, instruction manuals, audio-visual aids, multimedia facilities are present.

This training is expensive as the company needs to arrange accommodation and transportation supports to the trainees. The advantage of such kind of training programme is that all the candidates are exposed to one training programme. So, they can be evaluated on common performance criteria. Audio-visual methods can present some simulated sales presentations. New recruits can listen to the experiences of successful salespeople, sales demonstration, etc.

Decentralized training programme This kind of a training programme is held in regional or field sales offices. Thrusts are given on 'on-the-job training', seminars, providing training instruction manuals to trainees. Field sales training widely uses decentralized training where trainees are sent to sales territories and training is given by field sales or territory managers during actual sales operations. Here, training methods are highly customized to suit the requirements of the territories.

This kind of training is less expensive because the regional or branch office conducts the training programme with lesser number of sales trainees. More scope of close interaction between the trainees and trainers is possible. But this has a number of disadvantages as well. First, the company may find it difficult to control the training programmes held in different locations. Second, the quality of the training programme may not be high because sales supervisors are busy with their work pressures. Third, differences in training–learning methods are obstacles to generate equally productive salespeople. Fourth, training expenses vary from one location to the other.

Combination of centralized and decentralized training programmes The best training programme is the one where centralized training equips the salespeople in-house to know the production process, R&D activities, human resource policies, organizational structure, etc. After completion of 'in-plant training', the sales recruits are sent to regional or branch offices to conduct 'on-the-job training' or 'field training'. In-house training provides a detailed knowledge and understanding of the selling job. They also learn the relations between sales jobs and sales performances. Furthermore, 'in-house training' develops knowledge and skills of the salespeople and help them to socialize with the organizational culture. Field training teaches them the application of knowledge and they get the opportunity to apply these skills which they have acquired during centralized training.

10.7 TRAINING METHODS—A DETAILED ILLUSTRATION

Selection of the right training method is vital. Before choosing a method, it is essential to know which method will offer the best skill and learning development to the trainees. The training method is also geared to generate the right attitude in the trainees that would enhance the acceptability of training.

The details of the training methods are explained below:

Lecture Methods

The lecture method, basically, presents the needed information on selling skills and techniques to the trainees. Sales trainees learn ideas about selling as a functional component, managerial practices of selling, different underlying problems of selling, creativity in selling, role of selling in cross-functional interaction, etc. A participative environment is created in the lecture method, where trainees can be actively involved by listening to the lectures, writing notes, asking questions, clearing doubts, and getting suggestions.

Often written materials and instruction manuals are handed to the participants. Some instructors take help of the audio-visual aids to animate the lecture sessions and arouse a deep interest among the trainees. Company executives, senior managers, professional trainers, guest lecturers with huge experience in the marketing discipline are invited to act as speakers in the lecture sessions.

Conference Training

Conference is a platform for discussing various issues on a topic. As a training medium, it provides the right ambience for interaction between the trainees and the trainers. It is a group meeting which has pre-planned items for discussion. The discussion can flow on multiple tracks revolving around the issue. The conference coordinator or the leader presents the connective link between these different points of discussion.

In sales training, conference method gives opportunity for an all-round discussion veering around specific product(s) or service(s) that sales trainees will sell in future. Sales management and territory management are also discussed in the conference proceedings. The entire session is controlled by a chairperson who sums up the discussion in the conference.

Case Study

Case study is a written description about a real life or hypothetical selling situation or a sales problem that is discussed in a classroom. The trainees have to sincerely listen to and understand the various issues in the case. After this, they need to relate to these issues with personal selling concepts and principles which they have already learnt before they take part in the case study. The case discussion tries to highlight the problem areas, diagnose the inputs of personal selling discipline and offer solutions to the problems. Salespeople are allowed to throw their views to gain confidence.

On-the-Job Training

On-the-job training (OJT) is a popular technique that gives opportunities to new employees to gather hands-on learning experience. In the selling context, newly recruited salespeople get a scope to observe the approaches of senior salespeople, sales supervisors when they interact with customers. These new salespeople are asked to minutely watch the discussion from where they can get an idea of how to deal with the present and prospective customers.

Next, the sales trainees are allowed to make sales calls in the presence of senior sales personnel. After the completion of calls, the seniors discuss the mistakes of the salespeople and advise on how to improve a specific sales situation. This, in fact, motivates the trainees to sell more, and learn from their faults.

Modern day training programmes are more interactive in nature. Particularly in the field such as sales, these newer methods have proved of immense use. Let us discuss some of these methods.

Audio-visual Oriented Training

These training methods are lively and interesting demonstration of films, power points, audio cassettes, videos, etc. It gives the trainees a chance to have a look at the charts, graphs, tables, slides, talk show, buyer–seller interaction, interview of a marketing expert or consultant, a meeting session with the dealers, some realistic buying–selling situations, etc. These methods, when integrated with lecture-based trainings, create a highly stimulating training environment where trainees get the opportunity to learn both theoretical and practical applications of selling.

Newly recruited salespeople are exposed to computer-based training (CBT), DVD systems or other multimedia applications that simulate unique buying–selling situations. These training devices, though expensive, are highly effective because of the practical orientation and the short learning time available. In fact, multimedia applications have revolutionized the simulated training methods where the sales trainees get advanced training through e-learning modules and e-performance support system (EPSS).

Videoconferencing is becoming popular today and is effective for long-distance communication. This training method combines video presentations and computer-aided questioning techniques. In this technique, questions are displayed on computers regarding how to manage a particular sales situation, how to take decisions in problem-oriented situations, etc. Web-based training and video conferencing are useful in a decentralized training technique where trainees stay geographically dispersed and both make possible the live demonstration combining audio and video effects.

Management Games

Computerized management games are used by some firms where trainees are divided into groups with each group having five to six participants. Games take place amongst these groups after creating a simulated marketplace situation. The competition judges the teams on the most effective decision taken on sales budget, selling expenses, sales turnover ratio, etc.

Role Playing

In role playing, an artificial environment of the realistic sales situation is created and salespeople are asked to sell a product to an imaginary prospect. Trainees are asked to assume the role of salespeople and prospects in rotations. So, the trainees find an opportunity to replicate the buying–selling session that they will face in real-life situations. Trainers closely monitor the session and guide the trainees on how to improve in different scenarios. The objective is to develop skills in trainees in managing and controlling the sales situations. Trainees also learn to handle problems.

10.8 EVALUATION OF THE TRAINING PROGRAMME—A PRACTICAL UNDERSTANDING

A training programme should be followed by a sound evaluation system to critically appraise the effectiveness of the training programme. In fact, evaluation is a part of the training programme. Armstrong (2001) viewed evaluation with respect to training as the comparison between the set objectives and the outcome of the training. Objectives are deterministic and outcomes are result-oriented behaviours. Armstrong termed objectives as criterion behaviour and outcomes as terminal behaviours.

A training programme has three important considerations to be kept in mind. These are monetary investment, time value of training, and magnitude of the training programme.

A return (outcomes) on investment on the training programme is the index of the monetary involvement. This can be studied by comparing the expected outcomes (say, the desired sales turnover for the first six months immediately after training) with actual sales performance. The sales turnover ratio is calculated to understand the return on investment.

The time value of training determines if the required change in knowledge and skill has been inducted within a fixed time period in a sales trainees or not. Time investment should be coupled with cost control to maximize value additions during training.

The magnitude of training programme encompasses the right training procedures and methods to become compatible with time limits and investment in training. Before setting an evaluation programme, four important questions are asked. These are the following:

1. What to measure? (e.g., communication efficiency)
2. How to measure? (e.g., interviewing the participants)
3. When to measure? (e.g., in the midst of the training programme or during on the job)
4. What conclusions to be drawn? This is vital because based on the reports of training, the company takes a decision on how to engage salespeople in the sales operations.

Kirkpatrick (1994) discussed the following four categories of training effectiveness measures. These are the following:

(a) Reaction
(b) Learning
(c) Behaviour
(d) Results

Reactions search for whether the training objectives are fulfilled in terms of lessons learnt. These can be better studied by interviewing the trainees or instructing them to fill in questionnaires specially designed for the purpose of evaluation.

Learning involves testing the trainees to know how much have they acquired from the training programmes. In other words, how much knowledge, skill and aptitude they have developed or absorbed from the training programmes. The measurement of success factors (the features which the trainee has acquired) say, job knowledge prior to the beginning of the training programme and after the training programme gives an indication of what has been counselled.

Behaviour means the outcome of the training programme that can be best judged by the changes in the behaviour of the trainee due to the training programme. The change in the behaviour can be judged from the job performance indexes. The sales supervisor can notice and bring to attention the change that can be seen in the behaviour of the trainee. Sometimes, customers also impart information on the behavioural changes of the salespeople. Information on these is helpful to appraise the effectiveness of the training programmes.

Results refer to whether the training programmes have improved the performance or not, based on some realistic measures of sales performance. Companies can, again, compare training outcomes against costs and checks whether the outcome surpasses their costs or not. Results are reflected through sales, profits, customers satisfactions, number of complaints received from the customers, customer retentions, customer relations, number of new customers developed, etc. These results are tracked down for a time period (usually one year) after the training programme to develop a better training module for the next year.

SUMMARY

Training is an activity to generate the best possible knowledge, skill, and attitude from new employees that contribute to the performance of the organization. So, it is an act of enhancing these attributes for carrying out the respective jobs successfully. Training is a systematic approach which is a part of the strategic marketing plan too.

Formal sales training includes planned sales training programme whereas informal sales training involves continuous development of salespeople on professional qualities.

The basic objective of sales training is to develop the all-round abilities of the salespeople so that they not only contribute to the job but also become psychologically involved with the organization. Sales training helps salespeople to do goal-directed efforts of which customer relationship building is an important part apart from generating target sales volume. The benefits of the sales training programme are immense.

The steps in the sales training programme are (a) identifying training needs, (b) setting training objectives, (c) evolving training methods, (d) designing sales training programme, and (e) evaluating the training effectiveness. Training needs are different at different stages of the salesperson's career cycle. From the perspective of place, training programme can be centralized, decentralized or be a combination of the two. The types of training programme are induction training, apprenticeship training, internship training, job instruction training, and literacy training. The various training methods are lecture based, conference, case studies, audio visual, management games, role playing, and on-the-job training. Evaluating the training programme is important to appraise the effectiveness of the training.

KEY TERMS

Career Cycle Career cycle is usually defined as a stepwise progression of career of a salesperson covering four stages, i.e., initial training or grooming, development, maturity and diminution.

Induction During induction, the new and inexperienced employees are acquainted with existing employees and efforts are made to develop their insights towards different functions of the organization.

Management Games Managemant games are forms of training method in which the employees are divided into groups and are tested on their qualities through managerial games.

On-the-Job Training (OJT) On the job training is a popular technique which gives opportunities to

new employees to gather hands-on learning experience. The newly recruited candidates get to observe the approaches of senior salespeople when they interact with customers.

Training Training is a method to induct skills, knowledge, and attitudes amongst new or present employees with a view to extract needful performances from them.

Training Programme Training programme helps in getting the employees more motivated and willing to fulfil their objectives. Various companies deign different kinds of training programmes for its employees to make them more efficient and achieve their targets.

CONCEPT REVIEW QUESTIONS

1. What is training? How is it relevant for new sales force?
2. What are the objectives of sales training?
3. What are the benefits of sales training programme?
4. Briefly explain the steps in sales force training.
5. How do you design a sales training programme?
6. Explain the various types of training. Examine how these are relevant to sales force training.
7. Briefly illustrate the different training methods. How these are applicable to sales force training.
8. Explain the sales force training evaluation process.

CRITICAL THINKING QUESTIONS

1. Illustrate the implications of career cycle of the sales force on the design of a sales training programme.
2. Senior salespeople do not require any training in the midst of their career cycles. True or False? Justify.
3. Sales managers would like to evaluate the effectiveness of sales training programme when it is underway. How is it possible?

PROJECT ASSIGNMENTS

1. Meet a senior HR personnel of a multinational FMCG firm and gather the following information using a questionnaire:
   (a) Types of training methods they apply on new salespeople
   (b) Proportion of 'on-the-job training' to 'off-the-job training'
   (c) Whether the company pursues centralized, decentralized training or a combination of both
   (d) Enquire about the training evaluation programme

2. Meet an HR Manager of a foreign bank that undertakes internship training to management students of reputed B-schools. Enquire about the procedures of internship training and training evaluation methods. To what extent does the company offers placements to the trainees.

REFERENCES

Armstrong, M. (2001), *A Handbook of Human Resource Management Practice*, 8th ed., Kogan Page, London.

Chhabra, T.N. (2002), *Human Resource Management: Concepts and Issues*, 3rd ed., Dhanpati Rai & Co. (P) Ltd, Delhi.

Havaldar, K.K, and M.V. Cavale (2008), *Sales and Distribution Management*, Tata McGraw-Hill Publishing Company Ltd, New Delhi.

Johnson, M.J., L.D. Kurtz, and E.E. Scheuing (1994), *Sales Management: Concepts, Practices, and Cases*, 2nd ed., McGraw-Hill Inc., New York.

Kirkpatrick, D. (1994), 'Kirkpatrick's Four-Level Training Evaluation Model', http://www.n.wlink. com~doncark/hrd/isd/kirkpatrick.html,accessed on 3 January 2011.

Rao, Subba R. (2009), *Essentials of Human Resource Management and Industrial Relations*, Himalaya Publishing House, Mumbai.

Shukla, Sonali (2006), 'In Pursuit of "the" Personality'. *Express Pharma*. Fortnightly insight for Pharma professionals, 16–30 June. http://www.expesspharmonline.com/2006063pharmalife01.shtml, accessed on 1 October 2010.

The Brandon Hall Research, Focus on Sales Training, http://www.brandon-hall.com, accessed on 25 January 2010.

http://www.itvarneews.net/newsph?j=645, accessed on 25 January 2010.

CASE STUDY

Sales Force Training in Pharmaceutical Industry

Selling as a profession in a pharmaceutical industry is a prestigious engagement for young people. This is because of the enormous potentialities of the industry from the growth and earning opportunities. This recession-proof industry always welcomes young and dynamic science graduates preferably from bio-science backgrounds, though pharmacy graduates get an edge over others. But this industry never turns back the general degree holders who have a flair for selling pharmaceutical products. People with a capacity to learn the nitty-gritty's of the profession and adapt to the specific selling skills of serving healthcare products and/or services are welcomed. The importance of this industry for the well-being of people has made it one of the most stable and rapidly expanding industries creating huge opportunities for job seekers.

Selling pharmaceutical products requires special features.

(Contd)

(Contd)

First, building relationships with general physicians, surgeons, medical officials of the government and non-government hospitals, distributors and retailers peddling in medicinal products is the ground reality to initiate selling endeavours for pharmaceutical products.

Second, getting up-to-date with the latest development in the pertinent medical field triggering innovations, product development, and improved formulations on a regular basis are given huge priority.

Third, acquiring complete knowledge of the impact of medicines on the treatment programmes, its consequential side effects and keeping the doctors and users aware of these is vital. This develops the reliability platform for the salespeople and the company they represent.

Fourth, the industry always accepts salespeople who have the right interpersonal skills, keeps promises, develops expertise, and ensures credibility in business transactions. Pharmaceutical companies include learning programmes for personal and professional developments in their training packages to inculcate all-round qualities needed for pharmaceutical products selling.

Sales training programme in pharmacy sectors have some contrasting specifications in comparison to other sectors. Because of the sensitive nature of the products, first the budding salespeople from the very beginning are trained to gather detailed product knowledge on drug constituents, compositions, application courses, benefits to the patients, stability of the medicines, side effects, and other information inputs leaving aside no loose ends or laxity in this regard.

Second, training programmes stress upon developing personality profiles, communication skills, a receptive frame of mind, assertiveness, confidence building, respecting ethics and values inherent in the profession.

Third, training programme impart managerial skills such as planning and organizing powers, team-building capacity, knowledge on the basics of team dynamics, relationship management skills, report writing ability, and understanding strategic issues.

Fourth, learning technical and operational issues of the job is given paramount thrust in training. This includes pre-selling preparations, enquiring physicians' chambers, contacting healthcare units to know the conditions of buying, estimating the nature of demand and getting clues of the conditions of buying in hospitals, network building in the distribution, and promotion of the products of the company, etc.

Fifth, acquiring knowledge of ethical and legal issues in selling pharmaceutical products and nurturing minds to arouse a strong desire

(Contd)

(Contd)

to serve society at large is the basic premise of this profession. In fact, this profession deserves loyalty, integrity, honesty, and value systems from the salespeople who should never detract from the norms and principles of business that are essential to generate a holistic society.

The applications of web-based training, management games, role playing have gained popularity in pharmaceutical industries as training media. But, whatever the training method is, identification of the training needs is crucial particularly at the individual level. It means organizations should make an effort to research the training needs of an individual recruit vis-à-vis that of all the trainees in a group.

In this context, companies lean towards psychometric tests to understand the training needs that would help both the bright performers as well as under performers by properly studying the strengths and weaknesses of the employees. A person can be mentored on the basis of psychometric testing (say, aptitude test) that works on exploring the limitations of the employees and then appropriate training measures are devised. The pharmaceutical alike IT sectors use psychometric instruments in hiring candidates. For training them, importance is given to mapping the behaviour of the selected candidates based on psychometric analysis.

Pharmaceutical majors such as Glenmark Pharmaceuticals, Nicholas Piramal, Eli:Lilly, Lupin, Dr. Reddy's Laboratories, Sun Pharma, etc. are some of the companies utilizing these tests on the selection and training of employees. Psychometric tests are also applicable for taking decisions relating to promotions. A striking feature of psychometric analysis is the development of human job analysis (HJA) that is based on human personality characteristic criteria such as dominance, influence, steadiness, and compliance (DISC). Under HJA, a comparison is made between a graph depicting the results of HJA and an ideal graph for a particular position. This shows the area of deficiencies and reveals weaknesses. Psychometric testing is a practical method to probe learning needs of employees and help to generate a training module to fulfil it.

Discussion Questions

1. Examine the specific features of sales force training in a pharmaceutical industry.
2. The training methods applicable in pharmaceutical industry have some special objectives to meet. Elucidate
3. The psychometric tests are getting popular in sales force training and evaluation, Justify.

Source: Shukla (2006).

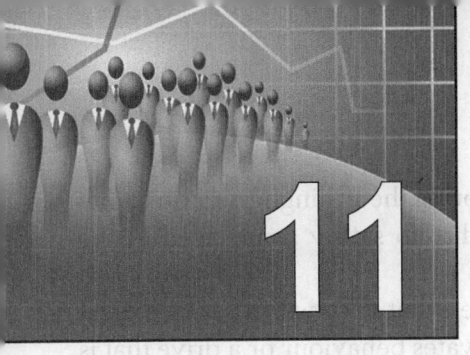

11 Sales Force Motivation

11.1 MOTIVATION—A CONCEPTUAL ILLUSTRATION VARIEGATED

The word 'motivation' was derived from the Latin word *movere* that denotes 'to move'. The word 'move' here means to psychologically stimulate an individual or a group to perform a specific task in a desired manner. In the context of personal selling, motivation is an effort to kindle a strong desire amongst salespeople to perform various activities involved in the job. Motivation is an activation process that encourages salespeople to use not only their knowledge and skills but also expend psychological resources (say, commitment to the job, motivation, etc.) to carry out the sales tasks effectively. Motivation aims to bring a sense of purpose, an immediacy to perform, a strong desire to excel, and an urge to show loyalty to the firm. It acts as a prime mover to energize salespeople to work to their potential towards a goal. Gupta (2000) defined motivation as the process of steering a person's inner drives and actions towards certain goals and committing his energies to achieve those goals.

Dalrymple and Cron (1995) defined motivation as the willingness of an individual to exert effort to achieve the goals of the organization while satisfying individual needs. They further stated a key management principle expressing the relationship between the role of motivation, ability of the work force, and opportunity to work to generate performance.

$$\text{Performance} = f(\text{opportunity to work} \times \text{ability} \times \text{motivation})$$

From the discussion so far, it is clear that lack of motivation, despite the presence of the other two factors cannot produce any effective job performance.

DeCenzo and Robbins (2000) defined motivation as the willingness to do something which is conditioned by the action's ability to satisfy some need of the individual.

Luthans (1989) defined motivation as the process that starts with a physiological or a psychological deficiency or a need that activates behaviour or a drive that is aimed at a goal or an incentive.

Schermerhorn Jr et al. (2005) referred to motivation as the individual force that accounts for direction, level, and persistence of a person's effort expended at work. By direction, he means that an individual can choose an effort when presented with a number of alternatives and decide how the effort will be spent. Level signifies the amount of effort a person puts in to reach the goal. Persistence refers to the length of time a person engages in a given action.

Lewthwaite (2007) stated that motivation for a manager is about providing people with the means to achieve their goals and also about ensuring that the goals of the individual and that of the organization are aligned to some degree.

Hence it can be said that motivation is the driving force that causes one to achieve goals. According to various theories, motivation may be rooted in the basic need to minimize physical pain and maximize pleasure, or it may include specific needs such as eating and resting, or a desired object, goal, state of being, ideal or it may be attributed to less apparent reasons such as altruism, selfishness, morality or avoiding mortality.

11.2 MOTIVATING SALESPEOPLE—OBJECTIVES AND BENEFITS

Motivation is expected to change the behaviour of the salespeople so that they can work more independently with confidence and self-respect. A salesperson working independently with confidence and self-respect is bound to perform better than a salesperson performing with lower confidence. Employees, or for that matter individuals perform the best when they are motivated. In the corporate world, employees are usually inspired through monetary rewards, promotions, and praises. As a result, employees feel good about their job which also makes them feel that they are valuable members of the company.

Many organizations use short-term incentives instead of major developments in compensation packages to motivate salespeople. In fact, small organizations may not be able to provide high compensations to salespeople and rely on short-term incentives to induce them to work smartly and effectively. For this sake, sales managers often resort to sales contests as short-term promotional tools to motivate salespeople. A sales contest is aimed at generating a sense of competition among sales force where a definite sales target is fixed and salespeople are required to achieve that within a stated time period and obviously high

Table 11.1 Objectives of motivation

Objectives to achieve	Meaning
Self-start	A good starter of a sales operation without taking any help
Self-plan	A good planner of a sales operation. Particularly, a salesperson can do tactical planning when confronted with a unique sales situation
Self-direct	A salesperson can perform without much or no supervision
Self-control	A salesperson can evaluate the faults or deficiencies and can make corrections

performers are rewarded. Sales managers also reward salespeople for displaying analytical or technical skills to contribute to sales performance. Awarding cash prize for excellent performance or allowing travel allowances for recreational tours for the salespeople and their family is not uncommon in many organizations.

The broad objectives of motivation are represented in Table 11.1.

Motivating employees help in the process of completing the task. Apart from this, certain other benefits of motivation are presented below:

1. Motivation triggers a sense of drive to initiate action and gives a mental push to the individuals to complete their task and move towards goal attainment. It spurs on the willingness to bring quality of effort in the work.

2. It generates willingness in an individual to bring quality in the work and accomplish tasks successfully

3. It prepares an individual mentally to confidently take up any challenge at work

4. It indoctrinates a spirit of zeal and enthusiasm amongst individuals for them to apply their inner potential to the fullest

5. It brings in acuity, steadfastness, and firmness in one's mind to act uninterruptedly towards a goal

6. It fosters supervision ability, managerial instinct, and leadership skills in the salesperson

So, in general it can be said that it is motivation and inspiration that actually drives the process of achieving results. Every individual has certain needs such as monetary or status, which if fulfilled can get the individual to work towards the prosperity of the whole organization.

11.3   NEED—A MOTIVATION BOOSTER

Motivation is an extension of the word 'motive'. Motive refers to the inner state of the mind of a person. It is a psychological impulse to obtain something which is not yet obtained. Pattanayak (2004) referred to motives as the expressed needs which could be conscious or unconscious. So, motive is the result of need deficiency that drives one to act towards goals that satisfy the need(s). Some needs are biological, called biogenic needs such as hunger, thrust, sex, etc. also termed as primary needs. Other needs are psychological known as psychogenic needs such as the need for recognition, self-esteem, love, etc. also called secondary needs. Therefore, it can be said that need is the subconscious state of motive and motivation is expressed in behavioural manifestation to show a tenacity to act towards a goal. Motivation answers the 'why' of human behaviour. In an organizational context, it lends reason to a goal-directed behaviour of employees where motivation of each employee is a contributing unit.

As discussed, motivation stems from the unsatisfied need that creates a state of tension and triggers goal-directed behaviour that ends with either goal accomplishment or unaccomplishment. Accomplishment leads to satisfaction and unaccomplishment breeds dissatisfaction. Satisfaction generates further motivation whereas dissatisfaction begets tension and the cycle repeats itself. Figure 11.1 represents the need–motivation–satisfaction/dissatisfaction relationship.

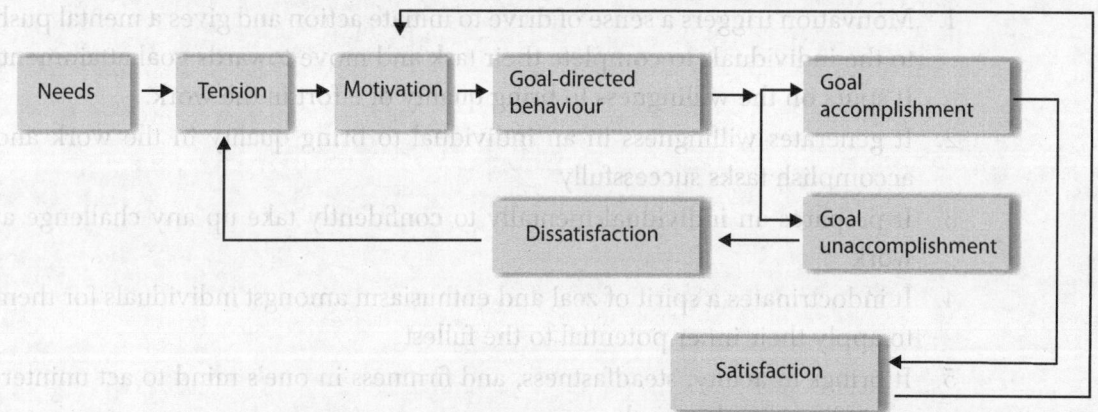

Figure 11.1 Need–Motivation–Satisfaction/dissatisfaction continuum

Motivation can be extrinsic or intrinsic in nature. The source of extrinsic motivation is from outside the job or the task itself. Here, some external factors not related to the job or task motivates one to act. So, extrinsic motivation related to some external incentives inspires one to derive job satisfaction. Examples include compensation, promotion, rewards, etc. Intrinsic motivation, on the other hand, comes from self-satisfaction with the job itself. The willingness to work eagerly and encouragingly comes from the intrinsic motivation that has nothing to do with external incentives. Intrinsic motivation stems from psychological incentives such as pleasure, pride, etc. that people derive from the job or task. Box 11.1 shows the qualities of a motivated salesperson.

> **Box 11.1   Qualities of a motivated salesperson**
>
> Following are the qualities of a motivated salesperson:
>
> (a) High on learning drives   (b) Attentive
>
> (c) Adaptive   (d) Self-confident
>
> (e) Co-operative   (f) Emotionally mature
>
> (g) Independent   (h) Competitive
>
> (i) Expressive   (j) Assertive
>
> (k) Persevering   (l) Insightful
>
> (m) Able to cope with failure   (n) Warm and sociable

Sekaran (2008) explained the three essential components of motivation. These are (a) level, (b) direction, and (c) persistence. Level means the degree of physical and psychological efforts that a salesperson applies to perform a job. Direction implies the choice of alternatives i.e., various job activities where the salespeople will put their efforts. Persistence decides a salesperson's tenacity to hold the enacted effort over time, especially in an odd situation.

11.4   MOTIVATION—A STRATEGIC PUSH TO INFLUENCE SALESPEOPLE

Motivating salespeople is an important component of strategic planning. Encouraging salespeople to exert more efforts and achieve the sales targets is the underlying reason for motivation. But some other allied objectives are also fulfilled by motivation. These are listed in the Exhibit 11.1.

Exhibit 11.1   Allied objectives fulfilled by motivation

Following are the allied objectives fulfilled by motivation:

(a) Salespeople are required to stay focused on building customer awareness, interest, and a sense of conviction on the company's products or services.

(b) Salespeople are asked to build customer relationships and loyalty where the after-sales service has a significant role.

(c) Salespeople are engaged in new customer development, old customer retention, developing distribution network, logistical support, and information gathering on inventories of customers, financial transactions, etc.

(d) Salespeople need to interact with different departments in an organization and provide feedback pertinent marketing information to them. For example, a salesperson can help in developing package designs that have become popular amongst present customers.

(e) Salespeople can take part in product development, giving valuable advice on cost control, human resource planning, mapping out business strategies, territory development, etc.

(f) Senior salespeople are required to assist organizations in selection and training of new sales force.

So, salespeople need to engage in a plethora of jobs, apart from pure selling. Needless to mention, not all the jobs are rewarding. On the contrary, these jobs are laborious and tiring, sapping huge mental energy of the salespeople. Loss of energy, weariness, tiredness, fatigue, exhaustion, listlessness, etc. often grip salespeople badly that affects their performances. Sometimes, these problems lead to psychosomatic disorder amongst salespeople which impact sales performances. The stereotyped nature of the jobs appear dull and uninteresting to them because of which their performance graphs take a nosedive. Here, lies the importance of sales force motivation. Motivation can be called a remedy to do away with the work-related problems that salespeople suffer. It is a medicine to liberate salespeople from physical and psychological complications and stress associated with the sales profession.

Before discussing the theories of motivation in detail, one should get a clear idea regarding motivation being a very good stress buster.

Stress and Motivation

In today's competition-nailed marketing scenario, organizations often fail to produce the right motivation programmes for salespeople with a view to reap expected contributions from them. Many organizations deliberately brush aside the difficulties of the market situation and mount pressure on the salespeople to reach apparently unattainable sales targets. Indeed, in-built psychological pressures within the organization to stay unperturbed in the vicious marketing environment is forcefully percolated down, from the top brass to grass-root level sales employees, as if shifting the responsibility and accountability will relieve the situation. The position of salespeople in this regard is extremely pathetic. As they work at the bottom line of the organization with none to share their huge workload, they often become the delicious soft targets of the top management to face hire and fire as if the medieval slave era still leaves some reminiscent to flash back.

Carrot and stick still rules large as ill-competition and pressure-cooker situation in the industry makes managers hard to accept social renaissance and accept competition on a friendly note. As a result, a highly pressing job situation squeezes out the confidence, mental energy, and tact pushing them to the maze of disproportionate stress that renders sagging salespeople totally bereft of the motivation and morale, and exhausts their potencies and efficiencies. Results often show a dramatic fall in the performance and productivity of the salespeople in many IT and IT-enabled service organizations, insurance firms, FMCG sectors, etc. that are sharply because of stress.

In fact, overload of work pressure puts them in extreme tyranny resulting in psychological trauma and physical disorders. It sounds incorrect if it is presumed that no organization is aware of the violent stress problems of salespeople and its repercussion on sales performance. Below are presented some of the common problems triggering stress amongst salespeople:

(a) Lack of clearly defined goals and responsibilities
(b) Lack of supervision and direction
(c) Extended working hours
(d) Faulty selection of salespeople
(e) No recognition for good performance
(f) Weak leadership
(g) Poor compensation packages
(h) No extra incentives for good performers
(i) Unreasonable sales targets to attain
(j) No direct communication between the top management and the salespeople
(k) Wrong distribution of sales force in sales territories

It is true that in today's complex and demanding business environment salespeople need to work for ten to twelve hours everyday and even more (in some cases Sundays are not spared) to do varieties of jobs. Meeting old customers to prolong business deals, developing new customers, preoccupation with sales target fulfilment consume a lion's share of the time and effort of the salespeople. Next comes sales meetings, completion of sales reports, preparation of customer database in data processor, etc. that encroach upon the total time available to the salespeople. Besides, salespeople invest time in product and package development, marketing research, conferences, sales meetings, and many such additional programmes that pump out their energy levels.

The vagaries and challenges of the jobs of salespeople are contrastingly different from other profiles and demand special attention from the management in terms of increased motivation and morale boosters. Simply financial incentives such as salaries, commissions, bonuses, and travelling allowances may not compensate for the heavy toll of energy and vigour on the salespeople. Non-financial incentives such as right working environment, right mentoring, rewards for good performance, deliverable sales targets, access in sales planning, participation in social and cultural programmes, etc. definitely compensate for the lost energy and desperation that ominously trail behind salespeople to vitiate their vitality and mental strength.

Moreover, a strong but empathetic supervision, verbal appreciation for work, patient hearing of the problems that they face in field selling, etc. can work wonders on the motivation of salespeople. A vibrant organization can cope with any challenge if a bunch of motivated salespeople act like brave warriors.

11.5 MOTIVATION THEORIES—APPLICATIONS TO SALES FORCE MOTIVATION

Since understanding the relationship between motivation and the performance of an individual or a group in an organizational setting is important, motivation has become a study of academic and professional interests. At the same time, researchers and theorists are working towards investigating to explore reasons and rationales behind motivation and how it pushes employees to work. Moreover, the relationship between motivation and other psychological variables including job performance and job satisfaction have turned out to be important issues of scholastic investigations. So far the theoretical developments on motivation have been categorized into classes as depicted in Figure 11.2.

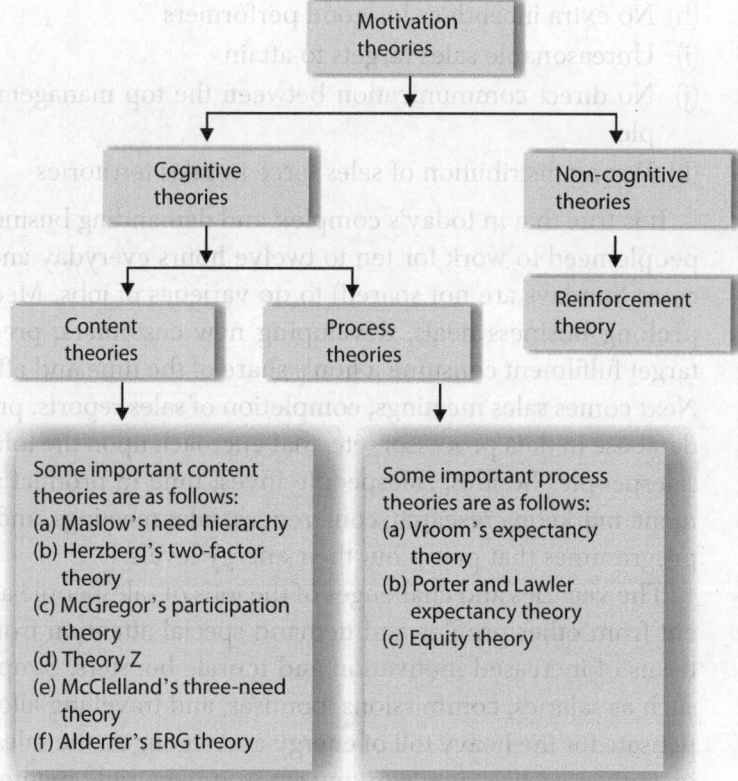

Figure 11.2 Classification of motivation theories

We will be discussing these theories in the following paragraphs.

11.5.1 Content Theories

Content theories focus on human needs (physical and psychological needs) and desires that compel individuals to behave in a way that mitigates their needs. What are these 'needs' that motivate people? These 'needs' form the basic features of the content theories. Exhibit 11.2 demonstrates how two giant companies in their respective fields have taken unique measures to motivate their people.

Exhibit 11.2   Motivation mantra

Kajaria Ceramics, a well-known ceramic tiles company in India, has a wide distribution network covering the sales and marketing officers, dealers, and sub-dealers. The company specifically stresses on enriching job content, great development opportunities, and enviable compensation packages to provide high degree of motivation to all HR units.

Eureka Forbes, India's number one multi-product and multi-channel company recruits young, dynamic, ambitious people. It encourages them to hone their potential status for direct selling jobs. The company's success is backed by a motivating work culture, great career prospect, and high rewards for its working force.

Source: Sales Jobs in Bangalore, Naukri Hub ™, http://www.naukrihub.com/job-opennings/sales-fmcg-india/bangalore.htm, accessed on 11 March2010.

Maslow's Need Hierarchy Theory

Abraham H. Maslow, a renowned American psychologist developed a conceptual model of motivation that postulates five-level needs that are arranged in a set of hierarchy to show the importance of different needs. It believes that human needs follow a hierarchical structure where psychological needs are at the bottom and self-actualization needs are at the top of the structure. Safety, social, and esteem needs are in the middle of it. Figure 11.3 exhibits these five categories of needs.

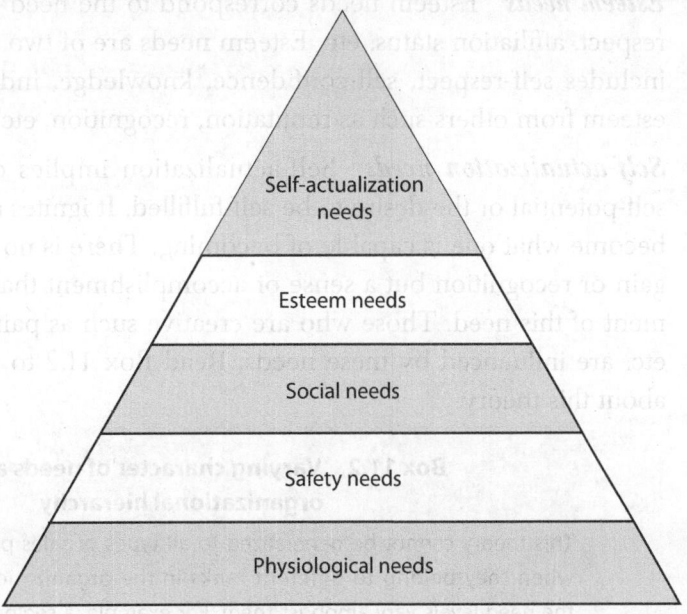

Figure 11.3   Maslow's need hierarchy

The theory states that the lower level needs are satisfied prior to fulfilling the higher level needs. So, physiological needs are satisfied first before safety needs appear. Again safety needs are met before one feels the need of fulfilling the social needs. These continue till an individual reaches the stage of the self-actualization need level. According to this, one higher-level need cannot be a motivating factor unless the preceding lower-level need is satisfied. Moreover, once a need is satisfied, it cannot be a motivating factor and it sparks the importance of the next order need. Therefore, it can be construed that according to the theory only unsatisfied needs act as motivators. It believes that satisfied needs cease their importance as motivating factors. A short description of the five order needs is given below.

Physiological needs   Physiological needs are the basic or biological needs that explain the basic requirements of human life for survival and maintenance such as food, clothes, shelter, etc.

Safety needs   Safety needs arise from the want of safety, security, and protection from dangers and uncertain environments. When people become apprehensive of their economic insecurity, fearful of own and family well-being, jittery of losing their job, etc. they feel the urge of satisfying the safety needs.

Social needs   Social needs relate to the need for love and belongingness. Humans have inherent needs to love or be loved, needs for social acceptance, and yearnings for affection and companionship.

Esteem needs   Esteem needs correspond to the need for power, achievement, respect, affiliation status, etc. Esteem needs are of two types (a) self-esteem that includes self-respect, self-confidence, knowledge, independence, etc. and (b) esteem from others such as reputation, recognition, etc.

Self-actualization needs   Self-actualization implies one's need for realizing self-potential or the desire to be self-fulfilled. It ignites an urge within oneself to become what one is capable of becoming. There is no involvement of material gain or recognition but a sense of accomplishment that emerges with the fulfilment of this need. Those who are creative such as painters, writers, musicians, etc. are influenced by these needs. Read Box 11.2 to understand a small note about this theory.

Box 11.2   Varying character of needs across organizational hierarchy

This theory cannot be generalized to all types of sales personnel especially when they belong to different ranks in the organization. This is because the need levels vary amongst them. For example, a senior salesperson might

(Contd)

(Contd)

> have higher social or esteem needs as their physiological and safety needs are met. This puts sales managers in a fix to design varied motivational packages to satisfy their needs equally. Though, it is seen that salespeople of the same rank generally express similar need patterns.

Exhibit 11.3 shows the application of Maslow's need hierarchy theory in sales force motivation. Sales managers must understand the needs of salespeople working at various organizational levels. A salesperson working at a lower order has a need to prove his worth and has to work towards confirming his footing in the company. To him, satisfying the safety and security needs are a big challenge. In contrast, a senior salesperson or a sales manager has a need for recognition and esteem. It is important to note that both cannot be motivated by the same means and a sales manager needs to be aware of such needs and ways to tackle them. The need hierarchy theory points towards varying needs that come across employees serving lower and higher ranks.

Exhibit 11.3   Application of need hierarchy theory

Physiological needs can be satisfied by monetary compensation. *Safety needs* can be fulfilled by assisting salespeople in goal achievement. Again, when salespeople feel insecure, sales managers can stand by their side and give them mental support and encouragement. They advise salespeople on action plans when they are unable to reach target sales. To enhance the satisfaction of *social needs*, sales managers emphasize on team selling to increase peer relationship and belongingness.

Moreover by organizing sales meetings, conferences, workshops, etc. sales managers can foster social mixing of salespeople. Promotions, salary raise, recognition, empowerment, affiliation, etc. meets the *esteem needs* of the salespeople. Salespeople are also encouraged to satisfy their *self-actualization* needs by allowing them the time and ambience to express their latent skills and dexterity in other fields. For example, a salesperson with writing ability is given a scope to write articles in the company newsletter or house organ. The organization can arrange sports meet, cultural functions, quiz contests, etc. to allow salespeople to participate in programmes to display their inner potentialities.

Herzberg's Two-factor Theory

Fredrick Herzberg (1966) developed the two-factor or dual-factor theory of motivation. According to him, various sources of satisfaction and dissatisfaction are classified into two groups. These are as follows:

Hygiene factors or dissatisfiers   These factors include company policy and administration, technical supervision, interpersonal relationships with peers and supervisors, salary, job security, personal life, and working conditions.

Motivation factors or satisfiers The satisfiers include achievement, recognition, advancement, opportunity for growth, responsibility, and the work itself.

In general, dissatisfiers are linked to job context and satisfiers to job contents. Job context provides the necessary support to work in an organization. It does not give any satisfaction to the workforce but its absence definitely gives rise to dissatisfaction amongst employees. Job contents, on the other hand, provide satisfaction to the employees as they clearly state the responsibilities that are to be fulfilled by the employees. It is seen that the absence of job contents generates dissatisfied employees who lack motivation. The relationship between these two factors and job satisfaction and dissatisfaction can be better understood from the following matrix (Figure 11.4).

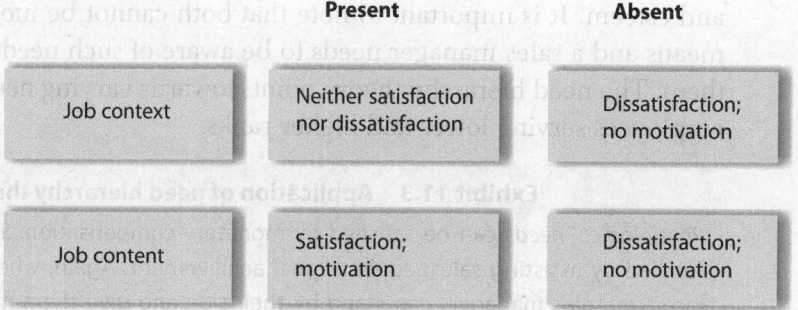

Figure 11.4 Relationship between job context and job content

It is also interesting to note from the above discussion that the reason for dissatisfaction in salespeople is linked to the absence of both hygiene and motivation factors. But it is also important to keep in mind that simply with the presence of good company, policy and administration, working conditions, etc. one cannot motivate sales force unless they get achievement, recognition, etc. in return. Therefore, it is advisable to maintain hygiene factors at least at a threshold level so that these factors do not distract job motivation.

Also, it can be generalized that these motivational factors incite salespeople to put in more efforts for organizational as well as their own development. It is believed that a company needs to generate a job environment that provides both job content and context to motivate employees for best results. Exhibit 11.4 illustrates such an example.

Exhibit 11.4   Motivation mantra of IBM

IBM is a company where job environment is a great source of inspiration to employees. At the same time, opportunity to grow in one's career is paramount. The company offers

---

(Contd)

(Contd)

challenges, potential, and access to different resources. So, IBM has rightly integrated job contexts and job contents to motivate employees. Here, salespeople are not only selling products but they also get the opportunity to sell some of the world's most innovative IT solutions.

Source: 'Are you ready for IBM?' http://www-05.ibm.com/employment/ch/professionals/job_aresa. html, accessed on 16 September 2010.

McGregor's Theory—Theory X and Theory Y

McGregor, a noted psychologist, is the main proponent of theory X and theory Y of motivation in the 1960's. Both the theories are based on certain assumptions of human behaviour. He also suggested the management's responsibility in each situation.

Following are the main assumptions of the theory X:

(a) Average people are basically lazy

(b) They dislike work and lack ambition

(c) They are indifferent to organizational goals

(d) They are mainly oriented towards meeting physiological and safety needs

Following are the main responsibilities of theory X:

(a) The management should direct, motivate, and control the behaviour of people. The management should show the threat of punishment for non-compliance with the work done

(b) The management should exercise close supervision and stricter control

(c) The management should follow an autocratic type of leadership style

External control is needed to motivate salespeople to work on the desired path because salespeople are assumed to be somewhat immature and irresponsible. Close supervision and procreating a fearful and panicky environment can drive the employees towards their goal. High centralization of decision-making and stringent leadership style are the right prescriptions for the salespeople who always try to avoid work, if they can.

Similarly, assumptions of theory Y are as follows:

(a) Average people do not dislike work

(b) They know how to apply self-direction and self-control, and show commitment towards their objectives. This is because of the reward linked with the job

(c) They do not shun job responsibility

(d) They have the capacity to show imagination, ingenuity, and creativity in their jobs

And, responsibilities of theory Y are as follows:

(a) The management exercises decentralization in decision-making and delegation of authority

(b) The management creates scope for job enrichment and finds ways to extract effective and efficient performances from the employees

(c) The management shows concern for the satisfaction of not only psychological and safety needs but also social, esteem, and self-actualization needs

So in short, the theory assumes the salespeople to be co-operative, responsible, and hardworking. Management can take up participative leadership and delegation of authority as means to motivate the sales force. It is supposed that salespeople are capable of self-direction and self-control. The management takes steps to satisfy both the lower- (say, by money) and higher-order (say, by recognition) needs of the salespeople.

Willian Ouchi's Theory Z

Theory Z was originally developed by Willian Ouchi in 1981 and was published in the book *Theory Z: How American Management can meet Japanese Challenge.* It is an integrated model of the Japanese and American management practices. It is also called the hybrid model of motivation. Japanese management believes in group effort, group decision-making, and social cohesion in the organization. The American management, on the other hand, emphasizes on individual freedom in decision-making. The distinguishing features, keeping in mind both the American and Japanese management, of theory Z are presented as follows:

(a) There should be trust, integrity, and openness amongst organizational participants such as employees, management, work group, union, and supervisors

(b) Employees have a strong loyalty and interest in team work

(c) A strong bond between the employees and the organization keeps retrenchment, etc. at bay for a lifelong existence of the organization

(d) Due recognition is given to employee participation in decision-making, particularly in matters that affect them

(e) An integrated organization talks about job rotation which in turn brings interdependence of tasks and team spirit

(f) Organizational control system should be informal

(g) The leader should coordinate the efforts of the employees in order to develop common culture and to this end the leader encourages communication, debate, and analysis.

The theory focuses on mutual trust, strong cooperation, and mental bonding between salespeople and sales managers to cause successful performance.

A sales manager's role is to coordinate the activities of salespeople. They can seek the suggestions of salespeople to manage the sales activities. This means that salespeople are given additional importance in the organization to make them more jobs involved. Their views are often listened to in decision-making. This approach definitely improves the sense of commitment and belongingness amongst salespeople within the organization. They become more emotionally involved within the organization and so perform better.

McClelland Three-Need Theory

David C. McClelland, a prominent personality in the field of psychology from Harvard University used thematic apperception test (TAT) and identified three types of needs. These are the following:

(a) Need for achievement (n Ach)

(b) Need for power(n Power)

(c) Need for affiliation (n Affiliation)

Table 11.2 talks about the important human characteristics of all the three types of needs.

Salespeople with high 'n-ach' show a strong drive to overcome challenges and are self-starters. This implies that they need no major external incentives to work on their jobs and achieve results. They can take moderate risks and choose activities that give them immediate and accurate feedback. To them, accomplishing a task provides more intrinsic satisfaction as they do not bother much about the material rewards. They are very open in their communications.

Salespeople with high 'n-power' are very influential and want to control the group. They become successful in managerial positions.

Salespeople with high 'n-affiliation' are hungry for social acceptance. They like to work as members of a team that is working for a common goal.

Table 11.2 Useful human characteristics vis-à-vis the type of needs

Type of need	Human characteristics
N Ach	People show a drive to excel and grow and want immediate feedback of their performance. They find accomplishing a task intrinsically satisfying and preoccupy themselves with the task until the goal is reached. People like to take moderate risks
N Power	They show a drive to influence, dominate, and control others. For that sake they can take risk
N Affiliation	They want to belong to a cohesive group. They like companionship and believe in mutual understanding. They are motivated by tasks that involve social interaction with peers

Salespeople differ in terms of achievement orientation, power drives, and social interaction potentials. Sales managers should develop motivation programmes in such a way that all these three types are benefited. High n-ach with low n-power or low n-affiliation salespeople needs to enhance their leadership qualities and group cohesion. Again, high n-power salespeople cannot succeed without flexible and empathetic minds. Similarly, high n-affiliation salespeople should enhance self-dependence and self-control.

Alderfer's ERG Theory

Claytron Alderfer (1969) came up with this theory in line with Maslow's need hierarchy which showed a reduction in the number of levels from five to three. The motivation theory, that he formulated, related to the satisfaction of three needs which are as follows:

(a) Existence needs (E)
(b) Relatedness needs (R)
(c) Growth needs (G)

The *existence needs* are concerned with the satisfaction of physiological and safety needs. This is tantamount to the satisfaction of the first and second level needs of Maslow's need hierarchy. The *relatedness needs* put importance on the interpersonal and social relations which finds resemblance with the satisfaction of the third and fourth level needs of Maslow's need hierarchy. The *growth needs* are related to the individual's intrinsic desire for personal development. This complies with the satisfaction of the fifth level needs of the same.

Though the same logical deduction for sales force motivation can be drawn from Maslow's need hierarchy. But, the ERG theory does not fit exactly with the framework of Maslow's need hierarchy.

The points on which Alderfer differed from Maslow views are discussed as follows:

1. ERG limited the number of need categories to three. These are existence, relatedness, and growth.

2. ERG theory did not plead that the satisfaction of lower-order needs stimulated the start of the next higher-order need.

3. ERG believed that salespeople may both move up or down the various stages of needs. It follows the frustration–regression process which states that in case an individual is unable to satisfy a certain level of need, he can either regress or move down to the next level of need.

4. They believe that more than one need may arise at the same time. As there are no clear demarcations amongst different needs, salespeople can make an effort to satisfy them at different levels simultaneously.

So, more than one level of need can motivate salespeople at the same time. Salespeople can be motivated by existence (say, money), relatedness (say, social relationship), and growth (say, a desire for personal development) needs to act in a manner that the organization wants them to at the same time. All these work in tandem to motivate sales force.

11.5.2 Process Theories

Process theories involve how motivation acts upon people, i.e., dynamics of motivation, interplay, and interaction of different motivation stimuli. How people cook different motivational inputs is an internalized process. Needless to mention, the efforts of people to satisfy needs are goal-bound.

Vroom's Expectancy Theory

Victor Vroom (1964) hypothesized that in order for a person to be motivated towards achieving a goal, his effort, performance, and motivation must be linked. He proposes three variables to account for this, which he calls valence, expectancy, and instrumentality.

Valence refers to the strength of an individual's preference for a particular outcome. It denotes the values or attractions of an outcome that results from efforts to the person in terms of reward. Expectancy refers to the probability of an effect that a particular action or an effort will have on the performance. Instrumentality refers to the perception of the relationship between performance and reward, and relates to the outcome of the job performance. It refers to the probability a person assigns to each performance–outcome alternative.

All the three variables, according to the theory, are linked to motivation.

$$\text{Motivation} = \text{Valence (V)} \times \text{Instrumentality (I)} \times \text{Expectancy (E)}$$

The theory, also, focuses on three types of relationships (refer to Figure 11.5):

Effort–performance relationship   Here, expectancy variable plays the influencing role as expectancy determines the strength of belief that a particular effort or action gives rise to a performance. (This is also called the first level outcome.)

Performance–reward relationship   Here, instrumentality plays the influencing role. It yields perception that says that favourable performance will produce expected rewards which will satisfy needs.

Reward–personal goal relationship   Here, valence plays the influencing role. The valence may be positive, negative or zero. A positive valence means the person desires outcome. The negative valence means the person avoids having negative consequences such as stress, layoffs, etc. Zero valence indicates that a person appears indifferent to the outcome.

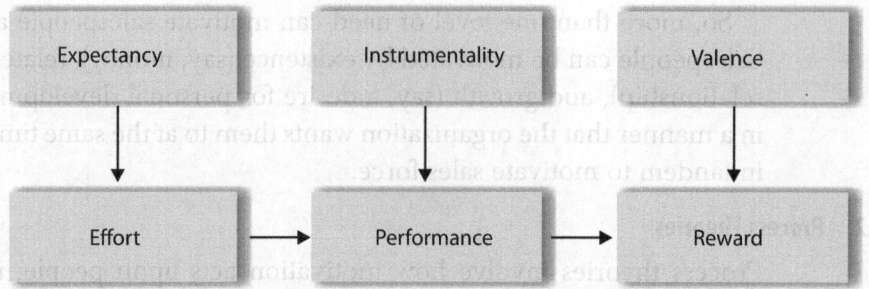

Figure 11.5 Framework for Vroom's model for motivation

Porter and Lawler Expectancy Theory

Porter and Lawler (1968) made an extension to the earlier expectancy model developed by Vroom. The theory infers that performance results from the effort, ability, and role perception of the individual and leads to various outcomes or rewards. Some rewards are extrinsic (e.g., salary, promotion); some are intrinsic (say, self-esteem, job satisfaction).

Effort is spent on the basis of perceived effort–reward probability and the value of the reward (valence). An individual evaluates the equity or fairness of rewards comparing against his efforts expended and performance achieved. Depending on the perception of equitable reward, satisfaction occurs. The degree of satisfaction again moderates the effort or energy that is due for the individual to spend for his performance in further tasks. Figure 11.6 shows a shorter version of Porter and Lawler model.

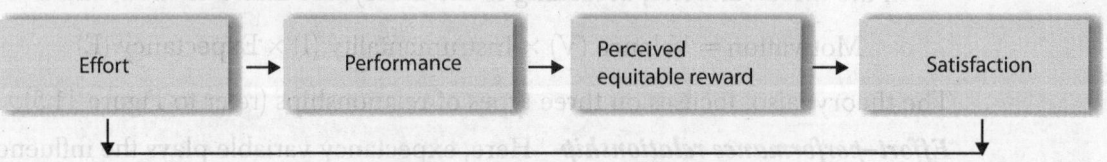

Figure 11.6 Porter–Lawler model

An employee always expects justice and fairness in treatment from the top management. They want their worth in performance to be rewarded justifiably. It often happens that good salespeople (obviously, on performance factor) are treated equitably with poor salespeople in salary raise, promotions or rewards which creates a great deal of frustration and disappointment for the top performers. Salespeople with years of experience, seniority in age, knowledge, and skill are wrongly placed in the same sales positions with the new and young salespeople; it becomes an injustice on the part of the management. Ideally, the younger should never be given equal status with the older; rather the seniors should be placed in the higher ranks.

During recruitment, selection or preparation of wage and salary structure, top-level managers sit in a meeting to decide on promotion or punishment of salespeople where they always consider contributions of the employees/candidates on an individual basis. They should not overindulge a high achiever nor should they undermine his performance. When the sense of inequity comes in the salesperson's mind, it definitely distorts his satisfaction.

Equity Theory

J. Stacy Adams (1965) was the proponent of the equity theory of motivation. Inputs and outcomes are the main variables of this theory. The theory is based on the assumption that employees are motivated by a desire to be equitably treated on inputs they invest and outcomes they receive in their workplace. These inputs are time, effort, education, special knowledge, training, experience, etc. and outcomes are pay, promotion, recognition, social relationships, personal development, etc.

An individual compares his (say person A) outcome–input ratio with the ratios of others in the organization. The following comparison can be drawn from this theory to study the extent of motivation and satisfaction of employee A.

$$\frac{\text{A's outcomes}}{\text{A's inputs}} = \frac{\text{Others' outcomes}}{\text{Others' inputs}}$$

Here, 'A' perceives his outcomes–inputs ratio as equitable to the others and hence feels satisfied and motivated. Inequity comes in when the ratios are not equal. If the ratio of A is significantly lower than the same of others, A will feel dissatisfied and frustrated. On the contrary, if the ratio of A is significantly higher than that of others, A would feel guilty. Therefore, the perceived equity creates motivation for an employee and the perceived inequity leads to tension within him. The degree of tension is proportionally related to the magnitude of inequity.

11.5.3 Non-cognitive Process

Under this theory, it is believed that the behaviour and experiences of the past are the stimulators of motivation. This can be further supported by the reinforcement theory.

Reinforcement Theory

B.F. Skinner, a sagacious psychologist propounded the reinforcement theory of motivation. It says that behaviour is the outcome of the past consequences. This means that people learn from their past experiences, previous knowledge, etc. and use it to rework on the behavioural disposition; so that they can control future consequences.

Similarly, salespeople learn from their mistakes that they have rendered in the past; rewards and punishments they have received and previous dealings with superiors, subordinates, and peers within the organization; and customers, distributors, competitors from external environment. They use these earned experiences to shape their future behaviours and take decisions on how to act in a particular situation. These reinforcements may be positive or negative. Positive reinforcement (say, reward) entails repetition of behaviour and negative reinforcement (say, punishment) spurs avoidance of behaviour. They help them act accordingly in different situations and accomplish goals effectively.

SUMMARY

Motivation has been defined by many a psychologists, academicians, etc. in various ways. The essence of their views is that motivation is a willingness to apply efforts to achieve the organization's goal and the satisfaction of the individual's needs. Motivation in an important function of sales forces management. A self-motivated salesperson can perform independently with self-direction and control. Motivation answers the 'why' of human behaviour. Motivation is intimately connected to the unsatisfied need. An unsatisfied need creates tension for an individual that drives him to show goal-directed behaviour, which drives the person to get motivation. Motivation can be extrinsic (e.g., money) and intrinsic (e.g., pleasure in work).

Motivation is a strategic incentive to the sales-people to work more for the organization. Motivation theories are propounded by many eminent psychologists. The broad classification of all the theories is two: cognitive theories and non-cognitive theories. Cognitive theories are further classified to two: content theories and process theories. Content theories are linked to the 'what' of motivation and process theories are linked with the 'why' of motivation. Under the non-cognitive approach, reinforcement need theory is discussed. This theory relates past consequences as the predictors of present behaviour. Different content and process theories are worthy of discussion and provide valuable insights and interrelationships of variables causing motivation. The applications of these theories in sales force motivation are immense.

KEY TERMS

Content Theories Content theories focus on human needs which compel people to behave in a way that mitigates needs.

Existence Needs The existence needs are concerned with the satisfaction of physiological and safety needs.

Growth Needs Growth needs are related to the individual's intrinsic desire for personal development.

Hygiene Factors/Dissatisfiers These factors include company policy and administration, technical supervision, interpersonal relationships with peers and supervisors, salary, job security, personal life, working conditions, status that are linked to the job

context and in the absence of which an employee gets dissatisfied.

Maslow's Need Hierarchy Maslow's need hierarchy postulates five-level needs which are arranged in the set of hierarchy to show the importance of different needs. These needs are physiological, safety, social, esteem, and self-actualization.

Motivation Motivation is a process which encourages people to carry out their tasks effectively. Motivation aims to bring a sense of purpose, an immediacy to perform, a strong desire to excel, and an urge to show loyalty to the firm.

Motivation Factors or Satisfiers The satisfiers include achievement, recognition, advancement, opportunity for growth, responsibility, the work itself that are linked to job content and in the presence of which the employee is satisfied and content.

Process Theories Process theories, basically, revolve around how motivation acts upon people to move towards their goals.

Related Needs Related needs give importance to interpersonal and social relations.

CONCEPT REVIEW QUESTIONS

1. Define motivation. How is it relevant to sales force?
2. What are the objectives for sales force motivation?
3. What are the benefits of sales force motivation?
4. What are the indexes of a motivated salesperson?
5. Discuss Maslow's need hierarchy theory of motivation and examine its application in sales force management.
6. Examine the relevance of Herzbers's two-factor theory in sales force motivation.
7. Explain Vroom's theory of motivation and its utility in developing motivation programmes for sales employees.

CRITICAL REVIEW QUESTIONS

1. A company fails to motivate senior salespeople despite attractive salaries and other incentives and that are substantially high compared to the prevailing compensation packages in the industry. Sales performance shows a nosedive and the company is at a point of crisis. What do you suggest?
2. Do you think rewards and recognitions given to good performing salespeople badly affect the morale of the lesser performing ones that ultimately affect the sales productivity of the organization?

PROJECT ASSIGNMENTS

1. Meet the sales managers of a consumer durable and courier organization and collect information on their sales force motivation programmes. Then meet ten salespeople of each company to know the job satisfaction levels. Prepare a note on the impact of motivation programmes on the satisfaction levels. Compare the situation between two industries.
2. Interview 20 salespeople working in the IT and IT-enabled eervice organizations on their degree of satisfaction on various need hierarchy levels proposed by Abraham Maslow. Review the results and critically analyse the application of the theory in real-life sales force motivation.

REFERENCES

Adams, J.S. (1965), 'Inequity in Social Exchanges' in L.Berkowitz (ed.), *Advances in Experimental Social Psychology*, Academic Press, New York, pp. 267–99.

Dalrymple, D.J., and W.L. Cron (1995), *Sales Management: Concepts and Cases*, 5th ed., John Wiley & Sons Inc., New York.

DeCenzo, A.D., and P.S. Robbins (2000), *Personnel/Human Resource Management*, Prentice Hall of India Pvt. Ltd., New Delhi.

Gupta, C. B. (2000), *Management Theory and Practice*, Sultan Chand & Sons, New Delhi.

Herzberg, F. (1966), *Work and Nature of Man*, The World Publishing Co., New York.

Ingram, N.T., W.R. LaForge, A.R. Avila, H.C. Schwepker Jr, and R.M. Williams (2007), *Sales Management: Analysis and Decision Making*, South-Western Cengage Learning, United States.

Lewthwaite, J. (2007), *Managing People for the First Time: Gaining Commitment and Improving Performance*, Viva Books Private Limited, New Delhi.

Luthans, F. (1989), *Organizational Behaviour*, 5th ed., McGraw-Hill Book Company, New York.

Pattanayak, B. (2004), *Human Resource Management*, 2nd ed., PHI, New Delhi.

Porter, L.W., and E.E. Lawler (1968), *Managerial Attitudes and Performance*, Richard D. Irwin Inc., Homewood, Illinois.

Schermerhorn, Jr R.J, G.J. Hunt, and N.R. Osborn (2005), *Organizational Behaviour*, Wiley-India, New Delhi.

Sekaran, U. (2004), *Organizational Behaviour: Text and Cases*, 2nd ed., Tata McGraw-Hill Publishing Company Limited, New Delhi.

Vroom, V.H. (1964), *Work and Motivation,* John Wiley and Inc., New York.

CASE STUDY

Dwindling Sales

Josephine Electronics Ltd (JEL), manufacturing and marketing batteries of wall clocks began its journey in 2001 from Bengaluru. Batteries were designed to produce standardized products and meet technological specifications which were comparable to the recognized indigenous and international manufacturers of batteries. The company was much aware of the vast retail market space concomitant with accelerating market growth. At the same time, it kept abreast of hostile market competition getting more teeth with each passing year.

The company with moderate strength on infrastructure and human resource went on to run its operations in four major cities—Bengaluru, Chennai, Trivandrum, and Kochi. The company engaged one sales manager along with four salespeople in each city to execute sales and marketing operations. Customers for this company comprised of clock manufacturers, retailers, and watch repairing boutiques.

There was a mixed bag of market response up to 2004 with Bengaluru and Kochi devouring the toast of success in terms of hairline variances between sales targets and actual sales but Chennai and Trivandrum lagged a little causing worry to the company. On the whole, the aggregate sales turnover for a beginner such as Josephine Electronics was satisfactory.

In the year 2004–05, a different story was seen altogether; as sales began to plummet in Bengaluru and Chennai and that of Kochi and Trivandrum experienced a steep downward fall. Figures (A and B) illustrate the sales trends of Bengaluru and Kochi to understand the sales situations. The reason for choosing these two cities was only because of the fact that Bengaluru showed the most promising sales growth and

(Contd)

Kochi was the most bothering to the company in terms of generating satisfactory sales.

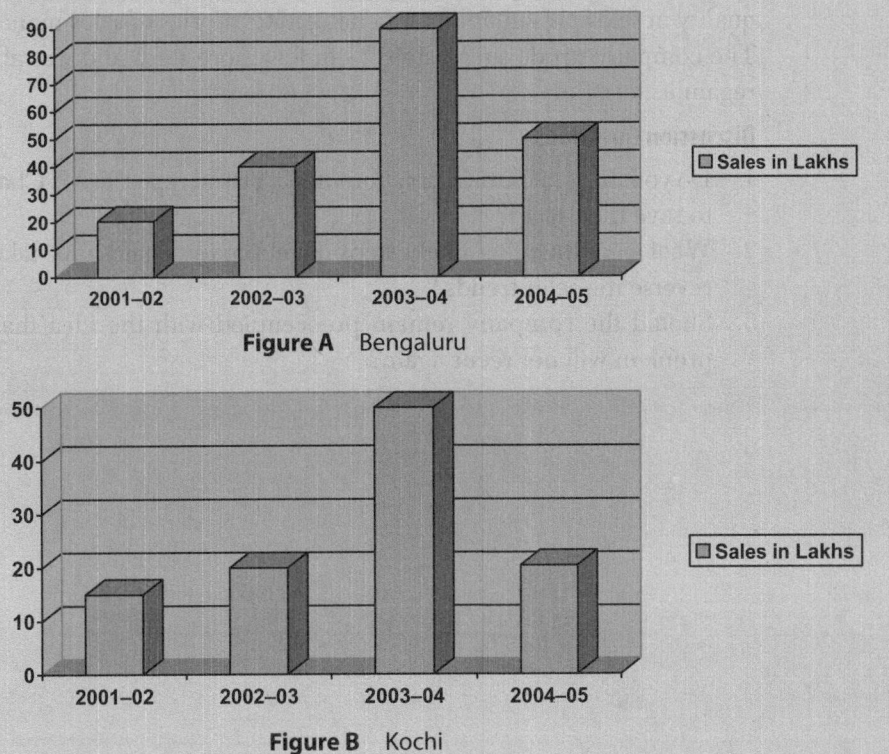

Figure A Bengaluru

Figure B Kochi

The vice president (marketing) of the company, Mr Chandra, immediately called the four sales managers to the company headquarter to hold an emergency meeting. In the meeting, they were instructed to spot out the reasons and submit the reports within a week. Later, a thorough review of the situations revealed that the main reason for this change in the sales figure was the lack of motivation of the salespeople, particularly on the commission structure in the compensation package.

Immediately, the company enhanced its commission rate from 5 to 7 per cent for every thousand rupees additional sales over ₹50, 000 in a month. The sales, still, did not show any expected upward trajectory. The company appointed a marketing research firm to investigate the reasons and the research findings showed that lack of motivation was due to weak leadership too.

On the analysis of these reports, Mr Chandra was deeply dismayed and decided to make a radical turnaround in sales force planning

(Contd)

along with the facelift of sales management. For example, the company provided laptops to salespeople to bring in enhancement of the quality of sales presentation and changed territories of sales managers. The company strode successfully with few more steps and was able to regain its lost glory.

Discussion Questions

1. Do you think sales mangers submitted a biased report to Mr Chandra to save their faces?
2. What were the other likely steps the company could have taken to reverse the sales trends?
3. Should the company remain preoccupied with the idea that the problem will not recur again?

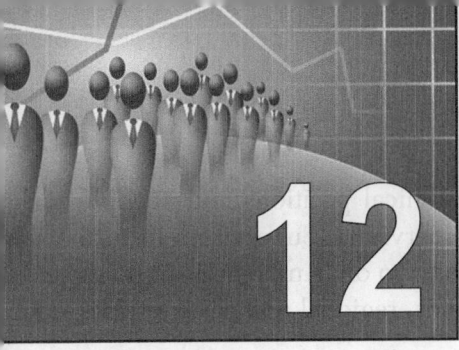

12 Directing the Sales Force

LEARNING OBJECTIVES

After reading this chapter, you will be able to

- understand the basic features and the role of leadership in direction
- understand the relationship between leadership and motivation
- gather ideas on the qualities of a sales leader
- understand in detail the different theories of sales leadership and their implications on sales leadership behaviour
- discuss the futuristic approach to sales leadership
- develop an understanding of the different leadership styles and how they influence the performance of salespeople

12.1 DIRECTION—CONCEPT AND UNDERSTANDING

Directing is a managerial function. It aims to set the desired norms, customs, disciplines, and work attitudes in someone's behaviour in an organization. In the selling context, directing the sales force implies influencing their behaviour in a way that can act towards achieving the organizational goals. It also purports to satisfy the individual's goal as well. Thus, an effective and efficient direction helps the sales force to work towards the stated goal. And so, effective and efficient directions are the index of the quality of management.

Pearce II and Robinson Jr (1989) defined directing as communicating to others what their responsibilities are in achieving the company plan, as well as providing an organizational environment in which employees can become motivated to perform well.

Haynes and Mukherjee (2001) defined directing as getting people to focus their attention on achieving the objectives of the organization.

In a sales organization, directing is a process where sales managers train, motivate, and communicate the right instructions to the salespeople to work towards a prefixed goal at the expense of the optimal utilization of a company's resources. Other functions such as planning, organizing, motivating, coordinating, and controlling are also effected through the function of directing. Directing is a critical management function.

Specific issues in direction with sales management in perspective are discussed as follows:

1. Directing pervades all strata across all hierarchical positions. Salespeople act according to the direction of the sales supervisors. Supervisors in turn receive instructions from the sales managers and so on. An organization has to also follow the direction of local civic bodies, regional as well as central governments on various regulatory issues.

2. Communication is the central link in direction. Save proper communication, direction becomes meaningless. In case any selective distortion happens in communications with the sales force, the entire sales planning process becomes ineffective. Again, sales managers should patiently hear the problems in selling. These, if any from the salespeople, can help them to rework on the sales plans. As communication is a two-way process, feedback assists in the evaluation of the directing process.

3. Direction should have a motivational element. Insipid direction cannot motivate the sales force. Employees do not find much expectation or inspiration towards completing their jobs under such direction. Direction should be influential enough to stimulate the sales force to show maximum willingness to do the required job.

4. Directing should be authoritative. A sales manager must be empowered with the capacity to direct the sales force. So, a manager requires certain administrative qualities such as technical knowledge, skill, ability, and an analytical mind to guide and inspire the sales force.

5. Directing is preceded by right decision-making on any process or activity. Direction on an improper decision can have a negative impact. Before a sales manager directs the employees, he must be assured of the accuracy of the decisions.

6. Direction has leadership function as well. Leadership adds vision, objectivity, and thrust to direction. It also induces employees to be psychologically involved with the job. The nature of direction is authoritative, whereas, leading is more participative and persuasive in nature. A manager as a leader should indoctrinate more responsibility and sensitivity within the employees and the organization as a whole in order to get the best results. Direction coupled with leadership does wonders in terms of the commitment of employees to the job and disposition of more goal-bound efforts.

Leadership adds visionary elements to direction. Direction means sending instructions to the work force but a leader not only communicates the instructions but also spearheads the execution of the job and asks the employees to follow suit. The way subordinates do the job is contingent upon how a leader thinks and acts. Direction implies application of power and authority but leadership requires influencing the capacity in addition to the two so that the employees show spontaneity in their efforts.

12.2   LEADERSHIP—A CONCEPTUAL CLARIFICATION

Leadership is an instrument to motivate employees. In the selling context, leadership motivates the salespeople to achieve the desired sales productivity. As motivation is a psychological force, leaders must know the mechanism to arouse the inner potentials of the salespeople and find its proper application for an accurate completion of the job. Salespeople are human beings and therefore, they differ not only in terms of skill levels but also on the psychological compositions that affect their degrees of application on the sales efforts. An effective leader can understand the subtle differences in the energy potentials from one salesperson to the other and manifest the right leadership quality to mould and shape the sales behaviour of each salesperson to produce the desired outcome.

Leadership is different from supervision. Supervision is giving instructions and directions to the employees. Leading is a purposeful involvement with the employees both physically and psychologically to utilize their strengths for a satisfactory job performance. A leader is more visionary than a supervisor. A leader trains and prepares his subordinates for the present and future jobs. A supervisor motivates the employees to complete the job as per the target level. A leader makes his subordinates understand by setting examples, i.e., a leader stays at the forefront of the work to show how work can be done effectively. A supervisor, however, instructs from the background on what work has to be done and how it is to be done.

A good leader is a friend, facilitator, and guide to the subordinates instead of being a boss, order giver, and instructor. But, a leader is active in taking disciplinary measures against errant workers. At the same time, the leader should show no miserliness to hand over awards and incentives to good performers.

Robbins (1996) defined leadership as the ability to influence a group towards the achievement of a goal.

Schermerhorn Jr et al. (2005) defined leadership as a special case of interpersonal influence that gets an individual or group to do what the leader wants done.

Haynes and Mukherjee (2001) distinguished between leading and leadership. Leading is a managerial function that influences and motivates employees to achieve the desired organizational objectives. Leadership is the process of influencing others towards goal achievement.

Misshauk (1979) defined certain basic components or characteristics of leadership. These are as follows:

(a) Leadership formulates some methods or means that are able to influence the behaviour of others; (b) Leadership sets its purpose of influence on the goal-directed behaviour of the employees.

He, further, referred to Ralfh Stogdill (1974), the essayist of the *Handbook of Leadership,* to identify the common leadership traits. Table 12.1 makes an endeavour to depict the basic personality traits that are in line with the above characteristics and outlines its manifestations by the sales managers as leaders.

Leadership is an important part of human resource development. Without it, employees become directionless. Exhibit 12.1 gives an overview of the need for leaders in the development of human resources in retail organizations. It presents the role of leadership in some prominent retail organizations of the world. Indeed, retail industry, at present, has been leapfrogging at an enviable growth rate. Simultaneously, employment potential of the industry has been rising exponentially as well.

Table 12.1 Personality characteristics of a leader—its manifestation in sales leadership

Basic personality traits	Manifested behaviours of sales managers as leaders
Capacity	Sales managers show high attention-getting strength, intelligence, and alertness in tackling salespeople. They have a strong capacity to assume responsibility and drive for the completion of jobs. Moreover, they show an innovative capacity to modify the sales plans and strategies under contingencies
Achievement	Sales managers have high degree of achievement orientation. They not only care for personal achievement but also lead salespeople to fulfil the goals of both the organization and the individual. So sales managers take recourse to skill development, knowledge sharing, and motivation to achieve performance
Responsibility	Sales managers show high responsibility and initiative by being actively involved with the salespeople towards job accomplishment. They set examples before the salespeople by displaying performance. Salespeople feel secure and comfortable working with such sales managers
Participation	A sales manager incites participation by activity and cooperation. They treat all salespeople alike and do not discriminate between the good and bad salespeople, at least, in their presence. They always try to reduce interpersonal stress amongst salespeople. A good sales leader can also meaningfully identify personal characteristics of salespeople and persuade them with the right motivation techniques
Status	Status determines the positional ranking in the authority that deserves esteem and respect from the subordinates. It also provides them with prestige and social recognition
Situation	A sales manager must understand the gravity and importance of a situation before they decide on the leadership style. They can influence the salespeople by being self-involved in field selling. In fact, this is part of the on-the-job sales training The acumen of situational understanding gives a leader the tools for mapping out-sales strategies

---

Exhibit 12.1   Retail organizations—need for leadership

Retailing, worldwide, has been witnessing elephantine growth. Globalization has opened new vistas for many major retail players to expand their operations in the far corners of the world as if the entire world has been steadied for retail revolution. Third-world nations including India have turned into major retail destinations for the world's who's who retail organizations such as Wal-Mart, Mc Donald's, Metros, etc. The country, India, once the paragon of unorganized retailing has taken a formidable stride to invite these retail majors. Meena (2009) reported that organized and modern retail together account for almost nine per cent of the total retail in India.

The organized retail sector is highly people-centric. In view of a large number of employees in the retail industries, HR (human resource) functions in the retail sector is of utmost importance. Managing HR functions such as recruitment and selection, training and development, motivation, compensation, and most importantly leadership, etc. is crucial in this business.

Leadership plays an important role in HR development in the retail business. Only right motivation by the leaders can produce efficient, enthusiastic, and highly job-involved salespeople. Because of the troubles and travesties of work pressure (e.g., long working hours, continuous customer interactions, maintaining liaison with peers and superiors, etc.), the motivation level of retail salespeople often suffers and poses a question to leadership. Effective leadership has been able to provide the right working environment, enlighten salespeople with the organizational culture, develop the right attitude, and morale to produce satisfactory job performance.

Therefore, it can be said that with skillful leaders and managers, an organization has greater chances of succeeding.

Sources: Berman and Evans (2005); Meena (2009).

12.3   LEADERSHIP AND MOTIVATION

First of all, a leader should be a self-motivated person, otherwise he cannot motivate others. Second, a leader must understand the organization's goal as well as the individual needs and demands of the employees that motivate them as a part of leadership behaviour. Third, he must develop insights in to how to make the right coherence between the various tasks and functions the employees perform and incentive schemes, both financial and non-financial, as motivation drivers in order to generate a smooth performance from them. Fourth, a leader must have the capacity to identify the ability and skill of each employee so that the right job is assigned to the right person and no working individual is overused or underused. So, unbiased approach to each in terms of workload distribution and apportioning incentives is the hallmark of leadership.

A sales manager as a leader should develop the right intensity of efforts among sales force. It should propel them in the right direction and encourage persistence for job performance. Sales leaders motivate the sales force by their own performances. For instance, they initiate the field sales operations by self-involvement and direct the sales force to follow suit. This is necessary, particularly for the new and young salespeople.

One important personality characteristic is that they never criticize weak salespeople (obviously, on performance parameters) in front of others or compare them with strong salespeople, rather they need to mentor weak performers on how to overcome the crises. Constructive criticism with suggestions to improve is one of the key aspects of sales force motivation. Again, they should not exaggerate praise for good performers so that they become overconfident and distract their performance levels. A sales leader instils team spirit or morale amongst salespeople and this enhances their motivation to a further degree.

Leadership is vital for human resource development in any organization. An effective leadership inspires employees to give cent per cent effort to their jobs and the organization grows rapidly.

12.4 QUALITIES OF A SALES LEADER

A leader is born or made with the combination of a large number of quality characteristics. It is difficult to mention all such quality factors. Table 12.2 makes an attempt to highlight some of the important leadership qualities that a sales manager should possess and how they can apply those qualities to draw out the desired sales performance from the salespeople and achieve organizational goals.

Table 12.2 Leadership qualities

Quality traits	Implications
Ability	To influence salespeople to behave in a desired manner
Creativity	To think out of box to solve problems. To cause variety in the sales plans and strategies whenever the situation demands
Initiative	To set examples by being self-starters
Self-confidence	To infuse a high degree of confidence amongst salespeople
Emotional stability	To remain unperturbed in unwanted situations
Fairness in treatment	To weigh both the organization's and the individual's interests justifiably
Integrity	To be true to one's core values and ideas and let other people trust those values and ideas
Openness	The ability to pay heed to new thoughts and ideas and find the opportunity of its application provided it benefits the organization

(Contd)

(Contd)

Quality traits	Implications
Dedication	The ability to spend time and efforts in unflinching ways till the goal is reached
Visionary	The ability to predict future situations and prepare contingency plans
Flexible	The ability to accept changes in the sales plans and policies under demanding situations
Communication skills	The ability to communicate ideas to salespeople in both verbal and written forms
Interpersonal skills	The ability to develop healthy and sustained relations with superiors, peers, and subordinates
Analytical skills	The ability to diagnose a situation and suggest alternative solutions and decide the best approach that solves the problem in a cost-effective manner
Administrative skills	The ability to set plans, formulate policies, draw strategies, organize efforts, coordinate and control the operations, and work within the budget constraints accurately and effectively
Decision-making skills	The ability to take prompt decisions with the available information and resources
Conceptual skills	The ability to draw lessons from academic discourses and research papers, and apply it for managerial purposes.
Consistency	The ability to adhere to the missions, values, and culture of the organization and work for the preservation of it.
Empathy	The ability to get along with others and show regards to the beliefs and sentiments of others
Objectivity	The ability to stay focused on the objectives to be fulfilled
Honesty	To be faithful to the organization and its members
Charisma	To be accepted by the peers and juniors because of ability and a lovable personality
Assertiveness	The ability to stand up for what is right without fear and without infringing the interests of others

12.5 LEADERSHIP THEORIES AT A GLANCE

Theorizing leadership is still under investigation and research. But attempts are on to develop a theoretical building block or normative postulations of leadership styles. So far, academicians, scholars, and researchers from the field of psychology, behavioural sciences, etc. have put forward some valuable insights on the theoretical developments of leadership along with their practical ramifications.

Table 12.3 provides a summary table of some prominent leadership theories and their meaning in the concept of sales leadership.

Table 12.3 Leadership theories

Name of the theory	Focus	Application in sales leadership
Great man theory	Leaders are born, not made	Sales leadership is an inborn quality
Trait theory	Leaders inherit traits	Sales leadership is an inherited quality
Behavioural theory	Leaders are made, not born	Sales leadership can be learnt
Managerial grid	Combination of concerns for people and work develop varying leadership styles	Sales leadership is backed by people and work orientations
Lewin's leadership theory	Leaders can be autocratic, democratic or laissez faire	Sales leadership might be authoritative, participative or free from both, i.e., salespeople are allowed to self-direct
Likert's leadership theory	Leaders can be exploitative authoritative, benevolent authoritative, consultative or participative in groups	Sales leadership finds a wide range from extremely stringent leadership to submissive but productive leadership
Hersey and Blanchard's situational leadership theory	Delegating, participating, selling or telling leadership style	Concerns for people and task determine sales leadership patterns
Path-goal theory	Directive, supportive, achievement-oriented or participative leadership Styles are chosen depending upon the situations	Situation has an important bearing on sales leadership style
Fiedler's least preferred co-worker (LPC) theory	Combinations of task-focus and people-focus produces varying degree of leadership styles	A high LPC sales leadership is more prone to relationship orientation and a low LPC sales leadership is biased towards task orientation
Transactional theory	Exchange relationship between the leader and the follower is the key	Sales leaders want the sales force to perform and get rewards, otherwise face adverse consequences
Transformational theory	Leaders inspire followers by learning core values and beliefs of the organization and make them understand how they can protect and improve the position by performance	Sales leaders want salespeople to learn and adhere to organizational culture. They are asked to work on broad organizational missions while serving the customers

12.6   HIGHLIGHT OF THE LEADERSHIP THEORIES—A PRACTICAL APPROACH

Early leadership theories focused majorly on what qualities distinguished good and bad leaders from each other. However, subsequent theories, today also look at other variables such as situational factors and skill levels. Some of these theories are being discussed as follows:

Great Man Theory

The basic features of the theory are as follows:

(i) Leaders are born and not made. This is a traditional concept.

(ii) When there is a pressing need, a leader comes into picture and takes care of the situation.

(iii) Leaders generally belong to an aristocratic background and they inherit leadership qualities from the root of the same. So clan and upbringing have a role in making a good leader.

(iv) The theory proposes that leaders are male.

The great man theory and sales leadership   Great sales leaders are born and not made. They descend from well-off family backgrounds. Practical and demanding sales situations bring out leadership qualities. But the theory has proved itself wrong in many situations. Today, it has been proven on many occasions that leaders are made as well. Moreover, females now occupy many pedestal positions (e.g., female CEO) in the organizations that show ample evidences for formidable leadership.

Trait Theory

The basic assumptions of this theory are as follows:

(i) People are born with inherited traits that contribute to leadership.

(ii) People with the right combination of leadership traits become good leaders.

(iii) People inherit both physical traits (e.g., height, weight, appearance, mannerism, intelligence, knowledge, etc.) and psychological traits (e.g., ambition, decision-making skill, self-confidence, judgemental ability, etc.) from their ancestors.

Trait theory and sales leadership   Stogdill (1974) critically analysed traits and skills of leaders. Figure 12.1 has made an attempt to show the traits–skills co-habitation of sales leaders. They inherit the traits and possess skills. Trait–skill combinations produce the effective leadership quality.

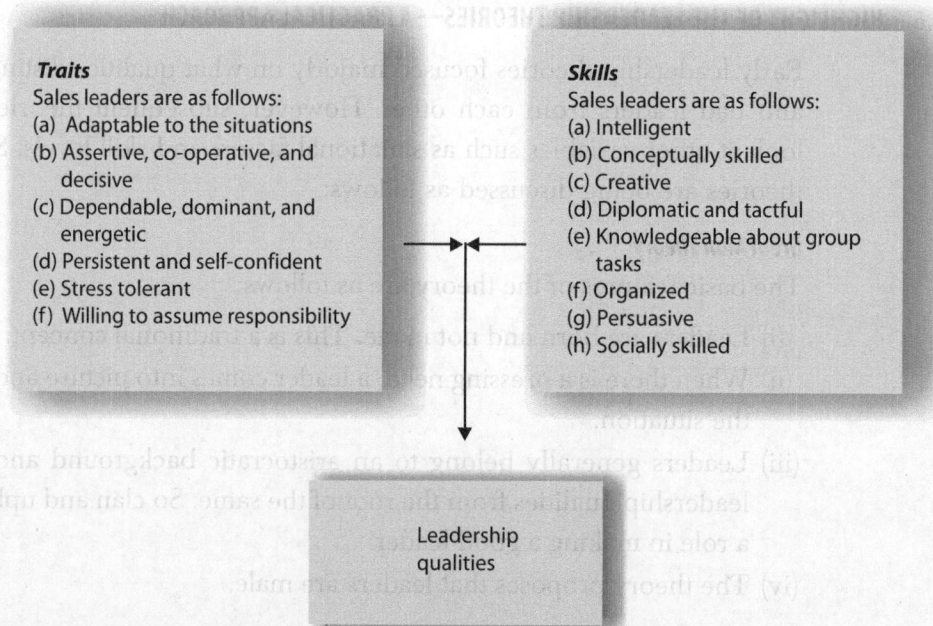

Traits
Sales leaders are as follows:
(a) Adaptable to the situations
(b) Assertive, co-operative, and decisive
(c) Dependable, dominant, and energetic
(d) Persistent and self-confident
(e) Stress tolerant
(f) Willing to assume responsibility

Skills
Sales leaders are as follows:
(a) Intelligent
(b) Conceptually skilled
(c) Creative
(d) Diplomatic and tactful
(e) Knowledgeable about group tasks
(f) Organized
(g) Persuasive
(h) Socially skilled

Leadership qualities

Figure 12.1   Trait–skill components of leadership

Behavioural Theories and Sales Leadership

These theories suggest the following:

(i) Leaders are made rather than born.

(ii) Individuals can learn behaviour that helps him to be an effective leader.

Two types of leader behaviour studies can be discussed—Michigan studies and Ohio state studies.

The Michigan studies, conducted by the Michigan University Survey Research Centre categorized leadership behaviour to two types, as follows:

(i) Employee-centred

(ii) Production-centred

Employee-centred leaders are more oriented towards the satisfaction of employees. They stress on interpersonal relationships amongst employees keeping in mind the individual differences among them. They have a genuine concern for employee welfare.

Production-centred leaders are more task-oriented and have a bias on how jobs can be completed well. They maintain close supervision. Michigan studies concluded that employee-centric leaders are able to produce more effective employees compared to production-centric.

Sales leaders who look after the satisfaction and well-being of salespeople therefore would be more successful and this will positively influence the sales productivity. Sales leaders who always drive the sales force to achieve sales targets and sales turnover would not be successful in providing job satisfaction to the sales force.

The Ohio state studies conducted by the Bureau of Business Research revealed the results after a series of studies. It identified two major dimensions of leadership.

These are as follows:

(i) Consideration

(ii) Initiating structure

Consideration defines the willingness of a leader to develop a likable relationship with the subordinates by showing regards to their feelings. So, consideration develops job relationship of a leader with others pivoted on mutual trust and respect for the subordinates' ideas.

Initiating structure refers to the extent to which a leader is able to articulate the role of his subordinates and clarify their tasks on the way to goal attainment. It, furthermore, defines the behavioural direction of a leader that includes the delegation of task and responsibility, channel of communication, decision flow, etc.

A leader who is high on both consideration and initiating structure is a successful leader compared to one who does not have one or both the characteristics.

Sales leaders should combine both the task or job assignments to the salespeople with appropriate direction. They keep a close tab on the personal feelings and opinions and create a sense of mutual trust between them and salespeople to fetch long-term success of the organization.

The Managerial Grid and Sales Leadership

Blake and Mouton (1964) proposed five styles of managerial grid that can be placed along two dimensions. These are as follows:

(i) *Concern for people:* It has people orientation. It focuses strongly on interaction with people.

(ii) *Concern for task:* It has task orientation. The focus is on organizational efficiency.

Table 12.4 presents five leadership styles and their characteristics, and their implications in sales leadership behaviour.

Table 12.4 Leadership styles and sales leadership

Leadership styles	Characteristic features	Implications in sales leadership
Impoverished management	Low concern for people–Low concern for task	Most imperfect and imprudent leadership approach
Authority compliance	High concern for task–Low concern for people	Strong importance is attached to the task with less people orientation
Country club management	Low concern for task–High concern for people	A familial environment is built with less emphasis on task. This may result in less efficiency
Middle of the road management	Medium concern for task–Medium concern for people	Lack of clear focus on both. Leader believes in adjustment
Team management	High concern for task–High concern for people	It results in highly motivated workforce who are dedicated to work

Lewin's Leadership Theory and Sales Leadership

Kurt Lewin and co-workers identified three different styles of leadership based on leadership–decision experiments in 1939. These three styles are autocratic, democratic, and laissez faire. Table 12.5 exhibits the characteristics of these three styles. It also tries to draw inputs from such styles for application in sales leadership.

Table 12.5 Lewin's leadership style

Leadership style	Characteristics	Applications in sales leadership
Autocratic	These leaders exercise central authority and structures in managing people. Subordinates have no role in decision-making. They are non-empathetic to followers. The subordinates are forced to become dependent on leaders. The autocratic leaders wish the followers to follow their path without any deviation.	Sales leaders ask salespeople to obey their directions in predetermined order and violations of it are dealt stringently by the leaders. These leaders do not bother about anything except sales target and they want salespeople to be their ardent followers. Emotional reactions or fellow feelings are hardly encouraged in such leadership style.
Democratic	Leaders take decisions after consultation with the followers. A subordinate is given freedom to express his/her views or opinions on the job contents and its operational procedures. So, cooperation and coordination of efforts are the bases of this leadership style. A democratic leader incites the followers to work as a team. He/She also encourages participative work culture.	A democratic sales leader gives importance to the suggestions of senior or experienced salespeople on sales planning and its execution. They extend a helping hand to the budding salespeople. They believe in team selling to achieve success.

(Contd)

(Contd)

Leadership style	Characteristics	Applications in sales leadership
Laissezfaire	The leaders are least involved in decision-making, rather they delegate authority to the subordinates to take decisive actions. Employees are only made aware of their tasks and responsibilities. Employees are assumed to work on self-motivation and control. Openness and individual freedom are the key to this leadership style.	Sales leaders give leeway to salespeople to draw the sales plans and the course of actions in their sales territories. But they keep a watch on whether any plans or actions are being inconsistent with the company's marketing goals. They provide instructions to the salespeople in categorical terms and mind their responsibilities. They leave the rest to the salespeople and do not interfere in their plans and procedures.

Likert System Four and Sales Leadership

Renesis Likert (1967), suggested four types of leadership systems leading to respective behaviours.

Table 12.6 portrays Likert's approach to leadership. It also describes the features of leadership and corresponding implications on the sales leadership behaviours.

Table 12.6   Four leadership styles

Type of leadership system	Characteristic features	Behavioural implications in sales leadership
Exploitative authoritative	(i) Low concern for people (ii) Enforce motivation by fear and threats (iii) Centralized decision-making (iv) Coercive control (v) Interpersonal relationship discouraged	Sales leaders act as tough task masters. They get results and for that sake, they can go to the extremes to manage salespeople. This style may be successful in short term but proves vain in the long term.
Benevolent authoritative	(i) Authoritative but not apathetic to the interests of the employees (ii) Reward for successful employees and punishment for unsuccessful ones (iii) Decision-making is mostly centralized albeit selective delegation	Sales leaders like to add a tinge of human value in their authoritative style of leadership. Salespeople feel sceptical of their leader's behaviour. Sales managers, on being sure, delegate few responsibilities to the senior salespeople.
Consultative	(i) Decision-making rests with the top management but suggestions of employees are listened with due care (ii) Scope for interpersonal interaction (iii) Some authority is delegated to employees	Sales leaders give importance to the views and ideas of the salespeople. The organization's environment is friendly and the salespeople feel committed to their jobs.

(Contd)

(Contd)

Type of leadership system	Characteristic features	Behavioural implications in sales leadership
Participative group	(i) Leaders and followers take decisions together. (ii) Complete delegation of authority to employees (iii) Informal relationship is given priority	Sales leaders repose complete faith and trust to the salespeople and delegate authority and responsibility to them. They delimit the relational boundary between them and the salespeople.

Hersey and Blanchard's Situational Leadership and Its Implication on Sales Leadership

Hersey and Blanchard's situational leadership theory suggests that successful leadership is achieved by choosing the right leadership style. Indeed, the theory rests on two major dimensions as follows:

(i) Concern for task
(ii) Concern for relationship with people

Table 12.7 shows various leadership styles, its characteristic features, and strategic application that fosters sales leadership.

Table 12.7 Task–relationship dyad—a source of leadership style

Leadership Styles	Characteristics	Strategic interpretation under sales leadership
Telling	High concern for task-Low concern for people	Sales leaders give suggestions to the salespeople who are less in ability and willingness.
Selling	High concern for task-High concern for people	Sales leaders show directions to the less able but willing salespeople on how to sell.
Participative	Low concern for task-High concern for people	Sales leaders give motivational support to salespeople who are able but lack enthusiasm.
Delegating	Low concern for task-Low concern for people	Sales leaders entrust upon the salespeople because they are capable and hold willingness and delegate duties and responsibilities to them.

Path–Goal Theory and Sales Leadership

The path–goal theory was proposed by House (1971). It is a contingency theory, emphasizing on the situational factors of leadership. It implies that the leader adjusts his behaviour according to the situations. It suggests four different leadership styles. These are the following:

(a) Directive leadership (The leader directs the subordinates)
(b) Supportive leadership (The leader extends cooperation and support to the subordinates)

(c) Participative leadership (The leader takes suggestions from the subordinates before decision-making)

(d) Achievement-oriented leadership (The leader sets challenges before subordinates and gears them to act confidently for excellent performance)

So, if leaders are able to associate the right leadership style with the situation, they can expect the right kind of job behaviour from the employees and their performance would also be satisfactory. The employees can also show high job motivation and derive job satisfaction by fulfilling the organization's goal. Figure 12.2 shows the schematic presentation of the path–goal theory.

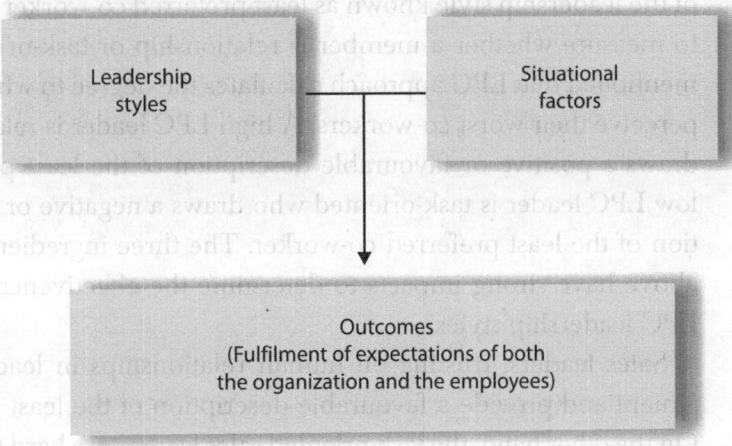

Figure 12.2 A schema of situational leadership approach

The path–goal theory finds immense application in sales leadership. Different sales situations direct sales leaders to choose the right leadership behaviour to generate the desired performance from the salespeople. In some situations, salespeople can give valuable suggestions (say, the needs and demands of the customers in a territory are better known to the salespeople rather than the sales managers) to the sales managers helping them take the right decisions. The sales managers as leaders can accompany salespeople in dealing with the major customers and give give them valuable suggestions on handling such customers. The sales managers always instil confidence in the salespeople particularly when the sales situations are challenging (say, highly competitive sales situations).

Fiedler's Least Preferred Co-worker (LPC) Theory and Sales Leadership

Fiedler (1967) developed the leadership theory based on the contingency approach. The approach suggests that a leader's ability to lead is dependent upon situational factors. Fiedler proposed the following three ingredients of leadership style:

(i) Leader–member relations: The relationship stands on mutual trust, confidence, and respect between the two.

(ii) Task-structure: Task-structure determines the degree of standardization and formalization to the assigned jobs.

(iii) Position–power: The ability of a leader by dint of authority to utilize power variables (e.g., rewards and punishments to members) to influence subordinates.

The theory states that effective group performance is contingent upon the proper fit between the leader's style of interaction with the subordinates and the situational perspectives. Furthermore, the theory suggests an operational measure of the leadership style known as least preferred co-worker (LPC) that is designed to measure whether a member is relationship or task-oriented. Luthans (1989) mentioned that LPC approach calculates the degree to which leaders favourably perceive their worst co-workers. A high LPC leader is relationship-oriented and draws a positive or favourable description of the least preferred co-worker. A low LPC leader is task-oriented who draws a negative or unfavourable description of the least preferred co-worker. The three ingredients of leadership listed above have strong impacts to determine the effectiveness of high LPC or low LPC leadership styles.

Sales leaders, trusting on human relationships in leadership behaviour are lenient and provide a favourable description of the least preferred salesperson. On the other hand, the task-oriented sales leaders are hard task masters and attach an unfavourable description of the least preferred salesperson.

Transactional Theory of Leadership—A Reference to Sales Leadership

The basic tenet of transactional leadership is direction and control of subordinates. Leaders apply coercive power that links performance as a yardstick to decide reward or punishment to the employees. Subordinates are expected to be blind followers of their leaders. Transactional theory, as the name suggests, develops an exchange relationship with the subordinates, i.e., rewards for good performance and punishment for the opposite. Transactional leaders give directions and motivate employees. They apprise subordinates of their roles and responsibilities. Here, leadership is demonstrated in supervision style, guiding employees on day-to-day operations. Leaders set standards before the employees and provide clear work structures and instructions, and ask employees to follow the established paths.

Transactional sales leaders, as it is understood, want their salespeople to work to their stated direction to meet sales targets. Meeting the target is the main objective for salespeople which lead them to receive rewards, otherwise salespeople have every reason to worry about their future in the organization. Sales managers can face the same consequences in an organization that acts on a chain of command and centralized decision-making. Relationship between salespeople and sales leaders stand on exchange perspectives.

Transformational Leadership Theory—A Reference to Sales Leadership

Here, leaders from the beginning try to develop a sense of vision and mission of the organization in the subordinates so that the latter can perform for the organization from a bigger perspective. Leaders instil confidence in the subordinates, guide them about their responsibilities and the expectations of the organization from them, and cater to the intellectual stimulation for fulfilling the organization's goal. Transformational leadership, if successful, can lead employees to go beyond their capacity to perform and position their organization on the altar of pride and prosperity. So, a leader's role is to transcend the philosophy of unlimited strength and profound ability within the subordinates that, in its turn, acts as a morale booster among them. Rationality in problem solving, providing support and intelligence to the employees, inspiring them to work in a team, and protecting the core values and image of the organization are the nodal points of transformational leadership.

Transformational sales leaders can create a sensible leadership style by inculcating the oath of determination and performance beyond the capacity within the salespeople. A sales leader can develop an iconic or charismatic image by the way he guides and inspires salespeople, stands by them by giving important instructions, and injects a sense of togetherness within them.

So, from the above discussion on various leadership theories, it is clear that with a leader in the organization, the task of the employees as well as the entire organization becomes much simpler. There are a certain set of goals which are easily set and achieved through a leader directing, motivating, and managing his sales team.

12.7 SALES LEADERSHIP—A FUTURISTIC APPROACH

Leadership style has undergone a massive change in the present-day organization. Gone are the days when line managers used to put pressure on the workforce to fulfil the production or sales targets at any cost. Earlier, the business phrases such as situational leadership, participatory leadership, pro-people human resource policies, collective bargaining between employees and management were far from reality.

In the selling context, one example of irrational leadership from management can be cited. Sales potentials across sales territories vary from narrow to wide range but sales people in many companies are evaluated on the basis of performances, irrespective of territories they cover, given the assumption of equal sales opportunities in territories.

In traditional selling, target marketing, niche marketing, market positioning and repositioning, relationship marketing, etc. was beyond considerations of sales managers. Indeed, attaining sales productivity at the stare and glare of line or field sales managers were the usual course of practices of field sales personnel.

The legacy of oppressive leadership where autocracy ruled the roost of man management or bureaucracy that bound employees in the cobweb of rules and regulations has torn apart on the wake of sweeping changes of worldwide business environment. All of a sudden, the traditional leadership style has come to a point of obsolescence in view of the mind-boggling changes in the global business particularly after globalization of the economy. Management practices such as perfectionism, cost rationalization, total quality management (TQM), supply chain management (SCM), customer relationship management (CRM), corporate governance, etc. have become business drivers. Myopic business culture characterized by wealth maximization of owners or shareholders has given way to the equitable distribution of benefits to the stake holders including employees.

Now, a new look organization accepts new ideas, encourages innovation and continuous quality improvement, customer-centric business, more employee participation in corporate administration, and sensibly serving the interests of the stakeholders. HR perspective of the new age organization does not stand still. Employee motivation, communication, skill development, leadership, etc. are some of the HR areas where transformation takes place rapidly. For example, Poppen (2000) pointed out a change in the leadership profile of an organization where the traditional image of a line manager as a 'boss' gets transformed to an 'enabler' and as a 'judge' to a 'counsellor'. The enabling capacity of a manager is important to incite the work force to self-improvement and self-evaluation. As a counsellor, the manager constantly guides and mentors the work force to reach the organizational objectives.

So, a gigantic re-engineering in the leadership styles in view of currently whopping changes in the employee–employer relationship is on the way of progression to evolve a new look organization. Here, cross functional interactions and cross fertilization of ideas among functional units are given huge premium within the ambit of transformational leadership functions. In fact, transformation leadership is considered as the order of the leadership in the present-day organization.

An HR policy under sales management has been undergoing metamorphic changes in line with the above in the organization. Innovative changes in sales leadership in the presence of market quake factors such as digital revolution in the product-technology-process, guillotine-edged competition, sky-high quality expectations of customers, price wars among market players is the pressing need of the day.

Traditional leadership style was typified by the managers directing and controlling the sales force through giving rewards for their high performance and punishment for under performance. Task-driven leadership style ruled the roost where an individual salesperson used to get commands to achieve goals by any means. There was no room for lateral communication or information sharing, etc. It did not encourage support to salespeople, work emotions, work flexibility, fairness of treatments, team building, and seldom emphasized on situational factors, keeping salespeople in the dark on the company's futuristic approaches. This sort of orthodox leadership style began to take retreat in the new age organization, particularly under the impetus of globalization.

Today, salespeople are treated as specialists rather than generalists. An organization banks upon a salesperson's knowledge and skill in the specialized field (e.g., telecommunication, banking, etc.), real-time information sharing and virtual information networking, integration of sales and marketing department (other functions as well) to the entire organization by ERP (enterprise resource planning) with a view to reduce cost and increase profitability , use of CRM (customer relationship management) software in the DSS (decision support system) to tackle customer problems on a zero waiting time concept. So, the erstwhile leadership style has become a matter of just literary interest.

Primarily, a leader at present is to be a knowledgeable person in the respective field, otherwise leading a sales team comprising of highly potential salespeople will be a futile task.

Second, technical competency of the sales leader should be enriched with expertise and experience otherwise, salespeople cannot be handled with confidence and determination.

Third, a leader must keep in touch with latest innovations in the technical field as well as that of the organizational developments so that invoking changes in the sales planning and operations are not difficult.

Fourth, a leader should have the capacity to gauge the strengths and weaknesses of the competitors and map out the appropriate strategic plans to anchor his company on the rock solid position.

Fifth, the interpersonal, analytical, and decision-making skill of a sales leader should be unquestionably strong.

Last but not the least, the global mindset of a leader, his perception of global market and competition, and his ability to develop global marketing strategies to counter challenges of globalization can be the trump card to steer the organization in the leading position of the global business landscape.

SUMMARY

Directing, a managerial function, sets norms, customs, disciplines, and work attitude in the employee's behaviour in an organization. Directing is relevant in sales force management to influence the behaviour of the salespeople. Directing is a communication process. Salespeople act according to the direction of the sales managers. Directing should have a motivational element. Directing should be authoritative. Directing should be backed by right decision-making, otherwise no positive results can be yielded for the organization.

Directing has a leadership function. Leadership is an instrument to motivate employees to accomplish the desired job to the satisfaction of both the organization and the individual. Leadership involves purposeful involvement with the employees both physically and psychologically. Leadership, in the selling parlance, is an ability to influence salespeople to the sales and marketing goals. The basic personality traits determining the leadership behaviour are capacity, achievement, responsibility, participation, status, and situation. Leadership is important in human resource development. Basic leadership qualities are ability, creativity, initiative, self-confidence, emotional stability, etc. Leadership theories are prescriptive of different leadership behaviours and styles. These theories are traditional, behavioural, situational, participative, directive, supportive, autocratic, democratic, transactional, transformational, etc. Leadership can be people- or task-oriented. Leadership can be based on exchange relationships or transcendental, inculcating core values and missions of the organization within the sales force. Today, the scenario of leadership has become very different from that of the old one.

KEY TERMS

Direction   Direction is a managerial function that aims to set the desired norms, influences the behaviour of the salespeople in a way that can act towards achieving the organizational goals. It also purports towards satisfying an individual's goal.

Leadership   Leadership is an instrument that helps in motivating an individual. It is defined as the ability to influence a group towards realizing a goal.

Least Preferred Co-worker (LPC)   Least preferred co-worker is a scale that is designed to measure if a member is relationship-oriented or task-oriented. It is supposed to calculate the degree to which a leader favourably perceives the attitudes of his co-workers.

CONCEPT REVIEW QUESTIONS

1. Define direction. What are its features?
2. How is direction related to leadership?
3. How is leadership related to motivation?
4. What are the basic qualities that a sales leader should possess?
5. Explain the trait theory of leadership and its application in the sales force motivation.
6. Explain managerial grid and its implications on sales leadership.
7. Explain Likert system four leadership style. Draw reference from it to explain how a sales leader with varied characteristics can influence the salespeople to achieve the organizational goal?

8. Distinguish between transactional leadership and transformational leadership on approaches and motivational influences on salespeople.

CRITICAL REVIEW QUESTION

1. A sales supervisor needs to acquire some special qualities to be a sales leader, although the roles are the same. Illustrate the commonalities of the characteristics of the two and the specificities of a sales leader on quality traits.
2. Today, sales organizations demand more of transformational leadership style to guide and motivate salespeople rather than transactional leadership. Critically justify.

PROJECT ASSIGNMENTS

1. Approach the salespeople of a product- and service-based organization with the questionnaire prepared on the basis of six quality factors (pick those factors from the text) describing sales leaders. Evaluate the quality of leadership of the sales managers by interviewing them. Use a 5-point scale in this regard where 1 signifies very insufficient; 4, sufficient; 3, neither; 2, sufficient; and 1 indicates very sufficient.
2. Meet sales managers of a (i) FMCG firm, (ii) consumer durable firm, and (iii) a private health insurance firm. Collect information from them on the following:
   (a) Leadership style in their firms
   (b) Motivation policies
   (c) Leadership–motivation vis-à-vis supervision–motivation relationships
   Based on the information collected, make a comparative review of the contributory influences of the above on the sales force performance. influences of the above on the sales force performance.

REFERENCES

Berman, B and R.J. Evans (2005), *Retail Management: A Strategic Approach*, 9th ed., Prentice-Hall of India Pvt. Ltd, New Delhi.

Blake, R.R., and J.S. Mouton (1964), *The Managerial Grid*, Gulf Publishing Company, Houston.

Fiedler, F.E. (1967), *A Theory of Leadership Effectiveness*, McGraw-Hill, New York.

Haynes, W. and S. Mukherjee (2001), *21st Century Management*, New Central Book Agency (P) Ltd, Calcutta.

House, R.J. (1971), *A Path-goal Theory of Leader Effectiveness*, Administrative Science Quarterly, vol.16, pp. 321–338.

Likert, R. (1967), *The Human Organization*, McGraw-Hill, New York.

Luthans, F. (1989), *Organizational Behaviour*, 5th ed., McGraw-Hill Book Company, New York.

Meena, S.R. (2009), 'Human Resource Management in Retail Sector: An Overview', *Advances in Management*, vol.2 (6), June, pp. 45–47.

Misshauk, M.J. (1979), *Management—Theory and Practice*, Little, Brown and Company, Boston.

Pearce II, A. J., and B.R. Robinson Jr (1989). *Management*, McGraw-Hill Book Company, New York.

Poppen, C.A.H. (2000), 'From Boss to Enabler: Shifting Priorities in HR', *Rajagiri Management Journal*, vol 1(1), March, pp. 19–20.

Robbins, P.S. (1996), *Organizational Behaviour*, 7th ed., Prentice-Hall of India Pvt. Ltd, New Delhi.

Schermerhorn, Jr, R.J., G.J. Hunt, and N.R.Osborn (2005), *Organizational Behaviour*, Wiley-India, New Delhi.

Sekaran, U. (2004), *Organizational Behaviour: Text and Cases*, 2nd ed., Tata McGraw-Hill Publishing Company Limited., New Delhi.

Stogdill, R.M. (1974), *Handbook of Leadership: A Survey of Literature*, Free Press, New York.

--- CASE STUDY ---

Vinyl Chemicals Ltd

Vinyl Chemicals Ltd (VCL), a Faridabad-based company, entrenched itself venerably in the business of lubricating oils, branded as Lubeol X and Lubeol 2T, aimed for the automobile sectors. The two-decade old company, in spite of experiencing staggering situations since foundation, steadied its progress till 2007 with an annualized sales growth of 11 per cent on an average. But, all of a sudden, the world economy plunged into a whirlwind of global recession, shaking off the company like others vociferously. In fact, the meltdown in the automobile sector left a huge toll on the envious sales trends and the company went into a state of deep turmoil. But at the fag end of 2009, the gloom of the economy began to fade with the resurrection of hope as companies at large have started the course of revival. Companies have started to bring back their past glories. But, surprisingly, VCL is not hopeful as the company does not find any sign of recovery and many loyal customers of yesteryears switched flanks to join its rival firms. Many automobile dealers have shown cold shoulder to VCL. The sales growths in the first two quarters of 2010 was mere 3.5 per cent and 4 per cent compared to that of 2009 respectively. In July 2010, the company approached, Ultra Solution, a marketing consultancy firm in New Delhi to investigate the reasons for the downfall.

The research firm has not been able to find any particular reason in quality or price differentials among various brands available and VCL's. The company seems to have a capable marketing infrastructure, warehousing facility, number of salespeople, connection with distributors, etc. At this moment, the research firm decided to get feedback from customers, both present and past to spot the dilemma. In fact, Ultra Solution wanted to undergo a holistic survey where salespeople, sales managers, and customers were separately interviewed. Some of these excerpts of the responses from salespeople, territory sales managers, and customers are presented below. The interviews were carried out in strict confidence.

From salespeople:

(a) Sales managers are not co-operative and when trivially short of targets, sales managers behave rudely

(Contd)

(b) Sales managers consume more time in completing official formalities before delivery of the products

(c) There is no discussion regarding the problems in selling faced by the salespeople in the sales meetings

(d) Sales managers seldom visit the customers

(e) Customers raise time objections in delivering the products

(f) Sales mangers entrust inexperienced salespeople in handling a few most profitable customers

(g) Sales mangers criticize them but do not suggest solutions

(h) For petty mistakes sales managers take an upper hand on them

From sales managers:

(a) Salespeople of rival firms are more proactive

(b) Salespeople are getting lazy

(c) Customers do not complain anything to us

(d) Customers are leaning more towards rival brands particularly 'Chemion'

(e) Salespeople are weak in developing customer relationships

(f) The company is somewhat lukewarm to their demands, particularly on perks. Sales managers of competing firms are given handsome incentives besides regular salaries

(g) Selection of sales force was somewhat faulty where we had no major role

(h) Few of the salespeople are really unmanageable

From customers:

(a) Lead time (time between placing an order and actual delivery) is high

(b) Neither sales managers nor salespeople visit them frequently

(c) Salespeople do not explain the problems (such as poor delivery, rare follow-up after sales, etc.) precisely

(d) Other firms are punctual in replenishment of our stocks

(e) We expect better deals from the VCL, particularly responsive behaviour

It is evident from the findings that a blame game has started amongst the three parties where customer views are to be treated seriously because their interests and issues are to be obliged with alacrity. But, it is true that there is a lack of cohesion between the salespeople and the sales managers. Managerial inattention to customers appears to be prominent.

(Contd)

Discussion Questions

Put yourself in two positions, first, the head of the consultancy firm and second, as a CEO of VCL and answer the following questions:

1. As a head of Ultra Solution:
   (a) Where are the lacunae of the recent problems of VCL?
   (b) What suggestions would you offer to the company?

2. As a CEO of VCL, you will trust on the report of VCL. But based on the excerpts of interviews,
   (a) What are the strategic action plans do you think imminent to arrest the situation?
   (b) Would you suggest radical changes in the sales force management?

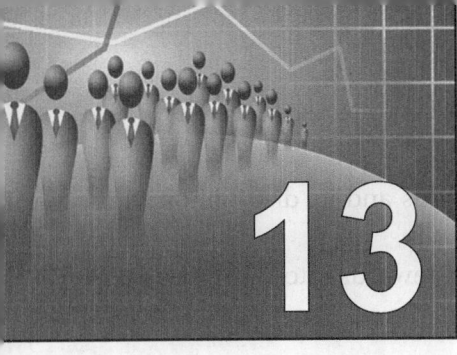

13 Sales Force Compensation

LEARNING OBJECTIVES

After reading this chapter, you will be able to

- understand the concept, definition, and types of compensation
- explain the basic features of sales force compensation plan
- comprehend the factors affecting the compensation plan designed for a sales force
- understand the insights of requirements and the aims of the compensation plan
- understand the characteristics of sales force compensation plan from strategic perspectives
- understand the steps in developing the compensation plan
- recognize different methods of compensation and their advantages and disadvantages
- explain the role of non-financial compensation for sales force motivation
- understand the strategic compensation system

13.1 COMPENSATION—CONCEPT, DEFINITION, AND TYPES

Compensation is defined as the money received by employees from the organization on account of the performance they render. When the employee receives the money in terms of salary or wage, it is known as direct compensation. When the employee receives benefits such as health insurance, medical benefits, travel allowances, etc. these are known as indirect compensations. Compensation is an integral part of an employee s sustenance and survival which has a motivational element also. An organization always wants to draw an effective compensation plan to make their employees content and motivated. An effective compensation plan fulfils the expectations of the employees and satisfies them. At the same time, it works towards the overall fulfilment of an organization's objectives.

Flippo (1984) defined compensation as the adequate and equitable remuneration of personnel for their contributions to the organizational objectives.

Foulkes and Livernash (1989) defined compensation as the payment of wages and salaries including incentive, bonus payments, and benefits to employees in exchange of work.

Agarwala (2007) defined compensation as the sum total of all forms of payments and rewards provided to the employees for performing tasks to achieve organizational objectives.

In a broad sense, compensation is a kind of employee reward. An organization lays an effective reward system management that works for the selection of rewards and its distribution to the employees.

Ingram et al. (2007) categorized organizational rewards into two types as follows:

(a) Compensation rewards

(b) Non-compensation rewards

Compensation rewards are offered to employees in return for their acceptable performance. Again, compensation rewards can be of two types—financial and non-financial. Financial rewards are given in terms of money such as salaries, commissions, etc. and non-financial rewards are non-monetary but no less attractive than financial rewards such as opportunity for growth, recognition, etc.

Non-compensation rewards relate to the favourable work situations and employee welfare, for example, a healthy job environment, consulting salespeople on sales plans, assigning a salesperson to an attractive territory. etc.

Agarwala (2007) mentioned two types of financial compensations, direct and indirect. Direct financial compensations include salaries, commissions, etc. Indirect financial compensations are pensions, insurance, paid time-off work, etc. Direct and indirect compensations are collectively called extrinsic rewards. Intrinsic rewards for employees are recognition, praise for job performance, etc.

13.2 SALES FORCE COMPENSATION PLAN—AN ILLUSTRATION

A compensation plan refers to the determination of the right compensation schemes and application of it to the sales force to bring a balance between compensation and the sales force performance. The basic purpose of the plan is to establish an equitable and fair distribution of salaries or wages, and other incentives amongst working personnel in a way that maintains equity between proportionate performance contribution of an employee and compensation received. So, a well-laid out compensation plan keeps away dissonance in compensation structure and policies.

It should be *judiciously devised* so that no single employee feels deprived and thinks compensation packages as unjustified. Otherwise, an experienced or skilled salesperson can feel under-compensated. The compensation plan, at the same time does not make room for overcompensation for young or rookie salespeople. Compensation is part of the organization's cost. So, one precondition for a sound compensation plan is that the total compensation should be decided at a level to be *consistent with the total earnings* of the firm and it does not violate the sales and profit objectives of the firm. Figure 13.1 shows the basic features of a compensation plan.

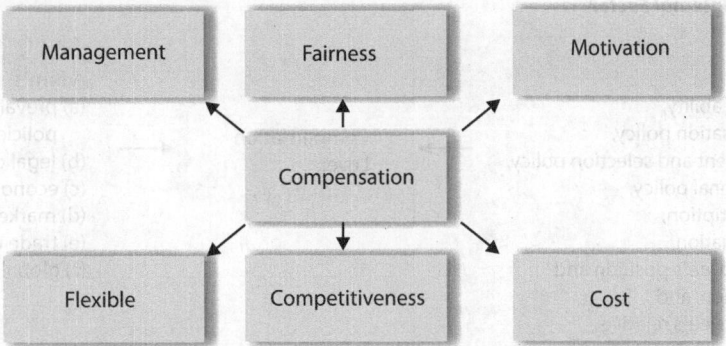

Figure 13.1 Basic features of a compensation plan

Motivation of employees is the central objective of compensation. In the selling context, it stimulates salespeople to work with more vigour and spirit. Cost is the guiding component of motivation. As compensation itself is a cost, it must be within the manageable level of the total profit and sales volumes of the firm. It regards the prevailing compensation level of the industry and is very much in congruence with the compensations offered by the competing firm.

A leading firm may even offer compensation above that of the average industry level to the sales force. It is flexible to meet the future changes in the compensation level. Future changes may imply company growth, sales turnover, increase of market share, etc. Secondly, it is flexible to accommodate the individual employee's increase of compensation. The compensation is impartial in all senses so that the right compensation for the right employee is decided. Here lies the fairness of compensation. It is commensurate with the financial capacity of the firm if it meets its requirements.

A compensation scheme is manageable in cases where its various elements such as salary, commission, fringe benefits, etc. are controllable and differences of it amongst employees are well-maintained to the satisfaction of both—the employees and the employer. Moreover, the coordination of compensation and financial power of the firm needs to be managed effectively as well.

13.3 FACTORS INFLUENCING COMPENSATION PLAN

Compensation level is influenced by a host of factors. Some factors are internal in nature and others are external. Internal factors are company-specific that relate to the company's resources, abilities, policies, etc. External factors are those that operate outside the organization, i.e., the external environment that have an effect on the compensation plans. Figure 13.2 represents the influence of these factors on the compensation level.

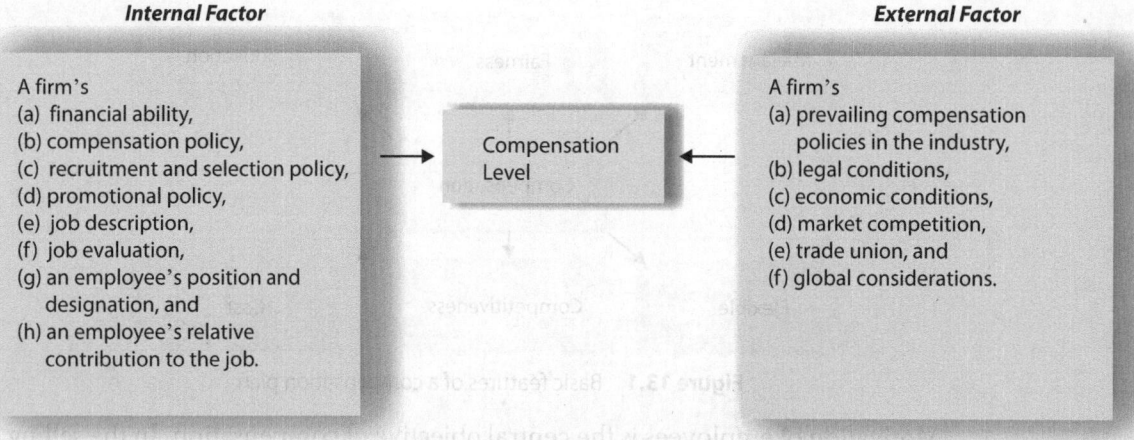

Internal Factor

A firm's
(a) financial ability,
(b) compensation policy,
(c) recruitment and selection policy,
(d) promotional policy,
(e) job description,
(f) job evaluation,
(g) an employee's position and
    designation, and
(h) an employee's relative
    contribution to the job.

Compensation
Level

External Factor

A firm's
(a) prevailing compensation
    policies in the industry,
(b) legal conditions,
(c) economic conditions,
(d) market competition,
(e) trade union, and
(f) global considerations.

Figure 13.2 Compensation level

Internal Factors

The internal factors are discussed in brief as follows:

Financial ability   A firm's liquidity position, returns on investment, financial outlay, etc. indicate the long-term financial capacity of a firm. A company's financial strength should be such that even in uncertain situations, it can adhere to the compensation policies and pay uniformly to all its employees.

Compensation policies   A company's compensation policies are determined by the number of employees working, number of permanent employees, number of casual staff, etc. Moreover, whatever policies the company follow (say, only salary schemes or performance-based incentive schemes) should have a relationship with the total remuneration volumes of the company.

Recruitment and selection policy   This influences the number of people that are on the payroll. The compensation policies should take into account the number of new employees inducted and the number of employees that are retired or have left.

Promotional policy   Compensation plans should be consistent with various managerial or non-managerial ranks and promotion from one rank to the next should be coupled with reasonable rise in salaries and other benefits.

Job descriptions   The volume of job (sales volume), its importance, and characteristics are related to the compensation level assigned to a job position.

Job evaluation   The worth of the job in terms of contributions in financial terms to an organization is related to the compensation level. For example, the contribution of a salesperson in selling a high unit value item such as a turbine or furnace to the firm is immense and therefore, the concerned employee needs to be suitably compensated.

An employer's designation and position An executive or managerial position definitely deserves higher pay level. Secondly, a senior in position demands a higher remuneration package than that of the junior employee.

An employee's relative contribution Here, merit of the employee is a decisive factor in finalizing his pay package. A high performing salesperson in a rank can deserve special attention in terms of incentives or rewards.

External Factors

The external factors including a compensation plan are discussed as follows:

Prevailing compensation policies in the industry Every industry has a trend to offer compensation to its salespeople and it is safe for a firm to follow the industry trend. This is especially true for medium and small companies with limited financial strength. But efficient salespeople, once they prove their worthiness, can bargain for better salaries or commissions. There is no difficulty in putting them on premium compensation packages in large companies.

Legal conditions As companies operate within the legal frame of governments, they need to strictly observe the legal policies and regulations of the governments. The government has legal stipulations on the minimum wages act or provisions for fringe benefits. But, many companies often violate these norms and engage salespeople on a meagre pay package and exploit them.

Economic conditions These are important pay level determinants. It is a customary practice in the industry circuit that with the rise in inflationary conditions, the companies escalate the level of the dearness allowance so that the employees can cope up with the rising price level. Similarly, under recessionary condition, the company itself remains in a depressed condition and percolate down the same to the employees. Therefore, employees are forced to remain with their existing pay package for a long time unless the gloom is over. Sometimes, one can see a reduction in the compensation as well and this is not an uncommon practice.

Market competition It is a great trigger to manage employees tactically on the compensation packages. Under highly competitive situations, the companies deploy strategies to sustain or survive in the chaotic situation and here, skilled employees become valued resources of the organization. The company wants to retain them desperately by giving them attractive pay levels to prevent sudden attritions. The efficient employees also can play their cards to compel reluctant companies to augment their pay levels.

Trade unions It often plays a mediating role in the company's decision to fix up different pay levels for employees along various positions. This is true in public sectors and large private sector firms. In small- or medium-sized firms, trade unions are generally non-existent and employees are forced to swallow the salary or wage levels as determined by the company.

Global considerations   These are important when the company establishes any subsidiary units in foreign nations or send their employees abroad to work on international projects or businesses. It is essential, therefore, for the company to understand the cost of living, tax structure, social or cultural norms, etc. of a nation that has strong relationships with compensation levels.

Ingram et al. (2007) noted that individualism is a prized practice than collectivism in work operations in the industry of some nations. Some other nations believe working in a team. So, the compensation for salespeople working as a team (e.g., salespeople engaged in team selling) is expected to be different than individual employees who are solely entrusted to perform a piece of job. Unites States is a follower of individualism where as, Japan is a strong votary of collectivism.

Criteria for Sound Compensation Scheme

A compensation scheme needs to follow some basic criteria or requirements. These are important for both the organization and salespeople for peaceful coexistence under one roof. It should serve the interests of both the parties equitably. Exhibit 13.1 furnishes the essential requirements of a compensation scheme that are designed for salespeople.

Compensation of sales force is a vital aspect of sales force management. It not only meets the basic needs of salespeople but also fulfils social and esteem needs, according to Maslow's need hierarchy.

Exhibit 13.1   Criteria for a sound compensation scheme

Following are the criteria for a sound compensation scheme:

1. It must ensure a guaranteed income to the salespeople who are in the payroll of the organization.
2. It should match a salesperson's qualification and experience.
3. It must precisely mention the fringe benefits, if any given to the salespeople. Fringe benefits include indirect compensations such house rent allowance, fuel allowance, tour allowance, etc.
4. It should be stated in simple form so that it is understood by the salespeople. The fixed and variable components of remuneration should be shown separately. The objective is to present the scheme in a lucid manner which salespeople can comprehend at a glance
5. There must be fairness of treatment for all the salespeople with a view to remove any conflict between the senior and junior salespeople and also amongst peers. A principle of equity should be maintained in its fixation.

(Contd)

(Contd)

6. It should show direction for increment with the year that will indicate salary raise both on the fixed and variable components of salaries of the salespeople.

7. The plan must get support and should be prepared in cognizance with the top management.

8. In this digital age, compensation is prepared electronically using software tools where performance records of salespeople are stored on databases that can be retrieved on an annual basis. Moreover, compensation schemes and structures are also readily available on stored computer files and calculation of remunerations can be made in a limited time with accuracy. So, skilled and efficient people who have expertise in the use of software and database management support expect a higher pay and are high in demand.

13.4 AIMS AND CHARACTERISTICS OF A COMPENSATION PLAN—A STRATEGIC INITIATIVE

Compensation plan is a part of strategic marketing plan. It is the line managers and their subordinates who are ultimately responsible for the implementation of these plans. A sound compensation plan should be consistent with the strategic marketing plan because it is linked to sales force motivation, coordination, and control. Satisfaction with the compensation schemes stimulates the salespeople to exert more selling efforts and achieve better results. Managers, too, can lead and supervise salespeople easily. Box 13.1 shows what a good compensation plan aims to fulfil.

Box 13.1 Aims of a good compensation plan

Following are the aims of a good compensation plan:

(a) To increase the enthusiasm and motivation of the salespeople

(b) To instil a sense of commitment in the salespeople towards their jobs

(c) To inject an atmosphere of team spirit and morale within the salespeople

(d) To develop a stable sales force and reduce the chances of attrition of sales force

(e) To retain the efficient sales force for a long run

(f) To co-ordinate and control the sales force successfully

(g) To attract efficient salespeople from the competing firms

(h) To increase the loyalty of the sales force to the firm

(i) To increase the quality of interaction of the salespeople with customers

(j) To improve the sense of confidence of customers on the sales force and the organization

(k) To create a dedicated sales force who leaves no stone unturned to reach the organization's goal

A good compensation plan is crucial for the financial health of the firm. It consolidates the position of the firm on both the financial and human resources.

Moreover, it establishes an image of the firm in the broad societal environment and employees, being happy, carry the image to everywhere in the society. The important characteristics of the compensation plan are summarized as follows:

Characteristics of a Good Compensation Plan

Following are the characteristics of a good compensation plan:

1. It is consistent with the position held by a salesperson and the job description laid down for such a position.
2. It decides the right salary and other benefits befitting the position and is at least in conformity with the prevalent salary structure for such a position in the industry.
3. It acts as a catalyst to improve the productivity of the organization.
4. Money is a great motivator. It acts in this direction. It provides satisfaction and security to the sales force.
5. It helps to improve the financial health of the employees, organization, and the society at large.
6. It does not distract the team spirit and the group cohesion within the sales force.
7. It helps to generate a hearty and a cordial relation between the salespeople and the sales managers.
8. It is simple and very easy for the salespeople to understand. The sales managers find no difficulty to apprise them on the plan.
9. It is flexible so that future changes in the compensation structure can easily be accommodated.
10. One of its components (particularly variable part such as commissions, bonuses, etc.) has a direct relationship with the sales force performance.
11. It helps to retain the existing sales force particularly those who perform satisfactorily for the firm. Alternatively, it keeps the competing firms away to pull out the efficient salespeople.
12. It is in sync with the sales and profit objectives of the firm.
13. It is acceptable to both the salespeople and the employers.
14. It generates a positive correlation between compensation and motivation, and motivation and performance.
15. It provides salespeople with a direction for individual goal-fulfilment.
16. It enhances the job involvement and the commitment to the job.
17. It increases the sense of belongingness of the salespeople to the company.
18. It acts within the contours of the strategic marketing plans of the company.

13.5 STEPS IN COMPENSATION PLAN—A DEVELOPMENTAL PROCESS

A compensation plan should be well thought out and balanced. This means it aims to satisfy both the employees and the employers justifiably. Moreover, it is formulated keeping in mind the broad organizational objectives. It fits well with the strategic initiatives of the company. Figure 13.3 shows a schematic presentation of the steps in developing a compensation plan.

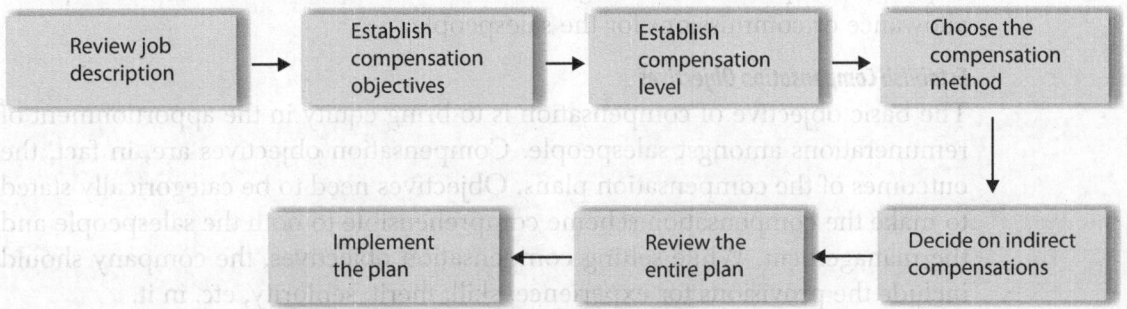

Figure 13.3 Steps in developing a compensation plan

All these steps have been explained in detail as follows:

Review Job Description

Analysing job description is the starting point of developing a compensation plan. Careful analysis of the features of job description helps a company decide the pay level of the salespeople holding the job title mentioned in the job description. A detailed profile of the job description is discussed in Chapter 8. A job description gives a clear picture of the characteristics of the primary and secondary job responsibilities.

The company should decide the compensation level for the salespeople considering the importance and volume of the jobs listed in the job description. Education and experience are two important qualities of the salespeople and the company should not hesitate to value these factors while formulating the compensation level. Suitable adjustments in this regard should be incorporated in the job description and the compensation levels. So, accurate job evaluation from the job description ensures fairness of compensation.

Job evaluation is a method of precise adjustment of compensation with the jobs prescribed in the job description. Job evaluation is the assessment of the relative worth of the components of job responsibilities and duties so that the formal appraisal of expected and enacted job performance of salespeople can easily be made. The objective is to ascertain the level of knowledge, skill, experience needed to perform the tasks in the desired and actual manner. A comparison can also be made to decide on the promotion and subsequent increment of remunerations. Merits should get a special emphasis in fixing the compensation level.

Management should see that a meritorious salesperson should not be undervalued in the scheme of the compensation plan. The type of products to be dealt and the markets to be served have a significant connotation with the remunerations offered. A slow selling but high-unit cost item (e.g., turbine) demands extremely deft and laborious selling efforts and deserve attractive compensation for the salespeople. Again, a highly competitive market where a salesperson needs to push more persuasive selling efforts to cut competition should draw special allowance or commissions for the salespeople.

Establish Compensation Objectives

The basic objective of compensation is to bring equity in the apportionment of remunerations amongst salespeople. Compensation objectives are, in fact, the outcomes of the compensation plans. Objectives need to be categorically stated to make the compensation scheme comprehensible to both the salespeople and the management. While setting compensation objectives, the company should include the provisions for experience, skill, merit, seniority, etc. in it.

These objectives are to be goal-directed and should be able to tackle any complications that may arise in the present or future circumstances. For example, a sudden decline in the sales volume needs additional time and effort from the senior sales personnel to overcome the situation or an unexpected rise in sales due to the hard and painstaking efforts from the salespeople can expect additional disbursement of indirect compensations to encourage sales employees and boost their morale. As a result salespeople can put in more diligence for economic advancement of the firm. Objectives should not be some rigid and conventional statements. Instead, they should include variability factors in the market such as new product–market situations, competition, new-market development, etc. and relate it to the performance of salespeople and their compensation levels.

Compensation objectives, again should aim to fulfil the personal goals of the salespeople which can be understood by the satisfaction of the sales force within and outside the organization. The job involvement, achievement, and affiliation motives, etc. are the indexes of a salesperson's satisfaction within the organization. A salesperson's quality of life (say, personal life, family life, social life, etc.) is an index of his satisfaction outside the organization. Bhattacharya (2007) reported that Cognizant Technology Solutions design their compensation packages to help their employees grow and develop in every sphere of life.

Three pivotal aspects of compensation objectives are operations, control, and measurability. Objectives should not be non-practical so that these cannot be implemented. Suppose, the management attaches a hefty market-share level as a yardstick to allow commissions to the salespeople that are absolutely unattainable. This will mar the basic spirit of the salespeople and adversely affect their performances.

Second, these objectives should have inherent controlling features that the management can use to steer the compensation scheme on the right path. For example, the sales performance is definitely an index of compensation but at the same time selling expenses should not be ignored. Performance–expense ratios give a definite projection of the actual performances of the salespeople.

Third, performances should be measurable for them to be operational in nature. For example, order–call ratio, sales–selling expenses ration, sales–gross profit ratio, etc. are estimated to appraise the performances of the salespeople, which obviously act as an important decider of the compensation levels, particularly the variable components of it.

Establish Compensation Levels

Establishing the compensation level is the third step in the compensation plan. The objective of this is to establish a right compensation level for a group of salespeople belonging to a common rank. Rank and compensation level, therefore, have a strong association. The management should be careful to fix an appropriate compensation level for senior and junior salespeople, sales trainees and salespeople, sales executives and sales representatives, etc. But at the same time, one should also review the plan so that a wide discrimination, between the seniors and the juniors, does not intrude the compensation plan.

Before setting the level, salespeople should be made aware of the different components of the compensation i.e., the fixed part (e.g., salaries), variable part (e.g., commissions and bonuses), deferred part (e.g., provident fund, gratuity, etc.). In general, a company follows the present average industry trend of compensation level for a rank because it is safe and tested. However, if the company wants to exceed the average limit, it must take precautions to examine the fit between the compensation and company's sales or profit goals.

For a stable market where the company has secured returns on investment, slightly higher compensation level does not affect the company's financial strength. But, a company might feel unsteady in settling a compensation plan for highly unpredictable or threatening market situations. This may happen due to competitive aggression, fall in market demands, etc. This is why strategic compensation plan is thought out. It basically takes into account future environmental situations and draws a long-term compensation plan that can safeguard against any odd situation in the market. For example, under inflationary condition, with the rise in price level, a certain percentage increase of dearness allowance benefits the salespeople without disturbing the sales or profit targets. In this regard, a slight modification of price level of the company's products or services can be made because inflation triggers a general rise in the price level of all commodities in the market.

Methods of Compensation

Direct compensation is a major part of the compensation plan. A company can choose from the following compensation plans to match compensation levels for salespeople:

(a) Straight salary

(b) Straight commission

(c) A number of combination plans such as salary and commission, salary and bonus, and commission and bonus.

Salary is the fixed sum of money paid to the salespeople generally on a monthly basis. Under commission, salespeople are paid a percentage of the sales or gross profits they generate for the firm. Commission is given on the basis of the total volume of work done irrespective of the time spent for the completion of the job.

Bonus is a payment paid to the salespeople for achieving desired results that fulfil the organization's goals. Bonus is a kind of reward that the management pays to the salespeople over salaries or commissions or both due to some achievement that the company feels rewarding. So, it is a subject matter of the management's discretion. Management decides the basis for bonus payment (say, a certain percentage of salary). It also decides the mode of payment (say, annually).

Combination plans, at present are very popular. It ensures a stable income for the salespeople provided that salary is one component of the plan. It provides a variable income to the salespeople also in terms of commissions and/or bonuses. The variable part depends on the salesperson's performance level. Combination plans motivate salespeople because of multiple compensation elements. However, it demands more management time and effort to run the combination plan.

Deciding Indirect Monetary Compensation

The indirect monetary compensation is a monetary reward that is not direct such as salary or commission. It includes retirement pension, gratuity, payment from insurance plans (e.g., medical insurance, group life insurance, disability compensations, thrift savings plan, paid holiday, paid vacations). These together are called fringe benefits. Indirect compensation is a great source of attraction for efficient salespeople. It helps the company to hold the existing salespeople and attract new salespeople of competing firms offering fewer benefits. A company's salespeople bear a sense of security and satisfaction from the fringe benefits. They do not hesitate to perform with huge motivation and the company at the end excels.

Review the Compensation Plan

Drawing out a plan is one part of the plan and implementation is the other. In between the two, an important requirement is the viability of the plan. So, a compensation plan should be thoroughly checked before its implementation. The basic requirement of a plan is its aim to fulfil the compensation objectives.

This is the first and the foremost decision in the compensation plan. Second, financial resource of the firm must facilitate plan implementation and its continuation for a long time. Third, the plan can absorb shocks such as sudden spurt of inflation or recession, tough market competition, change in the regulatory mechanisms (say, change in the indirect tax structure stipulated by the central or state government), etc. So, the company should make provision for a contingency plan along with the main plan to counter adverse consequences in the business environment. Fourthly, the company should make budgetary allocation to meet the annual increment of salaries, commission or bonus payments.

Before the announcement of commission or bonus rates, they must ensure that these will not negatively affect a company's financial health. The rates must be commensurate with the sales volume achieved or profits earned. In this regard, previous experience of the company with the similar product or service or marketing research on industry situations on rate structure or annual increment of salaries, etc. can help a company to pre-test the entire plan before it is introduced. So, before execution, the plan should be verified to see that it meets an organization's sales and profit goals. Also, it is important to note that it covers all compensatory expenses adequately. Last but not the least it must act within the budgetary estimates of the company for a financial year.

Implementation of the Plan

Here, the crucial decision that the company has to take is whether it will implement it for all salespeople such as executives, juniors, seniors, trainees, commission agents, etc. or for a selected group as a test case. The company takes a decision to implement it for salespeople working in two/three territories and if successful makes it operational for all salespeople. Once introduced, it must continue for a long term and effectively use contingency plans in case of urgency.

Starting from conception to the development and implementation, a compensation plan is designed to serve employees for their all-round welfare. In turn, it pays back to the organization in multiples of what the organization spends. But, what is important is stretching the compensation cost in a calculated manner, so that it never exceeds a company's sales budget. Exhibit 13.2 presents how WIPRO, an illustrious name in the Indian industrial scene has developed a unique compensation package for its employees.

Exhibit 13.2   WIPRO—a saga in employee compensation

WIPRO has set an example by setting multifarious compensation schemes for its employees. In fact, the company has the track record of being consistent and positive towards

(Contd)

(Contd)

the well-being of its workforce including salespeople. The benefit it offers in the name of compensation and other facilities is highly lucrative and comparable to the best pay package of any other reputed company. The compensation schemes that the company plans and implements are applicable to its entire staff irrespective of their positions. But what WIPRO expects from its employees is the performance that is worth the compensation received. WIPRO is quite open-handed in handing both financial and non-financial compensations to the employees.

Some of the dotted features of WIPRO's compensation schemes besides conventional compensations are as follows:

(a) Full medical assistance programme for its employees and its family members

(b) Facilitating self-development programme by providing educational assistance plan. It even allows sabbatical leave to deserving employees for higher studies that will enrich one's profession

(c) Offers interest-free loans to cover housing deposits or purchase of two wheelers

(d) Offers contingency loans for marriage, illness or death of a close family member

(e) Offers stock options as a part of employee empowerment to employees (WIRO employee stock option plan, WESOP).

(f) Credit card facility

(g) Engages an external agency to take care of the domestic chores such as payment of bills, personal travel booking, etc. for the employees

(h) To provide shuttle services for employees to reach the development centres, canteens, cafeteria, etc.

The list is quite long. In fact, what WIPRO is doing for its workforce is worthy of discussion. The basic philosophy that saliently pervades in each dotted feature of its compensation is to consider its employees as the greatest assets in the organization.

Source: 'Life@Wipro', http://www.wipronfra.com/lifeatwipro.html, accessed on 28 April 2010.

The success of the company on productivity or performance depends a lot on the right selection of compensation method that motivates as well as satisfies the sales force. Otherwise, the company might have to face failure.

There are a number of compensation methods, which are broadly classified. Every method has its own advantage and disadvantage. Each has its application in specific selling situations and is applicable to a particular category of sales force as well. Hence, a manager needs to consider all variables before choosing a salary method. A detailed discussion on each method is made as follows:

Straight Salary

Straight salary is the commonest form of all compensation schemes. It involves paying a fixed sum of money to salespeople for performing certain duties over a given period of time. The amount paid is not related to how much a salesperson performs or the quality of performance. It is paid at regular intervals (commonly on monthly basis). So, it is neither based on the unit of time nor on the volume of work. It is a fixed sum paid to salespeople regardless of their performance, fluctuation of business or economic conditions. The method has some advantages and disadvantages. These are illustrated as follows.

Advantages   Following are the advantages of straight salary:

1. It provides a sense of security to the salespeople.
2. It ensures stability of income to the salespeople, thus allaying fear of fluctuation in earnings.
3. It helps to develop a loyal sales force.
4. An attractive salary plan resists high turnover of salespeople.
5. It enhances a sense of belongingness of the salespeople to a company.
6. It is safe to new salespeople or sales trainees who are assured of a steady income as opposed to straight commission.
7. The method is simple to understand, to keep intricate calculation under straight commission or combination plan, and is economical in application.
8. Salespeople feel more committed to their jobs.
9. Salespeople pay more attention to retain old customers than generate new customers.
10. Salespeople can concentrate more on the satisfaction of customer needs. As a result, customers feel more loyal towards the company.
11. Salespeople can give more attention to non-selling activities such as marketing research, territory development, developing distribution network, etc. Salespeople working on commissions alone generally avoid these jobs.
12. Sales managers can exercise close control and supervision on the salespeople.

Disadvantages   Following are the disadvantages of straight salary:

1. It has no provision to pay any incentives to the salespeople. This may restrain salespeople to take additional initiative and drive in personal selling jobs
2. The selling expenses are not related to sales volume. Thus, regardless of the sales volume, selling expenses are incurred by the company
3. The method offers equal treatment to both high and low performing salespeople. As a result of inequitable distribution of compensations, efficient salespeople feel disappointed
4. The scheme may not attract highly efficient salespeople from competing firms

5. It seriously lacks motivational push for potential and energetic salespeople
6. It may discourage salespeople to offer additional efforts, particularly for hard selling items
7. Hard working salespeople may not find this method attractive

Box 13.2 talks of situations where the straight salary method is suitable.

Box 13.2   Application of straight salary method

Following are the applications of the straight salary method:

(a) It is effective for sales trainees or newly appointed salespeople

(b) The company can adopt this scheme when it has a stable market position or assumes a leading position in the market

(c) When the brand names of the company's products are well-established they seldom need any promotional push to reach the target customers

(d) When salespeople are engaged mostly in non-selling jobs such as collecting information from the market, follow-up after sales, concept selling, educational selling, customer relationship building, missionary selling, etc.

(e) The company introduces a new product or a product line in the market

(f) When the salespeople are engaged in team selling

(g) The company wants to go for extensive prospecting drive

(h) The market reaches a saturation point and the salespeople are engaged in routine selling

(i) The company wants to enter a new geographical territory

(j) The product is technically complex and a long-term negotiation period is needed to complete the sale

(k) A lot of pre-selling through advertising and post-selling through follow-up calls to allay consumer fears on product use become crucial to increase customer base

(l) When products are sold through distributors or retailers where in-store merchandising and display are important

---

Straight Commission

Here, salespeople are compensated on the basis of the percentage of sales or gross profits that they produce for the firm. Salespeople are rewarded for the volume of sales or profits they generate which is compensated over time. Thus, compensation is directly related to performance of the salespeople. A percentage of commission (called commission rate) on sales volume in rupees or quantity is the base of determining the compensation. This is determined by the company management. Box 13.3 shows some of its applications.

The term for payment of compensation is also a management decision area. For example, the management may decide to pay the compensation after it receives the payment from the customers for the order served by the salespeople. Insurance companies, real estate firms, industrial distributors, etc. engage salespeople on commission basis. Companies that engage salespeople to work on door-to-door selling engage salespeople on commission basis. The method has certain advantages and disadvantages. These are discussed as follows.

Advantages   Following are the advantages of straight commission:

(a) It acts as a great motivator for salespeople who are high achievers in terms of sales performance

(b) It differentiates high performing salespeople from mediocre or low performing ones

(c) There is an unlimited opportunity for efficient salespeople to earn money

(d) As there is a close relation between performance and reward, the management feels no such pressure to incur selling costs

(e) Selling cost is related to sales volume. Selling costs are incurred when sales volumes pick up

(f) Salespeople can work freely because the management has no or lesser degree of control and supervision unlike pure salary scheme

(g) The method is easy to understand and economical to operate

(h) Salespeople know that their performance speaks of their earnings. So, they cannot complain to the management for any underpayment

(i) Salespeople would not resent against any pressure selling jobs

Disadvantages   Following are the disadvantages of straight commission:

(a) Loss of control over the activities of salespeople may render this scheme untenable

(b) Salespeople may show fewer interests to sell those goods that are slow selling or less profit making

(c) Rather, salespeople may concentrate easy selling items or high profit per unit selling items

(d) Salespeople may persuade the customers to buy expensive variants of any product despite the availability of economical product items serving the same purpose of the customers

(e) Salespeople may take up aggressive selling approach that can adversely affect the image of the company

(f) Salespeople may lack a sense of belongingness to company

(g) Salespeople can divulge valuable information of the company to outside sources

(h) Salespeople may not pay attention to the non-selling activities (e.g., after-sales service)

(i) Salespeople may not be interested in building long-term relationships with the customers

(j) Salespeople do not find any certainty of their income. When the economic environment is adverse (say, recession) earnings are small

(k) Salespeople would not be interested in a developed market

Box 13.3 shows the applications of the commission method.

Box 13.3 Applications of the commission method

Following are the applications of the commission method:

(a) When the company wants to relate selling expenses to sales volume

(b) When the financial capacity of the company is weak

(c) When the non-selling activities are not important

(d) When the company appoints part-time salespeople

(e) When the company wants to do overseas selling of its items

(f) When the financial strength of the company is weak

Combination Plans

Combination plans include putting together two to three compensation options. The purpose of the compensation plan is to iron out the demerits of one plan by the merits of the other. It creates an integrated advantage to both the company and the salespeople that is more than the advantages of one single plan. Thus, it ensures a regular income and an incentive for selling over a predetermined level. The plan has the capacity to benefit both the company and the salespeople. The company can expect high sales productivity from the salespeople who are motivated by the incentives to work harder for the company.

Combination plans falls into following three categories:

(a) Salary and commission

(b) Salary and bonus

(c) Salary plus commission and bonus

Salary and commission is the most popular of all the combination plans. The plan is developed on the basis of adding a certain percentage of the salary as commission with the salary to determine the total compensation. Alternatively, a suitable percentage division of the total compensation into salary and commission is the basis of this method. Salary constitutes the fixed part and commission, the variable part of the total compensatory amount. The right proportion of the two makes the scheme attractive to the salespeople and acceptable to the company.

When the company wants to operate selling operations with a moderate to small budget but at the same time desires to yield maximum efforts from salespeople, salary and bonus scheme is effective. Bonus is subject to managerial discretion. The time of bonus payment is contingent on the managerial decision. The bonus amount is decided on a certain percentage of salary of an employee. But under commission, a certain predetermined percentage of volume of the sales or amounts sold or the total profits are given as commission to the workforce. When the management decides to pay bonus, it considers a salesperson's overall performance which is evaluated not only on sales figure but also on customer satisfaction, customer relationship, after-sales service, etc.

The percentage of bonus payment is generally not known to salespeople in advance unlike commission. When a company does a lot of pre-selling activities such as advertising, it lessens the role of the salespeople to develop customer awareness or persuasive selling effort. Under such a situation, salary plus bonus is a better option than salary and commission. Again management can control selling expenses in salary and bonus better than the salary and commission scheme. Though the bonus percentage is not declared earlier, still salespeople can get some idea of the company's bonus payment from the past records or old experiences.

The salary plus commission and bonus plan combines the three in a way that overcomes the demerits of each and generate more benefits for both the salespeople and the company. *Salary* gives security to the salespeople. It also helps the management to have a certain control on the sales force. Commission adds on the income of the salespeople. It is a strong performance-linked incentive. It benefits the company by getting additional productivity. *Bonus* acts as an incentive to motivate the salespeople and the company gets a more committed and loyal sales force. But, the crucial part of the plan is to determine the share of each element to the total compensation i.e., determining the right proportion of the salary, commission and bonus to finalize actual compensation of salespeople. For slow selling items (e.g., boilers, industrial equipments, etc.), this scheme can be effective. A salesperson does both the selling and the non-selling (e.g., after-sales services) activities giving equal importance to both. So, for high-priced or unit-value products, the scheme can get satisfactory results, benefiting the sales force and the company together. Advantages and disadvantages of the combination plans are mentioned as follows.

Sales quota is often treated as a benchmark to determine bonus level for salespeople. Realistic and achievable sales quota acts a great motivator for salespeople. Moreover, when the bonus is linked with such sales quota, motivation level increases manifold. The scheme is known as sales quota bonus plan. A sales quota is defined as the sales target for salespeople to achieve within a given time period.

Kumra (2008) reported (based on the research on pharmaceutical industries) that from optimum bonuses and sales quota plans, firms can maximize their profits and give salespeople adequate incentives. Balancing selling costs against salespersons' motivation vis-à-vis satisfaction is a challenging task to the organization.

Advantages The advantages of the salary plus commission and bonus plan are as follows:

(a) It provides a stable income as well as additional income due to financial incentives
(b) Salary gives the salespeople a sense of security and confidence, and the incentives stimulate their desires to earn more by generating more sales
(c) A part of the income varies with sales productivity. Incentive part brings flexibility to the scheme
(d) Combination plans tackle differences in the sales potentials across territories better as compared to a singe plan
(e) Efficient salespeople are benefited by this scheme
(f) The combination scheme is ideal for energetic and diligent salespeople
(g) The scheme can be made flexible by suggesting different combinations of components for different salespeople such as sales trainees, salespeople working for two to three years in a company, senior salespeople, etc.

Disadvantages The disadvantages of the salary plus commission and bonus plan are as follows:

(a) The plan is not simple to understand and is difficult to operate
(b) Selling costs vary across different selling situations therefore, establishing performance–reward relationship and comparing these across selling situations are difficult
(c) Sales managers may find it difficult to control the sales operations
(d) The plan requires constant recording of sales turnover. It may appear cumbersome to the sales managers
(e) The plan requires high actuarial practices
(f) It demands high administrative costs
(g) Finding out the composition of the plan may be a problem. To decide what should be the fixed and variable components of the plan, what are their proportions, etc. are time-taking and laborious
(h) As sales vary across territories, sales turnover are also different. So, evaluation and comparison of sales force performance on common performance standards are difficult. Therefore, combination plans lead to unequal income of the salespeople

(i) The salespeople may underestimate the non-selling activities

(j) When the sales target level is fixed at a high level for salespeople to attend and earn commissions, it discourages salespeople to do their best

(k) Frequency of incentives payment should be shorter, otherwise, it may despair salespeople seriously. Long-term deferred payment of incentives may frustrate salespeople

Box 13.4 shows the application of the combination plans

Box 13.4   Application of combination plans

Following are the applications of the combination plan:

1. The company operates in a highly competitive market and wants a stable sales force to counter competition. An attractive combination plan can serve the purpose to this end.

2. The product faces a stage of maturity or decline in the product lifecycle and the company wants its sales force to avert the falling trend of sales by undertaking more promotional efforts to retain existing customers. A sound combination plan can influence salespeople to work towards this end.

3. For technically complex products or products of high quality, salespeople are expected to deal with the customers intelligently and sensibly. A good combination plan can act as a motivator for the salespeople to apply themselves in the desired way.

4. The company can use this scheme at the launching stage of a product to encourage sales force to work hard to create high awareness cum sales level spearheading a good start of the product lifecycle.

5. Sales managers can use this scheme to evaluate proficiency on selling amongst salespeople. This can help the management to decide on the promotional matters for the salespeople.

13.6   COMPENSATION SCHEMES—A NON-FINANCIAL APPROACH

Non-financial compensation follows the financial one to motivate salespeople. In fact, usually salespeople do not bother much about the financial compensation because they eventually obtain it after a fixed time period. Non-financial compensation appears to be more interesting than their counterpart. So, from the motivational point of view, non-financial compensation aggrandizes the interest and enthusiasm of salespeople. Some common non-financial compensation schemes are described as follows.

Career Advancement through Promotion

It is regarded as a valued and awaited reward for salespeople working in a company for substantive periods and expecting promotions to the next higher positions. Many companies have career advancement schemes as policy decisions that promote salespeople regardless of vacancies as a consequence of working in a particular position for a particular period of time. But claimants for promotions in some cases are many because salespeople working in the same positions for more or less the same time periods and aspiring for promotions are sometimes many. In such situations, the company takes promotional interviews to lift the deserving candidates to higher positions.

But, given the limited opportunity in higher ranks, the management should formulate more objective-based promotional policies where performance records, important customer reports, punctuality, integrity, etc. to the company are thoroughly scrutinized to offer promotions to the candidates. The suitability of a candidate to higher positions is an important decision question. Generally, all-round ability in selling of the candidates is observed closely to take decisions on promotions. Promotion means putting additional responsibilities on the candidates. Here, job enrichment is crucial. Through job enrichment, the company adds more tasks, activities, and responsibilities to the salespeople. At the same time, salespeople get more independence to accomplish their tasks.

Recognition

Salespeople aspire eagerly for this non-financial reward too to get solid footings within the company. Praise from management, peers, customers, other departmental staff provides a huge sense of satisfaction to the salespeople. Salespeople, when receive accolades or kudos from the management, consider it as a great recognition in their hard fought career. A salesperson may even be rewarded with a gift or other kinds in a banquet party, get together platform or annual cultural programmes of the company.

Recognition may be formal or informal. An affectionate pat on the back from a senior or a management staff or a hug from seniors is informal recognitions that motivate salespeople. Formal recognition employs offering prizes, medals, performance certificates in a banquet party or company socials, sending successful salespeople to national or international conferences, etc.

Selling Expenses

These are reimbursements made to the salespeople for the expenses they incur legitimately on the job. Typical reimbursement expenses are travelling, lodging, telephones, customer entertainments, etc. The salesperson submits the expense accounts to the finance department of the company after being duly verified and countersigned by the sales managers. In many situations, salespeople submit exaggerated expense accounts to gain unethically more than the actual expenses. This is why salespeople are asked to submit bills, receipts, vouchers, and expense statements to show the legitimacy of their expenses.

Overcharging by fictitious expenses heads and amounts (called padding) simply drains out redundant funds from the company's coffer. The company takes every step to prevent padding and for this reason the company fixes an expense quota or expense budget ceiling to control undue expenses by salespeople.

Fringe Benefits

Fringe benefits are a type of compensation made in addition to normal financial compensations such as salary, commission, etc. A list of fringe benefits is presented as follows:

(i) Medical benefits: Payments for medical reimbursement policies, running medical expenses for sales employees and their close and dependent family members, annual health checkups, hospitalization benefits, etc.

(ii) Retirement benefits: Pensions, provident funds, gratuities, group insurance, etc.

(iii) Company stock options: Ability to buy the company's shares at reduced prices

(iv) Leave travel concessions

(v) Paid vacations, etc.

Perks

Some companies pay their executives and managers special privileges as a mark of their position, power, prestige, and social affiliations they enjoy within and outside the company. These privileges are termed as perks. For example, free cars, fuel charges, car parking facilities, personal secretaries, drivers, bungalow at moderate rentals, room furnishings, etc.

Sales Contests

Sales contests are temporary incentives programmes designed by the management to offer some attractive incentives such as prizes or other monetary or non-monetary rewards for achieving some short-term goals or objectives in both selling and non-selling activities by the salespeople. The main objective of it is to motivate strongly the salespeople to serve the interests of both—the company and the individual. The company wants to influence salespeople to work towards sales goals and for this sake, the company organizes contests amongst salespeople. This can happen within the sales team to incite group competition or among salespeople for showing individual performance.

The organization also runs sales contests on performance-related to non-selling activities. For example, a salesperson is rewarded for showing high customer relationship skills. In this regard, customer viewpoints can be collected in confidence on their satisfaction levels with the dealings of salespeople. Again, contests can take place based on how many customer calls are received for order after the salespeople visit them. The total volume of orders in monetary terms or quantity can be a point of contest amongst salespeople.

Sales contests are high stimulators for salespeople to work harder and smarter. Winning a sales contest provides a high confidence level and a sense of accomplishment amongst salespeople.

13.7 STRATEGIC COMPENSATION SYSTEM SCS—AN IMPERATIVE TO SALES FORCE MANAGEMENT

Strategic compensation system (SCS) is yet another innovative system that has become a part and parcel of human resource management of an organization. In fact, employee motivation and control, the two essential components of human resource management are highly influenced by SCS. SCS has been defined as the right selection of compensation tool, developing it in line with the compensation objectives and application of it with an aim to attain broad strategic pursuits of the compensation. The essential condition for SCS is that it must fit well with the resource capabilities of the firm. The major goals the SCS are as follows:

(a) To distribute compensations equitably amongst employees so that reasonable differences in pay levels exist between the junior and senior employees, skilled and unskilled workforce.

(b) To design and develop the compensation packages in a manner that fulfils the objectives of the firm and the employee's personal goals.

(c) Compensation is a motivational tool. Therefore, SCS aims to correlate the employee performance and compensation in a way that it acts as an engine to boost motivation and the morale of the employees.

(d) The controlling aspect of compensation is important in the sense that an organization needs to evaluate the performance of the employees and put control whenever the performance deviates from the benchmarks

(e) To reward employees who perform according to the set standards established by the company.

Compensation is a reason for obligation the employees to serve the company. It enables the management to send direction to the workforce and awakens its sense of accountability for the work done. SCS acts as a facilitator to shape compensation plans. This is applicable to the sales organization as well. Salespeople are, to some extent, characteristically different from employees working in production or other departments. The specific features of SCS for salespeople are as follows:

1. Salespeople can work not only on straight salary system but also on different combination plans such as salary plus commission, or salary plus bonus, etc. Production employees may earn wages and bonuses but the basic difference is the yardstick to judge the incentives for salespeople that is more rigorous.

How much sales volume they will attain or profits they ensure for the company determines their incentive levels.

2. The percentage of commissions offered to salespeople is an important decision area. SCS should suggest a balanced commission percentage and other incentives that motivate salespeople to work hard and cause high sales productivity.

3. Compensation is a product of multiple units. Basically, it has a fixed basic component. It has a variable component also. A sound SCS makes the components flexible. It means these can be changed or adjusted over time. This is relevant to sales force because they are asked to move from one sales territory to the other and are required to face varied market conditions, different customer bases and competitive situations. So, they expect suitable modifications of their compensation levels when they cover difficult sales territories. SCS should have provisions for it.

4. SCS should bestow competitive advantage to the firm. This can be better understood when the company is able to retain skilled salespeople and trigger self-motivation and social esteem within them.

5. SCS should have provisions for team-based incentives when the salespeople work as a team. Here, team performance is a deciding factor to adjudge the compensation levels. But, the striking point is that a team consists of both the efficient and moderately efficient salespeople. An efficient salesperson may not work to the potential or show individual performance in a team. But when a company requires a team effort for sales operation (e.g., selling, commissioning and servicing furnace or turbine to the industrial customers) team dynamics is an important behavioural issue. A skilled salesperson joins the team. This may cause disappointment for the salesperson to work with mediocre salespeople. So, management must work up the task to oversee equitable opportunities for performance and distributing compensations proportional to the performances. So, a salesperson's earnings while working in a team should be consistent with the relative contribution to team's overall performance. This should be done without disturbing the team harmony or morale.

IT and ITES (IT enabled sectors) offering a wide range of services such as business process outsourcing, knowledge process outsourcing (KPO), software and hardware consultancy projects are worth mentioning for their lucrative compensation packages and high incentives.

Top-notched companies such as Microsoft, Oracle, Satyam, Infosys, IBM, etc. are quite successful in attracting and retaining talented employees including sales and service personnel. The same is happening with the telecommunication sector.

Bigwigs such as Bharati Airtel, Reliance Communications, Nokia, Siemens, LG, etc. offer competitive packages to attract and hold talented human resources.

What is more important in those sectors is performance. It is the key to determine the stability of workforce. Companies are whole hearted in offering bounties of incentives, paid vacations, housing allowances, vehicles and other attractive perks but what it expects from employees are performances at par expectations of the organizations. These companies are quite successful in their compensation systems. Their proven track records and employee contributions speak volumes for it. In fact, the mystery of success, to some extent, is giving major importance in strategic compensation system. SCS is deemed to be an adjunct of strategic human resource management (SHRM).

SUMMARY

Compensation is defined as the money received by employees on account of the performances they render for a firm. When the employees receive salaries or wages, these are known as direct compensations. When they receive benefits such as health insurance, medical benefits, travel allowances, etc. these are known as indirect compensations. Compensation is a motivational tool. The organization uses it to motivate salespeople so that they give their best efforts to fulfil organizational objectives. At the same time, it aims to serve an employee's personal goals. Motivation is a kind of reward.

A compensation plan refers to the determination of the right compensation policies and application of it to the workforce to bring a balance between the compensation and performance offered by salespeople. The basic purpose of the plan is to ensure equitable and fair distribution of compensations amongst salespeople. The six basic features of

compensation are management, fairness, competitiveness, flexible, motivation, and cost.

Compensation plan is affected by factors both internal and external to the firm. The steps in developing the compensation plan are reviewing the job description, establishing compensation objectives, establishing compensation levels, choosing the compensation method, deciding on indirect compensation, reviewing the entire plan, and implementing the plan. The major compensation methods are straight salary, straight commission, salary plus commission, salary plus bonus, and salary plus commission plus bonus. The last three are combination plans. Each method has its advantages and disadvantages. The company offers salespeople non-financial incentives such as career advancement through promotion, recognition, selling expenses, fringe benefits, perks, and sales contests.

KEY TERMS

Bonus Bonus refers to the extra pay that an employee receives due to his good performance or an organization's achievement.

Compensation Compensation is defined as the remuneration that an employee receives from an

organization on account of providing their services to it.

Compensation Plan Compensation plan refers to the determination of the right compensation schemes and application of it to the sales force to bring a balance between the compensation and sales force performance.

Commission Commission is usually given to an employee on the basis of the total volume of work done irrespective of time spent for the completion of the job.

Salary Salary is a form of periodic payment from an employer to an employee, which may be specified in an employment contract.

Strategic Compensation System Strategic compensation system is an innovative system which helps in the right selection of the compensation tool. It is developed on the line of the compensation objectives and application from company to company.

REVIEW QUESTIONS

1. Define compensation. What are its basic properties?
2. What are the aims of a compensation plan?
3. Distinguish between direct and indirect compensations.
4. What are the characteristics of a sound compensation plan?
5. What are the steps in developing a compensation plan? Explain each step with its contribution to the plan.
6. Explain the straight salary compensation scheme. What are its advantages and disadvantages?
7. Examine the applications of combination compensation schemes. What are its merits and demerits?
8. Explain various non-monetary compensation schemes that a company offers to salespeople.

CRITICAL REVIEW QUESTIONS

1. A company wants to introduce salary plus commission scheme for one group of salespeople and salary plus bonus for other group as compensation measures. Salespeople of both the groups are equivalent i.e., they belong to the same position in the company and have more or less similar demographic characteristics. Which scheme do you think will motivate the salespeople more?
2. A company wants to draw out talented salespeople from the competing firms and as a step towards it, the company fixes up high starting salary that other firms cannot afford. The scheme is not pre-planned and the company apprehending it may adversely affect its economic condition. But the company wants to play a gamble. It floats this scheme because it wants to break away the customer base of the competing firms and for this sake it will exploit the relationships the migrating salespeople have developed while working with rival firms.
   In fact, the company wants to destroy the strengths of other firms. Obviously, such a phenomenon, if happens, will lead to unhealthy war among firms. Do you support the company's approach given the consequence that the company becomes successful at the cost of the competing firms? As a sales manager of a firm, what precautions would you take to stop sudden turnover of efficient salespeople?

PROJECT ASSIGNMENTS

1. Contact customer relationship managers of a (i) nationalized bank and (ii) private bank. Meet them to know the following:
   (a) Compensation schemes for them
   (b) The non- compensatory supports including fringe benefits
   (c) Promotion linked compensation schemes
   (d) Retirement benefits

Compare and contrast the two organizations on compensation plans. Comment on the broad objectives of the compensation plans.

2. Contact salespeople of three FMCG firms—large, medium, and small—working in the same sales territories. Based on sales turnover, the companies can be categorized on size. Information on sales turnover roughly can be known from the salespeople themselves or from the territory managers posted there. Even distributors can provide the needed information on it. Collect information from a sample of salespeople of each company and know their compensation level by explaining them your academic interests. Also, collect information on their levels of satisfaction, number of working years, and promotion-linked salary increment Comment on the type of compensation plans of the three and suggest whether there exists any relationship between the size and compensation plan of a company. Also, link the satisfaction levels with the compensation levels and size of the firm.

REFERENCES

Agarwala, T. (2007), *Strategic Human Resource Management*, Oxford University Press, New Delhi.

Bhattacharya, S. (2007), 'Strategic Compensation Management: Concept and Practices', *HRM Review*, November, pp. 37–41.

Ceriello, R.V., and C. Freeman (1991), *Human Resource Management Systems: Strategies, Tactics and Techniques*, Lexington Books—An imprint of MacMillan Inc., New York.

Flippo, B.E. (1984), *Personnel Management*, 6th ed., McGraw-Hill Book Company, New York.

Foulkes, K.F., and R.E. Livernash (1989), *Human Resource Management: Cases and Text*, Prentice-Hall, Englewood Cliffs, New Jersey.

Ingram, N.T., W.R. LaForge, A.R. Avila, H.C. Schwepker Jr, and R.M. Williams (2007), *Sales Management: Analysis and Decision Making*, 6th ed., South-Western Cengage Learning, New Delhi.

Kumra, R. (2008), 'Salesperson's Preferences Toward Sales Quota Bonus Plan: A Study of Indian Pharmaceutical Industry', *Decision*, vol. 35(1), June, pp. 111–27.

http://paayroll.naukrihub.com/compensation/Imdian-industry, accessed on 6 May 2010

CASE STUDY
Compensation Dilemma

Integrating sales force compensation to sales potentials of territories vis-à-vis sales quotas is a common and controlled attempt of an organization to manage compensation costs. In fact, strategic compensation plans (SCPs) strictly vouch for an optimal balance between sales revenues, and sales and distribution costs for a long term. Any planned compensation package always tries to achieve two ends—one, that the compensation expenses are in line with the estimated expenditure patterns on salaries, commissions, dearness allowances, bonuses that are apportioned in the overall sales budget for a financial year. Two—It should make salespeople contented and motivated enough to apply them more enthusiastically. Another important aspect of SCP is to make the organization prepared to withstand any slack in market demands or loss of customers so that the expenses do not eat away the revenue components.

(Contd)

Farguson Equipments Corporation (FEC), headquartered in Vadodara, is not a strong practitioner of SCP. The company is in a business of selling and servicing medical equipments all over India. It prepared a compensation package for its sales executives in force two years ago and was cruising along with it nicely, i.e., sales executives were seen to be demonstrating a progressive pace in meeting sales targets and the company was in sound economic health. In fact, the company even had a firm control on the sales and distribution costs and a steady rise of net profits, and return on investments (ROI) which marked the progress chart of FEC.

But for the last six months, the company has been experiencing otherwise. The sales turnover which remained steady for the initial two months have been showing a little downward trend leaving a trail of despondence from director (marketing) lately. On the whole, the business is somewhat sluggish. But the industry leader Dolphine Mediotronucs Ltd, based in New Delhi has made subtle modifications in compensation schemes that pay dividends to their sales managers. In a bid to reverse the trend, FEC has adopted a tactical ploy to introduce performance-based incentives. This is a bonus-based compensation scheme that entails cash prizes of ₹ 15, 10, and 5 thousand for the top three sales performers respectively. But unfortunately, this ploy proved wrong and so no sign of recovery is in sight. The company as a measure to address the situation has collected the compensation formula of Dolphine Mediotronics. Tables (A) and (B) presents the compensation items of the two companies for junior sales executives.

Table (A) FEC's breakup of compensation

Items	Rupees(₹)
Basic salary	30,000 p.m.
Dearness allowances @ 15%	4500 p.m.
House rent allowances (consolidated)	5000 p.m.
Fuel allowances—60 litres of petrol p.m.	3000 p.m. approx
Medical allowances (employee and spouse)	12,000 every year

Table (B) Dolphine mediotronic's breakup of compensation

Items	Rupees(₹)
Basic salary	30,000 p.m.
Dearness allowances @ 18%	5400 p.m.
House rent allowances (consolidated)	5000 p.m.
Fuel allowances—80 litres of petrol p.m.	4800 p.m. approx.
Medical allowances (employee, spouse, and children)	15,000 per year

(Contd)

(Contd)

Besides this, Dolphine Mediotonics also announces a raise in dearness allowances at least twice in a year. On the contrary, the FEC declares 5 per cent commission for every sales executive for meeting sales targets but has freezed the dearness allowance for the next two years. The compensation plans of the two firms results in a difference of ₹4000 to 5000 per month draws between sales executives and of course, the sales executives of Medoitronics are gainers. This has brewed a fume amongst sales executives in FEC who have not been able to accept the compensation policy of the company by heart and soul. Indeed, this leaves a cascading effect in their sales performances and the company has been feeling a pinch of it. To bounce back, the company has taken another tactical move to gift a Hero Honda two-wheeler to each sales executive but the situation remains same and the expected sales becomes elusive as yet. The company has decided to convene a meeting with sales executives to discuss the situations and know their demands.

Discussion Questions

1. As a director (marketing), what are the items you would include in the meeting's agenda?
2. Should the company detract from one year freeze of dearness allowance?
3. What compensation plans would you suggest to breeze the pay differences of ₹4000 to 5000 between your company's sales executives and that of Dolphine Mediotronics?

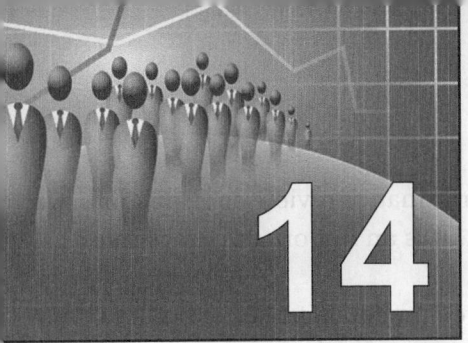

14 Sales Force Performance

14.1 PERFORMANCE APPRAISAL—CONCEPTS, DEFINITIONS, AND OBJECTIVES

Performance appraisal is integral to the management of sales force. It gives a clear indication whether the salespeople have achieved the stated sales goals and objectives, and if the sales organization has acted towards achieving corporate goals and objectives. Good performance means the company's ability to excel and stay rooted in the marketplace and poor performance indicates unsteady and unstable economic health of it. Without performance appraisal, the company cannot predict its current state of economic conditions or competitive positioning in the market.

Mandell and Rosenberg (1983) mentioned that performance appraisal encompasses periodic evaluation of the sales force performance in order to ensure smooth functioning of the organization and keep problems away from it. Performance appraisal lends objectivity in performance evaluation. Sales managers can continually monitor sales force performance through it.

Performance appraisal is basically an evaluative process. Evaluation stands on two important factors:

(a) Setting predetermined standards
(b) Comparing actual performance with the set standards.

The first factor is decided at the planning stage of the organizational decision-making which reflects the objectives of the firm more precisely. The second one is a post-performance review, which means getting results of evaluation that entails measuring the variations between what should be and what has been done. This is known as performance review or evaluation. Popularly, it is known as performance appraisal. It is an important part of sales force management.

Performance appraisal is a process that is developmental in nature too. It not only evaluates performance but also identifies reasons for the gap between the desired and the actual performance, and prescribes corrective actions to revamp the performance to the expected level. In case of sales organization, the purpose of performance appraisal is to explore the deficient areas of sales performance where corrective actions can be taken to improve future results.

Stoner and Wankel (1986) defined performance appraisal as a continuous process of giving feedback to the subordinates about how well they are doing their work for the organization.

Anderson (1983) illustrated performance appraisal as the process of reviewing an individual's performance and progress in a job and assessing the potential for future performance.

Pattanayak (2004) referred performance appraisal to all those procedures that are used to evaluate the personality, performance, and potential of its group members.

Dessler (2007) defined performance appraisal as the process of evaluating the current and/or past performances of employees relative to their performance standards.

Sales managers evaluate the performance of sales force basically on two grounds: (a) to measure the productivity of salespeople and (b) to control salespeople when results show deviations from pre-established benchmarks of performance. The first one relates to effectiveness and efficiency of the sales force performance. Effectiveness means whether the sales force is able to reach the stated goals. Efficiency means the success of the sales force in comparison to the costs incurred and the goals attained. The second one relates to taking corrective actions when productivity or performance of a salesperson shows deviations from the expected performance.

So, in short, the management of any firm should take the initiative to measure the sales effectiveness and sales efficiency of salespeople on one hand and also take control measures to enable salespeople to move on the right performance track. The basic objectives of performance appraisal are furnished as follows:

(a) To identify the deficient areas of salespeople that act as bottlenecks in achieving the desired performance

(b) To diagnose the problem areas of performance that salespeople face in their assigned tasks

(c) To guide salespeople on how to overcome the barriers of performance

(d) To generate information to develop future plans for performance improvement

(e) To suggest suitable remedies (skill development, assertiveness training, mentoring programmes, etc.) to generate expected future outcomes from salespeople

(f) To use it as an instrument to
  (i) ascertain future training and development needs of salespeople,
  (ii) change the recruitment and selection policies of the firm,
  (iii) improve the method and style of supervision and guidance of the salespeople, and
  (iv) moderate the compensation policies of salespeople.

(g) To capitalize it to improve effectiveness and efficiency of the organization

Furthermore, sales managers evaluate the performance of the sales force both formally and informally. When sales managers have some planned performance goals to achieve, they set standards for salespeople that compare the actual results with the pre-established standards. This is known as formal performance appraisal. Informal appraisal means evaluating performance without much objectivity. It relates to some sort of regular interaction with the salespeople to get their feedback on efforts and getting an idea of how they perform.

14.2 PERFORMANCE APPRAISAL—CRITERIA AND BENEFITS

Performance appraisal needs suitable methods or techniques to evaluate employee performance. Reports on performances help managers to decide on whether to continue, or modify their plans of achieving pre-assigned objectives. Whenever performances are satisfactory in line with the stated goals or objectives, managers move ahead with the plans; otherwise they need to identify the loopholes. Loopholes may relate to plans or implementation mechanisms. So, without the right performance appraisal procedures, it is difficult for managers to understand the sources of the problems, if any. Therefore, the process of performance appraisal is crucial for diagnosing the problems and rectifying the errors. It also helps them to avoid wrong future decision-making. Box 14.1 shows the essential criteria/pre-requisites for a performance evaluation.

> **Box 14.1 Criteria for performance evaluation**
>
> Following are the criteria for performance evaluation process:
> **Systematic:** A step-by-step procedure
> **Formal:** Work on specific objectives

(Contd)

(Contd)

Result oriented: It yields definite results

Directions: Employees are made aware of the specific goals and means of attaining them

Understandable to employees: If understandable, employees can repose faith on the procedure and results

Realistic: It must be based on operational performance parameters (i.e., measurable). Moreover, the results should not be drawn on evaluation of a sample of employees or estimated data

Vision for improvement: Results give future projections for further improvement

Periodic: Evaluations are made at regular time intervals

Flexible: Can be changed under different measurement situations (e.g., a change can be inducted in progress rating scales for salespeople to sales executives by adding or altering performance criteria without violating validity or reliability of the scale)

Encouraging: It encourages employees to take part in performance appraisal

Strategic fitness: Employee development has a strategic insight. Therefore, the procedure should fulfil strategic human resource planning of the firm

Fair: It should be free from bias

Accuracy: Results should be accurate else further decisions based on such results will be inaccurate

Performance of sales managers has a tangible effect on the performance of the sales force. Starting from sales planning, strategic thinking, action programming to performance goal setting, and reviewing sales performance, the competence and accuracy of managerial efforts largely affect sales force performance appraisal. Exhibit 14.1 shows how a renowned firm such as Hewlett Packard made use of strategic human resource planning to garner success in the ever-expanding computer industries.

Exhibit 14.1   SHRM at its best to contribute performance

Hewlett-Packard, a successful name in the computer industry, has made successful application of strategic human resource management to generate an overwhelming performance. Apart from its supremacy in technological in its products (personal computers, printers, etc.), the firm's steady progress can be attributed to organizing and planning human resources for its strategic implementation in highly competitive personal computer markets across the globe. As an outcome of these strategic plans, the sales force too is organized into teams that keep a constant vigil on the customers' requirements.

One necessary feature that the SHRM keeps in mind while working on the sales force is that it encourages

(Contd)

(Contd)

(a) the development of a conglomerate of small ventures, each responsible for their own success,

(b) setting up cross-functional teams that focus on different customer segments, major accounts
or application systems, and

(c) substantial autonomy to each strategic business unit to pursue their own product and
market development.

These gestures by the HR department may appear small but are good enough to provide
the sales force enough motivation for them to excel and succeed.

Source: Walker Jr et al. (2006)

Welhrich and Koontz (2005) opined that the best criteria of managerial performance is setting goals intelligently, planning programmes that will help accomplish and achieve goals successfully. These are possible only when managers go by consistent, integrated, and comprehensible planning process with an aim to reach specific objectives. So, problems at the helm of the affairs definitely have deleterious impacts on lower-level staff and achieving the expected performance level from them is a questionable issue.

Performance appraisal caters immense benefits to the organization. Actually, performance appraisal decides the economic health of the firm. It examines the accuracy of organizational planning and the implementation process. Some benefits of performance appraisal are listed as follows:

1. It helps in determining a salesperson's contribution to the organizational performance.
2. It makes salespeople aware of what is expected from them in terms of duties and responsibilities.
3. It enables sales managers to systematically measure the performance of the sales force.
4. It helps sales managers to take corrective actions (sales force control) when actual performance of the salespeople do not meet the performance standards being set during sales planning.
5. It guides sales managers to make assessments of the sales plans and policies when the salespeople are at no fault so far as their individual or group performances are concerned.
6. It assists sales managers to review compensation plans for salespeople.
7. It aids sales managers to make further evaluations of job descriptions or job specifications of the salespeople.
8. It can bring suitable changes in the staffing process of salespeople in the firm.
9. It helps sales managers to change the training programmes for sales people.
10. It assists sales managers to decide on the sales force promotion, demotion, transfer, etc.

11. It not only measures performances but also give clues on how to improve the performances.

12. It benefits salespeople to identify their strengths and weaknesses on the basis of their different performances.

13. It makes sales managers aware of their company's current standing in the market positions vis-à-vis competitors and facilitates the performances of sales managers.

14. It improves the personal relationship between salespeople and sales managers if it is constructive.

15. It imparts a good lesson to less the successful or unsuccessful salespeople on how to improve the performance.

16. It acts as a huge source of motivation to successful salespeople.

14.3 STEPS IN SALES FORCE PERFORMANCE APPRAISAL—AN ELABORATION

Performance appraisal is a step-wise process. It starts with setting the goals and objectives of the organization and ends with taking proper measures to control any deviated behaviour as per the set standards. It establishes standards of performance and compares the actual performance against these standards. It also suggests the controlling measures to rectify errors in achieving the performance. Figure 14.1 shows the steps in performance appraisal.

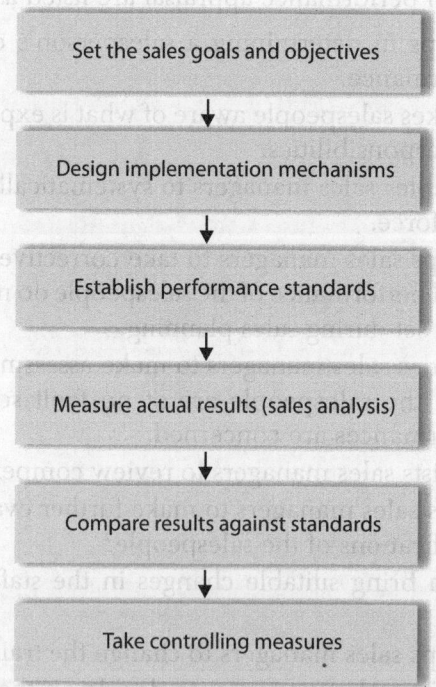

Figure 14.1 Steps in the sales force evaluation process

Setting Sales Goals or Objectives

Setting the sales goals or objectives is the starting point of sales force evaluation plan. This basically helps one to understand what a company desires to achieve. For example, a company has planned a target sales of rupees one crore in a territory within a time period of one year. The essential criteria for setting sales targets are as follows:

It must be attainable Goals must be set keeping in mind that they are reachable otherwise plans will not fructify.

They should be realistic in nature Resources, skills, competencies, and opportunities in real terms within and outside the firm should be available. An unrealistic sales goal can deter salespeople to show zeal to perform.

Goals should be quantifiable Goals should be translated into sales quota that provides quantitative specifications to sales targets, such as sales volumes in rupees or quantities.

Results are measurable When goals are stated in quantitative terms, it is expected to be measurable and analysable.

Designing Implementation Mechanisms

Implementation mechanisms imply how salespeople achieve targets. For example, a company manufacturing inverters can associate sales targets of its salespeople with the total ordering and reordering values of inverters in monetary terms. This process can be carried out at various dealer points in a geographic area every six months. So, for this company the total sales turnover of all the dealers in a place within six months is the index of actual performance of a salesperson. Moreover, shorter credit terms, better credit control, inventory level of dealers, promotional pushes at dealer level, prompt delivery schedule by reducing the lead time (difference between dates of actual order placed and serving the orders), deft handling of distribution functions, etc. are some of the non-selling performance criteria that are adjudged important for the evaluation of sales force performance.

Performance of salespeople hinges more upon how they handle an account. It encompasses (i) how quickly and accurately they apprise the potential customers, (ii) how quickly they procure orders and fulfils them, (iii) how precisely they can convert the sales orders to monetary benefits to the company. Broadly, salespeople act as an interface between the customers and the company. They not only help the company to build economic relationships with customers but also induce customers to develop long-term relationships with it.

To strengthen ties with the customers, a salesperson, during transactions, tries to make value additions for the customers in a better way compared to the competitors. Value additions are intrinsically possible by supplying quality products.

At the same time, a salesperson wants to provide some advantages such as credit facilities, easy availability of the products, quick solutions to the problems of the customers, etc. that also adds some values to the customers. Indeed, the result of an effective performance of the salesperson is a satisfied customer. This is one side of the performance coin. But, from the company's point of view, the ability of the salesperson to manage credit facilities by providing shorter credit terms and controlling credits are important so that cash flow never becomes a problem to the company and returns on investment stay on the expected levels of the company.

Moreover, a salesperson should undertake logistical functions for smooth functioning of the physical distributions. All these, together, contribute to the company's sales productivity. So, a salesperson should meet both ends, i.e., customer satisfaction and company's economic interests.

In short, a salesperson can make sense to sales performance if he ruminates the following:

(i) Never lose a good customer at the gain of a company

(ii) Never develop and retain a bad customer at the cost of the company

Establishing Performance Standards

Performance standards are expressed in quantitative and qualitative terms. Quantitative terms are sales revenues, gross or net profits, expense levels, order-call ratio, market share etc., number of new customers developed, etc. Qualitative terms are managerial ability, stability of the customer base, customer-relationship skills, development of selling skills, personality development, etc. Quantitative terms decide standards or targets for which quantifications are possible. The qualitative terms, on the other hand, involve qualitative ratings of salespeople by managers or by subjective evaluations (say, developing a consensus opinion of the yearly performance of the salesperson) or objective assessments (say, written tests or interviews, etc.) Exhibit 14.2 shows common quantitative performance factors used by a company.

Exhibit 14.2   Quantitative performance standards

Following are the quantitative performance standards:

(a) Sales volume in rupees or quantities (obtained from the past sales trend or sales forecasting, market potential studies, sales tracking of the products of the competitors):

  (i) by products

  (ii) by customer groups

  (iii) by territories

(Contd)

(Contd)

(b) Profits:

    (i) Gross or net profits (profit margins established from previous profit trends after making suitable corrections considering market competitions, change in market demands, market and sales potentials, and other contingent factors):

- by products
- by customer groups
- by territories

    (ii) Gross margin ratio which is defined as the ratio of gross margin to the total sales in a territory

    (iii) Net profit ratio which is defined as the ratio of net profit to the total sales in a territory

(c) Sales orders:

    (i) Order: Call ratio: A salesperson needs to maintain a balance between the number of calls and the number of orders procured. Higher number of calls add expenses to the firm. If the number of orders is not consistent with it, the graph of a salesperson's performance takes a dip.

    (ii) Number of orders procured: This is estimated by checking (i) number of customers developed and (ii) volume of sale orders acquired in monetary terms. For example, if the number of customers is large and the volume of orders is less it is an unsatisfactory performance.

    (iii) Order value (expressed in sales volume): The sales volume in monetary terms should meet the expected target level.

(d) Accounts:

    (i) Number of old accounts held: Salespeople should keep in mind that retaining a customer is more important than generating a customer. Hence, they should never attain a new client at the expense of losing an old one.

    (ii) Number of new accounts added: The added accounts strengthen the customer base. Higher the number of new accounts better is the performance considered.

    (iii) Number of existing accounts lost: The attrition of customers entail erosion of customer base.

(e) Selling expense ratios:

    (i) Selling expenses : Total sales: Selling expenses should be kept minimum in comparison to the sales volume.

    (ii) Field selling expenses: Total selling expenses: A large percentage of field selling expenses escalate the selling costs. So, the salesperson should try to keep them as low as possible.

    (iii) Average selling expenses per call: This is an index of the call efficiency. Higher average selling expenses per call indicates inefficiency.

(f) Number of calls per day: This refers to the number of calls a salesperson attempts.

(g) Cost per call: This indicates the cost of a call that a salesperson makes. Higher the cost with no positive results means poor performance.

(Contd)

(Contd)

> (h) Call frequency ratio: It is defined as the ratio of the number of actual calls to the number of accounts held.
>
> (i) Market share analysis: It is defined as the ratio between the percentage of the company's sales to the total industry sales in a geographic area, territory, region or at a national level.
>
> (j) Sales coverage effectiveness index: It is calculated as the ratio of the number of customers to the number of prospects in a territory.

Needless to mention that the quantitative base actually shows the true projections of sales performance displayed by the salespeople because these are quantitative estimations and, therefore, more objective and result oriented. In contrast, qualitative bases are subjective and so direct measurements are not possible. This involves cases where sales managers use psychological inventories previously developed by noted academicians and social science researchers or are self-developed to get an attitudinal measurements of salespeople. Some of the tests used are Rathus assertiveness schedules, McClelland's achievement motivation scale, etc. Consideration of qualitative bases is important because these ultimately impact on the quantitative factors of performance. But precautions should be taken while evaluating qualitative performance bases because of their subjective natures and chance of bias in their measurements.

Exhibit 14.3 shows the qualitative performance standards used by the company.

> **Exhibit 14.3   Qualitative performance standards**
>
> Following are the qualitative performance standards:
>
> (a) Knowledge on
> - (i) products or services dealt with
> - (ii) company policies
> - (iii) competition
> - (iv) distribution channels
> - (v) customer behaviours: economic, social, psychological
>
> (b) Individual skills
> - (i) selling skill
> - (ii) customer relationship skill handling skill
> - (iii) communication skill/ presentation skill
> - (iv) problem-solving skill
> - (v) analytical skill
> - (vi) managerial skill
> - (vii) interpersonal skill
>
> (c) Personal and personality factors
> - (i) personal appearance
> - (ii) industriousness
> - (iii) cooperation
> - (iv) stability of mind

(Contd)

(Contd)

(v)	tact	(vi)	empathy
(vii)	assertiveness	(viii)	achievement motivation
(ix)	ego drive	(x)	conscientiousness
(xi)	agreeableness	(xii)	punctuality, etc.

Measure Actual Results (Sales Analysis)

Sales analysis is an essential instrument for evaluating sales performance. A careful study of the quantitative estimates stated in the preceding step tells managers what is intended from salespeople and what they have achieved. Organizations might have plans for sales targets by products or product lines, customer types (large, medium, and small customers) or territory wise. Whatever the company's plans are, sales analysis reveals sales effectiveness or sales efficiencies, collectively determining the sales productivity.

Decenzo and Robbins (2000) recounted sales effectiveness referring to goal achievements and efficiency evaluating ratios of inputs consumed to outputs achieved. So, efficiency has cost consideration. *The Westburn Dictionary of Marketing* edited by Baker (2002) defined efficiency as a performance to evaluate the relationship between sales volume or value and individual or total selling costs. Understanding efficiency is important because it indicates a company's ability to effectively utilize its resources. Profitability is also an indicator of performance. Profitability is the ability of the firm to maximize sales revenue at the minimum of cost. As revenue is a balancing factor between profit and cost (profit = revenue-cost) so, either ability to control costs or maximize revenue is important to ensure profitability.

In short, sales effectiveness and sales efficiency are two vital parameters of sales analysis. If the company fixes thirty per cent market share to achieve its target within the time period and if it is successful, then we say that the company has high sales effectiveness. On the other hand, the company desires to achieve certain target outcomes (say sales, number of orders, number of new customers, etc.) as predetermined earlier. The company is said to have high sales efficiency when for each unit of investment of selling efforts and selling costs yield satisfactorily and correspond to the target outcomes. So, sales analysis precisely entails productivity analysis, profitability analysis, and cost analysis to interpret the company's sales performance. Moreover, these three analyses supplement each other and reciprocate sales analysis. Finally from these, conclusions the sales performances are drawn. Figure 14.2 shows the reciprocal determinisms among them. A detailed discussion on this is made in Chapter 16.

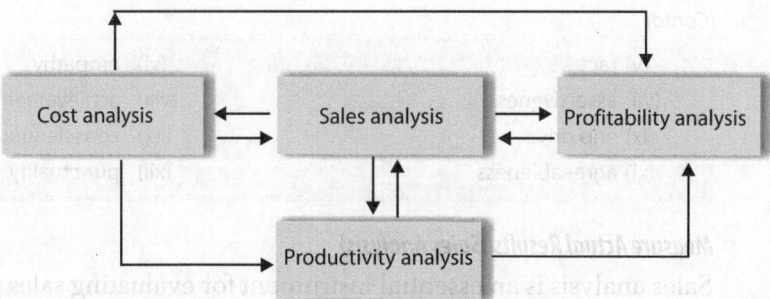

Figure 14.2 Sales analysis—an integrated process

Compare Results against Standards

Comparing results against standards is in fact the actual evaluation of performance of salespeople. Sales managers compare the actual results with the performance standards on products or product lines, customer types or territories and draw conclusions on the progress of selling by individual or group. These comparisons brings into fore whether remedial measures are needed to improve the organizational performance and, if needed, what should be the corrective actions and if not, what should be the future plans of the organizations to hold or improve the current performance.

Take Corrective Actions

Taking corrective actions is last but most important step in performance appraisal. Whenever the results of performances are dissatisfactory, it becomes a serious concern for the organization. It is advisable to measure the performances of the sales force periodically to track their progress and spot deficiencies. Sooner the loopholes in the sales performance are uncovered better it is for the managers to deal with the symptoms of weak performance.

There are certain policies, if followed, would decrease the number of problems being faced. First, sales managers should provide some short-term target levels particularly for new salespeople. Second, they should clearly state the target levels and make sure that the salespeople have understood their tasks and outcomes. This is important as one can be sure that the salespeople have understood what is to be achieved and so can accordingly work towards it. This also helps the sales managers to easily track down their performance graphs.

So, for effective performance appraisal, sales managers should take initiates to develop performance appraisal system and make it clearly known to the salespeople. And, it is also important for the salespeople to ventilate their problems (understood from the shortfall of intermediate target levels) to their superiors that can be looked into immediately to iron out the crises. Table 14.1 exhibits some of the common problems encountered by sales organization/employees while performing sales.

Table 14.1 Some Common Problem Areas in Sales Performance

Product-related problems	Price-related problems	Distribution-related problems	Promotion-related problems	Sales force-related problems	Sales managers-related problems
For old products:	(a) Price is not commensurate with the quality (b) Customer rejection due to high perceived price (c) Customer rejects due to low-perceived price as low price is index of poor quality (d) The customer wants to extend the credit terms that the company cannot afford (e) The customer wants more price-offs for long-term buying. This is beyond a company's capacity	(a) The customer wants the company to bear the transportation and delivery costs (b) The company has to compensate the cost due to loss of materials during transportation (c) The customer wants to maintain minimum inventories and keep the company always on its toes for uninterrupted supply of product(s) (d) The customer wants the company to buy back unsold items	(a) The customer wants the company to carry out promotional costs alone (The problem is felt in large scale while working with distributors or retailers) (b) The promotional supports of the company is too negligible to persuade target customers (c) Competitors are high in promotional intensities (d) The company does know through word-of-mouth whether the promotion is doing good to the company or not	(a) Salespeople feel inconvenient during customer interactions (b) Impractical call plans, call frequencies are not high for covering major customers. (c) Fail to impress customers (d) Huge selling expenses debar salespeople to fulfil call plans (e) Loss of customers due to poor customer relationship skills (f) Travelling problems (g) Getting not much time to interact with customers (h) Lack of cohesion while engaged in team selling	(a) Faulty sales plans and policies (b) Improper sales forecasting (c) Unable to send right instructions to the salespeople (d) Poor sales supervision and guidance (e) Lack of knowledge in market diagnostics (f) Too much authority to salespeople (g) Too much pressure from top-level management leaves no room for thinking independently on sales plans or mapping out strategies. (h) Too much target orientation distract efforts for market/customer developments (i) Need to operate with limited sales budget
(a) Customer's perception that the quality of the good is poor (b) Poor working performance of the product (c) Short life (d) After-sales service is poor					
For new products:					
(a) Customer's indifference (b) Does not meet the customer's decided specifications (c) Does not fit with the other components in the finished product (d) Customer is satisfied with present supplier(s)					

14.4 SALES FORCE CONTROL—A NECESSARY ADJUNCT OF PERFORMANCE APPRAISAL

Controlling the performance is an integral part of the sales force evaluation process. Before carrying out this process, managers should know the reasons and the degree of variations of performances from the set standards. This is because unless the symptoms of poor performances are identified, no corrective actions can be taken. Organizations have various control measures at their disposal and the successful applications of such measures not only brings into light the actual lacunae that are responsible for under-performance but also prepares the organizations to avert performance-related problems in future. Some popular control measures are as follows:

(a) Sales audit
(b) Management information system
(c) Management by exceptions

Sales Audit

Sales audit is a comprehensive, periodic, constructive, and unbiased review of sales operations on post-facto basis i.e., after the fact survey. It reveals the following:

(i) What decisions were taken at the planning and implementation stages?
(ii) How these affect the sales operations?
(iii) What changes are to be brought in to improve the situations?

Sales audit starts with the investigation of the impact of environmental factors, both internal and external, on sales performance. It looks into what steps the organizations have taken to manage those factors? And, whether they have considered that the performance standards under depressed economic situations would be different from that under normal situations while carrying out corrective measures.

Say, the organization has introduced new incentive schemes to motivate salespeople to work hard for performance achievement. The sales audit will tell whether this incentive would have any impact on the performance level of the employees. Sales audit makes a detailed review of the sales plans, objectives, programmes, strategies, methods in finer details. It also investigates the job descriptions, staffing procedures, sales force motivation, compensation, and managerial controls. It further probes customer demands, strengths and weaknesses of competitors, customer buying behaviour, sales budgets, problems with products, promotional expenditures, distribution plans, pricing impacts, quality of after-sales service, etc. After a thorough diagnosis, sales auditors suggest

(i) whether the company should maintain the present position, i.e., status quo,
(ii) whether the company should change the performance standards, and
(iii) in case (ii) is accepted, what steps should be taken to meet the performance standards.

Management Information System

Management information system is a more preventive measure for controlling performance. It is an integrated system specially designed to help the managers to forecast, plan, implement, and control the organizational activities. Pearce II and Robinson Jr (1989) reported that MIS can address problems that are known and understood in advance. In today's digital age, with companies getting flooded with lot of information everyday; managing information has become vital. With an information system in hand, this voluminous information can be easily managed. Technology has a big hand in taking decisions in business and management.

According to Kotler (1988), MIS in marketing parlance consists of four components. These are (i) internal reporting system, (ii) marketing intelligence system, (iii) marketing research system, and (iv) analytical marketing system.

Internal reporting system deals with the actual sales, total order placed, inventory levels, bill receivables and payables, number of new customers acquired or old customers retained, etc. in a time period. So, MIS has a database support system to store all types of relevant data from where managers can retrieve the specific dataset to address decision-making situations.

Marketing intelligence system reports everyday information on market situations such as latest customers, competitors, and sales updates.

Marketing research deals with a specific marketing problem and starts with definite objectives to achieve. It gathers data, analyses it, and solves marketing problems. It suggest managers what specific actions to be taken.

Analytical systems provides an analytical tool such as statistical techniques or management models to solve the marketing problems.

So, MIS not only solves problems but also warns managers of the impending problems and gives the right direction to sort out the problem. Exhibit 14.4 shows how Cisco systems have been successful with establishing information network.

Exhibit 14.4   Cisco Systems—the success story

Cisco Systems, a leading name in internet networking across the globe has been glorified by over a decade of rapid growth, dotted with the innovation of many non-standard items, and processes. Cisco sales organization has brought in huge acceleration in performance by the application of web portals that lend salespersons all the important sales tools such as online services, quick access, retrieval, and application of information to manage their businesses at extreme precisions. The programme that has made Cisco's sales performance on the roll is e-sales.

E-sales is a highly dynamic, personalized web portal that helps salespeople to manage information and serve customers. The e-sales programme is run on a common strategy that is poised to meet the customers' needs and expectations. The success of Cisco's e-sales initiatives can be attributed to

---

(Contd)

(Contd)

> (i) consistent data capture,
>
> (ii) accuracy in handling myriads of data,
>
> (iii) keeping non-productive tasks (e.g., follow up on credit sales) at bay,
>
> (iv) constantly feeding manufacturing, marketing, finance departments, etc. more pertinent and timely data to expedite their business solutions,
>
> (v) a terrific booster to sales force motivation because of exponential annual sales growth.
>
> *Source:* Gist and Mosher (2005)

Management by Exceptions

In management by exceptions managers emphasize upon those problems which are bigger in gravity or intensity, ignoring those that are ignorable and self-manageable if the larger problems are thoroughly addressed. Managers are always on the lookout where significant deviation of the actual performance from the standard takes place. Whenever deviations are noticed, corrective actions are taken. This will save the management time and huge cost. So, the basic objective of this method is to pinpoint the critical areas of discrepancies and overhaul it without delay.

14.5 PERFORMANCE APPRAISAL METHODS—A SPECIAL REFERENCE TO SALES FORCE

Methods of performance are broadly classified into two types, traditional and modern. Traditional methods rely on how the traits or characteristics of salespeople contribute to sales performance. Modern methods consider salespeople as part of a performance appraisal system and in some cases they are allowed to offer suggestions in further developing these systems as well. Moreover, employee self-appraisal has become a common place in many organizations. Figure 14.3 shows the classification of performance appraisal methods.

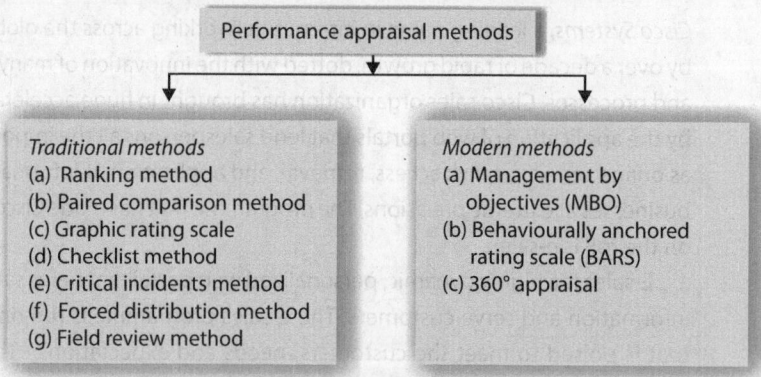

Figure 14.3 Classification of performance appraisal methods

14.5.1 Traditional Methods

Following are the traditional methods of performance appraisal:

Ranking Method

Here, salespeople are compared on the level of their performance regardless of the type of work they perform. They are judged on a common set of factors. No assessment is made on the basis of a salesperson's individual traits or personal characteristics. Therefore, the rank arranges salespeople in terms of best performance, next best till the least performing salesperson is reached. The ranking can also be done in ascending order of performance.

The main drawback of the method is that the actual degree of difference in the performance of two employees is not possible to judge. Moreover, if salespeople are ranked based on subjective judgment of some attributes, the results may not project the actual ranking of salespeople on merits.

Paired Comparison Method

Paired comparison method is a type of ranking where two salespeople are considered at a time and compared on a common criterion. If there are n number of salespeople, the total number of comparisons that are possible is $n(n-1)/2$ under this method. So, if there are 10 salespeople, then the number of paired comparisons possible is 45. This comparison continues till no salesperson is left. Here, the selection of performance criteria for comparing salespeople is very important. Selection of the rater is also important.

This method is more reliable compared to the ordinary ranking method. But, the comparison is very tedious for a large number of salespeople and the rater may make mistakes due to boredom or fatigue. For example, if this method is carried out on 10 salespeople, there will be 45 pairs of comparisons to be done and the rater may find it difficult to conduct so many. Human error, therefore, can intrude to render the evaluation process unsuccessful

Graphic Rating Scale

In graphic rating scale, some specific factors that influence the performance of the employees are identified before comparing salespeople. The rater does this comparison on a graphic scale that presents the list of factors and a scale presenting numerical values in sequence, representing the degrees of presence or absence/good or bad, etc. of such factors in the scale.

Scales can be continuous or discreet. In continuous scale, the factors are evaluated continuously representing different degrees of comparisons with the rater putting a mark somewhere in the continuum depending on his appraisal of a salesperson on a specific factor. For example, for a factor, persuasive ability, the following continuous scale can be constructed. Refer to Figure 14.4.

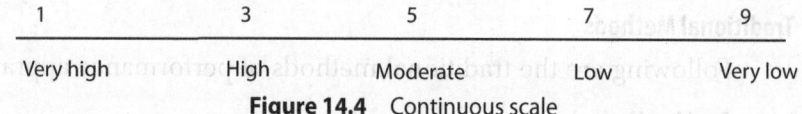

Figure 14.4 Continuous scale

Under discreet arrangement, a scale representing different points for degrees of comparison on a factor is used. The rater is asked to choose a specific point or he is asked to put a tick mark on a specific category of comparison. Here, there is no opportunity to select any point on the scale because there is no continuum; rather points on the scale are discreet. However, for quantitative estimations, some numerical weights in an order are assigned to each category. For example, in an evaluation of testing the company knowledge of salesperson, the following discreet scale can be constructed. The rater has no freedom to exercise opinion between bad and very bad or good and very good. Refer to figure 14.5.

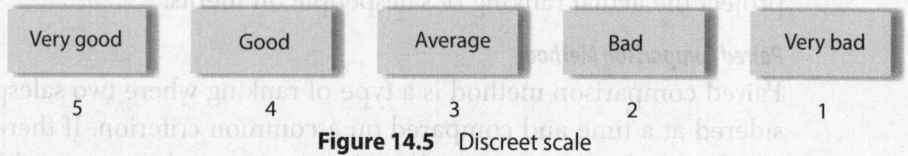

Figure 14.5 Discreet scale

Graphic rating scales are easy to construct and administer. However, the rater applies subjective judgments to compare salespeople and therefore, bias in evaluation cannot be entirely ruled out.

Checklist Method

In the checklist method, some common attributes describing the characteristics of salespeople and influencing sales performance are chosen. Often, the attributes are expressed in the form of statements. A rating scale is attached with the characteristics so that the rater can evaluate a salesperson in it based on its characteristic features mentioned sidewise. Table 14.2 is an illustration of such scale.

Say, the rater evaluates a salesperson on 5 for company knowledge, 4 for product knowledge, 2 for diligence, 3 for selling skills, 2 for customer-relation skills, and 3 for motivation. The total score for a salesperson is 19. The total score

Table 14.2 Illustration of checklists

Attributes/Characteristics	Excellent (5)	Good (4)	Fair (3)	Bad (2)	Very Bad (1)
(a) Product knowledge					
(b) Company knowledge					
(c) Diligence					
(d) Selling skill					
(e) Customer relations skill					
(f) Motivation					

Table 14.3 Weighted checklists

Attributes/ Characteristics	Relative weight	Excellent (5)	Good (4)	Fair (3)	Bad (2)	Very bad	Score
(a) Product Knowledge	0.3						
(b) Company knowledge	0.2						
(c) Diligence	0.2						
(d) Selling skill	0.1						
(e) Customer relations skill	0.1						
(f) Motivation	0.1						
Total weight	1						

has a potential to attain a maximum score of 30 (5×6) and a minimum score of 6 (6×1). The average score is $30 + 6/2 = 18$. So, the salesperson getting score 19 has scored more than average on performance characteristics.

An improved version of the scale is checklist with each attribute getting a weight or importance value assigned after consultation with the experts in the relevant. In this case, some senior sales managers of two/three similar firms can be requested to distribute a total score, say one among different attributes. Each attribute is given an average weight (averages of all sales managers) indicating its relative importance. Table 14.3 represents such a scale.

Say, a rater provides scores of 4, 4, 3, 3, 2, and 2 for attributes (a), (b), (c), (d), (e), and (f) respectively. The actual score for company knowledge will be $4 \times 0.3 = 1.2$. Similarly, the product knowledge will get a score of $4 \times 0.2 = 0.8$, diligence $3 \times 0.2 = 0.6$, selling skills $3 \times 0.1 = 0.3$, customer relation skills $2 \times 0.1 = 0.2$, and motivation $2 \times 0.1 = 0.2$. The summated score will be 3.3. The range of the total score is from 5 to 1. So, the salesperson getting a score 3.3 has moderately higher value of performance characteristics.

Critical Incident Method

The critical incident method requires the rater to record significant events, called critical incidents that happen when salespeople are involved in sales activities. The essence of the method is to ascertain critical events that make the differences between performance and no performance. To illustrate, a sales manager has recorded the following as critical incidents for a salesperson:

(a) He is quite bright in prospecting activities
(b) He is not smart in handling customer complaints
(c) His demonstration skill is exceptional
(d) He gets tired whenever, he receives any adverse comments from customers
(e) He reports to his supervisor in time
(f) He writes his call reports well

Objective assessment of each can be made by attaching a 5-point scale (as shown in the checklist method) with each statement to know the degree of presence or absence or the good or bad of each characteristic. The sales manager can later discuss the problems with the salesperson on where he should improve more and how to convert negative characteristics to positive.

The important feature of this method is to find out critical incidents that are not easy. Secondly, proper recording of the events is necessary otherwise the rater might have problems of recalling. Bias may creep in the method particularly when negative incidents are more focused than positive ones.

Forced Distribution Method

In the forced distribution method, a distribution scale is developed encompassing different grades that have two extremes, extremely good and extremely bad, connected by good, average and bad. Grades are distributed as follows:

Very bad : Below 10 per cent
Bad : Below 20 per cent
Average : 20 per cent to 40 per cent
Good : 40 per cent to 60 per cent
Very good : Above 60 per cent

However, different combinations of gradations can be used. The rater is asked to evaluate salespeople on a specific performance criterion or aggregate performance considering the above distribution and the result indicates the grade of salespeople. Say, a salesperson is rated 25 per cent on communication skill, 40 per cent on selling skill, 50 per cent on persuasive capacity, 30 per cent on personality, and 30 per cent on emotional maturity. Needless to mention, here the company considers these five characteristics to determine the overall performance of the salespeople. So, the performance rating of the salesperson is 35 per cent. So, the salesperson is treated as average. The method is simple and can eliminate bias to a large extent. The flexibility of the gradation eases the task of the rater to appraise performance.

Field Review Method

In the field review method, the rater interviews the field sales managers and supervisors to know how salespeople perform in the field. The latter are asked about both quantitative and qualitative performance criteria and how salespeople fare on both. For example, the rater asks about progress on sales volume, selling expenses, order procurements, number of calls made, etc. as regards to the respective target levels.

Similarly, the rater asks about the strengths and weaknesses on communication efficiency, conceptual skills, managerial potency, job motivation, ego drives, etc.

The method makes a holistic appraisal of performance of the salespeople. What is important is the development of the right performance questionnaire containing the actual performance bases that are appropriate to a particular selling situation. So, prior to performance appraisal, raters should make an in-depth study on it and only after being sure about the validity and reliability of the measuring instrument, they should go for field survey.

14.5.3 Modern Methods

Here are the modern methods of performance appraisal.

Management by Objectives (MBO)

The management of objectives method, propounded by Drucker (1954) is a potentially powerful tool for performance evaluation. MBO can be described as a process that begins with the joint setting of goal by managers and employees in an organization, identifying the responsibility areas of each employee keeping in view the goals expressed in measurable terms and later applying them as guidelines during performance appraisal of employees. So, MBO consists of the following steps:

Set organizational goal(s)   Long-term goals should be set keeping in mind the compulsions of the internal and external environments of the organization.

Joint goal setting   After thorough deliberation of the preceding step and sales tasks to accomplish, sales managers and salespeople (management and subordinates), establish short-term performance targets. Sales managers clearly explain the role, tasks expectations and responsibilities of salespeople after both the parties reach an agreement on the specific activities to perform to reach short-term goals. It also precisely states how managers can help salespeople to achieve their goals.

Preparation of action plans   After setting goals, detailed resource requirements and methods of selling are developed. Moreover, how resources will be utilized is also explained. Authorities and responsibilities are clearly defined in line with the job descriptions. Even, job descriptions are modified if the situations demand so. Periods of performance review are also determined.

Performance review   It involves tracking progress of sales performance on a periodic basis. This is important to find out the lacunae in the sales operations and managers should intervene to remedy the situations. This is necessary to streamline the work flow in the desired goal direction. Feedbacks are also communicated to salespeople to make them aware of their mistakes and suggest what actions can be taken to do away with the wrongs.

Formal appraisal   This is done at the end of a specific period decided at the planning stage. Results of performance are compared with organizational goals.

Deviations, if found are thoroughly analysed and if found irreparable, managers turn towards goal redefinition and actions revisits, and modifications. The process is recycled again.

MBO, if properly planned and executed throw tough challenges to the competitors. It eases the communication flow between managers and subordinates. As goals are jointly set, salespeople have little grievances against management when their performance falls short of expectation.

Behaviourally Anchored Rating Scale (BARS)

The starting point of behaviourally anchored rating scale is the job analysis. The results of job analysis define the specific behaviour that a salesperson should display to reach predetermined sales goals and objectives. In fact, BARS points out the critical areas of performance in jobs and analyses job behaviours and performance relationships of a specific job situation (here, selling situation). In the process, it identifies the critical areas of job performance that helps to classify the job behaviours to highly effective and lowly effective behaviours.

It goes without saying that highly effective behaviour contributes to performance significantly than the lowly effective ones. The objective is to know which behaviours are responsible for the desired results. Keeping the results of this analysis as benchmark, the rater evaluates salespeople in a real life spelling situation and identifies the specific characteristics that he has already studied during job analyses and measures it, and compares the observation with BARS. So, the BARS consist of the following steps:

(a) Analyse the characteristics and behavioural areas of the job.

(b) Identify the critical behavioural areas and categorise them to most-effective behavioural and least-effective behavioural factors. This is better known from previous empirical research findings in the similar area or from interviewing salespeople or sales supervisors working in the relevant fields about the critical incident areas of effective and ineffective job behaviours affecting performance in different degrees.

(c) These critical incident areas are reviewed and refined to a small group of performance dimensions and each dimension is given the right definition.

(d) Another group of salespeople or supervisors who have experience of handling the jobs are given the performance dimensions to review and rate on a 1 to 10 scale, value approaching 10 indicating more effectiveness of performance behaviour and value approaching 1 meaning low effectiveness of performance behaviour.

(e) Finally, a few performance dimensions with their individual rating scales define the BARS.

360° Appraisal

360° appraisal gives a holistic impression of the sales force performance. Under this method, salespeople are appraised by a number of individuals including salespeople themselves (self-appraisal) who happen to be the stake holders of the firm and come in close contact with salespeople and whose good or bad are associated with sales force performance. Salespeople can be evaluated by sales managers, peers, distributors, and themselves. Figure 14.6 shows a diagrammatic presentation of 360° appraisal.

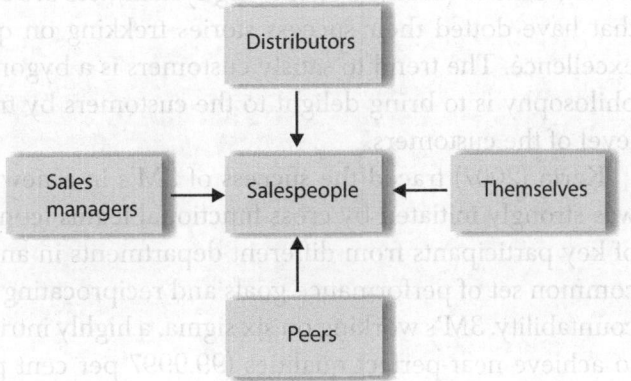

Figure 14.6 360° appraisal of sales force performance

Questionnaire-based interviews are taken from the assessors systematically to collect data on performance determining factors. Before the final implementation of questionnaire, pretesting of it is done by making a pilot survey on a small group of salespeople. It is a very comprehensive survey and can reduce bias in appraisal to a significant extent. Moreover, continuous feedbacks of performance data to salespeople make room for correction of errors.

Critics are sceptical on self-performance evaluation under this method. But the errors that are self-identified can be redressed quite easily. It is true that bias may intrude during self-evaluation and that is why more than one individual evaluates and judges the performance to develop a pooled performance score for the salespeople. This is assumed to have a greater degree of precision and least error.

14.6 SALES FORCE PERFORMANCE APPRAISAL

Managing performance in an environment of global competition and unprecedented technological advances is a daunting task for the organization. Rapid increase of customer base, varieties of customer tastes and preferences, razor-edge competition, etc. drive organizations to usher in qualitative orientations in its visions, missions, goals, and programmes to sustain in today's chaotic business milieu. Various quality improvement techniques such as total quality management (TQM), six sigma quality control measures, business process reengineering (BPO), JIT (just in time) inventories and many such innovative practices have crept in the organizations. Indeed, organizations should not stop at quality improvement but strive to attain business excellence that can reach an organization to a very formidable position of stability and growth.

The success of Titan (quartz revolution), LG (high definition TV), Levi's (premium jeans), Microsoft (software), Xerox (office automation), Amul (operation flood), Gillette (innovative shaving system), etc are some of the many examples that have dotted their success stories trekking on quality wagons for business excellence. The trend to satisfy customers is a bygone culture. Today's business philosophy is to bring delight to the customers by transcending the satisfaction level of the customers.

Kerin (2007) traced the success of 3M's in a new product development that was strongly initiated by cross-functional teams (constituted by a small number of key participants from different departments in an organization) generating a common set of performance goals and reciprocating each other with mutual accountability. 3M's working on six sigma, a highly intricate but disciplined process to achieve near-perfect qualities (99.9997 per cent perfection) in their deliverables is a symbol of business excellence. This is invariably the 3M's 'delight the customer' programme.

True, organizational orientation is imperative to stay tuned with the upheavals of the globalization forces. At the same time, customer orientation is a big issue that the organization confronts. Customer orientation compels organization to take up reengineering drives to respond to the ever-changing customer demands with time. Kumar (2002) pointed out that reengineering aims at improving the organizational efficiency by bringing necessary changes in the organizational process. Finally, it facilitates the value addition to the products/services to benefit the customers and organizations in the long run.

Need-based changes concomitant with the demands of the customers were welcome in the organization. But what if these changes are not rightly translated to performance due to reasons attributed to poor salesmanship. Despite quality enhancement, organizations cannot reap any benefits if salespeople fail to generate the right customer education and interests to respond to the organization's call. The disappointing sales performance can be attributed to the following:

1. Salespeople are unable to read the nuances of dynamics of change due to cognitive incompetence.
2. Salespeople are incapable to understand the technological advances behind the products or services and they suffer setback in selling particularly when technology is the USP to persuade target customers.

3. Salespeople are unable to communicate the features–benefits trysts of products or services that would have given significant mileage in selling success.

4. Salespeople are psychologically oriented to think themselves as the members of the marketing departments only in the organization. The system approach of marketing says that the success is reasoned by concerted efforts by all departments in the organization working towards cost-quality-price-delivery-customer satisfaction in a synergistic manner. Salespeople therefore should perceive themselves as members of the organizational team represented by all departmental units. Salespeople ought to take part in product development, cost control, quality achievement besides their routine selling jobs.

5. The abating commitments of salespeople to the organizations they work is an apprehending feature. At times, they are unable to overcome the switching call from the competing firms even for the marginal gain of monetary incentives. In fact, this is a burning problem of many a organizations to retain experienced salespeople for long terms because of the constant attempt by rival firms to scoop away the vital salespeople by luring them with incentives and perks.

6. Comfortable with routine and disquieting with complex selling situations are the perennial problems with many salespeople. Salespeople, being human beings, have different mental capacities and faculties and, therefore, act differently in different buying–selling situations. Where plain order taking and serving is the primary task, salespeople have no difficulties. But whenever, they are asked to deal with variety seeking or complex buying situations, they do not live up to the expectations.

   Again, where buying authority is vested with not an individual but a cluster of individuals (in many industrial firms, production manager, purchase manager, and R&D manager jointly take buying decision), satisfying all the members of the buying unit is very difficult. Each member has an own interest to satisfy (e.g., R&D managers focus on quality issues and purchase manager on price discounts). A salesperson faces a messy affair in such a situation and cannot overcome the problem.

7. A salesperson's behavioural problems can adversely affect the organizational performance. A salesperson, being a human being has sentiments, emotions, value systems, attitudes, personal opinions, etc. Salespeople under a bad phase in his own life or organizational life may go into deeper straits of depression but another salesperson under an identical scenario, never becomes unnerved and accept the eerie situations as challenges by dint of two important personal qualities—tact and resilience. Organization houses many salespeople of varying capacities but ultimately it suffers in terms of performance bottlenecks.

An organization under present global context cannot accept all these as granted and ought to take controlling measures to revert the downturn of performance. But before it takes up any steps to rejuvenate the sales force, managers must make some self-appraisals of (a) whether there is any lacunae in sales plans and policies, (b) whether there are any drawback in the sales force recruitment and selection policies, (c) whether there is any divergence in the sales force training programme, (d) whether there is any negligence or overstepping in the sales force supervision and guidance, and (e) whether there is any wrong in the performance appraisal programmes.

If the answers of the above are affirmative, an organization should investigate the reasons underlined in the inabilities of the salespeople to accomplish sales goals. The problems owing to salespeople are classified into (a) behavioural, (b) technical, and (c) improvisational. Behavioural problems relate to sales force motivation, communication, coordination, interpersonal relations, etc. Technical problems mean lack of product knowledge and expertise in product handling and applications. Improvisational problems relate to the inability to convert prospective customers to actual customers, retain existing customers and instil interests in customers on the company's products/services due to lack of communication and customer-relationship skills

An organization cannot start the sales force development programme from the scratch in the mid way. Therefore, it is advisable to empower senior sales personnel to supervise and guide new and young sales force and appraise their performances from time to time. Second, the senior sales personnel or supervisors accompany them in covering major customers and closely watch them while interacting with customers. Later, the seniors can discuss their mistakes and suggest how to improve. To address behavioural problems, sales managers can scrutinize the compensation programmes to find whether problems emanate from the dissatisfaction of the salespeople with pay packages. Assertiveness training can be arranged for personality development among salespeople. Similarly special training on communication skill development, simulations, management games, role playing, etc. can be organized to remove inertia within salespeople. Learning non-verbal communication should be a part of training session. Salespeople should undergo rigorous technical training after they join the organizations by which they acquire technical knowledge and applications on products/services.

Today, organizations are vulnerable to competition. Globalization poses immense challenge to the organization to perform. Therefore, total overhauling of human resource development programme is the order of the day. Sales force, as critical human resource, should be given special attention because they will finally convent the organization's effort to performance.

=== **SUMMARY** ===

Performance appraisal is an evaluative process. It rests on two important factors—setting performance standards and comparing actual performance with standards. Performance appraisal is also a developmental process. It not only works on rectifying errors but also suggests methods for performance improvement. It is a process of reviewing an individual's performance and assessing the potential for future performance. The essential objectives of performance appraisal are to identify deficient areas of performance and guides salespeople on how to overcome these areas. Performance appraisal assesses future training needs, staffing process, compensation schemes for salespeople.

Performance appraisal should be systematic, formal, result oriented, realistic, etc. It makes salespeople aware of what are expected from them. It improves the interpersonal relationships between sales managers and salespeople. The steps in performance appraisal are (a) setting the sales goals and objectives, (b) designing the implementation mechanism, (c) establishing performance standards, (d) measuring sales results, (e) comparing results against standards, and (f) taking controlling measures.

Sales force control is a necessary adjunct of performance appraisal. This is possible by the application of sales audit, management information system, and management by exception. Performance appraisal can be made by traditional and modern methods. Some of the traditional methods are ranking method, paired comparisons, critical incidents method, etc. Modern methods include management by objective, (MBO), behaviourally anchored rating scale (BARS), etc.

KEY TERMS

Management by Objectives (MBO) Management by objectives is a powerful tool for evaluating performances. MBO can be described as a process that begins with the joint setting of goal by managers and employees in an organization, identifying the responsibility areas of each employee keeping in view the goals expressed in measurable terms and later applying them as guidelines during performance appraisal of employees.

Performance Appraisal Performance appraisal is defined as the periodic evaluation of the performance of sales force in order to ensure smooth functioning of the organization. It lends objectivity while evaluating the performance.

Performance Standards Performance standards can be expressed in both qualitative as well as quantitative terms. It helps to benchmark the performance of an employee or the organization.

Sales Analysis Sales analysis is defined as an essential instrument for evaluating sales performance. It involves a careful study of all the factors before actually analysing an employees' performance.

Sales Force Control Sales force control is a necessary part while evaluating the performance of an employee to be objective and fair. Sales audit, management information system, and management by exceptions are a few controls used by managers in their companies.

CONCEPTUAL QUESTIONS

1. What is performance appraisal? What are its objectives?
2. What are the criteria of effective performance appraisal?
3. What are the benefits of performance appraisal to the (a) organization and (b) sales force?

4. What are the steps in performance appraisal? What is the importance of sales analysis in performance appraisal?
5. What are the quantitative and qualitative bases of performance appraisal of the sales force?
6. What is sales audit? How does it help in performance appraisal?
7. Explain two traditional and modern methods of performance appraisal
8. What is MBO? How is it evolved for performance appraisal?
9. What is BARS? State its application in performance appraisal.

CRITICAL REVIEW QUESTIONS

1. The evaluative part of performance appraisal is more predominant than the development part. Do you agree? Illustrate your answer with reasons.
2. Traditional methods of performance appraisal seldom involve sales force in developing the performance appraisal procedures but modern methods regard sales force as opinion givers in developing performance appraisal system. Why is it so?

PROJECT ASSIGNMENTS

1. Meet marketing/sales managers of a pharmaceutical, professionally managed courier and an industrial organization, and obtain the following information:
   (a) What they mean by performance appraisal?
   (b) How they apply it?
   (c) What criteria they use it for performance appraisal?
2. Contact sales manager(s) of a firm who do network marketing to reach customers and gather information on the following:
   (a) Its method of operation
   (b) Its features of sales plans
   (c) Its performance appraisal system specially for sales force
   (d) Its qualitative performance factors
   (e) Future of network marketing

REFERENCES

Anderson, G.R. (1983) *A Dictionary of Management Terms*, Macdonald and Evans Ltd, Estover, Plymouth.

Baker, J.M. (2002), *The Westburn Dictionary of Marketing*, Westburn Publishers Ltd, http://www.westburnpublishers.com/marketing-dictionary/S/Sales-efficiency.aspx accessed on 13 January 2011.

Decenzo, A.D., and P.S. Robbins (2000), *Personnel/Human Resource Management*, 3rd ed., Prentice-Hall of India Pvt. Ltd, New Delhi.

Dessler, G. (2007), *Human Resource Management*, Prentice-Hall of India Pvt. Ltd, New Delhi.

Drucker, P.F. (1954), *The Practice of Management*, Harper & Row, New York.

Gist, P.E., and P. Mosher (2005), 'Changing Sales Force Behavior to Achieve Performance', *Marketing Mastermind*, February, pp. 31–6.

Kerin, R.A., S.W., Hartley, E.N. Berkowitz, and W. Rudelius (2007), *Marketing*, 8th ed., Tata McGraw-Hill Publishing Company Limited, New Delhi.

Kotler, P. (1988), *Marketing Management: Analysis, Planning, Implementation and Control,* 6th ed., Prentice-Hall, Englewood Cliffs, New Jersey.

Mandell, I.M., and L.J. Rosenberg (1983), *Marketing,* 2nd ed., Prentice-Hall of India Private Limited., New Delhi.

Memoria, B.C. (1984), *Personnel Management,* Himalaya Publishing House, Mumbai.

Pattanayak, B. (2004), *Human Resource Management,* 2nd ed., Prentice-Hall of India Pvt. Ltd, New Delhi.

Kumar, R.S. (2002), *Managing Indian Brands: Marketing Concepts and Strategies,* Vikas Publishing House Pvt. Ltd, New Delhi.

Pearce II, J.A., and R.B. Robinson Jr (1989), *Management,* McGraw-Hill Book Company, New York.

Stoner, J.A.F., and C. Wankel (1986), *Management,* 3rd ed., Prentice-Hall of India Ltd., New Delhi.

Walker Jr, O.C. , J.W. Mullins, H.W. Boyd Jr, and J.C. Larreche (2006), *Marketing Strategy: A Decision-focused Approach,* Tata McGraw-Hill Publishing Company Limited, New Delhi.

Welhrich, H., and H. Koontz (2005), *Management: A Global Perspective,* 11th ed., Tata McGraw-Hill Publishing Company Ltd, New Delhi.

CASE STUDY

Bottlenecks in Sales Performance

Mr Kripal Desouza, senior sales manager of Asian India Ltd, was one of the unhappiest men of the world at the dawn of 2004. He was in a lot of trouble and was unable to find a solution to avert the critical phase of his career. His once adored and vaunted managerial skills and leadership qualities were being questioned.

Asian India Ltd, founded in the year 1976 in Ghaziabad, U.P., is in the business of manufacturing electronic weighing machines in the categories of 30, 60, 100, and 500 kg. Before this company came into existence, another company named Trevor Weight and Scale Company Ltd stared manufacturing electronic weighing machines. Indeed, before Asian India Ltd came into being, customers depended heavily on imported weighing machines to serve their purposes. Since the mechanical weighing machines commanded the market till 1980s, Asian India Ltd saw it as a big opportunity to plunge in the market. It proved to be a bright start for them and progressed steadfastly. They were able to capture a sizable portion of the market by the end of 1990s (20 per cent of market share). Meanwhile, many national and international companies came into the arena and the customers started to disperse among them.

But, there was no doubt that Mr Desouza was a man behind the success of Asian India Ltd. The company sailed along nicely till the midst of 2003, despite knife-edged competition. But sudden erosion of market share at the end of this year left wrinkles in the otherwise

(Contd)

(Contd)

ironed forehead of Mr Desouza. Since his joining in the company, he had worked very hard to bring smiles to the company's fortune. The success of Mr Desouza owed much to the making of a well-nurtured sales team comprising of three senior and four young salespeople with Mr Desouza at the helm. Each salesperson was given independent sales targets to meet in his sales territory but the team was in charge of pre-selling and post-selling activities, particularly after-sales services. The salespeople acted satisfactorily and the team cohesion was intact.

Initially, Desouza was of the idea that the company's downturn was because of the upcoming of many international brands taking advantage of free market economy in India. These players were selling their products at a comparatively cheaper price because of which customers became price sensitive. But it was also true that a sizable section of customers had a demand for high quality–high priced products and therefore the reasons for the dip in the sales remained unfolded. So now, he started believing that probably the team-selling approach was not active. He immediately went through the sales performances of salespeople by crosschecking annual sales contributed by senior and young salespeople for the last three financial years. One result of the average sales volumes in numbers in the 60 kg category of the machine explained by the senior and young salespeople is furnished as follows.

Number of machines sold

(Numbers in the bracket in the average sales targets in numbers)

Average sales	2000–01	2002–03	2003–04
Senior salespeople	385 (450), 85.55%	325 (450) 72.22%	290 (450) 69.44%
Junior salespeople	455 (480) 94.8%	402 (480)83.75%	369 (490) 75.3%

The figures in percentages were quite indicative of the moderate to poor sales performance by seniors as compared to junior salespeople. In other categories of machines, the sales made by seniors were also of low order. The results therefore, demanded immediate intervention of senior manager like Mr Desouza. He convened a meeting inviting seniors and juniors. He again sat together with the two groups separately in which he wanted to know the reasons for the sorry state of performances from seniors and the factors encouraging impressive performances from juniors.

Discussion Questions

1. What were the plausible points Mr Desouza discussed with his team in the combined and separate meetings?
2. Did he require a change in sales force planning? Comment.

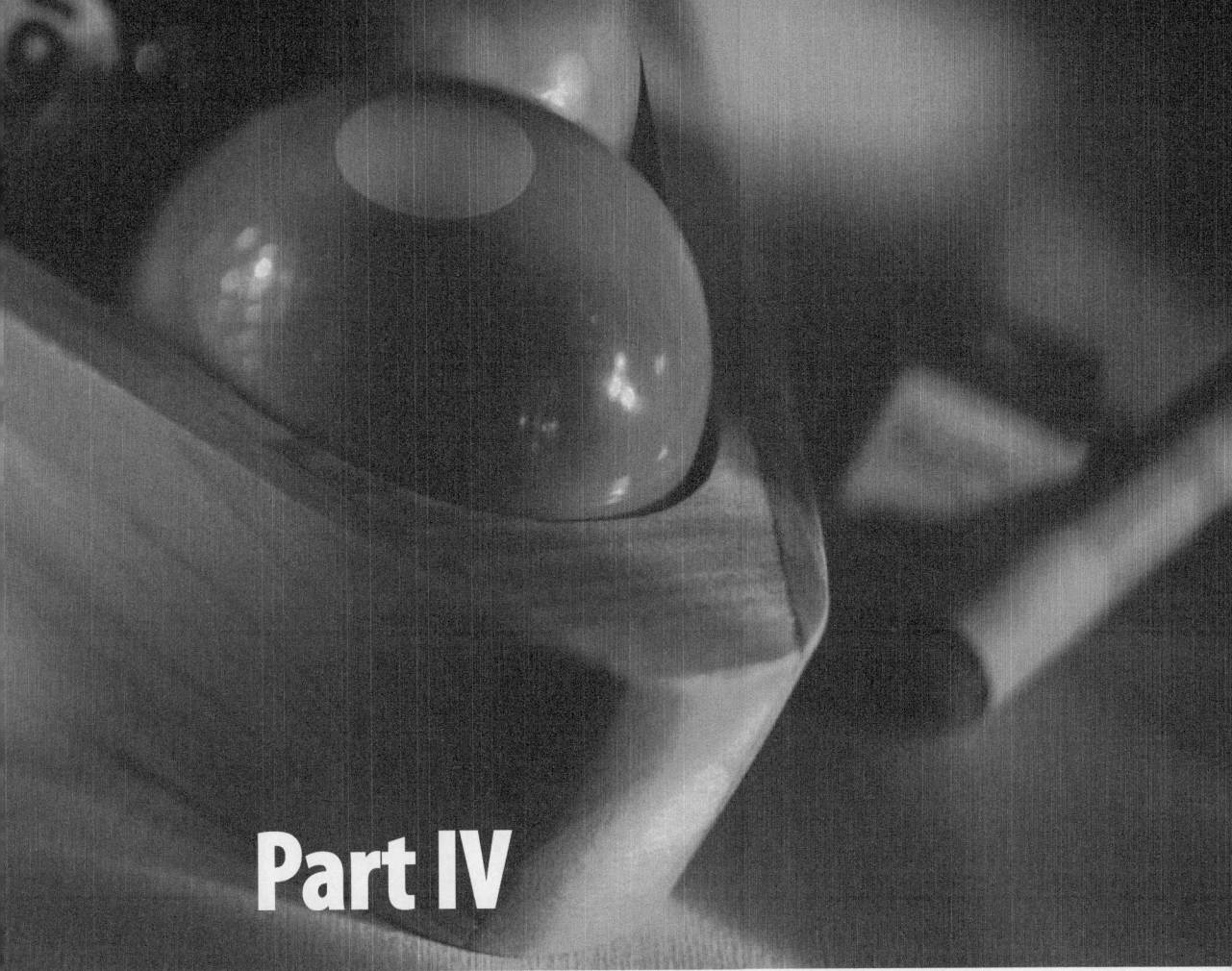

Part IV

Financial Aspects of Sales

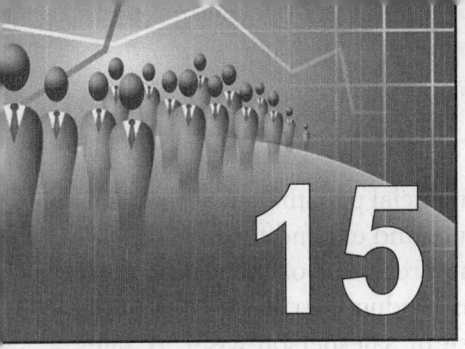

15 Sales Budgeting and Forecasting

LEARNING OBJECTIVES

After reading this chapter, you will be able to

- understand the basics of sales budget
- get acquainted with the general expense heads
- understand the approaches and important features of sales budget
- define the objectives along with the benefits of sales budget
- understand the steps of sales budgeting
- explain the basics of sales forecasting
- develop insights on the importance of sales forecasting
- gather ideas on the approaches and the methods of sales forecasting

15.1 SALES BUDGET—AN INTRODUCTORY APPROACH

A sales budget can be defined as a detailed plan that presents the expected sales for a particular period. It can be expressed both in the units of cost and production. It is a formal document of a firm that expresses the projected revenues and expenditures of a firm within a time schedule. It is an integral part of the organizational plans. The more accurate a sales budget is, higher are the chances of an organization succeeding. In simple terms, it is considered as the key to the entire planning, including the financial plans of an organization.

The fructification of a financial plan depends on the orchestration of an organization's tasks and budgets. Budget, in simple sense, is a planned statement for allocation of funds to accomplish tasks within a specified time. Right estimations of future revenues and costs are the necessary ingredients of a budget. Budget has a provision for monitoring the success or failure, i.e., performance of tasks in terms of comparisons of the following:

(a) Estimated revenues and actual revenues
(b) Estimated costs and actual costs

These comparisons are the basis for controlling future operations of the business and taking corrective actions.

Dominiak and Louderback III (1985) opined that a budget captures and reflects the results of the planning decisions in a formal and integrated way. Thus, budget is a tool to make plans operational, move on the right path, and render activities move according to the plans.

Spiro et al. (2003) defined budget as a tool, a financial plan that an administrator uses to plan for profits by anticipating revenues and expenditures.

A sales budget is a detailed articulation of the break ups of the selling costs across selling units. Selling units are expressed as products, territories, functions (selling and non-selling), persons (customer-wise or salesperson-wise). A sales budget furnishes projected sales revenues and expenses on a weekly, monthly or yearly basis which is part of the sales plans. It gives them a clear indication on how funds will be utilized for each selling unit. It also underscores the line of direction on how the selling activities will be controlled.

The important aspect of budgeting (the procedure for setting budgets) is proportionate distribution of funds across selling units according to the objectives or goals and demands or potentials of each unit. The overall budget must correspond to the organization's missions and objectives. A sales budget decides the budget of other units of the organizations such as production budgets, labour budgets, purchase budgets, etc. It mentions different expense heads and projected selling expenses under these. Box 15.1 gives an idea about the general expense heads or categories. The lists can be enlarged.

Box 15.1 General expense heads

Following are the general expense heads:

(a) Sales force compensations:
   (i) Fixed expenses such as salaries
   (ii) Variable expenses such as commissions, bonuses, etc.
(b) Promotional expenses such as advertisements, preparation of booklets, sample preparations, power point presentations, etc.
(c) Travelling expenses
(d) Logistical expenses such as inventory costs, delivery costs, etc.
(e) Stationery expenses such as preparation of call registers, diaries, writing aids, etc.
(f) Telephone expenses

Dalrymple and Cron (1995) mentioned that sales budget is essentially a set of planned expenses that is prepared on an annual basis. Sales budget has two important wings (i) revenue goals and (ii) expense ceilings.

Still et al. (1994) defined sales budget as a document consisting of estimates of an operating period's probable dollar and unit sales and the likely selling expenses in a year.

15.2 SALES BUDGET—BASIC APPROACHES

A sales budget is the master plan that shows how to balance the sales volume and selling expenses in the sales operations. It is a controlling tool to maintain parity between revenue and expenditure for a specified period of time, usually one year. This is prepared during the stage of sales planning. Sales managers use sales forecasts as an auxiliary component to fix up sales and profit targets for a particular time horizon and estimated costs, called projected costs, to articulate selling expenses and combine the two to plan the sales budgets. They also show the break up of projected selling costs for different products or product lines, territories, customer groups, sales functions, sales projects or programmes, etc. separately. The basic aim of a sales budget is to meet the 'profit objectives' of the firm manoeuvring the future revenue generations within the confines of the expense ceilings.

There are, generally, two approaches of sales budgets:

(i) Top-down approach
(ii) Bottom-up approach

In a top-down approach, the top management decides on the promotional goals and budgets which are communicated to different sales/marketing departments along with disbursal of funds. Budget preparations on percentage of sales, competitive parity or affordability methods fall under the top-down approach. In the bottom-up approach, the sales/marketing departments are asked to set their budget levels according to their goals and communicate it to the top management level where, finally, these are aggregated. Objectives and tasks method is a bottom-up approach. Figure 15.1 exhibits these two approaches.

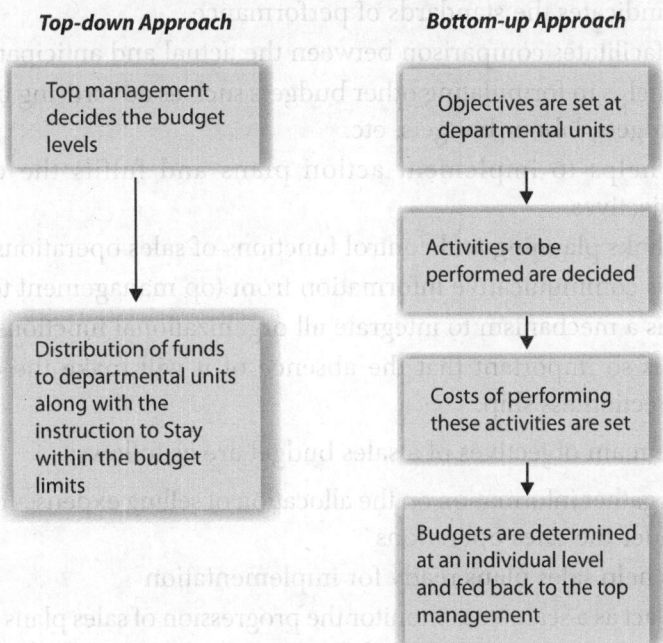

Figure 15.1 Approaches for setting budgets

15.3 SALES BUDGETS—FEATURES, OBJECTIVES, AND BENEFITS

Sales budget has multiple features and therefore meets multiple objectives. Its contributions to sales plans, operations, performance measurements, controlling sales operations, etc. are immense. It occupies a central position in a firm's business. An organization without a sales budget means a reckless ship groping in a treacherous harbour. A sales budget caters profuse benefits to the organization. From handling financial transactions to meeting selling expenses, sales budgets are a real guide to the organization.

The basic features of sales budgets are listed as follows:

1. It is an offshoot of a sales plan. It is a part of the planning process.
2. Budget is a part of the operational plan because budget is made for planned actions.
3. It takes into account allocation and utilization of the company's resources.
4. It has a time limitation. The length of time varies from firm to firm.
5. It arranges provisioning of funds for different heads of expenditure.
6. It is laid down at the top management level.
7. It begins with sales forecasts.
8. It gives an indication of future results such as anticipated sales volumes, sales revenues or profits, etc.
9. It is a device to control costs.
10. It indicates the standards of performance.
11. It facilitates comparison between the actual and anticipated results.
12. It helps in formulating other budgets such as advertising budgets, production budgets, labour budgets, etc.
13. It helps to implement action plans and fulfils the company's selling objectives.
14. It links planning and control functions of sales operations.
15. It is communicative information from top management to lower-level staffs.
16. It is a mechanism to integrate all organizational functions.
17. It is so important that the absence of it will make the organization like a directionless ship.

The main objectives of a sales budget are as follows:

(a) To gather information on the allocation of selling expenses of different activities under the sales operations
(b) To help sales plans ready for implementation
(c) To act as a scanner to monitor the progression of sales plans when it is on course of execution on a periodic basis

(d) To caution sales managers not to act beyond the confines of sales plans

(e) To watch that the activities are undertaken on the pre-planned routes

(f) To act as a watchdog of sales performance keeping continuous tabs on deviations, if any, of actual sales from the target sales

(g) To lend a precise idea of the anticipated future sales in numerical terms

(h) To act as a guide to control and coordinate different sales activities

(i) To set standards of performance for various sales activities separately and as an organization as a whole

(j) To provide a check on the expenditure pattern of different activities

The major benefits of sales budgets are summarized as follows:

1. It helps in the deft and economical handling of financial resources.
2. It makes sales plan purposeful and goal-directed.
3. It coordinates different activities under sales operations in terms of budgetary allocations proportionate to the needs for the accomplishments of those activities.
4. It regulates the expenditure patterns of selling activities and confirms that the expenditure never supersedes allocated funds.
5. It gives an indication of the priority of selling activities. Most important activities deserve highest allocation of resources and least important, lowest allocation.
6. It gives an assurance to the sales managers that they work on predetermined plans.
7. It acts as a controlling tool to bring back unwanted expenditures within the budgetary estimates.
8. It gives prior signal to the sales managers to arrange monetary and other resources before taking any action.
9. It helps the organization to prevent unnecessary wastage of resources.
10. It influences sales managers to do sales forecasts and thus inspires to study market demands, factors affecting demands, market potentials, sales potentials, market competition, etc. The information on it helps the company to scan the economic environment of the business that is necessary for sales planning.
11. It aids in developing strategic plans for business.

15.4 FACTORS INFLUENCING SALES BUDGETS

Sales budget is a complex subject. An organization before contemplating to develop sales budget delves into factors that influence it, otherwise it loses its utility. Some of these factors are as follows:

Market size   Market size has an effect on the magnitude of sales budget. If the company wants to function in a small territory, the budget will be comparatively small compared to that designed for covering large geographical units. Market size, itself, depends on the location of the customers. If the customers are geographically dispersed, the budget level is also high. In contrast, for geographically concentrated customers, the same will be low.

Company's intention to curb selling expenses   It, obviously, affects the volume of sales budget. This happens when (i) the company has a stable market, (ii) the company is in a tight financial position, (iii) competitors reduce the intensity of sales campaigns and sales budgets as well, (iv) the company wants to prune unworthy selling expenses, etc.

Company's financial resources   The company's financial resources has a bearing on the volume of sales budgets. If a company has strong equity markets, healthy debt positions or attractive returns on investment in the immediate past, the liquidity position of the company is good and it can think of apportioning a large sum for sales budget.

Market potential   Market potential indicates the maximum demand response in a geographical unit within a specified period of time, given the environmental and competitive situations. It is believed that higher the market potential, higher would be the opportunity for the company to build the markets and the larger would be the sales budget. The market potential relates to the strength of demand and its applicability to the industry as a whole. The company, as a player in the industry, wants to have a larger percentage of served markets by cutting competition. And for this sake, it can enhance its sales budget.

Sales potential   Sales potential relates to the maximum demand response for a company under identical conditions mentioned in factor (d). This means that the sales potential is high or low depending on a company's strengths and weaknesses or other factors mentioned so far. A low sales potential is not conducive for the allocation of resources under sales budget. But, an ambitious company can try to afford higher budgets if the market potential is very high and take some risks to expand its business.

Production efficiency   Production efficiency affects and is affected by the sales budget. If the company's sales target does not match the production target, the company faces a crisis. In fact, the sales budget is a trigger for the production budget. If the later is small due to production inefficiency, the sales budget is negatively affected. For an attractive market situation, the company desires to augment sales budget and expects high production budget for the manufacturing unit that would help in improving the production efficiency.

15.5 STEPS IN DETERMINING SALES BUDGET

Setting the sales budget is a multi-step process which is a part of the sales plan. The process starts with planning the sales, in broader sense, finalizing the corporate plan. As personal selling is part of promotion, therefore, sales budgets are inclusive of promotional budgets. Sales managers also make use of past sales records to understand the trend of sales in the near future and concomitant selling expenses. The steps in developing a sales budget is shown in Figure in 15.2.

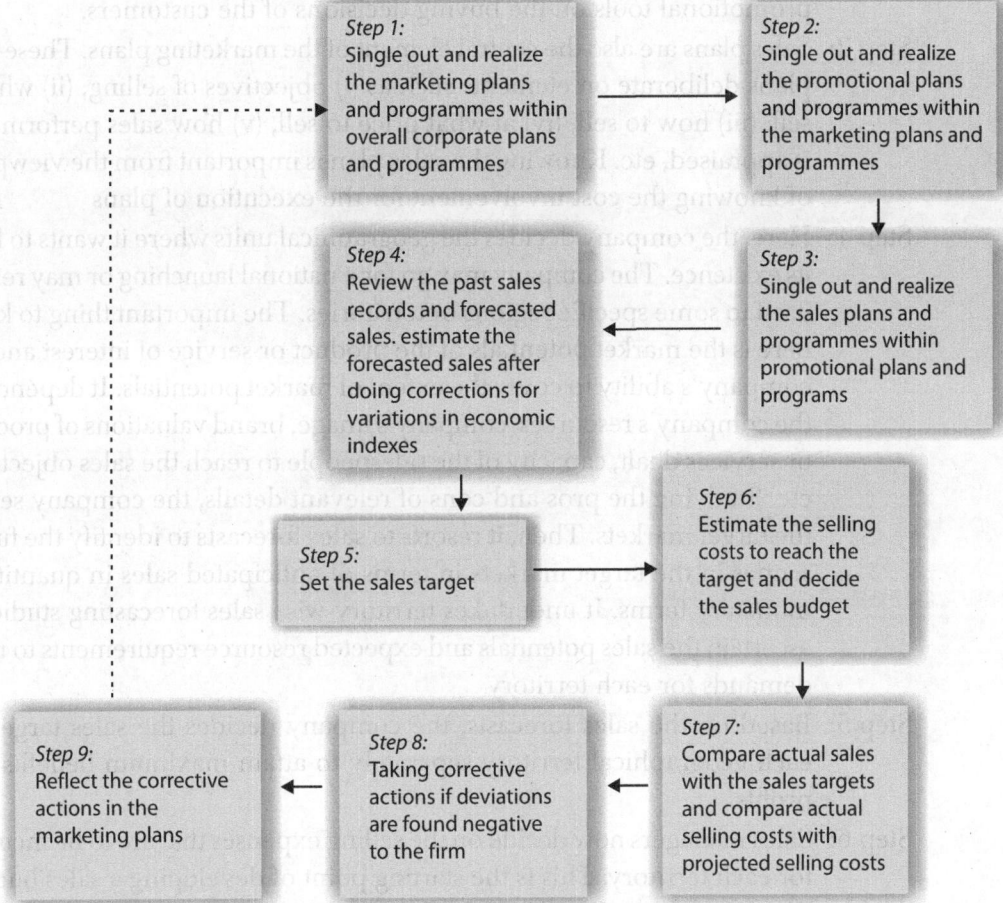

Step 1:
Single out and realize the marketing plans and programmes within overall corporate plans and programmes

Step 2:
Single out and realize the promotional plans and programmes within the marketing plans and programmes

Step 4:
Review the past sales records and forecasted sales. estimate the forecasted sales after doing corrections for variations in economic indexes

Step 3:
Single out and realize the sales plans and programmes within promotional plans and programs

Step 5:
Set the sales target

Step 6:
Estimate the selling costs to reach the target and decide the sales budget

Step 9:
Reflect the corrective actions in the marketing plans

Step 8:
Taking corrective actions if deviations are found negative to the firm

Step 7:
Compare actual sales with the sales targets and compare actual selling costs with projected selling costs

Figure 15.2 Steps in developing sales budget

Step 1: The first and the foremost step, while forming the budget, is to decide on the marketing plans that occupy a major part of the corporate plans. These marketing plans elaborate on the marketing goals and objectives, strategies encompassing different elements of the marketing mix such as market segmentation schemes, positioning strategies, distribution channel decisions, pricing strategies, etc. of a firm. These plans are actually made to outperform competitors and serve customers satisfactorily without affecting the profit objectives or margins.

Step 2: Deciding on the promotional plans is the next step which also happens to be a major part of the marketing plans. Here, the company attempts to develop the right promotional mix that would aid it to reach the target customers with the right kind of communication and promotion. Therefore, an emphasis should be given to understand the impacts of promotional tools on the buying decisions of the customers.

Step 3: Sales plans are also the central element of the marketing plans. These sales plans deliberate on elements such as (i) objectives of selling, (ii) what to sell, (iii) how to sell, (iv) at what price to sell, (v) how sales performance is appraised, etc. Knowing the sales plan is important from the viewpoint of knowing the cost involvement for the execution of plans

Step 4: Here, the company decides the geographical units where it wants to have its existence. The company may go for a national launching or may restrict itself to some specific regions or territories. The important thing to know here is the market potentials of the product or service of interest and the company's ability to cover the extent of market potentials. It depends on the company's resources, company's image, brand valuations of products or services dealt, capacity of the salespeople to reach the sales objectives, etc. Studying the pros and cons of relevant details, the company selects the target markets. Then, it resorts to sales forecasts to identify the future scopes in the target markets in terms of anticipated sales in quantity or monetary terms. It undertakes territory-wise sales forecasting studies to ascertain the sales potentials and expected resource requirements to meet demands for each territory.

Step 5: Based on the sales forecasts, the company decides the sales target for each geographical territory separately to attain maximum benefits and profits.

Step 6: Sales managers now decide on the selling expenses that are to be incurred for each territory. This is the starting point of developing a sales budget. The company selects a method that can precisely determine the sales budget for the firm. The budget helps taking a decision about resource generations and allocations amongst target markets. It reflects the territory-wise sales targets, projected sales revenues, and selling costs for every unit.

Step 7: The sales budget has a provision to compare data on actual sales with the estimated ones and actual selling costs with the projected ones. So, the sales managers get a chance to review their sales performance and selling expenses.

Step 8: Appraisal reports manifest the extent of deviations from the desired performance levels. If no such deviations are found, the company is deemed to be quite on targets. If deviations are negative to the firm, the company revisits the sales budgets and identifies reasons for deviations. The company, after which, takes rectification measures in the sales budget.

Step 9: Being assured of the efficacy of corrective actions, these are included in the marketing plans and the process is repeated. The feedback is expressed as dotted lines to show the recycle of the process.

15.6 METHODS OF DETERMINING SALES BUDGETS

The method of setting the sales budget is a vital part of the budgeting process in every organization. Selection of the right method is important because it is only the right method that can fix the actual sales budgets to fulfil a company's sales goals. Again, the method varies from company to company even for the same product depending on the company's past sales records, financial capacity, competitive positioning of the product or desire to match objectives and tasks.

Following are the methods of determining sales budgets:

Percentage of sales method This is a common method of determining sales budget. It can consider one of the following three bases.

1. A fixed percentage of the last year's sales revenue is set aside for sales budget for the coming year.
2. A fixed percentage of the projected sales figure of the period of interest (planned period) can also be used as the budget. Projected sales are determined by sales forecasting.
3. The average sales of the last few years (say, three years) can also be used as a base and a certain percentages of it can be treated as sales budget.

These percentages may be decided on the basis of information on the average percentages prevailing in the industry.

Advantages Following are the advantages of this method:

1. The method is simple and easy to calculate.
2. It maintains a balanced relationship between sales revenues and selling expenses.
3. It is proved effective for established products or stable marketing environment.

4. If all the competing firms follow more or less the same percentage figures and base year, competition in the market will be healthy and will lend stability to the market.

Disadvantages Following are the disadvantages of this method:

1. It lacks logic because the method suggests that the sales budgets increase proportionately with the increase in sales revenues and vice-versa. Actually, the opposite should hold true. Sales budget should be increased when the sales decline and relaxed in the opposite situation.

2. The percentages are subject to approximation. This means that what should be the right percentages on sales that would match a company's economic situation or help reach sales objectives are not easy to know.

3. The method is not applicable for new or innovative products.

4. For fluctuating market situations, the method is suicidal.

Competitive parity method Here, the budget of a company is determined by comparing its budget with the budget that the competitors are spending. The company follows the budget level of leading competitor (s) and reflect the same in its budget. So, the sales budget of the competitors is treated as the base or reference point. The company may use average percentages of selling expenses incurred by the industry as a whole on the sales in the last year to determine its current budget. Information on the spending of competitors can also be gathered from company websites, annual reports, news from trade associations or trade journals, etc.

Advantages Following are the advantages of this method:

1. It is comparatively a safe practice

2. It reflects the collective wisdom of the industry and as a result sales budget is expected to be optimal or close to the optimal

3. If all the competitors follow more or less similar budget levels, it prevents marketing warfare and brings stability to the industry

Disadvantages Following are the disadvantages of this method:

1. It is less practical because sales problems of companies are different and so are the sales objectives. Therefore, budgets should be different.

2. There is no assurance that a competitor's spending policy is correct.

3. It is not possible to collect information in advance and the budget level of a competitor for the next year.

4. If the budget level is determined on wrong information of the competitors, it can destabilize the market.

5. If all the firms have the same intensity of promotions, then a firm cannot single out from the rest to reach target customers with informative or persuasive messages meaningfully.

Objectives and tasks method   This involves determining budget based on the pre-planned sales objectives, tasks, and costs. The method consists of three steps.

1. The company decides its sales objectives.
2. The company decides on the tasks to achieve those objectives.
3. The company estimates how much money will be needed to accomplish these tasks. This is treated as the sales budget.

Advantages   Following are the advantages of this method:

1. It has an element of realism because its bases are sales objectives and tasks.
2. It is flexible in the sense that changes in the marketing environments are reflected in the sales objectives and tasks, and therefore budget estimates are assumed to be correct.
3. It gives sales managers a chance to make periodic review of budgets.

Disadvantages   Following are the disadvantages of this method:

1. Formulating the right sales objectives and tasks require sales managers to possess sufficient knowledge and wisdom because any wrong information would mar spending decisions.
2. There might be some difficulties in understanding what are the major sales objectives.
3. As communication is a series of steps such as creating awareness, arousing interests, prompting actions, etc. sales managers may have problems in determining spending patterns for each communication objective to fulfil.
4. It ignores past sales figures, forecasted sales, and competitors' budgets, etc., which are assumed to be vital inputs to budget preparation.

What you can afford method   The budget is fixed at a level that the company is able to bear or afford in the coming year. A company takes decisions on sales budget depending on its capacity to spend. It rests on the maxim 'cut your coat according to your clothes'.

Advantages   Following are the advantages of this method:

1. The method is simple and easy to administer.
2. It is safe because it never exceeds a company's limits to spend.
3. It is flexible because it is adjustable.

Disadvantages Following are the disadvantages of this method:

1. This method lacks planning process and there is no guarantee that the apportioned amounts will serve the objectives of budgeting.
2. The budget does not follow any guideline except the management's arbitrary discretion of deciding budget levels.

15.7 INTELLIGENT BUDGETING—AN ILLUSTRATION

Budgeting is a strategic exercise. Today, every company is on a route to hover on cost control as means to size the unnecessary flab on sales budgets. But it is also important to allot the right amount of budget for various activities. For instance, in some cases artful and effective choice of promotional tools can sideline many popular brands but hefty media penetrates target consumers successfully. Exhibit 15.1 is an evidence of it.

Exhibit 15.1   A new budgetary experience

Sula Vineyards, a firm with tremendous performance backup, unwavering promise, and prospect is India's first white wine business. It has a promotional budget of different sorts such as conventional media-print, audiovisual, etc. which are out of reach for people due to legal implications. The company has spruced up sampling as a promotional tool to reach target consumers. In fact, target groups have got an opportunity to get a first-hand taste and generate an impression about it. Sula, one of the recognized brands has got huge success where sampling and word-of-mouth communication have moved side-by-side and, therefore fatty promotional budgets have been kept in check.

Thus, selling expenses can be intelligently managed and sales budget can be restricted to a moderate degree. Same happened with The Elan Company. The company, manufacturer of frozen yogurt, made optimal selling expenses by resorting to product sampling and in-store demonstration to reach target consumers.

So, a company can depend on unconventional yet popular promotional means to reach prospective customers speedily and economically instead of weighty and expensive mass media.

Sources: Choudhury and Gupta (2006); Johnson et al. (1994)

15.8 SALES FORECASTING—A PRELIMINARY INTRODUCTION

Forecasting is an enabler in solving managerial decision-making problems. Solutions to economic and business problems heavily rely on forecasting future business phenomena. In fact, planning, policymaking, strategizing, budgeting, etc. are all decision-making areas that depend on forecasting the future conditions. As future is apprehended to be uncertain, forecasting is of immense importance to the firm. Where future is certain, albeit a utopia in present-day business environment, forecasting finds no need. The more the uncertainties of future outcomes, the more is the need for sales forecasting. Thus, forecasting helps to explore the future events and makes an objective assessment of the future happenings and gives estimates of business variables (such as human resource requirements, market potentials, etc.) that have both qualitative and quantitative meanings.

Kapoor (2004) reported that forecasting involves examining a variety of quantitative and qualitative data, weighing them against each other and drawing conclusions. Forecasting provides a groundwork for making future plans and programmes. According to Samuelson and Nordhaus (1992), a good forecast sheds light on the economic ups and downs ahead and prepares decision-makers to adapt their actions to economic conditions for best results.

Stoner and Freeman (1994) defined forecasting as the process of using past events to make systematic predictions about future outcomes and trends.

William et al. (1985) defined forecasting as a formal process of predicting future events that will significantly influence the effectiveness of a given strategy.

Sales forecasting is a pivotal activity for every organization as carrying out forecasting accurately and then inserting the necessary changes in the sales plans and programmes as per the forecasted results affects the result of a project. Sales forecasting is the starting point of sales budgets preparation. It gives an opportunity to project the expected market demand of the firm's products or services and later compare it with how much the firm is able to cater. Thus, it enables firms to compare the desired sales performance with actual figures and also directs it to take controlling actions if the deviations are unacceptable to the firm. Sales forecasting contributes to an organization's sales plans, policies, strategies, budgets, quotas, and targets. The other processes which are also get positively affected by it are product planning and schedules, staffing, inventory, and logistical policies, promotional mix, capital outlays, cash flow, working capital decisions, and the performance standards.

Forecasting is a weapon in the armoury of the strategic tools for business managers. It has immense potential to guide business firms by showing the path that happens to be safe or reasonably less disturbed compared to other ways. Since time immemorial, forecasting has been a popular practice to envision future situations such as weather, rainfall, crop productions, industrial progress, and prediction of environmental disasters that have critical effects on society. It has a strategic significance also. It can gauge the attacks of enemies from internal or external sides of a nation and pre-empt the causes of such aggressions before it takes shape. From the corporate viewpoint, forecasting is deemed to be a strategic initiative.

From cans to canons, business firms in today's juncture use forecast as a vital force to steer business functions on the right path. This is essential because of the complex nature of business environment characterized by technological leap-frogging, digital breakthroughs, relentless surge of customer demands, volcanic competition, and so many externalities. Forecasting has different meanings in an unperturbed and shifting economic environment. In a seamless environment having no such gross aberrations of its conditions from equilibrium combinations, forecasting is a cakewalk. No challenges, no threats, no impediments, no further opportunities make business a routine sojourn and predicting the future is just a linear extrapolation of the present with cent per cent precision. In fact, in static environment, prediction is a matter of arithmetical progression. But, unwavering environment is an imaginary conceptualization. Rather, its discussion is passé. Environment, in pragmatic sense, is dynamic. It has upswings and downswings. Its changes are difficult to plot on a plane.

Clay (2004) viewed that accurate forecasting can help companies manage their sales well and plan with confidence. Forecasting has a time dimension. Generally forecasting is made either short term or long term. Sales forecasts for shorter durations mean forecasting for a month, three months or one year. While long-term forecasts are made for three to five years or even more. Chandra (1993) recounted that short-term forecasts are helpful in facilitating working capital planning and cash budgeting whereas the long term ones can be used for investment planning. Short-term forecasts are made keeping in mind the intermittent changes (such as drop in market shares) in marketing environments and task for tactical initiatives. Long-term forecasts are important to fructify strategic plans, staffing decisions, compensation programmes, etc.

The broad objectives of sales forecasting are shown as follows:

(a) To decide on sales targets and sales quotas for salespeople and sales territories

(b) To determine sales budgets, aid in sales planning, and formulate sales strategies

(c) To attain proper control of inventories of finished products

(d) To set up performance standards and understand the growth of past sales

(e) To identify sales opportunities and know the strengths and weaknesses of competitors

(f) To research out sales and market potentials of the firm and to get an idea of the profit potentials of the firm

(g) To gather idea of the image or goodwill of the firm

(h) To help in product planning and development, devising distribution, promotion, and pricing policies

(i) To understand the nature and volume of selling expenses in the past and predict these for the future

(j) To help the organization to set production targets and to decide on capital budgeting, investment, and working capital management decisions

(k) To assist an organization in sales force recruitment, selection, and compensation decisions and to help in the performance appraisal of sales force

The following Exhibit 15.2 takes the readers through the importance and contribution of sales forecasting in retail sector.

Exhibit 15.2   Retail sector—trends and trajectories

The retail sector provides a dynamic environment where prediction of the future is a mountainous task. It is a growing sector experiencing unpredictable contingencies such as competition, fresh investments, strategic alliances, innovations, rising consumer expectations, etc. Competition is precisely fierce between unorganized and organized sectors and even within the sectors of each. Innovation encores such as online retailing, e-commerce, use of wireless LANs, mobile POS terminals, etc. pervade retail scenes. The quality of service in retail business has got momentum.

Retail business was mostly dominated by the unorganized retail outlets till the dawn of the new millennium. Opening of Indian economy has made a remarkable turnaround in the retail sector, particularly, with the pouring of huge FDI (foreign direct investment) in retail sector. The forays of Wal-Mart, Metro, K-mart, etc. in India are true indicators of investment-savvy retail sector in India. What have prompted these retail giants to embark in India is a matter both academic and business interests. To resolve the mystery, some pertinent questions can be raised as follows:

(a) What are the pasts of the Indian retail sector?

(b) What are the present situations of it?

(c) What is likely to be ahead in this sector?

Past: Retailing was never dreamt of as an organized movement, as it is today. It always had a fragmented industrial format, largely controlled by the private independent owners and distributors. The retail operations had been managed largely by stockiest, distributors, wholesalers, retailers, C&F (carry and forwarding) agents, etc. The traditional formats were dominated by hawkers, grocers, street markets, kiosks, point of purchase (POP) stores. Shoppers seldom found total assortments under one roof. Moreover, narrow retail space, limited retail ambience, poor deliver policies, shoddy packaging, unscientific queuing, no parking place, shallow merchandise mix, etc. were the haunting features of the traditional retail business.

Present: The retail sector has come to an age which involves large consumer base, high disposable personal incomes of people, booming middle class, media blitz, burgeoning youth segment who are exposed to international brands and have an urge to catch up with the international taste and flavour. These have given lifeblood to retail business to flourish

---

(Contd)

(*Contd*)

in an unexpected proportion. Moreover, technology has given a huge boost to the retail sector at present. The growth of online retailing, electronic data interchange (EDI), retail information system, wireless scanning, etc. are some of the major technological advances that have bestowed retail sector a cutting-edge position in the global market.

Future: Retail sector has a very bright future ahead. Besides its contribution to employment generation, growth of GDP (35 per cent of India's GDP) and FDI, the cohabitation and competition amongst domestic and multinational players and unorganized retail businesses have drawn everyone's attention. In fact, this sector has become a paradise of revenue generation and foreign exchange earnings. Indeed, big companies have been spreading its retail operations very fast. For example, Wal-Mart by its efficient supply chain and distribution expertise in combination with large merchandise mix aims at sustainable triple digit annual growth over the next 5–10 years (Sahoo and Mishra 2008).

Thus, a retail player has to wear the modern format of retailing in order to make sense of its business in the years to come.

15.9 SALES FORECASTING—FACTORS AND FUNDAMENTALS

Basically, sales forecasting is the prediction of future sales. It is an effort to estimate what a firm's future sales are likely to be. Marketing research is a means to do sales forecasting studies. Marketing research provides information on past sales trends, anticipated future sales, studies and analyses change in business or economic indexes such as customer demands, competitive conditions, price variations, industrial productions, capacity and facility utilizations, etc. that affect future revenue generations and have an impact on investment and cash flow decisions. The accuracy of sales forecasting depends on the precision of statistical data on various business or economic parameters influencing market potentials and growth rate.

Sales potentials of a firm rests within the periphery of market potentials and are influenced by how the firm manages its internal resources and capitalizes it to explore market opportunities. The following factors are noticed and analysed to examine their impacts on outcomes of forecasting.

Unexpected fluctuations in business or economic environments do not help or make the trend analysis of past events simple. An efficient researcher should have prior knowledge of different combinations of environmental factors and their impacts on sales forecasting. Analytical tools are also available to counter these factors to reach good estimates of forecasting.

Factors influencing sales forecasting are as follows:

Fluctuations in business environment For example, cyclical or seasonal fluctuations in business

Future state of economy For example, price rise, entry of foreign firms, changes in demand, market and sales potentials, interest rate fluctuations, foreign exchange reserves, etc.

Political conditions of a nation For example, change of government, external trade relations with foreign nations, etc. have some impacts on political stability which, in turn, impacts on economic policies, foreign policies, etc.

Market characteristics For example, tastes and preferences of consumers, buying powers, market competitions, terms and conditions of the distributors, etc have an impact on market demands and potentials too.

Situational factors For example, unpredictable future events such as natural calamities, large-scale economic recession, wars, etc. have an impact on market stability and should be considered in forecasting.

In short, one can say that, sales forecasting is a type of marketing research because it fulfils the basic characteristics of marketing research. It involves collection of data relating to marketing, its analysis, and drawing conclusions on the future outcomes. Green and Tull (1986) while discoursing the role of sales forecasting in marketing research underlined two major reasons for forecasting: (i) It helps to identify the problems and (ii) It helps to solve the problems.

Sales forecasting, thus, relies on factual data on past sales events that are analysed to predict future circumstances. The nature and type of data (say, accounting records, sales proceeds, etc.) has a strong influence on the precision of predictions. Listed below are some fundamentals of past data that can help to reach the actual estimation of future events.

Fundamentals for collecting data for sales forecasting are as follows:

1. Availability of data from primary and secondary sources: Primary source produces primary data such as experience of customers, distributors, company salespeople, etc. They are asked to give opinions of future outcomes. Secondary data collected from secondary sources include gathering information on trade statistics, company annual reports, company websites, etc. to get an idea of future results or outcomes. Second, data from few years ago to immediate past should be available to make accurate projections of future.

2. Authenticity of data: Data that is collected should be actual and reliable. In fact, the sources from where data is collected should be genuine and believable.

3. Cost of collecting data: Data should be collected at an optimal cost. Value of data or information should outweigh the cost of collection.

4. Availability of good researchers: Skilled and experienced researchers are required to collect and analyse the data.

5. Selection of forecasting method: Right method should be chosen to analyse the findings and report results.

The correctness of sales forecasting, thus hinges on the collection of relevant and reliable raw data, past and future market conditions and application of right analytical tools to synthesize information that help sales managers to work on sales forecasting. Moreover, the reports of sales forecasting should be delicately compiled to sales plans documents and sales budget proposals. To what extent, these reports are errorless will determine the accuracy of managerial decisions. For example, to what extent sales budgets timely and truly act upon the outcomes of sales forecasts determine the right accumulation and distribution of resources to accomplish sales tasks and goals.

The importance of sales forecasting are listed as follows:

1. It integrates past, present, and future performances of the business and insures future prospects of the business.
2. It studies the market trends, tracks the upswings and downswings of market demands, competitive threats, marketing infrastructures such as media supports, logistics, supplies, etc.
3. It helps in estimating sales budgets to meet selling expenses and determines the sales quota (including area-wise) for each salesperson.
4. It helps in production planning, production scheduling, inventory planning, purchase policies, distribution planning, setting promotional budgets, etc.
5. It is important in staffing, setting training needs and budgets, delegation of tasks, planning sales operations, cost control, cost containment and curtailment, etc.
6. It helps in fixing performance standards and helps in comparison of actual performance against standards.
7. It aids in taking new product launching decision, sales territory expansion decision, product positioning decision, target market entry decision, etc.
8. It facilitates decisions on strategic alliances, mergers, acquisitions, franchising operations, international market entry, long-term financial plans, credit policies, debt–equity ratios, returns on investment, etc.
9. It is important to assess company image and the image the company is likely to achieve.
10. It helps in assessing and improving relationships with present and prospective customers.
11. It creates an investment-friendly environment in the firm and increasing the effectiveness and efficiency of sales operations.
12. It aids in SWOT analysis, i.e. identifying strengths and weaknesses of the firm as well as opportunities and threats in the market.

15.10 APPROACHES OF SALES FORECASTING

Sales can be forecasted in two ways—top-down approach and bottom-up approach.

15.10.1 Top-down Approach

A firm starts from the forecast of the total market (say, national market). This forecast is for a specific industry engaged in manufacturing a specific product group or product line (say, baby foods or cosmetics). Company X finds the sales forecast by estimating the total demand for a product in the national market. If the firm wants to do its business in the national market, then it determines the expected market share of the total market it would like to achieve (for a new product) or will be able to achieve (for an existing product). This is the top-down approach. Figure 15.3 outlines this approach in a nut shell.

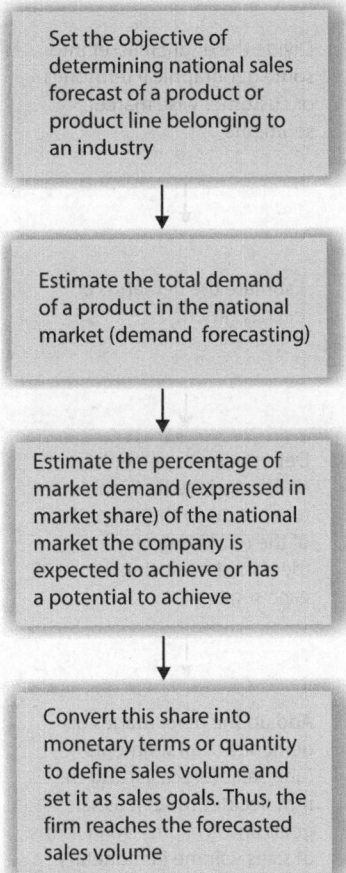

Figure 15.3 Top-down approach

However, if the firms want to operate in a geographic area, then it should find out the percentage of market share of the national market that is explained by the territory of interest and estimate the total sales in that territory and the firm's expected share in it. After this, convert the firm's estimated market share into sales volume. This is the sales forecast in that territory.

15.10.2 Bottom-up Approach

The bottom-up approach is the opposite of the top-down approach. Here, the entire market (say, the national market) is divided into some segments. Each segment may represent territory or customer groups. Territories might be regions, districts or cities. Customer groups can be major, moderate or minor customers depending on their sales turnover, order size, etc. After this estimate the forecast of each segment and then aggregate the forecasts of all segments to reach at national forecast of the product or product line. Refer to Figure 15.4 for the broad outline of the approach.

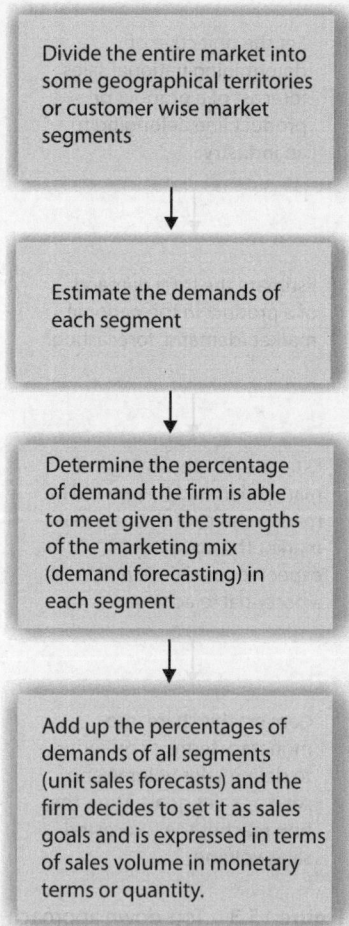

Figure 15.4 Bottom-up approach

15.11   METHODS OF SALES FORECASTING

Forecasting methods can be qualitative and quantitative. Qualitative methods are subjective in nature where the opinion of the experts is given importance while estimating the future sales. Quantitative methods imply objective or mathematical analysis of factors predicting sales. Quantitative methods provide more accurate forecasts than qualitative ones. A tabular classification (Figure 15.5) of forecasting methods is shown as follows:

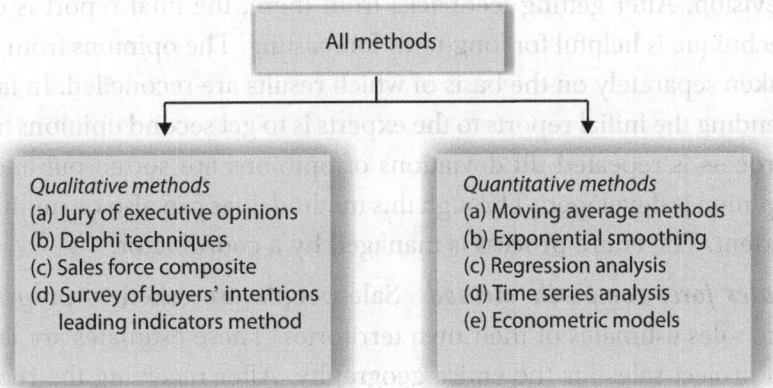

Figure 15.5 Classification of forecasting methods

Qualitative Methods

Following are the quantitative methods of sales forecasting:

Jury of executive opinions   The jury of executive opinions is based upon the collective judgments of a jury of executive panel. Top-level executives in an organization are consulted while estimating the possible future sales of a product or a group of similar products after which an average of all these estimates is calculated. This is in fact a pooled judgment of sales for a definite time period in future. Opinions are pooled and averaged out and finally reconciled in a group meeting.

This is a quick method of sales forecasting because data is easily available within the organization. Only those in the organization are approached who are well-informed about the industry and factors, internal and external to the organization, influencing sales. The closer the opinions of the executives are the more reliable is the estimate. In contrast, when opinions vary significantly, the estimate cannot be depended upon. Executives should be serious enough in having their opinions and should apply their minds in the prediction.

But the method is not scientific and the executives opine on guesswork. Often executives have their own personal workloads and may not find it interesting. Also, the estimates of sales, product- or territory-wise are difficult to get by this method.

Delphi method A group of experts is chosen who are requested to give their views on the projection of sales in the future time period. Experts are selected from various fields such as industries, government agencies, research institutions, trade associations, distribution houses, etc. They are requested to review competition, customer tastes and preferences, general business conditions, etc. and report how these will influence the results.

These reports are then processed, analysed, and sent back to the experts for revision. After getting feedbacks from them, the final report is compiled. This technique is helpful for long-term forecasting. The opinions from the experts are taken separately on the basis of which results are reconciled. In fact, the idea for sending the initial reports to the experts is to get second opinions from them. The process is repeated till deviations of opinions are sorted out and a consensual opinion is developed. Through this method, bias can also be minimized to a great extent. The entire process is managed by a coordinator.

Sales force composite method Salespeople are asked to prepare a report on the sales estimates of their own territories. These estimates are later aggregated to project sales for the entire geography. After receiving the reports, these are checked and verified for final projections. For a limited number of customers in a territory and industrial products, this method is very practical.

The estimate calculated from this method is expected to be very close to the actual figures because salespeople hardly overstate the estimates to avoid huge sales quota which would adversely affect their performance. Salespeople, here, get a chance to interact with the prospective buyers before they start sales operations. So, the initial recognition to buyers is a bonus to the salespeople.

The company entrusts senior salespeople, particularly those who are engaged in field selling, to find sales potentials. But they may devote less attention to the forecasting jobs, if they are busy with the pressure-selling situations. In such cases, they either might not do it or do it casually, in which case, the results will be wrong. Sometimes salespeople intentionally report some figures that best suit them to accept as sales quota, as result of which, organizations lose a part of their revenues in those territories. Some salespeople overstate the sales estimates from share over ambition and in this case, the company's selling expenses mount up with less productive results. So, an initial training of salespeople regarding methods of sales forecasting is important before, they do it in fields.

Survey of buyers' intentions The method suggests selecting a sample of buyers and questioning them about their intentions to purchase a particular product.

This information is then extrapolated to the total population of buyers to estimate probable future sales. The validity of this method depends on

(a) how accurately the sample is chosen;
(b) how accurately the questionnaire is constructed to get information from the samples; and
(c) how accurately the sales are estimated from the sample results.

Many companies select a panel of consumers and interact with them at regular intervals about buying intentions. They are also asked on various other issues such as product quality, their satisfaction with price level, after-sales service, etc. Even suitable suggestions can be obtained on how to improve features or cause changes in the deficient areas to improve sales. The method is suitable for buyers and industrial products because the procedure is manageable unlike the situations where the number of buyers is very high.

Leading indicators method The method suggests identification of key factors that are called indicators that influence sales. The trends or time series of the leading indicators are studied to see their impacts on sales. In fact, these series are combined to see their joint impacts on sales. For example, GDP, industrial production, whole sales price index, quality of life, etc. can be leading indicators to influence sale of a product or product line.

A leading indicator may contain some underlying indicators to influence it. Study of an economic indicator involves examining the statistics or trends of it. These leading indicators change to cause change in the business environment. Similarly, leading indicators (say, demand, personal disposable income, etc.) are responsible for the change in sales. Forecasting study, therefore, implies estimation of combined impacts of leading indicators on sales of a product under study.

Quantitative Methods

Following are the quantitative methods of sales forecasting:

Moving average method The method suggests drawing an average of the sales of a number of years to predict the sales of a coming period. The objective is to smooth out the fluctuations and provide a close estimate of the forecasted sales. This method can be better understood from the following:

Period	Sales
1	S_1
2	S_2
3	S_3

Therefore, the sales in period 4 will be

$$S_4 = \frac{S_1 + S_2 + S_3}{3}$$

S_4 is a three-yearly moving average. If this is policy of the company to three-yearly moving average every time, then, the average sales in period five will be

$$S_5 = \frac{S_2 + S_3 + S_4}{3}$$

So, the sales of the preceding three years are considered to forecast the sales of the year of interest. This is a very simple method and the calculation for this is easy too. When the market is stable for a considerable period of time, it gives an accurate estimate of sales. Alternatively, this can be construed that when factors influencing sales are common for previous three years (for calculating three-year moving average), this method gives accurate projection of sales.

Exponential smoothing method It is similar to the moving average method. In moving average, the sales of previous years are given equal importance but in exponential smoothing, the recent past sales are given more weight than the earlier pasts. The objective is to smooth out fluctuations in the time series for accurate estimation of sales forecast.

The general equation of exponential smoothing is as follows:

Next year's sales = a(this year's sales) + $(1-a)$ (this year's forecasts)

where,

a is a constant, and is called the smoothing constant or weight

where a = weight for the current year's sales

$(1-a)$ = Weight for the immediate preceding year

If $a = 1$, then, the forecasted sales is equal to sales of the current year. If $a = 0$, then current year's forecast is equal to next year's forecast. No adjustment is needed.

The range of the value of 'a' is from 0 to 1. For practical reasons, the value of a is chosen between 0.1 to 0.4. Similarly, the observations for the preceding second year, third year, etc. may be considered. A practical illustration is discussed as follows to understand the concept better:

The sales and forecasted sales for the year 2000 is shown below. Say, $a = 0.4$

Year	Sales (lakh)	Forecasted sales (lakh)
2000	50	45

So, the forecasted sales for the year 2001 = $0.4 \times 50 + (1 - 0.4) \times 45 = 47$

Time series analysis A time series is a sequence of values, a variable assumes corresponding to different time periods. Data on sales, industrial production, revenues or profits are arranged in a sequence with respect to time period produces a time series. Say, ten years annual sales, when arranged chronologically against years give us a time series. A time series of sales represents four basic elements of variations in sales. These are

 (i) trends,
 (ii) seasonal variations,
 (iii) cyclical variations, and
 (iv) irregular factors.

Trend (T) represents long-term increment or decline in the sales. It is the long-term movement in time series.

Cyclical variations (C) represent the ups and downs in the business and are better understood by studying the nature of the business cycle. Ups in business cycle mean prosperity and downs mean recession. Twists and turns in the cycle take place in a regular sequence. Time series over an extended period of time indicate cycles. Exponential smoothing can detect cyclical variations satisfactorily.

Seasonal variations (S) represent periodic movements over a time period, usually one year. For example, climatic changes, festival periods, Christmas occasions, etc. take place every year at a particular time period and these influence sales for some products. The sales of garments, consumer durables pick up during festival times. Seasonal variations can be understood when data in the time series are presented monthly or quarterly. Seasonal variations take place in a definite time of a year and when the sales data are assumed to pick up for some products during that period and therefore, percentages of the total sales are high. If past data are indicative of it, then percentages of sales during previous years can be used to predict future sales.

Irregular factors (I) are unexpected events such as wars, natural calamities, strikes in the organization, etc. that cannot be predicted in advance.

These four factors are combined to calculate the estimate.

Thus, Sales $= T \times C \times S \times I$

Projection of sales is made by extrapolating the trends with adjustments of cyclical and seasonal variations. The irregular factors cannot be anticipated in advance and therefore certain allowances are given in the future sales trend by provisioning contingency plans.

Regression analysis Regression analysis is a statistical method that is used for representing the linear relationship between two or more variables. If a relationship between two variables exist, then the value of one variable can be predicted given the information on the value of the other variable. This method can be used in sales forecasting to measure the relationship between a firm's sales and other economic or demographic indicators.

Dillon et.al (1987) defined regression analysis as the procedure that determines how much of the variation in the dependent variable can be explained by the independent variables. Four questions are pertinent in this regard as follows:

 (i) Is the relationship linear?
 (ii) How strong is the relationship, i.e. how well can we predict the dependent variable from the value of independent variables?
(iii) Whether the relationship is statistically significant?
(iv) Which independent variable contributes more in explaining the variation of the dependent variable?

Suppose, the personal income and education are indicators for the sale of personal computers to households, it can be assumed that sales go up with increase in personal income and education. But what is important is whether the regression model with sales as dependent variable and personal income and education as independent variables are linear. This can be understood when the change in the independent variables causes a constant absolute change in the dependent variable. Second, what is the degree of relationship? For example, if the income rises by 20 per cent and the average education rises by 10 per cent, what will be the per cent increase of sales? Third the researcher should test the statistical significance of the model. Otherwise, the certainty of relationship will be in question. Fourthly, which variable, personal income or education contributes significantly to sales than the other?

Econometric Models

Econometric models are mathematical models describing the economic relationship between variables, say the relationship between demand and the disposable income. Studies of these relationships help managers to take economic decisions. Econometrics determines how different economic variables interact and affect one another. So far as application of econometrics in sales forecasting is concerned, forecasters study the past relationships between sales and the sales determining variables such as household incomes, spending patterns, consumption behaviour, etc. After this they predict how changes in these variables would affect sales in future by statistical analysis.

However, these relationships are assumed to be based on theoretical rationales rather than full empirical understandings. Green and Tull (1986) viewed that econometric models are less empirical than correlative models.

SUMMARY

Budget is a formal document to show projected revenues and expenses of a firm within a time limit. A sales budget is a detailed articulation of breakups of selling costs across selling units where selling units are products, territories, customers, etc. A sales budget is the master plan to balance sales volume and selling expenses. Its basic aim is to attain profit objectives managing sales revenues within the defined selling expenses.

Basically, there are two approaches of setting sales budget. These are (i) top-down approach and (ii) bottom-up approach. Sales budget is a part of the operational sales plan. In fact, it makes sales plan ready for implementation. It helps to set the sales performance standards and provides a check on the expenditure patterns. It assists in handling financial resources that is beneficial to the firm. The factors that influence sales budgets are market size, company's financial resources, market potentials, sales potentials, etc. The methods that are popular in setting sales budgets are percentages of sales, competitive parity, objectives and tasks, and affordability.

Sales forecasting is the prior stage of sales budgeting. Solutions of business and economic problems rely on sales forecasting. It is the process of using past events to make systematic prediction on future results. It helps a company to decide on sales targets and sale quotas for salespeople. Fluctuations of business environment, economic uncertainty, political conditions, etc. impact sales forecasting. Methods of sales forecasting are classified into qualitative and quantitative. Qualitative methods are subjective and hinge on opinions of experts. Quantitative methods are objective. The later tries to identify the factors affecting sales and tries to build mathematical relationship between sales and these factors.

KEY TERMS

Bottom-up Approach In bottom-up approach, the sales/marketing departments set their budget levels according to their goals and communicate it to the top management level.

Forecasting Forecasting involves examining and weighing a variety of quantitative and qualitative data against each other before drawing conclusions.

Sales Budget Sales budget can be defined as a detailed formal plan that presents the expected sales for particular period.

Top-down Approach When following the top-down approach, it is the top management that takes all the important decisions which are then communicated to different sales/marketing departments along with disbursal of funds.

CONCEPT REVIEW QUESTIONS

1. Define sales budget. What are its objectives?
2. What are the benefits of sales budget?
3. Explain the steps in setting sales budget.
4. What is sales forecasting? Why is it important to the firm?
5. What are the factors influencing sales forecasting?
6. What are the main approaches of sales forecasting?
7. Discuss the qualitative methods of sales forecasting.
8. What do you mean by time series? How does it help in sales forecasting?
9. Compare and contrast the moving average and exponential smoothing methods of sales forecasting.

CRITICAL REVIEW QUESTIONS

1. Sales forecasting gives direction to the sales organizations about the future plans of operations and sales budgeting provides the necessary inputs to accomplish what are recommended in the plans. Thus, coordination of the two is must for achieving performance in the sales organization. As a sales manager of a firm how can you attain this coordination?
2. Discuss the possible flaws in sales budgeting and forecasting methods that can render these ineffectual.

PROJECT ASSIGNMENTS

1. Approach two marketing research firms that do sales forecasting for their clients' products. Enquire about the sort of problems they encounter in sales forecasting. How do they manipulate cyclical and seasonal variations during forecasting sales?
2. Meet sales managers of organizations manufacturing (i) pesticides, (ii) industrial equipment, and (iii) food cereals. Ask them how they feel about the importance of sales budget. How do they link sales budgets to sales forecasts?

REFERENCES

Chandra, P. (1993), *Financial Management: Theory and Practice*, 3rd ed., Tata-McGraw Hill Publishing Company Ltd, New Delhi.

Choudhury, P.K., and A. Gupta (2006), *Successful Promotions Build Successful Brands*, Universities Press, Hyderabad.

Clay, J. (2004), *Successful Selling Solutions*, Viva Books Private Limited, New Delhi.

Dalrymple, D.J., and W.L.. Cron (1995), *Sales Management: Concepts and Cases*, John Wiley & Sons Inc., New York.

Dillon, W.R., T.J. Madden, and N.H. Firtle (1987), *Marketing Research in a Marketing Environment*, Times Mirror/Mosby College Publishing, St. Louis.

Dominiak, G.F. and J.G. Louderback III (1985), *Managerial Accounting*, Kent Publishing Company, Boston.

Green, P.E., and D.S. Tull (1986), *Research for Marketing Decisions*, 4th ed., Prentice-Hall of India Private Limited, New Delhi.

Johnson, E.M., D.L. Kurtz, and E.E. Scheuing (1994), *Sales Management: Concepts, Practices and Cases*, McGraw-Hill Inc., New York.

Kapoor, D.C. (2004), *Marketing and Sales Management*, S.Chand & Company Ltd, New Delhi.

Prabha, G.L., and A. Basser (2007), 'Emerging Retail Trends in India', *Indian Journal of Marketing*, vol. XXXVII (12), December, pp. 23–27.

Sahoo, D., and H.G. Mishra (2008), 'Organized Retail in India: A Case Study of Wal-Mart', *Indian Journal of Marketing*, vol. XXXVIII (1), January, pp. 35–43.

Samuelson, P.A. and W.D. Nordhaus (1992), *Ecomomics*, 14th ed., McGraw-Hill Inc., New York.

Spiro R.L., W.J. Stanton, and G.A. Rich (2003), *Management of a Sales Force*, Tata McGraw-Hill Publishing Company Limited, New Delhi.

Still, R.R., E.W., Cundiff, and N.A.P. Govoni (1994), *Sales Management: Decisions, Strategies and Cases*, Prentice-Hall of India Private Limited, New Delhi.

Stoner, J.A.F., and R.E. Freeman (1994), *Management*, 5th ed., Prentice-Hall of India Private Limited, New Delhi.

Williams, J.C., A.J. Dubrin, and H.L. Sisk (1985), *Management and Organization*, South-Western Publishing Co., Cincinnati.

(Contd)

CASE STUDY

Rural Blues

Mr Deep Sanyal is the marketing manager of Orient Food and Beverage Company Ltd. The company has its registered office in Kolkata and has been mainly concentrating its business in the eastern region. The company has its manufacturing plant in Kalyani, North 24 Parganas, with its distribution networks all over West Bengal. The company manufactures baby foods as its principal product branded as 'Crysol'. It has developed sales territories based on geographical divisions and each district in West Bengal is treated as a territory.

The company has appointed territory managers to oversee the sales and marketing operations in each district. The last fifteen years have seen the company sailing along nicely despite competition from recognized national and multinational brands. Mainly, two districts in West Bengal, Burdwan and Hooghly, so far have shown somewhat lower sales compared to other districts. The rate of sales growth was averaging at merely 3 per cent annually till 2006 but still there was a steadiness of sales growth. But from 2007 onwards the sales fluctuations were noticeable and bothered Mr Sanyal, an experienced marketing man having acumen on financial fundamentals also.

However, Mr Sanyal was very much aware of the turns and twists of the baby food markets. He wanted to take stock of the situation and initiate some precautionary actions. He also wanted to draw a future plan for the company to withstand the strong inflationary trends of the economy and aggression of multinational firms creating volatility in the market.

The data from the sales turnovers of the two districts, Burdwan and Hoogly, clearly indicated that the variations in sales for the last two years were getting wider compared to the previous years. Mr Sanyal decided to get to the root of the problem. He knew that birth rate is a strong determinant to influence the growth of sales in baby foods and generate target customers. Again, birth rate has an impact on demographic compositions of a place. The difference in birth rates among geographies is one such reason to cause variations in sales. At the same time, difference in income distributions among households and attitude towards products also contribute to the fluctuations in sales.

Another important factor stirs Sanyal's mind. In rural belts, families would rear cattle as mothers preferred cow's milk for their babies. They would not prefer packaged baby foods. Apart from the emotional aspect, some religious sentiment also drives the mothers to feed cow's milk. But, simultaneously, advertisements in mass media and increased awareness

(Contd)

(Contd)

of mothers had a gradual impact and resulted in changed attitudes. The families have now started realizing that the combination of nutrients in the baby foods supplements the usual diet of their children.

These questions are pertinent because large sections of Burdwan and Hooghly districts are rural even though massive urbanization of the rural bases is prominent. The migration of people from rural to urban spaces has gradually resulted in the decline of rural population density. The farming communities, particularly the young members, have started moving on to some other urban-oriented occupations.

The ghost of competition also looms large in Sanyal's mind. Multinational companies by their financial muscles have made deep inroads in rural India and stood in the way of domestic firms to get a share in the agrarian markets. But, Sanyal is a man of determination. He knows that baby food markets will be more competitive in the years to come. He needs to overhaul the situations with more strategic manoeuvrings. He calls upon the territory heads with the financial statements of last two years in the districts of Burdwan and Hooghly.

The territory heads came to Mr Sanyal with the financial statements.

Table A and B, portrays the financial statements of the two territories based on the sales of baby foods as follows.

Table A
Burdwan District

HEADS	₹ (000) in 2007–08	₹ (000) in 2008–09
Estimated sales	200	207
Estimated costs of goods sold	120	132
Actual sales	168	157
Actual costs of goods sold	127	128
Gross profits	41	29
Net profits	37	26

Table B
Hooghly District

HEADS	₹ (000) in 2007–08	₹ (000) in 2008–09
Estimated sales	180	195
Estimated costs of goods sold	137	138
Actual sales	156	156

(Contd)

(Contd)

Actual costs of goods sold	132	137
Gross profits	24	19
Net profits	18	16

Discussion Questions

1. Analyse the findings and delineate the sales situations of the company in the two districts.
2. Suggest Mr Sanyal so that he can make a recovery from the present crises.
3. Assuming nine per cent inflation every year henceforth, how should Mr Sanyal plan so that it reflects in the sales budget?

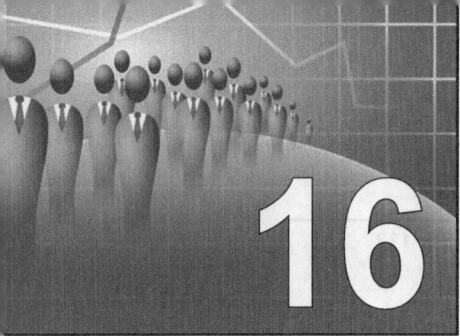

16 Sales and Cost Analysis

16.1 SALES ANALYSIS—CONCEPTS AND FEATURES

Sales analysis is a systematic review and critical investigation of sales operations with an objective to evaluate its efficiency and effectiveness. Basically, it is a tool to appraise sales performance. So, the extent to which the sales force is able to fulfil a company's sales objectives is the primary objective of sales analysis. Obviously, time is a factor that is set for salespeople to attain their sales goals within definite time horizons. Therefore, it can also be said that sales analysis is a method of gathering, classifying, and analysing sales data of a specific time period and comparing it with the expected sales volume.

Expected sales figure is the estimated sales volume evolved by sales forecasting techniques. It is always done with reference to the cost incurred else the performance evaluation remains incomplete. Thus, sales analysis is not merely studying and reporting of actual sales results but also drawing comparison of sales with costs incurred and profits earned during a time horizon. Reeder et al. (1998) viewed that sales analysis acts as an early warning system for spotting decelerating or rapidly growing sales.

Morris (1992) defined sales analysis as breaking down of sales, costs, and profit levels by products, product line, territory, customer segments, salespeople, and distributor types to generate a complete frame of sales performance in a geographic area within a limit.

Evans and Berman (2007) defined sales analysis as a detailed study of sales data to appraise the appropriateness and effectiveness of a marketing strategy.

Kotler (2003) defined sales analysis as consisting of measuring and evaluating the actual sales in relation to goals.

Features of Sales Analysis

Sales analysis has multiple features. The more the company is aware of the features, the better it can pursue it. A brief description of the features is listed as follows:

1. It is a comprehensive study made to evaluate sales performance.
2. It is an integral step of sales audit.
3. It gives accuracy in sales forecasting.
4. It is important to be able to control sales activities.
5. It reveals the strengths and weaknesses of sales plans.
6. It helps to understand the efficacy of sales budget.
7. It is necessary to study the sales effectiveness and efficiency of sales operations.
8. It is necessary to study the cost effectiveness and efficiency of sales operations.
9. It is a tool to measure the sales productivity and undertake profitability analysis.
10. It is important to understand the sales potential of a geographic area.
11. It is important to classify territories into high, moderate and low sales potential units
12. It guides in detecting the sales problems in an area.
13. It helps to estimate a company's actual market share (percentage of total industry sales) and relative market share with respect to leading competitors.
14. It is a part of strategic sales management programme. By continuous monitoring of sales, the company can decide whether it acts towards achieving sales goals and objectives.

16.2 SALES ANALYSES AT INDIVIDUAL UNITS—A REVIEW

A company always desires to break up sales in different selling units. By selling units, we mean salespeople, product or product line, customer groups or territories. A company is interested in getting sales figure for each product or product line individually. Another company wants the same for each customer group or territory. This helps a company to make comparative review of sales performances across sales units. A brief review of features of sales analysis for each sales unit is illustrated as follows.

Salespeople as a Unit

Following are the features of sales analysis for salespeople:

1. Sales analysis reports performance of salespeople.
2. It establishes a benchmark for performance of the salespeople.
3. It keeps salespeople informed of their strengths and weaknesses in selling activities.

4. It helps salespeople to probe into areas (e.g., weak persuasive skills, poor call planning, etc.) where they are to improve upon to reach sales targets.

5. It helps sales managers to improve sales force planning, staffing, training, and setting compensation programmes.

6. It helps sales managers to review the distribution of selling tasks and responsibilities.

Product/Product Line as a Unit

Following are the features of sales analysis for product or product line:

1. It gives quantitative estimations of sales productivity for each product/product line.

2. It gives sales proceeds, selling expenses, profit margins for each product/product line.

3. It provides a comparative result of product-wise sales accruals, cost involvement, profit margins, and contributions to company's market share.

4. It shows how sales plans and strategies work for each product/product line to contribute to the sales goals or objectives.

5. It helps sales managers by prioritizing the products, i.e. which product should be given additional importance in terms of selling efforts.

6. It helps in taking managerial decision in terms of product development, product line extension, product pruning, etc.

Customers as a Selling Unit

Following are the features of sales analysis for customers:

1. It gives a clear picture of customer-wise sales revenues, selling costs, and profit contributions.

2. It gives customer-wise information on sales turnover, sales productivity, and sales efficiency.

3. It helps to chalk out definite sales plans and programmes for each customer group.

4. It helps to set call plans, personal selling time, and call frequencies for each customer group.

5. It aids in studying customer-wise satisfaction level.

6. It helps in formulating sales budget for each customer group.

Territory as a Selling Unit

Following are the features of sales analysis for territory:

1. It gives territory-wise sales opportunities, competition, and sales potentials.

2. It helps in forecasting sales and determining sales budgets for each territory.

3. It helps to control sales performance for each territory.

4. It assists in better customer planning and coverage for yielding good sales results.
5. It helps to understand territory-wise selling expenses, cash flows, and profit contributions.
6. It facilitates sales mangers to design promotional plans for each territory.
7. It assists sales managers to decide about the number of sales plans to be engaged in each territory.
8. It helps to allocate quota amongst salespeople.

16.3 METHODS OF SALES ANALYSIS—A CONCISE DESCRIPTION

Generally, by analysis one means the comparison or an evaluation of a process or result of any act or performance with the predetermined standards. Sales analysis follows a similar principle.

Organizations resort to different analytical techniques to undertake sales analysis. Some of which are mentioned and discussed as follows:

(a) Sales variance analysis
(b) Unit-based sales variance
(c) Sales effectiveness index
(d) Sales growth
(e) Market share analysis

Sales Variance Analysis

A variable assumes different values with time when it is manipulated. But, it is assumed to possess a standard value or expected value and its actual value centres around the expected value. Similarly, sale of a product varies with time and has an expected value as decided by the sales managers. Sales analysis relies on the deviation of the actual value from the expected or the standard values. The expected value of sales is reflected in the sales budget and is called budgeted sales value. If the actual value touches the expected or exceeds it, the situation is favourable to the firm. If it is opposite, then the situation becomes unfavourable.

Some common methods of sales variance analysis are illustrated as follows:

(i) **Sales variance or sales value variance:** This variance is based on sales turnover. This is computed by comparing actual sales with budgeted sales. It is expressed as follows:

Sales value variance = Actual sales value – Budgeted sales value

where,   Value = Quantity sold × Selling price (price per unit sold)

So,

Sales value variance = (Actual quantity sold × Actual selling price)
                       – (Budgeted sales quantity or quota × Target selling price)

If
Actual selling price = target selling price,
Sales value variance = Actual sales value – Budgeted sales value

Then,
Sales value variance = (Actual quantity sold – Budgeted quantity sold) × Selling price

Sales value variance can be expressed in two ways as follows:

- Sales price variance = (Actual selling price – Budgeted selling price) × Actual quantity sold
- Sales volume variance = (Actual quantity sold – Budgeted quantity) × Budgeted selling price

(ii) **Variance of profit margin:** The method is based on the difference between the actual profit and the budgeted profit. Here, the difference of actual profit and standard or budgeted profit is the measure of sales variance, called sales margin variance. Thus,

Sales margin variance = Actual profit – Budgeted profit

If the actual profit is greater than or equal to budgeted profit, the situation is favourable to the firm. If it is otherwise, the satiation is unfavourable.

Sales margin variance has two forms as follows:

(i) **Sales margin price variance:** Sales margin price variance shows the effect on profit for change in the selling price and other factors remain at standard.

Sales margin price variance = (Actual margin per unit – Budgeted margin per unit) × Actual quantity sold

(ii) **Sales margin volume variance:** Sales margin volume variance shows the difference between the actual sales units and the budgeted sales units.

Sales margin volume variance = (Actual sales volume – Budgeted sales volume) × Budgeted margin per unit

Table 16.1 Sales results across sales units

Sales unit	Classification	Budgeted sales	Actual sales	Deviation (+/–)	Percentage of budgeted sales (in per cent)
Territory	North	20	23	3	115
	South	18	18	0	100
Salesperson	Mr X	16	14	-2	87.5
	Mr Y	16	18	2	112.5
Customer	Major	25	22	-3	88
	Minor	15	16	1	106.6
Product	Economy	30	28	-2	93.3
	Premium	40	35	-5	87.5

Unit-based Sales Variance

This is a study of sales variance for each unit separately and drawing meaningful conclusions on it. Table 16.1 shows the unit-wise budgeted and actual sales in a financial year of a company. It also analyses the deviation and presents the percentage achievement of actual sales targets.

Following are the remarks that can be drawn from the analysis:

(i) **Territory as a unit:** Both the north and the south territories have reached the expected sales targets but the north has the distinction of exceeding the target level (115 per cent of the budgeted sales). South has just managed to achieve the sales goal. It is expected that the company will enhance the target sales from the next financial year in the south.

(ii) **Salesperson as a selling unit:** Mr Y's sales performance is comparatively higher than that of Mr X. Mr Y has superseded the expected benchmark of the sales turnover but Mr X is quite short of achieving the target. It is a cause of concern for the sales manager since both the individuals work in the same sales territory. In case, two individuals work in different territories, they are bound to have different turnovers, or rather, their performance levels. The sales manager should reward Mr Y for his excellent performance and at the same time try to find out the reasons for Mr X's failure.

(iii) **Customer as a unit:** The expected target level has not been fulfilled from the major customers, while the small customers have been more responsive to the company's product. The sales manger could have been happier if the sales results showed the opposite. In fact, major customers contribute more to the company's sales revenue and therefore deserve more attention.

(iv) **Product as a unit:** Both the economy and the premium variants of the product are quite short of targets. Indeed, the variance is more in premium type compared to the economy category. The expected profit margin is more in the premium type than in the economy one. Therefore, reasons must be attributed for poor sales results for both, especially for the premium product.

Sales Effectiveness Index

Sales effectiveness expresses the ability to sell more so that the overall sales revenues and consequent profits move up to reach their budgeted values. The following equations are used to measure sales effectiveness index.

$$\text{Sales effectiveness index} = \frac{\text{Actual sales}}{\text{Budgeted sales}} \times 100$$

If,

Actual sales = budgeted sales, the sales effectiveness index is 100

Actual sales > budgeted sales, the sales effectiveness index is more than 100

Actual sales < budgeted sales, the sales effectiveness index is less than 100

Table 16.2 Sales effectiveness index (Figures are in lakhs)

Previous year's sales	Budgeted sales of the year	Actual sales of the year	Increase/Decrease in actual sales from the previous year	Expected increase in sales from the previous year
14	20	18	4	6

Sales effectiveness index can also be measured in the following way and is illustrated by an example (Table 16.2).

$$\text{Sales effectiveness index} = \frac{\text{Expected increase} - \text{Actual increase/decrease}}{\text{Actual increase or decrease}} \times 100$$

Thus,

$$\text{Sales effectiveness index} = \frac{6 - 4}{4} \times 100$$
$$= 50$$

Sales Growth

This is also a tool for sales analysis. This is measured by dividing the sales of a time period by sales of the previous time period. Both time periods are equal in length. This is a measure of sales performance index also.

$$\text{Sales performance index} = \frac{\text{Sales of a time period}}{\text{Sales of the previous time period}} \times 100$$

In this method, the selection of time period is important. For example, a quarterly time period is more meaningful than a year because fluctuations in demands can be easily traced. It is better to project four quarterly results of sales growth in a year than one yearly growth.

Market Share Analysis

Market share is a measure of sales analysis too. This measure is important to know how a company performs in relation to its competitors. It has two measures:

(i) **Overall market share:** Overall market share refers to a company's total sales in a definite time period as a percentage of the total industry sales in which the company belongs.

(ii) **Relative market share:** Relative market share is expressed in terms of a company's market share with respect to that of a market leader.

Now, suppose if the market leader's share is assumed to be 100, then what is the market share of the company? Say, in a year, the market leader has a sale of ₹10 lakhs and the company's sale during the same period is ₹6 lakhs. Then, the relative market share of the company is 60 per cent. Again, market share of a company can be expressed as a percentage of total sales of the top three competitors. If the company's sales is 6 lakhs in a year, and the top three competitors have sales of 6, 8, and 10 lakhs respectively in the same period, then, the company's relative market share is $6/24 \times 100 = 25$ per cent.

16.4 SALES QUOTA—A TOOL FOR SALES ANALYSIS

Defining the sales quota is the basis for conducting a sales analysis. Sales quotas are set for different market segments, products or product lines, customer groups, and salespeople depending on the characteristics of sales organizations. Quota is an organizational goal-setting process. It is a step to determine the realistic sales target that is consistent with the organizational goals. A quota is a quantitative standard being allocated to the sales units and is expressed in absolute terms. Quota can be set for sales volume in rupees, gross profits, net profits, returns on investment, contribution margins, and selling expenses.

Similarly, quota can be expressed in quantity also such as pieces, kilograms, or tons particularly for sales volume. So, analysis of quota is a crucial part of sales analysis because it compares the actual sales with the target sales, actual profits (gross and net) with target profits, actual expenses (selling and non-selling) with budgeted expenses. Quotas can be fixed for a number of sales calls, number of orders, number of customers and prospects to be generated, number of sales demonstrations to render, number of cold calls to do, etc. These are called input quotas. Quotas for sales volumes, profits, etc. are called output quotas.

So, quota is the benchmark, which sales managers use to perform sales analysis. It is an instrument to evaluate performance of the salespeople. Comparison of quota and the actual sales help sales managers to plan future sales operations, forecasting of projected sales and revision of sales targets and preparation of sales budgets. Box 16.1 provides a list of important dos and don'ts for sales quota.

Kotler (2003) defined sales quota as the sales goal set for a product line, company division or sales representative. This is basically a managerial tool for defining and stimulating sales efforts.

Kurtz and Boone (2009) defined sales quota as the specified sales or profit targets that the firm expects salespeople to achieve.

Stiffler (2006) defined sales quota or any other quota as a numerical target expressed either in absolute terms or as percentage of some overall sales goal.

Box 16.1 Dos and don'ts of sales quota

Following are the dos and don'ts of sales quota:

(a) Do not fix up sales quota on guesswork or hunches.

(b) Clearly state the following:
   (i) What is to be sold?
   (ii) Where to be sold (geographic area)?
   (iii) How long to be sold (time period)?
   (iv) How much to be sold?

(c) Sales quota should not be set by averaging sales of the last three or four years or by dividing the total sales by the number of salespeople.

(Contd)

(Contd)

(d) Attention must be given to the ability of a salesperson while assigning a quota to him.

(e) Quota should be based on facts and figures.

(f) Units of the quota should be clearly stated to the salespeople. For example, sales volume in rupees is assigned as quota.

(g) Growth or decline in business must be kept in mind at the time of deciding the quota.

(h) A company should provide all types of sales supports (financial support, sales kits, samples, etc.) to help salespeople to meet the quota.

(i) A salesperson should not only be given the sales quota but also the expense quota.

(j) Salespeople should be apprised of other selling (e.g., missionary selling) and non-selling tasks (e.g., new customer development) along with sales quota.

16.5 METHODS FOR SETTING SALES QUOTA

There are different ways of measuring sales quota. The selection of a method depends on the objective of the company in which it wants to proceed for sales, evaluate sales performance, and analyse cost.

Following are the different methods of measuring sales quota:

Sales Volume Quota

Sales volume quota is the most common method used for deciding on the sales quota. It suggests 'how much to fix up' (quantity) and the 'time period to attain' (time frame) for sales quota. Sales quota can be fixed according to the following;

(i) Sales in monetary terms (rupees, dollars, etc.)

(ii) Sales in units (number of pieces)

(iii) Sales in quantity (kilograms, pounds, etc.)

This method also considers time as a condition for deciding a sales quota. The company also decides on sales unit as the base for assigning quota. It has already been said that by sales units we mean territory, product or product line, customer group, etc. The starting point of setting this quota is past sales and sales potentials. The sales figures of the last two to three years are followed and the percentage increase or decrease in sales is tracked down. In some cases, the last year's sale is given major prominence. In other cases, the average of the last three years' sales data may be considered and over it the expected sales growth is added based on forecasted sales.

Sales potential can also be treated as a base for deciding the quota. Sales potential is the maximum attainable sales volume in a given territory within a definite time period. However, the sales potential study requires complete knowledge of the customers' demands, strengths and weaknesses of competitors, etc.

Sometimes quota is set on point basis. A company may consider sales of ₹ 10,000 as a point for a product or sales of 50 kilograms as a point. This point basis can help sales managers to evaluate performance of salespeople quite easily. A company may attach bonus plans to the point-linked quota. Say, a salesperson is given 10 points of a product as a quota and sales of one additional point may mean 2 per cent of salary as a bonus. While distributing quota to the salespeople, sales managers should take care to assign equal workload to salespeople. It should not be so that some salespeople are given easy selling items or easily attainable quota (soft quota) and the others are given difficult items to sell or hardly attainable quota (hard quota).

Financial Quota

Companies use gross margin or net profit as the quota to achieve results within a predetermined time period. Budget quota can also take into consideration the selling expenses as well. So, sales managers fulfil two objectives at a time.

One, they directly evaluate the sales performance of the organization in terms of profits earned.

Second, they can verify the actual sales expenditure comparing it with estimated or budgeted expenses. Here, profit earned and expenses incurred across different sales units can be compared.

Companies can set financial quota when they handle both low and high margin products. Generally low-margin items are easy to sell whereas high-margin products require strong selling efforts. Salespeople feel comfortable with low-margin products. But high-margin products contribute more to the net profits of the organization. So, when the financial quotas are distributed amongst salespeople, it should be kept in mind that

(i) efficient salespeople should be given charge to handle high-margin products and

(ii) during comparison of quota with actual results, types of products handled (low or high margin) should be kept in mind or else comparison amongst salespeople would be injudicious.

Activity Quota

Activity quotas are set in terms of sales activities. The company determines the important sales activities that are communicated to the salespeople. Following are some of the activities treated as activity quotas:

(iii) Number of sales calls to the present and potential customers

(iv) Number of new customers procured

(v) Number of sales demonstrations made

(vi) Number of intermediaries handled

(vii) Number of installations or commissioning works completed in customer premises (particularly for large industrial items such as furnace, boiler, etc.)

(viii) Number of missionary-selling activities undertaken

Activity quotas are quite common in use for industrial equipments, pharmaceutical products, insurance selling, etc.

Combination Quota

Combination quota refers to the application of two or three quotas, discussed so far, together in the organization. This is useful where both selling and non-selling activities are given due importance. For conducting the selling activities, sales volume or financial quota are usually referred to. Salespeople are required to do a number of non-selling activities such as prospect generation, opening up distribution outlets, missionary selling, etc. where activity quotas are assigned to them. The combination quota needs delicate handling and control from sales managers. Pharmaceutical companies can use it for their medical representatives for better performance evaluation.

16.6 COST ANALYSIS—CONCEPTS AND OBJECTIVES

Cost analysis is the review and evaluation of a company's cost data and its comparison with the anticipated cost data furnished in the annual budget. As regards to cost analysis in sales organization, it is the detailed examination of selling costs and their impacts on the sales volume and profit margins. Systematic collection, categorization and comparison of cost elements, and how these contribute to the profits are the basic aims of cost analysis. It is essential for cost control in organizational activities and it also acts as a tool for managerial decision-making. It helps in proper implementation of managerial decisions. In fact, both sales and cost analyses are instruments for identifying unexpected problems.

Selling cost is an integral part of sales budget. 'What', 'where', 'how', and 'when' costs which will be incurred are the elements of sales budget. Moreover, cost is a determinant of price and revenues of the firm. Cost controls the profit margins. A part of the costs is an operational component and is spent in undertaking a firm's day-to-day activities. These are called operating costs, for example, travelling costs.

Selling costs have direct and indirect elements. Direct selling costs are directly linked with personal-selling jobs such as sales force commission, customer entertainment costs, etc. Indirect costs have no direct association with personal-selling activities such as marketing research costs, sales office expenses, etc.

Lal (2006) made a classification of costs to expired costs and deferred costs.

Selling overheads refer to those indirect costs that are connected with selling activities. Examples include salaries and commissions of salespeople, advertising costs, etc. *Distribution overheads* are separate from selling overheads such as freight and insurance costs, packing costs, etc. These are those expenses that are incurred during delivery of the product after sales are made.

Expired costs are called expenses. They are incurred for the generation of a firm's revenues.

Deferred costs are spent with a view to accrue benefits in future time periods such as plant, machineries, etc.

Fixed and variable costs are common classification of costs. Fixed costs do not vary with sales volume such as office rents. Variable costs change with the sales volume such as sales force commission, distribution costs, etc.

During addition of existing business operations, a company may consider marginal costs, which means change in total cost that crop up from producing and marketing additional unit of a product. Box 16.2 gives salient objectives of cost analysis.

Box 16.2 Objectives of cost analysis

Following are the objectives of cost analysis:

(a) It is important for proper allocation of costs to different selling units (e.g., territory, customer group, etc.) or marketing functions (advertising, distribution, etc.).

(b) It aids in forecasting future sales and preparation of sales budgets.

(c) It helps to know various cost components such as fixed and variable costs, direct and indirect costs, controllable and un-controllable costs, etc.

(d) It helps to determine sales productivity and profitability of the enterprise.

(e) It helps to understand whether costs are incurred within the expense budget.

(f) It is important to decide on the price of a product particularly when the firm desires to set price that covers variable costs and a part of fixed costs, and generate a fixed profit margin per unit sales.

(g) It facilitates control of the sales operations. It is very important for a firm that is struggling for survival.

(h) It helps to estimate the gross and net profits, profit margins, and break-even sales volume of the firm. It gives a clear indication of the recovery of costs from sales operations.

(i) It is important for a firm that strives for cost leadership. It is an attempt to achieve lowest-cost position in the industry.

(j) It enables management to spot and compare trouble areas in different market segments.

16.7 COST CONTROL—AN IMPORTANT OBJECTIVE OF COST ANALYSIS

Controlling costs is an important objective of cost analysis. A company can progress only when it has a firm control over cost elements. Some of the prominent areas are discussed where sales managers can effectively take measures in controlling selling costs.

Spot the redundant expense items The redundant items unnecessarily enhance costs and detract the profit consequences of it. For example, over sizing of sales force in a territory, undue administrative overheads can increase costs beyond projected cost levels.

Route plans Route plans and travelling plans for salespeople are important areas of cost control. These are designed in a manner so that the majority of customers are adequately covered. Time and money should be distributed as compared to the size of the customer. With small customers who do not contribute much to the company's sales revenue, the manager should keep in mind not to devote much time or money on them.

Travelling costs Travelling costs are linked to route plans. Faulty or lengthy route plans amount to cost increment and destroy profit margins. Travelling cost is a major part of selling costs.

Time schedules Time schedules must be consistent with the call plans. Prospective or actual customer appointment time, face-to-face time with the customers, covering a predetermined number of customers a day, managing follow-up after call time and after sales time, etc. are crucial in time scheduling. If daily call plans are not complied with, controlling selling costs lead to problems. An intelligent salesperson can handle the presentation and demonstration time before the customer with right precision.

Product/service quality Product or service quality is a matter of perception to customers in many occasions. However, maintaining product or service specifications are corroborative of their qualities. Salespeople can reduce personal selling time to a major extent, if customers develop quick first-hand impressions of the product/service quality. This can reduce the bargaining scope of customers as well. Ultimately, customers can be brought to the company's favour and sales can be generated. So, quality of an offer can facilitate order taking from customers which have positive effects on the company's selling costs.

Proper selection and training of salespeople Proper selection and training of salespeople can reduce the selling costs to a respectable degree. In fact, the objective of the firm is to select potentially strong candidates who can serve the company well. Second, they can absorb the training materials quickly and successfully. Ultimately, the firm will be benefited by their performances. But, cost of selection, training, and compensation should never outweigh their performance contributions.

Cost of sales force supervision   Cost of sales force supervision should be controlled by judicious administration of the sales tasks. It should be neither exaggerative nor diminutive. Right supervision and control of sales force can reduce the selling costs to a substantive level.

Planing promotional budget carefully   Most profitable products should be given enough attention in terms of promotional efforts and costs than less profitable items. Promotional costs should be cleverly apportioned amongst different product items based on their importance.

Control of costs of logistics   Control of costs of logistics include control of warehousing costs, transportation or product delivery costs, loss of materials during transportation, material-handling costs, loading and unloading costs, etc. which need effective manoeuvring and control. These can reduce the selling costs to an exorbitant volume.

Box 16.3 shows some important areas of cost to be considered while setting the budget.

Box 16.3   Areas of cost

Following are the different areas of costs:

(a) Average costs per sales call

(b) Field sales cost as a percentage of total sales costs

(c) Travelling costs, outstation food and lodging costs to salespeople

(d) Pre-selling costs such as cost of generating leads, telecommunication costs, stationary costs, etc.

(e) Customer entertainment costs, e.g., gifts

(f) Cost of samples

(g) Costs of presentation kits such as video clippings, charts, graphs, etc.

(h) Promotional costs such advertisements, product literatures, manuals, catalogues , and price lists

(i) Cost of processing sales orders

(j) Costs of keeping sales records, documents, etc.

(k) Cost of mailing invoices, sales letters, etc.

(l) Post-selling costs such as follow-up after sales costs, after-sales service costs, technical service expenses to guide customers

(m) Sales force compensation costs

(n) Sales office rents, taxes, depreciation, etc.

(o) Costs of participation in industrial fares and exhibition

(p) Sales meeting costs

(q) Marketing research costs

(Contd)

(Contd)

(r) Cost of delivering the products

(s) Warehouse rents and staff salaries

(t) Packing costs

(u) Freight and insurance costs

Exhibit 16.1 furnishes three glaring examples of three notable organizations and reports how these have used cost control as a strategic measure to succeed in their respective business fields.

Exhibit 16.1 Three success stories

1. Xerox Corporation

Xerox Corporation, a Fortune 500 global document management company (Wikipedia, free encyclopaedia, accessed on 01 July 2010) manufactures a wide range of photocopiers, colour and, black and white printers, digital production printing presses and related consulting services and equipments, etc. It has evolved a unique inventory planning policy to control costs of their products including supplies of the parts and chemicals for its copying machines. The company, a well-articulated name in every nook and corner of the world (both in domestic and industrial scenarios), stocked those items locally which have regular dealings and keeps the remaining inventories in selected regional warehouses. This was recommended in the distribution policies where products are shipped from regional warehouses to sales branches via airfreight to maintain speedy and successful customer services. The company by this very thought of cultivating logistical control is reported to have saved millions of dollars in logistical costs.

2. Hammond Valve Corporation

Hammond Valve Corporation, manufacturing valves to cater to plumbing, heating, cooling, and other industrial practices are opening up additional warehouses in order to reduce the order cycling time drastically. Albeit it enhanced logistical costs but additional sales revenues were so improved that it compensated for the excess costs of physical distribution and profits soared overwhelmingly. The company is a name in the industrial circuits of valves due to excellent customer services.

3. Wal-Mart

Cost leadership is a means to attain competitive advantage in the industry. The company that has better control over costs can gain maximum by enjoying advantage of economy of scale in production and distribution. Wal-Mart has achieved this cost leadership through satellite-based distribution system. The company is able to keep store location costs to a minimum by positioning stores on low-cost land in the outskirts of small- and medium-sized towns. The company, thus, maintains its competitive advantage quite convincingly.

Sources: Reeder et al. (1998). Based on materials found in the following:

'New Strategies to Move Goods', *Business Week*, 24 September 1966 for the first case and *Principles of Marketing* by Martin Zober (1970), Allyn & Bacon Inc., Boston for the second case.

Dessler, G. (2005), *Human Resource Management*, Prentice-Hall of India Private limited, New Delhi for the third case.

16.8   METHODS OF COST ANALYSIS

Cost analysis is fundamental to understand the efficiency of the firm. In a sales organization, cost analysis is crucial because generation of sales and profits ultimately rests on the selling efficiency. Some common methods of cost analysis are discussed as follows:

Gross Profit and Net Profit Ratios

Gross profit and net profit ratios are indicators of the profitability of the enterprise. These ratios tell how much a company earns as profits for each rupee of sales. These reflect a firm's ability to control costs and the acceptability of its products in the market.

$$\text{Gross profit margin} = \frac{\text{Gross profits}}{\text{Sales}} \times 100$$

or

$$\text{Gross profit margin} = \frac{\text{Sales} - \text{Cost of goods sold}}{\text{Sales}} \times 100$$

$$\text{New profit margin} = \frac{\text{Net profits after taxes and interests}}{\text{Sales}} \times 100$$

Thus, gross profit ratio indicates the profitability of sales after direct costs of sales are subtracted from them. Here, overhead costs (sales and distribution overheads, administrative overheads, etc) are excluded. Net profits include deduction of all costs from sales.

Expense Ratios

The relationship of different expenses to sales is expressed as expense ratios. These are the indexes of the economic efficiencies of the firm. Higher the expense ratio, lesser is the economic efficiency. Some expense ratios are given as follows:

$$\text{Operating ratio} = \frac{\text{Costs of goods sold} + \text{Other operating expenses}}{\text{Sales}} \times 100$$

If operating ratio is 75 per cent, that means the total operating expenses occupy 75 per cent of sales receipts. The remaining 25 per cent is reserved for paying interests, taxes, dividends, and future operations.

$$\text{Costs of goods sold ratio} = \frac{\text{Costs of goods sold}}{\text{Sales}} \times 100$$

If the costs of goods sold ratio is 80 per cent, then 80 per cent of the sales receipts is spent for cost of goods sold. In other words, it can be construed that

80 per cent of the sales is consumed or would be consumed for meeting selling and distribution expenses, taxes, interests, dividends, etc.

Break-even Analysis

Break-even analysis is a point where a company's sales volume covers costs and is at a state of no profit–no loss. It is important to know whether sales equate costs or not as it gives an idea to the firm regarding its progress.

$$\text{Break-even sales (in units)} = \frac{\text{Total fixed costs}}{\text{Price} - \text{Variable cost per unit}}$$

$$\text{Break-even (sales)} = \frac{\text{Total fixed costs}}{1 - \dfrac{\text{Variable cost per unit}}{\text{Price}}}$$

Break-even analysis helps to understand the production and sales volume that the company should target, analyse the cost structure, and decide on the forecasted sales and sales budgets.

Achieving Target Profits

Achieving target profits is a variation of the break-even analysis. Break-even point suggests the target volume of sales that ensures no profit–no loss situation for the firm. By incorporating the desired profit component in the break-even analysis, the required sales volume can be reached. The following equations can help to associate target profits, costs, and the sales volume to achieve target profits.

$$\text{Target profit} = (\text{Unit sales to achieve target profit} \times \text{Contribution margin per unit}) - \text{Fixed costs}$$

where, Contribution margin = Sales price per unit – Variable cost per unit

So, $$\text{Sale in units} = \frac{\text{Fixed costs} + \text{Target profit}}{\text{Contribution margin per unit}}$$

Preparation of Income Statement

This method considers the following variables while preparing the income statement:

(i) Total sales in units, (ii) Selling price,
(iii) Total fixed costs, (iv) Variable cost per unit,
(v) Selling and administrative expenses.

Now,

Sales – Cost of sales = Gross margin

where, Cost of sales = Cost of production + Selling and distribution overheads

and

Gross margin – Selling and administrative expenses = Income

For instance,

Total sales = 10,000 units,
Selling price = ₹10,
Total fixed costs = ₹20,000,
Variable cost per unit = ₹6, and
Selling and administrative expenses = ₹15,000

Therefore,

Fixed cost per unit = ₹2 (20,000/10,000)
Total sales = 10,000 × 10 = ₹100, 000
Cost of sales = (2 + 6) × 10,000 = ₹80, 000
Gross margins = 1,00,000 – 80,000 = ₹20, 000
Income = 20,000 – 15,000 = ₹5,000

Selling and administrative expenses include sales force salaries and commissions, administrative expenses, sales force travelling expenses, advertising expenses, cost of insurance, supplies and telephone, warehousing expenses, shipping expenses, etc. These are also called operating expenses. Figure 16.1 shows how profit margins are computed from gross sales.

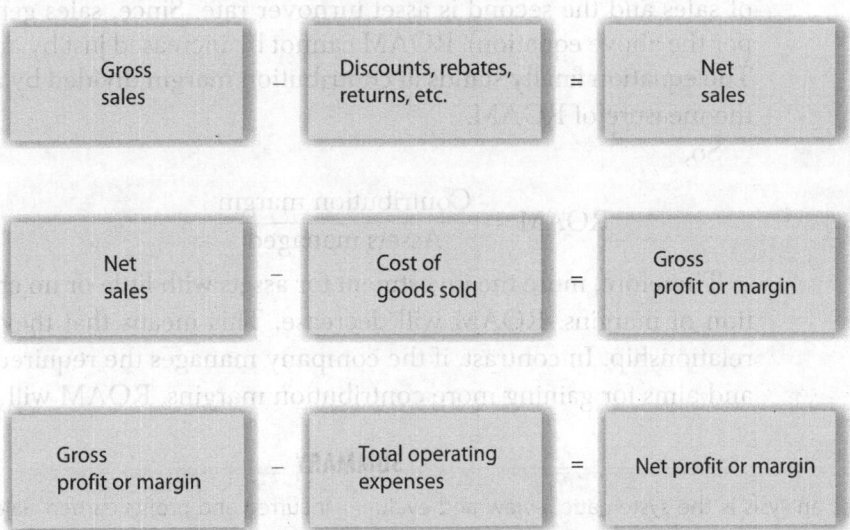

Figure 16.1 Step-wise flow of gross sales to net profits

Return on Investment (ROI) and Return on Asset Managed (ROAM)

Both ROI and ROAM are measures of efficiency of sales operations in a territory. ROI is a measure of efficiency by relating output (profit) to input (investment). So, sales efficiencies of different territories can be compared by their respective returns on investment.

$$\text{ROI} = \frac{\text{Net profit}}{\text{Sales}} \times \frac{\text{Sales}}{\text{Investment}}$$

The first ratio of the equation indicates return on sales. The second is investment turnover. It is clear from the equation that by an increase in sales, ROI cannot be increased as sales get cancelled out and the equation stands at net profit divided by the investment as a measure of ROI.

So,

$$\text{ROI} = \frac{\text{Net profit}}{\text{Investment}}$$

So, if investment can be controlled letting others to improve, the ROI will increase.

ROAM is a modified version of ROI. In ROAM, the net profit under ROI is substituted by the contribution margin and the assets employed and managed replace investment. So the equation is as follows:

$$\text{ROAM} = \frac{\text{Contribution margin}}{\text{Sales}} \times \frac{\text{Sales}}{\text{Assets managed}}$$

The first ratio of the equation indicates the contribution margin as a fraction of sales and the second is asset turnover rate. Since, sales get cancelled out (as per the above equation), ROAM cannot be increased just by an increase in sales. The equation finally stands at contribution margin divided by assets managed as the measure of ROAM.

So,

$$\text{ROAM} = \frac{\text{Contribution margin}}{\text{Assets managed}}$$

Therefore, more the investment for assets with little or no change of contribution of margins, ROAM will decrease. This means that they share an inverse relationship. In contrast, if the company manages the required volume of assets and aims for gaining more contribution margins, ROAM will increase.

───────────────────── **SUMMARY** ─────────────────────

Sales analysis is the systematic review and evaluation of sales operations to understand sales efficiency and effectiveness. It is gathering, classifying, analysing sales data of a specific time period and comparing it with expected sales volume. Sales analysis implies breaking down of sales figures across territories, products or product lines, customer groups and salespeople and subsequent cost incurred and profits earned. Sales analysis can be performed by studying the total sales variance, unit-based sales variance, sales effectiveness index, sales growth, and market share analysis.

Sales quota is treated as a tool for sales analysis which is also the sales goal for a product line, company division, or salesperson. Quota can be determined by sales volume, budget, activity, and

(Contd)

(Contd)

combination methods. Cost analysis is the review and evaluation of a company's cost data furnished in the annual budget. Selling cost is an integral part of sales budget. Cost control is an important objective of cost analysis. Cost analysis can be done through the analysis of gross and net profits, expense ratios, break-even analysis, achieving target profit, preparation of income statement and return on investment, and return on asset managed methods.

KEY TERMS

Cost Analysis   Cost analysis is the review and evaluation of a company's cost data and comparing it with the anticipated cost data furnished in the annual budget.

ROAM   ROAM is a modified version of ROI. In ROAM, the net profit under ROI is substituted by the contribution margin and the assets employed and managed replace investments.

Sales Analysis   Sales analysis is the systematic review and critical investigation of sales operations with an objective to evaluate its efficiency and effectiveness.

Sales Variance   Sales variance is the difference between the standard value or expected value of sales and its actual value.

Sales Quota   Sales quota is the specified sales or profit targets that the firm expects salespeople to achieve.

CONCEPT REVIEW QUESTIONS

1. Define sales analysis. Why is it important to a firm?
2. What are the features of sales analysis?
3. Explain at least three methods of sales analysis. Why you have chosen these methods?
4. What is the role of sales quota in sales analysis?
5. How are sales quotas determined?
6. Examine the importance of cost analysis in a firm.
7. How is cost analysis made in the sales organization? Explain at least three common methods of cost analysis.

CRITICAL REVIEW QUESTIONS

1. Ramesh, a salesperson of a chemical firm, has achieved 75 per cent of his sales quota in a territory where competition is too tough. Birat, another salesperson has achieved 95 per cent of his sales quota where the competition is feeble and the company has an edge over competitors. How will you evaluate their performance?
2. Sales analysis without consideration of cost is an important description of it. Justify.

PROJECT ASSIGNMENTS

1. Collect annual reports (last two financial years) of any business firm of your choice and identify the following information:
   (a) Gross sales
   (b) Net sales,
   (c) Sales and distribution overheads
   (d) Total selling expenses
   (e) Gross profits
   (f) Net profits

Perform a sales and cost analyses and comment on the selling efficiency and overall financial health of the firm.

2. Meet sales managers of one (a) textile and (b) software firm to know the items for sales and distribution expenses. Ask, further, what role do the salespeople play in controlling selling expenses.

REFERENCES

Evans, J.R., and B. Berman (2007), *Marketing Management*, Cengage Learning, Australia.

Kotler, P. (2003), *Marketing Management*, 11th ed., Pearson Education, Singapore.

Kurtz, D.L., and L.E. Boone (2009), *Principles of Marketing*, 12th ed., South-Western Cengage Learning, Australia.

Lal, J. (2006), *Advanced Management Accounting: Text and Cases*, S.Chand & Company Ltd, New Delhi.

Morris, M.H. (1992), *Industrial and Organizational Marketing*, Maxwell Macmillan International, New York.

Reeder, R.R., E.G. Brierty, and B.H. Reeder (1998), *Industrial Marketing: Analysis, Planning and Control*, Prentice-Hall of India Pvt. Ltd, New Delhi.

Stiffler, M.A. (2006), *Performance: Creating the Performance Driven Organization*, Wiley India, New Delhi.

CASE STUDY

Performance Evaluation—Taking Inputs from Sales Analytics

The company, *Megapipes Polyolefins Ltd*, engaged in manufacturing polypropylene pipes, has a captive market of rupees thirty-five crores annually. The company has been serving industrial customers, households, and institutional customers quite capably for the last ten years. It has geographical specializations, having headquartered in Mumbai with branch sales organizations in different states. At present, the company has one post vacant in the eastern region and the post is of a regional sales manager.

The regional sales manager in charge of the eastern region retired a month ago. Ashoke Chandra and Kajol Gupta, two successful territory sales managers, are claimants of this post. Ashoke is in charge of West Bengal and Kajol is managing the sales in Bihar. The company has decided to appraise sales performance and demographic compositions of the two before selecting one for this coveted post. Following are the performance track records of the two.

Sales quota (2008–09)

Sales volume	Quota (lakhs)	Actual sales (lakhs)
Ashoke	90	85
Kajol	86	79

(Contd)

(Contd)

Annual selling expenses (2008–09)

Selling expenses	Budgeted (Lakhs)	Actual (Lakhs)
Ashoke	15	14.5
Kajol	18	18

New customers acquired (2008–09)

New customers acquired	Target (Nos)	Actual (Nos)
Ashoke	15	14
Kajol	16	14

Old customer retention (2008–09)

Old customer retention	Target (100%)	Actual (100%)
Ashoke	100z	94
Kajol	100	90

Previous regional managers report (on a 5-point performance rating scale where 1 means poor performance and 5 excellent performance)

Performance rating	Maximum score	Actual
Ashoke	5	4
Kajol	5	4.5

Demographic compositions (based on the last degree achieved and percentage of marks, age, and years of experience)

Demographic compositions	Last degree achieved and percentage of marks	Age (years)	Years of experience
Ashoke	MBA (Marketing), 78%	47	17
Kajol	MBA (Marketing), 74%	49	19

In order to get the overall performance scores, the company has decided to assign grade points to different qualification criteria. A point of 10 is distributed among those criteria to define weights of each. The weights are as follows.

Sales quota–3; Selling expenses–1.5; New customers–2; Old customer retention–1.5; Performance reports–1; Demographic compositions–1.

Furthermore, the company has assigned activity points in a way, where 10 units (rupees, numbers, percentages, performance ratings or

(Contd)

(*Contd*)

demographic information) are equal to one. For example, sales quota of 30 lakhs is equal to 3.

Discussion Questions

1. Evaluate the performances of Ashoke and Kajol based on the above criteria.
2. Whom do you suggest as the most potential candidate for the post of regional manager?
3. Comment on the reliability of such measure.

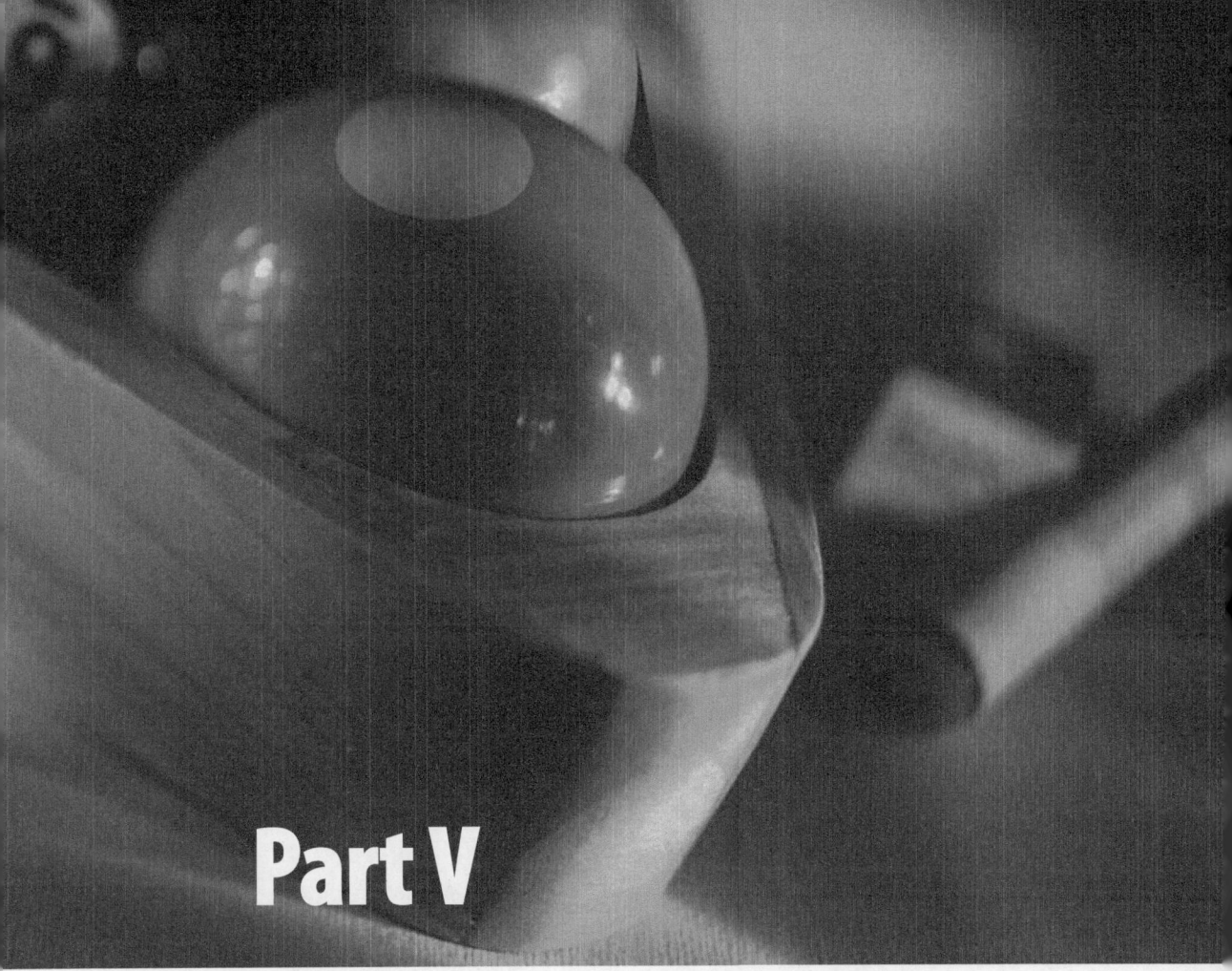

Part V

Strategy and Modern Approaches

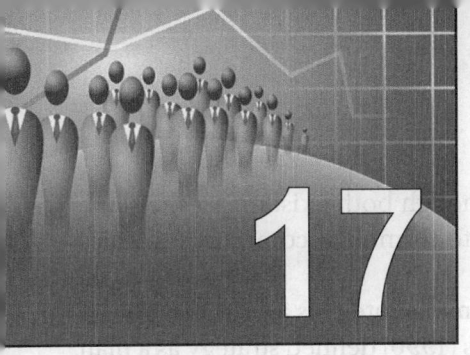

17 Sales Strategy

17.1 STRATEGIC ORIENTATION OF SELLING—AN INTRODUCTION

Strategic orientation is essential for a firm to confront the marketing challenges in today's competitive business environment. In fact, strategic orientation is a deliberate and sustained attempt of the firm to formulate strategic plans to acquire competitive advantages over competing firms. HUL's competitive advantage is that it has a strong product portfolio that hones strong quality perception and dots across wide price points over economy to premium products. The philosophy of consistent quality, rich tradition, unwavering trust that the Tata groups of companies have created amongst people definitely caters competitive advantage to their products and services.

Every firm has some strategic plans that encompass participation of all the business units. Usually, a multi-product firm has several business units called strategic business units or SBUs and each of these business units have their own strategic interests as they serve a specific customer group. Each SBU is built around a product or a service for which separate plans, objectives, strategies, and operations are devised. Setting common goals and strategies despite the presence of product differentiation and varied-market fundamentals (demand–supply, situations, competitive conditions, etc.) across market segments can jeopardize a firm's future prospects. Companies such as HUL, P&G, ITC, etc. handle diverse products in their product portfolios where each product group has its own division, mission, goal, customer, competitors, and strategies. In short, it can be said that one

SBU is different from the other in all respects though both exist under the same umbrella of the organization and any attempt to formulate common strategies can be counterproductive to the firm.

A strategy is a result of business plans. In a sense, strategy is a plan that guides an organization's actions. Dalrymple and Parsons (1990) defined strategy as a plan of action designed to achieve long-term goals of the organization. Alternatively, we can say that strategy is backed by effective planning. Planning embossed with strategic elements is known as strategic planning. A strategic plan mentors decision-making and implementation of business plans to achieve organizational objectives.

Koudri (2004) emphasized that a strategic plan should guide actions and decisions, providing a sense of purpose, energy, and direction. Moreover, it is a means of communication and coordination of efforts throughout the organization. In the case of selling, strategic plans are made in order to make the organizations customer-oriented. A strategic sales plan not only involves a quick understanding of market opportunities, threats, and target markets but also the strengths and weaknesses of the competitors. It irons out the myopic interest of selling that advocates profit generation as the sole aim of the firm. In fact, strategic sales plan blurs the line of distinction between the sales and marketing goals imbibing the philosophy of marketing in the veins of selling.

Once the strategic sales plans are clearly formulated, sales managers get themselves engaged in the procurement of resources (e.g., finance, human resources, etc.) and develop a suitable marketing mix covering all its elements. Mehta (1980) viewed that a plan covering the components of marketing mix such as product policy, pricing, distribution and promotion, especially advertising and personal selling, has to be worked out keeping track of the sales goals and the forecasted sales. Again, strategic sales plan cannot produce desired goals unless the activities it proposes are coordinated effectively to act towards the goals. It must respond positively to the present and anticipate future market conditions.

17.2 ENVIRONMENTAL ANALYSIS—A PRE-REQUISITE FOR STRATEGIC PLAN

Planning starts with the anticipation of future environmental situations and more precisely, the events that are expected to happen in the future. Planning suggests the course of actions and sets performance standards to compare the actual results with the expected outcomes to check whether the organization is moving in the right direction and towards its objectives. Kurtz and Boone (2009) viewed that planning provides a blueprint for actions and defines checkpoints to trace out the progress of the actual performance by comparing it with predetermined set of standards. Kotler and Armstrong (2006) defined strategic planning as the process of developing and maintaining a strategic fit between the organization's goals and capabilities, and its changing marketing opportunities. Strategic planning aims to cater the right intelligence and direction to the organization to make optimal utilization of resources to achieve goals, keeping in mind the specific situations and conditions of the business environment.

So it can be said that environmental analysis is the primary condition in devising strategic plans that entail environmental scanning and monitoring as well. Scanning involves researching all environmental factors and their interactions to spot the specific opportunities and threats of the organization, whereas, monitoring is the continuous follow-up of the changes in the environmental factors. Kumar (2002) viewed that monitoring a consumer drift involving significant shift in the consumer preferences, competitive actions, technological advances, investment behaviour of the firms, etc. is important for companies to achieve their goals. Exhibit 17.1 tracks down an important drift in two-wheeler category initiated by Kinetic Honda in the early 1990s.

Exhibit 17.1   Market drift in two wheelers

It was seen that the two-wheeler industries plunged into depression in the first half of the 1990s at the time of uncharacteristic buying behaviour of the consumers towards two-wheeler purchase. Kinetic Honda unveiled the reason for this apparent inertia by the consumers. Kinetic Honda introduced scooters with electronic start which further proved that kick starting a bike was not always a soothing experience for the consumers. In fact, the innovative two-wheelers triggered the emergence of a new market segment, i.e., women who gleefully accepted a product that so far was found in the male-dominated markets.

Source: Ramaswamy and Namakumari (2003).

Rising income of the middleclass, spurt in electronic media, trend of the young generation to emulate western lifestyles, increasing number of working women, burgeoning rural markets, etc. have given pace to this market drift. So, without environmental studies, tracing the drift is not possible.

Aswathappa (2007) viewed environmental scanning as the general surveillance of all the environmental factors and their interactions amongst themselves with a view to identify early signals of possible environmental changes. Continuous assessment of market trends (expressed in terms of customer expectations, demands, competitive actions, socio-economic changes, technological progress, regulatory frameworks, etc.) makes an organization adaptive as well as responsive. A responsive firm cannot waste time in sensing the changes and takes necessary measures to overcome the problem areas. An adaptive firm shows pro-activeness to cause changes in its earlier missions, goals, strategies, and business policies to create a viable fit with the new market conditions.

Changes may be invoked in the product, process, organizational structure, etc. For example, Xerox developed new products by coordinated efforts initiated through multidisciplinary teams that cut across all the functional tasks. Bolo (2008) viewed that Godrej adopted a participative management model peeling off its earlier model of management hierarchy that is well supported by team spirit and employee improvement programmes. This is a classic example of change management.

In a multi-product multi-market firm, sales strategies of one product–market variant should not interrupt with that of the other. Rather, these should complement each other to the benefit of the optimal resource utilization. Second, the strategies at corporate level (the top-level management), business level (mid-level management), and operational level (line-management level) should act interdependently to work towards the goals. It is the top-level management (e.g., chief executive officer of the manager) who devise overall corporate missions, goals and objectives, policies, etc. and establish directions for the way the corporate will move in future to sustain and improve growth of the firm. Business-level managers (regional-sales managers) take charge of the different products or geographical divisions, and formulate strategies and policies that best address the present industrial situations characterizing customer demands, competitions, government regulations, etc. Operation level or line managers (e.g., field-sales managers) are responsible for the execution of business plans who report to the mid-level managers and the later finally becomes accountable to the top level.

Strategies at each level must be consistent with the other and in no way lose intensity and direction by the strategies of the other. Walker et al. (2006) underwent a study on how IBM with its multiple business units follows interdependent strategies cutting across corporate, business levels, and operational levels to generate huge success for the company. Marketing strategies assume significant roles in the operational level by which the company categorically divides its market into segments, defines target markets in the segments, designs promotional tools, and employs right pricing schemes for different product–market situations. From personal computer business to e-commerce engineering and consultancy services, corporate strategies show goals and directions, business strategies map out schemes to address competitions, and marketing strategies suggest an intelligent use of the knowledge and expertise of its personnel to spot-market opportunities, offer solutions to customer problems, and finally forge well-knit beneficial relationships with their customers. Box 17.1 lists the criteria to keep in mind while developing a sound sales strategy.

> ### Box 17.1   Criteria for sound sales strategy
>
> Following are the criteria for sound sales strategy:
>
> 1. Sales strategies should be well-defined and presented in unambiguous statements.
> 2. It should have a specific product–market focus, i.e., product(s), target market(s), customer segments, etc. are inclusive in the strategy statements.
> 3. It must work on the company's missions and objectives.
> 4. It must consider the company's available resources to make it operational.
> 5. It must suggest how resources are to be allocated to meet both the major and minor business opportunities.
> 6. It must give direction to establish the right marketing mix that works for strategic implementation of marketing actions.
> 7. It should have the right bites to outweigh any competitive actions.
> 8. It must act towards gaining competitive advantage to the firm.
> 9. Different sales strategies for different product–market combinations must reinforce each other to obtain synergistic benefits.

17.3   SALES STRATEGIES—SOME COMMON DRIVERS

There are a number of strategies available for the personnel to carry out their responsibilities and duties effectively But what is important is what leads to develop these sales strategies and how they affect an organization. The success of sales strategies depend on the identification and analysis of those factors that are treated as drivers of sales strategy formulation. Box 17.2 lists some of the common drivers of sales strategy that are discussed in detail as follows.

> ### Box 17.2   Common drivers of sales strategy
>
> Following are the common drivers of sales strategy:
>
> | | |
> |---|---|
> | (a) Tapping unconventional markets | (b) Niche marketing |
> | (c) Product positioning | (d) Making use of core competencies |
> | (e) Direct selling | (f) Cost leadership |
> | (g) Technological leadership | (h) Unique pricing |
> | (i) Sales force development | (j) Value for money offer |
> | (k) Customer service | (l) Team selling |
> | (m) Corporate image | |

Tapping Unconventional Market

Tapping unconventional market strategy involves exploring a new product–market situation by a company that is so far unnoticed by the other competing brands. Asian Paints was successful in breaking the common system of supplying paints in large containers of 500 ml by coming up with smaller-sized containers. Second, the company, also, underwent certain changes in its distribution mechanisms by adding retail dealership in its distribution network to reach small, medium, and large buyers.

Niche Marketing

Niche marketing involves marketing the products/services in a small but significantly profitable market segment. Identifying the niche market is crucial for successful niche marketing. Since a niche market is small in size, marketing communication is easy and if a product requires personal selling in this market, the company can entrust a limited number of salespeople to reach the target customers effectively. Formulating niche strategy needs some innovative approach from the company. A niche market can be created by exploring an unconventional market segment, technological breakthrough, product differentiation, etc. Such kind of a strategy can be seen when a tours and travel company offers an attractive price for couple vacationers. Some of the branded commodities such as rice, flour, etc. have also successfully created niche market segments.

Product Positioning

Product positioning is an act of fixing a prominent location of a product in a carefully chosen market. The firm decides the competitive advantage of a product and puts it in the market before competitors make any inroads. TTK group introduced its prestige range of frying pans in the non-stick category claiming the distinction of adding a coating based on DuPont's Teflon. Teflon is assumed to be a high quality non-stick material in the world.

Making Use of Core Competences

A firm can generate competitive advantage by identifying the core competence, i.e., a specific feature of the product that provides a unique strength to the offer and helps to stand out from all competing products. This is done so that no competitors can emulate its core competence. This concept, which is a technological competence, is owed to C.K. Prahlad and Gary Hammel.

Ramaswamy and Namakumari (1996) pointed out that corporations that enjoy core competence in the root technology/process/expertise keep gaining enduring advantages over its offers. A competitive advantage can be emulated but core competency cannot be. Miniaturizations of electronic products from Sony, chemical technology of DuPont are the company's respective core competencies.

Direct Selling

Direct selling involves selling the products directly to the customers where one-on-one interaction with the prospective customer is the key to achieving success.

Direct selling can develop a sales network where interested individuals can join to extend their network in terms of increasing their business revenues themselves or indirectly appointing others in the chain. Direct selling is successful in selling home utilities such as cosmetics, toothpastes, shampoos, etc. Companies such as Amway, Oriflame, Avon, etc. are some of the big ones that are operating with huge success using this approach. Marketing that includes direct selling as a means to reach a large customer base is known as multi-level marketing (MLM).

Cost Leadership

When a firm is able to be a low-cost manufacturer where other firms within its industry are unable to do so, the former is said to enjoy cost leadership. Saxena (1997) explained that cost advantage may result from several factors such as economies of scale in production and distribution, preferential access to raw material sources, strong intermediaries, patents, efficient value chain, etc. Texas Instruments, Dell, etc. are cost leaders in their respective fields.

Technological Leadership

A company can attain leadership through technological breakthroughs as well. Portable fax machines from Xerox, Via Voice speech recognition software from IBM have become pioneers as a result of their technological arenas. Technology can outweigh other disadvantages of a product (e.g., high price) and provide a competitive advantage.

Unique Pricing

A company can formulate a sales strategy depending upon the price level (either high or low) that its competitors are offering. High price (skimming-pricing strategy) gives the firm a chance to compensate initial costs at the launching period. High price also helps to carry a superior image of the product. Low price (penetration-pricing strategy) provides huge sales turnover and improve sales productivity. PepsiCo's Frito-Lay, a snack food brand rests on aggressive promotion and maintains a low price giving competitors no chance to encroach upon its market share. Good retailing also contributes heavily to the success of the brand.

Sales Force Development

Sales force development is part of sales strategy where better recruiting process, sales force selection, training, motivation, and compensation are compared with competing firms to draw good potential salespeople who are expected to cater to the desired sales performance. L&T recruits its engineers with excellent qualifications and deserve praise for executing its projects successfully. It also stays high on qualification criteria in recruiting salespeople.

Value for Money Offer

A sales strategy cannot succeed until customers accept the company's products ignoring other similar products available in the market. Customers justify their purchase by comparing the value of the offer with the price. If the perceived value is less than the price, the customer rejects it. On the other hand, if the perceived value equates price, the customer is satisfied. If the perceived value is more than the price, the customer is delighted.

Customer Service

Efficient customer service may also be one of the main components of sales strategy. Lending satisfactory service compared to other similar firms may prove to be productive. Servicing customers before, during, and after selling are equally important to satisfy and hold customers. Otis elevator has already made a mark in providing valuable services to the customers.

Team Selling

Building a sales team is important to respond to the multifarious requirements of the customers, particularly for complex products such as installation of computerized networks. This refers to a situation where a team of salespeople with different capabilities is needed. This is because, in certain situations, one individual is required for skill in catering software services while the other at customer training. Johnson et al. (1994) cited that AT&T, IBM, and other information management companies use team approach in developing effective sales techniques which involve sales support personnel.

Corporate Image

A strongly built up corporate image can be an effective tool for selling strategy. Bajaj, Hindustan Unilever, IBM, etc. are some of the names that have already created histories in business landscape. A company can intelligently synergize its product with the corporate image to generate profitable results.

17.4 STEPS IN STRATEGIC SALES MANAGEMENT—A SCHEMATIC OVERVIEW

To make personal selling more effective, the strategic sales management with proper steps should be pursued. Strategic sales management revolves around the right selection of target customers, right combination of marketing mix elements, and reaching target customers with it. Figure 17.1 shows the steps in strategic sales management.

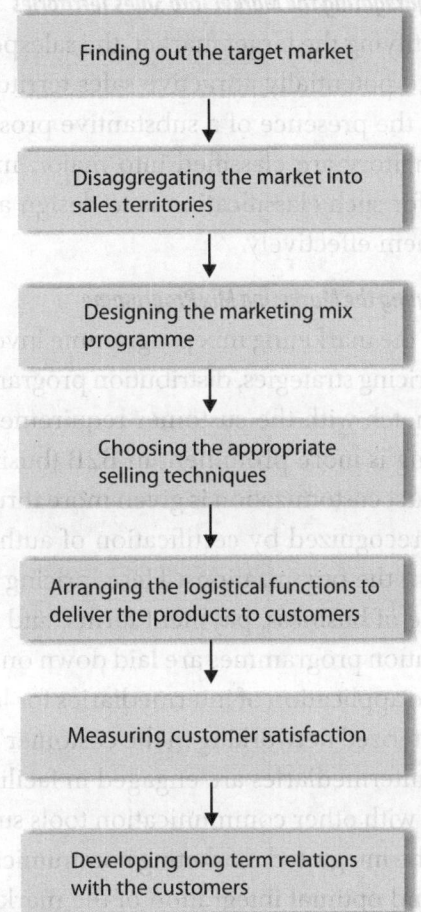

Figure 17.1 Steps in strategic sales management

Step 1: Finding the Target Market

It is important to know the following issues before the actual sale in order to achieve the best results:

(a) Who are the target customers?

(b) What are their demands (a study on market potential will reveal it)?

(c) What are their buying habits and patterns (a study of recent past trends of buying behaviour of customers will reveal it)?

(d) Competitive actions in the market

(e) Presence of market gap (an analysis of product positioning and marketing-mix policies of competitors will reveal it. The objective is to know whether there are any untapped market niches that competitors have not explored)

Step 2: Disaggregating the Market Into Sales Territories

After identifying the target market, the salespeople need to break down the entire market into potentially attractive sales territories where each territory is characterized by the presence of a substantive prospective customer. These customers in each territory are classified into major, moderate, and minor accounts. The objective for such classification is to design appropriate marketing programmes to serve them effectively.

Step 3: Designing the Marketing Mix Programme

Designing the marketing mix programme involves preparing appropriate product policies, pricing strategies, distribution programmes, and finally some promotional plans to match with the customer requirements satisfactorily. As we know, personal selling is more prominent in B2B (business-to-business) selling, but in this case, product customization is given more thrust. Otherwise usually, standardized products (recognized by certification of authorized agencies such as ISO) have demands in the organizations. Here, pricing strategies are formulated based on the volume of business, payment terms, and financing supports, etc.

Distribution programmes are laid down on direct business-to-business logistics without the application of intermediaries for large items (e.g., a server installation for computerized networking in the customer's office). For standardized products, however, intermediaries are engaged in facilitating transactions. Personal selling combined with other communication tools such as advertising, trade promotion, etc. form the integrated marketing communication (IMC) which results from cost effective and optimal integration of the marketing mix elements.

Step 4: Choosing the Appropriate Selling Technique(s)

Once, the marketing mix has been finalized, the sales managers decide on the appropriate selling techniques to be used depending on the nature of the products, seniority of sales personnel, selling kits available to make effective presentation of the company's products, etc. Senior salespeople are entrusted to deal with technically complex products (e.g., electronic weighing machine for industrial use). Demonstration of products with free samples, power point presentations, documents containing sales histories of the products, etc. are important tools to persuade prospective customers.

Step 5: Arranging the Logistical Functions

Logistical functions is part of distribution management that includes collection of orders from customers, order processing, and finally delivering the products at the predetermined time and place. Whether products are distributed through intermediaries or directly to the customers, enquiring about stock positions, proper packaging, making shipping arrangements, and ensuring availability of the products to the distributors or end users are important.

Step 6: Measuring Customer Satisfaction

It is crucial for consumers to be satisfied to develop relationships with the customers. This is important as it can keep the competitors' products at bay and can make customers brand loyal. Satisfaction determines how far a product's performance is able to meet the customer demands. Also, satisfied customers may be strong influencers to generate more customers.

Step 7: Developing Long-term Relationship With Customers

Developing long-term relationships with the customers is possible by creating mutual trust with them. Customers by nature are sensitive to the deals as proposed by the salespeople and if their expectations are diminished, the company starts losing customers. Therefore, whatever has been promised during the pre-selling, selling, and post-selling stages to the customers should be fulfilled consistently. Satisfaction from both the sides, buyers and sellers, is the key to long-term relationship between the two.

17.5 UNDERSTANDING COMPETITION—ESSENTIAL FOR SELLING STRATEGY

Competition is welcome, if it engages organizations to improve upon their product performance and satisfy customers more than their expectations. Competition can improve the quality of life, enhance industrial progress, and cause social well-being. On the other hand, competition is worse if it acts in the opposite manner.

Sales strategy is shaped and influenced by the type of market competition. When there is no competition, formulating a sales strategy is simple because the company feels no such competitive resistance from other companies in the same industry either because other companies are weak or have no existence. Barring this, if a company faces competition from others, it needs to be more careful in formulating a strategy. The nature of competition varies from one product–market situation to the other. In general a company can operate under the following competitions:

(a) Pure competition

(b) Monopolistic competition

(c) Oligopolistic competition

Pure competition exists when

(i) the number of sellers is large,

(ii) one seller cannot influence the other on pricing terms,

(iii) there are no differences amongst products apart from their brand names, i.e., products meant to satisfy specific customer demands are homogeneous, and

(iv) free entry or exit in the industry at will without legal hassles characterizes this competition.

Pure competition is a condition that finds no markets to rule in the real world. Presumably, it can be argued that no seller can drive home the advantage by pushing a product by personal selling. Buyers are informative about the various offers and justify the purchases on price comparisons. Promotional tools cannot stimulate customers to select a particular brand. Even product distribution, where buyers and sellers come in close proximity, cannot be the deciding element in pushing a brand.

Monopolistic competition exists when

(i) there are large number of firms in an industry,

(ii) firms produce commodities similar to one another but these are not identical,

(iii) the situation is between pure competition and monopoly, and

(iv) competition can spiral more due to entry of more competitors in the market.

Here, a firm (e.g., cosmetics, toiletry products manufacturing units) tries to create a point of differentiation in its offer from others by a specific product feature (e.g., attractive packaging) or distinct distribution scheme (e.g., direct selling) or attractive price. Finding the right marketing opportunities and skills in planning and implementation of marketing strategies are important for a firm to make a dent. The ability to create product differentiation and designing appropriate promotional schemes can also help a firm prove a point in terms of success.

Personal selling strategy can be intelligently used to stimulate middlemen to exert more efforts. Advertising and personal selling efforts can be combined in the right proportion to get more customer attention and reach customers through promotional push by the middlemen.

Oligopolistic competition exists when

(i) the number of firms must be more than two but not many,

(ii) there are a number of buyers,

(iii) each firm's price of a product is influenced by the prices of all the other sellers on the same or similar products,

(iv) a condition may arise where one or a few firms constantly set prices and others follow it. The former is called price leader and others are price followers, and

(v) the competitive moves of one firm affect all the others.

This is an aggressive competitive situation. Immediate and appropriate response to the changes of product features, distribution types or price variations initiated by one competitor is the key for other firms to survive in the market. But, before emulating changes, the following firms must ensure the beneficial effects of it, otherwise it may be counterproductive. Personal selling can assume a significant role to scan the competitors' activities, obtain additional supports at various levels of distribution network and assure full cooperation from dealers and distributors. Both personal selling and advertising can be central in the marketing strategies of the firm. Tires, aluminum, steel industries, etc. face this sort of a competitive situation.

17.6 MARKETING STRATEGY—A TRIGGER OF SALES STRATEGY

Marketing strategy lays the foundation of sales strategy. Marketing strategy is an instrument to attain marketing objectives of the firm. It formulates the game plan to combat competitors and uses sales strategy to generate a platform for effective sales operations. It utilizes sales strategy to perform boundary spanning activities to include more sales territories, more number of customers, and expansion of distribution network to produce more wealth for the firm. All these come into effect when the company has adequate resources to execute the strategies. Second, the company also has strategic intensities to baffle the competitors. According to Porter, five vital forces decide the intensity of competition. These are (a) entry barriers, (b) bargaining power of suppliers, (c) bargaining power of customers, (d) threats of substitute products, and (e) industry rivalry

So, marketing strategy is the brain behind sales strategy. Marketing strategy directs sales strategy to decide the sales objectives, build sales territories, recruit, select, train and compensate sales force, and measure sales performance. Personal selling is the medium to generate sales. Advertising plays a catalytic role to stimulate personal-selling activities. Sales strategy is designed to execute a firm's marketing strategy. Figure 17.2 shows the interconnectedness between the sales and marketing strategy.

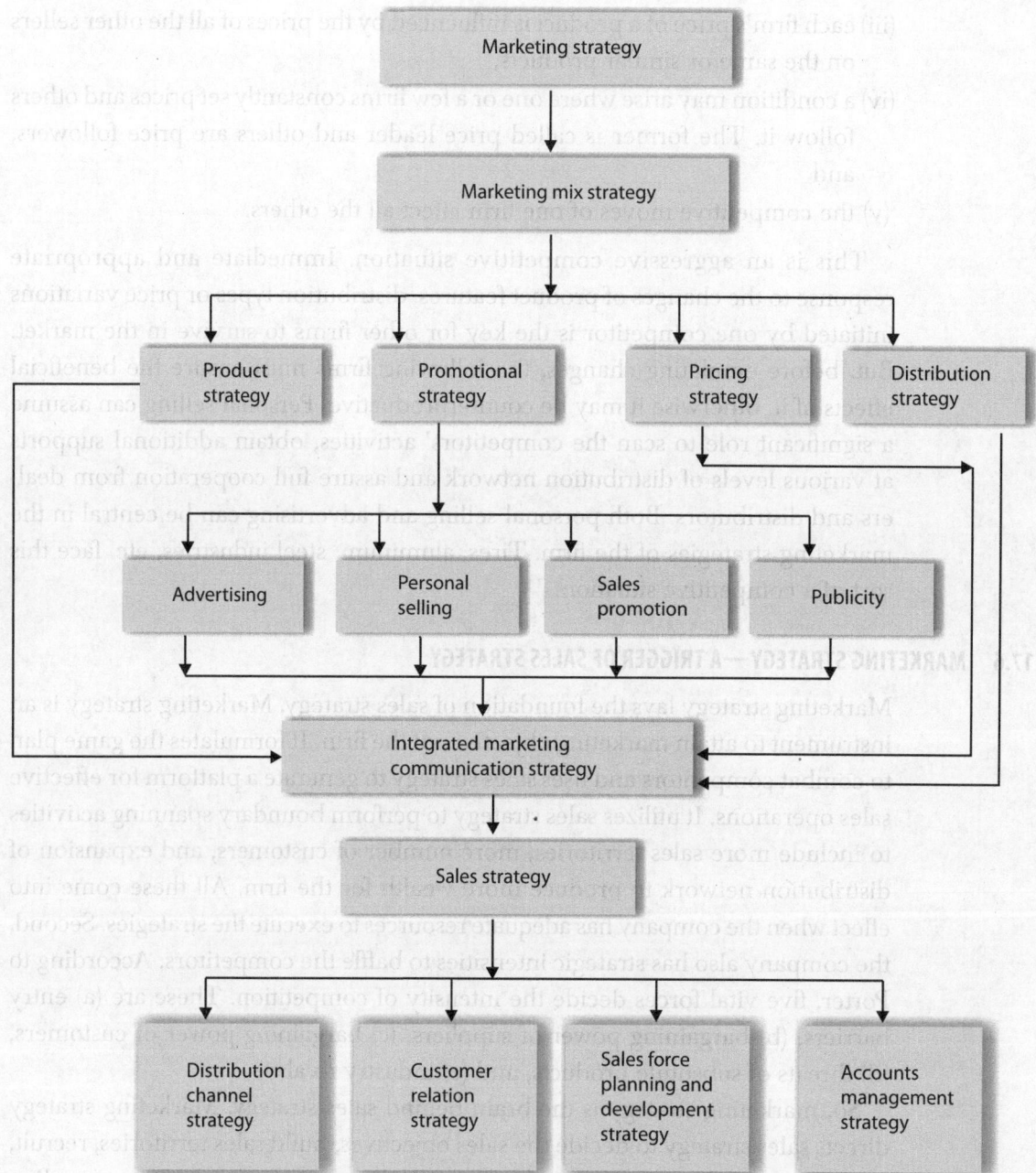

Figure 17.2 Model-link between marketing and sales strategy

It is evident from Figure 17.2 that marketing strategy provides direction and guidance to formulate the marketing mix strategy combining four components such as product, distribution, pricing, and promotion strategies. Promotional strategies need the application of promotional tools such as advertising, personal selling, sales promotion, and publicity to meet the company's communication objectives. The promotional tools, when act in a combination to fulfil certain communication objectives, integrated marketing communication takes place.

A company formulates integrated marketing communication strategy depending on the nature of product, competition, marketing strategies of the firm, etc. and judiciously combines two to three communication tools to reach target audiences with the message. Sales strategy takes inputs from the communication strategies and uses it along with product, pricing, and distribution strategies to attain sales effectiveness. Sales strategy, also, takes into account the requirements of individual accounts. Therefore, accounts management strategy is a part of sales strategy that acts for individual account or account groups.

To meet the account demands effectively, sales strategy recommends the proper selection and deployment of sales force who act on sales plans and programmes. Therefore, sales force planning and development strategy is laid down within the framework of sales strategy. Sales strategy suggests how target customers can be effectively reached at a cost that is within the limit of estimated distribution costs. Selection of the right marketing channel is an important consideration. Therefore, distribution channel strategy is inclusive of sales strategy.

Sales strategy is not just expected to work for a single transaction but for a series of transactions. To do this, continuous rapport with the customers is important. Here, congenial customer relationship plays a crucial role for a company to prolong business relationships with customers. Sales strategy stresses upon customer relationship strategy for business continuity and stability.

17.6.1 Sales Strategy—Focus on Customer Relationship

Relationship is the key to success in any business. The organization might be technologically excellent and replete with resources but the absence of any meaningful relationship with internal customers (employees) and buyers (external customers) can spell doom for the organization. Strategic sales management cannot ignore this part of personal selling. Under traditional selling practices, meeting customer satisfaction at a profit to the organization was the motto and very little attention was imparted to customer service. The organization mainly acted upon profit motive and the achievement of sales target. Thrust was more upon exchange relationships rather than giving thought to the need for approaching the same customer again and again for repeated business.

But one point that was not understood in traditional selling despite fulfilling all the conditions of the marketing mix combinations was holding on to a customer that was not rest assured. It is then that the need for relationship selling came to fore. Relationship selling is the base for developing effective customer relationship.

Factors that should be understood while developing effective customer relationship are as follows:

1. A customer justifies a product based on how beneficial it is for him. Benefit is usually defined as the outcome from product value. In case, there is incongruence between the price and value, not favouring the customer; he does not hesitate to go for the competing brand. Therefore, product value can be calculated using the following formula.

$$\frac{\text{Perceived benefit}}{\text{Cost}}$$

The more the perceived benefits as compared to the cost, the more will be the value of the product to the customer. A customer may justify the purchase of a bike based on its mileage against fuel consumption.

2. A customer not only gives stress on core benefits of the product (e.g., cooling, storing, and preserving capacities as in a refrigerator) but also to the associated benefits (e.g., warranty, service supports, duration of warranty, etc.). The competition of firms may take place not on core features of the product but the degree of augmented benefits of one over the other.

3. Keeping the 80:20 principle in mind (20 per cent of all customer account for 80 per cent of the sales) can be useful for the companies. Major customers should be given large attention but not at the cost of losing a few minor customers. It might be possible that three to four small customers can contribute more sales revenue to the firm than a single major customer. Proper sales planning and guidance to salespeople is needed to handle both the major as well as the small customers.

4. Sales strategy gets its meaningful application only under right salesmanship. Proper sales force development, motivation, and control of sales functions are important to nurture the quality of salesmanship within salespeople.

5. Development of sales territories, organization of sales tasks, allocation of duties and responsibilities amongst salespeople contribute positively towards sales performance. Sales strategy statements should give the right direction to this end. The application of strategy without direction makes it barren and ineffective.

6. Commitment to customers to provide whatever is promised to offer during pre-selling, imparting customer education on product use and application during selling, getting continuous feedback from customers in post-selling period can develop healthy relationships between the organizations and the

customers. Sometimes, the valued customers are requested to give their advice on the quality improvement of the product.

So, customer relationship is an important element of strategic sales management. It is a strategic intent. Sales managers should choose the right approach to develop customer relationships. Business with customers may come to an end as soon as the exchange is over but the relationship may last for long if the sellers take initiatives. A stable relationship removes all psychological barriers for the sellers to request for a second or a third time business with the existing buyers.

Customer relationship management is a customer-centric business philosophy that permeates from the marketing department to other departments. For example, a customer-centric production department becomes active in meeting the demands of the customers in time. R&D department becomes sensitive to the quality control of the product that benefits customers at the end. Finance department gives a go ahead call to the marketing department with the financial supports for meeting promotion and distribution expenses. Thus, CRM philosophy renders the entire organization to be customer-centric. A firm following this philosophy chants and breathes for the customer's well being and relates it to the social well being. If CRM is successful, the society will reward the organization with the opulence of wealth.

17.6.2 Sales Strategy—Distribution as an Implementation Channel

Distribution includes a wide range of activities such as physical handling, transportation of goods to the customers, order processing, managing inventories of finished goods, making arrangements for the transfer of ownership from buyers to sellers, etc. Some of its functions are intertwined with the selling functions. Salespeople procure orders from customers, process and facilitate distribution functions to serve customers at the right place, time and form, satisfying conditions for transfer of ownership. So, the elements of distribution functions integrate among themselves to maintain a balance between the sales and distribution planning.

Sales objectives of the firm are designed to inform, persuade, and implement sales plans whereas distribution objectives aim to fulfil what is claimed to offer to the customers during personal selling communication and promotion. Sales and distribution objectives are set explicitly to find some logistical functions that work for the attainment of both the objectives. Figure 17.3 exhibits these functions and show how these integrate both the sales and distribution plans and objectives.

Selling and distribution have some common objectives to pursue which can be substantiated by some functional commonalities between the two as well. Following are the areas where sales and distribution move towards common goals:

1. Analysing the needs of the customers require attention from the sales and distribution functions. Without sound understanding, the sales department cannot develop sales plans or formulate sales strategies. Similarly, without

knowing the customers' demands and service requirements, selection of distribution channel, finding out inventory positions, determining distribution expenses are not possible.

2. Distribution such as sales is a communication function. Channel members take responsibility of informing target customers about the market offers and conditions for business transactions.

3. Both the salespeople of the firm and the distribution channel members work on order taking, processing, and accomplishment of orders.

4. Both sales and distribution are components of strategic marketing plan.

5. Sales and distribution complement each other to complete the transaction. Salespeople stimulate demand amongst customers and pull them towards distribution centres where transaction takes place. So, sales without distribution means nothing to the buyers and sellers.

6. Sales and distribution are legal functions. Both need to follow some legal formalities in business transactions. Whatever has been promised to the customers through personal selling have legal bindings and the distribution functions must obey such guidelines.

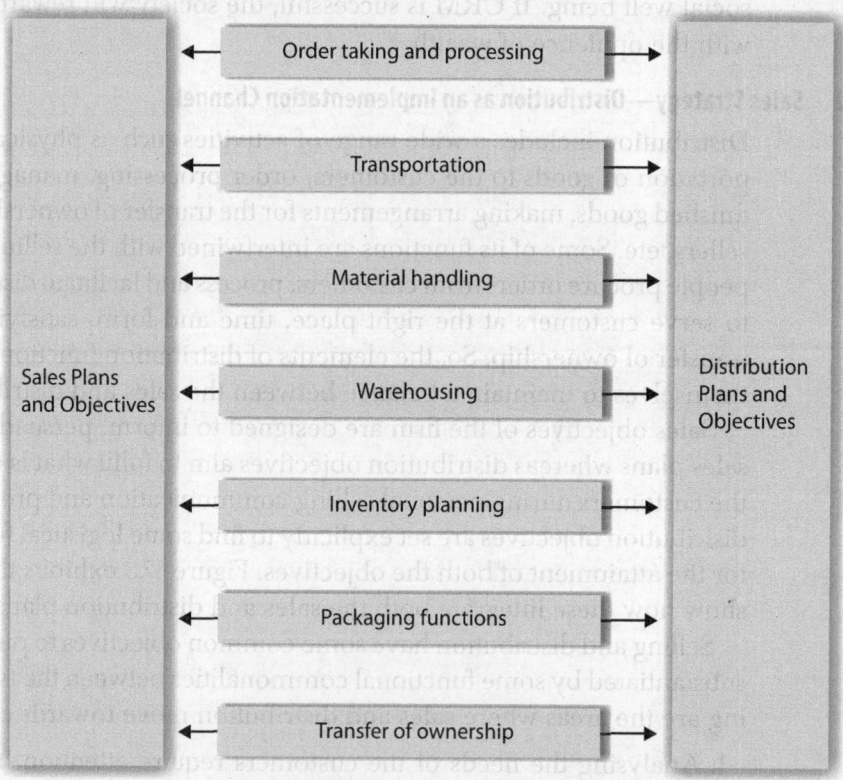

Figure 17.3 Logistical function integrating sales and distribution functions

Exhibit 17.2 shows how Asian Paints has coordinated both the selling and the distribution functions to reach stellar height in the paint industry. Indeed, these two are important strategic elements to endow the company with the right marketing approaches that act towards the company's goals and missions.

Exhibit 17.2 Asian Paints—a symbol of strategic excellence

Asian Paints, India's leading paint company has sparked revolution in the distribution of its products. The company manufactures and distributes paints within a range that serves different customers with varying preferences and offers customers to select their products through colour vending machines. It banks on information technology to manage its supply chain.

Excellent inventory management, updating of stocks, material handling have eased the logistical operations. Moreover, it has started retail distribution of paints to cater to small and medium customers who instead of asking for bulk orders, demand for small quantity of paints (less than 500 ml containers.). The company has explored a huge market potential of paints in rural segments, and has expanded its distribution network in rural belts. Country-wide distribution network of retailers and dealers have made the company reachable in both domestic and industrial customers. High advertising intensity of its products in popular media channels have created high top–of-the-mind awareness amongst potential customers.

Source: http://www.indiahousing.com/asian-paints.html, accessed on 22 July 2010.

17.7 SALES STRATEGY—SOCIAL RESPONSIBILITY ISSUES

Strategic sales management would be sustaining and efficacious if the sales goals and objectives are laid down with social responsibility in the backdrop. In fact, sales managers should not forget to make use of the term 'sales' in the myopic version of marketing. Indeed, they should engage in marketing activities while fulfilling social objectives along with corporate objectives as their principle tasks. On the fulfilment of social objectives within the confines of the company's capabilities, it can expect to grow both economically and socially. At the same time, it is true that a company survives on revenue generations and profit earnings, and the social responsibility issues cannot ignore this part because the company's financial health is an insurance of the stakes of investors, employees, distributors, vendors, government, etc.

An organization should act upon societal and social goals. Societal goals consider customers as part of the society and considers serving them with honesty and integrity as a means of contributing to the social progress. Social objectives of a firm work on some social causes. In India, Tata group, a great practitioner of corporate social responsibility (CSR) bestows a large part of its profits to the social development programmes through philanthropic trusts. Sharma quoted from Drucker (1954) to mention that, 'The enterprise is an organ of society and its actions have a decisive impact on the social scene. It is, thus, important for the management to realize that it must consider the impact of every business policy and business actions upon society.'

Sales managers can perform social responsibilities by integrating their functions with social causes. Box 17.3 presents some of the major social responsibility areas of sales managers.

Box 17.3 Social responsibility areas

Following are the social responsibility areas:

1. Imparting quality of the product or service commensurate with its price which must pervade across customer-oriented organizations. Before finally committing to the customers, sales managers must ensure that customers can get their money's worth.

2. Product safety is an important concern for product use or application. Customers should never be led to a point of harm or danger when they use a machine or equipment. Improper product design, poor manufacturing quality, etc. can lead to such problems. Sales managers before finally delivering the products to the customers must ensure product safety.

3. Raising the points of demerits along with the merits during sales presentation should be instructed to the salespeople. Salespeople should not try to camouflage the flipsides of the product to the customers under the sheds of strong points. Sales managers should properly guide and instruct salespeople.

4. Passing the buck is a serious offence in sales transaction. Sales managers are often accused of making stinted sales plans that suggest passing on high promotional costs or packaging costs to the shoulders of innocent customers. This is a serious allegation against sales managers, if followed.

5. Taking no care of the customers after the products are sold to them is again a serious breech of condition and trust on the buyer–seller relationship. Sales managers must be aware of it.

6. Organizations should not be engaged in breeding unfair and unjustified business climate and the competitive environment to destroy the health and equilibrium of the market. Unjustly hoarding the products, deceptive advertisements, supplying banned products, adulterated products, unsafe and unhygienic packaging, dumping, etc. are such practices. Sales managers cannot escape blame on such vindictive issues.

Sales managers should strictly add directly and indirectly the social responsibility issue in their strategy statements. Their decisions, plans, policies, actions must encourage those issues and the subordinates should learn to preach and deliver the organization's philosophy of caring and nurturing greater causes of customers. Adhering to the social norms and ethics should be the benchmark of strategic sales management. Social responsibility should be treated as a strategic obligation of the firm.

17.8 THE SEED FOR SUCCESS

Relationship marketing is the cornerstone of customer orientation in today's marketing environment. It is a philosophy of the marketers to visualize the buying–selling relationship as a focal point of business transaction. It aims to develop a permanent bonding between the buyer and the seller that ultimately shapes the society and the economy at large. Customer relation is a customer-retention marketing strategy. It treats marketing not as a single opportunity to serve customers but as a medium to generate series of interconnectedness with the customers through the multitude of buying–selling situations.

Transactional marketing is the flipside of relationship marketing. Under the transactional marketing approach, marketers plan and control their efforts on individual transactions. Here, every transaction is assumed to be new and has no such bearing with the previous or the next transaction.

An organization, pursuing transaction marketing, rethink and rebuild business criteria for every next transaction. An organization's commitment is limited to the delivery of the right product at appropriate time and place. Once the customers accept it and reciprocate with price, business is assumed to be over. Under relationship marketing, every transaction is the driver of the next transaction. Series of successful transactions create long-term relationships between the buyers and sellers.

An organization pursuing relationship marketing treats each customer as a stakeholder of it and therefore, it must pay back to the customer satisfactorily without distorting its strategic pursuits in attaining expected sales goals. Indeed, relationship marketing directs organization to stay affirmed in offering values to customers through its products/services during every transaction where a customer's perception of product(s)/service(s) value must equate or exceed the price the customers pays. The result is a sense of trust and confidence of the customer to the organization. So, the essence of relationship marketing is to procreate a win–win situation for both the organization and customer irrespective of the volume of transaction. Successful relationship marketing binds customers to the organization both economically and psychologically. Moreover, it acts as a catalyst to generate new customers where word of mouth from the existing customers become great inducements. Product customization, providing meaningful core, and augmented services of the product to the customers, giving constant and proper attention to the customers including both tangible and intangible benefits of the product, following up even after sales when the customer does not inform about his experience with the product bestows the pillars for rock-solid relationship between the buyer and the seller.

Relationship marketing is a collaborative relationship between the buyer and the seller. It is a two-way process buttressed by shared efforts and values, mutual interests, and win-win exchange attitude and behaviour. It is, furthermore, unstinted and unwavering confidence and commitment from both the parties in addition to the above conditions that bolsters such relationships. The figure that follows depicts how relationship marketing gets its proper significance in the presence of commitment and confidence. These two are the result of nurturing the shared values, shared efforts, and mutual trust over a period of time. Refer to Figure 17.4.

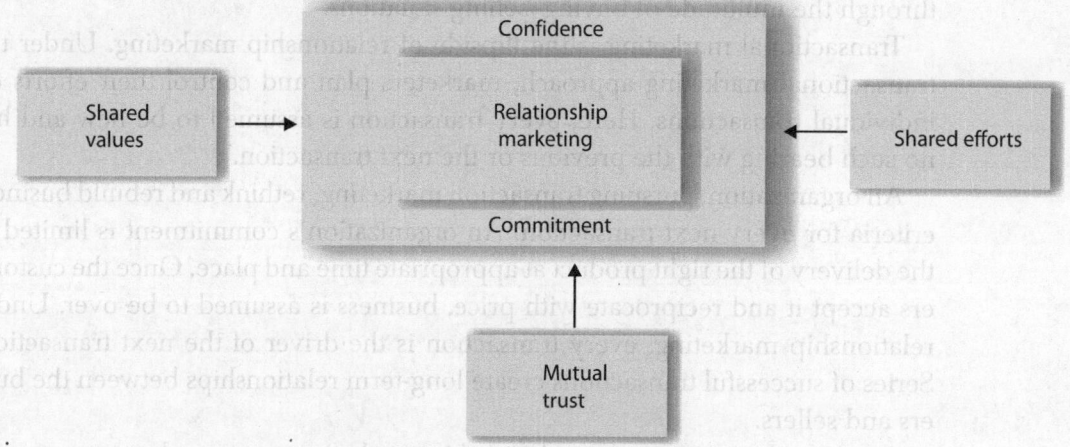

Figure 17.4 Relationship marketing

Hallmark Card Inc. (founded in 1910) has become the epitome of success in the personal expression industry. For 100 years, Hallmark cards have turned into connecting links for sharing good wishes, courtesy, love, affection, respect, and many more expressional dispositions. Mohamed and Sagadevan (2002) noted that the company has more than 40,000 products being sold through nearly 45,600 outlets.

Moreover, these products are manufactured in more than thirty languages and distributed over more than hundred countries. The company has created history behind making its name almost generic in greeting cards. Besides cards, it manufactures calendars, gift wraps, albums, stickers, party goods, Christmas ornaments, and many such valued products. The reasons for success are continuous creativity and innovation in its products, nurturing customer values, and also caring and sensible employees who are passionate enough to respect the sentiments of the people.

Hallmark is a strong case of integrating company, customers (both internal and external), distributors, etc. and regrouping its efforts to leverage a plethora of data generated at the point of sales, analyse it, and capitalize it for competitive advantage. The company helps people to unite in the spirit of love and respect for each other. It mediates very esthetically in the exchange of expressions among people. Hallmark focuses on customer-specific culture and continuously tracks information on it. It has vast customer information database and instructs every sales point to send more information on customers. The information generating efforts of the company has made it closer to the customers. Indeed customer orientation buzzes around the company, its products and its mission to spread feel-good relationship among expression sharing people.

SUMMARY

Competitive business environment needs strategic orientation in selling to confront marketing challenges. Strategic orientation in selling is a deliberate and sustained attempt of the firm to develop strategic plans to find an admirable position in the market by outwitting competition. A multi-product firm should have strategic plans for each business unit (strategic business unit or SBU). SBU is built around a group of similar products. A strategy is a result of a business plan which is also the framework to guide the organization's action.

A strategic plan in selling needs quick understanding of the marketing environment, analysis of strengths and weaknesses of a firm, and its competitors and characteristics of target market. Strategic plan brings closer selling and marketing by injecting the philosophy of marketing in selling.

Executing strategic sales plan are futile if activities that it porpoises are not coordinated effectively. They provide a blueprint for selling actions.

Strategic sales plan is the process of emanating and maintaining a viable fit between an organization's goals and its resource capabilities given in a particular marketing opportunity. Sales strategy varies across types of market competition. An effective sales strategy must emphasize on building strong customer relationships. Sales strategy should recommend right distribution channels to implement it as well. Indeed, sales and distribution are intertwined. Sales strategy cannot ignore social responsibility issues. Sales managers should add social responsibility issues within their strategic plans.

KEY TERMS

Cost Leadership   Cost leadership is a position where a firm is able to be a low-cost manufacturer where other firms within its industry are unable to do so.

Direct Selling   Direct selling involves selling the products directly to the customers where one-on-one interaction with the prospective customer is the key to achieve success.

Relationship Marketing   Relationship marketing is the cornerstone of customer orientation in today's marketing environment. It is a philosophy of marketers to visualize the buying–selling relationship as a focal point of business transaction.

Strategic Planning Strategic planning is the process of developing and maintaining a strategic coherence between the organization's goals and capabilities, and its changing marketing opportunities.

80:20 Principle 80:20 principle signifies that 20 per cent of all customer account for 80 per cent of the sales.

CONCEPT REVIEW QUESTIONS

1. What is the importance of sales strategy?
2. Explain the importance of 'SBU' in effective strategic sales plan.
3. Why is environmental analysis important before formulating sales strategy?
4. Examine the nature of competition that affect strategic sales plan.
5. Why is customer relationship included in strategic sales management?
6. Sales and distribution functions complement each other for sound sales performance. Justify.
7. Social responsibility is an important consideration in strategic sales management. Examine.

CRITICAL REVIEW QUESTIONS

1. In today's competitive market scenario, a firm should not distinguish between sales and marketing strategies, i.e., formulate sales strategies that do not have marketing elements and marketing strategies that do not have sales elements. Justify.
2. Corporate social responsibility of a firm raises tremendous storm in the cup of strategic sales management in today's business climate. Strategic sales management should intelligently induct it in its mission statements. Elucidate.

PROJECT ASSIGNMENTS

1. Consider three multinational firms operating in India and study their strategic business units and respective marketing mix elements. Portray the strategic issues of one unit of each firm. Meet sales managers of (i) Travel and tourism company and (ii) Transportation company. Collect information on their service attributes, consumer perceptions of their service qualities, and logistical considerations. Give a brief sketch of their strategic pursuits from sales and marketing strategic standpoints

REFERENCES

Aswathappa, K. (2007), *Essentials of Business Environment,* Himalaya Publishing House, Mumbai.

Bolo, B. (2008), *Cover Story,* 4Ps, 29 August–11September, pp. 80–81.

Dalrymple, D.J., and L.J. Parsons (1990), *Marketing Management: Strategy and Cases,* 5th ed., John Wiley & Sons, New York.

Drucker, P.F. (1954), 'Management by Objectives (MBO)', *The Practice of Management,* Harper & Row, New York.

Johnson, E.M., D.L. Kurtz, and E.E. Scheuing (1994), *Sales Management: Concepts, Practices and Cases,* McGraw-Hill Inc., New York.

Kotler, P., and G. Armstrong (2006), *Principles of Marketing,* Prentice-Hall of India Private Limited, New Delhi.

Koudri, J. (2004), 'Business Strategy—A Guide to Effective Decision-making', *The Economist* in association with Profile Books Ltd, London.

Kumar, S.R. (2002), *Managing Indian Brands: Marketing Concepts and Strategies*, Vikas Publishing House Pvt. Ltd, New Delhi.

Kurtz, D.L., and L.E. Boone (2009), *Principles of Marketing*, 12th ed., South-Western Cengage Learning, Australia.

Mehta, S.C. (1980), *Marketing: Environment, Concepts and Cases,* Tata McGraw-Hill Publishing Company Limited, New Delhi.

Mohamed, H.P., and A. Sagadevan (2002), *Customer Relationship Management: A Step-by-Step Approach,* Vikas Publishing House Pvt. Ltd, New Delhi.

Ramaswamy, V.S., and S. Namakumari (2003), *Marketing Management, Planning, Implementation and Control,* 3rd ed., Macmillan India Limited, Delhi.

Saxena, R. (1997), *Marketing Management,* Tata McGraw-Hill Publishing Company Limited, New Delhi.

Walker, Jr, O.C., J.W. Mullins, H.W. Boyd, Jr, and J.C. Larreche (2006), *Marketing Strategy, A Decision-focused Approach,* Tata McGraw-Hill Publishing Company Limited, New Delhi.

CASE STUDY

Strategic Selling at Its Best

Ramesh Talwar has been working as a sales executive in a medium-sized automobile components manufacturing company, named Trans Equipments Ltd for the last ten years. The company manufactures gaskets, pedal pads, etc. for four wheelers. Recently it has started manufacturing wind shield wiper assemblers. The company mainly works with large car dealers and caters to replacement markets in the automobile parts and components.

Ramesh, being an experienced sales executive, is given the charge of developing the business of wiper assemblers. He has already earned the trust and confidence of his boss. He has good communication skills and a persuasive capacity to bring in favour even the hard-nut-to-crack prospective buyers. Ramesh's ability to develop a tryst with prospective buyers can be understood from the following conversation of Ramesh with a senior purchase manager of Avian Car Distributors located in New Delhi. The conversation has been secretly tape recorded by Ramesh in order to train the new joinees about how to persuade a prospective buyer in a new product selling situation. Here, an excerpt of the interaction is presented.

Ramesh: Good morning, Sir. My name is Ramesh Talwar. I am the senior executive of Trans Equipments Ltd (handing a business card to senior purchase manager (SPM) of Avian Car Distributors). We have been in the business of automobile components for the last fifteen years. Presently, we are manufacturing wind shield wiper assemblers and I would like to show a sample to you.

(Contd)

SPM: But … currently we are buying this from another supplier who has been consistently delivering it to us. Moreover, the quality and reliability of the products are excellent.

Ramesh: I know your company has a reputation to carry out business with trusted suppliers. Therefore, I am not here to sell our products but to introduce it in the automobile industries. If you will give some time, I would like to tell you how our product is somewhat different from others.

SPM: How is it?

Ramesh: Principally, our product is more light and sleek than others because it is made of reinforced fibre unlike the light metals that are used by others. Moreover, you will get smoother operation and durability in our product. (Intelligently, he hands a piece of product to SPM.)

SPM: Are you are expecting us to change our supplier? That is not possible. Moreover, it is troublesome to change suppliers.

Ramesh: Sir, I am not requesting you to change. But our product needs some acquaintances in the industry and that is why I am here. Second, where will I get a bigger platform like here to introduce my product? I am, in fact, looking for an opportunity for demonstrating my product to you.

SPM: It is not possible now. I have an urgent meeting to attend now …

Ramesh: Well Sir, if it is not possible right now, I would like to try introducing our product some other time, when you have the time.

SPM: See, a demonstration is not possible now. But tell me, what are the additional benefits that your product would be able to generate?

Ramesh: Our product is unique in the sense that its parts are easily detachable. Therefore, there are no such maintenance hazards. Second, due to lighter weight and fibre body, you will get zero sound operation. Third, its resilience is high and its hardness is comparable to that of the metallic body. Fourthly, it has extremely high-weather resistance. Fifth, we offer two years replacement warranty in case you find any difficulties.

SPM: Are you so sure of it?

Ramesh: All our products are standardized as per the ISI specifications. Moreover, these are all tested and approved both by our own R&D department and external research agencies. I can show you the test reports on it.

SPM: Why are you not directly selling your products to the car manufacturers?

(Contd)

Ramesh: I appreciate your question. In fact, in future we have plans to do so. But currently, we are not looking into meeting the demands of the car manufacturers. In future, we plan to cater both to the new and replacement markets.

SPM: But, I hope you know that our company has huge demands for these? Will you be able to supply?

Ramesh: Yes of course, Sir! We will definitely try our best. Will you please communicate your requirements?

SPM: Approximately ten thousands wipers monthly.

Ramesh: Please be assured that we can make it. Our monthly production targets are about fifty thousand pieces.

SPM: OK, let me talk to our MD about your proposal.

Ramesh: Thank you, Sir. It is really nice of you. For your convenience, may I leave two pieces of wipers at your disposal?

SPM: Okay.

Ramesh: Please check its fitness with the cars. If you have any difficulty please give me a call. I will come as soon as possible to look into the matter.

SPM: I will send you our views soon. But, you keep in mind our monthly targets.

Ramesh: Thank you, Sir.

Discussion Questions

1. From the above interaction, can you identify the points of strategic manoeuvrings, where Ramesh has dealt successfully?
2. What specific sales strategy on the whole, has Ramesh played as a trump card to lubricate the tough stand of the senior purchase manager?

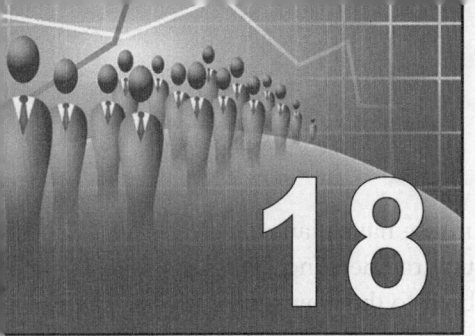

18 Modern Selling Approaches

18.1 DYNAMICS OF SELLING—TRACING ITS TRADITIONAL ROOTS

Selling has been regarded as an important business activity since the traditional age till date. In fact, since time immemorial, selling has been regarded as being integral to business and has become an indispensable aid to the growth and survival of business organizations. It is treated as an engine of the organization that cycles it through both static and turbulent times.

The practice of selling is always dynamic. Selling in the primitive age (around 10,000 BC) wrested on the exchange and transaction (mainly barter system) of agricultural and handicraft products. With the inception of the monetary system, barter system was gradually replaced. Selling has been undergoing changes with time as forces defining dynamics of business environment propels it to change. One such force was the industrial revolution. The Industrial revolution sparked radical changes in business ushering in mass production, distribution of products, and new ways of doing production, communication, transportation, etc. To facilitate delivery of goods, producers hired intermediaries from whom buyers could purchase goods from the nearest locations. Traders peddled through streets and lanes to sell commodities to the customers. But what was noticeable in business was its concentration in the hands of a few producers who did not give much opportunity to the buyers to opt for alternatives or bargain on business terms and conditions. A few sellers ran monopoly to rule over naïve buyers emanating in the sellers' markets. In fact, this was the reality of the business environment in the pre-industrial revolution stage.

But the industrial revolution opened the doors of competition as many producers began to pour in with production of the same or similar commodities and buyers found scope to voice their interests or disinterests in the selection of goods and negotiate on pricing and other terms. Suddenly, the business economy transformed from the sellers' markets to the buyers' markets and this emerged markedly, particularly during the pre-Second World War regime. These buyers' markets initiated the need for sales orientation in the organizations. It viewed that the customers would not show any responsive buying behaviour to collect goods from the markets without high-pressure selling efforts and aggressive promotions from the organization. It forced traders to bend from their terms and conditions in the fear of getting lost in the competition. Gradually, the focus of the customers got shifted to quality and performance of the products. They began to adore the innovative features of the products.

The discerning and discretionary attitudes of customers led to the emergence of selling concepts which held the view that organizations would require to do aggressive promotions and have persuasive skills to draw customers to their folds. Thus, the selling concept was based on the premise that customers will not buy products or services (particularly of unsought nature) even in small quantities unless they are persuaded to do so. In some situations, the salespeople used to put in aggressive promotional efforts to coax customers to buy. The concept further believed in the fact that customers are sensitive to their buying decisions and cannot be tempted into buying until and unless they find something unique in the product or benefit promises in the products and/or services. This has happened because buyers are of the view that only quality products and services can uphold their quality of living standards.

However, the concept was geared towards increasing the sales revenues and earning profits rather than meeting customer demands. Companies used to manufacture those products that could be sold but did not pay attention to satisfy customer needs or satisfaction. But with the rise in the number of business firms and concomitant competition, manufacturers understood the market realities and leaned towards producing those goods that could satisfy customers. In fact, the attitudinal changes of business firms took place after the World War II when rejuvenation of the industrial world took place.

Manufacturers, gradually, sensed that without understanding the needs and expectations of the customers, products could not be manufactured and sold profitably. This had been further stimulated by the soaring discretionary income of customers and freedom for customers to choose or reject the goods. This led to the emergence of the marketing concept which replaced the 'produce and sell' approach of business and aroused the need for marketing research, product design and development, proper distribution and promotion of products, setting prices commensurate with values the products bear, and the need for long-term relationships with the customers. Customer satisfaction becomes the only way to ensure profit earning of the firms.

So, selling since its inception has been witnessing diversity in markets, customers, competition, demands, buying practices, and needs transformation in its way of functioning. It appears to be a never-ending process as changes are incessant in the business environment. So, what is assumed to be an updated selling practice today will soon become traditional. In fact, forces that enable changes in the selling practices are highly pervasive and influencing, and therefore a continuous tracking of its transformation is crucial to businessmen, marketing professionals, and academicians in the relevant field.

18.2   FORCES OF ORIENTATION—TRADITIONAL TO MODERN SELLING

Modern selling is an imperative under turbulent business environments. In fact, the impulse of globalization that have swept the socio-economic architecture of the globe has necessitated the shift from traditional to modern selling both in home and in the international markets. This is mandatory in view of the integration of economies and societies triggering divergent consumer preferences, varied-business opportunities and threats, and atypical geopolitical conditions. Furthermore, digital revolution and internationalization of business are two gigantic forces that have compelled organizations to morph from traditional to modern selling. Some of these orientations that act as catalytic forces behind transition from traditional to modern selling are discussed as follows:

Marketing Orientation

Anticipating customer needs and demands, and fulfilling them to the best of their ability is the crux of marketing orientation. Simultaneously, an organization's interest of meeting the sales and profit objectives follow in no uncertain terms. To begin with marketing, a company must constantly watch changes both in the micro and macro environmental forces such as customers, competitors, suppliers, public, marketing intermediaries, etc. (collectively termed as micro-environmental forces) and physical, economic, technological, social, cultural, legal environments influencing the organization (collectively termed as macro-environmental forces). In fact, analysing the marketing opportunity amidst these forces is the starting point of modern marketing.

In the marketing parlance, the following three things are important and should be kept in mind:

First, the objective is to find gaps or niches in the marketplace where the products can be profitably positioned.

Second, identifying market segments and target customers within the segments is essential to reach the marketing goals and objectives. A two-wheeler manufacturer must understand the needs and demands of women and men bikers, i.e., market segments and design sleek, small, self-start, gearless bikes for women bikers and somewhat heavy, powerful, two/four stroke bikes for adult male segments.

Third, informative advertising, product differentiation (i.e., introducing specific features and benefits that competing products do not have), brand positioning (i.e., creating a psychological aura surrounding the product that helps it to occupy a position in the psyches of the customers), competitive pricing, and selective distribution of a company's products are important strategic devices that foster modern marketing.

LG's effort to create an emotive connection between technology and customers (the ad integrates the idea of the golden eye and the digitally yours slogan) definitely lends a strong mileage in brand association and enviable sales turnover of LG's televisions testify it. So, the success undoubtedly can be attributed to meaningful product differentiation and brand positioning. Exhibit 18.1 presents the differentiation story of Spencer's, the flagship brand of RPG Group.

Exhibit 18.1   Spencer's—a symbol of innovative retailing

Spencer's, one of the largest retail malls in India, decided to offer food and bakery services to the customers by the extension of its retail services and provide retailtainment (retail + entertainment). In fact, the company planned to create a food court in each of their large format stores.

Spencer's effort of how to cater refreshments coupled with the delight to customers along with professional retail services is commendable and quite differentiable.

Source: Chabra (2008), 'So, Are You a Foodie?', *4Ps*, vol. III (9), pp. 18, 12–13 October.

Customer Orientation

Modern selling sustains on customer orientation. It implies envisaging the business from the perspectives of the customers. Customers are treated as the nerve centre of the organization. Every organizational activity, function, and operation gears towards customer welfare. Modern selling believes that profit consequences will be automatic if the needs and aspirations of the customers are met satisfactorily.

In today's business environment, customers are quite accessible to both the domestic and international brands. So, as the choices to customers are wide and open, they can show more discerning behaviour in the product or service selection. Customers can dare to be choosy. As a result, sellers need to understand the pace and complexity of the buying behaviour in a more intelligent and pragmatic way. For example, the tendency of the customer to buy liquid mosquito repellent instead of mats or coils should moderate the critical thinking process in the minds of mosquito repellent manufacturers.

Modern selling also stresses more on concept selling in comparison to earlier selling processes. For example, the concepts of value for money (Wheel detergent) or all features in one (Colgate Total) are successfully entrenched in the minds of the customers by the manufacturers before they have pushed in the products. Exhibit 18.2 gives a vivid description of how a distinguished company such as Tata has made a delicate strategic makeover to win the hearts of young generation by its 'Jaago Re' campaign. Needless to mention, youth is a large population segment as well as customer group of products or services in India.

Exhibit 18.2   A spirited call to the young generation

Tata, as a brand, has occupied a remarkably successful niche in the minds of the customers in the field of information technology to tea. The company is distinguished because the brands have a global outlook but is capable of meeting local demands as well. The company knows that its brand value is constantly changing with time and is accustomed to take significant measures to brand value augmentation keeping track with the future market situations.

The company, furthermore, has understood that young generations are the heartthrobs of the society. Establishing a mental association with young generation is not only important for the expansion of business but also would be consistent with the patriotic image of it. Somehow, the company was of the perception during 1990s that it needs to get closer to the youths. Since then, to win the minds of the youths, it has started the 'Jaago Re' campaign. Second, it has floated Tata crucible quizzes and Tata jagriti yatra youth programme.

So, what is clear from the above write-up is that the vibes of young Indians have penetrated the social infrastructure of the nation. It has further changed the behavioural trends that had been reflected in buying and consuming products and services. Tata has risen to the task to listen them.

Source: Radhakrisnan, S. (2010), 'OK Tata, Brand Equity', *The Economic Times*, 25 August.

Marketing Mix Orientation

Modern selling thrives on judicious combinations of the marketing mix composition that has been proliferated from traditional 4Ps (product, price, place, and price) to include packaging, physical environment, product positioning, people, process, probe (it signifies marketing research), and more. From the effort to extend marketing mix, it is clear that the service component of marketing, once a neglected arena, is being given major thrust. Kotler (2003) rightly pointed out that the 4Ps are too simplistic to cover the needs and satisfactions of the customers and referred to Lauterborn (1990) to mention the importance of the 4Cs that include customer cost, customer solution, customer convenience, and communication. Modern selling, therefore, revolves more around improving service quality to enhance customer base and loyalty and become better as compared to competitors.

Parasuraman et al. (1988) viewed that service quality has turned out to be a key management issue and central to competitiveness. From the perspective of sales management, technical quality of service is very important. It speaks about accuracy in meeting product specifications from physical, morphological or chemical standpoints as it depends on the nature of the product. So, practitioners of modern selling must transgress from the conventional marketing mix and train them to learn the marketing skill in the light of customer experience and satisfaction.

The following exhibit 18.3 shows how the Essar group has come forward to institutionalize the customer experience management.

Exhibit 18.3   Aegis—a venture with a broad mission

Aegis, a BPO of the Essar Group has ventured out to open an institute of customer experience management to educate company executives about the limitations of right customer management skills. In this effort, The Indian Institute of Management, Indore has joined hands with Aegis. The objective of the training programme is to make business more customer-lifecycle oriented with less emphasis on its transaction orientation. The inherent philosophy is to lay stress on counseling students to aim at servicing a customer through his lifecycle rather than transacting a product or service. Here, the 3Cs that were taught to students were customer centrality, customer experience, and customer lifetime value. Students would also be getting evaluated based on the aptitudes on it too.

Source: Kar, S.(2010), 'Filling the Service Demand Gap, the Strategist', *Business Standard*, Kolkata, 23 August, p. 3.

Global Orientation

The era of globalization has made significant inroads in the ideology of the modern selling approach. It goes without saying that globalization has ushered in the opening of an economy of a nation and integrating it with the global economy. So, it has pushed the global business environment and spurred a revisit in the contemporary selling approaches. Global business milieu has initiated an integral marketing culture transcending from nation to nation. This has been quite evidenced by the phenomena of media explosion, e-commerce, e-marketing, e-bay (person-to-person online trading), web conferencing with customers, BPO (business process outsourcing), virtual marketing, etc.

Indeed IT revolution has brought plenty of options to buyers and sellers to interact without personal contacts as well. Modern selling just anchors upon the IT surges to reach millions of customers at the shortest possible time and promises quick delivery of products, receiving customer complaints, servicing customers at the earliest, and online monetary transactions. A company today can establish its business network in an alien nation without setting any manufacturing unit there. Again, it has a number of options such as licensing, direct selling, franchising, joint ventures, setting up BPO units, etc. to undergo global operations. For example, Coca Cola has expanded its operations globally by connecting it with bottling plants through licensing arrangements.

On the other hand, NIIT, McDonald's, etc. have franchising operations to mop up global operations. Companies such as Avon, Amway, Oriflame, etc. pursue direct selling, a major type of non-store retailing, to reach to the customers directly with their products. Nike, the noted multinational company, has outsourced its business operations by getting its products manufactured by independent sub-contractors situated in different corners of the world without compromising with quality, specifications, and the marketing acumen of its products (Cherunilam 2008). Hero Cycles Ltd and Honda, too, have forged a joint venture to establish a third organization to manufacture and market two wheelers. This venture has achieved commendable success in terms of market dominance and customer loyalty.

Environmental Orientation

Environment has never impacted the organization in a way unlike the same in the present day. Therefore, environment is a huge concern for modern selling. The earlier external environment was a major thrust area in governing business strategies. Now internal environment is given much importance along with the external one to lay down business plans and strategies. In fact, a company's business environment confronts both the internal and external forces to influence its ability to run in a desired way. Figure 18.1 shows the components of internal and external forces affecting a company's business. External forces are classified into macro- and micro-environmental forces.

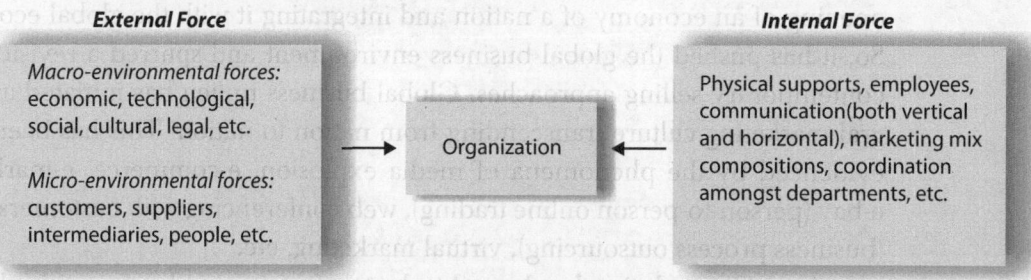

External Force

Macro-environmental forces: economic, technological, social, cultural, legal, etc.

Micro-environmental forces: customers, suppliers, intermediaries, people, etc.

Organization

Internal Force

Physical supports, employees, communication(both vertical and horizontal), marketing mix compositions, coordination amongst departments, etc.

Figure 18.1 Components of internal and external forces

So, one can say that environmental analysis is a pre-requisite for modern selling. By investigating the demand and supply situations in the market, competition, the buying power of customers, technology used in manufacturing and distribution of products, social and cultural contexts of people such as languages, customs, traditions, taboos, ethos, etc. the laws and regulations of the government in one hand (macro-level studies) and researching the market segments, target markets, availability of suppliers, distributors, people's views on the company (micro-level studies) on the other hand, a company can understand the sales opportunities, anticipate future selling situations, and choose pre-emptive changes in the selling strategies.

Modern selling suggests that a company must adapt and accommodate with the changing business environment and exploit the sales opportunities to the best of a company's potential. For example, the upsurge of the rural markets in India in terms of increased standard of living and accession of the electronic media has led many organizations to find new business opportunities and guide its sales force to capitalize it effectively. At the same time, a company also studies its strengths and weaknesses by diagnosing its internal environment and enlightens its internal customers (employees) by developing appropriate HR policies.

Similarly, FMCG companies are gradually drifting towards sachet versions of the products, use of tetra packs, etc. to reach the consumers satisfactorily. Such changes are made possible by investigating market trends, the purchasing power of common consumers, and the product trial mentality of many consumers. Again consumers are showing affinity to herbal products, credit cards, designer dresses, tourism products, etc. and presenting mammoth opportunities to the firms to design and sell those products to target consumers.

Managerial Orientation

As sales occupy a major part of marketing, sales management commands a major part of marketing management. By sales management, precisely we understand

(i) how to manage personal selling jobs,

(ii) how to manage sales force.

The first part (i) can be effective if the second part (ii) is well-planned, organized, and executed effectively. So, the thrusts of sales management are in the following:

(i) Planning HR policies for sales and marketing department that are capable of achieving sales and marketing objectives

(ii) Setting up the organizational structure and procedures to implement plans

(iii) Recruiting and selecting the sales force who are able to meet the standards set in the job specifications and perform duties and responsibilities mentioned in the job descriptions

(iv) Training and developing sales force so that it can resolutely perform according to the organization's plans and objectives

(v) Motivating sales force to instil encouragement and confidence where both financial and non-financial incentives can be utilized judiciously

(vi) Evaluating the sales force to monitor its activities

(vii) Controlling its activities whenever discrepancies in its activities from the expected course of actions are noticed

Modern sales management does not differ significantly from the traditional one but certain developments are genuinely sought for. In modern selling, sales plans and policies are not only geared towards fulfilling the sales goals and objectives but also customer retention and relationship developments for the long-term interest of the company. Salespeople are managed in this direction. For some products (e.g., electrical appliances), salespeople are instructed to do value-added selling where customers can easily understand how much benefits they can accrue from the purchase against how much costs they can save.

Moreover, modern selling demands salespeople to work as a team who can provide complete solutions to the customers' problems. So, team-based selling is getting prominence in sales organization. Sales managers in present-day selling also participate with salespeople in personal selling jobs, particularly, for selling high-unit value items (e.g., computerized weighing machine) or dealing with major customers. Job analysis in modern day is not restricted just to profiling duties and responsibilities of the salespeople. The competencies, skills, knowledge, and behaviour of salespeople, too, are given significant emphasis. Managers feel that the right selection of sales force can automatically ensure the fulfilment of expected sales performance. Dessler (2007) rightly referred to the need for competency-based job analysis that involves describing the jobs in terms of measurable and observable behavioural competencies. Again, performance management takes a major role in evaluating and controlling the sales force.

Traditional selling was more keen on measuring the sales performance rather than its management. Today, salespeople are given scope for self-performance measurement. In fact, peer-performance review, subordinate-performance review, in addition to superior performance appraisal (360° appraisal) are followed by many firms. Significant improvements in training and development have also taken place. Computerized training, web-based training, video conferencing with trainees, simulated training, etc. are some of the modern techniques of training that are being adopted by the companies. Therefore, reengineering (radical change in managing sales force with rethinking and revisiting the present practices) brings in significant changes in sales management practices in view of the emergence of modern methods of managing the sales force.

Table 18.1 Difference between transactional and relationship selling

Transactional selling	Relationship selling
Thrust is on single transaction	Thrust is on serving customers through endless transactions
Quick order taking and fulfilling	Creating an environment of mutual trust and respect to facilitating order placing from customers and fulfilling it from the sellers side according to the agreed upon terms and conditions.
Profit earning without giving no or limited attention to the problems of the customers	Creating a win-win situation for the buyer and the seller
The sellers value addition in terms of profit earned is the sole motto	Sharing values optimally from the business by both the buyer and the seller. The buyer's value is related to deriving expected benefits from the product at an acceptable cost and the seller's value is related to generating customer satisfaction at a desired profit
Emphasis is on profit maximization	Emphasis is continuing the business with buyers profitably
It focuses on profit earning by maximizing the sales volume	It focuses on understanding the customer needs and demands both in quality and quantity, and deals it properly. If these are properly attended, profit generation would not be a problem
Lacks strategic foresight and therefore losing customers is a common phenomenon	Backed with well-knit strategic sales plans and therefore customer retention is easy. Overcoming competition is not a problem.

Customer Relationship Orientation

Under traditional selling, relationship selling believes in long-term connection with customers which is based on mutual trust, co-operation, and understanding. This is completely unlike the transaction-selling approach. Transactional selling, basically, aimed at persuading target customers to take part in the buying situations and salespeople who are more interested in bringing the customers to their side and closing the sales as soon as possible. Under relationship selling, salespeople act proactively to understand the needs of the customers and try earnestly to solve their problems by suggesting the right product/service. Moreover, they take additional interest in the installation of products in the premises of the customers, educate customers in product usage and applications, solve post-sales problems such as repair and maintenance, difficulties in repeat purchase, etc. Table 18.1 presents a comparative review of the transactional and relationship selling.

Entrepreneurship Orientation

It has been seen that modern selling thrives more in entrepreneurial business environment. An entrepreneurship orientation is typified by

(i) risk-taking propensity,

(ii) innovativeness,

(iii) ability to explore business opportunity,

(iv) achievement motivation,

(v) ability to face risk and uncertainty,

(vi) futuristic,

(vii) interpersonal skill,

(viii) hunger to get prompt feedback, and

(ix) team building.

A sales manager needs to possess the above-mentioned qualities to manage salespeople successfully in the present-day business environment where opportunities and threats exists in an intertwined manner. A sales manger must be able to detect signals of the two at an earliest before threats loom large and opportunities get exploited by the competitors. Moreover, he should have a vast capacity to coordinate resources—material, money, human resource, allocate it to capitalize the sales opportunities before competitors and, fructify sales plans. A sales manager like an entrepreneur can gauze future plans, respond to changes in business environment and bear risk in advancing the organization economically. So, sales managers are expected to uphold the spirit of entrepreneurship in modern selling whatever the circumstances they confront.

18.3 E-COMMERCE—A DIGITAL ROUTE TO CONTEMPORARY PERSONAL SELLING

E-commerce is a branch of e-business. E-business is an electronic means of conducting a company's business. E-business entails creating the right electronic platform (environment) to contact prospective customers, cognize them about the company's history and mission, past and present business performance, future plans for extension of business as well as business plans that are ought to be known to them. It gives an elaborate picture of the products or services available, their benefits to the customers, buying procedures, service availabilities, ways of payments, etc. E-business finds use of electronic means such as intranets (networking that connects employees–employees and employees–employer within a company), extranets (networking company and its suppliers, distributors, and other stakeholders outside) and internet. Internet is a pervasive computer network connecting every user to other through the World Wide Web (WWW), shortly termed as the Web. It is a way of accessing the internet. Internet is a strong interactive multimedia tool whereby people can work with user supportive web pages and addresses. Shurtey (2000) cited that e-business involves using the internet technology to transform the way the key business processes are performed.

E-commerce first came into the business scene in the late 1970s with the facilitation of commercial transaction resting on EDI (electronic data interchange) and electronic data transfer (EDF) technologies. Later on (1980s), introduction of ATMs (automated teller machines), telephone banking, and use of credit cards were further developments of e-commerce. E-commerce operation thrives under well-built, maintained and updated customers, and other databases including suppliers, intermediaries, etc. and timely and accurate analysis, synthesis and retrieval of the processed data for the purpose of interacting, transacting and establishing relationships with them In fact, the emergence of data mining and data ware housing in the 1990s was a significant step to bolster e-commerce operation.

Data mining and data warehousing are technological developments of e-commerce to smoothly and efficiently perform customer relationship management (CRM) practices. CRM makes use of sophisticated software and analytical tools to ease buyer–seller interactions and exchanges. Data mining and data warehousing are techniques to manage voluminous data relating to business process and transaction. Data mining helps in extracting useful data and information from the vast computer network. Data warehousing involves preparing detailed, comprehensive, organized, integrated, and easily accessible databases on customers, suppliers, distributors, production centres, inventories, etc. From CRM perspective, data mining and data warehousing are two important aids to use customer-related information and respond to customer queries. Quick retrieval of the needed information to disseminate the right information and get feedback from the customers is just a matter of mouse click, today. So CRM gets huge benefits from these two.

E-commerce also relates to the transaction part of e-business, where the company sells its products or services using web-based platforms. It uses internet as a technology to make rapid response to customer demands. Thus, it executes the selling and facilitates payments for all items purchased from the customers using electronic means.

Kotler and Armstrong (2006) defined e-commerce as the buying and selling processes supported by electronic means, primarily the internet.

Evans and Berman (2010) defined e-commerce as revenue generating internet transactions.

Keegan (2002) defined e-commerce as selling goods and services over the Internet, both business-to-consumer (B2C), consumer-to-consumer (C2C), and business–to-business (B2B).

Nayyar (2003) defined e-commerce as the production, advertising, sales, delivery, and payment realization for products and services via telecommunication network.

So, e-commerce involves buying and selling of products or services using electronic systems and internet as a principal communication tool. In fact, e-commerce uses internet as technology to enable customers, both present and prospective to

(i) consult company websites,

(ii) choose right products or services that are promoted in those websites,

(iii) interact and exchange information with the company using online platforms such as video conferencing, web meeting, e-mailing or social networking sites,

(iv) selection of payment mode such as e-banking, credit cards, etc.

(v) settle terms with the company regarding the delivery of products or services and payment procedures,

(vi) acknowledge the receipt of goods and services to the marketers by sending an e-mail, and

(vii) e-mail your feedback after the use of the bought items.

The box 18.1 represents the application of e-commerce in the real estate business.

Box 18.1   E-commerce finds application in property selling

Application of e-commerce in realty is not uncommon today. Realtors and prospective buyers interact on e-commerce platforms with no need for face-to-face personal interactions. Banks, financial institutions use online auctions of properties that are on default in terms of long outstanding dues in loan repayment by customers and properties that are declared as non-performing assets (NPA). In fact, the problem had blown to disproportionate volumes during the meltdown of the economy in the recent past.

These properties are displayed on company websites along with documents and physical inspections which are arranged for the prospective customers. In case of auctioning of properties, the company trains new internet bidders and arranges bidding on a scheduled date and time. Today, e-selling of land, commercial properties and residential premises is getting popular. Moreover, quick access to property information, quick processing of property papers, electronic payments, chance of price recovery, transparent deals, etc. mark the merits of e-selling of properties.

Source: Mondal, A. (2010), 'Going…Going….Click', Times Property, *The Times of India*, 14 August.

Benefits of E-commerce

Following are the benefits of e-commerce:

1. Geographical distance between the buyer and seller is no more a problem with the introduction of e-commerce. Reaching a business firm or customer from

one continent to the other is just a click and portal exercise away. Companies doing business through websites or the brick and click companies can conduct business transactions on e-commerce with no physical or personal proximity to customers.

2. E-commerce is highly convenient to customers. Customers do not have to exhaust energy by physical movements. They can simply trek through company websites where detailed information on products or services is available. They can download order forms, fill in, and send them through fax. They can compare different company websites and make a choice of the product or service. They need not bear the monotony of long queuing in stores and face, buying hassles or drudgery from time wasting undue deliberations of salespeople. For example, prospective customers of airlines can compare airlines websites on flight schedules, fares, service facilities, refund policy for cancellation, etc. before buying tickets online.

3. E-commerce has opened up doors of globalized retailing (e.g., Amazon. com). Order placing, procuring, processing, and dispatching can be made in a customer-friendly manner.

4. E-commerce helps to reduce sales and distribution costs of the company. Today websites emulate the role of salespeople and companies can run their sales operations on a few or no salespeople. Companies are getting paperless as the stores can process, retrieve, and distribute information electronically. So, e-commerce is able to bring in huge transaction efficiency, negligible supervision, and controlling costs.

5. Because of the personalized and interactive nature of communication, companies can get quick feedback from the customers and make arrangements to sort out customer problems. It hastens quick interaction with suppliers, distributors, marketing researchers, insurers, legal consultants, production centres, besides customers.

Limitations of E-commerce

Following are the limitations of e-commerce:

1. Actual product demonstration and gathering hands-on-experience are not possible because of the physical inaccessibility.

2. It is acceptable to those who have knowledge on computer handling, internet operations, web browsing, e-mailing, electronic fund transfer, etc. Thus, it is not affordable for the poor or the illiterate customers and difficult for some who are not very comfortable working on computers.

3. E-commerce demands substantial initial investment. Developing data mining and data warehousing, CRM, e-marketing, opening up websites, preparing electronic catalogues and brochures, placing banner ads on portal sites, listing

in search engines, developing the right IT infrastructure involve huge start up and maintenance costs. Again, presenting multimedia messages by combining visuals, graphics, charts, tables, animations, videos, etc. is a technically complex job. The company needs technically proficient personnel. They are often a scarcity.

4. Fears on privacy issues haunt customers working on e-commerce. Unauthorized access to customers' computer systems or networks flaunting security mechanisms (called hacking), illegal downloading of customers' documents, forging of their credit card passwords, computer source codes, destroying their computer software by viruses, etc. are some real threats to customers.

5. Internet connectivity and downloading are problems due to slow operations of the systems which often confound customers to get immediate access to websites and work on it.

18.4 WEB-BASED SELLING—CONCEPTS AND APPLICATIONS

Web-based selling makes goods, services or ideas move across B2B (business to business), B2C (business to customer), C2C (customer to customer), and C2B (customer to business) efficiently at the click of a mouse. So, web-based selling needs application of e-commerce which, in turn, capitalizes the power of the internet, considered as a revolutionary development in the field of communication technology. It needs support from digitized resources such as data mining, data warehousing, digital signatures, mobile telecommunications, electronic data interchange (EDI), interactive voice recognition, etc.

Web-based selling is also known as online selling. B2B online selling takes place on trading networks, auction sites, barter sites, etc. Corporate customers consult corporate sellers to identify their goods or services, their features and benefits, and buying formalities. Under B2C e-commerce, customers visit company websites to take informed choices of products or services and buying decisions. Under C2C, customers can buy or exchange goods using popular retail websites or auction websites (e.g., Amazon.com, e-bay, etc.) Amazon.com has achieved mammoth success by capitalizing the power of the internet to sell its large spectrum of products such as books, music, consumer electronics, toys, videos, gifts, etc. by company websites and online auctions.

C2B is a platform by which customers take initiatives to contact business firms and send post-purchase feedback. For example, for booking and cancellation of hotel rooms, tour packages or music albums, customers contact respective sellers to buy these items. Ever-increasing popularity and spread of internet has made high penetration of web-based selling amongst customers. This has been further proliferated by the increasing interests and affordability of the customers towards buying computers with internet facilities. Increase in computer literacy and the ease of buying for customers without taking any trouble of physically attending stores or distribution outlets have also added to this ever-increasing popularity. Customers get the opportunity to directly interact with selling firms or speak to its call centres and gain information on the company's offers. A call centre is engaged as an official link or network of the company to send (called outbound calls)and receive calls (called inbound calls) of customers to handle customer inquiries, arrangements for the delivery of products or services, outsourcing operations, etc. across borderless geographies by the grace of internet on round the clock basis (24×7).

Contacting call centres, customers can get detailed product information, testimonials, information on additional or new product, and marketing intelligence. In fact business process outsourcing (BPO) units do identical jobs of call centres by handling customer relation management (CRM) services. BPOs or call centres demand technically equipped, and hard working workforce who should be internet savvy, ought to have strong soft skills, can work for extended time period, and interact with varieties of customers of different countries.

Web-based selling by the application of internet offers not only a high degree of personalized interaction but also meets individual needs and demands. Kourdi (2004) viewed that the internet has the ability to capture, store, and disseminate detailed information about customers and their preferences, and direct companies to take quick and practical decisions on it. It, thus, provides a high degree of business benefits to the firms in terms of transaction cost efficiency. It saves time and cost in delivering the products. It benefits customers in terms of lower product acquisition efforts and emotional gains from self-satisfaction for directly dealing with the companies and getting quick feedback on their enquiries. Thus, it reduces significantly the lead time for sales. Customers can choose what they want and the way they want by online or telephonic conversations. The company therefore is also benefited by reduced chance of rejection and return shipments.

Web-based selling helps companies to reach customers with loads of information at a speed quite comparable to the speed of light. Moreover, customers can concentrate only on the concerned information that is helpful to them. They can focus only on those offers which they are interested in. From a company's side, it can quickly spot business opportunities and track customers needs and wants. The Web also helps a company to cut costs. Zimmerer and Scarborough (2007) viewed that the Web can reduce costs in generating sales leads, providing customer support, and distributing marketing materials.

At times, complaints are labelled against web-based selling as human elements of personal selling lack in it. There is no scope for face-to-face interaction and thus, the method lacks personal touch. However, allowing customers to gather interactive experience by video conferencing or communicating through social networking sites, a personalized environment in selling can be created.

Social networking sites help both the customers and the organizations to share their information with others and also enable an individual-to-individual interaction at a personal level. Information on activities, interests, opinions, events, likings or disliking, etc. can be exchanged between business-to-business or business-to-customers by being connected with the online community.

Exhibit 18.4 displays a successful online business transaction in the business of image marketing.

Exhibit 18.4 Imagesbazzar.com—a revolution in image marketing

Imagesbazaar, the world's largest collection of creating images with Indian face has a reservoir of over nine lakh images and a client base of over seven thousand in more than forty-five countries. The images find application in advertising, marketing and publishing needs, and are used in brochures, catalogues, posters, stickers, multimedia, websites, advertisements, billboards, etc. The company also gives opportunity to the clients to search, purchase, and download images depending on their needs.

Source: 'Search, Buy & Download Indian Images', 4Ps, *Business and Marketing*, vol. V (20), 22 October–4 November 2010.

The exhibit above precisely indicates the need for designing an effective corporate website for promoting a company's products. More attractive the website, the more it can increase web traffic density and generate participation of customers in searching the variety of information of a particular company and its products. Online advertising plays an important role in information dissemination and persuasion as well. A user-friendly website with lesser number of instructions is an exciting medium for users who can view information with a little effort. For multi-page websites, sitemaps or search features should be clearly indicated to facilitate quicker navigation.

Companies are always searching for newer ways to design catchy web advertisements. Generally, online classified ads, online text ads, banner ads, social network advertising, e-mail advertising, etc. are getting popular in depicting suitable texts, visuals, graphics, animation, etc. Again the combination of two or three elements (e.g., text and visuals) intelligently can produce hotspot web advertising.

Cell phones have also opened the doors of interactive advertising that facilitate sending personalized messages to the recipients only to persuade them to reply with a feedback message. So, interactive advertising incites more of the two-way communication that is possible in cell phones, internet, telephone, etc. Exhibit 18.5 maps the development of mobile technology by a company who has already established itself within a short time.

Exhibit 18.5   Tata DoCoMo—honing technology to perfection

Tata DoCoMo, a joint venture between the Tata Group and the NIT DoCoMo is the first private operator to introduce the third generation mobile services. In fact, the 3G technology has brought in ultra-fast internet, video conferencing, mobile TV on the mobile screen. This has, therefore, ushered in a new vista for mobile advertising, mobile video, and mobile computing. Hayzlett (2010) pointed out that mobile advertising is worth watching with innovations in mobile devices and marketing. He also cited an estimate of some experts that forecasts $30 billion industry of mobile marketing in the next few years.

Source: 'Tata DoCoMo Announces Rates for 3G', Corporate, *The Economic Times*, 10 November 2010, p. 6.

Again, many companies opt for multi-channel distribution policies where web-based selling might be one such route. So, both online and offline marketing are followed by a company to distribute the same product to target customers. McDaniel et al. (2006) defined it as multiple distribution that involves a producer who chooses two or more channels to sell the same product to target markets. For example, Avon, a direct supplier of health and beauty products for women sells its products through multiple channels such as on the Web, directly from company to customers, from the company representatives to customers, and gives opportunities to customers to procure it from Avon Salon & Spa.

Online selling, therefore, unveils a new era of direct selling. Direct selling involves delivering the target customers without using intermediaries. More customized selling is possible through this approach. In this type, telemarketing is a popular method where a company performs planned and structured calls using telephones to customers, present and prospective, to perform pre-selling, selling, and post-selling (getting customer's feedback and arranging after-sales services). Pre-selling incites customers to take initiatives for inbound telemarketing where potential customers contact company either on toll free or paid telephone calls. Otherwise, the company makes outbound telemarketing where it contacts its customers to conduct selling jobs.

Home shopping is also a popular medium where the role of telecommunication media (such as internet, television, etc.) is prominent. Here, products or services are advertised in media and customers are requested to directly contact a company or its agents to deliver the products to customer homes or customers are requested to collect it from nearby sales points. Exhibit 18.6 presents how online transactions can give birth to the state of the art home shopping experience to customers.

Exhibit 18.6   Star CJ Alive—a stride to delightful home shopping

The joint venture between Star-Network India and South Korean home shopping company CJO Shopping, named Star CJ Alive, a 24-hours home shopping channel invites call for products through their call centres that are routed to the franchises who deliver. The specialty of these call centres is that they focus more on services for customers unlike other shopping networks. The IT system is used to connect franchises that assists channel to track order deliveries. Their logistics partner provides online tracking of deliveries.

Source: Kar, S. (2010), 'Shopper's Star', The Strategist, *Business Standard*, 6 September, p. 4.

18.5 SOCIAL MEDIA—A NEW VISTA TO MODERN SELLING

Social media as marketing channel is sprawling at an exponential rate. It spurns out enormous business space prodding on 'online community' where companies and customers actively participate in the 'buying–selling' process from their respective locations without shifting an inch. An effective social media helps the organization to share marketing intelligence with community members and persuade customers to respond quickly to its products or service with seconds to spare. Moreover spreading of real-time information from one user to the other via internet or word of mouth, a company can capitalize the efficacy of viral marketing (word-of-mouth communication with intensity). So, once a company is successful in social networking with the current customers, they automatically create new customers for the company and the community proliferates. A company can capitalize the community to encourage users to listen and interact amongst themselves where not only the customers but also, the business partners, suppliers, distributors, business professionals, management students or business enthusiasts engage in the community.

Indeed, the expansion of the number of users everyday sounds an alarm bell to the conventional media such as television, outdoor, etc. to add concern about the audience reach. The popular social media such as Facebook, Linkedin, Twitter, etc. have already created milestones in social networking. Facebook has more than 500 million users, Linkedin 75 million users, and Twitter, 65 million users, who send 65 million tweets each day (Hayzlett 2010). In fact applications of social media find variety of business opportunities. Social media are being effective for selling automobiles, FMCGs, entertainment products, wellness products, travel, etc. Brands such as Pepsi, MTV, General Motors, Blackberry, Ford Motors, and many others have made use of social media to reach target groups. Pepsi has developed four lakh fan bases on its Facebook alone. Ford Motor has decided to select Facebook to display the much popular next-gen explorer on Facebook. So, companies in large numbers are joining social media networking as a part of their marketing strategies. They list their products and services on social sites that can exploit e-commerce to run their shows.

Ticket Buddy, the online ticketing company has introduced a Facebook application that allows users to pre-book movie tickets without making any payment. Retailers such as clothing company (e.g., nine West) have been leveraging social networking that allows consumers to shop for clothing from virtual shelves.

So innovations are galore in online retailing and shopping. Traditional media are gradually taking backseats due to skyrocketing costs of applications. And non-traditional media such as mobile telephony, social networking, etc. are pivoting their positions. Cost of application is definitely a factor that has brewed mass excitation among firms, small or large to route some of their advertising expenses for non-traditional media. E-commerce finds channel in mobile telephony by the grace of 3G boom. Companies who have been associated with social networking sites are pursuing to develop fan bases and a large percentage of it can be transformed into customers by subtle uses of online advertising and user friendly e-commerce applications.

SUMMARY

Selling, as a concept, in general was based on the premise that customers would not buy products or services unless they are persuaded to buy it. Under, traditional selling traders peddling through streets and lanes to sell their commodities were the only type of sellers seen. But it underwent transformation as the seller's market left space to buyer's market as a result of creeping competition in the industry and buyers asked for quality products. The old concept was geared towards increasing sales revenue and earning profits rather than meeting customer demands. Modern selling holds the opposite view. It believes in understanding customer needs and demands, and how economically and effectively they can be reached with the products or services.

Again, the worldwide changes of the socio-economic environment as a result of globalization have forced organizations to adopt the modern selling approach. So, a change in the orientation of the traditional to modern selling is backed by orientations in market, customer, marketing mix, global business environment, customer relationship, and entrepreneurial ventures.

Digital revolution has also become a major driver of modern selling. E-business, e-commerce, digital revolution, social networking, etc. have entered to rejuvenate the practices of modern selling. E-business is the electronic means of conducting a company's business. E-commerce involves both buying and selling supported by electronic selling. Web-based selling, which is coming up in big way, needs application of e-commerce to perform selling through electronic medium. Social networking, encouraging person-to-person interaction through social websites has made deep inroads in modern selling.

KEY TERMS

Direct Selling   Direct selling involves delivering to the target customers without using intermediaries.

E-commerce   E-commerce involves buying and selling of products or services using electronic systems and internet as a principal communication tool.

Internet   Internet is a strong interactive multimedia tool whereby people can work with user supportive web pages and addresses.

Relationship Selling   Under relationship selling, salespeople act proactively to understand the customer needs and try earnestly to solve their problems by suggesting the right product/service offers.

Transactional Selling   Transactional selling basically aims at persuading target customers to take part in the buying situations and salespeople who are more interested in bringing customers to their side and closing the sales as soon as possible.

Web-based Selling   Web-based selling makes goods, services or ideas move across B2B (business to business), B2C (business to customer), C2C (customer to customer), and C2B (customer to business) efficiently at the click of the mouse.

CONCEPT REVIEW QUESTIONS

1. How is traditional selling different from modern selling?
2. What are the forces of orientation that influence modern selling? Explain at least two such forces.
3. Distinguish between transactional and relationship selling.
4. Define e-commerce. What changes has it brought in the business organization?
5. What are the benefits of e-commerce?
6. What are the limitations of e-commerce?
7. What is web-based selling? What are its uses?
8. How have web-based sellings improved selling practices in an organization?

CRITICAL REVIEW QUESTIONS

1. Web-based selling and e-commerce complement each other in modern selling. Do you agree? Justify.
2. Social networking has opened up a new vista in modern marketing. Analyse.
3. Online selling has made a serious dent on the so called selling profession. Argue.

PROJECT ASSIGNMENTS

1. Visit websites of one multinational FMCG and a consumer durable company that have online marketing channels in addition to conventional channels. Collect information on how products can be purchased using online channels.
2. Visit a company's websites that performs online auctioning of antiques. Collect information on how can the company be reached with a purpose to buy such products?

REFERENCES

Charba, P. (2010), 'Does Media Matter to Indian Businesses?', 4Ps, *Business & Marketing*, vol.V(21), 5 November–18 November, pp. 61–5.

Cherunilam, F. (2008), *International Business: Text and Cases*, 4th ed., (Revised), Prentice-Hall of India Private Limited, New Delhi.

Dessler, G. (2007), *Human Resource Management*, 10th ed., Prentice-Hall of India, New Delhi.

Evans, J.R., and B. Berman (2010), *Marketing 8e—Marketing in the 21st Century*, Biztantra, New Delhi.

Hayzlett, J. (2010), 'Where Will Marketers Put their Money in 2011?', 4Ps, *Business & Marketing*, vol. V(20), 22 October–4 November, p. 32.

Joshi, P., and S. Shinde (2010), 'Time for "Social" Shopping', Digital Consumer, *Business Standard*, 23 August, p. 11.

Keegan, W.J. (2002), *Global Marketing Management*, 7th ed., Prentice-Hall of India Private limited, New Delhi.

Kotler, P. (2003), *Marketing Management*, 11th ed., Pearson Education, Singapore.

Kotler, P., and G. Armstrong (2006), *Principles of Marketing*, 11th ed., Prentice-Hall of India Private Limited, New Delhi.

Kourdi, J. (2004), 'Business Strategy—A Guide to Effective Decision Making', *The Economist*, Profile Books Ltd, London.

Kulkarni, M.V. (2009), *Marketing Management*, 9th ed., Everest Publishing House, Pune.

Lauterborn, R. (1990), 'New Marketing Litany: 4P's Passe; C-Words Take Over', *Advertising Age*, 1 October, p.26.

McDaniel, C., C.W. Lamb, Jr, and J.F. Hair, Jr (2006), *Introduction to Marketing*, Thomson, South-Western, Australia.

Nayyar, S.K. (2003), 'Contract Management', *International Business and Contract Management*, Vrinda Publications (P) Ltd, Delhi.

Parasuraman, A., V. Zeithamal, and L.L. Berry (1988), 'A Multi-Item Scale for Measuring Customer Perception of Service Quality', *Journal of Retailing*, vol.64 (1), pp. 12–37.

Shurtey, S. (2000), *E-business with Net.Commerce*, Prentice-Hall PTR, New Jersey.

Zimmerer, T.W., and N.M. Scarborough (2007), *Essentials of Entrepreneurship and Small Business Management*, 4th ed., Pearson Prentice-Hall, New Delhi.

CASE STUDY

A Great Entrepreneur

Adi Venkatesh, founder and CEO of a five-year old Bengaluru-based Cyberspace Marketing Corporation also engaged in the marketing of the designer apparels, came up with the idea of integrating its company with a social shopping channel named 'My Shopping Cart'. This channel acts as an integrator between business houses and shoppers on line (B2C architecture). It also allows web space to each firm to encourage shoppers to navigate on the electronic brochures, catalogues, etc. on the array of its products. Through this, shoppers can spot out the selected items and book their orders without making any payments at the initial stage. Only on the receipt of orders that are dispatched by the company, do the shoppers pay the price.

Adi was in the business of selling designer dresses for men. He named his brand 'Smart'. He also contacted prospective shoppers using social media and established his boutiques in two metro cities, Bengaluru and Hyderabad. These collection centres for shoppers were called

(Contd)

(Contd)

the 'Smart Selection'. Adi involved one master tailor each to handle customer fitting oriented-problems and one delivery boy each to deliver the finished product. Figure A represents the distribution channel of Adi's company.

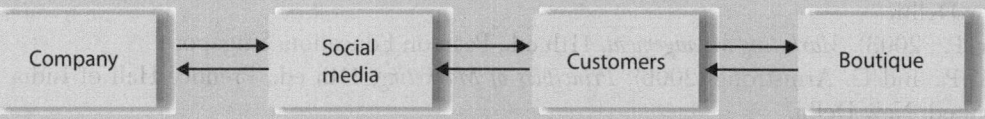

Figure A Channel configuration

The reversible interactions shown in the figure above between two parties indicate scope for reciprocal interactions between them. The payment procedures through this had the following options:

(a) On spot payment to delivery boy in the homes of the shoppers
(b) Collecting the materials from the boutiques and making cash payments or swapping credit cards
(c) Making online payments using credit cards

The business with social media worked steadily for six months since September 2009. But a personal hitch between Adi and the owner of the social media company scrambled the ties between the two.

Adi was a very resolute person. In March 2010, an idea struck in his mind regarding launching an independent website in the name of his company. And soon, he launched a website by assigning a tag 'Smartsite'. The strategy was to save recurring promotional costs in earlier procedure that was eating a huge pie of the company's profits. Adi's strategy initially paid no dividends. This was obvious because customers were still accustomed with the social media to get them connected with the company. Second, getting an audience reach such as social media was not possible for the new website. But Adi was an entrepreneur. He knew that an entrepreneur had to stride on thorny paths and find success only after much toil and grind.

In fact, Adi scrapped the relationship with social media strategically. Results in the beginning were abysmal. Sales were cut down to one fourth of the sales in the initial thirty days of its independent operations compared to that of the last thirty days when the company worked with the social media. The next month saw not much improvement. The third month was a repetition of the preceding month's sales results.

Adi knew that every new business venture had a gestation period where the business had to incur some losses with a hope that a breakeven

(Contd)

(*Contd*)

point will be reached and the positive trend in business will appear. But somehow he felt that there was something wrong in the new venture. He understood that his website was getting lost in the plethora of websites. He posted advertisements in two national dailies consecutively for two days highlighting details of the products, website address, mode of access, etc. He also attached coupons with it to offer ten per cent discounts on the price on the products at the time of delivery. Surprisingly, fortune turned to Adi's side and the company's sales began to pick up at the rate equal to the average rate of sales of last three months with social media. Adi' venture after some efforts paid back with loads of success. At present, Adi is sailing along with his website and business smoothly.

Discussion Questions

1. Do you think that social media as a channel of marketing is not an economically viable means of reaching target customers in the long term?
2. Should Adi have started with personal website from the beginning?
3. What according to you is the future of social networking sites as business facilitators?

Index